# Japanese

## A Comprehensive Grammar

*Japanese: A Comprehensive Grammar* is a complete reference guide to modern Japanese grammar.

Accessible and systematic, it explores the complexities of the language thoroughly, filling many gaps left by other textbooks.

Clear grammar points are put in context using examples from a range of Japanese media. The emphasis is firmly on contemporary Japanese as spoken and written by native speakers.

Key features of the book include:

- coverage of colloquial and standard Japanese
- extensive cross-referencing
- detailed index of Japanese and English terms
- up-to-date real examples of current usage
- greater emphasis on structures that learners find particularly confusing.

Written by experts in their fields, *Japanese: A Comprehensive Grammar* will prove a lasting and reliable resource for all learners of Japanese.

**Stefan Kaiser** is Special Professor at Kokugakuin University, Japan, and Emeritus Professor at the University of Tsukuba, Japan.

**Yasuko Ichikawa** was previously Professor at the International Center, University of Tokyo, Japan.

**Noriko Kobayashi** was previously Professor at the University of Tsukuba, Japan.

**Hilofumi Yamamoto** is Associate Professor at the Tokyo Institute of Technology, Japan.

*Routledge Comprehensive Grammars*

Comprehensive Grammars are available for the following languages:

Bengali
Cantonese
Catalan
Chinese
Danish
Dutch
Greek
Indonesian
Modern Welsh
Modern Written Arabic
Polish
Slovene
Swedish
Turkish
Ukrainian

# Japanese

*A Comprehensive Grammar*

Second edition

**Stefan Kaiser,
Yasuko Ichikawa,
Noriko Kobayashi and
Hilofumi Yamamoto**

 Routledge
Taylor & Francis Group

LONDON AND NEW YORK

First published 2001
by Routledge

Second edition published 2013
by Routledge
2 Park Square, Milton Park, Abingdon, Oxon OX14 4RN

Simultaneously published in the USA and Canada
by Routledge
711 Third Avenue, New York, NY 10017

*Routledge is an imprint of the Taylor & Francis Group, an informa business*

© 2013 Stefan Kaiser, Yasuko Ichikawa, Noriko Kobayashi,
Hilofumi Yamamoto

*British Library Cataloguing in Publication Data*
A catalogue record for this book is available from the British Library

*Library of Congress Cataloging-in-Publication Data*
Japanese : a comprehensive grammar / Stefan Kaiser ... [et al.].
    p. cm. – (Routledge comprehensive grammars)
  Text in English and Japanese.
  Includes bibliographical references and index.
  1. Japanese language–Grammar.  I. Kaiser, Stefan.
  PL533.J36 2012
  495.6'82421–dc23

                                                    2012014794

ISBN: 978-0-415-68739-3 (hbk)
ISBN: 978-0-415-68737-9 (pbk)
ISBN: 978-0-203-08519-6 (ebk)

Typeset in Sabon and Gill Sans
by Graphicraft Limited, Hong Kong

# Contents

## 22 Nominalizations 519

## 23 Conjoining 536

# Tables

# Symbols and abbreviations used in the text

| | |
|---|---|
| ✐ | (before example) made-up example |
| × | (before example) ungrammatical example |
| [] | (in example) addition to original text to assist understanding |
| [] | (in entry or subentry, etc.) occasionally used to mark the extent of a grammatical structure |
| [] | after entry: gives the grammatical class (sometimes meaning) of entry, e.g. **wa** [focus particle]. When referring to other entries, the [] part is attached only if it is needed to specify that entry, i.e. where there is more than one entry of the same form, i.e. **wa** [focus particle], **wa** [final particle], but **-ba**. |
| '. . .' | marks translation of entry (in examples it also marks quoted speech) |
| ". . ." | marks literal translation of entry (in examples it also marks direct speech) |
| * | used for footnotes in tables, etc. |
| ' | an emphatic way of ending a word, exclamation, sentence-final particle, etc. |

| | |
|---|---|
| adj. | Adjective |
| adv. | Adverb |
| AN | Adjectival noun |
| caus. | Causative |
| C | Counter |
| dem. | Demonstrative |
| fin. | Finite forms |
| imp. | Imperative |
| *lit.* | literally (literal translations are given in ". . .") |
| MJ | Mixed-Japanese vocabulary |
| N | Noun |

| | |
|---|---|
| neg. | Negative |
| NJ | Native-Japanese vocabulary |
| N-mod. | Noun-modifying forms (also: N-modifying) |
| NP | Noun phrase |
| num. | Number |
| P | Particle |
| pass. | Passive |
| pos. | Positive |
| pot. | Potential |
| pred. | Predicate |
| pref. | Prefix |
| pres. | Presumptive |
| pron. | Pronoun |
| Q | Question |
| S | Sentence (this can stand for a sentence, or a clause) |
| SJ | Sino-Japanese vocabulary (Japanese words of Chinese origin) |
| suf. | Suffix |
| V | Verb |
| VN | Verbal noun |
| WJ | Western-Japanese vocabulary (loanwords from Western languages) |

# Acknowledgements

The idea for the first edition of this book was suggested back in 1992 by Sarah Butler, then working at Hodder & Stoughton. An initially anonymous reviewer, Nic Tranter, made many useful suggestions, most of which were taken on board.

For the second edition, thanks are due to Samantha Vale Noya (assistant editor), who provided the idea for the new format. We were lucky to have a copy editor of Tessa Carroll's calibre, whose knowledge of Japanese and thorough reading resulted in a much improved book. Thanks are also due to the production editors, Cathy Hurren and then Anna Callander, and my partner Sue Henny, who ably organized the index, just like last time. Any shortcomings are of course the sole responsibility of the authors.

Stefan Kaiser

# Introduction

A comprehensive grammar of Japanese can take many forms; this book uses actual or real examples from sources such as the Japanese media and other databases, and attempts to illustrate Japanese grammar by plentiful use of such examples. Made-up examples (marked by ✐) are used only sporadically in cases where no appropriate real examples could be obtained.

Using real examples implies that not much control can be exercised over vocabulary; the intended reader therefore is expected to have some knowledge of Japanese and its representation in writing, either in the mixed *kanji/kana* script, or in the romanized version given under the original for those not fluent in regular Japanese writing. Each example also has an English translation and, where useful, a literal translation.

The first edition of this book was arranged by items listed in alphabetical order, some of which were grammatical categories such as 'adjectives' or 'nouns', while others were Japanese language items such as **aida** or **tara**. For the second edition, examples and items have been updated, edited and added, but the most visible change has been to rearrange the book around grammatical categories only, so as to make it conform better with most people's notion of a grammar, more or less in the traditional Western order, i.e. starting with nouns.

The Japanese language, which is spoken by 120 million Japanese, and is being learned as a foreign language by over three and a half million people all over the world, has markedly different characteristics from European languages (although statistically speaking, verb-final languages like Japanese are known to be the most common type amongst the languages of the world, pipping verb–object order languages such as English to the post). Features arising from this language type are that modifiers precede the modified. Thus adjectives and adverbs always precede the nouns and verbs they modify (or qualify). This characteristic also extends to the equivalent of relative clauses in European languages. Where you have an English clause like 'the book which I read yesterday', where the information about 'book' follows, usually by means of a relative pronoun, in Japanese the order is 'yesterday read book', which makes it an instance of noun modification. In other words, the notion of 'relative clause' exists only in translation equivalent.

Japanese does not easily fit the grammatical categories of European languages. What we have termed 'Tense and Aspect Endings', for instance, includes one use of **tokoro**, which is originally a noun meaning 'place' or 'situation'. As an aspect marker, this item (formally a noun) is modified by verb forms such as non-past, in which case it means 'about to (do)', or past forms, in which case the meaning is 'just have (done)'. The same **tokoro** also crops up under 'Modal Endings', where, modified by verbs, and followed by past forms of the copula, it indicates the meaning of something 'nearly (happening)'. The same **tokoro** is also found under 'Conjunctive Particles', where it means 'as' or 'just when', used with various case particles attached.

The term 'structural noun' is occasionally used in this book used to characterize items like **tokoro** and others, which are used as grammatical items while still retaining noun-like features (i.e. being preceded by noun-modifying forms and followed by case particles).

Like **tokoro**, many other grammatical items have several functions or meanings, but in most cases separating the functions complicates things unnecessarily. Therefore, items are often subdivided into a number of meanings or uses.

Chapter headings unfamiliar to eyes attuned to the grammar of European languages include the frequent appearance of 'particle', as in Case Particles, Phrasal Particles, Adverbial Particles and Sentence-Final Particles. This is a convenient, if not really well-defined, way to refer to items with grammatical function that do not quite fit traditional grammar. In addition, there are Honorific and Humble Forms, but these are sufficiently well known as a notable characteristic of Japanese.

## A note on romanization

In accordance with common practice, the so-called syllabic nasal (in *hiragana*, written ん) before a vowel (or semi-vowel, like **y**) is followed by an

apostrophe, as in **jin'in** ('personnel') or **kin'yū** ('finance') to distinguish these words from otherwise identical sequences like **jinin** ('resignation') or **kinyū** ('filling [a form]'), etc. Naturally, these pairs are also pronounced differently.

Note the similar symbol ', which in the absence of an established romanized equivalent is used to mark what amounts to a kind of emphatic way of ending a word, exclamation, sentence-final particle, etc. In *hiragana*, this is effected by つ, the so-called 'small tsu'). ねっ, for instance (an emphatic variant of ね), is rendered as **ne'** (pronounced somewhat like English 'net' stopping just before pronouncing the final 't').

# Chapter 1

# *Nouns*

Nouns in Japanese do not inflect for case, gender or number (but see 1.2.2 and 1.3). Their grammatical function is indicated by case particles (see 2). In Japanese writing, most nouns are written in *kanji*. For predicative use, nouns require the copula (see 7.5).

## 1.1 Types of noun

Generally, subgroups of nouns such as common nouns, abstract nouns, and proper nouns are often distinguished; in Japanese, however, this is a matter of meaning only. On the other hand, there are different strata of vocabulary in Japanese, which, though not exclusive to nouns, most typically exhibit the distinction between the four strata of vocabulary typical of Japanese – Native, Sino-Japanese, Western-Japanese and Mixed formations. Some of these distinctions are also reflected in the way nouns are written, i.e. Western-Japanese nouns and parts of Mixed-Japanese nouns are written using *katakana*, while the remainder is usually written in *kanji*.

Although the distinction is not reflected in the form of the noun, animate nouns and inanimate nouns are distinguished in that they select different existential verbs. Another type of nouns that can be distinguished are relational nouns, which are used where English uses prepositions such as above, behind etc. to indicate a location. We can also distinguish time nouns, verbal nouns, honorific/humble nouns, and personal nouns.

### 1.1.1 Native-Japanese (NJ) nouns

Native-Japanese nouns (in length, single-morpheme words can range from one to five or six syllables/*kana* letters) are either written in *kanji*, *kanji* + *kana*, or *kana* alone (the hyphens show the boundaries between morphemes):

| 鵜 | u | 'cormorant' |
| 目 | me | 'eye(s)' |
| 川 | kawa | 'river(s)' |
| 山 | yama | 'mountain(s)' |
| 命 | inochi | 'life' |
| 山登り | yama-nobori | 'mountaineering' |

### 1.1.2 Sino-Japanese (SJ) nouns

Sino-Japanese words have entered the language at various stages, beginning from about the eighth century. They also played a major part in the modernization of the language in the nineteenth and twentieth centuries, when new terminology entering from Europe was coined in Japan using Chinese character (*kanji*) roots. Almost all Sino-Japanese words are written in *kanji*, with one *kanji* being the equivalent of one morpheme or unit of meaning. One morpheme corresponds to a (short or long) syllable, (in some cases two syllables: **aku** 'evil', **ichi** 'one', etc). Some SJ words consist of one *kanji* only, but the vast majority are made up of two or more.

| 胃 | i | 'stomach' |
| 悪 | aku | 'evil' |
| 点 | ten | 'dot', 'point' |
| 線 | sen | 'line' |
| 計 | kei | 'total' |
| 研究 | ken-kyū | 'research' |
| 発見 | hak-ken | 'discovery' |
| 料理 | ryō-ri | 'cooking' |
| 河川 | ka-sen | 'rivers' |
| 山岳 | san-gaku | 'mountains' |
| 山岳地帯 | san-gaku-chi-tai | 'mountainous area' |
| 天文学 | ten-mon-gaku | 'astronomy' |
| 経済成長 | kei-zai-sei-chō | 'economic growth' |

Note the use of (usually) two-*kanji* SJ terms in written or formal (including scientific) contexts, such as **ka-sen** and **san-gaku**, which are near-equivalents of the (one-*kanji*) Native-Japanese words **kawa** and **yama** in 1.1.1. The Native-Japanese words can have both specific and generic meanings depending on the context, whereas the Sino-Japanese terms have generic meanings only. The SJ terms are also used in further compounding, such as **san-gaku-chi-tai** in the above list.

## 1.1.3 *Western-Japanese (WJ) nouns*

Most relatively recent Western-Japanese words (especially after World War II) come from English (older words from Portuguese/Spanish, Dutch, German, French and other languages, which entered the language through various forms of cultural contact, are also still used). Recent WJ items include Japanese creations, so-called Japlish or Janglish, which are made up by combining English roots. WJ words are adapted to the Japanese sound system, and are written in *katakana*.

### 1.1.3.1 *WJ nouns from languages other than English*

| | | |
|---|---|---|
| パン | **pan** | 'bread' (from Portuguese) |
| コップ | **koppu** | 'cup' (from Dutch) |
| シャンソン | **shanson** | 'chanson' (from French) |
| ゲレンデ | **gerende** | 'ski slope' (from German) |
| イクラ | **ikura** | 'salmon roe caviar' (from Russian) |

### 1.1.3.2 *WJ nouns from English*

| | | |
|---|---|---|
| ケーキ | **kēki** | 'cake' |
| マッチ | **matchi** | 'match(es)' |
| ゴルフ | **gorufu** | 'golf' |
| テレビ | **terebi** | 'television' |
| ボクシング | **bokushingu** | 'boxing' |

| 1.1.3.3 | *'Japlish' creations or uses of nouns* |

| ワンマンカー | **wanmankā** | 'one man car', i.e. driver only (bus etc.) |
| カンニング | **kanningu** | 'cunning', i.e. cheating in an exam |
| スピード・ダウン | **supīdo daun** | 'speed down', i.e. slow(ing) down |

*Note* – not all WJ words are written in *katakana*. Some items that used to be written in *kanji* are now also written in *hiragana* (煙草・たばこ **tabako** 'tobacco', じゅばん **juban** 'underwear (for kimono)', both from Portuguese), and a few others are occasionally written in *kanji*, otherwise in *katakana*: 珈琲・コーヒー **kōhī** 'coffee', 具楽部・クラブ **kurabu** 'club', 頁・ページ **pēji** 'page'.

| 1.1.3.4 | *Mixed-Japanese (MJ) nouns* |

If we limit the discussion to words made up of two items (the most common compound type), a Mixed-Japanese word can be any of the six possible combinations:

| NJ-SJ | 掛け金 | **kake-kin** | 'insurance premium' |
| NJ-WJ | 赤ワイン | **aka-wain** | 'red wine' |
| SJ-NJ | 残高 | **zan-daka** | 'bank account balance' |
| SJ-WJ | 鉄パイプ | **tetsu-paipu** | 'iron rod' |
| WJ-NJ | ガス漏れ | **gasu-more** | 'gas leak' |
| WJ-SJ | ジェット機 | **jetto-ki** | 'jet aeroplane' |

## 1.2 Apposition of nouns and noun reduplication

### 1.2.1 *Apposition of nouns*

The relationship between items (usually two, but sometimes three or more) that are lined up referring to the same entity is called apposition. There are two ways of doing this with nouns, by means of **no**, and by zero.

*Note* – in Japanese, the main noun is always the second one, whereas in English the order is reversed.

*Apposition by* **no**

a 大学生の娘
  **daigakusei no musume**
  My daughter, a university student

b 母親のみさ子さん
  **hahaoya no Misako-san**
  Misako, the mother

c 高校生の二男
  **kōkōsei no jinan**
  my second son, a high-school
  student

d 横綱の白鵬
  **yokozuna no Hakuhō**
  Hakuhō, the grand (Sumo)
  champion

1.2.1.2 *Apposition by zero*

a 妻子あるロッセリーニは、女優イングリッド・バーグマンと恋に
  落ち、彼女をハリウッドの映画界から奪った。
  **Saishi aru Rosserīni wa, joyū Inguriddo Bāguman to koi ni
  ochi, kanojo o hariuddo no eigakai kara ubatta.**
  Rossellini, who was married with children, fell in love with Ingrid Bergman,
  the actress, and took her away from Hollywood's world of film.

## 1.2.2 Noun reduplication

A few Native-Japanese nouns, such as 人 **hito** (人々 **hitobito** 'people'), 国
**kuni** (国々 **kuniguni** 'countries'), 山 **yama** (山々 **yamayama** 'mountains'),
店 **mise** (店々 **misemise** 'establishments', 'shops') can indicate a kind of
plural (indicating an unspecified amount only, i.e. these cannot be counted)
by reduplication, but this is limited to a very small number of nouns, most
of which are given here. Note that the repeat sign used for *kanji*, 々, is
used in writing to indicate that the second *kanji* in the *same* word is
repeated, i.e. it is not applied where the same *kanji* appears in a compound
as the first element of another word. Therefore **minshushugi** is written
民主主義, *not* 民主々義, because **minshushugi** 'democracy' is a compound
consisting of **minshu** 'people governing' and **shugi** 'principle' or '-ism').

Reduplication is not limited to nouns only; it includes pronouns (我々
**wareware** 'we'), and adverbs (次々に **tsugitsugi ni** 'one after another'), etc.

a 「家々、木々、山々」と題した作品がある。
  **'Ieie, Kigi, Yamayama' to daishita sakuhin ga aru.**
  There is a work entitled 'Houses, Trees, Mountains'.

## 1.3 Plural suffixes

### 1.3.1 -domo

-domo is mostly attached to first-person pronouns (see 5.4). Attached to nouns, -domo forms a plural which has a ring of contempt. In example b, the implication is that the other cats are useless or inferior, compared to the old cat.

a ジェシーらはそこで銃をとり、悪党どもに反撃を始めるのだ。
   **Jeshī-ra wa soko de jū o tori, akutō-domo ni hangeki o hajimeru no da.**
   At that stage, Jesse and his men take their guns and begin to fight the baddies.

b 夜、猫どもが古猫にその極意を聞く。古猫はそれぞれ腕自慢の猫たちの至らぬところを教え、・・・
   **Yoru, neko-domo ga furuneko ni sono gokui o kiku. Furuneko wa sorezore udejiman no neko-tachi no itaranu tokoro o oshie,...**
   At night, the cats ask the old cat about the secret [of catching rats]. The old cat tells the cats, each of whom takes pride in her abilities, where they fall short, and...

### 1.3.2 -gata

To express an honorific plural, -gata (rather than -tachi, see 1.3.4) is usually attached to the title of persons of higher social status (**sensei** 'teacher', 'professor', 'member of parliament', 'politician', etc.) and forms of address ending in -**sama** (honorific equivalent of -**san**). However, -**tachi** can also be used.

a 大学の先生方は美しい自然を強調していたが、それだけでは人は来ない。
   **Daigaku no sensei-gata wa utsukushii shizen o kyōchō shite ita ga, sore dake de wa hito wa konai.**
   The academics at the university were stressing the beautiful natural surroundings, but that's not enough to attract people [= students].

b 教科書、副読本、副教材は市販のものではなく先生方の手作りだ。
**Kyōkasho, fukudokuhon, fukukyōzai wa shihan no mono de wa naku sensei-gata no tezukuri da.**
Textbooks and supplementary texts and materials are not commercial products but handmade by the teachers.

c どうか、ここにおられる奥様方も安心していただきたい。
**Dōka, koko ni orareru okusama-gata mo anshin shite itadakitai.**
We also want you wives who are here not to worry [about your husbands getting the sack].

d …そのとき非常に印象に残ったのは、先生方や守衛さんら多くの人々が、私が日本人だと分かると、数年前にプリンスがおられたが非常にジェントルマンだ、と言っていたことです。
**…sono toki hijō ni inshō ni nokotta no wa, sensei-gata ya shuei-san-ra ōku no hitobito ga, watashi ga Nihonjin da to wakaru to, sūnenmae ni purinsu ga orareta ga hijō ni jentoruman da, to itte ita koto desu.**
…what impressed me very much at the time was that many people such as the professors and the porters, once they realized I was Japanese, told me that some years ago the prince was here and that he's a real gentleman.

### 1.3.3 -ra

Attached to nouns (and also demonstrative pronouns, 5.4.3). -ra indicates plural; attached to nouns only, -ra can also indicate the leading member of a group.

### 1.3.3.1 Plural

a 泰の息子らはまだ大学生だ。
**Yasushi no musuko-ra wa mada daigakusei da.**
Yasushi's sons are still university students.

b 関連企業の社長らはまだ若い。
**Kanren kigyō no shachō-ra wa mada wakai.**
The presidents of [the] affiliated businesses are still young [so they can't be promoted to main firm president].

c ···地元の竜馬ファンら約四十人が参加。

**...jimoto no Ryōma fan-ra yaku yonjū-nin ga sanka.**

...about 40 local Ryōma fans took part.

*Noun-**ra** 'noun' and those associated with 'noun'*

Like -**tachi** (see 1.3.4), -**ra** can also indicate the idea of 'N and those associated with N'.

a 男はそのまま逃走したが、経営者の「泥棒」という声を聞いた···
中学校二年、川端直樹君 (14) ら中学生五人が自転車や駆け足で
男を追跡、西へ約二百メートル離れた路上で取り押さえ
た。···経営者や川端君らにけがはなかった。

**Otoko wa sono mama tōsō shita ga, keiei-sha no 'dorobō'
to iu koe o kiita ... chūgakkō ni-nen, Kawabata Naoki-kun
(jūyon)-ra chūgakusei go-nin ga jitensha ya kakeashi de
otoko o tsuiseki, nishi e yaku nihyaku-mētoru hanareta rojō
de toriosaeta. ... keiei-sha ya Kawabata-kun-ra ni kega wa
nakatta.**

The man took flight, but five middle-school pupils, [including] the
second-year Kawabata Naoki (14), who heard the proprietor's shout
of 'Thief!' pursued him by bicycle and on foot, and overpowered
him on the road about 200 metres to the west. ... the proprietor
and Kawabata and his group were not hurt.

**-tachi**

The suffix -**tachi** is attached to nouns (and pronouns, see 5.4) to indicate
plural, mainly for humans. It can also indicate the idea of 'person *X* and
those associated with *X*'.

*Plural*

Like other plural suffixes, -**tachi** is optional, i.e. 1.3.4.2 and 1.3.4.3 could
equally be formed without -**tachi**.

The fact that **ōku no hito** is still much more common than **ōku no hito-tachi**
seems to indicate that this type of plural is still an optional, perhaps even
a stylistic device.

a 多くの人が祖国のために命をささげた。
**Ōku no hito ga sokoku no tame ni inochi o sasageta.**
Many people gave their lives for their country.

b 多くの人々が賛成していることも聞いた。
**Ōku no hitobito ga sansei shite iru koto mo kiita.**
I also heard that many people approve [= of moving the capital].

1.3.4.2 | *Human nouns*

a 価格破壊の主役はやはり女性たちだ。
**Kakaku hakai no shuyaku wa yahari josei-tachi da.**
The protagonists of [fixed] price destruction are after
all women.

b 世界の"鉄人"たちが集まり、体力の限界に挑戦する。
**Sekai no 'tetsujin'-tachi ga atsumari, tairyoku no
genkai ni chōsen suru.**
The world's 'iron men' gather and test the limits of their
strength.

1.3.4.3 | *Non-human nouns*

-tachi is also these days attached to animals (the film/book *Silence of the
Lambs* became **Hitsuji-tachi no Chinmoku** 羊たちの沈黙 in Japan) and
even plants. In magazine headlines even nouns like **mise** 'shop', 'restaurant'
and kēki 'cake' appear with -tachi attached, but this new convention does
not extend to running text.

a 中でも、ひときわ目を引くのはフラミンゴたちだ。
**Naka de mo, hitokiwa me o hiku no wa furamingo-tachi da.**
What particularly attracts attention amongst these are the
flamingoes.

b 島大陸マダガスカルの奇妙な植物たち
**Shima-tairiku Madagasukaru no kimyō na shokubutsu-tachi**
The strange plants of the island continent Madagascar
[Title of an article in サイエンス, a Japanese edition of
*Scientific American*]

| *Noun-**tachi**: 'noun and those associated with noun'*

This used to be regarded as the typical use of **-tachi**, but is increasingly becoming rare compared to the plural-type usage.

a しかし天心たちはすぐ立ち直った。
   **Shikashi Tenshin-tachi wa sugu tachinaotta.**
   But Tenshin and those around him [= his pupils] recovered
   immediately.

## 1.4  Personal nouns: addressing family and others

As with non-family, instead of personal pronouns other forms of address/ reference are frequently used (see 5.3).

An important distinction in use depends on whether one is *addressing* others, or *referring* to them.

When referring to others, an ingroup–outgroup distinction is also applied. This distinction requires that, towards outgroup listeners, members of one's own group are referred to without hon. pref. (**o-/go-**) and/or personal suf. (**-san/-sama**, etc.), as in examples 2 b, d, f and h–j. However, note the use of the words for mother/father(**o-**)**tōsan/chan**/(**o-**)**kāsan/chan**, and also **papa/mama**, by parents towards their children like first-person personal pronouns (example 2 c), where this rule does not apply. Wives/husbands also commonly use (**o-**)**tōsan**/(**o-**)**kāsan** and variants to refer to their marriage partners (example 2 a). Also, children need to learn the address/ reference distinction, and often fail to distinguish them (example 2 g) (see 5.3).

The choice between **o-** and **go-** depends on whether the word the prefix is attached to is Native-Japanese or Sino-Japanese vocabulary (see 1.1). Exceptions include **o-jōsan** and **o-bot-chan**.

Where names are used for addressing, the general rule is to attach **-san**, etc. for seniors, and nothing (except for intimate children, etc., **-chan/-kun**) for those junior to the speaker.

*Note 1* – older-generation husbands also use **oi** ('say', 'hey') to address their wives (example 2 l), and wives (or girlfriends) often use **nē** ('I say') towards their husband (boyfriend), in a variety of intonations (example a).

a 「ねえ、入るんならこっちのホテルがいいな」。平日の午後
　 七時、連れの男性と腕を組んでいた若い女の子が嬌声
　 （きょうせい）をあげた。

**'Nē, hairu n nara kotchi no hoteru ga ii na'. Heijitsu no gogo
shichi-ji, tsure no dansei to ude o kunde ita wakai onna no
ko ga kyōsei o ageta.**

'Look, if we go to [a love hotel], then I'd like this one'. Around 7 p.m.
on a weekday, a young girl who had been walking arm in arm with
her male companion, raised her voice coquettishly.

*Note 2* – when there is no need to make the in-/outgroup distinction or to
use honorifics, as in narrative text or when referring to historical or fictional
figures, the terms in the first column in Table 1.1 (but not the ones in
brackets) are used, *excepting* the words for husband and wife, where only
**tsuma** and **otto** are normally used, although depending on such situational
factors as the speaker–listener relationship, formality, etc., the terms in the
last columns are also used (example 2 a).

### 1.4.1 Family address

a お父さん、お母さん、長い間ありがとうございました。
**Otōsan, okāsan, nagai aida arigatō gozaimashita.**
Father, mother, thank you for all [you've done] all these years.

b なあオヤジ、早く隠居しなよ。
**Nā oyaji, hayaku inkyo shi na yo.**
Come on, dad, retire soon, will you.

c おふくろ、死ぬなよ。
**Ofukuro, shinu na yo.**
Mum, don't die!

### 1.4.2 Family reference

a 今夜はお父さん帰ってこないの。
**Konya wa otōsan kaette konai no.**
Tonight hubby's not coming home.

b 「父は解剖学の偉大な先生だった」という。
**'Chichi wa kaibōgaku no idai na sensei datta' to iu.**
She says 'Father was an eminent anatomist'.

c どんなことがあっても、お父さんとお母さんは守ってやる。
**Donna koto ga atte mo, otōsan to okāsan wa mamotte yaru.**
No matter what happens, daddy and mummy will protect you.

d 親父の墓には既におふくろが入っている。
**Oyaji no haka ni wa sude ni ofukuro ga haitte iru.**
Mum is already interred in dad's grave.

e おふくろに花束を!
**Ofukuro ni hanataba o!**
Flowers for mum!

f ···男子生徒が「おふくろに教えてやろう」と喜んでいた。
**···danshi seito ga 'Ofukuro ni oshiete yarō' to yorokonde ita.**
...a male pupil rejoiced, saying 'I'll tell mum [that the nutritional value
of spinach is in the roots]'.

g 「もう少ししたら、シベリアのおばあさんの所に行く」という。
**'Mō sukoshi shitara, Shiberia no obāsan no tokoro ni iku' to iu.**
'Soon, I'll go to my grandmother's place in Siberia', he said.

h 昨年、主人と離婚しました。
**Sakunen, shujin to rikon shimashita.**
Last year, I got divorced from my husband.

i ···家内と一緒に住むつもりです。
**···kanai to issho ni sumu tsumori desu.**
I intend to live [there = in the official residence] with my wife.

j 家族を食わせないといけないし。
**Kazoku o kuwasenai to ikenai shi.**
I also need to feed my family.

k 奥さんがご主人の会社の車で買い物に行くなどというのも、さほ
ど珍しいことではなかった。
**Oku-san ga go-shujin no kaisha no kuruma de kaimono ni iku
nado to iu no mo, sahodo mezurashii koto de wa nakatta.**
It wasn't that unusual [in the old days] for the wife to go out
shopping in the husband's company car.

l 「おい、仕事で疲れているんだから早くなんとかしてくれよ」 ―、
幼い我が子がむずかると夫が妻に文句を言う。
**'Oi, shigoto de tsukarete iru n da kara hayaku nan to ka shite
kure yo' --, osanai waga ko ga muzukaru to otto ga tsuma
ni monku o iu.**
'Hey, I'm tired from work, so do something about him right away',
the husband complains to the wife when their little son gets fretful.

15

**Table 1.1** Address forms: family

| Relation | Speaker's family | Addressing | Listener/third person's family |
|---|---|---|---|
| | Referring (*my …*) | | Referring (*your …, someone else's …*) |
| family | 家族 <br> **kazoku** | — <br> — | ご家族 <br> **go-kazoku** |
| parents | 両親 <br> **ryōshin** | — <br> — | ご両親 <br> **go-ryōshin** |
| father | 父、おやじ・親父 <br> **chichi (oyaji)** | （お）父さん* <br> おやじ・親父（さん） <br> **(o-)tōsan\*,** <br> **oyaji(-san)** <br> パパ <br> **papa, dad(dy)** | お父さん <br> **o-tō-san** |
| mother | 母、おふくろ <br> **haha (ofukuro)** | （お）母さん* <br> **(o-)kā-san\*** <br> おふくろさん <br> **ofukuro-san** <br> ママ、マミー <br> **mama, mamī** | お母さん <br> **o-kā-san** |
| older brother | 兄 <br> **ani** | （お）兄さん* <br> **(o-)niisan\*** | お兄さん <br> **o-niisan\*** |
| older sister | 姉 <br> **ane** | （お）姉さん* <br> **(o-)nēsan\*** | お姉さん <br> **o-nēsan\*** |
| younger brother | 弟 <br> **otōto** | (name) <br> (name) | 弟さん <br> **otōto-san** |
| younger sister | 妹 <br> **imōto** | (name) <br> (name) | 妹さん <br> **imōto-san** |
| brothers (& sisters) | 兄弟 <br> **kyōdai** | — <br> — | ご兄弟 <br> **go-kyōdai** |
| sisters | 姉妹 <br> **shimai** | — <br> — | 姉妹 <br> **go-shimai** |
| child(ren) | 子ども <br> **kodomo** | (name) <br> (name) | お子さん <br> **o-ko-san** |
| son(s) | 息子、倅 <br> **musuko (segare)** | (name) <br> (name) | 息子さん、 <br> お坊ちゃん <br> **musuko-san,** <br> **(o-)bot-chan** |

**Table 1.1** (*cont'd*)

| Relation | Speaker's family | Addressing | Listener/third person's family |
|---|---|---|---|
| | Referring (*my* …) | | Referring (*your* …, *someone else's* …) |
| daughter(s) | 娘<br>**musume** | (name)<br>(name) | 娘さん、お嬢さん<br>**musume-san, o-jōsan*** |
| grandfather | 祖父<br>**sofu (jī-san)** | （お）じいさん*<br>**(o-) jī-san*** | おじいさん<br>**o-jī-san** |
| grandmother | 祖母<br>**sobo (bā-san)** | （お）ばあさん*<br>**(o-) bā-san*** | おばあさん<br>**o-bā-san** |
| grandchild | 孫<br>**mago** | (name)<br>(name) | お孫さん<br>**o-mago-san** |
| uncle | 叔父・伯父<br>**oji** | おじさん*<br>**o-ji-san*** | おじさん<br>**o-ji-san** |
| aunt | 叔母・伯母<br>**oba** | おばさん*<br>**o-ba-san*** | おばさん<br>**o-ba-san** |
| cousin | いとこ<br>**itoko** | (name)<br>(name) | （お）いとこさん<br>**(o-)itoko-san** |
| nephew | 甥<br>**oi** | (name)<br>(name) | 甥ごさん<br>**oi-go-san** |
| niece | 姪<br>**mei** | (name)<br>(name) | 姪ごさん<br>**mei-go-san** |
| husband | 主人、旦那、夫、ハズ、ダーリン<br>**shujin (danna, otto, hazu, dārin)**<br>surname | あなた、ねえ、お父さん、パパ、<br>**anata, otōsan, papa**<br>name | ご主人、だんなさん*<br>**go-shujin, danna-san*** |
| wife | 家内、ワイフ、母さん、妻、女房<br>**kanai (waifu, kāsan, tsuma, nyōbō)** | おい、お母さん、ママ、<br>**o-kāsan, mama** | 奥さん*<br>**oku-san*** |

*Note* *-**chan** often replaces -**san** when referring to others' children, and when children address their kin. Instead of -**san**, the superpolite -**sama** can be used for reference to others' kin.

Some of the above forms, such as **oyaji** and **ofukuro**, are only used by men in informal contexts.

## 1.4.3 Non-family address

Where a title (**sensei** 'teacher', 'MP', or **daijin** 'government minister') can be used, names are often avoided. Where names are used, suffixes like -**sama**, -**san**, -**kun** and -**chan** are usually attached.

a このことについての大臣の考えは。
**Kono koto ni tsuite no daijin no kangae wa.**
What are your [= the minister's] thoughts on this?

b 先生、こんなに暑くては授業できないよ。打ち切ろうよ！
**Sensei, konna ni atsukute wa jugyō dekinai yo. Uchikirō yo!**
Sir, if it's this hot we can't have classes! Let's finish!

c キャディーさん、こっちへ寄って。
**Kyadī-san, kotchi e yotte.**
Caddy, come over here.

d A君もぜひ遊びに来て下さい。
**A-kun mo zehi asobi ni kite kudasai.**
You [= A-kun] too please do come and visit.

## 1.4.4 Personal suffixes

### 1.4.4.1 -san and -sama

Attaching the suffix -**san** (and its very formal equivalent -**sama**) to family names or given names (especially those of Westerners) is the most common form of addressing people.

-**sama** is also used as a more formal equivalent of -**san** in **mina-san** (**mina-sama**) 'everyone' and **o-kyaku-sama** (**o-kyaku-san**) 'guest(s)', 'customer(s)'.

a それでは白石さん、支払いをお願いします。
**Sore de wa Shiraishi-san, shiharai o onegai shimasu.**
Well then, Mrs Shiraishi, please pay up.

b リンダさんは週に二回学校に行っているので、代わりにマイクさんが哺乳瓶で赤ちゃんに母乳をあげる。
**Rinda-san wa shū ni ni-kai gakkō ni itte iru no de, kawari ni Maiku-san ga honyūbin de akachan ni bonyū o ageru.**
As Linda goes to school twice a week, Mike gives the baby a bottle feed instead.

c 温かく見守り、応援してくださった皆様に感謝の気持ちでいっぱ
いです。

**Atatakuku mimamori, ōen shite kudasatta mina-sama ni
kansha no kimochi de ippai desu.**

I'm full of gratitude to all the people who have followed [my career]
with interest and have urged me on.

*Note* – on the use of **-sama** for addresses: **-sama** (never **-san**) is attached
to the name of the addressee on envelopes. In this case, it's attached to
company names as well as people's names (other suf. include the more
formal **-dono** (殿), and **onchū** (御中); the latter can be used only for companies, not individuals).

| 1.4.4.2 | **-kun** |

**-kun** is generally used for boys only (for both address and reference), by
close male friends, especially if they've been friends since schooldays,
and by senior males (or females) for more junior males, e.g. by teachers
in school or university, and even by the speaker in the Diet for MPs
(example b).

a 小学校から帰った春樹君（11）はコンピューターの画面をの
ぞいた。

**Shōgakkō kara kaetta Haruki-kun (jūichi) wa konpyūtā no
gamen o nozoita.**

Haruki-kun (11), who had come back from primary school, looked at
the computer screen.

b 河村君、君はねぇ、一年間謹慎するくらいの反省が必要だろう。

**Kawamura-kun, kimi wa nē, ichinen-kan kinshin suru kurai no
hansei ga hitsuyō darō.**

[At the Diet:] Mr Kawamura, you should repent and be on your best
behaviour for a year or so.

| 1.4.4.3 | **-chan** |

**-chan** is to address and refer to younger siblings, also by friends of the
family. In the media, **-chan** is used to refer to children of up to 6 years of
age. Women and young children also commonly attach it to cute animals,
e.g. **panda-chan**.

a 彩子ちゃんは移植手術を受けることなく、この世を去った。
**Ayako-chan wa ishoku shujutsu o ukeru koto naku, kono yo o satta.**
Ayako-chan left this world without receiving a transplant operation.

b まったく、お兄ちゃんの影響力の大きさにはまいるぜ。
**Mattaku, onii-chan no eikyō-ryoku no ōkisa ni wa mairu ze.**
It really amazes you how strong the older brother's influence is!

| 1.4.4.4 | *Within the family* |

In the family, too, personal name + suffix is also used (especially towards children), and (o-)tō-san/chan 'daddy' and (o-)kā-san/chan 'mummy', as well as 'papa' and 'mama', are used by children towards their parents (and between parents) like first-person pronouns.

a どんなことがあっても、お父さんとお母さんは守ってやる。
**Donna koto ga atte mo, o-tōsan to o-kāsan wa mamotte yaru.**
No matter what happens, daddy and mummy will protect you.

b ママ、もう現場に戻りなよ。
**Mama, mō genba ni modori na yo.**
Mummy, go back to [your] work now.

## 1.5 Animate and inanimate nouns

This is a distinction between persons and animals on the one hand, and plants and things on the other. In existential sentences, the verbs **iru** and **aru** (with some exceptions, see 7.4.1) distinguish the two types.

a 外に女性がいる。
**Soto ni josei ga iru.**
There's a woman outside.

b 共通の浴場がある。
**Kyōtsū no yokujō ga aru.**
There is a bath for shared use.

## 1.6 Relational nouns and structural nouns

### 1.6.1 Relational nouns

Relational nouns are nouns that indicate a position that is relative in time or space. They are often preceded by other nouns + **no**, or noun-modifying forms of V/Adj, and in turn can modify other nouns with **no** attached, or predicates by means of other case or adverbial particles.

Relational nouns often translate as a preposition in English and include the following: **aida** 'between', **ato** 'after', **hidari** 'left', **mae** 'in front', **migi** 'right', **naka** 'inside', **shita** 'below', **tonari** 'next to', **ue** 'above', 'on top', **ushiro** 'behind', etc.

a 山の上の静かな寺だ。
**Yama no ue no shizuka na tera da.**
It is a quiet temple on the top of the mountain.

b ちょっと上の会議室まで来てくれませんか。
**Chotto ue no kaigi-shitsu made kite kuremasen ka.**
Could you come to the conference room upstairs for a moment?

c テーブルの上にコーヒーカップを置く。
**Tēburu no ue ni kōhī kappu o oku.**
They put coffee cups on the table.

d あらしの後の静かな朝。
**Arashi no ato no shizuka na asa.**
A quiet morning after the storm.

e もう少し後にしていただきたい。
**Mō sukoshi ato ni shite itadaki-tai.**
I'd like to request you to put it off a little longer.

f 頭の中がぴかぴかと光った。
**Atama no naka ga pikapika to hikatta.**
There was a flash of light inside my head.

### 1.6.1.1 aida

As a relational noun, **aida** is attached to other nouns by means of the case particle **no**, with the meaning of 'between', 'among', 'through'. Like other relational nouns, **aida** itself attaches such case (and/or other) particles as are required by the valency of the verb (see 7.2).

Note also the set phrases **kono aida** (この間) 'the other day', **kono kan** (この間) 'during this period/time' (example a; the reading of the *kanji* 間 can be determined by the context only, i.e. when the meaning is *not* 'the other day' it can be read **kan** or **aida**).

a ゴレ島は十六世紀前半から十九世紀半ばまで約三百年間、西アフ
  リカ各地の奴隷を集め、送り出す基地として使われていた。
  この間、アフリカから連れ出された奴隷は数千万人といわれる。

  **Gore-tō wa jūroku seiki zenhan kara jūkyū seiki nakaba made
  yaku sanbyaku-nenkan, Nishi Afurika kakuchi no dorei o
  atsume, okuridasu kichi to shite tsukawarete ita. Kono kan,
  Afurika kara tsure-dasareta dorei wa sū-senman-nin to iwareru.**

  Gore Island was used for about 300 years from the first half of the
  16th century to the middle of the 19th century as a station for
  gathering slaves from all over West Africa and sending them on.
  The number of slaves taken from Africa during that time is said
  to be 20 or 30 million.

b 夫人との間に一男三女がいる。

  **Fujin to no aida ni ichi-nan san-jo ga iru.**

  With his wife, he has one son and three daughters.

c 日本人のあいだに気まずい空気が漂った。

  **Nihonjin no aida ni kimazui kūki ga tadayotta.**

  An awkward feeling among the Japanese hung in the air.

d 大気と海、陸地のあいだを水がどのように循環するかを調べるこ
  とが気候の解明につながる。

  **Taiki to umi, rikuchi no aida o mizu ga dono yō ni junkan
  suru ka o shiraberu koto ga kikō no kaimei ni tsunagaru.**

  The investigation of how water circulates between the air and the sea
  and land will lead to a clearer understanding of the climate.

---

| 1.6.1.2 | **ato** |

**ato** (usually written 後) is a relational noun meaning 'after'. It can be used by itself, usually with **wa**, in the sense of 'all that remains is . . .', combining with demonstrative pron. such as **sono** in the form **sono ato** 'after that', or attaching to a noun in the form N **no ato** 'after the N'.

Note the use before amounts, **ato** + number (+ counter), where **ato** is usually
written in *hiragana*.

| 1.6.1.2.1 | Noun/demonstrative pronoun **no ato** |

| 1.6.1.2.1.1 | *Noun* **no ato** |

This translates as 'after a/the N'.

a あらしの後の静かな朝。
  **Arashi no ato no shizuka na asa.**
  A quiet morning after the storm.

b シャンプーの後、ブラシをあて、耳を掃除してツメを切るのが
  一般的なコース。
  **Shampū no ato, burashi o ate, mimi o sōji shite tsume o kiru
  no ga ippan-teki na kōsu.**
  [Dog beauty parlour:] After a shampoo, the normal service consists of
  brushing, cleaning the ears and cutting the claws.

| 1.6.1.2.1.2 | **sono ato** |

This expresses the idea of 'after that', 'thereafter'. Note that this can also
be read **sono go**, in which case the meaning is 'since' or 'subsequently' (for
an example of **sono go**, see 24.1 e).

a 万一、夫が死亡した場合、借金やその後の生活が心配です。
  **Man'ichi, otto ga shibō shita baai, shakkin ya sono ato no
  seikatsu ga shinpai desu.**
  In the event that my husband should die, I'd be worried about debts
  and how to support myself thereafter.

| 1.6.1.2.1.3 | **ato** + NUMBER (+ COUNTER) |

In this combination, **ato** means 'another'. Note that **ato ippo** in example
b literally means "one more step". For number + counter, see 4.

a 投票日まであと一週間。
  **Tōhyōbi made ato isshūkan.**
  It's one more week to election day.

b 征服まであと一歩のところでリタイアした。
  **Seifuku made ato ippo no tokoro de ritaia shita.**
  He turned back with only a short distance (*lit.* "one more step")
  to go before conquering [the mountain].

23

## 1.6.1.3 mae

**mae** is a noun indicating a relative position, either in time or space 'in front of', 'before'. Like other nouns, it can be used after another noun (usually in the form N **no mae** (**ni**)), but it can also attach directly, like a suffix, especially after nouns of time. **mae** can also attach to clauses, in the sense of 'before doing' (1.6.1.3.2 below).

### 1.6.1.3.1 Noun (no) mae

a 一週間前に新築したばかりだったという。
   **Isshūkan mae ni shinchiku shita bakari datta to iu.**
   [Earthquake:] They say that the [destroyed] building had been completed only a week ago.

b クリスマス前にも送還される。
   **Kurisumasu mae ni mo sōkan sareru.**
   They will be deported as early as before Christmas.

c 下宿でも近所の商店でも、ラジオの前には人がいる。
   **Geshuku de mo kinjo no shōten de mo, rajio no mae ni wa hito ga iru.**
   In apartment houses and the shops in the vicinity, there are people in front of the radio.

### 1.6.1.3.2 Clause verb mae

a なぜ死を選ぶ前に、救いを求めなかったのか。
   **Naze shi o erabu mae ni, sukui o motomenakatta no ka.**
   Why didn't he seek help before choosing death?

b 内容を説明する前に、参加した顔ぶれを見た方がその目的が分かりやすい。
   **Naiyō o setsumei suru mae ni, sanka shita kaobure o mita hō ga sono mokuteki ga wakariyasui.**
   Before explaining the content [of the conference], it's easier to understand its purpose by looking at what sort of people were there.

## 1.6.1.4 naka

The relational noun **naka** is similar in meaning to the English prepositions 'among', 'in', 'inside'.

a 男性の中には磨かない人もいるが、・・・

**Dansei no naka ni wa migakanai hito mo iru ga ...**

Among men, there are people who don't brush [their teeth], but ...

b ・・・心の中では泣いているときがあるのです。

**...kokoro no naka de wa naite iru toki ga aru no desu.**

...there are times when I cry inside (my heart).

c タイムカプセルの中に入り込んだような錯覚を覚えさせる。

**Taimukapuseru no naka ni hairikonda yō na sakkaku o oboesaseru.**

[The exhibition] makes you feel as if you have entered a time capsule.


1.6.1.5 **uchi**

As a relational noun, **uchi** indicates the idea of 'among', 'of' or 'during'.

a このうち六人が死亡している。

**Kono uchi rokunin ga shibō shite iru.**

Of these, six have died.

b このうち六巻までをゲーム化した。

**Kono uchi rokkan made o gēmu-ka shita.**

Of these [= volumes of a novel], they have turned as many as six volumes into game software.

c そのうち二本が今月になって花を咲かせた。

**Sono uchi nihon ga kongetsu ni natte hana o sakaseta.**

Two of these trees have blossomed this month.

d 仕事も電子メディアを使うとなると、朝のうちはA社のため、昼からはB社の仕事ということも。

**Shigoto mo denshi media o tsukau to naru to, asa no uchi wa A-sha no tame, hiru kara wa B-sha no shigoto to iu koto mo.**

If one were to use electronic media at work too, one might work for company A in the mornings and company B in the afternoons.

e 歌い手さんでも、だんだん上手になってくると、歌詞がはっきりしてきますでしょ。最初のうちはなに言ってるかわからなくても。

**Utaite-san de mo, dandan jōzu ni natte kuru to, kashi ga hakkiri shite kimasu desho. Saisho no uchi wa nani itteru ka wakaranakute mo.**

As they get more proficient, singers' pronunciation gradually gets clearer, doesn't it. Even if one can't understand what they say at first.

Structural nouns are nouns that are used as grammatical items (modal endings, conjunctive particles etc.), but retain their 'noun-ness' in that they are preceded (and often followed) by the same forms that precede and follow nouns, i.e. noun-modifying forms precede them, and forms of the copula follow. Structural nouns include items such as **aida** (see 26.2.7), **ato** (26.2.5), **baai** (see 26.2.2), **gotoshi** (see 9.5.8), **hazu** (9.6.2), **tokoro** (see 9.1.2.5 and 26.2.10), **tsumori** (see 9.2.4), **wake** (see 9.6.4), **yō** (see 9.5.6).

## 1.7 Time nouns

### 1.7.1 toki

As a noun, **toki** 'time' is written with the *kanji* 時 or in *hiragana* (とき), whereas as a conjunctive particle it nowadays tends to be written in *hiragana* only (see 26.2.1). However, the distinction is not always clear, there being examples of the time noun **toki** that are translated as 'when' or 'the time when'. Being formally a noun, when **toki** is modified by a clause in such sentences (examples c–f), it acts as a relative clause head noun, just like any other noun.

a こんな時に歌なんて ⋯⋯。
**Konna toki ni uta nante ...**
Singing at a [difficult] time like this? [That's hard to believe.]

b 何であの時、入院なんかしたんだろう。
**Nande ano toki, nyūin nanka shita n darō.**
Why did I get myself hospitalized that time, I wonder.

c とうとうユニホームを脱ぐときが来た。
**Tōtō unihōmu o nugu toki ga kita.**
Finally the time has come to take off the uniform [= retire].

d 借金は15年前に家を新築したときのローンの残り。
**Shakkin wa jūgonen mae ni ie o shinchiku shita toki no rōn no nokori.**
The debt is the remainder of the loan [taken out] when we rebuilt our house 15 years ago.

e 人間生きていればつらい目にあうときも落ち込むときもある。
**Ningen ikite ireba tsurai me ni au toki mo ochikomu toki mo aru.**
As long as one is alive, there are times when things are hard and times when one feels down.

f 学生と接しているときが一番楽しいという教員はいっぱいいる。

**Gakusei to sesshite iru toki ga ichiban tanoshii to iu kyōin wa ippai iru.**

There are many teachers who feel that the time when they are in contact with the students is the most enjoyable of all.

g 赤ん坊の時に抱かれた記憶もなく、父の愛情を実感できずにいた。

**Akanbō no toki ni dakareta kioku mo naku, chichi no aijō o jikkan dekizu ni ita.**

I have no memories of being cuddled when I was a baby, and was unable to realize my father's love.

---

| 1.7.2 | **koro** |

Like **toki**, **koro** is used as a time noun, and as such can be modified by verbs, adjectives and noun + **no**, and attach case, adverbial and other particles.

Compared to **toki**, **koro** indicates an approximate time, but often also translates as 'when', like **toki**. Note the common combinations **osanai koro** 'when very young', **chiisai koro** 'when small', **wakai koro** 'when young (late teens to early twenties)', **kodomo no koro** 'when young' (see the following examples).

---

| 1.7.2.1 | *Adjective/verb* **koro** |

a 「わしら若いころはもどしながら勉強したもんじゃ」と年寄り。

**'Washira wakai koro wa modoshinagara benkyō shita mon ja' to toshiyori.**

'When we were young, we used to learn [drinking] while throwing up', said an old man.

b アメリカは幼いころから、テレビの中にあり、行かなくても分かる。

**Amerika wa osanai koro kara, terebi no naka ni ari, ikanakute mo wakaru.**

America was on TV from the time we were small, and can be understood without going [there].

c 大学に入ったころ、まだ海外渡航が自由化されていなかった。

**Daigaku ni haitta koro, mada kaigai tokō ga jiyū-ka sarete inakatta.**

When I entered university, we weren't free to go abroad yet.

*Noun/demonstrative pronoun* **no koro**

a 私の子どものころを、教えておきたいのです。

**Watashi no kodomo no koro o, oshiete okitai no desu.**

I want to tell about the time when I was a child.

b 三十八億年前のことだ。このころの海水の量や化学組成は現在と
あまり違いはなかった。

**Sanjūhachioku-nen mae no koto da. Kono koro no kaisui no
ryō ya kagaku sosei wa genzai to amari chigai wa nakatta.**

3,800 million years ago. At this time, it wasn't much different from
now with regard to things like the amount of sea water and
[the world's] chemical make-up.

**-goro**

-goro is a voiced variant of **koro**, used like a suffix that attaches to nouns
of time, indicating a point of time (including seasons) that is approximate.
As with other time expressions, the particle **ni** can optionally be attached
to **-goro** (see 2.4.13).

a 今月十五日ごろに妻を殺した疑いが持たれている。

**Kongetsu jūgonichi-goro ni tsuma o koroshita utagai ga
motarete iru.**

He is suspected of having killed his wife around the 15th of this
month.

b 二日午前零時三十二分ごろ、関東南部で地震があった。

**Futsuka gozen reiji sanjūnifun-goro, Kantō Nanbu chihō de
jishin ga atta.**

Around 12.32 a.m. on the 2nd, there was an earthquake in the South
Kanto area.

c 朝は六時ごろには起きて学校に向かい、授業が終わった後は下宿
でスペイン語の勉強に打ち込んだ。

**Asa wa rokuji-goro ni wa okite gakkō ni mukai, jugyō ga
owatta ato wa geshuku de Supeingo no benkyō ni
uchikonda.**

In the morning he got up by around 6 and went to school [to teach],
and after the end of classes he immersed himself in the study of
Spanish in his room.

d （同日）午前二時から三時ごろ、ドーンと物が倒れるような音
   がした。

   **(Dōjitsu) gozen niji kara sanji-goro, dōn to mono ga taoreru
   yō na oto ga shita.**

   Between about 2 and 3 a.m. (on that day), there was a sound as if
   something had toppled over.

e 出生数急増の背景には一九九〇年ごろから始まったウェディング
   ・ブームがある。

   **Shusseisū kyūzō no haikei ni wa senkyūhyaku kyūjū-nen-goro
   kara hajimatta uedingu būmu ga aru.**

   Behind the sudden increase in births there is the wedding boom that
   started around 1990.

## 1.8 Honorific and humble nouns

Honorific and humble nouns can be divided into nouns referring to a person,
nouns referring to people's actions, and nouns that are used as euphemisms.

### 1.8.1 *Nouns referring to a person*

#### 1.8.1.1 *Without honorific prefix*

To refer to a person, the honorific equivalent of **hito, kata,** can be used in
the singular, and the reduplicated **katagata** for the plural (see 1.4, 5.3).

a 大変健康な方だ。
   **Taihen kenkō na kata da.**
   He is a very healthy person.

b 観光関係者の方々、ご参考になっただろうか。
   **Kankō kankeisha no katagata, go-sankō ni natta darō ka.**
   [Advice on how to advertise a local area for sightseeing] Has [our
   advice] been useful for you people in the sightseeing business?

#### 1.8.1.2 *With honorific prefix*

The honorific prefix **o/go-** (the choice is mainly conditioned by the type
of noun attached to, i.e. **o-**NJ and **go-**SJ (see 16.1.1)) can be attached to

N in the sense of 'your N', and also to reflexive pronouns like **jishin** to make them honorific (example c).

For address and reference, these prefixes are also attached to some family terms (see 5.3).

a 今、初盆を迎え、ご親族のもとへあなたはひとときお帰りになっ
ておられるのだろうと思います。

**Ima, hatsubon o mukae, go-shinzoku no moto e anata wa
hitotoki o-kaeri ni natte orareru no darō to omoimasu.**

Now, on the occasion of your first Bon festival, I believe that you have
returned for a short time to your family.

b 三世代同居時代には嫁は姑（しゅうとめ）に「お食事でござい
ます」と告げたが、核家族では「ご飯よ」でも済んでしまう。

**Sansedai dōkyo jidai ni wa yome wa shūtome ni 'o-shokuji de
gozaimasu' to tsugeta ga, kakukazoku de wa 'go-han yo' de
mo sunde shimau.**

In the times when three generations lived under one roof, the wife
would say to the mother-in-law 'Your dinner is served', but in the
nuclear family 'Dinner!' is sufficient.

c ご自身に対する警備が厳しすぎると感想をもらされたこともある。

**Go-jishin ni taisuru keibi ga kibishi-sugiru to kansō o
morasareta koto mo aru.**

He [= member of the Imperial family] once commented that he felt
that he (*lit.* "Honorific himself") was being guarded too strictly.

## 1.8.2 | *Nouns referring to a person's actions or belongings*

These are typically used in **o/go-V-stem ni naru** and **o/go-V-stem suru**,
where V-stem is a verbal noun (see 1.9). With **o/go-V-stem ni naru/kudasai**,
the verbal refers to the subject's actions, and with **o/go-V-stem suru** to an
action the subject performs for a second/third person (see 16.1.1, 16.2.1).

## 1.8.3 | *Nouns used as euphemisms*

These are mostly nouns that have to do with eating, drinking, the toilet,
etc. in general, i.e. they do not refer to anyone's action. Typically, these
nouns attach the prefixes **o-** or **go-**, and some also contain honorific verbs.
They fall into three main groups as follows:

o-cha 'tea', o-hashi 'chopsticks', o-miyage 'gift', o-tearai 'toilet', o-sake 'alcoholic drink', o-kane 'money', o-tsuri 'change'.

go-fujō 'toilet', go-han 'food', 'meal'.

o-meshimono (this is honorific for kimono) 'apparel', mesu being an irregular honorific verb for kiru).

## 1.8.4 Nouns used when speaking to children ("motherese")

Mothers and other, usually female, siblings of small children often use 'children's talk' when conversing. Examples include parts of the body like o-meme 'eyes' and o-tete 'hands' (instead of me and te), nouns that are normally used to denote an action (even when suru is not attached), such as an'yo (suru) 'walk', nenne (suru) 'sleep/go to sleep', o-shikko (suru) 'pee'. The last one has gained common currency, even among men (in informal situations).

## 1.9 Verbal nouns

Verbal nouns are similar to English –ing forms such as *swimming* in that their meaning incorporates an action; thus they can attach the verb suru 'do' and in this form they can be used like verbs.

There are two ways of forming verbal nouns.

1 by detaching suru from a Sino-Japanese or Western-Japanese suru noun.
2 for many verbs, by forming the stem form (see 7.1.2.3).

## 1.9.1 Sino-Japanese/Western-Japanese/Native-Japanese suru nouns

Many nouns that indicate an action can attach the verb suru to form verbal nouns. This is especially common with SJ, but also WJ and some NJ nouns.

Sino-Japanese:

| | | |
|---|---|---|
| hakken 'discovery' | → | hakken suru 発見する 'discover' |
| kenkyū 'research' | → | kenkyū suru 研究する 'do research' |
| ryōri 'cooking' | → | ryōri suru 料理する 'cook' |
| setsumei 'explanation' | → | setsumei suru 説明する 'explain' |

*Note* – Verbal nouns that have the meaning of 'become' in their **suru** form have an adjectival meaning in their **-te iru** form:

| | | |
|---|---|---|
| **antei suru** 'become stable' | → | **antei shite iru** 'be stable' |
| **dokuritsu suru** 'become independent' | → | **dokuritsu shite iru** 'be independent' |
| **hattatsu suru** 'become developed' | → | **hattatsu shite iru** 'be developed' |

In their **-ta** form (**antei shita** N, etc.), these can be used to modify other nouns (see 6.6.7).

Native-Japanese:

| | | |
|---|---|---|
| **yama-nobori** 'mountaineering' | → | **yama-nobori suru** 山登りする 'climb mountains' |

Western-Japanese:

| | | |
|---|---|---|
| **bokushingu** 'boxing' | → | **bokushingu suru** ボクシングする 'box' |
| **kanningu** 'cheating in an exam' | → | **kanningu suru** カンニングする 'cheat in exam' |

Verbal nouns can insert adverbial particles (**wa, mo, sae, sura, bakari,** etc.) for emphasis between the noun and **suru** (see 9).

a いい仕事さえすれば、論文発表の機会はいくらでもある。
  **Ii shigoto sae sureba, ronbun happyō no kikai wa ikura demo aru.**
  As long as you do good work, you'll have plenty of opportunities to present papers.

### 1.9.2 Using verb-stem of many verbs

Forming the verb-stem (the noun form of many verbs) is possible with most verbs.

Verbal nouns are especially common in the pattern [V-stem **ni iku/kuru**] (see 2.4.10).

### 1.10 Nominalizing suffixes

Besides plural suffixes (1.3) and personal suffixes (1.4.4), there are suffixes that convert adjectives or verbs into nouns.

## 1.10.1 Adjective into noun

### 1.10.1.1 -sa

Adjective-root + **sa**/**na**-adjective (minus copula) + **sa** convert an adjective or **na**-adjective into a noun. This is a very productive formation, being possible with practically any adjective or **na**-adjective. **-sa** nominalizations are used in sentences that require a noun as predicate, i.e. equational, cleft and noun sentences (see 22), or for occupying the noun-slot in noun+case particle combinations, as in examples d–e.

a 六十九歳とは思えない若々しさだ。(cf., 若々しい **wakawakashii** 'youthful')

**Rokujūkyū-sai to wa omoenai wakawakashi-sa da.**

He's so youthful that it's hard to think he's 69 (*lit.* "it's a youthfulness which makes it hard …").

b 日本では考えられない速さだ。(cf., 速い **hayai** 'speedy')

**Nihon de wa kangaerarenai haya-sa da.**

The speed [of establishing a shareholding company] is unthinkable in Japan.

c ただし、大画面テレビはもう一つの問題を浮かび上がらせる。日本の住宅の狭さだ。(cf., 狭い **semai** 'small')

**Tadashi, dai-gamen terebi wa mō hitotsu no mondai o ukabiagaraseru. Nihon no jūtaku no sema-sa da.**

However, there's another problem with large-screen TVs. It's the smallness of Japanese homes.

d 安さだけでは顧客に満足してもらえない時代になった。(cf., 安い **yasui** 'cheap')

**Yasu-sa dake de wa kokyaku ni manzoku shite moraenai jidai ni natta.**

It's (*lit.* "become") an age where cheapness isn't enough to satisfy customers.

e サッカーの陽気さは、祈ったあとの迷いのない陽気さだ。(cf., 陽気な **yōki (na)** 'exuberant')

**Sakkā no yōki-sa wa, inotta ato no mayoi no nai yōki-sa da.**

The exuberance of soccer is an exuberance that knows no wavering, like that after praying.

| 1.10.1.2 | -mi

Some adjectives proper also have noun forms ending in -**mi**. These are derived by adding -**mi** to Adj-root. Examples include **tsuyomi** 'strength', **yowami** 'weakness', **kayumi** 'itch'.

Whereas the -**sa** forms are simple nominalizations, the -**mi** forms tend to have some idiomatic meaning. Compare the examples below for the difference between **tsuyosa** 'strength' (example a) and **tsuyomi** 'strength', 'strong point' (example b).

a 常緑樹の緑は、厳冬を乗り越える命の強さを象徴するのだそうだ。

**Jōrokuju no midori wa, gentō o norikoeru inochi no tsuyosa
o shōchō suru no da sō da.**

The green of evergreen trees is said to symbolize the strength of life
in getting through severe winters.

b 日本のサッカーに慣れているのも強みだ。

**Nihon no sakkā ni narete iru no mo tsuyomi da.**

One of his strong points is that he is used to Japanese soccer.

| 1.10.1.3 | Adjective-**ku**

A very small number of adjectives also has a noun form which uses the
stem form, ending in -**ku**. This is limited to a select number of adjectives
that relate to distance, time, and amount, **tōku** 'distance', **chikaku** 'vicinity', **furuku** 'of old' and **ōku** 'plenty'.

*Note 1* – in its noun form (as opposed to its adjective -**ku** use, see Notes 2 and
3), ōku is used only to modify other nouns by means of **no** in the sense of 'many'.

**tōku**, **chikaku** and **furuku** can also attach other case or adverbial particles
besides modifying other nouns by means of the **no**.

*Note 2* – these forms can of course also be used as conjunctive form
equivalents of Adj. (see 21.1.1).

*Note 3* – **chikaku** can also be used as an adverb in the sense of 'soon'.

a 女性は近くの銀行で現金を引き出した後、息子の家まで歩いて行
くところだったという。

**Josei wa chikaku no ginkō de genkin o hikidashita ato,
musuko no ie made aruite iku tokoro datta to iu.**

The woman says that she was about to walk to her son's house after
having withdrawn some cash from a nearby bank.

b 近くにいるより遠くから見たほうが目立つ。

**Chikaku ni iru yori tōku kara mita hō ga medatsu.**

It [= the clock] is more impressive when seen from a distance rather
than close to.

| 1.10.2 | *Verb → noun*

| 1.10.2.1 | **-kata**

Attached to V-stem, -kata converts the verb it is attached to into a noun
with the meaning of 'way of doing'.

a これが一番おいしい食べ方です。

**Kore ga ichiban oishii tabe-kata desu.**

This is the best way of eating [it].

b これがこの国でのやり方だ。

**Kore ga kono kuni de no yari-kata da.**

This is the way things are done in this country.

c 百貨店には百貨店の売り方がありますから。

**Hyakkaten ni wa hyakkaten no uri-kata ga arimasu kara.**

Department stores have their own way of selling things, you know.

d 英語による俳句の作り方について講演会などを催す。

**Eigo ni yoru haiku no tsukuri-kata ni tsuite kōenkai nado o
   moyōsu.**

They give classes in how to compose haiku in English.

e 養蚕農家の減り方はすさまじいほどだ。

**Yōsan nōka no heri-kata wa susamajii hodo da.**

The rate at which silk farmers are disappearing is appalling.

| 1.10.2.2 | **-yō**

-yō converts a verb (V-stem) into a noun. It is used in three ways, as set
out in the following sections.

Verb-stem-**yō**

The combination means 'way of doing'.

a 同店の栗原美弥子さん（46）は「今日の光（こう）ちゃんは本当
の笑顔を見せてくれた」と手放しの喜びようだ。

**Dōten no Kurihara Miyako-san (yonjūroku) wa 'Kyō no
Kō-chan wa hontō no egao o misete kureta' to tebanashi
no yorokobi-yō da.**

Ms Miyako Kurihara (46) of the same store is overjoyed, saying,
'Today, Kō-chan had a really radiant look'.

b 姫路っ子は古くからお城とともに生きてきた。それぞれの時代を
守りぬいてきたなじみのお城が一躍「世界の宝」にリストアッ
プされたのだから、その喜びようは推して知るべしである。

**Himeji-kko wa furuku kara o-shiro to tomo ni ikite kita.
Sorezore no jidai o mamori-nuite kita najimi no oshiro ga
ichiyaku 'sekai no takara' ni risutoappu sareta no da kara,
sono yorokobi-yō wa oshite shiru-beshi de aru.**

The inhabitants of Himeji have lived with their castle for a long time.
As the familiar castle, which has watched over the various ages, has
suddenly been listed a 'world treasure', you can imagine their delight
(*lit.* "way of showing joy").

Verb-stem-**yō ga nai**

In the negative, the meaning is 'there is no way of doing'.

a おカネがないのだから、ほかに考えようがない。

**Okane ga nai no da kara, hoka ni kangae-yō ga nai.**

[Issuing deficit government bonds:] Since we don't have any money,
there is nothing else that can be considered.

b 気候だけは手の打ちようがない。

**Kikō dake wa te no uchi-yō ga nai.**

Whatever else, about the weather there is nothing one can do.

c 初耳だ。コメントのしようがない。

**Hatsumimi da. Komento no shi-yō ga nai.**

This is the first time I've heard about this. I can't comment.

d ビビッドのつづりが分からない、いやその前に何語かわからない
  ので意味の確かめようがない。

  **Bibiddo no tsuzuri ga wakaranai, iya sono mae ni nanigo ka
  wakaranai no de imi no tashikame-yō ga nai.**

  I have no way of checking the meaning of 'bibiddo', because I don't
  know how it is spelt, and before that I don't know [from] what
  language it comes.

| 1.10.2.2.3 | **Verb-te shiyō ga nai** |
| --- | --- |

Note that **shiyō** itself is a combination of **shi** (V-stem of **suru**) + **yō**. The
literal meaning is therefore "there is no way of doing (anything about)
V-ing", i.e. 'can't help doing'.

a 涙が流れてしようがない。

  **Namida ga nagarete shiyō ga nai.**

  I cannot help tears running down [my face].

*Note* – the expression **shiyō ga nai** (often contracted to **shō ga nai**) and
its partial synonym **shikata ga nai** are extremely common by themselves,
meaning 'it can't be helped', 'there's nothing that can be done', 'never
mind', etc.

# Chapter 2

# Case particles

Case particles indicate the semantic or logical relationship of nouns or nominal elements they follow with other parts of a sentence.

## 2.1 ga

**ga** generally marks the subject of a sentence (but with certain predicates it translates into English like an object).

**ga** is often contrasted with the adverbial particle **wa**, and the distinction in usage between the two is said to be one of the most difficult problems facing the foreign learner of the language (see 11.3).

Depending on the type of sentence, **ga** also contrasts with some other case particles (see 2.1.4, 2.1.5).

The various uses of **ga** as a subject marker relate to its basic meaning, which can be characterized as perception. This in turn derives from the fact that **ga** used to be a genitive particle. This use is still found in some place names, and other fossilized uses.

a 霞ヶ関
   **Kasumigaseki** (*lit.* "barrier of haze", name of an area in central Tokyo; ヶ is an alternative way of writing **ga**)

b 我が家
   **wagaya**
   Our home (*lit.* "I + genitive particle + house")

When used with a following verb instead of a noun, the combination also functions like a noun phrase, i.e. **yuki ga furu** means 'snow falling' or 'the falling of snow', perceiving a phenomenon or event piecemeal. **wa**, on the other hand, splits a sentence in two, the second half being a considered judgement of the first (see 11.3, 11.3.12).

### 2.1.1 | With one-place verb/adjective

With a one-place (i.e. intransitive) verb, or adjective, **ga** marks the subject of a spontaneous happening or phenomenon (examples b–e).

a 涙が出た。(= spontaneous happening)
**Namida ga deta.**
Tears came to my eyes (*lit.* "tears came out").

b 空が暗くなった。
**Sora ga kuraku natta.**
The sky darkened.

c 頭が混乱してきました。
**Atama ga konran shite kimashita.**
I'm confused (*lit.* "my head has got confused").

d 時間が止まったようだった。
**Jikan ga tomatta yō datta.**
It was as if time had stopped.

e 日本海側では雪が降った。
**Nihonkai-gawa de wa yuki ga futta.**
On the Japan Sea side, it snowed (*lit.* "snow fell").

### 2.1.2 | With ellipted ga

Colloquially, **ga** is often ellipted.

a 今夜はお父さん帰ってこないの。
**Kon'ya wa otōsan kaette konai no.**
Tonight, hubby's not coming home.

### 2.1.3 | With ellipted predicate

Where the context makes it clear what the meaning is, the predicate can be omitted.

a しかし、だれが、なぜ。

**Shikashi, dare ga, naze.**

But who [did this], [and] why?

**ga *in potential sentences***

**ga** in a potential sentence usually marks the NP that would be marked by **o** in its non-potential counterpart. In English, this translates as the object of the potential verb.

The potential verb **dekiru** originally means 'to happen', so potential sentences can be seen to be related to the basic (= spontanous happening) meaning of **ga**.

Note that in potential sentences also using the comparative **hō ga** (example c), **ga** is used twice in a sentence. The object particle **o** can also be used with potential verbs (example d), which gives it a more objective ring.

a 勝つゴルフが出来ない。

**Katsu gorufu ga dekinai.**

I can't play winning golf.

b もう暑いところでは研究ができない。

**Mō atsui tokoro de wa kenkyū ga dekinai.**

I can't do research in hot climates (*lit.* "places") any more.

c ワイドな画面の方が動きが楽しめるためだ。

**Waido na gamen no hō ga ugoki ga tanoshimeru tame da.**

This is because movement can be enjoyed better on a wide screen.

d 露天ぶろのように入浴を楽しめる。

**Rotenburo no yō ni nyūyoku o tanoshimeru.**

One can enjoy the bath like [being in] an outside bath.

**ga *in desiderative sentences***

In desiderative sentences (**hoshii/-tai**), **ga** marks the object of desire (see 9.2), again as a spontanous indication of the speaker's wish.

In English, this translates as the object of a desiderative verb. Alternatively, the object of desire in these sentences can be marked by **o** (see 2.2.3, 9.2), which gives the sentence a more objective ring.

a 何か、刺激がほしい。
**Nani ka, shigeki ga hoshii.**
I want some stimulus.

b 本を五、六冊書く時間がほしい。
**Hon o go, roku-satsu kaku jikan ga hoshii.**
I want the time to write five or six books.

c ほかの仕事がやりたい。
**Hoka no shigoto ga yari-tai.**
I want to do a different job.

d すごく大きい。早く飛行機が見たい。
**Sugoku ōkii. Hayaku hikōki ga mi-tai.**
It [the airport]'s so big. I want to see the aeroplanes soon.

e 海外の反応が早く知りたい。
**Kaigai no hannō ga hayaku shiritai.**
I want to find out quickly about reactions abroad.

f 「肉やお菓子が食べたい」と笑う。
**'Niku ya o-kashi ga tabe-tai' to warau.**
'I want to eat meat and cakes', she laughs.

g いっしょに笑い、いっしょに泣けるような結婚がしたい。
**Issho ni warai, issho ni nakeru yō na kekkon ga shitai.**
I want a marriage where we can laugh and cry together.

---

**2.1.6** | **ga *in passive sentences***

In a passive sentence, **ga** marks the NP that would be marked by **o** in its active counterpart (see 12).

a また、インド洋でも海水温度の上昇が報告されている。
**Mata, Indoyō de mo kaisui ondo no jōshō ga hōkoku sarete iru.**
Furthermore, in the Indian Ocean a rise in the sea temperature has been reported.

b 僕ひとりが認められたんじゃない。
**Boku hitori ga mitomerareta n ja nai.**
I wasn't the only one to receive recognition.

| 2.1.7 | **ga** *marking the preceding subject noun/noun phrase* |

**ga** has been explained as providing emphasis to the noun or noun phrase it is attached to (shown in [ ]); when comparing **ga** and **wa** in subject position, **wa** has the effect of subduing the noun/NP it is attached to by focussing on the predicate, and in that sense **ga** is *comparatively* more concerned with the item it is attached to (see 11.3, 11.3.12 for details).

a これが一番おいしい食べ方です。
   **[Kore] ga ichiban oishii tabekata desu.**
   This is the best way of eating [it].

b ほとんどが家庭の主婦だ。
   **[Hotondo] ga katei no shufu da.**
   Almost all are housewives.

c 警察庁によると、今年に入っていじめが原因と推定される子供の自殺
   事件は未遂を含め計八件起きた。このうち六人が死亡している。
   **Keisatsu-chō ni yoru to, kotoshi ni haitte ijime ga gen'in to
   suitei sareru kodomo no jisatsu jiken wa misui o fukume
   kei hakken okita. Kono uchi [rokunin] ga shibō shite iru.**
   According to the police agency, this year there has been a total of
   eight cases of child suicide, including attempted ones, which are
   assumed to have been caused by bullying. Six of them have died.

d キャベツ、タマネギ、ニンジン、ハクサイなどが主な品目だ。
   **[Kyabetsu, tamanegi, ninjin, hakusai nado] ga omo na hinmoku da.**
   Cabbages, onions, carrots, Chinese cabbage, etc. are the main items.

| 2.1.8 | **ga** *in comparative/superlative sentences:*
*marking the preferred item (= subject)* |

Similar in effect to its use in 2.1.7, **ga** marks the item singled out as having some property or quality to a larger/the largest extent in comparative (often together with **hō**) and superlative sentences (see 6.7.1.1, 6.7.2.3).

| 2.1.8.1 | *Noun* **ga** |

a 豚肉より牛肉の方が安い。
   **Butaniku yori gyūniku no hō ga yasui.**
   Beef is cheaper than pork.

b 牛肉が豚肉より安い―。
   **Gyūniku ga butaniku yori yasui--.**
   Beef is cheaper than pork.

c 今が一番、仕事がおもしろい時期だ。
   **Ima ga ichiban, shigoto ga omoshiroi jiki da.**
   Now is the time when work is most interesting.

d お客様が一番正直です。
   **O-kyaku-sama ga ichiban shōjiki desu.**
   Customers don't lie (*lit.* "are the most honest").

---

2.1.8.2 | *Adverbial clause-**te ga***

**ga** can attach to an adverbial clause ending in the conjunctive form, which can function in the same way as a noun phrase, i.e. occupies the noun slot in comparative/superlative sentences. The -**te** clause (underlined) indicates a state (see 6.6.3.3).

a やっぱり夫婦そろってが一番？
   **yappari fūfu sorotte ga ichiban?**
   After all, husband and wife [= going to the movies] together is best?

---

2.1.9 | **ga *attached to question word in subject position***

In questions that have a question word as subject, the Q-word always attaches **ga**, never **wa** (there are some exceptions to this, but this is limited to set expressions such as **nani wa nakutomo** 'in any case', **nani wa tomo are** 'whatever else', or 'above all', etc.). Example a shows the latter case.

a ズボンの二本の足をストラップ（布ベルト）で結んだらどうなる
   か？何はともあれ歩きにくくなることだけは確実だ。
   **Zubon no nihon no ashi o sutorappu (nuno-beruto) de**
   **musundara dō naru ka? Nani wa tomo are aruki-nikuku**
   **naru koto dake wa kakujitsu da.**
   What happens if you tie the two trouser legs together with a strap (a cloth belt)? Whatever else, it becomes more difficult to walk.

After Q-words, much like the use of **ga** in 2.1.7 and 2.1.8, the effect has been explained as emphasis on the Q-word (where/what/who, etc). Strictly speaking, it is however the whole [Q-word **ga** N/V] phrase. Note also the combinations [Q-word **mo ga**] 'every', and [Q-word **ga** . . . -**te/de mo**] (see 5.2).

43

b 何が問題なのか。
**Nani ga mondai na no ka.**
What is the problem?

c 背景には何があるのか。
**Haikei ni wa nani ga aru no ka.**
What is in the background [to this]?

d アジア女性の何が日本人に受けているのだろうか。
**Ajia josei no nani ga Nihonjin ni ukete iru no darō ka.**
What is it about Asian women that makes them popular with the Japanese?

e 「ユキヒコ、バーカ」「何がバカだよっ」。
**'Yukihiko, bāka' 'Nani ga baka da yo"**
'Yukihiko, you fool!' 'What do you mean, "fool"?'

f 一体だれがカネを払ってると思ってるんだー。
**Ittai dare ga kane o haratteru to omotteru n da--.**
Who the hell do they think is paying! [= we are!]

g 経済はだれがやっても同じでしょ。
**Keizai wa dare ga yatte mo onaji desho.**
The economy should be the same, no matter who runs it.

h だれが見てもよくわかる自然な人事をやる。
**Dare ga mite mo yoku wakaru shizen na jinji o yaru.**
His staff appointments are natural, understandable by all.

i 中古部品をだれが買うのか。
**Chūko buhin o dare ga kau no ka.**
Who is going to buy second-hand parts!

## 2.1.10 *(Noun ni) ga aru/iru: ga in existential/locational sentences*

This indicates existence or location (see 2.4.4, 2.4.5, 7.6.1.9). From the 'existence' meaning, a 'possession' meaning flows naturally, as can be seen from the literal translations of examples a and b. Perception of existence is something that can be understood from the basic nature of **ga**.

a 妻と二男がいる。
**Tsuma to ninan ga iru.**
[He has] a wife and two sons. (*lit.* "there is/are a wife and two sons")

b この発言には重みがある。
**Kono hatsugen ni wa omomi ga aru.**
This statement has weight. (*lit.* "In this statement, there is weight")

c 著書に「日本児童演劇史」などがある。
**Chosho ni 'Nihon jidō engekishi' nado ga aru.**
Among his books is 'A history of child acting in Japan'.

d 三階には宿泊客共通の浴場がある。
**Sangai ni wa shukuhaku-kyaku kyōtsū no yokujō ga aru.**
On the third floor is a bath for shared use by lodgers.

## 2.1.11 ga in 'double-subject' (noun wa noun ga) sentences

This is a common sentence type in Japanese (see 7.6.1.8), and is known as a 'double-subject' sentence, because both **wa** and **ga** mark NPs that are like grammatical subjects.

However, the first NP-**wa** is more like a topic which is followed by a [NP-**ga** predicate] comment (see 11.3.8). The second NP also can look like an object in English translation, as in example 2.1.12 a.

a 古代は個人が主体だった。
**Kodai wa kojin ga shutai datta.**
In antiquity, the individual was central.

b スペインと浜松は共通項が多い。
**Supein to Hamamatsu wa kyōtsūkō ga ōi.**
Spain and Hamamatsu have a lot of things in common.

c イタリアとギリシャは統計がない。
**Itaria to Girisha wa tōkei ga nai.**
For Italy and Greece, there are no statistics.

d 今年のプレゼントは、パパがカシミヤのマフラー。
**Kotoshi no purezento wa, papa ga kashimiya no mafurā.**
For this year's [Christmas] present, hubby [gets] a cashmere muffler.

## 2.1.12 ga in 'double-subject' (noun wa noun ga) sentences with ellipted noun wa

a 空が好き。体を動かすのが好き。人と話すのがもっと好き。
**Sora ga suki. Karada o ugokasu no ga suki. Hito to hanasu no ga motto suki.**
'[I] like the sky. [I] like moving my body. Talking with people [I] like even more.'

## 2.1.13 ga *marking the subject in a noun-modifying clause*

The subject of a noun-modifying clause is usually marked by **ga** or **no** in both complement clauses (2.1.13.1) and relative clauses (2.1.13.2) (see 22, 2.3.2). This use of **ga**, where **ga** connects a noun or NP with a following verb, with the combination (shown in [ ]) modifying a following nominalizer such as **koto,** or another noun, is again in line with the basic meaning of the particle.

### 2.1.13.1 *Complement clauses*

a 「生存者がいたことは幸運だった」と話している。

  **'[Seizonsha ga ita] koto wa kōun datta' to hanashite iru.**

  They are saying, 'It was lucky that there were survivors'.

### 2.1.13.2 *Relative clauses*

The first example below has first a N-modifying clause (in [ ]) marked by **ga**, then another N-modifying clause (in [ ]) marked by **no**.

a 誰も彼が来たことに[気のつく]者はいなかった。

  **Dare mo [kare ga kita] koto ni [ki no tsuku] mono wa inakatta.**

  There was nobody who noticed that he had come.

b 外国人犯罪が増える 最大の背景は日本の豊かさだ。

  **[Gaikokujin hanzai ga fueru] saidai no haikei wa Nihon no yutakasa da.**

  The biggest reason why crimes by foreigners are on the increase is Japan's affluence.

## 2.1.14 ga *marking a nominalized clause*

Like **no, ga** can also mark a nominalized clause (complement or relative clause) that occupies subject position in the sentence (see 22, 2.3.2).

a いい演奏をするのが私の仕事だ。

  **[Ii ensō o suru no] ga watashi no shigoto da.**

  Giving a good performance is my job.

b いじめの責任者探しもさることながら、子供の世界で何が失われ
たかを見詰めることが大事ではないか。まず、[目を向けるべ
きなの] が都市である。

**Ijime no sekininsha-sagashi mo saru koto-nagara, kodomo
no sekai de nani ga ushinawareta ka o mitsumeru koto ga
daiji de wa nai ka. Mazu, [me o mukeru-beki na no] ga
toshi de aru.**

It's one thing to look for those responsible for bullying, but it's also
important to take a hard look at what has gone missing from the
children's world. What we need to direct our attention to first are
the cities.

c [何より印象的なの] が、カメラの位置が低いことだ。

**[Nani yori inshō-teki na no] ga, kamera no ichi ga hikui
koto da.**

What's interesting above all is the low position of the camera.

## 2.2 o

The basic function of **o** is marking the object of the sentence, but there
are also some uses where it is interchangeable with **ga** (2.1.4 and 2.1.5),
and with verbs of motion (2.2.4 and 2.2.5).

### 2.2.1 Marking the object

The basic function of the case particle **o** is to mark the object of verbs,
and certain **na**-adjectives. Note that **na**-adjectives like **suki/kirai**, which
usually require [NP-**ga**] can take [NP-**o**] instead (see 6.5.3).

#### 2.2.1.1 In complete sentences

a 腕時計を見せてくれ。

**Udedokei o misete kure.**

Show me [some] wristwatches.

b ドラフトで三人の投手を獲得した。

**Dorafuto de san-nin no tōshu o kakutoku shita.**

In the draft they acquired three pitchers.

47

c 音楽の偉大さを感じた。
**Ongaku no idaisa o kanjita.**
I felt the power of music.

d きっかけは「人を好きになって、恋をしたから」。
**Kikkake wa 'hito o suki ni natte, koi o shita kara'.**
It all began 'because I grew fond of someone, and fell in love'.

---

2.2.1.2 | With ellipted **o**

Colloquially, **o** can be ellipted (omitted). In writing, sometimes a comma is used to indicate this, but in speech there is usually no pause.

a 何、話しましょうか‥‥‥。
**Nani, hanashimashō ka ...**
What shall I talk about? ...

b あなた、ドレス買ってもいい?
**Anata, doresu katte mo ii?**
Darling, is it OK if I buy a dress?

---

2.2.1.3 | With ellipted predicate

With ellipted (omitted) predicate, the implication is one of request or wish for realization.

a 国際化と「アメリカ化」との差別化を。
**Kokusai-ka to 'Amerika-ka' to no sabetsu-ka o.**
A distinction [should be] made between internationalization and 'Americanization'.

b 教師にこそ、もっと自由をと言いたい。
**Kyōshi ni koso, motto jiyū o to iitai.**
Especially to the teachers I'd like to say that they should give themselves more freedom.

---

2.2.2 | **In potential sentences**

The object of a potential verb can be marked with **o** instead of the more usual **ga** (see 2.1.4, 14).

a　なぜ調和を保てるのか。

**Naze chōwa o tamoteru no ka.**

Why can they [= body cells] maintain the balance?

---

**2.2.3** | *In desiderative sentences*

The object of a desiderative sentence can be marked with **o** instead of the more common **ga** (see 2.1.5, 9.2).

In the following examples, **ga** could be used instead of **o** in example a without any change in meaning, but not in b, d and e, where the V is one of 'wishing', which is more strongly transitive in nature. In examples d and e, **o** is marking nominalized clauses (see 22).

a　ピアノを習いたい。

**Piano o narai-tai.**

I want to learn the piano.

b　…この地の利を生かしたい。

**…kono chi no ri o ikashi-tai.**

…we want to make the best use of the benefits of the area.

c　テレビでも研究が紹介され、「出演者の一人がこのシステムをほ
　　しいと話していた」。

**Terebi de mo kenkyū ga shōkai sare, 'Shutsuen-sha no hitori
　ga kono shisutemu o hoshii to hanashite ita'.**

The research was taken up on TV too, and 'one of the people on the
　programme said he wanted this system'.

d　平和が続くことを祈りたい。

**Heiwa ga tsuzuku koto o inori-tai.**

I hope that the peace will last.

e　意欲的な試みが続くことを期待したい。

**Iyoku-teki na kokoromi ga tsuzuku koto o kitai shitai.**

I'd like to hope that this enterprising experiment will continue.

---

**2.2.4** | *Marking the object of a verb of motion*

**o** here indicates the route by which the action of the verb takes place. In English, this often translates as a preposition 'through', 'across', 'along', etc.

Compare this to the case particle **de**, which indicates the place where the action happens without any implication that it involves passing through or following a route (see 2.5.1.1).

a 夜道を歩くのは不安だが、···
**Yomichi o aruku no wa fuan da ga ...**
Walking the street at night makes me feel uneasy, but ...

b 一日平均七百台の車がここを通る見込み。
**Ichinichi heikin nanahyaku-dai no kuruma ga koko o tōru mikomi.**
It is expected that an average 700 cars per day will pass through here.

---

### 2.2.5 | Marking departure point of a verb of motion

o can also mark the departure point ('out of', 'from') of the action of a verb of motion (see 2.7.4, 2.8).

a 部長に頭を下げて、部屋を出た。
**Buchō ni atama o sagete, heya o deta.**
I bowed to the department head and left the room.

b 起きてから家を出るまでの所要時間は女性の方が長い。
**Okite kara ie o deru made no shoyō jikan wa josei no hō ga nagai.**
As for the time [required] from getting up to leaving the house, women take longer.

---

## 2.3 | no

no is a case particle that can be used either as genitive (or associative) particle between nouns and noun-like units, or subject marker in noun-modifying clauses (see also 6.4).

### 2.3.1 | Genitive or associative particle

#### 2.3.1.1 | Noun 1 no noun 2

Used to modify a following noun (N2) with a preceding noun (N1), N1 no describes N2 in a variety of meanings, including location (example a), ownership (example b), authorship (example c), place of production or provenance (example d), material made of, genitive proper (example e), and many more. This is why **no** is sometimes called an 'associative particle', i.e. a particle that connects nouns and noun-like units in a wide variety of meanings; most typical is perhaps the meaning shown in 2.3.1.10 – examples of apposition of the two nouns. Note that the main (or modified) noun is always N2.

*Note* – there are examples where there is more than one N + **no**, i.e. N1 **no** N2 **no** N3 (example i), or even N1 **no** N2 **no** N3 **no** N4 (example j).

a 駅の電話
  **eki no denwa**
  a/the phone at the station

b 私の宝物
  **watashi no takaramono**
  my treasure

c 大江健三郎の小説
  **Ōe Kenzaburō no shōsetsu**
  a/the novel by Kenzaburo Ōe

d 日本のカメラ
  **Nihon no kamera**
  a Japanese camera

e 日本人の主食
  **Nihonjin no shushoku**
  the staple food of the Japanese

f 女の弁護士
  **onna no bengoshi**
  a female lawyer

g ユニホームの野茂投手
  **yunihōmu no Nomo tōshu**
  pitcher Nomo in uniform

h 税金の問題
  **zeikin no mondai**
  the tax problem(s)

i 日本の住宅の狭さ
  **Nihon no jūtaku no semasa**
  the smallness of Japanese homes

j ・・・結婚した後のC子さんの最近の話題は、夫や子供など「家庭ネタ」ばかり。

…**kekkon shita ato no C-ko-san no saikin no wadai wa, otto ya kodomo nado 'katei-neta' bakari.**

…C-ko's recent conversation topics since she got married are all 'domestic' ones about her husband and the children.

---

**2.3.1.2** | *Noun 1* **no** *noun 2 (noun 1/noun 2 = time noun)*

Either N1 or N2, or both, can be time nouns.

a 来年の10月ごろ
**rainen no jūgatsu goro**
around October of next year

b 日曜の正午すぎ
**nichiyō no shōgo sugi**
past noon on Sunday

c 最近の若者
**saikin no wakamono**
the young of recent times

d 現在の状態
**genzai no jōtai**
the present state

---

**2.3.1.3** | *Noun 1* **no** *noun 2 (noun 2 = verbal noun)*

Here, N2 being a verbal noun, an action is implied (= English V-ing).

a この工場ではハムの製造を行っている。(cf., 製造する **seizō suru** 'make')
**Kono kōjō de wa hamu no seizō o okonatte iru.**
In this factory they make (*lit.* "engage in the making of") ham.

b 引っ越したばかりで、部屋の整理ができていない。(cf., 整理する **seiri suru** 'put in order')
**Hikkoshita bakari de, heya no seiri ga dekite inai.**
As he has just moved, the room hasn't been put in order (*lit.* "the ordering of the room hasn't been achieved").

---

**2.3.1.4** | *Noun 1* **no** *noun 2 (noun 1 = noun of quantity (+ counter))*

Apart from numerals and/or counters, some adverbs of degree can also be used in this way (see 4, 10.2.2).

a 100円の切手
**hyakuen no kitte**
a hundred-yen stamp

b 10歳の子供
**jussai no kodomo**
a 10-year old child

c 一台の新車
**ichidai no shinsha**
a/one new car

d 60ワットの電球
**rokujūwatto no denkyū**
a 60W light bulb

e 一つの試み
**hitotsu no kokoromi**
an/one experiment

f たくさんのプレゼント
**takusan no purezento**
many presents

---

2.3.1.5 **X-bun no** Y (Y = number): indicating a fraction

Literally, the meaning is "Y out of X parts", and is used to indicate a fraction (see 4.4).

a 三分の二
**sanbun no ni**
two-thirds

b 十分の一
**jūbun no ichi**
one-tenth

c コップ半分の水を「半分しかない」と考えるか「半分もある」
と思うか。
**Koppu hanbun no mizu o 'hanbun shika nai' to kangaeru ka
'hanbun mo aru' to omou ka.**
Whether to think of half a cup of water as 'only half', or to feel that
'there's as much as half'.

---

2.3.1.6 Demonstrative pronoun **no** noun

Instead of N1, a demonstrative pronoun is used, which in Japanese functions similarly to a noun (see 5.1).

a ここの家の主人
**koko no ie no shujin**
the master of this house

b これらの問題
**korera no mondai**
these problems

| 2.3.1.7 | *Noun 1* **no** *noun 2 (noun 2 = relational noun)* |

The meaning of **no** N2 is similar to preposition + noun in English (see 1.6).

a 箱の中のりんご
**hako no naka no ringo**
(the) apples in the box

b テーブルの上にコーヒーカップを置く。
**Tēburu no ue ni kōhī kappu o oku.**
He puts the coffee cup on the table.

| 2.3.1.8 | *Noun 1* **no** *noun 2 (noun 2 = nominalized verb/adjective)* |

| 2.3.1.8.1 | Noun 1 **no** noun 2 (noun 2 = verb-stem-**kata**) |

**-kata** nominalizes a verb in the sense of 'way of doing' (see 1.10).

a はしの持ち方を練習する。
**Hashi no mochi-kata o renshū suru.**
They practise (*lit.* "the way of") holding chopsticks.

b 山口のやり方はよくない。
**Yamaguchi no yari-kata wa yokunai.**
Yamaguchi's way of doing things is no good.

| 2.3.1.8.2 | Noun 1 **no** noun 2 (noun 2 = adjective-root/**na**-adjective-**sa**) |

**-sa** nominalizes adjectives (see 1.10).

a 旅行かばんの重さを計る。 (cf., 重い **omoi** 'heavy')
**Ryokō kaban no omo-sa o hakaru.**
They check the weight of the travel bag.

b 東京の物価の高さには驚く。 (cf., 高い **takai** 'high')
**Tōkyō no bukka no taka-sa ni wa odoroku.**
One is amazed at the high level (*lit.* "height") of prices in Tokyo.

c 最後に強調したいのは、市民の声の重要さだ。 (cf., 重要（な）
**jūyō** (na) 'important')
**Saigo ni kyōchō shitai no wa, shimin no koe no jūyō-sa da.**
Lastly, what I'd like to emphasize is the importance of the citizens'
voice.

| 2.3.1.9 | *Noun 1* **ya** *noun 2* **nado no** *noun 3* |

Here, N3 is modified by a NP consisting of two nouns linked by **ya** and **nado** in the sense of 'N like . . .', 'N such as' (see 23.2.3, 11.6).

a パステルどフィンガー・ペイントなどの新製品
**pasuteru ya fingā peinto nado no shin-seihin**
new products like pastels and finger paint

b ピカソどゴッホなどの絵が飾られている。
**Pikaso ya Gohho nado no e ga kazararete iru.**
Paintings by Picasso and [Van] Gogh, among others, are displayed.

| 2.3.1.10 | *Noun 1* **no** *noun 2 (noun 1 = noun 2 (apposition))* |

N1 and N2 refer to the same entity; as the main N is N2, [N1 **no**] modifies it, giving further information as to its status, identity, etc. This device, which functions like an apposition, is used when the speaker or writer assumes that the listener or reader doesn't know this information (see 1.2.1).

a 弟の正夫君
**otōto no Masao-kun**
Masao-kun, the younger brother

b 電子部品メーカーの村田製作所独自製品を次々と開発している。
**Denshi buhin mēkā no Murata Seisakusho dokuji seihin o
tsugitsugi to kaihatsu shite iru.**
Murata Seisakusho, the electrical parts manufacturer, is rapidly
developing products unique to them.

| 2.3.1.11 | *Noun 1 particle* **no** *noun 2: 'condensed' noun-modifying phrase* |

Where a statement contains a noun + particle combination indicating the direction or place of action, or participants, etc. in the action (particle = case particle other than **ga/o**, including also phrasal particles such as **to shite** 'as'), this can be 'condensed' to a noun-modifying phrase [N1 particle **no**] N2.

*Note* – where P in the modifying phrase is **ni**, it gets regularly converted to **e** (see 2.6.3).

a 友だちへの手紙　　　　　　　　(←友だちに手紙を書く)
**tomodachi e no tegami**　　　　　**tomodachi ni tegami o kaku**
A/the letter to a/the friend　　　(←write a letter to a friend)

b 父からの電話　　　　　　　　　(←父から電話があった)
**chichi kara no denwa**　　　　　　**chichi kara denwa ga atta**
A phone call from father　　　　(there was a phone call from father)

c 海外でのボランティア活動　　　(←海外でボランティア活動をする)
**kaigai de no borantia**　　　　　**kaigai de borantia katsudō**
　　**katsudō**　　　　　　　　　　　**o suru**
voluntary activities abroad　　　(engage in voluntary activities
　　　　　　　　　　　　　　　　abroad)

d お父さんへのプレゼントはベルトに決めたの。
**Otōsan e no purezento wa beruto ni kimeta no.**
As for the present for father, we decided on a belt.

e 人との親しい付き合いは、五千年程度のウマやネコに比べるとず
っと長い。
**Hito to no shitashii tsukiai wa, gosennen teido no uma ya
neko ni kuraberu to zutto nagai.**
[Dogs:] Close relations with man have been much longer compared to
horses or cats, which [have been] only about 5,000 years.

f 教師としての立場からいろいろ注意をしなければならない。
**Kyōshi to shite no tachiba kara iroiro chūi o shinakereba naranai.**
From the standpoint of a teacher, one must pay attention to a variety
of things.

---

2.3.1.12 | *Indirect quotation* **to no** *noun*

An indirect quotation + quotation particle **to** serves to modify a following
noun by means of **no** in the sense of 'that', 'to the effect that', 'stating
that' (see 21.1.2, 7.6.4.2.2).

a 解散すべきとの強い意見があった。
**Kaisan subeki to no tsuyoi iken ga atta.**
There were strong views, stating that it [= the Diet] should be dissolved.

b 来る必要はないとの返事を受け取った。
**Kuru hitsuyō wa nai to no henji o uketotta.**
I received an answer to the effect that there was no need to come.

| 2.3.1.13 | *Verb-***te no** *noun*

The modified noun indicates an action that took place as a result of the action of the modifying V-**te** phrase, 'after doing V'.

a いろいろ考えての自殺だったのだろう。
**Iroiro kangae-te no jisatsu datta no darō.**
It probably was a suicide [that took place] after considering a variety of things.

b 親と話し合っての決定です。
**Oya to hanashiat-te no kettei desu.**
It is a decision [made] after consultation with my parents.

| **2.3.2** | **Marking subject in a noun-modifying clause**

**no** commonly marks the subject in a noun-modifying clause (shown below in [ ]), which can be a complement clause or relative clause. In this use, **no** can be replaced by **ga** (see 2.1.13, 22).

a 母の作る料理が一番おいしい。
**[Haha no tsukuru] ryōri ga ichiban oishii.**
The food that mother makes is the tastiest.

b イワシのおいしい季節になった。
**[Iwashi no oishii] kisetsu ni natta.**
The season when sardines are tasty has started.

c フランス語のわかる人は少なくない。
**[Furansugo no wakaru] hito wa sukunakunai.**
There are quite a few people who understand French.

| **2.4** | **ni**

The case particle **ni** indicates location, direction (see 2.6), goal, purpose and other indirect objects. In English translation, **ni** often translates as a preposition ('to', 'for', 'over', etc.).

*Note 1* – the combination **ni no** N does not exist (see 2.5).

*Note 2* – the adverbial form of the copula also takes the form **ni**; when used after N, this **ni** is commonly seen in the combinations N **ni suru** and N **ni naru** (see 7.6.1.10).

| 2.4.1 | *With three-place verbs* |

Many three-place verbs (see 7.2) take the case frame **ga-o-ni**, where **ni** marks the indirect object. The ga-phrase, and sometimes the o-phrase are ellipted. When the **ni**-phrase is moved to the beginning of the sentence (is fronted), it often attaches **wa** (example a and c, see also 11.3.1.2).

a 契約者には腕時計などを贈る。
   **Keiyakusha ni wa udedokei nado o okuru.**
   To the contractors, [they] send wristwatches and suchlike.

b 官僚に任せてはおけない。
   **Kanryō ni makasete wa okenai.**
   We can't leave [things] to the bureaucrats.

c プロジェクトには六百人程度をあてる方針だ。
   **Purojekuto ni wa roppyaku-nin teido o ateru hōshin da.**
   The policy is to assign about 600 people to the project.

| 2.4.2 | *With two-place verbs* |

A number of two-place verbs construct with the case frame **ga-ni** (the ga-phrase is often ellipted).

| 2.4.2.1 | *Verbs of motion* |

**ni** marks the goal of a verb of motion or the part (including also nouns of time, example e) affected by its action.

a 学校に行きたい。
   **Gakkō ni ikitai.**
   I want to go to school.

b 来春、東大に移る。
   **Raishun, tōdai ni utsuru.**
   Next year, he will move to Tokyo University.

c まずふろに入りたい。
   **Mazu furo ni hairitai.**
   First, I want a bath (*lit.* "want to enter a bath").

d 足に血が飛び散っていたよ。

**Ashi ni chi ga tobichitte ita yo.**

He had blood splashed over his legs (*lit.* "Blood had splashed over his legs").

e 四月に入ると一転してコメが売れなくなった。

**Shigatsu ni hairu to itten shite kome ga urenaku natta.**

Now we've entered April, rice is suddenly not selling any longer.

---

**2.4.2.2** *Other two-place verbs*

These include **oku** 'put', **oyobu** 'reach', **niru** 'resemble' (see 7.2).

a どこに大画面テレビを置くのか。

**Doko ni daigamen terebi o oku no ka.**

Where does one put a large-screen TV [in a small Japanese home]?

b しかし、まだ洪水は全域に及んでいない。

**Shikashi, mada kōzui wa zen'iki ni oyonde inai.**

However, the flood is not affecting the whole region yet.

c 米国に似てきた。

**Beikoku ni nite kita.**

[The market] is now similar to the US.

*Note* – the V (要る・いる iru) 'need' takes **ni** to mark what something is needed 'for' (example d).

d ザックの詰め方にはコツがいる。

**Zakku no tsumekata ni wa kotsu ga iru.**

Packing a rucksack requires skill. (*lit.* "skill is needed for packing a rucksack.")

---

**2.4.3** **With ellipted predicate**

With ellipted (= omitted) predicate, the implication is that the action of the missing verb has happened (see 27.2).

a より高い背に、より小さな足に。

**Yori takai se ni, yori chiisa na ashi ni.**

[women have developed] taller figures and smaller feet.

b 近畿地方、2日続きの肌寒い朝に。

**Kinki chihō, futsuka tsuzuki no hadazamui asa ni.**

The Kinki region [has faced] the second cold morning in succession.

*Stative location*

With stative verbs, **ni** expresses stative location (for dynamic location see 2.5). Stative location can be expressed in two ways, using the pattern (**wa-**) **ni** V, or **ni-ga** V.

2.4.4.1 *Noun* **wa** *noun* **ni** *predicate*

a 経団連は東京にある。
   **Keidanren wa Tōkyō ni aru.**
   The Keidanren (Federation of Economic Organizations) is in Tokyo.

b 答えはこのページの右下にあります。
   **Kotae wa kono pēji no migishita ni arimasu.**
   The answer is [found] at the bottom right of this page.

2.4.4.2 *Noun* **ni** *noun* **ga** *predicate*

This indicates existence or location (see 2.1.10, 7.4.1).

a 外に女性がいる。
   **Soto ni josei ga iru.**
   There is a woman outside.

b 三階には宿泊客共通の浴場がある。
   **Sangai ni wa shukuhaku-kyaku kyōtsū no yokujō ga aru.**
   On the third floor is a bath for joint use by lodgers.

2.4.5 *Noun* **ni** *noun* **ga/wa aru/iru (+ negative): possession**

This indicates possession. **iru** is normally used with animate subjects, and **aru** with inanimate ones (but see 7.4.1 for exceptions).

2.4.5.1 *With* **iru**

a ぼくにはどうしてお父さんがいないの。
   **Boku ni wa dōshite otōsan ga inai no.**
   Why don't I have a father?

b 夫人との間に一男三女がいる。
**Fujin to no aida ni ichi-nan san-jo ga iru.**
With his wife, he has one son and three daughters.

## 2.4.5.2 | With **aru**

Note especially examples c and d, where the relation between N **ni** and N **ga** (both inanimate) is not one of 'having', but 'including'.

a この発言には重みがある。
**Kono hatsugen ni wa omomi ga aru.**
This proposal has weight.

b イタリアでは大統領に解散権がある。
**Itaria de wa daitōryō ni kaisanken ga aru.**
In Italy, the president has the right to dissolve [parliament].

c 地場産業に織物がある。
**Jiba sangyō ni orimono ga aru.**
Local industry includes textiles.

d 代表作に「桜川」「花軍」「雨月物語」などがある。
**Daihyōsaku ni 'Sakuragawa' 'Hanaikusa' 'Ugetsumonogatari'
nado ga aru.**
Representative works include *Sakuragawa*, *Hanaikusa* and
*Ugetsu Monogatari*.

## 2.4.6 | *. . . noun* ni aru/nai

Attached to a noun phrase indicating a state or tendency, the resulting meaning is 'be/not be in a state of . . .', 'have a tendency to', etc.

a 例えばWASPは少子化傾向にある。
**Tatoeba WASP wa shōshika keikō ni aru.**
For instance, WASPs (= White Anglo-Saxon Protestants) have
a tendency to have fewer children.

b 四国への企業進出も足踏み状態にある。
**Shikoku e no kigyō shinshutsu mo ashibumi jōtai ni aru.**
The advancement of businesses into Shikoku too is in a state of
stagnation.

**2.4.7** *Noun* ni *noun* ga *verb-potential/noun* ga *noun* ni *verb-potential*

With **dekiru** and other potential verbs, **ni** indicates the agent (person or personalized entity who can do the action) of the verb. Both [**ni-ga** V-pot.] and [**ga-ni** V-pot.] are used (see 14).

a 本当に自分に仕事ができるのか。
  **Hontō ni jibun ni shigoto ga dekiru no ka.**
  Can I really do the work [properly]?

b 自分たちに何ができるか考えたいのです。
  **Jibun-tachi ni nani ga dekiru ka kangaetai no desu.**
  We want to think about what we can do.

**dekiru** 'come into being, acquire' also constructs the same way:

c 絵を描くことを通じて、二人には多くの友人ができた。
  **E o kaku koto o tsūjite, futari ni wa ōku no yūjin ga dekita.**
  The couple have made many friends through their painting.

**2.4.8** *Noun* ni *verb-passive (or pseudo-passive)*

Here, **ni** marks the agent of a passive sentence 'by'; with spontanous passive verbs like **shireru** 'become known' it translates as 'to' (see 12.7).

a 漠とした不安に襲われる。
  **Baku to shita fuan ni osowareru.**
  One becomes gripped by a vague feeling of unease.

b 時代の流れに取り残され、滅びのふちに立っている。
  **Jidai no nagare ni torinokosare, horobi no fuchi ni tatte iru.**
  They [= kiwis] have been left behind by the passage of time, and are on the verge of extinction.

c マスコミに知れたら大変だ。どの位の価値があるんだ。
  誠意を見せろ。
  **Masukomi ni shiretara taihen da. Dono gurai no kachi ga aru n da. Sei-i o misero.**
  If it [= leaked patient info] becomes known to the media, there will be trouble [for you = hospital]. How much is it worth [to you]? Make me a decent offer!

## 2.4.9 | Noun (noun = person) ni verb-causative

In some types of causative sentences, **ni** marks the person who is made or allowed to do the action of the verb (see 13.1, 13.2).

a 今は女子にも男子と同じように教育を受けさせる時代。

**Ima wa joshi ni mo danshi to onaji yō ni kyōiku o ukesaseru jidai.**

Now is an age when people give girls an education in the same way as boys.

## 2.4.10 | Verbal noun ni iku/kuru

Verbal noun **ni iku/kuru** indicates the purpose of the action of the verb 'go/come to do' (see also verbal nouns, 1.9).

a またぜひ働きに行きたい。

**Mata zehi hataraki ni ikitai.**

I very much want to go to work again.

b 今日は息子と娘の分を買いに来ました。

**Kyō wa musuko to musume no bun o kai ni kimashita.**

Today I've come to buy some [pillows] for my daughter and son.

c 念願かなってお礼参りに来るかたも多いですよ。

**Nengan kanatte o-rei mairi ni kuru kata mo ōi desu yo.**

There are also many who come to worship because they had their prayers answered!

*Note* – the combination **asobi ni kite kudasai** (*lit.* "please come to play") is a commonly used idiom in the sense of 'please visit us' (example d).

d A君もぜひ遊びに来て下さい。

**A-kun mo zehi asobi ni kite kudasai.**

You (A-kun) too, please come and visit.

## 2.4.11 | Verb I ni verb 2-potential-negative (between repeated identical verbs)

In this use, **ni** + V2, which is in the negative potential form of the same verb as V1, adds emphasis to V1 (see also 28.2).

a 泣くに泣けないよ。
**Naku ni nakenai yo.**
It's too sad even to cry (*lit.* "I can't even cry").

b 言うに言われないつらい時間を過ごしたことは事実。
**Iu ni iwarenai tsurai jikan o sugoshita koto wa jijitsu.**
It's a fact that I experienced an indescribably hard time.

c バブル期に購入した持ち家は当面は売るに売れない状態。
**Baburu-ki ni kōnyū shita mochi-ie wa tōmen wa uru ni urenai jōtai.**
The situation is that for the time being people just can't sell the houses they acquired during the bubble period.

### 2.4.12 *Verb* ni wa + *adjective*

The adjectives used are evaluatory adjectives like **yoi/ii** 'good', **benri** 'convenient', **fuben** 'inconvenient', etc.; the resulting meaning is 'good/convenient/inconvenient etc. for'.

a 老い、病、死について考えるにはよい時期である。
**Oi, yamai, shi ni tsuite kangaeru ni wa yoi jiki de aru.**
It's a good time to think about old age, sickness and death [= Bon festival].

b 本格的な誘致活動を進めるにはよいタイミングだ。
**Honkaku-teki na yūchi katsudō o susumeru ni wa yoi taimingu da.**
It's good timing for promoting full-scale activities for attracting [visitors to the theme park].

c 「すぐに読みたい」という読者には不便だ。
**'Sugu ni yomitai' to iu dokusha ni wa fuben da.**
For readers who want to read [a book] straight away it's inconvenient [= mail order of books].

### 2.4.13 *Time expression* ni

With time expressions, **ni** indicates a fixed time 'at', 'on', as opposed to a relative time (see 10.2.3.2).

a 詳細は一月二日に明らかになる見通しだ。
**Shōsai wa ichigatsu futsuka ni akiraka ni naru mitōshi da.**
Details are expected to become clear on January 2.

### 2.4.14 *Time/amount* ni *number + counter*

This indicates 'once per time/amount', 'X out of Y'. When **wa** is attached to number + counter, the implication is one of 'at least' (examples b and c) (see 11.3.6).

a イチゴの収穫は一年に一回。
**Ichigo no shūkaku wa ichinen ni ikkai.**
The strawberries are harvested once a year.

b 人は生涯に一回は家を建てる。
**Hito wa shōgai ni ikkai wa ie o tateru.**
A person builds a house at least once in life.

c ウチのお父さんは、とある映画仲間のサークルに入っている。月に一度は会合があって翌日は必ず二日酔いだ。
**Uchi no otōsan wa, to-aru eiga nakama no sākuru ni haitte iru. Tsuki ni ichido wa kaigō ga atte yokujitsu wa kanarazu futsukayoi da.**
My husband is a member of a certain film club. They have a gathering at least once a month, and on the day after he always has a hangover.

d 持ち株会加入者数は約二百四十九万人。これは上場企業従業員の五人に二人に当たる。
**Mochikabukai kanyūsha-sū wa yaku nihyaku yonjū kyūman-nin. Kore wa jōjō kigyō jūgyōin no gonin ni futari ni ataru.**
The number of people who have joined shareholding societies is about 2,490,000. This amounts to two out of five employees of listed enterprises.

### 2.4.15 *Noun* ni

Certain verbs, such as the ones in the examples below, take **ni** to mark the cause of their action. This variously translates as 'at', 'due to' 'because of N' (see 7.2).

a 暑さに音を上げたのは人間だけでない。
**Atsusa ni ne o ageta no wa ningen dake de nai.**
It's not only humans who suffered from the heat [= broiler chickens too laid fewer eggs].

b 思わぬハプニングに場内が沸いた。
**Omowanu hapuningu ni jōnai ga waita.**
The audience got excited at the unexpected happening.

| 2.4.16 | *Verb/verbal noun* ni wa |

Certain verbs (including verbal nouns), including the ones in the examples below, take **ni wa** to mark the purpose or cause of their action, which translates as 'for', 'in order to' (see 7.2).

a 地図を見るには磁石が欠かせない。
   **Chizu o miru ni wa jishaku ga kakasenai.**
   To look at a map, a compass is a must.
   (**kakasenai** = negative causative of **kaku** 'to be lacking')

b 山口組の東京進出には、関東の暴力団も神経をとがらせて
   いる。
   **Yamaguchi-gumi no Tōkyō shinshutsu ni wa Kantō no
   bōryokudan mo shinkei o togarasete iru.**
   Kanto [area] gangster organizations are getting nervous (*lit.* "making
   their nerves sharp") because of the advance of the Yamaguchi-gumi
   into Tokyo.

| 2.4.17 | *Noun (noun = person)* ni wa |

This indicates the idea of 'for' (see also 3.1.9).

a 彼にはカネがすべて。
   **Kare ni wa kane ga subete.**
   For him, money [is] everything.

| 2.4.18 | *Noun (+ counter)* ni *noun (+ counter)* |

This is used like a conjoining particle to enumerate items in the sense of 'plus', 'and' (see 23.2).

a 所持品はシャツ一枚に、スプーン一本と皿一枚だけ。
   **Shojihin wa shatsu ichimai ni, supūn ippon to sara ichimai
   dake.**
   [His] belongings [are] only one shirt, plus one spoon and one plate.

b エメラルドグリーンの海に白い砂浜。
   **Emerarudo gurīn no umi ni shiroi sunahama.**
   An emerald-green sea and a white sandy beach.

## 2.5 de

The basic function of the case particle **de** is to mark the location or means of an action. It often translates into an English preposition ('in', 'at', 'by', 'with', 'for', etc.). Some further uses are given below.

Note that before nouns, [ni no N] is not possible, instead [**de no** N] is used. In other words, **de no** N *can* in this case express a stative location (see 2.4), although this is limited to nouns that have verbal or adjectival meaning (see 2.5.1.2 for details).

For the combinations **de** + **yoi/ii/jūbun**, etc. see 25.2. See also 11.1.2.5 d.

### 2.5.1 Active or stative location

Depending on whether the predicate is dynamic or stative, **de** indicates active or stative location. In English, both translate as 'in', 'at'.

#### 2.5.1.1 Noun **de** predicate: active location

This indicates the place where the action of the verb takes place.

a もともとレストランで食事するのは好き。
  **Motomoto resutoran de shokuji suru no wa suki.**
  I've always liked eating in restaurants.

b 大阪大学で発酵工学を学んだ。
  **Ōsaka daigaku de hakkō kōgaku o mananda.**
  He studied fermentation engineering at Osaka University.

#### 2.5.1.2 Noun **de no** noun: active or stative location

This indicates the place to which an action or state applies. Note that this is limited to nouns that have verbal or adjectival meaning implied, and would require the particle **de** anyway.

a 店頭での人気も上々だ。(cf., 店頭で人気が上々だ **tentō de ninki ga jōjō da**)
  **Tentō de no ninki mo jōjō da.**
  Its popularity in the shops is also great (cf., *is popular* in the shops).

b これがこの国でのやり方だ。
**Kore ga kono kuni de no yarikata da.**
This is the way things are done in this country.

### 2.5.2 | *Means or method of action of verb*

With action verbs, the meaning is 'by', 'with', 'through', etc., whereas with verbs of information the meaning is 'from' or 'through' some medium of communication.

### 2.5.2.1 | *With action verb*

a 軽いうえ、家庭の洗濯機で洗える。
**Karui ue, katei no sentakuki de araeru.**
It's light, and moreover one can machine wash it (*lit.* "wash by machine") at home.

b 情報はカネでは買えない。
**Jōhō wa kane de wa kaenai.**
You can't buy information with money.

c 風邪は、ウイルスの飛沫（まつ）感染で伝染する。
**Kaze wa, uirusu no himatsu kansen de densen suru.**
Colds spread through viral droplet infection.

### 2.5.2.2 | *With verbs of information: source of information*

With verbs of information like **shiru/wakaru**, etc., **de** can indicate the source of the information, or the means by which one learns/understands something.

a 報道で知っているだけだ。
**Hōdō de shitte iru dake da.**
I only know it from the news.

b ・・・アンケート調査で分かった。
**...ankēto chōsa de wakatta.**
...became clear through a survey.

## 2.5.3 | Indicates basis for judgement

This translates as 'according to', 'by', etc.

a 高さは推定で約六十センチ。
**Takasa wa suitei de yaku rokujus-senchi.**
The height is about 60cm by estimate.

b 新鮮なのが一目で分かる。
**Shinsen na no ga hitome de wakaru.**
You can see it's fresh at a glance.

c 金子さんの観察では、男性よりも女性の方が冷静だ。
**Kaneko-san no kansatsu de wa, dansei yori mo josei no hō ga reisei da.**
According to Kaneko-san's observation, women are more cool-headed than men.

## 2.5.4 | Noun de shirareru

With the passive form of the verb **shiru** 'to know', this indicates what something/someone is 'known for'.

a 誠実な人柄で知られる。
**Seijitsu na hitogara de shirareru.**
He is known for his sincere personality.

b 自家製豆腐の料理で知られる店だ。
**Jikasei tōfu no ryōri de shirareru mise da.**
It's a restaurant that is known for its dishes of homemade bean curd.

## 2.5.5 | Noun (noun = time expression) de

This indicates the time or period over which action of the verb takes place/ is completed 'in', 'over', 'as of'.

a この一年で二倍に膨らんだ。
**Kono ichinen de nibai ni fukuranda.**
In the past year, it [the number of buyers for foreign parts] has doubled.

b 一月一日付で就任する。
**Ichigatsu tsuitachi-zuke de shūnin suru.**
He takes up the position as of January 1st.

c 組合数は二年連続で減少した。

**Kumiai-sū wa ninen renzoku de genshō shita.**

The number of unions decreased for two years in succession.

d 今年で四半世紀が過ぎた。

**Kotoshi de shihan seiki ga sugita.**

This year, a quarter of a century has passed.

---

| 2.5.6 | *Marks the extent of people involved in the action of verb* |

The noun to which **de** attaches can refer to either individuals or organizations.

---

| 2.5.6.1 | *Noun (noun = individual(s))* **de** |

Here, **de** means 'by' or 'with' when the noun refers to individuals.

a 自分の評価は、自分でするもの。

**Jibun no hyōka wa, jibun de suru mono.**

My own assessment is something I do myself.

b 従業員七十人でスタートする。

**Jūgyōin nanajū-nin de sutāto suru.**

We will start with 70 employees.

---

| 2.5.6.2 | *Noun (noun = organization)* **de**: *marks a topic* |

Although **de** can be interpreted as marking the place of action here, it is similar in use to the particle **wa** in that it is customary to mark the topic of the sentence with **de** if the topic is an organization. In other words, to mark organizations that are topics, **de** (**wa**) tends to be used rather than just **wa** (see 11.3.4).

a 同署などで原因を調べている。

**Dōsho nado de gen'in o shirabete iru.**

The said police station, among others, is looking into the cause.

b 同動物園では死因は老衰としている。

**Dō-dōbutsuen de wa shiin wa rōsui to shite iru.**

The said zoo views the cause of death [of the animal] as old age.

### 2.5.7 | Noun (noun = amount) de: unit or total

Here, **de** marks a unit or a total.

a　入場料は一回券で七百円。
**Nyūjōryō wa ikkai-ken de nanahyaku-en.**
The entrance fee is ¥700 for a single ticket.

b　全部で十八サイズある。
**Zenbu de jūhachi saizu aru.**
In all, there are 18 sizes.

### 2.5.8 | Indicates reason

In compound S (S1 **de** S2), **de** can indicate the reason for S2 (see 26.5).

a　ことしは天候不順で山にはなお雪が多いそうだ。
**Kotoshi wa tenkō fujun de yama ni wa nao yuki ga ōi sō da.**
This year, owing to bad weather, they say that there is still a lot of snow in the mountains.

*Note* – **de** (the conjunctive form of the copula) is often used in similar contexts (for an example, see 2.5.9).

### 2.5.9 | de [case particle] and de [conjunctive form of copula] compared

The case particle **de** must not be confused with the plain conjunctive form of the copula, especially as they can appear in similar-looking types of sentence (see 7.5). The latter usually appears in **wa-de**-type sentences which could be ended as an independent sentence with **da/desu/datta/deshita**, etc. Compare the following:

a　過熱するカメラブームで、多くの機種が登場した。
**Kanetsu suru kamera būmu de, ōku no kishu ga tōjō shita.**
In the mad craze for new cameras, many new models have appeared. (**de** = case particle)

b　1時間と答えた女性は65.0%で、男性の倍近い。
**Ichi-jikan to kotaeta josei wa rokujūgo-ten-rei pāsento de dansei no bai chikai.**
(The ratio of) women who replied 'one hour' was 65.0 per cent, nearly double that of men. (**de** = conjunctive form of copula, cf., b′ below)

b′ ✒1時間と答えた女性は65.0%だった。（これは）男性の倍近い。

**Ichi-jikan to kotaeta josei wa rokujūgo-ten-rei pāsento datta. (Kore wa) dansei no bai chikai.**

[The ratio of] women who replied 'one hour' was 65.0 per cent. [That is] nearly double that of men.

*Note* – in combinations like **de yoi/ii/jubun, de** is also the conjunctive form of the copula. (see 25.2).

## 2.6  e

The case particle **e** (written 〜) indicates a direction or goal 'to', 'towards'. It overlaps with the case particle **ni** to a considerable extent (see 2.4).

### 2.6.1 │ *With verbs of motion*

With verbs of motion, **e** can be used instead of **ni** to mark a core case (dative of direction). Whereas **ni** indicates the goal of a motion, **e** is said to be concerned more with the direction towards the goal, but in practice the two are often interchangeable (see 2.4).

*Note* – in all of the examples in 2.6.1, **e** can be replaced by **ni**.

A number of verbs typically take **ni**. These include verbs of arriving, putting and posture (**tsuku, oku, noru, suwaru, tatsu**) – but note examples a and b for exceptions!

This is also the case in the sense of beneficiary or recipient of an object or action, except when **no** is attached, in which case only **e no** is possible (see 2.6.3).

Verbs of entering and inserting (**hairu, ireru,** etc.) mostly take **ni**. However, despite what most textbooks say, they can also take **e** (examples c–e), without any change in meaning.

a さあ、そこへ座れ。

**Sā, soko e suware.**

Right, sit down there!

b 最近、教科書を家に持ち帰らずに、学校へ置いていく生徒が多い。

**Saikin, kyōkasho o ie ni mochikaerazu ni, gakkō e oite iku seito ga ōi.**

These days there are lots of pupils who don't take their textbooks home, but leave them at school.

c JRへ入るのは子供のころからの夢。
**Jeiāru e hairu no wa kodomo no koro kara no yume.**
Entering JR [Japan Rail] has been a dream since childhood.

d ペットを砂場へ入れないよう ・・・
**Petto o sunaba e irenai yō ...**
Do not let pets into the sandpit ...

e ・・・「中へ入れろ」と脅迫。
**... 'naka e irero' to kyōhaku.**
... he threatened him, saying 'Let me in'.

f 島へ渡るツアーは週一回で、毎回ほぼ満席という。
**Shima e wataru tsuā wa shū ikkai de, maikai hobo manseki to iu.**
They say that tours to the island take place once a week, and are
   more or less fully booked each time.

g この時期の経歴は空白だ。「実は大学へ行ったんです」。
**Kono jiki no keireki wa kūhaku da. 'Jitsu wa daigaku e itta n desu'.**
Her CV for this period is blank. 'Actually, I went to university'.

h 六月に名古屋へ着任した。
**Rokugatsu ni Nagoya e chakunin shita.**
In June, he arrived at his post in Nagoya.

i 組合員へは冷凍のまま供給する。
**Kumiai-in e wa reitō no mama kyōkyū suru.**
To co-op members they provide them [eels] frozen.

j 黒字はどうして生まれ、どこへ行ってしまったのか。
**Kuroji wa dō shite umare, doko e itte shimatta no ka.**
How did the surplus arise, and where did it go?

2.6.2 *With ellipted predicate*

With ellipted predicate, e also indicates direction or goal.

a 十一時半ぐらいにはベッドルームへ。
**Jūichiji-han gurai ni wa beddorūmu e.**
By about 11.30, [he heads] for the bedroom.

b ちょっと口にしては次々と灰皿へ。
**Chotto kuchi ni shite wa tsugitsugi to haizara e.**
He smokes them briefly, and then [stubs them out] in the ashtray one
   after the other.

73

In newspaper-style headlines, **e** indicates plans, or developments. In this use, **e** cannot be replaced by **ni**.

c パキスタン大統領が訪中へ。
**Pakisutan daitōryō ga hōchū e.**
Pakistani president set to visit China.

d タイ、ミャンマーから天然ガス購入へ。
**Tai, Myanmā kara tennengasu kōnyū e.**
[Plans] to buy natural gas from Thailand and Myanmar.

### 2.6.3 | Noun **e** no *noun*

To modify a noun, **e** is used instead of **ni**; the combination **ni** no N is not found, but it is not possible to explain every instance of **e** no as a conversion from **ni**, as examples c and d show.

a 新規分野への進出も探っている。(cf., 新規分野に進出する **shinki bunya ni shinshutsu suru**)
**Shinki bunya e no shinshutsu mo sagutte iru.**
They are also looking to expand into new areas.

b Eサイズから Lサイズへの切り替えを急ぎたい。(cf., Lサイズに切り替える **L-saizu ni kirikaeru**)
**E-saizu kara L-saizu e no kirikae o isogitai.**
We'd like to speed up the changeover from E size to L size.

c 記事への批判もあった。(cf., 記事を批判する **kiji o hihan suru**)
**Kiji e no hihan mo atta.**
There were also criticisms of the article.

d それは、日本への警告でもある。
**Sore wa Nihon e no keikoku de mo aru.**
This [= the polarization of political parties in the US] is also a warning for Japan.

### 2.6.4 | Noun **e** to *verb/verb phrase*

[N **e** to] is used to describe the manner in which some change (indicated by a verb/verb phrase of change) takes place. Again, **ni** to is not found (see 11.7).

a 文明はなぜか西へと回る。
**Bunmei wa naze ka nishi e to mawaru.**
For some reason, civilization moves westwards.

b パソコンがテレビへと変身を始めた。
**Pasokon ga terebi e to henshin o hajimeta.**
The PC has begun to change into a TV.

## 2.7 kara

**kara** marks the point of origin or departure of the action of a V 'from'.
It is mostly attached to N of time or place, or other N that can be used
with the idea of 'from . . . to'. **kara** is often used in combination with **made**
'to' or **e** 'towards' (see 2.10, 2.6). Note that unlike other case particles,
**kara** can be followed by **ga/o**.

### 2.7.1 | *Noun/demonstrative pronoun* kara

After time and place nouns or demonstrative pronouns, **kara** translates
as 'from', but after other nouns also variously as 'out of', 'compared to',
'against'.

a 小学校五年からサッカーを始めた。
**Shōgakkō gonen kara sakkā o hajimeta.**
He started soccer in year 5 of primary school.

b 三十日から試験運用を始める。
**Sanjūnichi kara shiken un'yō o hajimeru.**
From the 30th they will start a trial run.

c アラスカからホーン岬まで。
**Arasuka kara Hōn misaki made.**
From Alaska to Cape Horn.

d これからが一年中で一番水を多く使う時期だ。
**Kore kara ga ichinenjū de ichiban mizu o ōku tsukau
 jiki da.**
From now on is the time of year when [people] use the most water.

e クルマの街から生活者の街へ。
**Kuruma no machi kara seikatsusha no machi e.**
From a town for cars towards a town for those living there.

f 「技術を人から人へと伝えることは重要」と説明する。
**'Gijutsu o hito kara hito e to tsutaeru koto wa jūyō' to
 setsumei suru.**
'It is important to pass on know-how from person to person', he explains.

g 何枚からでも購入できる。
**Nanmai kara demo kōnyū dekiru.**
One can buy them [= shares] in any quantity [= there is no minimum].

h ただ全体からすれば女子はまだ少数派。
**Tada zentai kara sureba joshi wa mada shōsūha.**
[Government ministries are now hiring females] However,
seen against the total [of public servants], women are still in
the minority.

---

*Noun* **kara no** *noun*

In noun-modifying use, the meaning is the same as in 2.7.1.

a うち、九割近くは米国からの輸入品だ。
**Uchi, kyūwari chikaku wa beikoku kara no yunyūhin da.**
Nearly 90 per cent [of products] are imports from the US.

b 中東からの学生は減少した。
**Chūtō kara no gakusei wa genshō shita.**
Students from the Middle East have decreased in number.

---

| 2.7.2 | *Noun* **kara naru**

When the noun indicates a component, the meaning of **N kara naru** is
'consist of N'.

a 条例は十二条からなる。
**Jōrei wa jūnijō kara naru.**
The by-law consists of 12 articles.

b 解説編と実践編からなっている。
**Kaisetsuhen to jissenhen kara natte iru.**
It [= the manual] consists of a commentary and a practical part.

c 家庭という言葉は家と庭からなっている。
**Katei to iu kotoba wa ie to niwa kara natte iru.**
The word *katei* (home) consists of *ka/ie* (house) and
*tei/niwa* (garden).

d 市内料金は通話料と基本料からなっている。
**Shinai ryōkin wa tsūwaryō to kihonryō kara natte iru.**
The local charge consists of a call charge and a basic fee.

### 2.7.3 | *Noun* **kara tsukuru/dekiru**

Where the noun indicates a material, the meaning is 'made from', 'made of'.

a アルマニャックはブドウ酒から作った蒸留酒。
**Arumanyakku wa budōshu kara tsukutta jōryūshu.**
Armagnac is a distilled alcoholic drink made from wine.

b 日米関係は三つの柱からできています。
**Nichibei kankei wa mittsu no hashira kara dekite imasu.**
Japan–US relations consist of three mainstays.

*Note* – there are cases that look like **kara dekiru** at first sight (example c), but turn out to be a different use, belonging to 2.7.1, as **kara dekiru** is attached to a time N.

c 行事や呼び出しの原形もこのころからできたという。
**Gyōji ya yobidashi no genkei mo kono koro kara dekita to iu.**
The archetype of the *gyōji* and *yobidashi* [in Sumo] too came into being from that time, they say.

### 2.7.4 | *Noun* **kara** + *verbs of motion (deru/oriru)*

With verbs of motion like **deru** 'leave', 'come out' and **oriru** 'alight', 'come down', **kara** indicates the place one gets down from or leaves. The same verbs can also take the particle **o**. With some nouns, such as **doa, naka** and **toire**, only **kara** is possible. With others, e.g. **ie** 'house', the nuance is different in that **ie o deru** means 'leave home', whereas **ie kara deru** 'come/ go outside' (see 2.2.5, 2.8).

a 村から出て立派になるんだ。
**Mura kara dete rippa ni naru n da.**
You should get out of the village and make a career.

b 心配そうに家から出てきた人もいる。
**Shinpaisō ni ie kara dete kita hito mo iru.**
There were people who came out of their houses, looking worried.

c カプセルから降りたときはふらふらだ。
**Kapuseru kara orita toki wa furafura da.**
[Astronaut's training] When you step out of the capsule, you stagger.

d 二人の老人が中から出てきて話しかけてきた。
**Futari no rōjin ga naka kara dete kite hanashikakete kita.**
Two old men came out and started talking to me.

**2.7.5** *Indicating reason (koto kara, riyū kara, etc.)*

This is used with a limited number of nouns, such as **koto** and **riyū**, both meaning 'reason' in this context.

a 刺し身がハマチより日持ちすることから、高値で取引されて
  きた。

  **Sashimi ga hamachi yori himochi suru koto kara, takane de torihiki sarete kita.**

  Because it [= *kanpachi* fish] keeps fresh longer than *hamachi*, it has been traded at high prices.

b 健康上の理由から横山良一社長は取締役に退く 。

  **Kenkōjō no riyū kara Yokoyama Ryōichi shachō wa torishimariyaku ni shirizoku.**

  For reasons of health, president Yokoyama Ryōichi moves down to director.

c 東京の二店が好調なことから、全国展開を計画中だ。

  **Tōkyō no niten ga kōchō na koto kara, zenkoku tenkai o keikakuchū da.**

  Because the two stores in Tokyo are doing well, they are planning to expand nationwide.

d 経済制裁には、いくつかの理由から慎重論もある。

  **Keizai seisai ni wa, ikutsu ka no riyū kara shinchōron mo aru.**

  For several reasons, some are cautious about economic sanctions.

**2.7.6** *Noun/pronoun kara (noun/pronoun = person)*

When **kara** is attached to a personal noun or pronoun, it indicates the person who initiates an action, ventures an opinion, etc.

a 私から口を出すつもりはない。

  **Watashi kara kuchi o dasu tsumori wa nai.**

  I have no intention of interfering from my end.

b 私から言わせれば国連には三つの市民がいます。

  **Watashi kara iwasereba kokuren ni wa mittsu no shimin ga imasu.**

  According to my opinion (*lit.* "If you let me say it from my end"), there are three [types of] citizens in the UN.

### 2.7.7 | Indicating the agent in a passive sentence

In a passive sentence, **kara** indicates the agent 'by', which is more commonly indicated by **ni** (see 12, 2.4.8).

a 「ある青年は現地の人々から神様のように慕われていた」と驚く。
**'Aru seinen wa genchi no hitobito kara kamisama no yō ni shitawarete ita' to odoroku.**
'Some boys were idolized by the locals like gods', he said in amazement.

b 君から僕の転勤先のことを聞かれて、困ってしまいました。
**Kimi kara boku no tenkinsaki no koto o kikarete, komatte shimaimashita.**
I was perplexed when asked by you about where I have been transferred to.

### 2.7.8 | Idiomatic uses

This includes expressions like **kokoro kara** and **ima/kore kara**.

a 皆さんのご出席を心から歓迎します。
**Minasan no go-shusseki o kokoro kara kangei shimasu.**
I welcome the attendance of all of you from [the bottom of] my heart.

b これから行く。
**Kore kara iku.**
I'm coming (*lit.* "going") right now.

c これから演奏する曲は⋯
**Kore kara ensō suru kyoku wa...**
The piece we're going to play now...

d 「自分も今から死ぬつもりだ」と110番通報があった。
**'Jibun mo ima kara shinu tsumori da' to hyakutōban tsūhō ga atta.**
There was a call to an emergency number saying 'I intend to kill myself (*lit.* "die") now too'.

## 2.8 o and kara **with verbs of motion compared**

With **o**, the implication is 'to leave/alight from', whereas **kara** implies motion away from/out of, often by making an effort.

While many nouns can attach either **o** or **kara**, very few can attach only one of the two. An example of an exclusively **o**-marked NP is **kaidan o oriru** 'walk/come down the stairs'; an exclusively **kara**-marked NP is **taijūkei kara oriru** 'step off the scales'.

a しばらく部屋から出てこなかった。

**Shibaraku heya kara dete konakatta.**

He didn't come out of the room for some time.

b やがて海岸も姿を変え、漁師も一人二人と船を降りていった。

**Yagate kaigan mo sugata o kae, ryōshi mo hitori futari to fune o orite itta.**

Soon, the coast changed [in] appearance, and the fishermen left the boat in ones and twos.

c タクシーを降り集落を歩いていると女の人に出会った。

**Takushī o ori shūraku o aruite iru to onna no hito ni deatta.**

When I got out of the taxi and walked through the village, I came across a woman.

d 部屋から出ようとしなかった軽い痴ほう症の女性が車いすで食堂に出てきて食事をするようになった。

**Heya kara deyō to shinakatta karui chihōshō no josei ga kurumaisu de shokudō ni dete kite shokuji o suru yō ni natta.**

A woman with slight dementia, who had made no attempt to come out of her room, now appeared in her wheelchair in the refectory to eat.

### 2.9 yori

#### 2.9.1 yori *as equivalent of* kara

**yori** is used as a formal or written-style equivalent of the case particle **kara** 'since', 'from'. Note that in this use, **yori** is *not* followed by adjectives (see 2.7, 2.9.2, 6.7.1).

a 91年常務となり、92年4月より現職。

**Kyūjūichi-nen jōmu to nari, kyūjūni-nen shigatsu yori genshoku.**

In '91 he became managing director, and since April '92 he [has occupied] his current position.

b 昼はコースは一人三千円より、夜は五千円より。
   **Hiru wa kōsu wa hitori sanzen-en yori, yoru wa
      gosen-en yori.**
   At lunchtime, courses [are] from ¥3,000, at night from ¥5,000.

c 商品名は「前略、足の裏より」。
   **Shōhinmei wa 'Zenryaku, ashi no ura yori'.**
   The product name is 'Hello, from the sole of the foot'.

d 「映画 "赤い靴" より」ほか。
   **'Eiga "Akai Kutsu" yori' hoka.**
   'From the film *The Red Shoes*', and others.


### 2.9.2 | *yori in comparative sentences*

**N yori** literally means "compared to N", "more/less . . . than N", etc., and is used to indicate the standard of comparison (that which something/ somebody is being compared with) in comparative sentences (see 6.7.1).

For adverbial use of **yori** (**yori** + adjective) forming the equivalent to English comparative forms (see 6.7.2.1).


### 2.9.2.1 | *Noun yori (mo) + adjective*

Followed by adjectives, **yori** indicates comparison '-er than', 'more than'.

a 人のいのちは地球より重い、という。
   **Hito no inochi wa chikyū yori omoi, to iu.**
   They say that human life weighs heavier than the globe.

b 里が前より奇麗になった。
   **Sato ga mae yori kirei ni natta.**
   The village has become prettier than before.

c 必ず選手より早く来ます。
   **Kanarazu senshu yori hayaku kimasu.**
   He always comes earlier than the players.

d 彦根の初霜は平年より十日遅い。
   **Hikone no hatsushimo wa heinen yori tōka osoi.**
   The first ground frost in Hikone is ten days later than in
      average years.

| 2.9.2.2 | *Noun/verb* **yori** *(mo) verb* |

Followed by a verb, **yori** indicates that the action/state of the verb takes place 'compared to', 'rather than'.

a ボールが飛ばなくなったわけではない。体力より気力が落ちて
　いる。

　**Bōru ga tobanaku natta wake de wa nai. Tairyoku yori
　kiryoku ga ochite iru.**

　It's not that [I can't get the golf] ball to fly [the distance] any more.
　It's my mental rather than physical strength that's diminished.

b これまでより五モデル増える。

　**Kore made yori go-moderu fueru.**

　Compared to before, there will be five new models.

c 今は森を見るより木を見る時だ。

　**Ima wa mori o miru yori ki o miru toki da.**

　This is the time to look at the trees rather than the woods.

| 2.9.2.3 | *Noun* **yori** *(mo) noun (+ copula)* |

This is often used in slogans, sayings, etc. in the sense of 'rather than' (the copula is usually omitted).

a 対立よりも協調

　**tairitsu yori mo kyōchō**

　Co-operation rather than opposition

b 論より証拠

　**ron yori shōko**

　Proof [is] better than argument

## 2.10　made

As a case particle, **made** marks the endpoint of the action of the verb 'to'.
**Made** is usually attached to nouns of time or place, and often used in combination with **kara** 'from' (see 2.7; see also 2.10.1.3 for examples indicating a range, involving both **kara** and **made**). Note that like **kara**, **made** can also be followed by **ga/o**.

*Note 1* – there is also an adverbial particle **made** which indicates a degree or extent, and a case particle **made-ni** (see 11.2.4, 2.11).

*Note 2* – **made** can either replace the case particles **ga** and **o**, or attach them (**made ga, made o**).

| 2.10.1 | *Noun* made

| 2.10.1.1 | *Place noun* made *(+ particle)*

This indicates an endpoint in space 'to', 'until'.

a 駅まで歩いて五分。
  **Eki made aruite gofun.**
  It's a five-minute walk to the station.

b みんなで食堂まで下りていく。新聞をみんなでのぞき込んだ。
  **Minna de shokudō made orite iku. Shinbun o minna de nozokikonda.**
  They all went down to the canteen. They all looked at the newspaper.

c 両国からレインボーブリッジまでを往復する。
  **Ryōgoku kara reinbō-burijji made o ōfuku suru.**
  [The boat] makes a return trip from Ryōgoku to the Rainbow Bridge.

d あの丘陵の向こうまでが日本向けのカボチャ畑です。
  **Ano kyuryō no mukō made ga Nihon-muke no kabocha-batake desu.**
  All the way to the other side of that hill are fields of pumpkins for the Japanese market.

| 2.10.1.2 | *Time noun* made *(particle)*

This marks an endpoint in time 'to', 'until'.

a 2歳の時に宣教師の父と来日。高校までを日本で過ごす。完ぺきな日本語を話す。その後、フルブライト奨学生として日本に留学、米平和部隊のボランティアとして韓国にも滞在した。
  **Nisai no toki ni senkyōshi no chichi to rainichi. Kōkō made o nihon de sugosu. Kanpeki na nihongo o hanasu. Sono go, Furuburaito shōgakusei to shite Nihon ni ryūgaku, Bei-heiwabutai no borantia to shite Kankoku ni mo taizai shita.**
  At age 2, he came to Japan with his father, a missionary. He lived in Japan until high school. He speaks perfect Japanese. Later, he came to Japan as a Fulbright scholar, and had a stay in Korea as a volunteer in the US peace corps.

b ツリーは年明けまで展示される。

**Tsurī wa toshiake made tenji sareru.**

The Christmas tree will be on display until the New Year.

c 議論は夜遅くまで尽きない。

**Giron wa yoru osoku made tsukinai.**

The discussion continued till late.

d 政局不安も二月までは残る。

**Seikyoku fuan mo nigatsu made wa nokoru.**

The political instability will remain until February at least.

---

2.10.1.3 *Noun* **kara** *noun* **made**

In combination with the case particle **kara**, this indicates a range in space (with place nouns) or time (with time nouns) 'from . . . to' (see 2.7).

a 二月一日から三月十五日まで研究テーマを募集する。

**Nigatsu tsuitachi kara sangatsu jūgonichi made kenkyū tēma o boshū suru.**

We invite the submission of research topics from February 1st to March 15th.

b 切符は午前十時四十五分から午後一時四十分まで販売する。

**Kippu wa gozen jūji yonjūgo-fun kara gogo ichiji yonjup-pun made hanbai suru.**

Tickets will be on sale from 10.45 a.m. to 1.40 p.m.

c 温泉街の端から端まで雪に埋もれ、ひっそりとしている。

**Onsengai no hashi kara hashi made yuki ni umore, hissori to shite iru.**

The hot spring district looks deserted, covered in snow from one end to the other.

d 十階建てで地下一階から地上三階までが駐車場。

**Jukkaidate de chika ikkai kara chijō sangai made ga chūshajō.**

It's a 10-storey building, and B1 to 3F is parking.

---

2.10.1.4 *(Noun* **kara***) noun* **made no** *noun*

The meaning is the same when used to modify nouns ('from') 'to'.

a 40歳までの若手作家の発掘と育成が目的だ。

**Yonjus-sai made no wakate sakka no hakkutsu to ikusei ga mokuteki da.**

The purpose is to scout out and nurture young writers up to the age of 40.

b 二月に就任し今年六月末までの期間、教壇に立つ予定だ。

**Nigatsu ni shūnin shi kotoshi rokugatsu-matsu made no kikan, kyōdan ni tatsu yotei da.**

He plans to assume the post in February and to teach for the period until the end of June of this year.

## 2.10.1.5 Number (+ counter) **made**

This indicates the maximum amount that is possible or will be accepted 'up to'.

a 二百万円まで融資する。

**Nihyakuman-en made yūshi suru.**

They lend [people] up to two million yen [= educational loan].

b 一枚のはがきで三人まで応募できる。

**Ichimai no hagaki de sannin made ōbo dekiru.**

With one postcard up to three people can apply.

c 角度約五度までの坂道を登れる。

**Kakudo yaku godo made no sakamichi o noboreru.**

[Toy:] It can climb gradients of around 5 per cent.

## 2.10.1.6 Address, telephone number, etc., **made**

This is commonly used to indicate an address/telephone number., etc. to be contacted by potential customers etc.

a 電話は専用で06・362・1245まで。

**Denwa wa senyō de reiroku-sanrokuni-ichinīyongō made.**

(See 4.1.2.2 on lengthening of **ni** and **go**.)

By telephone, contact the dedicated line on 06-362-1245.

b 問い合わせは同支店（052・231・1115）まで。

**Toiawase wa dōshiten (zerogōnī-nīsan'ichi-ichiichiichigō) made.**

Please [direct] inquiries to the same branch (052-231-1115).

**2.10.2** *Verb* made

**2.10.2.1** *Verb*-ru made

After verbs, **made** indicates an endpoint or time of action 'until'.

a ふたをし、赤くなるまで蒸す。
**Futa o shi, akaku naru made musu.**
You put on the lid, and steam it [= crab] until it turns red.

b 死ぬまで公開はしない。
**Shinu made kōkai wa shinai.**
I will not make it [= the work of art] public until I die.

c 政府が何かをやるまで待つしかない ‥‥‥。
**Seifu ga nani ka o yaru made matsu shika nai …**
All we can do is wait until the government does something …

d 過労死と言われるような状態になるまで働いてきた。
**Karōshi to iwareru yō na jōtai ni naru made hataraite kita.**
He has worked himself into a condition similar to what's known as death from overwork.

e 二歳から十歳前後で死ぬまで、鹿の雌は毎年子を産む。
**Nisai kara jussai zengo de shinu made, shika no mesu wa maitoshi ko o umu.**
From the time they're 2 years old until they die around the age of 10, does (deer) produce offspring every year.

**2.10.2.2** *Idiomatic use:* **iu made mo nai/naku**

This combination is used in the sense of 'goes without saying'.

a ‥‥縦穴が、スキタイの古墳であることを証拠立てる粘土の層に突き当たった。すぐに本格的な発掘にとりかかったのは言うまでもない。
**… tateana ga, Sukitai no kofun de aru koto o shōkodateru nendo no sō ni tsukiatatta. Sugu ni honkaku-teki na hakkutsu ni torikakatta no wa iu made mo nai.**
… the vertical shaft hit a loam stratum that constituted proof that [we were dealing with] a Scythian burial mound. It goes without saying that we immediately started a proper excavation.

b ・・・米政府は最も（参入の）難しい市場と懸命に取り組んでい
  る。言うまでもなくそれは日本だ。

  **...Bei-seifu wa mottomo (sannyū no) muzukashii shijō to
  kenmei ni torikunde iru. Iu made mo naku sore wa
  Nihon da.**

  ...the US government is making efforts to grapple with the most
    difficult market (to penetrate). Needless to say, that's Japan.

## 2.11 made-ni

**made-ni** is a case particle that indicates the endpoint in time or space
over which an action extends, like **made** by itself. The difference between
**made-ni** and **made** is that **made-ni** is concerned with the cut-off point, i.e.
indicates a deadline when referring to the future, or the idea of 'up to
(now)' when used with past tense.

### 2.11.1 Noun/demonstrative pronoun made-ni

#### 2.11.1.1 Time noun/demonstrative pronoun made-ni

This phrase means 'by', 'up to'.

a 二、三日前までに予約が必要だ。
  **Ni, san-nichi mae made-ni yoyaku ga hitsuyō da.**
  Reservations need to be made no later than two or three days in
    advance.

b 来年二月末までに会社を清算する。
  **Rainen nigatsu-matsu made-ni kaisha o seisan suru.**
  We're going to liquidate the company by next February.

c これまでにも何度も足を運んだ場所だった。
  **Kore made-ni mo nando mo ashi o hakonda basho datta.**
  It was a place I'd been to many times till now.

d これまでに風俗店で働いたことはない。
  **Kore made-ni fūzokuten de hataraita koto wa nai.**
  Until now she has never worked in a nightclub.

e 往復はがきで九月十六日までに申し込む。
  **Ōfuku hagaki de kugatsu jūrokunichi made-ni mōshikomu.**
  One applies by return postcard by September 16th.

2.11.1.2  *Other nouns* **made-ni**

Although **daigaku** 'university' in example a is not a time noun as such, the implication nevertheless is one of time.

a 大学までに燃え尽きてしまったのかな。

**Daigaku made-ni moetsukite shimatta no ka na.**

He may have burnt out by [the time he reaches] university.

b 女性が多いが、ほとんど髪は肩ぐらいまでに短くしている。

**Josei ga ōi ga, hotondo kami wa kata gurai made-ni mijikaku shite iru.**

There are many women, but most keep their hair short to about shoulder length.

2.11.2  *Verb* **made-ni**

When attached to a verb, **made-ni** can follow a N-**suru**-type verb (verbal noun) in its noun form, i.e. without **suru**, or a verb in its plain non-past form. The meaning is 'until', 'before' or 'by'.

2.11.2.1  *Verbal noun* **made-ni**

a 景況回復までにはまだ時間がかかる。

**Keikyō kaifuku made-ni wa mada jikan ga kakaru.**

It'll still take time for the economy to recover.

b 党派問題の決着までに八回の投票が必要だったね。

**Tōha mondai no ketchaku made-ni hakkai no tōhyō ga hitsuyō datta ne.**

It took eight ballots for the faction problem to be settled, didn't it?

c 現在は二十八業者の加盟が決まっており、発足までに四十業者にする。

**Genzai wa nijūhachi gyōsha no kamei ga kimatte ori, hossoku made-ni yonjū gyōsha ni suru.**

At present, affiliation of 28 dealers has been agreed, and by start-up time we will make it 40.

### 2.11.2.2 Verb-ru made-ni

a 水は暖まるまでに時間を要し、冷めるのが遅い。

**Mizu wa atatamaru made-ni jikan o yōshi, sameru no ga osoi.**

Water requires time to heat up (*lit.* "until it heats"), and is slow to cool down.

b 決意するまでには二—三週間悩み抜いた。

**Ketsui suru made-ni wa ni kara san-shūkan nayami-nuita.**

He worried for several weeks before he made up his mind.

c そうなるまでに美術はおよそ百五十年ぐらいかかった。

**Sō naru made-ni bijutsu wa oyoso hyaku gojū-nen gurai kakatta.**

It took approximately 150 years for art to develop in that way [= expressionism].

## 2.12 to

The case particle **to** is used with a limited number of verbs whose action or state typically involves two or more participants (mutual or reciprocal action or state). Its basic meaning is 'with', seen also in the common phrase **to issho ni** 'together with' (example c), but depending on the verb it translates as 'to', 'from', and as an object (e.g. 'marry someone').

Here are some of the more common of these verbs: **au** 会う 'meet (with)', 'come across', **hanasu/hanashi o suru** 話す・話をする 'talk (with)', **kaidan suru** 会談する 'hold talks (with)', **kekkon suru** 結婚する 'marry', **kon'yaku suru** 婚約する 'get engaged (to)', **naka yoku suru** 仲良くする 'get on close terms (with)'. Note especially **chigau** 違う 'differ (from)' and **rikon suru** 離婚する 'get divorced (from)'. Note also compound verbs ending in -**au** (合う), which have the implication of 'mutually'.

*Note* – **au** 会う (example b) and **hanasu** can also take **ni** instead of **to**, with a different nuance of meaning (see 2.4).

a 問　当日は担当部長と会っているはずだが。

**Toi: Tōjitsu wa tantō buchō to atte iru hazu da ga.**

Q: On the day, you're supposed to have met with the department head in charge?

b 「(頭取に)会いたい」と話したという。
   **'(Tōdori ni) aitai' to hanashita to iu.**
   He is reported to have said that he wanted to see the CEO.

c 今でも日曜日は近所に住む父といっしょに過ごす。
   **Ima de mo nichiyōbi wa kinjo ni sumu chichi to issho ni
   sugosu.**
   Even now, he spends Sundays with his father, who lives in the vicinity.

d 娘さんと結婚します。
   **Musume-san to kekkon shimasu.**
   I'll marry your daughter.

e 昨年、主人と離婚しました。
   **Sakunen, shujin to rikon shimashita.**
   Last year, I got divorced from my husband.

f 住宅は家電や自動車と違う。
   **Jūtaku wa kaden ya jidōsha to chigau.**
   Housing is different from [things like] electrical appliances and cars.

g トイレで上司と会ったときには「逃げない」。
   **Toire de jōshi to atta toki ni wa 'nigenai'.**
   When he comes across his boss in the toilet, [he] doesn't 'run away'.

h 米国とは政治、経済的にぜひ仲良くしたいと思っている。
   **Beikoku to wa seiji, keizai-teki ni zehi nakayoku shitai to
   omotte iru.**
   We'd like very much to establish good political and economic relations
   with the US.

# Chapter 3

# *Phrasal particles*

Phrasal particles are called thus because they are combinations of a case particle and a verbal element in the conjunctive form (or V-stem in more formal or bookish style). They are often used after nouns in the form as [N **ni/o** V-**te**] in adverbial use, but some can also be attached to verbs. Some phrasal particles are also used to modify nouns, as indicated in Table 3.1.

In very formal writing, particularly business letters, some phrasal particles have polite versions ending in -**mashite**; **ni tsukimashite**, in particular, may be encountered for **ni tsuite**.

**Table 3.1** Major phrasal particles

| Meaning | Adverbial | Adv.-bookish | N-modifying |
|---|---|---|---|
| 'on the occasion of', 'when it comes to', 'in', 'for' | **ni atatte (wa/mo)** | **ni atari** | **ni atatte no** |
| 'contrary to' | **ni hanshite** | **ni hanshi** | — |
| '(extending) over' | **ni kakete (wa/mo)** | **ni kake** | **ni kakete no** |
| 'when it comes to' | **ni kakete (wa/mo)** | — | — |
| 'with respect to', 'about', 'as regards' | **ni kanshite (wa/mo)** | **ni kanshi** | **ni kansuru** |
| 'in lieu of' | **ni kawatte** | **ni kawari** | **ni kawaru** |
| 'in' | **ni oite (wa/mo)** | — | **ni okeru/ni oite no** |
| 'at (the time of)', 'in' | **ni saishite (wa/mo)** | **ni saishi** | **ni saishite no** |
| 'against', 'for', 'in' | **ni taishite (wa/mo)** | **ni taishi** | **ni taisuru/ni taishite no** |
| 'for' | **ni totte (wa/mo)** | **ni tori** | **ni totte no** |
| 'about' | **ni tsuite** | **ni tsuki** | **ni tsuite no** |

**Table 3.1** (cont'd)

| Meaning | Adverbial | Adv.-bookish | N-modifying |
|---|---|---|---|
| 'per' | — | ni tsuki | — |
| 'depending on' | ni yotte (wa/mo) | ni yori | — |
| 'by', 'through' | ni yotte | ni yori | ni yoru |
| 'surrounding', 'concerning' | o megutte | o meguri | o meguru |
| 'by', 'through', or marking object | o motte | — | — |
| 'through' | o tōshite | — | o tōshite no |
| 'as' | to shite | — | to shite no |

**3.1** **Phrasal particles incorporating** ni

3.1.1 **ni atatte**

This is equivalent to English expressions like 'on the occasion of', 'when', 'in', 'for'.

3.1.1.1 *Noun* **ni atatte** *(wa/mo)*

a 売却にあたって建物は除去する。
**Baikyaku ni atatte tatemono wa jokyo suru.**
At the time of selling [the land], they will remove the buildings.

b 再開にあたって付けられた厳しい条件をクリアしている。
**Saikai ni atatte tsukerareta kibishii jōken o kuria shite iru.**
We've cleared the strict conditions [= of stock increases] imposed on the reopening.

c 利用にあたっては財団の審査がある。
**Riyō ni atatte wa zaidan no shinsa ga aru.**
When using [the facility] one has to undergo (*lit.* "there is") screening by the foundation.

d 最高裁判決にあたっても、特別な感慨はないと言う。
**Saikōsai hanketsu ni atatte mo, tokubetsu na kangai wa nai to iu.**
He says that he has no particular feelings regarding the high court decision.

e その没後百年にあたって様々な書物が出版された。

**Sono botsugo hyakunen ni atatte samazama na shomotsu ga shuppan sareta.**

On the 100th anniversary of his death a variety of books were published.

---

| 3.1.1.2 | *Noun* **ni atatte no** *noun* |

a Jリーグ設立にあたっての手腕を高く評価されている。

**Jei-rīgu setsuritsu ni atatte no shuwan o takaku hyōka sarete iru.**

His clout in setting up the J-League is highly regarded.

---

| 3.1.1.3 | *Verb* **ni atatte** |

a 彼女はこの本を書くにあたってまずこう宣言する。「哲学という
言葉を一切用いることなく、哲学を語ることができるのでなけ
れば、それは哲学ではない」と。

**Kanojo wa kono hon o kaku ni atatte mazu kō sengen suru. 'Tetsugaku to iu kotoba o issai mochiiru koto naku, tetsugaku o kataru koto ga dekiru no de nakereba, sore wa tetsugaku de wa nai' to.**

Regarding the writing of this book, she proclaims the following. 'If you can't talk about philosophy without using the word "philosophy" at all, then that's not philosophy'.

---

| 3.1.1.4 | *Verb* **ni atari** |

a 番組供給サービスを展開するにあたり会員組織を発足する。

**Bangumi kyōkyū sābisu o tenkai suru ni atari kai-in soshiki o hossoku suru.**

In developing the programme supply service, they will set up a membership organization.

---

| 3.1.1.5 | **ni atari** *[phrasal particle] and* **(ni) atari** *(conjunctive form/verb-stem of* **(ni) ataru**) *compared* |

The phrasal particle **ni atari** is not to be confused with the conjunctive form of the verb **(ni) ataru** 'correspond (to)', 'fall (on)':

a 三—六月は産卵期にあたり、絶食しながら浅瀬に移動してくる。
**San kara rokugatsu wa sanranki ni atari, zesshoku shinagara
asase ni idō shite kuru.**
March to June being their spawning time, they stop feeding and move
to the shallows.

| 3.1.2 | ni hanshi(te) |

ni hanshi(te) indicates the idea of 'contrary to', 'inversely to' (see 3.1.8).

a 予想に反して裁判は長引き、原告のほとんどが今や五十代だ。
**Yosō ni hanshite saiban wa nagabiki, genkoku no hotondo ga
ima ya gojūdai da.**
Contrary to expectations, the trial dragged on, and most of the
plaintiffs are now in their fifties.

b 今回も気象庁の当初予想に反して強い勢力を保ったままになって
いる。
**Konkai mo kishōchō no tōsho yosō ni hanshite tsuyoi
seiryoku o tamotta mama ni natte iru.**
This time too, contrary to the initial expectations of the Weather
Agency, [the typhoon] has maintained its strength.

c 同社のレンジは機能に反して年々ボタン類が少なくなってきた。
**Dōsha no renji wa kinō ni hanshite nennen botanrui ga
sukunaku natte kita.**
Inversely to the [number of] functions of their microwave ovens,
the number of controls have decreased every year.

| 3.1.3 | ni kakete |

Attached to nouns of time or place, **ni kakete** indicates that the action or
state of the predicate extends over the time or area to which **ni kakete** is
attached '(extending) over', 'to'.

Whereas **made** (see 2.10) does not specify that the time or place it is
attached to is included in the mention, **ni kakete** does.

*Note* – when attached to other nouns, **ni kakete wa/mo** has a different
meaning: 'when it comes to', 'concerning'.

### 3.1.3.1 ni kake(te)

a 週末にかけて、雨の心配はないという。

**Shūmatsu ni kakete, ame no shinpai wa nai to iu.**

Over the weekend, there is no chance of rain, they say.

b カラスは春から初夏にかけて巣作りをする。

**Karasu wa haru kara shoka ni kakete suzukuri
o suru.**

Crows build their nests from spring to early summer.

c 台風が接近する夕刻にかけ、さらに影響が広夕る見込みだ。

**Taifū ga sekkin suru yūkoku ni kake, sara ni eikyō ga
hirogaru mikomi da.**

Over the evening hours, when the typhoon closes in, its influence is
expected to spread even wider.

### 3.1.3.2 ni kake(te) [phrasal particle] and (ni) kake(te) [verb-stem] compared

Note that **ni kake**(te), when *not* attached to a noun of time or place, can
also be the stem form of the verb **kakeru** 'put before' (a committee etc.),
which takes the particle **ni** to mark the committee, etc.

a 九月の都市計画審議会にかけ、早ければ来年度にも事業に
着手する。

**Kugatsu no toshi keikaku shingikai ni kake, hayakereba
rainendo ni mo jigyō ni chakushu suru.**

They will put it before the Town Planning Committee in September,
and may start work as early as next fiscal year.

### 3.1.3.3 ni kakete no noun

a 「年末にかけての増加に期待したい」と話す。

**'Nenmatsu ni kakete no zōka ni kitai shitai' to
hanasu.**

We hope for (*lit.* "wish to see") an increase over the
end-of-year [period].

b 特に関東から静岡県にかけての地域に出店を集中させる。
  **Toku ni Kantō kara Shizuoka-ken ni kakete no chiiki ni
  shutten o shūchū saseru.**
  They will especially concentrate outlets in the area from Kanto to
  Shizuoka prefecture.

c 女性の首から胸にかけてのシワ、たるみを防ぐ働きがある。
  **Josei no kubi kara mune ni kakete no shiwa, tarumi o fusegu
  hataraki ga aru.**
  [The cream] has the effect of preventing the wrinkles and sagging
  extending over the area from a woman's neck to décolletage.

---

## 3.1.3.4 | ni kakete wa/mo

The sense here is 'when it comes to'.

a 正直さ、率直さにかけては、マレーシアが一番だった。
  **Shōjiki-sa, sotchoku-sa ni kakete wa, Marēshia ga ichiban
  datta.**
  When it comes to honesty and openness, Malaysia came out on top
  [of the APEC politicians].

b しかしサービスにかけては日本の書店はとてもかなわない。
  最近オープンした比較的大きな書店にはまず、いすがある。
  **Shikashi sābisu ni kakete wa Nihon no shoten wa totemo
  kanawanai. Saikin ōpun shita hikaku-teki ōkina shoten ni
  wa mazu, isu ga aru.**
  However, when it comes to service, Japanese bookshops are no match
  at all [for US ones]. In a relatively large bookshop that opened
  recently, there are chairs, for starters.

---

## 3.1.4 | ni kanshi(te)

**ni kanshite** indicates the idea of 'concerning', 'about', 'with respect to', 'as
regards'.

The difference between **ni kanshite**, **ni tsuite** and **o megutte** is that whereas
**ni kanshite** is attached to some topic or problem that is to be dealt with
or considered/talked about, **ni tsuite** more narrowly refers to the topic of
some communication. **o megutte**, on the other hand, usually refers to
something that people argue about (see 3.1.10, 3.2.1).

$\boxed{3.1.4.1}$ **ni kanshi(te) (wa/mo)**

a 国際協力に関して、日本は予想以上に期待されている。
**Kokusai kyōryoku ni kanshite, Nihon wa yosō ijō ni kitai
sarete iru.**
As regards international co-operation, expectations toward Japan are
greater than expected.

b 景気対策に関し「この二、三日中に大枠を示したい」。
**Keiki taisaku ni kanshi 'kono ni, sannichi-jū ni ōwaku o
shimeshitai'.**
. . . with respect to measures to revive the economy, [he said], 'I'd like
to give an outline within the next two or three days'.

c また農薬の使用などに関しても調査する。
**Mata nōyaku no shiyō nado ni kanshite mo chōsa suru.**
We will also survey the use of agricultural chemicals.

$\boxed{3.1.4.2}$ **ni kansuru** *noun*

a カネに関する悩みは尽きない。
**Kane ni kansuru nayami wa tsukinai.**
There's always something to worry about where money is concerned.

b フランスで日本に関する本は多く出ている。
**Furansu de Nihon ni kansuru hon wa ōku dete iru.**
In France many books on Japan are published.

$\boxed{\textbf{3.1.5}}$ **ni kawatte**

**ni kawatte** indicates that some thing (or person) replaces some other thing/
person 'in lieu of', 'replacing'.

$\boxed{3.1.5.1}$ **ni kawatte/ni kawari**

a 自家用車にかわってバスを市民の足として定着させようと懸命だ。
**Jikayōsha ni kawatte basu o shimin no ashi to shite teichaku
saseyō to kenmei da.**
They are trying hard to establish the bus to replace the private car as
the citizens' means of transport.

b 楽器に代わり自動車が盟主の座に一一。浜松を中心とする静岡県西
  部地区で、こんな話をよく耳にする。

**Gakki ni kawari jidōsha ga meishu no za ni--. Hamamatsu o
chūshin to suru Shizuoka-ken seibu chiku de konna hanashi
o yoku mimi ni suru.**

The car has replaced musical instruments as the leading product
[of the area]. This is something you hear often in the western
region of Shizuoka prefecture centring on Hamamatsu.

---

| 3.1.5.2 | ni kawaru *noun*

When modifying a noun, the verb form (**ni**) **kawaru** 'in place of' is used.

a マニュアルに代わるものがいる。
  **Manyuaru ni kawaru mono ga iru.**
  We need something in lieu of a manual.

b ソ連の脅威に代わる「新しい脅威」が姿を現している。
  **Soren no kyōi ni kawaru 'atarashii kyōi' ga sugata o
  arawashite iru.**
  A 'new menace' is manifesting itself in place of the Soviet menace.

---

| 3.1.6 | ni oite

**ni oite** can be regarded as a written or formal equivalent of **de** 'in', 'at',
although it is not always replaceable with **de** (see 2.5).

When modifying a noun, both **ni okeru** and **ni oite** can be used (the former
is far more common).

---

| 3.1.6.1 | ni oite (wa/mo)

a 私は、人生と文学において渡辺一夫の弟子です。
  **Watashi wa, jinsei to bungaku ni oite Watanabe Kazuo no
  deshi desu.**
  I am, in life and in literature, a pupil of Watanabe Kazuo.

b 今後も番組製作においては著作権を尊重していく。
  **Kongo mo bangumi seisaku ni oite wa chosakuken o sonchō
  shite iku.**
  In the future too we will respect copyright in producing our programmes.

c やはり恋愛においても女性が優位なのではないか。

**Yahari ren'ai ni oite mo josei ga yūi na no de wa nai ka.**

As you might expect, women are dominant in love, too, aren't they?
[= men wearing wedding rings to show they're faithful to their
women]

---

3.1.6.2 | **ni okeru** *noun*

a トルコにおける成人識字率は約80%。

**Toruko ni okeru seijin shikiji-ritsu wa yaku hachijup-pāsento.**

The adult literacy rate in Turkey is about 80 per cent.

b 問題は中国におけるハイテクのレベルだ。

**Mondai wa chūgoku ni okeru haiteku no reberu da.**

The problem is the level of hi-tech in China.

---

3.1.6.3 | **ni oite no** *noun*

a 必要なことは研究開発においての柔軟性だ。

**Hitsuyō na koto wa kenkyū kaihatsu ni oite no jūnan-sei da.**

What's necessary is flexibility in research development.

---

**3.1.7** | **ni saishi(te)**

Although (like other phrasal particles) **ni saishi(te)** is attached to nouns,
these are VN (usually two-*kanji* SJ words), i.e. have verbal meaning 'built
in'. **ni saishite** indicates the idea of 'at (the time of)', 'in', 'in case of' that
action (see 1.9).

a 従来、選挙に際して「党」か「人」かがよく問題になった。

**Jūrai, senkyo ni saishite 'tō' ka 'hito' ka ga yoku mondai
ni natta.**

In the past, 'party' versus 'person' was often a problem
in elections.

b 売却に際し、地価下落に泣かされたところも少なくない。

**Baikyaku ni saishi, chika geraku ni nakasareta tokoro mo
sukunaku nai.**

At the time of selling, quite a few places suffered from the drop in
land prices.

c フランス入国に際し、政治亡命の申請などはしていないという。

**Furansu nyūkoku ni saishi, seiji bōmei no shinsei nado wa
  shite inai to iu.**

They say that at the time of entering France, he didn't apply for
  political asylum.

d 入居に際しては保証金として十万五千円を町に支払う。

**Nyūkyo ni saishite wa hoshōkin to shite jūman gosen-en o
  machi ni shiharau.**

At the time of occupation, you pay the town ¥105,000 as security.

### 3.1.8 | ni taishi(te)

**ni taishite** indicates that some action or state is directed 'against'or 'towards'
the N to which **ni taishi(te)** is attached. In meaning, **ni taishite** ranges from
'against' to 'towards', 'for', 'in', 'in contrast to', etc. Before nouns, both
**ni taisuru** and **ni taishite no** are used.

Note the difference to **ni hanshite**, which is much narrower in meaning and
use 'contrary to' (expectations etc.) or 'in inverse proportion to' (see 3.1.2).

a 男は調べに対し黙秘を続けているという。

**Otoko wa shirabe ni taishi mokuhi o tsuzukete iru to iu.**

The man is said to be keeping silent in the face of the questioning.

b 働くための都会に対し、地方は自然がいっぱい。

**Hataraku tame no tokai ni taishi, chihō wa shizen ga ippai.**

In contrast to the big city, [which is] for work, the regions are full of
  nature.

c 記者団に対しては一切沈黙を通した。

**Kishadan ni taishite wa issai chinmoku o tōshita.**

He maintained total silence to the press.

### 3.1.8.1 | ni taisuru noun

a 子供に対する愛情はもちろんある。

**Kodomo ni taisuru aijō wa mochiron aru.**

Of course I have love for my children.

b 通貨に対する信認も大切だ。

**Tsūka ni taisuru shinnin mo taisetsu da.**

Faith in the currency is important too.

c 公共事業の先行きに対する不安も強い。
**Kōkyō jigyō no sakiyuki ni taisuru fuan mo tsuyoi.**
There is also a strong feeling of unease regarding the future
[prospects] for public works.

3.1.8.2 | **ni taishite no** *noun*

a 都知事に対しての評価はまだ分からない」。
**To-chiji ni taishite no hyōka wa mada wakaranai.**
The rating of the metropolitan governor is still unknown.

**3.1.9** | **ni totte**

Attached to nouns and pronouns indicating persons (or organizations), **ni
totte** indicates that some action or state takes place 'for' the person(s) or
organization(s).

3.1.9.1 | **ni totte**

a 僕にとって大学は自由研究の場です。
**Boku ni totte daigaku wa jiyū kenkyū no ba desu.**
For me, the university is a place for unfettered research.

b 道路は生き物にとって「死のワナ」なのだ。
**Dōro wa ikimono ni totte 'shi no wana' na no da.**
Roads are a 'death trap' for living things.

c しかし、旅行者にとっては歩きやすい街だ。
**Shikashi, ryokōsha ni totte wa arukiyasui machi da.**
However, for the traveller it is a town that is easy to walk [around].

d こうした展開は北朝鮮にとっても得策ではない。
**Kō shita tenkai wa kita chōsen ni totte mo tokusaku de wa nai.**
This development is not good for North Korea either.

3.1.9.2 | **ni tori**

a 私にとり音楽監督は初めて。
**Watashi ni tori ongaku kantoku wa hajimete.**
It's a first for me to be a musical director.

3.1.9.3 **ni totte no** *noun*

a 欧州企業にとってアフリカは、いわば日本企業にとってのアジアだ。
   **Ōshū kigyō ni totte Afurika wa iwaba Nihon kigyō ni totte no
   Ajia da.**
   For European business Africa is so to speak [what] Asia [is] for
   Japanese business.

3.1.10 **ni tsuite**

**ni tsuite** is used with predicates of communicative activity (talking, writing, thinking, etc.), and indicates what that activity is 'about' or 'on'. It is similar in meaning and use to **ni kanshite**, but **ni kanshite** is more widely used in the sense of 'concerning' (see 3.1.4, 3.2.1, 22.3.2.3.14).

As the first example shows, **ni tsuite** (but not **ni kanshite**) can be used for titles of theses and essays etc. (for more about differences between these phrasal particles, see 3.1.4).

3.1.10.1 **ni tsuite**

a 「海外における女性の職場環境について」という作文を提出した。
   **'Kaigai ni okeru josei no shokuba kankyō ni tsuite' to iu
   sakubun o teishutsu shita.**
   She submitted an essay entitled 'On the work environment of women
   overseas'.

b その件についてはノーコメントです。
   **Sono ken ni tsuite wa nō komento desu.**
   On that matter, it's no comment.

c 消費税についてはどうお考えですか。
   **Shōhizei ni tsuite wa dō o-kangae desu ka.**
   What are your thoughts on the consumption tax?

3.1.10.2 **ni tsuki**

This is a bookish variant of **ni tsuite**, and should not be confused with **ni tsuki**, which is a separate phrasal particle (see 3.1.11).

*Note* – **ni tsuki** can also be the conjunctive form of the verb **tsuku** 'reach', 'arrive', 'take up a position', etc., which also takes the particle **ni**.

a 地球環境問題解決の緊急性につき繰り返す必要はない。
   **Chikyū kankyō mondai kaiketsu no kinkyū-sei ni tsuki
   kurikaesu hitsuyō wa nai;**
   There is no need to reiterate the urgency of solving the earth's
   environmental problems.

b このような事態となったことにつき、大変遺憾に存ずるとともに
   深くおわびを申し上げる。
   **Kono yō na jitai to natta koto ni tsuki, taihen ikan ni zonzuru
   to tomo ni fukaku owabi o mōshiageru.**
   [= finance company employee indicted for illegal goings-on:] We deeply
   regret that this has happened, and offer our sincerest apologies.

3.1.10.3 **ni tsuite no** *noun*

a コンピューターについての会話はスムーズだ。
   **Konpyūtā ni tsuite no kaiwa wa sumūzu da.**
   His conversation about computers is well informed.

3.1.11 **ni tsuki**

Used between units or amounts, the phrasal particle **ni tsuki** indicates '(unit/
amount) per', 'for (unit/amount)'. Attached to other nouns, it means 'owing to'.

3.1.11.1 *Unit/amount* **ni tsuki**

In this use, **ni tsuki** means 'unit/amount per', 'for unit/amount'. See also
2.4.14 for expressions like 'times per period', etc.

a 一回につき三百円だ。
   **Ikkai ni tsuki sanbyaku-en da.**
   It's ¥300 a go.

b 一びん六百ccにつき、一キログラムのトマトを使っている。
   **Hitobin roppyaku cc ni tsuki, ichi kiroguramu no tomato o
   tsukatte iru.**
   For one bottle [of] 600cc, they use one kilogram of tomatoes.

| 3.1.11.2 | *Other noun* **ni tsuki**

Attached to nouns other than units or amounts, **ni tsuki** indicates a reason 'owing to'.

a 私には「長期間留守につき、ゆっくり仕事できます。ゴッソリ
   持っていって」と聞こえてしまって⋯
   **Watashi ni wa 'Chō-kikan rusu ni tsuki, yukkuri shigoto
   dekimasu. Gossori motte itte' to kikoete shimatte ...**
   To me, [= the recorded message giving dates of absence from home]
   sounds like 'Owing to my extended absence from home, you
   [= the burglar] can work at your leisure. Take plenty' ...

b 「マリンジャンボ」が大好評につき、急きょ導入が決まったもの
   で、デザインは同じだ。
   **'Marin Janbo' ga dai-kōhyō ni tsuki, kyūkyo dōnyū ga kimatta
   mono de, dezain wa onaji da.**
   It was suddenly decided to introduce [this aircraft] because of
   the popularity of the 'Marine jumbo'; the design is the same.

| 3.1.12 | **ni yotte**

**ni yotte** expresses two meanings: the means or cause through which an action or development takes place ('through', 'of', 'in accordance with', 'due to'), and, in sentences with predicates of change or difference, **ni yotte** (**wa/mo**) means 'depending on'.

*Note* – **ni yotte** and **ni yoru to** are often confused by English speakers because they sound similar, and both are translated as 'according to'. They are *not* interchangeable. **ni yoru to** expresses source of information, while **ni yotte** expresses basis of difference.

| 3.1.12.1 | **ni yotte**

This indicates a means or cause 'through', 'with', 'owing to'. After nouns indicating a wish or request, the meaning is 'in accordance with'.

| 3.1.12.1.1 | **ni yotte** (means or cause)

a イベントによって連帯感が生まれる。
   **Ibento ni yotte rentaikan ga umareru.**
   Solidarity is created through [staging] events.

b 湿気によって壁にはカビが発生する。

**Shikke ni yotte kabe ni wa kabi ga hassei suru.**

Owing to the humidity, mould grows on the walls.

c 透明度を高めることによって国民の理解は深まるだろう。

**Tōmei-do o takameru koto ni yotte kokumin no rikai wa
fukamaru darō.**

Through increasing transparency, the understanding of the people
should deepen.

d 告別式は故人の希望により行わない。

**Kokubetsu-shiki wa kojin no kibō ni yori okonawanai.**

In accordance with the wishes of the deceased, no funeral will
be held.

---

| 3.1.12.1.2 | **ni yoru** noun

a 電話による相談も受ける。

**Denwa ni yoru sōdan mo ukeru.**

They also accept consultations by telephone.

b また、日本刀によるマキやワラの裁断も実演する。

**Mata Nihontō ni yoru maki ya wara no saidan mo jitsuen
suru.**

They also demonstate the cutting of firewood and straw [sheaves]
with Japanese swords.

---

| 3.1.12.2 | **ni yotte (wa/mo)** *predicate of change/difference*

With predicates of change/difference, **ni yotte (wa/mo)** and **ni yori** mean
'depending on'.

a 紫外線の影響の表れ方は生物の種によって異なる。

**Shigaisen no eikyō no araware-kata wa seibutsu no shu ni
yotte kotonaru.**

The way the influence of UV rays appears differs according to
the type of organism.

b 高さはコンテナの数により変わる。

**Takasa wa kontena no kazu ni yori kawaru.**

The height [of the warehouse] differs depending on the number of
containers [it holds].

c 内定者数は業種により明暗が分かれた。
**Naitei-sha-sū wa gyōshu ni yori meian ga wakareta.**
The number of informal [job] offers differed according to business
type.

d 商品によってはカウボーイより安かった。
**Shōhin ni yotte wa kaubōi yori yasukatta.**
Depending on the item, it was cheaper than Cowboy
[= a cheap chain store].

## 3.2 Phrasal particles incorporating o

### 3.2.1 o megutte

**o megutte** means 'surrounding', 'concerning', 'about', usually marking the
object of some dispute (for differences between **ni kanshite, ni tsuite** and
**o megutte**, see 3.1.4).

Note that in the noun-modifying form **o meguru** it can also mean 'surrounding' in a physical sense.

### 3.2.1.1 o megutte/meguri

a 一人の娘をめぐって産みの母と育ての母が壮絶な争いを展開する。
**Hitori no musume o megutte umi no haha to sodate no
haha ga sōzetsu na arasoi o tenkai suru.**
Over their only daughter, the real mother and the foster mother
are fighting a bitter battle.

b 来年の春闘をめぐり、鉄鋼労連が揺れている。
**Rainen no shuntō o meguri, tekkō rōren ga yurete iru.**
Concerning next year's spring offensive, the steel workers' association
is wavering.

### 3.2.1.2 o meguru noun

a 水俣病をめぐる紛争は、袋小路に陥っている。
**Minamata-byō o meguru funsō wa, fukuro kōji ni ochiitte iru.**
The dispute concerning Minamata disease has reached a dead end
(lit. "entered a dead-end alley").

b 日米の金融政策をめぐる環境は全く違う。

**Nichibei no kin'yū seisaku o meguru kankyō wa mattaku
chigau.**

The environments surrounding monetary policy in Japan and the US
are totally different.

### 3.2.2 | o motte

**o motte** is a combination of the case particle **o** and the conjunctive form
of the verb **motsu** 'have', 'hold', but it can be regarded as a written or
formal equivalent of the case particle **o** (marking an object) or **de** (marking a means). There are also some idiomatic uses (see 2.2, 2.5).

### 3.2.2.1 | Marking an object

Here, **o motte** can be replaced by **o**.

a 今の議論は何をもって空洞化というのかあいまいだ。

**Ima no giron wa nani o motte kūdō-ka to iu no ka aimai da.**

In the current debate it is unclear what is meant by hollowing out.

### 3.2.2.2 | Marking a means

Here, **o motte** can usually be replaced by **de**. Note the combination **o motte
shite mo** in example b, which is a written-style equivalent of **de mo**.

a ハイテクの裏をかいた知能犯罪。ハイテクをもって制するべ
きだ。

**Haiteku no ura o kaita chinō hanzai. Haiteku o motte
seisuru-beki da.**

It's a crime that's outsmarted hi-tech. It should be controlled by means
of hi-tech.

b 美しいステンドグラスは現代の技術をもってしても複製でき
ない。

**Utsukushii sutendogurasu wa gendai no gijutsu o motte shite
mo fukusei dekinai.**

The beautiful stained glass cannot be replicated even by modern
technology.

*Idiomatic uses*

Here, **o motte** means 'with', 'with effect from'.

a 愛情をもって育てて欲しい。
   **Aijō o motte sodatete hoshii.**
   We'd like people to raise them [= the plants] with love.

b 本日をもって総辞職することとしました。
   **Honjitsu o motte sō-jishoku suru koto to shimashita.**
   I have decided that we resign en masse with effect from today.

<hr>

**3.2.3** **o tōshite**

**o tōshite** is a combination of the case particle **o** and the conjunctive form of the verb **tōsu** 'let or make pass through'; it indicates the medium (object, activity, organization) 'through' which an action or state takes place.

After an expression of time (examples e and f), the meaning is 'throughout'.

a 日本人学校の中には、スポーツを通して現地との交流を図ってい
   る学校もある。
   **Nihonjin gakkō no naka ni wa, supōtsu o tōshite genchi to no kōryū o hakatte iru gakkō mo aru.**
   Among overseas Japanese schools, there are some which attempt exchange with the locals through sports.

b ただ、モノを通してのつながりは表層的なつきあいでしかない。
   **Tada, mono o tōshite no tsunagari wa hyōsō-teki na tsukiai de shika nai.**
   However, a connection through [material] things is merely a surface relationship.

c 同署では、「教室を通して防犯意識を高めてほしい」と話している。
   **Dōsho de wa 'Kyōshitsu o tōshite bōhan ishiki o takamete hoshii' to hanashite iru.**
   The said police station is saying, 'We want [schools] to raise crime prevention awareness in (*lit.* "through") the classroom'.

d 最大のコンピューター通信網「インターネット」を通して、
   世界のどこからでも特許の全文を参照できる。
   **Saidai no konpyūtā tsūshinmō 'intānetto' o tōshite, sekai no doko kara demo tokkyo no zenbun o sanshō dekiru.**
   Through the Internet, the largest computer communications network, one can refer to the whole text of the patent from anywhere in the world.

e ビールの種類は年間を通して飲めるタイプとシーズンごとに出す
  タイプの二つ。
  **Bīru no shurui wa nenkan o tōshite nomeru taipu to
  shīzun-goto ni dasu taipu no futatsu.**
  There are two kinds of beer: the type you can drink throughout the
  year, and the type that's brought out seasonally.

f ここ数年、クジラは日本の近海でほとんど一年を通して見られる
  ようになった。
  **Koko sūnen, kujira wa Nihon no kinkai de hotondo ichinen o
  tōshite mirareru yō ni natta.**
  For the past few years, one has been able to see whales in the seas
  near Japan almost all year round.

## 3.3 Phrasal particle incorporating to

### 3.3.1 to shite

**to shite** indicates the status or capacity of a thing or person 'as'. **to shite**
must not be confused with the conjunctive form of the phrase **to suru** 'to
regard/view as', especially as they can appear in identical-looking contexts
(see 3.3.1.2 d and e for examples).

### 3.3.1.1 to shite (wa/mo)

a 日本は加工貿易の輸出立国として生きてきた。
  **Nihon wa kakō bōeki no yushutsu rikkoku to shite
  ikite kita.**
  Japan has existed as a country based on the exports of
  the manufacturing trade.

b 中国の古典文学の研究者としても知られ、「水滸伝」「古今奇観」
  などを翻訳した。
  **Chūgoku no koten bungaku no kenkyūsha to shite mo
  shirare, 'Suikoden' 'Kokon Kikan' nado o hon'yaku shita.**
  He is also known as a researcher on Chinese classical literature, and
  has translated [works] such as *Suikoden* and *Kokon Kikan*.

c 本来は抑えだが、先発として起用する。
  **Honrai wa osae da ga, senpatsu to shite kiyō suru.**
  Originally, he is a stopper, but we'll use him as a starting pitcher.

d 政界から引退後はエコノミストとして活躍、多くの著作を残
している。

**Seikai kara intai-go wa ekonomisuto to shite katsuyaku, ōku
no chosaku o nokoshite iru.**

After his retirement from the politicial world he was active as an
economist, and has made [his mark with] many books.

| 3.3.1.2 | **to shite no** *noun* |

When used to modify a noun, **no** is attached to **to shite**.

a しかし選手としての実績はない。

**Shikashi, senshu to shite no jisseki wa nai.**

However, he doesn't have any record as a player.

b 実際、今の大阪市には住宅地としての魅力は余り感じられない。

**Jissai, ima no ōsaka-shi ni wa jūtakuchi to shite no miryoku
wa amari kanjirarenai.**

In fact, one doesn't feel much attraction to present-day Osaka city as
a residential area.

c 投資先としての中国の魅力は何よりも巨大な国内市場にある。

**Tōshisaki to shite no Chūgoku no miryoku wa nani yori mo
kyodai na kokunai shijō ni aru.**

The attraction of China as a place for investment lies above all in its
vast domestic market.

*Note* – there is also a phrase **to suru,** which means 'to view as', 'deal with'
(examples d and e).

d 大阪府警淀川署は強盗事件として男の行方を追っている。

**Ōsaka-fukei Yodogawa-sho wa gōtō jiken to shite otoko no
yukue o otte iru.**

The Yodokawa police station of the Osaka prefectural police views it
as a case of burglary and are looking for the man.

e 主として開発問題をテーマとし、推定だがその数は四千から六千
にのぼる。

**Shu to shite kaihatsu mondai o tēma to shi, suitei da ga sono
kazu wa yonsen kara rokusen ni noboru.**

[NGOs] deal mostly with development issues, and their number is
estimated at four to six thousand.

## Chapter 4

# Numbers and counters

## 4.1　Numbers

Japanese uses two sets of numbers, Native-Japanese and Sino-Japanese, although they are not usually used as 'pure' sets.

*Note* – numbers and number–counter combinations (see 4.2) behave like nouns in that they can be modified by noun-modifying demonstrative words (example a).

a 戦後は遊郭も消滅、店々は旅館などに姿を変えていく。その夜、泊まった「旅館みよし」もそんな一つ。

**Sengo wa yūkaku mo shōmetsu, misemise wa ryokan nado ni sugata o kaete iku. Sono yoru, tomatta 'Ryokan Miyoshi' mo sonna hitotsu.**

After the war, the red-light district ceased to exist, and the establishments changed into inns. The Miyoshi Inn, where we stayed that night, is one of these.

### 4.1.1 │ *Counting things*

When counting things, the combination number+counter is usual, where the Sino-Japanese and Native-Japanese numbers below (plus some variations) are used to form number–counter combinations (see Table 4.1).

| | I | 2 | 3 | 4 | 5 | 6 | 7 | 8 | 9 | 10 |
|---|---|---|---|---|---|---|---|---|---|---|
| SJ: | **ichi** | **ni** | **san** | **shi** | **go** | **roku** | **shichi** | **hachi** | **kyū/ku** | **jū** |
| NJ: | **hito-** | **futa-** | **mit-** | **yo(t)-** | **itsu-** | **mut-** | **nana** | **yat-** | **kokono-** | **tō** |

Numbers for 10 and above are basically Sino-Japanese (except for **tō**, which can be used by itself to count things):

| | |
|---|---|
| 10 ... | **jū, jūichi, ni, san, shi (yon), go ...** |
| 20 ... | **nijūichi, ...** |
| 30 ... | **sanjū, ...** |
| 40 ... | **yonjū (shijū), ...** |
| 50 ... | **gojū, ...** |
| 60 ... | **rokujū, ...** |
| 70 ... | **nanajū, ...** |
| ... | |
| 100 ... | **hyaku, nihyaku, sanbyaku, yonhyaku, ...** |
| | **roppyaku ..., happyaku ...** |
| 1,000 ... | **sen, nisen, sanzen ...** |
| 10,000 ... | **ichiman, niman, sanman ...** |
| 100,000 | **jūman, nijūman ...** |
| 1,000,000 | **hyakuman, nihyakuman ...** |
| 10,000,000 | **issenman, nisenman ...** |
| 100,000,000 | **ichioku, nioku ...** |

### 4.1.1.1 | Counting things approximately

#### 4.1.1.1.1 | Adjoining numbers

This can be done by using two adjoining numbers (in writing, these usually have a comma (or occasionally a hyphen) between them, but are pronounced as one unit). They are mostly used with counters, excepting **ni, san**, which is also used in the form of **ni, san no** noun in the sense of 'several' (see 4.2).

a ···二、三の疑問点を提示したい。
   **...ni, san no gimon-ten o teiji shitai.**
   ...I wish to raise a couple of queries.

#### 4.1.1.1.2 | By prefixes, adverbs or adverbial particles

The Sino-Japanese prefix **sū-** 'several' and the adverb **yaku** 'approximately', precede the number (but see below for how **sū-** can be inserted between number and counter), whereas the adverbial particles **gurai/kurai** and **hodo** follow number (+ counter) (see 11.5.1.1, 11.5.2.1).

a 「一人または数人」とあれば、二人でもいいわけだが、最大値は
   分からない。
   **'Hitori mata wa sūnin' to areba, futari de mo ii wake da ga,
   saidai-chi wa wakaranai.**
   If it [= the advert] states 'one or several people', then two people are
   OK, but one doesn't know the maximum figure.

Note how 数 sū- can be inserted between number (units of ten and above) and counter in the sense of 'unit-odd'.

b 2–3年のうちに20数巻をそろえる方針だ。

**Ni kara san-nen no uchi ni nijū-sū-kan o soroeru hōshin da.**

Their aim is to complete the set of all 20-odd volumes in two or three years.

c 花は二十日間くらい咲く。

**Hana wa hatsuka-kan kurai saku.**

The flowers bloom for about 20 days.

d 免許は三十万円ほどで取得できる。

**Menkyo wa sanjūman-en hodo de shutoku dekiru.**

A licence can be obtained for about three hundred thousand yen.

<br>

**4.1.1.2** *Amounts involving* **nan-/iku-** *'how much/how many'*
*+ ka/mo/demo*

The question words (+ counter) **nan-/iku-** combine with the particle **ka** (indefinite amount 'a lot', 'lots', etc.), **mo** (+ negative predicate, small amount 'no . . .', 'not many', etc.) and **demo** (/verb-**te mo** 'any') (see 5.2 and Table 5.2, 26.3.1.5).

a 電気を止められたことも何度もある。

**Denki o tomerareta koto mo nan-do mo aru.**

The electricity has been cut off many times.

b 何歳になってもダイビングを続けていくつもりでいる。

**Nan-sai ni natte mo daibingu o tsuzukete iku tsumori
de iru.**

He intends to continue diving regardless of age.

<br>

**4.1.2** **Counting in sequence**

**4.1.2.1** *Counting aloud*

For counting out aloud, the Sino-Japanese set is the more common. Note the common Native-Japanese alternatives for the near-homophones (in rapid speech at any rate) **shi** and **shichi**.

1 **ichi**, 2 **ni**, 3 **san**, 4 **shi** (**yon**), 5 **go**, 6 **roku**, 7 **shichi** (**nana**), 8 **hachi**, 9 **kyū/ku**, 10 **jū**.

4.1.2.2 | *Phone and account numbers*

Phone numbers are read more or less like counting out aloud, but there are some specific rules.

**rei** rather than **zero** is used; **yon** and **nana** are obligatory instead of **shi** and **shichi**; the single-syllable **ni** and **go** are obligatorily lengthened to **nī** and **gō**, and the longer variant **kyū** is obligatory rather than **ku**.

The (fictional) Tokyo phone numbers below, for instance, are normally read as follows (note the optional/more formal use of -**kyoku** 'exchange [number]' and -**ban** '[customer] number'):

(03) 123-4567: (**Tōkyō**) **reisan ichinīsan(-kyoku)**
(**no**) **yongōrokunana(-ban)**

(03) 987-6543: (**Tōkyō**) **reisan kyūhachinana(-kyoku)**
(**no**) **rokugōyonsan(-ban)**

Phone numbers for businesses etc. are often given with *kana* attached that combine imaginative 'readings' of the number for mnemonic and/or advertising purposes. Such 'readings' use not only Native-Japanese and Sino-Japanese readings (with additional *kana* often thrown in), but 'English' pronunciation of the numbers too.

6   7 9       -3 6 2
ムリナク   スリムニ

**murinaku surimu ni**
'getting slim without effort'

To explain: **mu** (Native-Japanese 6 + **ri** thrown in), **na** (Native-Japanese 7), **ku** (Sino-Japanese 9) **suri** ('English' 'three') **mu** (NJ 6), **ni** (SJ 2)

Or, the number of a hair-transplant clinic:

10       -2 3 2 3
い～わ   ふさふさ

**ii wa fusafusa**
That's nice! tufty [hair]

Here we have **i** (Sino-Japanese **i(chi)** lengthened to **ii** 'nice' (～indicates a long sound), **wa** for 0 (**wa** is a Native-Japanese word for 'circle', used here for **wa** [final particle], and **fu** for Native-Japanese 2, **sa** for Sino-Japanese 3).

| 4.1.3 | *Superstition and numbers* |

Many hotels in Japan lack a 13th storey, which is a Western import. More traditionally, because of the homophony between 死 **shi** ('four', 'death') and 苦 **ku** ('nine', 'suffering'), hospitals have no wards 4 and 9, and hotels, etc. usually lack a fourth storey.

## 4.2 Counters

Numbers are typically used to count nouns, in similar fashion to English 'a *cup of* tea' or 'five *head of* cattle'. Although some nouns can be counted by numbers using the 'default' counters -**tsu** and -**ko** (see Table 4.1), many nouns require a specific counter in the combination [number + counter].

There is a multitude of counters in Japanese, and some books list a large number of them, including a counter for furniture (-**kyaku**). However, in everyday language -**tsu** or -**ko** is used for tables and chairs, and one can get by with a relatively small number, which are given in Table 4.1.

*Note 1* – there is also a number of items that are used to count money (¥ -**en**, $ -**doru**, £ -**pondo**, etc.) and others that are used with figures, such as % (**pāsento**) or the Japanese 10%-unit, -**wari**.

*Note 2* – there are some differences between the 'default' counters -**tsu** and -**ko**, i.e. -**tsu** is attached to Native-Japanese numbers up to 9 only, whereas -**ko** attaches only to Sino-Japanese numbers. -**tsu** can be used with abstract items such as thoughts, but -**ko** is limited to concrete objects only (such as landmines, example d).

a 外国では発言を慎むのが一つの考え方だ。
  **Gaikoku de wa hatsugen o tsutsushimu no ga hitotsu no kangaekata da.**
  One thought is that [Japanese politicians] refrain from making statements abroad.

-**hai** is mostly used for cupfuls and glassfuls, and -**hon** for tubular objects such as bottles (example 4.2.3 a), flowers, trees, pencils, hairs, etc., but also trousers and even phone calls (example 4.2.4 a). -**mai** counts flat objects such as sheets of paper, coins (for coins, -**ko** is also used), CDs, bills, tickets (example 4.2.3 b), but also doors (example 4.2.1 a), shirts, kimonos, etc.

Animals are counted with -tō or -hiki, with -tō being used for larger species, such as cows, horses and pigs. Note that the size does not matter, e.g. piglets and calves are still counted with -tō (examples b and c).

b 八頭の子ブタを出産させるのに成功した。
**Hat-tō no kobuta o shussan saseru no ni seikō shita.**
They succeeded in making it produce eight piglets.

c 二十ヘクタールの放牧場で成牛、子牛合わせて四十三頭を飼育
している。
**Nijū hekutāru no hōbokujō de seigyū, koushi awasete yonjūsan-tō o shi-iku shite iru.**
On the 20ha. dairy farm, they keep a total of 43 grown cattle and calves.

d 紛争地帯に埋められたままの地雷は一億一千万個に上る。
**Funsōchitai ni umerareta mama no jirai wa ichioku issenman-ko ni noboru.**
The [number of] landmines still buried in conflict areas amounts to 110 million.

*Note 3* – counters of time and measurement count themselves, i.e. they don't count other nouns.

e この一年で二倍に膨らんだ。
**Kono ichinen de nibai ni fukuranda.**
In the past year, it has doubled.

f 入場料は一回券で七百円。
**Nyūjōryō wa ikkai-ken de nanahyaku-en.**
The entrance fee is ¥700 for a single ticket.

*Note 4* – the counter of time, -ji, is used to indicate the time, but when 間 -kan is added, the hours are counted. Compare:

g 一時 **ichiji** 'I o'clock'
h 一時間 **ichijikan** 'I hour'

Other counters of time can be used in the sense of 'period of time' by themselves, and adding 間 -kan does not change that meaning, but makes it more explicit.

i ✎三十分待った。　**Sanjuppun matta.**　'I waited 30 minutes.'
j ✎三十分間待った。**Sanjuppun-kan matta.**　'I waited for (a period of) 30 minutes.'

Number + counter is used to count nouns in the following ways.

### 4.2.1 | Number + counter no noun

Numbers + counter can precede the noun, with the particle **no** attached.

a その奥に二枚のドアが見えている。
**Sono oku ni ni-mai no doa ga miete iru.**
Beyond her [= female figure in painting], two doors are visible.

### 4.2.2 | Number + counter + particle

#### 4.2.2.1 | One number only

a 三階には宿泊客共通の浴場がある。
**San-gai ni wa shukuhaku-kyaku kyōtsū no yokujō ga aru.**
On the third floor is a bath for joint use by lodgers.

#### 4.2.2.2 | Two numbers, separated by comma or hyphen: approximate numbers

Two consecutive numbers, usually separated by a comma (but pronounced as one unit), or less commonly by a hyphen (example c) are one way of expressing approximate numbers (see 23.1; see also 4.1.1.1 for other ways of expressing approximate numbers).

a だが、ここ五、六年で風向きが一変した。
**Daga, koko go, roku-nen de kazamuki ga ippen shita.**
However, in the past five or six years the situation has changed completely.

b 旅に出ると、人々は普通の五、六倍のお金を使う。
**Tabi ni deru to, hitobito wa futsū no go, roku-bai no okane o tsukau.**
When they go on a trip, people spend five or six times as much money as usual.

c 決意するまでには二―三週間悩み抜いた。
**Ketsui suru made-ni wa nisan-shūkan nayaminuita.**
He worried for several weeks before he made up his mind.

# Table 4.1 Common number and counter combinations

| Counter | Number | | | | | | | | | |
|---|---|---|---|---|---|---|---|---|---|---|
| | ichi<br>hito- | ni<br>futa- | san<br>mit- | shi<br>yo(t)- | go<br>itsu- | roku<br>mut- | shichi<br>nana | hachi<br>yat- | kyū/ku<br>kokono- | jū<br>tō |
| **doru**<br>($) | | | | yondoru | | | | | | |
| **en**<br>(¥) | | | | yo-en | | | | | | |
| **fun**<br>(minutes) | ippun | | sanpun | yonpun | | roppun | nanafun | happun<br>hachifun | kyūfun | juppun<br>jippun |
| **pondo**<br>(lb. or £) | | | | yonpondo | | | nanapondo | | kyūpondo | juppondo<br>jippondo |
| **hon**<br>(bottles, etc.) | ippon | | sanbon | yonhon | | roppon | nanahon | happon | kyūhon | juppon<br>jippon |
| **kagetsu**<br>(months) | ikkagetsu | | | yonkagetsu | | rokkagetsu | | | | jukkagetsu<br>jikkagetsu |
| **kai**<br>(storeys) | | | sangai<br>sankai | | | rokkai | nanakai | hachikai | | jukkai<br>jikkai |
| **ko**<br>(default counter) | ikko | | | yonko | | rokko | nanako | hakko | kyūko | jukko<br>jikko |
| **mai**<br>(flat objects) | | | | yonmai | | | | | kyūmai<br>kumai | |
| **nichi**<br>(days) | ichinichi<br>tsuitachi* | futsuka | mikka | yokka | itsuka | muika | nanoka<br>nanuka | yōka | kokonoka | tōka |
| **nin**<br>(humans) | | | | yonin | | | | | | |
| **nen**<br>(years) | | | | yonen | | | | | | |
| **pāsento**<br>(%) | ippāsento | | | yonpāsento | | | | | | juppāsento<br>jippāsento |

| pēji (pages) | ippēji | | | yonpēji | | roppēji | nanapēji | happēji / hachipēji | kyūpēji | juppēji / jippēji |
|---|---|---|---|---|---|---|---|---|---|---|
| ri (humans) | hitori | futari | | | | | | | | jikko |
| sai (years of age) | issai | | | | | | nanasai | hassai | | jussai / jissai |
| satsu (bound objects) | issatsu | | | yonsatsu | | | nanasatsu | hassatsu | kyūsatsu | jussatsu / jissatsu |
| shū (weeks) | isshū | | | yonshū | | | nanashū | hasshū | kyūshū | jusshū / jisshu |
| tō (large animals) | ittō | | | yontō | | | nanatō | hattō | kyūtō | juttō / jittō |
| tsu (default counter: NJ numbers only) | hitotsu | futatsu | mittsu | yottsu | itsutsu | muttsu | nanatsu | yattsu | kokonotsu | — |
| tsuki (months) | hitotsuki | futatsuki | mitsuki | | | | | | | |
| wa (birds) | | | sanba | yonwa | | | | | | juppa / jippa |
| wari (10% unit) | | | | yonwari | | | | | kyūwari | |

*Notes* * Only used in the meaning of *the first of the month*.

The table lists some common counters and the way they combine with numbers. Only those combinations which involve sound change, irregular formation or only one of two regular ways of formation are listed (the remainder is predictable, consisting of the numeral (**ichi, ni**, etc.) given at the top plus the form of the counter given in the vertical left column). Note, however, that the pronunciation, especially of the syllabic **n**, varies according to its phonetic environment; for instance, before **b** and **m**, it is pronounced as **m**. Combinations with **nan-** *how many* are the same as those with **san** *three*.

With counters expressing time (**fun, nen**, etc.), the suffix **-kan** can be added (optionally in the case of **byō, fun, nen, nichi** and **shū**) to indicate *duration of time*. For instance, **goji** on its own means *5 o'clock*, whereas **gojikan** means *five hours*. Note, however, that whereas the months of the year (January–December) are counted **ichi-gatsu, nigatsu**, etc., *one month* is **ikkagetsu**, to which **-kan** can be added. The days of the month from the 11th onwards are as follows, in so far as they are irregular:

| | | | |
|---|---|---|---|
| 14th | **jūyokka** | 20th | **hatsuka** |
| 19th | **jūkunichi** | 24th | **nijūyokka** |

*Noun (+ particle) [number + counter] verb*

Note that [number + counter] can also be placed between [noun (+ particle)] and verb.

a ✐ビールを三本ください。(cf., ビールをください)
**Bīru o san-bon kudasai.**
Three bottles of beer, please.

b 一番安い天井桟敷席を一枚買った。
**Ichiban yasui tenjōsajiki-seki o ichi-mai katta.**
I bought one ticket for an upper circle seat, which is the cheapest.


4.2.4 *Noun [number 'one' + counter] (+ particle)*

[Number + counter] can be sandwiched between noun and particle. Note that only the number 'one' is used in this sense, which in negative sentences has the implication of 'just one', 'a single . . .'.

a 離婚原因は夫の気ままで不安定な生活ぶり。「旅行に出かけると
いっては数カ月、家を空ける。その間電話一本ない。そんなこ
とが何度もあった」。
**Rikon gen'in wa otto no kimama de fuantei na seikatsu-buri.
'Ryokō ni dekakeru to itte wa sūkagetsu, ie o akeru. Sono
kan denwa ip-pon nai. Sonna koto ga nando mo atta'.**
The reason for the divorce was the husband's irregular lifestyle.
'He would say he'd go on a trip, and stay away from home for
months. During that time, there wouldn't be a single phone call.
That sort of thing happened many times.'

b 葉っぱ一枚を見ても仕方がない。
**Happa ichi-mai o mite mo shikata ga nai.**
There is no point looking at a single leaf [= satellite pictures need to
show more than that].

c レンズ一枚の価格は二万二千円。
**Renzu ichi-mai no kakaku wa niman nisen-en.**
The price for one lens is ¥22,000.

| 4.2.5 | *Number + counter with ellipted noun* |
|---|---|

Where the context makes it clear which noun they refer to, number + counter can be used without the noun they count.

a 精密なイラストは ··· 息をのむほど美しい。一枚を仕上げるのに
　一カ月くらいかかるそうだ。
**Seimitsu na irasuto wa ... iki o nomu hodo utsukushii.**
**Ichi-mai o shiageru no ni ikkagetsu kurai kakaru sō da.**
The accurate illustrations ... are breathtakingly beautiful. Apparently
　it takes about one month to finish one.

## 4.3　Ordinal numbers

Ordinal numbers are formed by adding the suffix -**me** (め・目) to the combinations number + counter, including the 'default' counter **tsu**-(つ) (see 4.1, 4.2).

| 一つ目 | **hitotsu-me** | 'the first' |
|---|---|---|
| 二人目 | **futari-me** | 'the second person' |
| 三人目 | **sannin-me** | 'the third person' |
| 二台目 | **nidai-me** | 'the second' (car, TV, etc.) |
| 三日目 | **mikka-me** | 'the third day' |
| 五枚目 | **gomai-me** | 'the fifth' (page, photo, etc.) |
| 十代目 | **jūdai-me** | 'the tenth' (generation) |
| 一回目 | **ikkai-me** | 'the first time' |

To Sino-Japanese number + counter combinations, the prefix **dai-** (第) can also be attached, which gives it a more formal ring that cannot be captured in translation:

| 第一回目 | **dai-ikkai-me** | 'the first time' |
|---|---|---|

To Sino-Japanese numbers without counter the suffix -**ban** is attached, often in combination with the prefix **dai-** (第), again for a more formal/ written-style ring. **dai-ichi** forms many other Sino-Japanese and Western-Japanese nouns by attaching noun elements such as -**i** 位 (第一位 'first rank'), -**bu** (部) (第一部 'the first part'), -**shū** (週) (第一週 'the first week'), **dankai** (段階) (第一段階 'the first stage'), **raundo** (ラウンド) (第一ラウンド 'the first round'), etc.

| 第一 | **dai-ichi** | 'the first' |
|---|---|---|
| 第一番 | **dai-ichi-ban** | 'the first', 'No. 1' |

| 一番 | ichi-ban | 'the first' |
| 一番目 | ichi-ban-me | 'the first one' |
| 第一番目 | dai-ichi-ban-me | 'the first one' |

a 毎月第一、三、五月曜日が定休。
**Maitsuki dai-ichi, -san, -go getsuyōbi ga teikyū.**
They're closed on the first, third and fifth Monday of each month.

b ベートーベン「交響曲第一番」などを演奏する。
**Bētōben 'Kōkyōkyoku Dai-ichi-ban' nado o ensō suru.**
They perform Beethoven's First Symphony and other [works].

*Note* – (**mazu**) **dai-ichi ni, dai-ni ni, dai-san ni**, etc. are also used in the sense of 'firstly', 'secondly', 'thirdly' when lining up arguments, etc. (example c, see also 24.7).

c まずリベラルと片仮名英語を使うのはなぜか。三つの理由が想像
できる。第一に、何となくイメージがいい。第二に、日本語訳
の自由主義は・・・長い間、マルクス主義との関係を清算できな
かった社会党にとっては抵抗があったのだろう。第三に、・・・
**Mazu riberaru to katakana eigo o tsukau no wa naze ka.**
**Mittsu no riyū ga sōzō dekiru. Dai-ichi ni, nan to naku imēji**
**ga ii. Dai-ni ni, Nihongo-yaku no jiyū shugi wa . . . nagai aida**
**Marukusu-shugi to no kankei o seisan dekinakatta Shakai-tō**
**ni totte wa teikō ga atta no darō. Dai-san ni, . . .**
To begin, why do they use *riberaru* [liberal] in *katakana* English?
One can imagine three reasons. Firstly, the image is somehow good.
Secondly, the Japanese translation **jiyūshugi** was not acceptable to
the Socialist Party, which for a long time was unable to get rid
of its association with Marxism. . . . Thirdly, . . .

**Dai-ichi** is also used to introduce a statement that qualifies (often with a negative form) what has been said before 'to begin with', 'for a start'.

d 第一、すぐれた人材が政界を目指さなくなる。
**Dai-ichi, sugureta jinzai ga seikai o mezasanaku naru.**
To begin with, able people will not aspire to politics any more.

e 愛知県内では三十一番目の「市」。
**Aichi-ken-nai de wa sanjūichi-ban-me no 'shi'.**
It's the 31st 'city' in Aichi prefecture.

f 一番目の仮説は、・・・
**Ichi-ban-me no kasetsu wa, . . .**
The first hypothesis is . . .

## 4.4 Fractions and percentages

Fractions are expressed by *X*-**bun no** *Y* (*Y* = number). Literally, the meaning is "*Y* out of *X* parts". (see 2.3.1.5)

a 三分の二
  **sanbun no ni**
  two-thirds

b 十分の一
  **jūbun no ichi**
  one-tenth

c コップ半分の水を「半分しかない」と考えるか「半分もある」
  と思うか。
  **Koppu hanbun no mizu o 'hanbun shika nai' to kangaeru ka
  'hanbun mo aru' to omou ka.**
  Whether to think of half a cup of water as 'only half', or to feel that
  'there's as much as half'.

For percentages, **pāsento** (per cent) can be added to a number, but for units of 10 per cent it is also usual to attach the suffix –**wari**, which can be followed by –**bu** to indicate percentage points. The prefix **yaku-** can be added to indicate the idea of 'approximately'.

a ラケットの約六〇パーセントが日本製だ。
  **Raketto no yaku rokujup-pāsento ga Nihonsei da.**
  Approximately 60 per cent of the rackets are made in Japan.

b 組織の兵士の三割は女性。
  **Soshiki no heishi no san-wari wa josei.**
  30 per cent of the organization's soldiers are women.

c （出荷が）昨年より一割五分少ない。
  **(Shukka ga) sakunen yori ichi-wari go-bu sukunai.**
  (Shipments) are down 15 per cent compared to last year.

# Chapter 5

# Demonstrative/interrogative words and pronouns

When used to point at things, demonstrative words/pronouns make a three-way distinction, which is based on proximity to the speaker or listener: **ko-** 'this' (near speaker), **so-** 'that' (near listener) and **a-** 'that over there' (distant from both). The endings attached differ according to whether what is referred to is a thing or place, is used by itself like a noun or to modify a noun, etc.

However, demonstrative words/pronouns are also used to refer to previous or following context, where the above three-way distinction does not apply in quite the same way – refer to the examples in 5.2.

Question (or interrogative) words + pronouns (beginning with the syllable 'do-', which is equivalent to English 'wh~') share the same endings as the ko-/so-/a- series (see 5.2, 18).

**Table 5.1 ko-so-a-do** sets of demonstrative pronouns and question words

|  | ko- | so- | a- | do- | meaning (**ko-**/**do-**) |
|---|---|---|---|---|---|
| N-equivalent | **kore** | **sore** | **are** | **dore** | 'this/which (one)' |
|  | **kochira*** | **sochira** | **achira** | **dochira** | 'this/which (direction)' 'this/which (one) of two' 'this/which (person)' |
|  | (**konata**) | (**sonata**) | **anata** | **donata** | 'you/who (polite)' |
|  | **koko** | **soko** | **asoko** | **doko** | 'this/which (place)', 'here/where' |
|  | **koitsu** | **soitsu** | **aitsu** | **doitsu** | 'this fellow' [male informal use] |
| N-modifying | **kono** | **sono** | **ano** | **dono** | 'this/which N' |
|  | **kōiu** | **sōiu** | **āiu** | **dōiu** | 'this/what kind of N' |
|  | **kōitta** | **sōitta** | **āitta** | **dōitta** | 'this/what kind of N' |
|  | **konna** | **sonna** | **anna** | **donna** | 'this/what kind of N' |

**Table 5.1** (*cont'd*)

|          | ko-        | so-       | a-       | do-        | meaning (**ko-/do-**) |
|----------|------------|-----------|----------|------------|-----------------------|
| Adverbial | **kō**     | **sō**    | **ā**    | **dō**     | 'like this/how'       |
|          | **konna ni** | **sonna ni** | **anna ni** | **donna ni** | 'this much/how much'** |
|          | **kono yō ni** |         |          | **dono yō ni** |                     |
|          | **konna fū ni** |        |          | **donna fū ni** |                    |

*Notes* * colloquially **kotchi, sotchi, atchi, dotchi**.
** indicating degree; cf., **ikura** 'how much (money)'.

Others include **dare** 'who', **dochira** 'which', **dore** 'which', **itsu** 'when', **ikura** 'how much (money)', **nani** 'what' (see 5.2 and Table 5.2).

One of the differences between **dore** and **dochira** is its use in comparative sentences, where **dochira** refers to a choice of two items, and **dore** of three or more (see 6.7).

## 5.1 Demonstrative words and pronouns

### 5.1.1 *Demonstratives: spatial/temporal reference*

Demonstratives are used to point at, or refer to, persons, places, times, and things. Note especially example c, where **kono** expresses the literal meaning of "these 22 years", i.e. 'the past 22 years'.

a 答えはこのページの右下にあります。
**Kotae wa kono pēji no migishita ni arimasu.**
The answer is [found] at the bottom right of this page.

b その時かけていただいた言葉は、今でも私の宝物のようになっている。
**Sono toki kakete itadaita kotoba wa, ima demo watashi no takaramono no yō ni natte iru.**
I still treasure the words people said to me at those times [when I needed help with my pottery].

c この二十二年間、元日だろうが外国に居ようが毎朝欠かさず六キロメートル歩いてきた。
**Kono nijūni-nenkan, ganjitsu darō ga gaikoku ni iyō ga maiasa kakasazu rok-kiromētoru aruite kita.**
For the past 22 years, I've walked 6km every morning without fail, be it New Year's Day, [at home] or abroad.

d 「飛んでいる飛行機を見ながら、『あの飛行機のエンジンはオレが
つくったんだ』って言ってみたいんですよ」。

**'Tonde iru hikōki o minagara, "ano hikōki no enjin wa ore ga
tsukutta n da" tte itte mi-tai n desu yo'.**

Looking at a flying aircraft, I'd like to say 'I made the engine of that aircraft'.

*Demonstratives: discourse reference*

One important use of demonstratives is to refer to previous or following
context.

*Preceding context:* **kono/sono/ano N, kore, sore, are,
kō iu, kō itta, konna, sonna, anna**

In general, the **a-** series is often used to refer to something that is shared
knowledge between speaker/listener, writer/audience, etc. (example i).

**konna/sonna/anna** sometimes refer back to previous context in a critical
way (example f, etc.).

Note also the use of **sonna** before personal pronouns (example h), and
relational nouns (example j), which is something you do not find in English.

a 三十八億年前のことだ。このころの海水の量や化学組成は現在と
あまり違いはなかった。

**Sanjūhachioku-nen mae no koto da. Kono koro no kaisui no
ryō ya kagaku sosei wa genzai to amari chigai wa nakatta.**

3800 million years ago. At that time, there wasn't much difference
from now with regard to things like the amount of sea water and
its chemical make-up.

b まさに世紀末を象徴するかのような「殺人本」ブーム。それを読
みたがる現代人の心理を探ってみた。

**Masa ni seiki-matsu o shōchō suru ka no yō na satsujin-bon
būmu. Sore o yomi-tagaru gendaijin no shinri o sagutte mita.**

There's a veritable [non-fiction] murder book boom, as if symbolizing
the end of the century. We've looked into the psychology of
contemporary people who want to read these [= murder books].

c あれ以来、島の活動のすべてが止まってしまって……。

**Are irai, shima no katsudō no subete ga tomatte shimatte ...**

Since that time [of the earthquake], all activity on the island has come
to a standstill ...

d わずか百何十円という鉄道やバス料金も、うかつに支払えない額
に違いない。・・・こういう人も大勢日本に来ているのだ。

**Wazuka hyakunanjū-en to iu tetsudō ya basu ryōkin mo,
ukatsu ni shiharaenai gaku ni chigainai....Kō iu hito mo
ōzei Nihon ni kite iru no da.**

No doubt, [for her] a train or bus fare of a mere hundred and
something yen is an amount that is not easily affordable...Lots of
people like this have come to Japan.

e 意識がはっきりしているのに身体が動かない、なにやら恐ろしい
ものが自分を襲ってくるような感じがする。こういった症状も
Kさんには見られた。

**Ishiki ga hakkiri shite iru noni karada ga ugokanai, nani yara
osoroshii mono ga jibun o osotte kuru yō na kanji ga suru.
Kō itta shōjō mo K-san ni wa mirareta.**

You can't move your body even though you are fully conscious,
and you feel as if something terrible is going to attack you.
That kind of symptom, too, was observed with K.

f 所管官庁がこんな認識では、特殊法人改革はできない。

**Shokan kanchō ga konna ninshiki de wa, tokushu hōjin
kaikaku wa dekinai.**

If the authorities in charge have such [= insufficient] understanding,
reform of special administrative corporations is impossible.

g 理想は屋外だけど東京にはそんな場所ないでしょう。

**Risō wa okugai da kedo Tōkyō ni wa sonna basho nai desho.**

The ideal [place for our rural dance] is outdoors, but in Tokyo there
isn't that sort of space, I think.

h 勝負どころでコースを間違えて、浅利純子（ダイハツ）に続く
2位。「わたしってまぬけですね」のセリフで、一躍全国区の
人気者となった。そんな彼女も今では堂々たる世界のトップラ
ンナーだ。

**Shōbu-dokoro de kōsu o machigaete, Asari Junko (Daihatsu)
ni tsuzuku ni-i. 'Watashi tte manuke desu ne' no serifu
de ichiyaku zenkokuku no ninkimono to natta. Sonna
kanojo mo ima de wa dōdō-taru sekai no toppu rannā
da.**

At the decisive moment she took the wrong route and ended up
second behind Asari Junko (Daihatsu). Her words 'I'm a bit thick,
aren't I?' made her instantly famous nationwide. She (*lit.* "that
sort of she") is now without question one of the world's top
runners.

i サッカーのワールドカップ、あれは国を代表する十一人の
決闘だ。

**Sakkā no wārudo kappu, are wa kuni o daihyō suru jūichinin
no kettō da.**

The soccer World Cup, that's a battle [fought by] 11 men representing
their country.

j そんな中、これほど大きくて目立つ時計も珍しい。

**Sonna naka, kore hodo ōkikute medatsu tokei mo
mezurashii.**

Among such [clocks at well-known meeting points], there are
few clocks that are so large and noticeable.

---

| 5.1.2.2 | *Following context:* **konna** |

**konna** can also be used to introduce things that are mentioned in the
following context:

a ある男子大学生がこんなことを言っていた。

**Aru danshi daigakusei ga konna koto o itte ita.**

A certain male university student said this:

b こんな趣旨の文書だ。

**Konna shushi no bunsho da.**

It's a document with this kind of content:

## 5.2 Interrogative pronouns or question words

Interrogative pronouns will be referred to mostly as **question words**
(**Q-words**). Q-words (those beginning with the syllable **do**-) form part of
the **ko-/so-/a-/do-** system (see 5.1). These, along with other question words
(beginning in **i**- or **na**-), are listed in Table 5.2.

On the left, question words are given, followed by combinations (where
applicable) with the particle **ka** (= indefinite pron.), **mo** (with positive verbs
'every', 'many', etc.), **mo** (with negative verbs, 'no' etc.), and **demo** ('any').
Note how **nani** usually changes to **nan** before the sounds b, d, g, k (usually
with the exception of the question particle **ka**), n, m, p (see also 4.2 (counters), where similar sound changes take place).

**Table 5.2** Question words + ka/mo/demo combinations

| Q word | meaning | + ka | Meaning | + mo | Meaning (pos.) | Meaning (neg.) | + demo | Meaning (pos.) | Meaning (neg.) |
|---|---|---|---|---|---|---|---|---|---|
| dare* | 'who' | dare ka [P] | 'somebody' | dare [P] mo*** | 'everybody' | 'nobody' | dare [P] demo | 'anybody' | 'nobody' |
| dochira/izure | 'which (of two)' | dochira ka [P] | 'either one' | dochira [P] mo | 'both' | 'neither' | dochira [P] demo | 'either' | 'neither' |
| doko | 'where' | doko ka [P] | 'somewhere' | doko [P] mo | 'everywhere' | 'nowhere' | doko [P] demo | 'anywhere' | |
| dore | 'which' | dore ka [P] | 'one' | dore [P] mo | 'every (one)', 'each (one)' | 'none' | dore [P] demo | 'any (one)', 'whichever' | |
| ikura | 'how much' | ikura ka | 'somewhat' | ikura mo | 'plenty' | 'not much' | ikura demo | 'any amount' | |
| ikutsu | 'how many' | ikutsu ka | 'some' | ikutsu mo | 'many' | 'not many' | ikutsu demo | 'any number' | |
| itsu | 'when' | itsu ka | 'sometime' | itsu mo | 'always' | 'never' | itsu demo | 'any time' | |
| nani | 'what' | nani ka [P] | 'something' | — | | 'nothing' | nan demo | 'anything' | |
| nando** | 'how many times' | nando ka | 'a few times' | nando mo | 'many times' | 'not…many times' | nando demo | 'any number of times' | 'not any number of times' |
| dō | 'how' | dō [P] ka | 'somehow' | dō [P] mo | 'somehow' | 'somehow' | dō [P] demo | 'any way' | |
| dōshite | 'why' | | | | | | — | | |
| naze | 'why' | naze ka | 'for some reason' | — | | | | | |

*When particles are present:*

| Q word | meaning | + ka | Meaning | + mo | Meaning (pos.) | Meaning (neg.) | + demo | Meaning (pos.) | Meaning (neg.) |
|---|---|---|---|---|---|---|---|---|---|
| dare ni mo | not …anybody | dare ka ni | somebody | | | | | | |
| dare kara mo | not …anybody | dare ka no | someone's | dare ka kara | from someone | | dare ka kara | from somewhere | |
| doko ni mo | nowhere | doko ka e | somewhere | doko ka de | somewhere | doko ka kara | | | |
| itsu made mo | always | dō (ni) ka | somehow | | | | | | |
| nan no …mo | no …at all | nani ka no | some | | | | | | |

*Notes* * For polite equivalent, replace **dare** with **donata**.

** Also **nankai** 'how many times', and any other **nan(i)** + counter combination can be used in the same way (see note to Table 4.1).

*** except **dare mo ga**.

| 5.2.1 | *Question word + ka* |

| 5.2.1.1 | *Question word +* **ka** |

Adding **ka** to question words (including Q-word + counter) gives the combination an indeterminate meaning 'some~' (with **dochira** and **dore**, 'one of'). Note that **dochira** can also be a polite equivalent of **doko** (see example 16.1.3c).

a　私生活もどこかで仕事に結び付く。
**Shi-seikatsu mo doko ka de shigoto ni musubitsuku.**
One's private life is also connected to work somewhere.

b　どっか行こうよ。(**dokka** = contraction of **doko ka**)
**Dokka ikō yo.**
Let's go somewhere.

c　何か、刺激がほしい。
**Nani ka, shigeki ga hoshii.**
I want some stimulation.

d　いくらか改善はされた。
**Ikura ka kaizen wa sareta.**
[Things] have been improved somewhat.

e　・・・食後、庭園でモリアオガエルの白い泡状の卵を見つけた。
どこからか鳴き声も聞こえたが、姿は見えない。
**. . . shokugo, teien de moriao-gaeru no shiroi awajō no tamago o mitsuketa. Doko kara ka nakigoe mo kikoeta ga, sugata wa mienai.**
After the meal, I found the white foamy eggs of the green frog. From somewhere I could hear its croaking, but couldn't see it.

f　何度かこの欄でも述べてきたが、大人の男性のシンプルな服が
少ない。
**Nando ka kono ran de mo nobete kita ga, otona no dansei no shinpuru na fuku ga sukunai.**
I have said this a number of times in this column, too, but there aren't many simple clothes for grown men.

g　左右どちらかに偏った凝りは要注意だ。
**Sayū dochira ka ni katayotta kori wa yō-chūi da.**
Stiffness in the shoulders that is limited to one side needs to be watched carefully.

h 行員同士が結婚しても、どちらかが退職する慣行はない。

**Kōin dōshi ga kekkon shite mo, dochira ka ga taishoku suru kankō wa nai.**

When bank employees get married, there is no custom that [requires that] one of them quit.

i 結婚すると二人のどちらかが生活保護の対象から外される。

**Kekkon suru to futari no dochira ka ga seikatsu hogo no taishō kara hazusareru.**

If they get married, one of them becomes ineligible for unemployment benefits.

5.2.1.2 **dochira ka to ieba/iu to**

This indicates a tendency 'more or less', 'rather', 'if anything'.

a 話し方はどちらかといえばとつ弁である。

**Hanashi-kata wa dochira ka to ieba totsuben de aru.**

His way of speaking is on the slow side.

b また、「男は仕事、女は家庭」という考え方に「賛成」または「どちらかといえば賛成」と答えたのは、夫が53%、妻が23%。

**Mata, 'otoko wa shigoto, onna wa katei' to iu kangae-kata ni 'sansei' mata wa 'dochira ka to ieba sansei' to kotaeta no wa, otto ga gojūsan-pāsento, tsuma ga nijūsan-pāsento.**

Also, 53 per cent of husbands and 23 per cent of wives replied 'agree' or 'more or less agree' to the proposition 'Men should work, and women stay at home'.

c 「どちらかといえば‥‥‥」という条件節を付ければ、世の中は大抵ネアカとネクラに分けられる。

**'Dochira ka to ieba . . .' to iu jōkensetsu o tsukereba, yo no naka wa taitei neaka to nekura ni wakerareru.**

If you attach the conditional clause 'if anything', the world can more or less be divided into cheerful and gloomy people.

5.2.2 *Question word + mo*

5.2.2.1 *With positive predicate*

This is used with two types of sentences: those where **mo** is attached to the question word (or an intervening particle), and sentences where **mo** is attached to the conjunctive form of verbs/adjectives and nouns directly.

131

| 5.2.2.1.1 | Question word (particle) **mo** (particle) |

The combination means 'every~', 'any~'.

a だれもが一度は抱きそうな夢だ。
**Dare mo ga ichido wa idakisō na yume da.**
This is a dream that everyone is likely to entertain once.

b 大手スーパーは、どこも似たような状況だ。
**Ōte sūpā wa, doko mo nita yō na jōkyō da.**
The large supermarkets are all (*lit.* "everywhere") in the same situation.

c どこまでも、仕事に徹した人生である。
**Doko made mo, shigoto ni tesshita jinsei de aru.**
It's a life that's devoted to work all the way.

d 男の集まりはいくらもあるが、女性はいつも疎外されがちだ。
**Otoko no atsumari wa ikura mo aru ga, josei wa itsumo sogai
sare-gachi da.**
There are plenty of men's get-togethers, but the women always tend
to be excluded.

e いつもと変わらない夕方だった。
**Itsumo to kawaranai yūgata datta.**
It was an evening no different from usual.

f 電気を止められたことも何度もある。
**Denki o tomerareta koto mo nan-do mo aru.**
The electricity has been cut off many times.

g 代わりのメーカーはいくらもある。
**Kawari no mēkā wa ikura mo aru.**
There's no shortage of alternative manufacturers.

| 5.2.2.1.2 | Question word verb/adjective-**te mo**/[noun] **mo** |

This indicates the meaning of 'no matter who/what/where' etc. (see 26.3.1.5).

a 世界のどこにいても仕事は出来ます。
**Sekai no doko ni ite mo shigoto wa dekimasu.**
You can work, wherever in the world you are.

b どんないじめもなくそう。
**Donna ijime mo nakusō.**
Let's get rid of any form of bullying.

c 経済はだれがやっても同じでしょ。
**Keizai wa dare ga yatte mo onaji desho.**
As regards the economy, it should be the same no matter who does [the job of PM].

d どんなに値段が高くてもかまわないから純国産米を分けて
欲しい。
**Donna ni nedan ga takakute mo kamawanai kara jun-kokusan-mai o wakete hoshii.**
We want you to supply proper homegrown rice, no matter how expensive it may be.

5.2.2.2 | *With negative predicate*

5.2.2.2.1 | Question word/number + counter (particle) **mo** (particle)

This has the meaning of 'no-one', 'nowhere', etc.

a 「私は芝居のうまい役者じゃありません」。「だれもそう思いませんよ」。
**'Watashi wa shibai no umai yakusha ja arimasen'. 'Dare mo sō omoimasen yo'.**
'I'm not an actor who's good on stage.' 'Nobody thinks so.'

b 将来はだれにもわからない。
**Shōrai wa dare ni mo wakaranai.**
The future is known to no-one.

c 死亡した五人はいずれも外傷などはなかった。
**Shibō shita go-nin wa izure mo gaishō nado wa nakatta.**
None of the five persons who died had any external injuries.

d 連休中は天気が悪くてどこにも行けなかった。
**Renkyū-chū wa tenki ga warukute doko ni mo ikenakatta.**
The weather being [so] bad, we couldn't go anywhere during the holiday weekend.

e 品質ではどこにも負けない。
**Hinshitsu de wa doko ni mo makenai.**
On quality, we won't be beaten by anyone [= any company].

f 残された時間はいくらもない。
**Nokosareta jikan wa ikura mo nai.**
There isn't much time left.

g 今は一人も残っていない。
**Ima wa hitori mo nokotte inai.**
There isn't even a single person left now.

Question word verb/adjective-(y)ō to

The meaning of this is 'no matter how' (see 9.1.2.3.2).

a いえ、どんなに速かろうと、ちゃんと歌詞が聞こえなきゃいけま
せん。
**Ie, donna ni hayakarō to, chanto kashi ga kikoenakya
ikemasen.**
No, you must be able to hear the words of the song, no matter how
fast the tempo is.

## 5.2.3 | *Question word (+ counter) + demo*

### 5.2.3.1 | *With positive predicate*

Attached to a Q-word (+ counter) (+ intervening case particle), and followed by a positive predicate, **demo** means 'every~', 'any~' (or, in the case
of **dochira demo**, 'either').

a 仕事はいくらでもあった。
**Shigoto wa ikura demo atta.**
There was any number of jobs.

b 不平等を探せばどこにでもある。
**Fu-byōdō o sagaseba doko ni demo aru.**
If one looks for inequalities, they are everywhere.

c 往復ともJR、航空機のどちらでも選択できる。
**Ōfuku tomo JR, kōkū-ki no dochira demo sentaku dekiru.**
For both the outward and inward journeys, you can select either Japan
Rail or aeroplane.

d 「どこへでも行くし、何でも撮る」と謙虚に答える。
**'Doko e demo iku shi, nan demo toru' to kenkyo ni kotaeru.**
'I'll go anywhere, and photograph anything', he answers modestly.

e 買ってくれるところがあれば、いつでも供給する。
**Katte kureru tokoro ga areba, itsu demo kyōkyū suru.**
If there's a place that'll buy, we'll supply any time.

f 日本を訪問した外国人が驚くのは街角の自動販売機の多さである。いつでも、どこでも、だれでも、酒やたばこなどを買うことができる。

**Nihon o hōmon shita gaikoku-jin ga odoroku no wa machikado no jidō hanbai-ki no ōsa de aru. Itsu demo, doko demo, dare demo, sake ya tabako nado o kau koto ga dekiru.**

What amazes foreigners who have visited Japan is the large number of vending machines on street corners. Anyone can buy alcohol and tobacco any time, any place.

g 何度でも訪れたくなる美術館に育てたい。

**Nan-do demo otozure-taku naru bijutsu-kan ni sodatetai.**

I want to make it an art gallery that people will want to visit any number of times.

---

| 5.2.3.2 | *With negative predicate* |

| 5.2.3.2.1 | Question word **demo** negative |

Attached to a Q-word, and followed directly by a negative predicate, **demo** means 'not any' (or 'neither', in the case of **dochira demo**) (see 11.2.3.4, Table 5.1).

a 一見、何でもなさそうな封筒。

**Ikken, nan demo nasasō na fūtō.**

An envelope that at first sight seems nothing special

b 政治力は未知数だけに、どちらでも構わない。

**Seiji-ryoku wa michisū dake ni, dochira demo kamawanai.**

As their political prowess is unknown, I don't mind either one [of the two candidates].

| 5.2.3.2.2 | Question word verb/adjective-**te demo**/noun **mo** |

The resulting meaning is 'no matter', 'any'.

a 全国どこの大学でも構わない。

**Zenkoku doko no daigaku demo kamawanai.**

I don't mind any university anywhere in the country (*lit.* "in the whole country").

| 5.2.3.2.3 | Question word **demo** positive predicate |
|---|---|
| | (in negative sentence) |

Here, the Q-word **demo** + positive predicate modifies a noun that is followed by a negative predicate.

a 確かに、周りには何でも相談できる人ってあまりいない。

**Tashika ni, mawari ni wa nan demo sōdan dekiru hito tte amari inai.**

It's true, there aren't many people around me with whom I can talk over anything.

b 欧州各国の進める政策を英国が何でも受け入れるわけではない。

**Ōshū kakkoku no susumeru seisaku o eikoku ga nan demo ukeireru wake de wa nai.**

It's not the case that the UK adopts all the policies that EU countries promote.

| 5.2.4 | *Idiomatic uses* |
|---|---|

| 5.2.4.1 | *Noun* **demo nan de mo nai** |
|---|---|

This is a way of emphasizing the negation of the noun 'by no means', 'definitely not!'.

a 一番困るのは民族主義でも何でもない。

**Ichiban komaru no wa minzokushugi demo nan demo nai.**

The biggest problem [in Russia] is by no means nationalism.

| 5.2.4.2 | **nani ga nan demo** |
|---|---|

**nani ga nan demo** works like an adverbial phrase in the sense of 'by any means', 'no matter what'.

a 何が何でも就職しなければという危機感は薄い。

**Nani ga nan demo shūshoku shinakereba to iu kikikan wa usui.**

There isn't much feeling of desperation of having to get a job no matter what.

5.2.4.3 | **nan demo ... sō**

**nan demo** serves to reinforce the meaning of the sentence ending **sō**, which indicates hearsay, in the sense of 'apparently' (see 9.5.2, 10.2.4.1).

a 何でもお小姓が鍵を開けて、将軍吉宗様自ら書状の封を切るそう
だな。
**Nan demo o-koshō ga kagi o akete, Shōgun Yoshimune-sama
mizukara shojō no fū o kiru sō da na.**
I understand that his assistant opens the lock [of the box], and the
Shogun Yoshimune himself breaks the seal of the letter.

## 5.3 Personal pronouns and suffixes

Japanese personal pronouns are noun-like in that they can be modified by demonstrative pronouns (for an example, see 5.1.2.1).

Japanese personal pronouns do not usually distinguish number (singular/ plural) in the first and second person, although the suffixes -**gata** (formal) and -**domo**, -**ra** and -**tachi** can optionally be used for plural (see 5.4, also 5.5). Table 5.3 gives the more common personal pronouns and suffixes.

As is evident from Table 5.3, there are some differences in use depending on the sex of the speaker, and more pronounced differences according to the formality of the relationship with the addressee (and to some degree the speech situation). Women generally use more formal forms than men.

Japanese pronouns are intimately tied up with hierarchy and levels of respect. For this reason, the use of personal pronouns is generally avoided in formal relationships and situations; instead name (family name + suffix of personal address) is preferred.

### 5.3.1 | *Personal pronouns*

5.3.1.1 | *First-person pronouns*

5.3.1.1.1 | **wata(ku)shi, boku, ore**

The *kanji* 私 is usually used for both **watakushi** and the less formal **watashi**, so in writing it is often difficult to decide which reading is intended. Apart from the level of formality, both can be said to be neutral, i.e. they can be used with strangers and acquaintances alike. However, when contrasted with male-only pronouns such as **boku**, which is used towards males or females and sounds more intimate than **watashi**, the implication is usually that the user of **watashi** is female (example b).

**ore** is the most informal first-person pronoun, used by males only.

a 夫の留守を喜ぶ妻は私だけじゃないらしい。
**Otto no rusu o yorokobu tsuma wa watashi dake ja nai rashii.**
It appears that I'm not the only wife to take delight in her husband's absence.

b 私作る人、僕食べる人、という時代はもう終わった。
**Watashi tsukuru hito, boku taberu hito, to iu jidai wa mō owatta.**
The age where people could say, 'I [female] do the cooking, I [male] do the eating' is already over.

c おれにも撮らせろよ。
**Ore ni mo torasero yo.**
[PM to cameraman:] Let me take one [= a picture] too.

5.3.1.1.2 **jibun** as personal pronoun

The reflexive pronoun **jibun** 'self' can also be used like a personal pronoun, in the sense of 'I' or, with **-tachi**, as 'we' (see 5.5).

a 自分が同性愛者とわかっても構わない。
**Jibun ga dōseiai-sha to wakatte mo kamawanai.**
I don't mind if people realize that I'm gay.

b 日本初の契約制スチュワーデス。「自分たちはパイオニア。」
**Nihon-hatsu no keiyaku-sei suchuwādesu. 'Jibun-tachi wa paionia.'**
Japan's first stewardesses on contract. 'We are pioneers' [they say].

5.3.1.2 *Second-person pronouns*

5.3.1.2.1 **kimi, omae, kisama**

**kimi** is an intimate-sounding form of address for males or females, used by older men, or by boyfriends towards girlfriends. **omae** is quite informal, used between men who grew up or went to school together. It is also used

**Table 5.3** Personal pronouns and suffixes

| speaker | referent | formal | ← | → | | | intimate |
|---|---|---|---|---|---|---|---|
| male | First person 'I' (personal pron.) | 私(わたくし) **watakushi** | こちら **kochira** | 私(わたし) **watashi** | 僕 **boku** | 俺 **ore** | わし **washi** |
| female | | 私(わたくし) **watakushi** | こちら **kochira** | 私(わたし) **watashi** | あたし **atashi** | うち **uchi** | |
| male | Second person 'you' (personal pron.) | (あなた) **anata** | (そちら) **sochira** | 君(きみ) **kimi** | おまえ **omae** | あんた **anta** | きさま **kisama** |
| female | | あなた **anata** | (そちら) **sochira** | | | あんた **anta** | |
| male/female | Second person 'you' (name + personal-address-suf.) | -様(さま) **-sama** | -さん **-san** | -君(くん) **-kun** | -ちゃん **-chan** | | |
| male/female | Third person 'he/she' (demonstrative pron. + N/personal pron.) | こ/そ/あの方 **kono/sono/ano kata** | こ/そ/あの人 **kono/sono/ano hito** | 彼/彼女 **kare/kanojo** | こいつ/そいつ/あいつ **koitsu/soitsu/aitsu** | | |
| male/female | Third person 'he/she' (name + personal-address-suf.) | -様(さま) **-sama** | -さん **-san** | -君(くん) **-kun** | -ちゃん **-chan** | | |
| male/female | Third person 'they' (demonstrative pron. + N/personal pron.) | こ/そ/あの方々 **kono/sono/ano kata-gata** | こ/そ/あの人-たち **kono/sono/ano hito-tachi** | 彼/彼女-等 **kare-ra/kanojo-ra** | こ/そ/あいつ-等 **koitsu/soitsu/aitsu-ra** | | |
| male/female | Third person 'they' (name + personal-address-suf.) | -様(さま) **-sama** | -さん **-san** | -君(くん) **-kun** | -ちゃん **-chan** | | |

by parents to their sons. **kisama**, also common in comics, is used in such male bastions as the army, sports teams etc., to subordinates or equals; in ordinary life, if you address someone with **kisama**, it signals that you're trying to pick a fight!

a　ところが面接官は「君、処女なの？」。
　　**Tokoro ga mensetsu-kan wa 'Kimi, shojo na no?'**
　　However, the interviewer [asked] 'Are you a virgin?'.

b　おまえに託したい。
　　**Omae ni takushitai.**
　　I want to entrust [the running of the company] to you [= my son].

c　「ほら、お前ももっと足を高くあげろよ」「オレは腹が出てる
　　から、お前みたいなわけにはいかないよ」。
　　**'Hora, omae mo motto ashi o takaku agero yo' 'Ore wa hara
　　ga deteru kara, omae mitai na wake ni wa ikanai yo'.**
　　'Hey, raise your leg a bit higher!' 'I've got a big belly, so you can't
　　expect me to do things in the same way as you!' [baseball training]

d　貴様ァ、こりゃ、何だ！戦場に野球をやりに行くつもりかァ。
　　**Kisamā, korya, nan da! Senjō ni yakyū o yari ni iku tsumori kā.**
　　Hey you, what is this [= practising baseball]! You going to war to play
　　baseball?

e　俺、貴様の昔に返ってゆっくり話し合いたい。
　　**Ore, kisama no mukashi ni kaette yukkuri hanashiai-tai.**
　　I'd like a leisurely chat [among us men], back on the old terms of *ore*
　　and *kisama*.

---

| 5.3.1.2.2 | **anata** |

This is taught to foreigners as equivalent to 'you', simply because it is the most neutral of the lot. However, Westerners are renowned in Japan for overusing **anata**, which still has strong connotations, namely:

(i)　Impersonal use: **anata** is used when the speaker/writer does not know what the social level of the person/s addressed is; this is especially common in adverts (appealing to people of all levels).

　　a　もう黙っちゃいられない！あなたのダイエット方法は大丈夫？
　　　　**Mō damatcha irarenai! Anata no daietto hōhō wa daijōbu?**
　　　　I can't keep silent any longer! Is your [= the reader's] method of
　　　　losing weight safe?

b 「あなたのお子さんなの」と突然、聞かれた。
   **'Anata no o-ko-san na no' to totsuzen, kikareta.**
   She was suddenly asked [by a stranger], 'Is that your child?'

c 日本ではあなたの絵が好きな人が多い。なぜだと思いますか。
   **Nihon de wa anata no e ga suki na hito ga ōi. Naze da to
   omoimasu ka.**
   [Interview with painter:] In Japan, there are many who like your
   paintings. Why is that, do you think?

(ii) Woman to husband: **anata** is also typically used by a woman to her
husband or lover (although less so by the younger generation).

a あなた、ドレス買ってもいい？
   **Anata, doresu katte mo ii?**
   Darling, is it OK if I buy a dress?

b かたや、「あなた、ご飯よ」のように、「妻が夫を指す代表的
   な代名詞」でもある。
   **Kataya, 'Anata, gohan yo' no yō ni, 'tsuma ga otto o sasu
   daihyōteki na daimeishi' de mo aru.**
   On the other hand, it [= **anata**] is also a typical pronoun by
   which the wife calls the husband, as in 'Darling, dinner's ready!'

(iii) Overuse by foreigners: **anata** is also a word used by foreigners in
situations where Japanese would normally avoid the use of a personal
pronoun. This misuse was pointed out in grammars of Japanese by
people like Aston and Chamberlain over a hundred years ago.

| 5.3.1.3 | *Third-person pronouns* |

| 5.3.1.3.1 | **kare(-ra/-tachi) and kanojo(-ra/-tachi)** |

These are originally translation terms for rendering 'he' and 'she' into
Japanese from works of Western fiction. They are very common now, and are
less unwieldy than **sono/ano hito**, etc. However, there are some restrictions
on their use: they are more commonly used by men and younger Japanese,
and are considered rude if used of social superiors. They are also commonly
used to refer to boyfriends (**kare** or **kareshi**) and girlfriends (**kanojo**).

a 彼女に振られたので、女の子の友達がいません。
   **Kanojo ni furareta no de, onna no ko no tomodachi ga imasen.**
   I got dumped by my girlfriend, so I haven't got any female friends.

**koitsu/soitsu/aitsu** are used pejoratively or to refer informally to close friends, colleagues etc., or when no politeness is required, as when one talks about the content of one's thoughts, as in example a.

The difference between **ko-/so-/a-** follows the usual pattern (see Table 5.1, 5.1).

a こいつには話せる、そんな雰囲気を持っている人間だったらいいな。
   **Koitsu ni wa hanaseru, sonna fun'iki o motte iru ningen dattara ii na.**
   I'd like the kind of person who feels like someone I can talk to.

b 「あいつもいいばあさんだ」と写真を見せてくれた。
   **'Aitsu mo ii bāsan da' to shashin o misete kureta.**
   'She's quite a granny', he said and showed me a photo.

5.3.1.4 | *Plural forms*

Some plural forms are given in Table 5.3 for third persons, but first- and second-person pronouns can also be made plural by attaching plural suffixes (see 5.4).

A special case is **wareware** (我々), which is normally used to define a group and often prefixes a noun (regardless of any comma in writing, it is pronounced as one unit in speech).

a 我々、監査役はあなたがた取締役を訴える権限があるのですよ。
   **Wareware, kansa-yaku wa anata-gata torishimari-yaku o uttaeru kengen ga aru no desu yo.**
   We auditors have the power to take you [company] chairmen to court!

## 5.4　Suffixes attached to personal pronouns

Note that these suffixes can also follow nouns, for which see 1.3.

5.4.1 | **-domo**

Attached to nouns that refer to persons, **-domo** indicates plural (see 1.3). When attached to first-person pronouns (usually **watakushi**), **-domo** has a humble ring.

*Note* – where the same plural is used twice in a sentence, the second one is sometimes formed by different means, for stylistic reasons (see 5.4.3).

| 5.4.1.1 | *First person* (**watakushi**)-**domo** |

**watakushi-domo** means 'we' and is used in formal situations, often by persons representing an organization (company, political party, hospital, etc.).

a 私どもは野に下りました。
**Watakushi-domo wa ya ni kudarimashita.**
We have become the opposition.

b 私どもでやりましょう。
**Watakushi-domo de yarimashō.**
We (= our company) will take it on.

c 私どもの店には膨大な数の、お客様が来店する。
**Watakushi-domo no mise ni wa bōdai na kazu no,
o-kyaku-sama ga raiten suru.**
An enormous number of customers visits our shop.

| 5.4.2 | -gata |

To express an honorific plural, -gata (rather than -tachi) is usually attached to the title of persons of higher social status (**sensei** 'teacher', 'professor', 'member of parliament', 'politician', etc.) and forms of address ending in -sama (honorific equivalent of -san). However, -tachi can also be used (see 5.4.4, 1.4).

a お開きのとき、高齢者たちは「あなたがたを愛している」と言いましたが、少年たちは無視しました。
**Ohiraki no toki, kōreisha-tachi wa 'Anata-gata o aishite iru' to iimashita ga, shōnen-tachi wa mushi shimashita.**
At the end [of the gathering], the old people said 'We love you', but the youths ignored it.

## 5.4.3 -ra

Attached to personal pronouns, -ra indicates plural.

a 彼ら、彼女たちの声を拾った。
   **Kare-ra, kanojo-tachi no koe o hirotta.**
   We've gathered their [= male and female] opinions (*lit.* "voices").

b 学生時代にリュック一つ担いで旅行したフィリピンやメキシコで
   出会ったのは、貧しくとも家族みんなで助け合って生きる人々
   の底抜けに明るい笑顔。…彼らの生活には、日本人が失った
   何かがある。
   **Gakusei jidai ni ryukku hitotsu katsuide ryokō shita Firipin
   ya Mekishiko de deatta no wa, mazushiku tomo kazoku
   minna de tasukeatte ikiru hitobito no sokonuke ni akarui
   egao.... kare-ra no seikatsu ni wa Nihonjin ga ushinatta
   nani ka ga aru.**
   What I saw in the Philippines and in Mexico, where I travelled in my
   student days with just a rucksack on my back, were the radiantly
   smiling faces of the people, who were poor but lived in families
   where everybody helped each other.... their lives have something
   that the Japanese have lost.

## 5.4.4 -tachi

Attached to pronouns, -tachi indicates plural, mainly for humans.

### 5.4.4.1 With personal and reflexive pronouns

With nouns, -tachi to indicate plural is optional (see 1.3), but with personal
and reflexive pronouns, it is mandatory. In other words, if -tachi is detached
in the examples below, the meaning changes from plural to singular.

a 僕たちは四年生です。
   **Boku-tachi wa yonensei desu.**
   We are fourth-year pupils.

b 私たち大人は考え直したい。
   **Watashi-tachi otona wa kangae-naoshi-tai.**
   We adults wish to reconsider.

c ･･･心のどこかでいつも思っていた。"私はあなたたちとは違う。
　　いつか女優になるんだ"って。

　　**…kokoro no doko ka de itsu mo omotte ita.**
　　**'Watashi wa anata-tachi to wa chigau. Itsu ka joyū**
　　**ni naru n da' tte.**

　　…always felt somewhere in my heart: 'I'm different from you people
　　[= teachers and fellow pupils]. One day I'll be an actress'.

d 人々は自分たちの生活を見つめ始めた。

　　**Hitobito wa jibun-tachi no seikatsu o mitsume-hajimeta.**

　　People have begun to reconsider their lives.

## 5.5　Reflexive pronouns

Like other Japanese personal pronouns, reflexive pronouns are noun-like
in that they attach case particles. Like nouns, they can also affix honorific
prefixes (for an example, see 16.1.3 b).

**jibun** can also be modified by demonstrative pron. such as **sonna** (example a).

a 同性愛への強い欲求をもちながら、そんな自分を責め、聖者の
　　ような禁欲生活を送るが、一方で推理小説と西部劇が大好き、
　　といった人なのである。

　　**Dōseiai e no tsuyoi yokkyū o mochi-nagara, sonna jibun o**
　　**seme, seija no yō na kin'yoku seikatsu o okuru ga, ippō de**
　　**suiri shōsetsu to seibugeki ga daisuki, to itta hito na no**
　　**de aru.**

　　He is the sort of person who, while having strong leanings towards
　　homosexuality, blames himself for being like that and leads a saint-
　　like life of celibacy, but on the other hand loves detective stories
　　and westerns.

Reflexive pronouns refer back to a person/persons that were mentioned
earlier, either in the same sentence, or previously. The major reflexive pron.
are **jibun** and **jishin**, both of which literally mean "self" and, depending
on which person they refer back to, translate into English as 'myself',
'yourself', 'himself', 'herself'.

**jibun** also has a plural form **jibun-tachi** as 'ourselves', 'yourselves' and
'themselves'. As with personal pronouns, when using **jibun**, plural must
be indicated by the plural suffix (see 5.4.4.1), although in some generalizing cases this is not applied (5.5.1.1).

jibun

5.5.1.1 | *Reflexive use*

Here, **jibun** refers back to a noun (in [ ]) previously mentioned in the same sentence. Note that in some instances (examples c–d) no plural suffix is used even though the noun is plural (or generic).

a 人々は自分たちの生活を見つめ始めた。
**[Hitobito] wa jibun-tachi no seikatsu o mitsume-hajimeta.**
The people have begun to look hard at their daily lives.

b 英国人にとって家は自分の城。
**[Eikoku-jin] ni totte ie wa jibun no shiro.**
For the Englishman, his home is his castle.

c 親が子供にやさしすぎるのは、自分に自信がないからである。
**[Oya] ga kodomo ni yasashi-sugiru no wa, jibun ni jishin ga nai kara de aru.**
The reason why parents are overly kind to their children is because they have no confidence in themselves.

d みなさんよくカラオケバーとかゴルフに行くけれども、そのほとんどは自分の会社関係の人と行くでしょう。
**[Minasan] yoku karaoke-bā to ka gorufu ni iku keredomo, sono hotondo wa jibun no kaisha kankei no hito to iku deshō.**
People often do things like going to karaoke bars or playing golf, but almost always they go with people associated with their company, right?

5.5.1.2 | *Used like a personal pronoun*

5.5.1.2.1 | Like an indefinite personal pronoun

In this use, **jibun** is used in the sense of 'one', 'their', etc.

a まず自分の必要カロリーを知ること。
**Mazu jibun no hitsuyō karorī o shiru koto.**
First, one needs to find out one's calorie requirements.

b 面白い本に、子供が自分から出会うことが大切。
**Omoshiroi hon ni, kodomo ga jibun kara deau koto ga taisetsu.**
It's important that the children find interesting books on their own initiative.

5.5.1.2.2 | Like a first-person pronoun (see 5.3.1.1.2)

This can be either singular or plural.

a 会社は自分をどう評価するのか。
**Kaisha wa jibun o dō hyōka suru no ka.**
How will the company evaluate me?

b 自分が同性愛者とわかっても構わない。
**Jibun ga dōseiai-sha to wakatte mo kamawanai.**
I don't mind if people realize that I'm gay.

c 日本初の契約制スチュワーデス。「自分たちはパイオニア。」
**Nihon-hatsu no keiyaku-sei suchuwādesu. 'Jibun-tachi wa
paionia.'**
Japan's first stewardesses on contract. 'We are pioneers.'

d なぜ、清輝君の心の叫びがわかってあげられなかったのか。
　自分が情けない。自分がくやしい。
**Naze, Kiyoteru-kun no kokoro no sakebi ga wakatte
agerarenakatta no ka. Jibun ga nasakenai. Jibun ga kuyashii.**
[suicide caused by bullying:] Why was I unable to recognize Kiyoteru's
silent cries? I'm ashamed of myself. I'm disappointed with myself.

### **5.5.2** | jishin

5.5.2.1 | *Reflexive pronoun*

jishin can be used as a reflexive pron. 'him/herself', 'themselves', etc. in
the same way as **jibun,** but this is limited to the written language.

a 女優の宮沢りえさんがテレビのコマーシャルで、自身の波乱に富
んだ人生をもじって使った言葉。
**Joyū no Miyazawa Rie-san ga terebi no komāsharu de, jishin
no haran ni tonda jinsei o mojitte tsukatta kotoba.**
It's an expression that the actress Miyazawa Rie used in a TV advert
as a joke about her own eventful life.

b 自身を評して「何でもしてみたがる好奇心の固まりのような
性格」とか。
**Jishin o hyōshite 'Nan demo shite mi-tagaru kōkishin no
katamari no yō na seikaku' to ka.**
Assessing himself, he says things like, 'My nature is curiosity
personified, wanting to try everything'.

147

5.5.2.2 | *Attached to a personal pronoun*

The combination of personal pronoun + **jishin**, depending on the pronoun used, means 'I myself', 'he himself', 'they themselves', etc. Note that after a plural suffix such as **-ra**, **jishin** is attached after the suffix (example c).

a 私自身は監督になろうとは思わない。

**Watashi jishin wa kantoku ni narō to wa omowanai.**

I myself have no intentions of becoming a coach.

b 彼自身、天才と狂気のはざまに生きたような人なので
ある。

**Kare jishin, tensai to kyōki no hazama ni ikita yō na
hito na no de aru.**

He himself [Wittgenstein] is a person who was born on the
borderline between genius and madness.

c 若手・中堅が真の大指揮者に育つか否かは、彼ら自身の
能力の問題ばかりではない。

**Wakate, chūken ga shin no dai-shikisha ni sodatsu ka ina
ka wa, kare-ra jishin no nōryoku no mondai bakari de
wa nai.**

Whether young and established conductors will develop into really
great ones isn't just a matter of their own ability.

5.5.2.3 | *Attached to* **jibun**

**jishin** attached to **jibun** is used like a personal pronoun, with the combination meaning 'I myself', 'he himself', etc.

a 自分自身はパソコンが苦手だが、「子供にいろいろな
刺激を与えてやろうと思って」と購入することにし
たという。

**Jibun jishin wa pasokon ga nigate da ga, 'kodomo ni
iroiro na shigeki o ataete yarō to omotte' to kōnyū
suru koto ni shita to iu.**

He himself is no good with personal computers, but says he decided
to buy one thinking he would like to provide his children with
a variety of stimuli.

b 二十八日の報道各社とのインタビューでは半年間を振り返って、
首相は「自分自身でも良くやってきたという気持ちがある」と
自画自賛。

**Nijūhachi-nichi no hōdō kakusha to no intabyū de wa
hantoshi-kan o furikaette, shushō wa 'jibun jishin de mo
yoku yatte kita to iu kimochi ga aru' to jiga jisan.**

Looking back on the [first] six months in the interview with the
assembled media companies, the PM sang his own praises, saying, 'I
myself feel that I've done pretty well'.

---

| 5.5.2.4 | *Attached to noun* |

The noun can be a personal noun (examples a and b), or noun referring
to an entity or group made up of persons, such as universities (example
c), or a country (example d).

a 子供を産む、産まないを含め、女性の体に関する判断は女性自身
が行うこと。

**Kodomo o umu, umanai o fukume, josei no karada ni kansuru
handan wa josei jishin ga okonau koto.**

Decisions regarding their own bodies, including whether to have a
baby or not, should be made by women themselves.

b 容疑者自身も事件で負傷しており、収容先の病院で逮捕された。

**Yōgisha jishin mo jiken de fushō shite ori, shūyōsaki no byōin
de taiho sareta.**

The suspect himself was injured, too, and arrested in the hospital
where he was interned.

c 真の改革に向けて何よりも必要なのは、大学評価を積極的に受け、
自らを改革していこうという大学自身の姿勢といえそうだ。

**Shin no kaikaku ni mukete nani yori mo hitsuyō na no wa,
daigaku hyōka o sekkyoku-teki ni uke, mizukara o kaikaku
shite ikō to iu daigaku jishin no shisei to iesō da.**

For real reform the most necessary thing is that the universities
themselves take the attitude of having [outside] assessment and
reforming themselves.

d まず日本自身が「居心地の良さ」と決別しなくてはならない。

**Mazu Nihon jishin ga 'igokochi no yosa' to ketsubetsu
shinakute wa naranai.**

First of all, Japan herself must say goodbye to 'feeling comfortable'.

## 5.6 Pronominals

### 5.6.1 no

**no** can be a pronoun that substitutes for a lexical noun, referring to a thing or a person (or animal) in the sense of 'the one(s)'. In this use, **no** is modified like any other noun by a noun-modifying clause, in the same forms that are used to modify nouns. **no** itself attaches the same case or adverbials particles that the lexical noun would.

a 大きいのは500円、小さいのは300円です。
**Ōkii no wa gohyaku-en, chiisai no wa sanbyaku-en desu.**
The big ones are ¥500, the small ones ¥300.

b きのう買ったのを見せて下さい。
**Kinō katta no o misete kudasai.**
Show me the one you bought yesterday.

c これを書いたのは林さんだ。
**Kore o kaita no wa Hayashi-san da.**
The one who wrote this is Hayashi-san.

*Note* – where **no** replaces the modified N in the sequence N **no** N, **no** is used only once:

d ✎山田さんのかさ
**Yamada-san no kasa**
Yamada-san's umbrella

e ✎このかさは山田さんのです。
**Kono kasa wa Yamada-san no desu.**
This umbrella is Yamada-san's.

### 5.6.2 mono/mon

In this use, **mon(o)** is similar to **no**.

a いくつかの選択肢の中から一番条件に合ったものを自然に選んだ
だけ。
**Ikutsu ka no sentakushi no naka kara ichiban jōken ni atta
mono o shizen ni eranda dake.**
From several choices, I just naturally selected the one that suited the conditions best.

# Chapter 6

# Adjectives

## 6.1   Adjectives proper: forms

Where necessary, 'adjective proper' is used to distinguish adjectives ending in -i from other adjectival expressions, especially **na**-adjectives, the other main group of adjectives.

The main adjective (proper) forms are as shown for **yasui** 'cheap' in Table 6.1. The final forms (1–5) can be used independently as predicates, and the noun-modifying forms (in their plain forms only, 1–4) to modify nouns.

Polite predicates are formed by attaching the copula **desu** (see 7.5) to the plain final forms. Note that there are two polite forms each for the negative forms **yasukunai** and **yasukunakatta**.

The adjective-stem is used as a written-style conjunctive form (see 25.1.1), for using adjectives as adverbs (see 10.1.1; with some adjectives, also as nouns, see 6.1.1.1.4), and to attach **suru/naru**, 6.1.1.1.3).

The adjective-root is used to attach the nominalizing suffixes -**sa** and -**mi** (see 1.10), and also the modal ending -**sō** (see 9.5.2).

### 6.1.1   Stem forms

Stem forms of adjectives are used as a written-style conjunctive form. Colloquially, Adj-**te** is used instead (see 25).

**Table 6.1** Basic adjective forms

**yasui** 'cheap'

|  |  | Plain | Polite |
|---|---|---|---|
| 1 Non-past: | (Adj-**i**) | **yasu-i** | **yasu-i desu** |
| 2 Past: | (Adj-**ta**) | **yasukat-ta** | **yasukat-ta desu** |
| 3 Negative: | (Adj-**nai**) | **yasuku-nai** | **yasuku-nai desu/yasuku arimasen** |
| 4 Neg. past: | (Adj-neg. past) | **yasuku-nakatta** | **yasuku-nakatta desu/yasuku arimasen deshita** |
| 5 Presumptive: | (Adj-(y)**ō**) | **yasukarō/yasui darō** | **yasui deshō** |
| 6 Stem: | (Adj-stem) | **yasuku** | — |
| 7 Root: | (Adj-root) | **yasu** | — |
| 8 Conjunctive: | (Adj-**te**) | **yasuku-te** | — |
| 9 Conditional: | (Adj-**ba**) | **yasukere-ba** | — |

N-mod. (plain only)

Fin.

6.1.1.1 | *Uses of adjective-stem*

6.1.1.1.1 | Written-style conjunctive form (See 25.1.1.)

a 札幌は日の出は早く、日没は遅い。
**Sapporo wa hinode wa haya-ku, nichibotsu wa osoi.**
In Sapporo, the sunrise is early, and the sunset is late.

6.1.1.1.2 | Attaches the negative endings **-nai** (**desu**) or **arimasen**

a あまりうまくない。
**Amari umaku-nai.**
It's not very tasty.

b 教師の待遇はよくありません。
**Kyōshi no taigu wa yoku arimasen.**
The treatment [=pay] of teachers isn't good.

6.1.1.1.3 | Attaches **suru** 'do' and **naru** 'become' (see 7.6.1.10)

a 暗くなると照明がともる。
**Kura-ku naru to shōmei ga tomoru.**
When [it] gets dark, the lights come on.

b 賃下げは労使関係を悪くするだけ。
**Chinsage wa rōshi kankei o waru-ku suru dake.**
Lowering wages just worsens industrial relations.

6.1.1.1.4 | Forms the noun form of certain adjectives

A small number of adjectives in their stem form can be used as nouns,
attaching case particles. These include **tōku** 'distant place', **chikaku** 'vicinity' and a few others (see 6.6.3.4).

a 「私はこの土地が好き。遠くへ出かけるなんて大嫌い」と言う。
**Watashi wa kono tochi ga suki. Tō-ku e dekakeru nante
daikirai to iu.**
'I like this land. I hate going away to faraway places', she says.

### 6.1.2 | (-)nai: *negative forms*

There is both a negative adjective **nai** 'there isn't' (i.e. the opposite of **aru** or **iru** 'there is'), and a negative inflectional ending -**nai**. Both inflect like adjectives, but note that the negative ending -**nai** has two conjunctive forms, -**naide** and -**nakute**, as shown in Table 6.2 (for differences in use see 25.6).

The negative forms of **nai** (**nakunai** etc.) are used as 'double negatives' (see 17.2), which cancel themselves out into positives. The adverbial particle **wa** is often sandwiched between **naku** and **nai**, etc. for emphasizing the negative.

a 明るい材料も少なくはない。
   **Akarui zairyō mo naku wa nai.**
   Bright [economic] data are not altogether absent.

**Table 6.2** Forms of the negative adjective **nai**/negative ending -**nai**

|  |  | Plain | Polite |
|---|---|---|---|
| Final N-mod. (Plain only) | 1 Non-past | na-i | na-i desu |
|  | 2 Past | nakat-ta | nakat-ta desu |
|  | 3 Neg. | naku-nai | naku-nai desu/naku arimasen |
|  | 4 Neg.-past | nakunakat-ta | naku-arimasen-deshita |
|  | 5 Stem | naku | — |
|  | 6 Root | na | — |
|  | 7 Conjunctive | naku-te/-nai-de | — |
|  | 8 Conditional | nakere-ba | — |

In colloquial language, especially male language in Eastern Japan, (-)**nai** is often pronounced as **nē**.

a ああ、二度と浮気なんかしっこねえ。(V-っこない = no way will V)
   **Aa, nido to uwaki nanka shikko-nē.** (V-kko nē = no way will V)
   Yeah, there's no way he's gonna cheat on his wife again.

*Note* – There are some lexical items ending in -**nai**, which do not have negative meaning, such as **sukunai** 'few' and **tsumaranai** 'boring'.

## 6.2  Some alternative forms added to adjective-root

### 6.2.1  -kare

-kare is an ending which is used in set phrases with pairs of opposite adjectives, like ōi/sukunai or hayai/osoi.

a 火山に限らず地下には多かれ少なかれ地下水が広く分布して
  いる。
  **Kazan ni kagirazu chika ni wa ō-kare sukuna-kare chikasui ga**
  **hiroku bunpu shite iru.**
  Water is widely distributed underground more or less everywhere,
    not only under volcanoes.

b 遅かれ早かれ人員の見直しが始まるのではないか。
  **Oso-kare haya-kare jin'in no minaoshi ga hajimaru no de wa**
  **nai ka.**
  Sooner or later, a reconsideration of personnel will surely begin.

### 6.2.2  -karō

This is an old-fashioned equivalent of the presumptive ending Adj-i **darō**
(see 9.1.2.2).

a 景気へのインパクトは小さかろう。
  **Keiki e no inpakuto wa chiisa-karō.**
  The impact on the economy ought to be small.

### 6.2.3  -ki

This is the classical equivalent of the noun-modifying (see 6.6) Adj-i ending. It is still used for a stylish effect, mostly in headlines or in the titles of movies or books. In titles of books and movies, **utsukushii** N and **subarashii** N almost invariably become **utsukushiki** N and **subarashiki** N. Certain combinations are best seen as idioms (example e).

a 種子島—宇宙と生きる美しき島
  **Tanegashima – uchū to ikiru utsukushiki shima** [= headline]
  Tanegashima – a beautiful island that lives together with outer space
    [= launching pad for rockets]

b 素晴しき日
**Subarashiki Hi**
*One Fine Day* (= title of 1996 Hollywood film)

c 四十五歳で社長に抜てきされた「若きエース」も、今年で在任
十四年。
**Yonjūgo-sai de shachō ni batteki sareta wakaki ēsu mo
kotoshi de zainin jūyonen.**
The 'young ace' who was chosen as company president at the age of
45 has this year been in his post for 14 years.

d 独身時代が長く、最近良きパートナーを得た。
**Dokushin jidai ga nagaku, saikin yoki pātonā o eta.**
Having been single for many years, she has recently found a congenial
partner.

e 古き良き時代のシャンソンを聞きたければ、日本にいけ、と言わ
れるほどだ。
**Furu-ki yo-ki jidai no shanson o kikitakereba, Nihon ni ike,
to iwareru hodo da**
People even say that if you want to hear chansons of the good old
days, go to Japan.

---

| 6.2.4 | -shi |

This is the classical equivalent of the Adj-**i** ending, final use. It is still used
for a stylish effect, especially in the classical use of the negative adjective
**nai**, which does not require any case particle and makes for a concise
sentence, usually in writing (see 17.1.1.2).

a 入会金なし。
**Nyūkaikin nashi.**
No joining fee.

## 6.3 na-**adjectives**

na-adjectives comprise a group of words which have adjectival meaning,
but grammatically are similar to nouns, which is why they are also sometimes called nominal adjectives. When modifying other nouns, they attach

na, and when used adverbially, **ni,** but when used as predicates they are followed by forms of the copula, just like nouns do (see 7.5).

A small number of adjectives (**atatakai/ataraka na, chiisai/chiisa na**) have competing -i and **na** endings.

a 静かな寺だ。
**Shizuka na tera da.**
It is a quiet temple.

b 奇麗になった。
**Kirei ni natta.**
(The village) has become pretty.

c 穴子はきらいだ。
**Anago wa kirai da.**
I don't like conger eel.

d 小さな政府
**chiisa na seifu**
small government

e 小さい政府
**chiisai seifu**
small government

## 6.4  no-**adjectives**

no-adjectives comprise a limited group of words which have adjectival meaning, but grammatically behave like nouns, i.e. they attach **no** when modifying nouns and forms of the copula (see 7.5). They include a few NJ words like **nama** 'raw' and **hadaka** 'naked' and also many onomatope words (see 6.6.6, 28.3).

### 6.4.1 | *Noun-modifying: no-adjective no noun (see 6.6.6)*

a 生のキノコもご紹介しておこう。
**Nama no kinoko mo go-shōkai shite okō.**
I will also introduce raw mushrooms.

---

**6.4.2**  *Adverbial use*

6.4.2.1  *no-*adjective **ni suru/naru**: *change of state*

In this use, **no**-adjectives attach **suru** or **naru** in their **ni**-form, to indicate a change of state (see 7.6.1.10).

a 裸になれば人間は皆同じ。
**Hadaka ni nareba ningen wa mina onaji.**
Without clothes (*lit.* "when they become naked") people are all the same.

b 就職活動とは、これまで生きてきた二十年が丸裸にされる
"成人式"。
**Shūshoku katsudō to wa, kore made ikite kita nijū-nen ga maru-hadaka ni sareru 'seijin-shiki'.**
Looking for work [after university graduation] is a 'coming of age ceremony', where you're stripped of the 20 years you've lived so far.

6.4.2.2  *no-*adjective **de**: *state*

This indicates a state in which the action of the verb takes place.

a 加熱料理にも向くが、生で食べるとナシに似た甘さと食感が
ある。
**Kanetsu ryōri ni mo muku ga, nama de taberu to nashi ni nita amasa to shokkan ga aru**
It [= yacon] is suitable for cooked dishes too, but when you eat it raw it has a sweetness and texture similar to a pear.

b 猛暑のせいか裸で寝るのが癖になった。
**Mōsho no sei ka hadaka de neru no ga kuse ni natta.**
Possibly because of the heatwave, I've developed the habit of sleeping naked.

**6.4.3**  *no-*adjective + copula: predicate use

(See 6.5.2, 6.6.6)

a 王様は裸だ。
**Ōsama wa hadaka da.**
The king has no clothes.

## 6.5 | Adjectival expressions: as predicate

Adjectival expressions can be used as predicates as follows: 1) adjectives proper by themselves, and 2) **na-** and **no**-adjectives with the addition of the copula (see 7.5).

### 6.5.1 | *Adjectives proper and (-)nai, -tai, hoshii, etc.*

#### 6.5.1.1 | *Adjectives proper*

Adjectives proper are *formally* distinguishable because their plain non-past form ends in -**i** (this form is also used for listing in dictionaries). There is, however, also a number of grammatical and lexical items that end in -**i**, i.e. that are formally adjectives (see 6.5.1.2).

Adjectives proper can be distinguished from **na-** and **no**-adjectives in *function* because they can form a predicate by their non-past and other final forms, whereas **na-** and **no**-adjectives require the addition of the copula.

a 恥ずかしい。
  **Hazukashii.**
  [I feel] ashamed.

b この学校にはサラリーマンの子供が多い。
  **Kono gakkō ni wa sararīman no kodomo ga ōi.**
  There are many children of company workers in this school.

#### 6.5.1.2 | *The negative/negative ending **nai**/-nai, and other grammatical items that are formally adjectives*

These include items such as -**tai** (see 9.2.1), **mitai** (see 9.5.1), **hoshii** (see 9.2.3), -**ppoi** (see 6.9.2), **rashii** (see 9.5.5), -**te hoshii** (see 15.7) (see also 17).

a そんなことはない。
  **Sonna koto wa nai.**
  That's not so.

b 私だって子供がほしい。
  **Watashi datte kodomo ga hoshii.**
  I too want children.

c 迫力はあるけど、うそっぽい。
**Hakuryoku wa aru kedo, uso-ppoi.**
It [= the depiction of hell] is powerful, but looks a bit fake.

| 6.5.2 | **na-** *and* **no-***adjectives* |
|---|---|

| 6.5.2.1 | **na-***adjective* + *copula* |
|---|---|

**na**-adjectives tend to be either NJ (often ending in -**ka** or -**ta**), S-J (mostly consisting of two *kanji*, or equivalent) or WJ words (see 1.1).

**na**-adjectives require forms of the copula (see 7.5) to form predicates.

a 海はまだ静かだ。
**Umi wa mada shizuka da.**
The sea is still quiet.

b 準備は快適だ。
**Junbi wa kaiteki da.**
Preparations are going well.

c 材料も作り方もシンプルだ。
**Zairyō mo tsukurikata mo shinpuru da.**
Both ingredients and preparation are simple.

| 6.5.2.2 | **no-***adjective* + *copula* |
|---|---|

Like **na**-adjectives (and nouns), **no**-adjectives require forms of the copula to form a predicate (see 6.6.6, 7.5).

a 王様は裸だ。
**Ōsama wa hadaka da.**
The king has no clothes.

b 信号は赤だった。
**Shingō wa aka datta.**
The traffic lights were (on) red.

| 6.5.3 | *Valency and adjectives* |
|---|---|

Valency is a term that refers to how many obligatory 'arguments' (or NPs) a predicate, in this case an adjective, takes (see also 7.2).

Adjectives are for the most part 'one-place', i.e. take only one NP, but some, like **hoshii** 'want' and **suki** 'like' (which usually translate as verbs in English), take two obligatory NPs (**wa/ni** and **ga/o**), as illustrated by the following example with **hoshii**, taking **ga** and **o** (see 9.2.3).

a 出演者の一人がこのシステムをほしいと話していた。
   **Shutsuensha no hitori <u>ga</u> kono shisutemu <u>o</u> hoshii to hanashite ita.**
   One of the people on the programme said he wanted this system.

## 6.6 Adjectival expressions: noun-modifying

Adjectival expressions (like adjectives proper, which are one type of adjectival expression), describe properties or qualities 'what sort/kind of'. As seen below, adjectival expressions include word classes like nouns, pronouns, verbs, adverbs, etc., that *function* like adjectives, i.e. describe or modify a noun that follows.

### 6.6.1 Specialized noun-modifying words

#### 6.6.1.1 Noun-modifying demonstrative pronouns and question words

Demonstrative words and pronouns include words like **kono** 'this', **sonna** 'that kind of'. Q-words include **dono** 'which?', **donna** 'what kind of?', etc. (for details see 5.1, 5.2).

#### 6.6.1.2 Other specialized noun-modifying words (**arayuru, iwayuru, saru**, etc.)

There is a small number of other specialized N-modifying words (**arayuru** 'every possible', **iwayuru** 'so-called', **saru** 'the past', **onaji** 'the same'; note especially the use of **onaji** where English would use 'alike', 'like' (example c).

a 私たちはあらゆる問題を話し合った。
   **Watashi-tachi wa arayuru mondai o hanashiatta.**
   We talked about all possible problems.

b 同じ年の夫とは三年前に知り合った。
   **Onaji toshi no otto to wa sannen mae ni shiriatta.**
   She met her husband, who is the same age, three years ago.

c どうやら同じ島国でも、英国人のような紅茶好き、というわけに
はいかないようだ。

**Dōyara onaji shimaguni de mo, eikokujin no yō na kōcha-zuki,
to iu wake ni wa ikanai yō da.**

It appears that even though [we're] an island nation like the UK,
we are not as fond of black tea as the British.

*Note* – **onaji** has other uses too, such as predicate + copula (example d).

d 経済はだれがやっても同じでしょ。

**Keizai wa dare ga yatte mo onaji desho.**

The economy should be the same, no matter who runs it
[= the country].

---

**6.6.2** | *Noun (including number + counter/pronoun)* **no** *noun*

---

**6.6.2.1** | *Noun 1* **no** *noun 2*

---

N1 includes N of time (see 1.7). The [N1 **no** N2] combinations (= NPs)
often, but not always, translate into English as 'N2 of N1' (see 2.3).

a 最近の若者
**saikin no wakamono**
the young of recent times

b ここの家の主人
**koko no ie no shujin**
the master/husband of this house

c 日本の政治
**Nihon no seiji**
Japanese politics
(*lit.* "Japan's politics")

d 日本のカメラ
**Nihon no kamera**
a Japanese camera

---

**6.6.2.2** | *Personal pronoun* **no** *noun*

---

Depending on the pronoun, personal pronoun **no** N translates into English
as 'my/your/his/her/our/their N'. But see 1.4 for differences in use of personal pronouns compared to English.

a 私の仕事
**watashi no shigoto**
my job

b あなたの車
**anata no kuruma**
your car

| 6.6.2.3 | *Number + counter* **no** *noun* |

Number + counter **no** is used to modify nouns that require a specific counter, whereas those that lack a specific counter use the 'default' counter -**tsu** (number + **no**). Note that a number can also occur after the noun it refers to, as in example b, where the structure is N + number + counter **no** N (see 4).

a 一つの地域
　**hitotsu no chiiki**
　one area

b レンズ一枚の価格
　**renzu ichi-mai no kakaku**
　The price of one lens

| 6.6.3 | *Adverb/adverbial clause* **no noun** |

| 6.6.3.1 | *Adverb*-**te no** *noun* |

These include a number of adverbs ending in -**te**, such as **subete** 'all', **hajimete** 'for the first time', **katsute** 'formerly' (see 10.1.5.1). Example c contains an adverbial clause (**umarete hajimete** 'for the first time since being born').

a すべての規制
　**subete no kisei**
　all restrictions

b はじめての住居
　**hajimete no jūkyo**
　my first house

c 生まれてはじめての体験だった。
　**Umarete hajimete no taiken datta.**
　It was [my] first experience ever (*lit.* "in my life").

| 6.6.3.2 | *Noun + phrasal particle*-**te no** *noun* |

Phrasal particles are often equivalent to prepositions in English (see 3).

*Note* – most, but not all, phrasal particles can take **no** (examples a and b).

a 選手としての経歴はすごい。
　**Senshu to shite no keireki wa sugoi.**
　His career as a player is formidable.

b このことについての大臣の考えは。
　**Kono koto ni tsuite no daijin no kangae wa.**
　What are your [= the minister's] thoughts on this matter?

| 6.6.3.3 | *Clause-te **no*** *noun: adverbial clause modifying noun* |

Here, an adverbial clause ending in the conjunctive form -**te** (underlined) modifies a following noun (or NP) by means of **no**. The noun/NP implies an action, and S-**te** indicates 'how' or 'in what state/condition', etc. the action takes place. Check the idiomatic translations (also underlined) below.

a お客さんあっての商売。
   <u>**Okyaku-san atte**</u> **no shōbai.**
   Business [is something that] <u>depends on the existence of customers</u>
   (= no business without customers).

b ザックを背負ってのベトナムひとり旅。
   <u>**Zakku o seotte**</u> **no betonamu hitori-tabi.**
   A solitary trip through Vietnam, <u>shouldering a rucksack</u>.

c それでも豊かさを求めての逃走は続く。
   **Sore demo <u>yutakasa o motomete</u> no tōsō wa tsuzuku.**
   But nevertheless the flight <u>in pursuit of affluence</u> continues.

d 三十歳を目前にしての決意である。
   <u>**Sanjussai o mokuzen ni shite**</u> **no ketsui de aru.**
   It's a decision [made] <u>with age 30 just around the corner</u>.

| 6.6.3.4 | *Adjective-stem **no*** *noun: **ōku no**, **chikaku no**, etc.* |

The stem form of adjectives, ending in -**ku**, can be used with a following **no** to modify a noun. However, this is possible with only a very small number of adjectives, such as **ōi** 'many', **chikai** 'near', **tōi** 'far' (see 6.1.1.1.4).

a 過熱するカメラブームで、多くの機種が登場した。
   **Kanetsu suru kamera būmu de, ōku no kishu ga tōjō shita.**
   In the overheating camera boom, many new models have appeared.

| 6.6.4 | *Adjectives proper + noun* |

Adjectives proper always end in -**i** in their plain non-past form, which is also used to modify nouns (this is also the form under which they are listed in dictionaries).

a 古い家屋
   **furui kaoku**
   old houses/an old house

b 新しい体験
   **atarashii taiken**
   a new experience

## 6.6.5 na-*adjective* na *noun*

### 6.6.5.1 Unconverted na-*adjective* na *noun*

na-adjectives require the noun-modifying form **na** of the copula (see 7.5).

a 静かな朝
**shizuka na asa**
a quiet morning

b 柔軟な発想
**jūnan na hassō**
a flexible way of thinking

### 6.6.5.2 Converted na-*adj* na *noun*

The suffix -**teki** converts a noun (often a two-*kanji* compound) into a na-adjective, which then modifies a noun in the same way as other adjectival nouns, i.e. by attaching **na** (see 6.9.1).

a 精神的な強さ (cf., 精神 'mind')
**seishin-teki na tsuyosa**
mental strength

b 理想的な男性 (cf., 理想 'an ideal')
**risō-teki na dansei**
an/the ideal male

*Note* – N-**teki** can also modify nouns directly, without **na**; the whole NP in this case is understood as a compound (examples c and d) (see 6.9.1.1.2).

c 政治的問題
**seiji-teki mondai**
political problems

d 社会的責任
**shakai-teki sekinin**
social responsibility

## 6.6.6 no-*adjective* + *noun*

no-adjectives are words with adjectival meaning that behave grammatically like nouns, i.e. they modify other nouns by means of **no**.

The main groups of **no**-adjectives are those NJ colour words that are not adjectives proper (i.e. do not end in -i), and all WJ colour words, plus also a few other NJ words such as **nama** 'raw' and **hadaka** 'naked', and a select number of onomatope (see 28.3).

a 白のタキシード姿の新郎
**shiro no takishīdo sugata no shinrō**
the groom in a white tuxedo

b ピンクのフラミンゴ
**pinku no furamingo**
pink flamingoes

c オレンジかピンクのポロシャツ
**orenji ka pinku no poroshatsu**
an orange or pink polo shirt

d 生のキノコ
**nama no kinoko**
raw mushrooms

e 蒸し暑い夜、上半身裸の男たちが道ばたで名物の「火鍋」をつつく。
**Mushiatsui yoru, jōhanshin hadaka no otoko-tachi ga michibata de meibutsu no 'hinabe' o tsutsuku.**
On a hot and humid night, men with bare torsos are eating the local speciality, firepot, by the roadside.

---

**6.6.7** | *Verb/verbal noun/adverb-ta noun*

**6.6.7.1** | *Verb-**ta**, or verbal noun **shita** noun*

Here, a verb or verbal noun that indicates a state in its -**te iru** form (as indicated in the examples below) modifies a noun by means of the -**ta** form (V-**ta**).

*Note* – no meaning of completion or past is present in this case (see 8.2, 22.1).

a 安定した生活 (cf., 生活が安定している **seikatsu ga antei shite iru** 'life is secure')
**antei shita seikatsu**
a secure life

b 発達した筋肉 (cf., 筋肉が発達している **kinniku ga hattatsu shite iru** 'muscles are well-developed')
**hattatsu shita kinniku**
well-developed muscles

c 「家々、木々、山々」と題した作品がある。(cf., 題している **daishite iru** 'has the title of')
**'Ieie, Kigi, Yamayama' to daishita sakuhin ga aru.**
There is a work entitled 'Houses, Trees, Mountains'.

d 自立した証券会社は育たない。(cf., 自立している **jiritsu shite iru** 'is independent')
**jiritsu shita shōkengaisha wa sodatanai**
Independent securities firms don't thrive.

e 「子供を家庭・地域に帰そう」を目指した学校五日制。
(cf., 目指している **mezashite iru** 'is aiming for')
**'Kodomo o katei, chiiki ni kaesō' o mezashita gakkō itsuka-sei/**
The five-day school system, which has the aim of 'returning the children to their homes and locality'.

6.6.7.2 *Adverb* **(to) shita** *noun*

Many onomatope adverbs (see 28.3) modify nouns by means of **to shita**,
or just **shita**. But note that there are also some onomatope which modify
N by means of **no**.

*Note* – despite the -ta form used, no meaning of completion or past is
present with **(to) shita**.

a ふとしたことから寺山修司を知った。(ふと **futo** 'suddenly', 'accidentally')
  **Futo shita koto kara Terayama Shūji o shitta.**
  By chance I got to know Terayama Shūji.

b 川床に座ると、ひんやりした風が頬をなでていく。(ひんやり
  **hin'yari** 'cool')
  **Kawadoko ni suwaru to, hin'yari shita kaze ga hoho o nadete iku.**
  When one sits down on the riverbed [platform], a cool wind
  caresses one's cheeks.

6.6.8 **Noun** *ga/no adjective/verb + noun*

Some N **ga/no** adjective/verb combinations have adjectival meaning as
lexical items. N **ga** adjective combinations include **se ga takai** 'tall', **atama
ga ii** 'intelligent', etc., and N **ga** V combinations are **settokuryoku ga aru**
'convincing' and **ninki ga aru** 'popular'.

In noun-modifying use, these can use either **ga** or **no**, although **no** is far
more common.

a 背が高い女性が多くなっているのに対応したもの。
  **Se ga takai josei ga ōku natte iru no ni taiō shita mono.**
  This [introducing larger sizes] is to deal with the fact that there are
  more tall women.

b 説得力のあるコーチになるだろう。
  **Settokuryoku no aru kōchi ni naru darō.**
  He should turn out to be a convincing coach.

**6.7** **Adjectival expressions in comparative sentences**

Comparison typically concerns itself with items that have some property
or quality to a larger or lesser degree than one or several others. That
property is usually expressed by adjectives and **na**-adjectives.

Unlike such English formations as cheap → cheap<u>er</u>/cheap<u>est</u>, Japanese has no comparative and superlative forms of adjectives as such. Comparison (including choice of alternatives) is therefore effected by different means, some of which are similar to the English regular formations 'more beautiful'/'most beautiful', i.e. adverbs of degree such as **motto** 'more' and **ichiban/mottomo** 'most' are used (see 10.2.2).

The case particle **yori** and the noun **hō** ('on the . . . side') also figure prominently in comparative sentences (see 2.9.2).

---

### 6.7.1 | Comparison using yori and/or hō ga

The most common way of making a comparison uses the particle **yori** 'more than', 'rather than' and/or the noun **hō** (usually marked by the case particle **ga**). In combination with **hō** ('side'), **ga** may be seen as a way of emphasizing the item it is modified by (example a literally translates as something like "Rather than pork, *beef* is cheap"). The combination indicates the alternative in a choice of two.

---

#### 6.7.1.1 | Y yori (mo) X no hō ga adjective: X (no hō) ga Y yori (mo) adjective

Both constructions mean 'X is [adjective]-er than Y'. Note that instead of adjectives, verbs (and verb forms with a stative meaning) can also be used.

Comparing the two word orders, *Y* **yori (mo)** *X* **no hō ga** Adj is the more usual (unmarked) one, *X* (**no hō**) **ga** *Y* **yori (mo)** Adj having the effect of emphasizing the comparison (compare examples a and b).

a 豚肉より牛肉の方が安い。
**Butaniku yori gyūniku no hō ga yasui.**
Beef is cheaper than pork.

b 牛肉が豚肉より安い―。食肉市場ではこんな逆転現象が起きている。
**Gyūniku ga butaniku yori yasui – . Shokuniku shijō de wa konna gyakuten genshō ga okite iru**
Beef is cheaper than pork –. This kind of reversal is happening in the meat market.

c 人のいのちは地球より重い、という。
**Hito no inochi wa chikyū yori omoi, to iu.**
They say that a human life weighs heavier than the earth.

d 金子さんの観察では、男性よりも女性の方が冷静だ。

**Kaneko-san no kansatsu de wa, dansei yori mo josei no hō ga reisei da.**

According to Kaneko-san's observation, women are more level-headed than men.

---

| 6.7.1.2 | *Time expression + particle* **yori** |

This combination means 'compared to'.

a 昨日より軟らかいよ。

**Kinō yori yawarakai yo.**

They [= pears] are softer than yesterday.

b これまでより五モデル増える。

**Kore made yori go-moderu fueru.**

Compared to before, there will be five new models.

---

| 6.7.1.3 | *Clause* **yori** |

Here, two options are considered, with the clause marked by **yori** judged to be the less preferable one 'rather than'.

a 今は森を見るより木を見る時だ。

**Ima wa mori o miru yori ki o miru toki da.**

This is the time to look at the trees rather than the woods.

b 会社に無理して勤めるより，好きなことで生活したい。

**Kaisha ni muri shite tsutomeru yori, suki na koto de seikatsu shitai.**

Rather than forcing myself to work at a company, I'd like to earn my living doing something I like.

---

| 6.7.1.4 | *Clause* **yori hoka** ... *negative* |

Followed by a negative form, this indicates that the option (the clause to which **yori hoka** is attached) is the only viable possibility 'there is no choice but'.

a 「株を持ち続けるよりほかに手はない」とあきらめ切った表情。

**'Kabu o mochitsuzukeru yori hoka ni te wa nai' to akiramekitta hyōjō.**

'There's no choice but to keep holding on to the shares', he said with an expression of total resignation.

b できたばかりの支店を軌道に乗せるためには、がむしゃらに働く
　よりほかない。

**Dekita bakari no shiten o kidō ni noseru tame ni wa,
gamushara ni hataraku yori hoka nai.**

In order to get a newly established branch going, there's no other
way than to work like mad.

---

Idiom: **nani yori (mo)**

Unlike other question words + **yori**, which express the idea of 'more . . . than',
question word + **nani yori (mo)** is an idiomatic expression with the meaning of 'above all', 'more than anything else'.

a 何より印象的なのが、カメラの位置が低いことだ。

**Nani yori inshō-teki na no ga, kamera no ichi ga hikui
koto da.**

What's impressive above all is the low position of the camera.

---

**6.7.2** | *Comparison with adverb (yori-, motto, ichiban) + adjective*

6.7.2.1 | **yori-***adjective*

In this use, **yori-** acts like a prefix, used as an equivalent to the comparative form 'more . . .', '-er' in languages like English.

The construction **yori**-adjective itself, and certain derived noun + verb/
adjective expressions with adjectival meaning such as **antei shite iru** 'be
secure', **settokuryoku ga aru** 'be convincing', **inpakuto ga ōkii** 'have a big
impact', etc. are said to have arisen under influence from Western languages.

a ゲームはよりリアルになっている。

**Gēmu wa yori-riaru ni natte iru.**

Games have become more real[istic].

b より高い背により小さな足に。

**Yori-takai se ni yori-chiisana ashi ni.**

[Women have developed] taller figures and smaller feet.

c 直接投資の方がよりインパクトが大きい。

**Chokusetsu tōshi no hō ga yori-inpakuto ga ōkii.**

Direct investment makes the greater impact.

d "より良いものをより安く" をモットーに飛躍を目指す。

**'Yori-yoi mono o yori-yasuku' o mottō ni hiyaku o mezasu.**

They aim for dramatic improvement with the motto 'Better things,
more cheaply'.

e 今後、着工へ向けてより説得力のある理由付けが求められそうだ。

**Kongo chakkō e mukete yori-settokuryoku no aru riyūzuke
ga motomeraresō da.**

In future, it is likely that a more convincing reason will be required
for new construction works.

---

| 6.7.2.2 | **motto** |

motto 'more' can be used to modify adjectives, but also a verb phrase such
as **o-shigoto nasaru** 'do work' (honorific). Note also the intensified version
**motto motto** (see 10.2).

a 体を動かすのが好き。人と話すのがもっと好き。

**Karada o ugokasu no ga suki. Hito to hanasu no ga motto suki.**

I like moving my body. Talking with people I like [even] more.

b もっともっとお仕事をなさってほしかったのに、本当に残念
です。

**Motto motto o-shigoto o nasatte hoshikatta noni, hontō ni
zannen desu.**

I wanted her [= late actress] to do lots more [good] work, but … it's
such a pity.

---

| 6.7.2.3 | **ichiban/mottomo** |

As can be seen from the examples, **ichiban** and **mottomo** (both meaning
'most') also modify verb phrases besides adjectives, in particular before
nouns, i.e. in relative clauses (examples b and c).

a 雪解け前の雪崩が一番怖い。

**Yukidoke-mae no nadare ga ichiban kowai.**

Avalanches before the thaw are the most frightening.

b 今が一番、仕事がおもしろい時期だ。

**Ima ga ichiban, shigoto ga omoshiroi jiki da.**

Now is the time when work is most interesting.

c 今年もっとも記憶に残った出来事はやはり猛暑だった。
**Kotoshi mottomo kioku ni nokotta dekigoto wa yahari
mōsho datta.**
What has remained most in my memory this year was the extreme
heat.

*Note* – there is also a conjunction **mottomo** (example d), which indicates
a qualification of what was said previously 'mind you', 'however'. This
is usually found at the beginning of a sentence, and is *not* followed by
adjectives or verbs (see 24.5).

d 私は今、日本の新聞六種類の他に、英字新聞を一つ、それからア
メリカの週刊誌二つ、東南アジアの英語の週刊誌を読む。もっ
とも全部読む訳ではない。
**Watashi wa ima, Nihon no shinbun roku-shurui no hoka ni,
Eiji shinbun o hitotsu, sorekara Amerika no shūkanshi
futatsu, Tōnan Ajia no eigo no shūkanshi o yomu.
Mottomo zenbu yomu wake de wa nai**
Besides six Japanese newspapers, I'm currently reading one English
newspaper, two US weekly magazines, and a Southeast Asian
English weekly. Mind you, it's not the case that I read them in
their entirety.

---

| 6.7.2.4 | **hodo** |

**hodo** (see 11.5.2) indicates the degree to which the following verb/adjective
(or copula) applies 'as much as' (also **gurai/kurai**, see 11.5.1). It is used
with negative or positive predicates.

a これほどうれしいことはありません。
**Kore hodo ureshii koto wa arimasen.**
Nothing could make me happier (*lit.* "There is no thing that is as
happy [for me] as this").

b 苦しい時ほど愛する対象が欲しいんです。それが証拠に独り
暮らしの老人がよく犬を飼っている。
**Kurushii toki hodo aisuru taishō ga hoshii n desu.
Sore ga shōko ni hitori-gurashi no rōjin ga yoku inu o
katte iru.**
One never wants something to love so much as in difficult times.
A good illustration of this is that old people living alone often
keep dogs.

6.7.2.5 | *X* **no naka de** *(wa/mo) + evaluatory predicate*

**naka de** indicates that of the entity to which **naka de** is attached, the part which follows (marked by the evaluatory predicate) is 'is relatively good/bad, etc. of/amongst/compared to *X*'.

a ✐三人兄弟の中で太郎が一番背が高い。
**Sannin kyōdai no naka de Tarō ga ichiban se ga takai.**
Of the three brothers, Tarō is the tallest.

b ポリエチレンはプラスチックの中でも最も分解しにくいものの一つ。
**Poriechiren wa purasuchikku no naka de mo mottomo bunkai shinikui mono no hitotsu.**
Polyethylene is one of the most difficult of plastics to degrade.

c 不況、不況と言うが全国の中では九州はまだ元気がいい。
**Fukyō, fukyō to iu ga zenkoku no naka de wa Kyūshū wa mada genki ga ii.**
Everyone is saying there's a recession, but Kyushu is still in good shape compared to the rest of the country.

6.7.2.6 | *(A* **to** *B* **to** *(+ particle))* **dochira**

Here, two items are lined up, joined by the conjoining particle **to** (repeated also after *B*). The question word **dochira** gives a choice between these two alternatives, literally meaning "*A* and *B*, which is -er?" (see 5, 21.1).

a ✐紅茶とコーヒーとどちらがいいですか。
**Kōcha to kōhī to dochira ga ii desu ka.**
Which would you prefer, tea or coffee?

b 人とサルとどちらが被害者なのだろう。
**Hito to saru to dochira ga higaisha na no darō.**
Who are the victims, one wonders, the people [of the village] or the [wild] monkeys.

c しょせん、権力抗争だとするとどちらが正しいとか正しくないとかいってみても始まらない。
**Shosen, kenryoku kōsō da to suru to dochira ga tadashii toka tadashikunai toka itte mite mo hajimaranai.**
Ultimately, if it's a power struggle we're dealing with, there's no point in arguing who's right or wrong.

| 6.7.2.7 | **dore** |

| 6.7.2.7.1 | *(A to B to C to ... N to)* **dore** |

Here, three or more items are lined up, joined by the conjoining particle **to** (repeated also after *N*). **dore** 'which of three (or more)' is used if the choice is of three or more items.

When followed by **mo** or **-te mo**, the implication is one of 'all' or 'whichever' (see 5.2).

*Note* – the conjoining particle **to** preceding **dore** can also be the adverbial particle **to** (example c) or the conjunctive particle **to** (example b), resulting of course in a different meaning. Generally, the written language (media etc.) often uses patterns that diverge somewhat from language textbooks (and from such made-up examples as example a)!

Note how in examples b and d the nouns are lined up in apposition, with commas between (see 23).

a  ✎すしとてんぷらとすきやきと、どれが一番好きですか。

   **Sushi to tenpura to sukiyaki to, dore ga ichiban suki
   desu ka.**

   Which do you like best, sushi, tempura or sukiyaki?

b  水泳、釣り、食事の準備、散策‥‥‥。雑誌のグラビアページを
   見ているとどれも楽しそうで、そのままキャンプ場でまねした
   くなる。(**to** = conjunctive particle)

   **Suiei, tsuri, shokuji no junbi, sansaku ... zasshi no gurabia pēji
   o mite iru to dore mo tanoshisō de, sono mama kyanpujō
   de mane shitaku naru.**

   Swimming, fishing, preparing meals, going for walks ... If one looks at
   the photo pages of magazines they all look such fun, so one feels
   like doing the same at the camp.

c  ラーメンが食べられる貴重な店。ギョウザ、チャーハン、カレー
   とどれもすごくおいしい。

   **Rāmen ga taberareru kichō na mise. Gyōza, chāhan, karē to
   dore mo sugoku oishii.**

   A rare place where you can eat *ramen* (soup noodles). *Gyoza*
   (dumplings), *chahan* (fried rice), and (Japanese-style) curry are all
   supremely tasty.

6.7.2.7.2 **X no naka de ... dore**

As in 6.7.2.7.1, the choice is between three or more items 'which amongst *X*'.

a 写った天体の中で、どれが銀河でどれが恒星かも自動的に識別で
きる。

**Utsutta tentai no naka de, dore ga ginga de dore ga kōsei ka
mo jidō-teki ni shikibetsu dekiru.**

It can also automatically distinguish which among the heavenly bodies
on screen are galactic and which are fixed stars.

*6.7.2.8* **hō**

**hō** is preceded and followed by the forms that precede and follow nouns.

The basic meaning of **hō** as a lexical noun (方) is 'area' or 'direction', but
as a structural noun, **hō** (usually followed by the case particle **ga**) indicates
choice of the preferred item or course of action.

This is effected by emphasizing the preferred item (by means of **hō ga**)
when two items, courses of action, etc. are (explicitly or implicitly) being
compared.

6.7.2.8.1 Noun/noun phrase **no hō ga**

Like any other noun, **hō** is attached to a noun (or noun phrase) by means
of **no**. Note also how **hō** can combine with **yori** (see 6.7).

a 野球よりサッカーの方が面白い。
**Yakyū yori sakkā no hō ga omoshiroi.**
Soccer is more interesting than baseball.

b 男性の方がお金にはルーズなようだ。
**Dansei no hō ga okane ni wa rūzu na yō da.**
[Compared to women] men seem to be more careless with money.

c 社会主義時代の生活の方がよかった。
**Shakaishugi jidai no seikatsu no hō ga yokatta.**
Life was better during socialist times.

d 年をとってからは町の方が暮らしやすい···
**Toshi o totte kara wa machi no hō ga kurashiyasui ...**
Once you're old, a town is easier to live in [than the country] ...

6.7.2.8.2 | Clause-verb **hō ga** adjective

Consisting of a clause ending in a verb modifying **hō** (given in [ ]), this can indicate the idea of 'doing . . . is adjective-er' or 'doing . . . would be adjective-er'.

a 家で寝転がってテレビでも見ている方が楽だし、お金もかからない。

**[Ie de nekorogatte terebi demo mite iru] hō ga raku da shi, o-kane mo kakaranai.**

Lying down at home watching TV is easier (than going to a show), and doesn't cost anything either.

b これだけ県費をつぎ込んでうまくいかない方がおかしい。

**[Kore dake kenpi o tsugikonde umaku ikanai] hō ga okashii.**

Considering all the prefectural funds going into [the project], it would be strange if it didn't succeed.

6.7.2.8.3 | Clause-verb/adjective **hō ga ii/yoi/mashi da**

Followed by evaluatory adjectives such as **ii/yoi** 'good' and **mashi** (na-adjective) 'preferable', this is used for recommending a course of action, or stating a preference 'you should', 'is better/preferable'.

Verbs often use the ending **-ta** (which indicates not past but completion here) before **hō**, but **-te iru** and **-ru** are also found (in the negative, **-nai** is used, for an example see 6.7.2.8.2 b).

a 医師に詳しく診てもらった方がいいだろう。

**Ishi ni kuwashiku mite moratta hō ga ii darō.**

You'd better have a thorough check-up from a doctor.

b 辞任するのなら早く辞任した方がよい。

**Jinin suru no nara hayaku jinin shita hō ga yoi.**

If he resigns, then he should do so soon.

c 財布のひもはやっぱり女性が握った方がいい？

**Saifu no himo wa yappari josei ga nigitta hō ga ii?**

Is it in the end better if women control the purse strings?

d 効率を考えると解体して何か新しい物を建てる方が簡単だ。

**Kōritsu o kangaeru to kaitai shite nani ka atarashii mono o tateru hō ga kantan da.**

When you consider efficiency, it's easier to dismantle them [= historic buildings] and build something new.

e 缶は持ち運ぶのに軽い方がいい。
**Kan wa mochihakobu no ni karui hō ga ii.**
Cans are better light, for carrying them around.

f 平凡でけっこう、平凡で幸せな方がはるかにいい。
**Heibon de kekkō, heibon de shiawase na hō ga haruka ni ii.**
Mediocre is fine, it's far better to be mediocre and happy.

g 毛皮を着るぐらいなら裸の方がまし。
**Kegawa o kiru gurai nara hadaka no hō ga mashi.**
I'd rather be naked than wear a fur.

| 6.7.2.8.4 | Clause-verb/adjective **hō** copula

This indicates a tendency, compared to other people or entities that are
not explicitly mentioned: 'on the . . . side', 'relatively', 'tend to'.

a 私なんかおとなしい方よ。
**Watashi nanka otonashii hō yo.**
I'm on the quiet side, you know.

b 自分からすすんで、新しい友だちをつくるほうですか。
**Jibun kara susunde atarashii tomodachi o tsukuru hō desu ka.**
Do you tend to go out of your way to make new friends?

## 6.8 Adjectival suffixes

### 6.8.1 Adjective-garu

-**garu** is an adjectival suffix that indicates that the feeling expressed by the
adjective is openly displayed, usually by persons other than the speaker.
The suffix -**garu** can be attached to the stem forms of Adj and **na**-Adj
(minus the copula) that express a feeling or attitude, to the stem form of
the desiderative ending -**tai** (which in turn attaches to V), and the stem
form of the adjective of desire **hoshii**. Note that -**garu** itself works like a
Group I verb.

#### 6.8.1.1 Adjective/**na**-adjective-stem-**garu**

Adj/**na**-Adj to which -**garu** attaches are limited to those that express a
feeling, i.e. **omoshiroi** (besides the meaning of 'interesting') also means 'to

177

show an interest in', and **fushigi na** 'to feel mystified'. **-garu** adds the nuance that the subject visibly or audibly displays such feelings.

a 子供たちが一番面白がったのは折り紙。
**Kodomo-tachi ga ichiban omoshiro-gatta no wa origami.**
What the children showed most interest in was origami.

b かわいがりようは子供並み。
**Kawai-gari-yō wa kodomo-nami.**
They lavish affection [on pets] as if they were their children.

c 国民がいやがることも必要があればやらなければならない。
**Kokumin ga iya-garu koto mo hitsuyō ga areba yaranakereba naranai.**
If necessary, we must also do things that the people express dislike for.

d かつて「安全と水はタダだと思っている」と外国人に不思議がられた日本人だが、水に関する限りこの言葉はもうあてはまらない。
**Katsute 'anzen to mizu wa tada da to omotte iru' to gaikokujin ni fushigi-garareta nihonjin da ga, mizu ni kansuru kagiri kono kotoba wa mō atehamaranai.**
In the past, foreigners used to be mystified at the Japanese, saying 'they think that safety and water come free', but with regard to water these words no longer apply.

---

| 6.8.1.2 | Verb-**tagaru** |

Attached to the Adj-root form of **-tai**, **-garu** forms the combination **-tagaru**. This usually indicates that a second person, or most commonly a third, 'want(s) to' (see 9.2). Note, however, example g, where the speaker uses **-tagaru** about himself!

a 君が辞めたがっているという話を聞いたのだけど。
**Kimi ga yame-tagatte iru to iu hanashi o kiita no da kedo.**
I've heard that you want to quit.

b 日本旅行の関係者はこの問題に触れたがらない。
**Nihon Ryokō no kankeisha wa kono mondai ni fure-tagaranai.**
The people at Japan Travel are unwilling to comment on this problem.

c うちの社員は技術者が大半で、設計も頑丈にしたがる。
**Uchi no shain wa gijutsusha ga taihan de, sekkei mo ganjō ni shi-tagaru.**
Our staff are mostly technicians, and therefore want to make designs sturdy.

d 親にも教師にもいじめの事実を隠したがる。

**Oya ni mo kyōshi ni mo ijime no jijitsu o kakushi-tagaru.**

[The children] want to hide the fact that they are being bullied
from both parents and teachers.

e あいつは部を出たがっている。

**Aitsu wa bu o de-tagatte iru.**

He wants to leave the section.

f 母親は「汚い言葉がはんらんしている」と、子供を競技場に行か
せたがらない。

**Hahaoya wa 'Kitanai kotoba ga hanran shite iru' to kodomo o
kyōgijō ni ikase-tagaranai.**

Mothers feel that the place is awash with foul language, and don't
want to let their children go to the stadium.

g 自身を評して「何でもしてみたがる好奇心の固まりのような
性格」とか。

**Jishin o hyōshite 'Nan demo shite mi-tagaru kōkishin no
katamari no yō na seikaku' to ka.**

Assessing himself, he says things like 'My nature is curiosity personified,
wanting to try everything'.

---

6.8.1.3 | **hoshi-garu**

Whereas the Adj of desire **hoshii** (see 9.2.3) usually indicates what first
persons (or second persons in questions) want, **hoshi-garu** (again, **-garu** is
attached to Adj-root) is used for the wants of third persons.

a ドイツのオーケストラは今、ドイツ人をほしがっている。

**Doitsu no ōkesutora wa ima, doitsujin o hoshi-gatte iru.**

German orchestras at present want [to employ] Germans.

b いま日本が、本当に子供をほしがっているのなら、アフリカや
東南アジアの子供たちをひきとって育ててもいいと思う。

**Ima Nihon ga hontō ni kodomo o hoshi-gatte iru no nara,
afurika ya tōnan ajia no kodomo-tachi o hikitotte sodatete
mo ii to omou.**

If Japan really wants [more] children now, I think people should adopt
and raise children from Africa or Southeast Asia.

c 「モノの時代からココロの時代へ」といわれるなかで、消費者が
　　特にほしがっているのはクルマや住宅などのモノだ。

**'Mono no jidai kara kokoro no jidai e' to iwareru naka de,
shōhisha ga toku ni hoshi-gatte iru no wa kuruma ya jūtaku
nado no mono da.**

In the midst of the supposed shift of emphasis of our age from
objects to spiritual matters, what consumers really want are objects
like cars and housing.

## 6.9 Adjective-forming suffixes

### 6.9.1 -teki

Attached to nouns (often two-*kanji* SJ compounds, and occasionally Western
loanwords), -**teki** converts the noun into a **na**-adjective. Depending on the
form of copula attached to -**teki**, it can modify nouns (in compound-like
combinations also without the copula), modify verbs etc. in adverbial use,
and act as a predicate.

#### 6.9.1.1 Noun-modifying

##### 6.9.1.1.1 -teki na noun (by means of copula-na)

a 根本的な疑問は残る。(cf., 根本 **konpon** 'basis')
　　**Konpon-teki na gimon wa nokoru.**
　　Basic doubts remain.

b 何より印象的なのが、カメラの位置が低いことだ。(cf., **inshō**
　　印象 'impression')
　　**Nani yori inshō-teki na no ga, kamera no ichi ga hikui koto da.**
　　What's most impressive is the low (*lit.* "lowness of the") camera angle.

##### 6.9.1.1.2 -teki noun (directly)

It is also possible to modify a noun directly with -**teki**; in these cases, the
combination acts like a noun compound.

a テレビなど刺激的文化の影響で、本らしい本の衰弱が目立つ。
　　(cf., 刺激 **shigeki** 'stimulus')
　　**Terebi nado shigeki-teki bunka no eikyō de, hon rashii hon no
　　suijaku ga medatsu.**
　　Under the influence of the stimulus culture such as TV, the decline of
　　proper books is conspicuous.

b ガムランは伝統的音楽の要素を持ちながら、現代音楽でもあるわけだ。(cf., 伝統 dentō 'tradition')

**Gamuran wa dentō-teki ongaku no yōso o mochinagara, gendai ongaku de mo aru wake da.**

So gamelan, while having elements of traditional music, is also modern music.

6.9.1.2 | **-teki ni** *(adverbial use)*

a 雨が降ったときは一時的に気温が下がることがある。
(cf., 一時 ichiji 'at times')

**Ame ga futta toki wa ichiji-teki ni kion ga sagaru koto ga aru.**

After it has rained, the temperature can drop temporarily.

b 米国とは政治、経済的にぜひ仲良くしたいと思っている。
(cf., 経済 keizai 'economy')

**Beikoku to wa seiji, keizai-teki ni zehi nakayoku shitai to omotte iru.**

We'd very much like to establish good political and economic relations with the US.

c 一人一人の労働時間が減っても、マクロ的には余暇消費の拡大には結びついていない。(cf., マクロ［経済］ makuro [keizai] macro[economics])

**Hitori hitori no rōdō jikan ga hette mo, makuro-teki ni wa yoka shōhi no kakudai ni wa musubitsuite inai.**

Even if each individual's working hours have decreased, this has not, in macro terms, been linked with an expansion in leisure consumption.

6.9.1.3 | **-teki da** *(as predicate)*

a 空港に着陸するときに眺めた美しい景色は印象的だった。
(cf., 印象 inshō 'impression')

**Kūkō ni chakuriku suru toki ni nagameta utsukushii keshiki wa inshō-teki datta.**

The beautiful scenery I saw when landing at the airport was memorable.

b アメリカ人の性行動はきわめて保守的なのである。
(cf., 保守 hoshu 'conservatism')

**Amerikajin no seikōdō wa kiwamete hoshu-teki na no de aru.**

The sexual behaviour of Americans is extremely conservative.

## 6.9.2 | -ppoi

-ppoi is a suffix that is attached to nouns and noun-equivalents such as a verb-stem. It converts the noun into an adjective that indicates a tendency, i.e. what things or people tend to be like. Some combinations are better dealt with as lexical items

### 6.9.2.1 | Noun-**ppoi**

Note the somewhat unusual example c, where a following noun such as **mono** needs to be assumed as omitted.

a 迫力はあるけど、うそっぽい。

**Hakuryoku wa aru kedo, uso-ppoi.**

It [= the depiction of hell] is powerful, but looks a bit fake.

b 内装は黒と黄土色、ステンレスっぽい銀色を基調に、おとなしくまとめている。

**Naisō wa kuro to ōdoiro, sutenresu-ppoi gin'iro o kichō ni, otonashiku matomete iru.**

The interior is finished soberly with black and ochre and silvery stainless steel as the main colours.

c そのバッグ、アメ横とかで売っている安物っぽいですね。

**Sono baggu, Ameyoko toka de utte iru yasumono-ppoi desu ne.**

That bag is one of those cheap [ones] they sell in places like Ameyoko, right?

d ステージも、ジャズというよりはソウルミュージックっぽい力強いもの。

**Sutēji mo, jazu to iu yori wa souru myūjikku-ppoi chikara-zuyoi mono.**

The performance is powerful, more like soul music than jazz.

### 6.9.2.2 | Lexical items

a 日本人は忘れっぽい。

**Nihonjin wa wasure-ppoi.**

The Japanese people forget easily.

b 上下とも黒っぽい服を着て、髪はオールバックだった。

**Jōge tomo kuro-ppoi fuku o kite, kami wa ōru bakku datta.**

He wore a black top and trousers, and his hair was combed back.

c 「怒りっぽい、飽きっぽい、骨っぽい」の「三ぽい」で知られる水戸っぽ気質。

**'Okori-ppoi, aki-ppoi, hone-ppoi' no 'san-ppoi' de shirareru mitoppo katagi.**

The Mitoite character is known for three qualities: 'irritable', 'fickle' and 'tough'.

# Chapter 7

# Verbs, valency, copula and sentence types

## 7.1 Verbs

Japanese verbs are inflected (for inflectional forms of verbs, see Tables 7.1–7.3 below).

The basic form of all Japanese verbs ends in -u, -eru or -iru, which is also the form they are listed under in dictionaries. According to the way they inflect, verbs can be divided into three groups, I, II and III.

### 7.1.1 Forms

#### 7.1.1.1 Group I verbs

These end in the syllables う・く・ぐ・す・つ・ぬ・ぶ・む・る (-u, -ku, -gu, -su, -tsu, -nu, -bu, -mu, -ru) in Japanese writing, but in romanization these endings can be analysed further as consonant-root + -u (買う kau, 沿う sou, etc. can be thought of as kaw-u, sow-u).

#### 7.1.1.2 Group II verbs

These end in -ru (following either i or e).

#### 7.1.1.3 Group III verbs

Irregular V (usually just two are distinguished, kuru 'come' and suru 'do') are included in this group. Note, however, that suru, apart from being used by itself, forms part of the widely used N-suru verbal nouns (see 1.9).

## 7.1.1.4 | Group II lookalikes

There are a few verbs that look like Group II on the basis of V-**ru**, but their V-**nai**, V-**te** forms clarify the issue:

**iru**　　要る 'need' 要らない・要って
　　　　**iranai/itte** (**ir-u**, Group I)

　　　　いる 'be there' いない・いて
　　　　**inai/ite** (**i-ru**, Group II)

**kaeru**　帰る 'return' 帰らない・帰って
　　　　**kaeranai/kaette** (**kaer-u**, Group I)

　　　　変える 'change' 変えない・変えて
　　　　**kaenai/kaete** (**kae-ru**, Group II)

　　　　代える 'substitute' 代えない・代えて
　　　　**kaenai/kaete** (**kae-ru**, Group II)

　　　　換える 'convert' 換えない・換えて
　　　　**kaenai/kaete** (**kae-ru**, Group II)

**hairu**　入る 'enter' 入らない・入って
　　　　**hairanai/haitte** (**hair-u**, Group I)

## 7.1.1.5 | Plain and polite forms

Verbs and other Japanese predicate or modifiers, etc. can be used as plain or polite forms; this choice is conditioned by factors such as the situation and the status (social/age etc.) of the listener in relation to the speaker, but in grammatical terms also by the item modified. For instance, a verb modifying a noun is as a rule plain (except in some hyperpolite styles), and many tense/aspect and modal endings follow only the plain form.

The main plain forms of the regular Groups I and II are as follows (for polite forms, -**masu** (see 7.1.2.4) is attached to V-stem). Forms 1–4 (final/N-modifying) can be used as predicates or to modify a following N. Forms 5–6 can be used by themselves as a predicate only, whereas 7–9 can be used only in subordinate clauses or with other forms attached (except in some colloquially shortened uses).

**Table 7.1** Group I and Group II verb forms (plain)

| | | Group I (consonant root) | | Group II (vowel root) | |
|---|---|---|---|---|---|
| | | kik-u | ka(w)-u | tabe-ru | mi-ru |
| | | (hear) | (buy) | (eat) | (see) |
| 1 Non-past | (V-ru) | kik-u | ka(w)-u | tabe-ru | mi-ru |
| 2 Past | (V-ta) | kii-ta | kat-ta | tabe-ta | mi-ta |
| 3 Neg. | (V-nai) | kik-ana-i | kaw-ana-i | tabe-na-i | mi-na-i |
| 4 Neg.-past | (V-neg.-past) | kik-ana-kat-ta | kaw-ana-kat-ta | tabe-na-kat-ta | mi-na-kat-ta |
| 5 Imperative | (V-imp) | kik-e | ka(w)-e | tabe-ro | mi-ro |
| 6 Presumptive/hortative | (V-yō) | kik-ō | ka(w)-ō | tabe-yō | mi-yō |
| 7 Stem | (V-stem) | kik-i | ka(w)-i | tabe | mi |
| 8 Conjunctive | (V-te) | kii-te | kat-te | tabe-te | mi-te |
| 9 Conditional | (V-ba) | kik-eba | ka(w)-eba | tabe-reba | mi-reba |

N-mod. ⟷

Fin. ⟷

**Table 7.2** Group I verb forms (plain) by root-final consonant

| Root-final consonant | V-ru | V-stem | V-ta | English |
|---|---|---|---|---|
| -s | hanas-u | hana*sh*-i | hana*sh*i-ta | 'to speak' |
| -ts | mats-u | ma*ch*-i | ma*t*-ta | 'to wait' |
| -k | kik-u | kik-i | ki*i*-ta | 'to hear' |
| -g | oyog-u | oyog-i | oyo*i*-*da* | 'to swim' |
| -n | shin-u | shin-i | shin-*da* | 'to die' |
| -m | yom-u | yom-i | yo*n*-*da* | 'to read' |
| -b | yob-u | yob-i | yo*n*-*da* | 'to call' |
| -r | kaer-u | kaer-i | kae*t*-*ta* | 'to return' |

**Table 7.3** Group III verb forms (plain)

| | | | | kuru ('come') | suru ('do') |
|---|---|---|---|---|---|
| N-mod. ↕ | Fin. ↕ | 1 Non-past | (V-**ru**) | kuru | suru |
| | | 2 Past | (V-**ta**) | kita | shita |
| | | 3 Neg. | (V-**nai**) | kona-i | shina-i |
| | ↓ | 4 Neg.-past | (V-neg.-past) | kona-kat-ta | shina-kat-ta |
| | | 5 Imperative | (V-imp.) | koi | shiro |
| | | 6 Presumptive/ hortative | (V-**yō**) | koyō | shiyō |
| | | 7 Stem | (V-stem) | ki | shi |
| | | 8 Conjunctive | (V-**te**) | kite | shite |
| | | 9 Conditional | (V-**ba**) | kureba | sureba |

### 7.1.1.6 | *Formation rules for Group I*

For -**u** substitute the endings -**ta**, -**i**, -**anai**, -**te**, -**e**, -**eba**, -**tara**, -**ō**; the final consonant doubles before -**t** (for **ka-u**, **so-u**, etc. the forms become more regular if we assume a root-final (**w**) consonant, as actually found in the V-**nai** form). There are some further irregularities, as shown in the italicized and underlined parts in Tables 7.1 and 7.2 above (all others are regular). The equivalent forms are used for all Group I verbs with identical root endings (**shin-u** is the only verb with a root ending in -**n**).

*Formation rules for Group II*

For -**ru** substitute the endings -**ta**, zero, -**nai**, -**te**, -**ro**, -**reba**, -**tara**, and **yō**.

## 7.1.2 | Uses of verb forms

### 7.1.2.1 | Verb-**ru**

#### 7.1.2.1.1 | Used by itself

V-**ru** (the non-past form of verbs) can be used by itself as a predicate to complete a sentence in the present, habitual present, future, and also narrative present. It can also express the speaker's intention (see 8.1).

Unlike Adj/**na**-Adj + copula sentences, which have adjectival meaning as predicates, and N + copula, which are equational in meaning, V-**ru** can express a variety of meanings as a predicate.

#### 7.1.2.1.2 | Items attached

The main items that are attached to V-**ru** *only* are -**beki** (but note the still-used classical variant **su-beki** instead of the regular **suru-beki**), and -**mai** (see 9.4, 9.3).

a 選挙で選ぶべきだ。
  **Senkyo de erabu-beki da.**
  [He] ought to be chosen by election. (note that the verb form is active in Japanese)

### 7.1.2.2 | Verb-**ta**

#### 7.1.2.2.1 | Used by itself

V-**ta** is the plain past ending. It can indicate both past and perfective (see 8.2).

#### 7.1.2.2.2 | Items attached

For items that commonly attach to -**ta**, see 8.2.

The V-**ta** base (i.e. the form remaining when -**ta** is detached) attaches the conjunctive particle -**tari** (see 26.7).

a たまの休日には本を読んだりゴルフに興じたりする。
**Tama no kyūjitsu ni wa hon o yondari gorufu ni kyōjitari suru.**
On his rare days off he does things like reading books and enjoying
golf.

b 例えば、盲導犬は人にほえたり、かみついたりすることがない。
**Tatoeba, mōdōken wa hito ni hoetari, kamitsuitari suru koto
ga nai.**
For instance, guide dogs don't do things like barking at people and
biting them.

c 特に慌てたりする同僚はいなかった。
**Toku ni awatetari suru dōryō wa inakatta.**
There weren't any colleagues who were particularly flustered.

| 7.1.2.3 | *Stem forms*

Stem forms of verbs are used as a written-style conjunctive (see 25) form
(colloquially, V-**te** is used).

| 7.1.2.3.1 | Uses of verb-stem

| 7.1.2.3.1.1 | *Written-style conjunctive form*

This is used in compound sentences only (see 7.6.5).

a ふたをし、赤くなるまで蒸す。
**Futa o shi, akaku naru made musu.**
You put on the lid, and steam [the crab] until it turns red.

b 二人組は車で逃走し、夫婦にけがはなかった。
**Futari-gumi wa kuruma de tōsō shi, fūfu ni kega wa nakatta.**
The gang of two took flight, and the couple were not injured.

| 7.1.2.3.1.2 | *Forming the noun form of verbs*

V-stem is also used as the noun form of many verbs. In particular, this is
used in the pattern V-stem **ni iku/kuru** (see 2.4.10).

a またぜひ働きに行きたい。
**Mata zehi hataraki ni ikitai**
I very much want to go to work again.

| 7.1.2.3.1.3 | *Items attaching to verb-stem* |

V-stem attaches to the endings -**masu** (polite) (see below), -**sō** (likelihood) (see 9.5.4), -**tai** (desiderative) (see 9.2.1) and -**nagara** (see 26.4.3), the final particle **na/na yo** (familiar imperative) (see 20.1.3), the polite imperative ending -**nasai** and **o/go** V-stem **kudasai** (see 20.1.5), the nominalizing suffix -**yō** and -**kata** ('way of -ing') (see 1.10.2), etc.

*Note* – **nasaru** and **kudasaru** have irregular stem forms, **nasai** and **kudasai**, which attach the polite ending -**masu** directly (see 16.3).

| 7.1.2.4 | *Polite verb ending* -**masu** |

Unlike honorific and humble forms, which are used of second or third persons (honorific), or first and third persons (humble), the polite ending –**masu** is used for the benefit of the listener, regardless of who is being spoken about.

For polite forms of V, the polite ending -**masu** is attached to V-stem, i.e. Group I **kiki-masu, kai-masu**, etc.; Group II **tabe-masu, mi-masu**, etc.; Group III, **shi-masu** and **ki-masu**.

-**masu** forms belong to the same polite style as the **desu**-form of the copula (see 7.5). They are usually restricted to the spoken language, in ordinary conversation with strangers or those who are not intimate.

-**masu** itself inflects as follows (forms in ( ) are archaic, but still occasionally encountered; the imperative -**mase** is used only with honorific verbs such as **irassharu** and **kudasaru** etc.):

| 1 | Non-past | -**masu** |
|---|---|---|
| 2 | Past | -**mashita** |
| 3 | Neg. | -**masen** |
| 4 | Neg-past | -**masen-deshita** |
| 5 | Imperative | -**mase** (-**mashi**) |
| 6 | Stem | — |
| 7 | Conjunctive | -**mashite** |
| 8 | Conditional | (-**masureba**) |

*Note* – the N-mod. use of -**masu** (-**masu** N) and the conjunctive form -**mashite** are largely restricted to the formal language of letters and speech-making.

Apart from its use as the equivalent of the -**nai** form, -**masen** is also used to make some modal endings polite: **kamoshirenai** → **kamoshiremasen**.

Likewise, the **-masu** form of the negative adjective **nai, arimasen,** is also applied to such endings as **ni chigai nai,** which becomes **ni chigai arimasen** (see 9.6.3).

## 7.2 Valency and arguments of verbs

Valency is a convenient term that refers to how many obligatory 'arguments' (or NP) a predicate (a verb or adjective) takes. For instance, **miru** 'see' requires a subject (the person who sees) and an object (what the person sees). The former is marked by the case particle **ga,** the latter by **o.** These arguments need not be present in any given sentence (see 27.2), but where not explicitly mentioned they are understood. (Of course, **miru** can appear with further NPs (e.g. where the action of **miru** takes place, marked by **de**), but this information is more peripheral, i.e. not obligatory for **miru**).

### 7.2.1 Valency and transitive/intransitive verbs

Some verbs take just one obligatory NP ('one-place V'); these are usually intransitive. Others take two NPs ('two-place V'), which are usually transitive. Yet others take three ('three-place V'), which are sometimes called ditransitive, e.g. **ageru** and other V of giving.

In the following example, **ageru** 'give' has NP-**ga** marking the subject (the person carrying out the action of the verb), NP-**ni** to mark the indirect object (the person who is the receiver of the action of V), and NP-**o** indicating the object, i.e. what is given.

a リンダさんは週に二回学校に行っているので、代わりにマイクさんが哺乳瓶で赤ちゃんに母乳をあげる。
**Rinda-san wa shū ni nikai gakkō ni itte iru no de, kawari ni Maiku-san ga honyūbin de akachan ni bonyū o ageru.**
As Linda goes to school twice a week, Mike gives the baby a bottle feed instead.

The case particle for one-place verbs is typically **ga** (subject), for two-place verbs **ga-o** (subject-object), and for three-place verbs **ga-o-ni** (subject-object-indirect object, also in the alternative order V **ga-ni-o**). In other words, the core case particles are **ga, o** and **ni.** Other case particles are generally more peripheral ('oblique' cases). However, **e** and **to** are used for core cases with some verbs: for instance, **iku** 'go' can take **e** instead of **ni** to indicate the goal of the action, and **kumu** 'team up' constructs with **ga** and **to** ('with').

## 7.3 Transitive/intransitive verb pairs

Japanese has a large number of verbs that come in (formally related) transitive/intransitive pairs (for a comparison of the use of transitive and intransitive V, see 28.5, 12–14 and certain aspectual endings: 8.3, 8.4).

Common pairs and their relation in form are shown in Table 7.4 (only one representative meaning is given).

*Note* – only very few pairs are identical in form (compare this to the large number of identical pairs in the English translations).

**Table 7.4** Transitive and intransitive verb pairs

| Intransitive verb | Transitive verb |
| --- | --- |
| *-aru* | *-eru* |
| **agaru** 上がる 'rise' | **ageru** 上げる 'raise' |
| **ataru** 当たる 'be hit' | **ateru** 当てる 'hit' |
| **atsumaru** 集まる 'be gathered' | **atsumeru** 集める 'gather' |
| **azukaru** 預かる 'be entrusted' | **azukeru** 預ける 'entrust' |
| **hajimaru** 始まる 'begin' | **hajimeru** 始める 'begin' |
| **kakaru** かかる 'hang' | **kakeru** かける 'hang' |
| **magaru** 曲がる 'be bent' | **mageru** 曲げる 'bend' |
| **mazaru** 混ざる 'be mixed' | **mazeru** 混ぜる 'mix' |
| **mitsukaru** 見つかる 'be found' | **mitsukeru** 見つける 'find' |
| **sagaru** 下がる 'hang' | **sageru** 下げる 'hang' |
| **shimaru** 閉まる 'close' | **shimeru** 閉める 'close' |
| **shizumaru** 静まる 'become calm' | **shizumeru** 静める 'calm' |
| **tomaru** 止まる 'stop' | **tomeru** 止める 'stop' |
| **tsumaru** 詰まる 'be stuffed' | **tsumeru** 詰める 'stuff' |
| **tsunagaru** つながる 'connect' | **tsunageru** つなげる 'connect' (ALSO **tsunagu** つなぐ) |
| | |
| *-u* | *-eru* |
| **aku** 開く 'be open' | **akeru** 開ける 'open' |
| **machigau** 間違う 'be mistaken' | **machigaeru** 間違える 'make a mistake' |
| **muku** 向く 'face' | **mukeru** 向ける 'point at' |
| **susumu** 進む 'advance' | **susumeru** 進める 'advance' |
| **tsuku** つく 'stick' | **tsukeru** つける 'attach' |
| **ukabu** 浮かぶ 'float' | **ukaberu** 浮かべる 'float' |
| **umaru** 埋まる 'be buried' | **umeru** 埋める 'bury' |
| **sodatsu** 育つ 'grow up' | **sodateru** 育てる 'bring up' |
| **tatsu** 立つ 'stand' | **tateru** 立てる 'erect' |

**Table 7.4** (cont'd)

| Intransitive verb | Transitive verb |
|---|---|
| ***-waru*** | ***-eru*** |
| kawaru 変わる 'change' | kaeru 変える 'change' |
| owaru 終わる 'end' | oeru 終える 'end' |
|  | (ALSO owaru 終わる) |
| tsutawaru 伝わる 'be transmitted' | tsutaeru 伝える 'transmit' |
| ***-ru*** | ***-su*** |
| amaru 余る 'be left over' | amasu 余す 'leave over' |
| kaeru 返る 'return' | kaesu 返す 'return' |
| naoru 直る 'be mended' | naosu 直す 'mend' |
| nokoru 残る 'be left' | nokosu 残す 'leave' |
| tōru 通る 'pass through' | tōsu 通す 'pass through' |
| wataru 渡る 'cross over' | watasu 渡す 'pass over' |
| ***-u*** | ***-asu*** |
| kawaku 乾く 'dry' | kawakasu 乾かす 'dry' |
| ugoku 動く 'move' | ugokasu 動かす 'move' |
| ***-eru*** | ***-asu*** |
| deru 出る 'come out' | dasu 出す 'put out' |
| ***-eru*** | ***-yasu*** |
| fueru 増える 'increase' | fuyasu 増やす 'increase' |
| hieru 冷える 'become cool' | hiyasu 冷やす 'cool' |
| moeru 燃える 'be burnt' | moyasu 燃やす 'burn' |
| ***-reru*** | ***-su*** |
| kakureru 隠れる 'hide' | kakusu 隠す 'hide' |
| kowareru 壊れる 'break' | kowasu 壊す 'break' |
| taoreru 倒れる 'collapse' | taosu 倒す 'knock down' |
| ***-eru*** | ***-u*** |
| kudakeru 砕ける 'be crushed' | kudaku 砕く 'crush' |
| nukeru 抜ける 'come out' | nuku 抜く 'pull out' |
| wareru 割れる 'split' | waru 割る 'split' |
| yakeru 焼ける 'be roasted' | yaku 焼く 'roast' |
| ***-iru*** | ***-osu*** |
| horobiru 滅びる 'be ruined' | horobosu 滅ぼす 'ruin' |
| ochiru 落ちる 'fall' | otosu 落す 'drop' |
| okiru 起きる 'get up' | okosu 起こす 'raise' |
| oriru 降りる 'come/go down' | orosu 降ろす 'take down' |
| sugiru 過ぎる 'pass' | sugosu 過ごす 'pass' |

**Table 7.4** (cont'd)

| Intransitive verb | Transitive verb |
|---|---|
| *Irregular* | |
| **hairu*** 入る 'enter' | **ireru** 入れる 'enter' |
| **kieru** 消える 'go out' | **kesu** 消す 'put out' |
| **mieru** 見える 'be seen' | **miru** 見る 'see' |
| **noru** 乗る 'get on' | **noseru** 乗せる 'put on' |
| *Identical* | |
| **fuku** 吹く 'blow, breathe' | **fuku** 吹く 'breathe' |
| **masu** 増す 'increase' | **masu** 増す 'increase' |

*Notes* * **hairu** is the usual pronunciation for 入る, but **iru** occurs in compounds 入口 **iriguchi** 'entrance' etc. and idioms 郷に入れば郷に従え (**gō ni ireba gō ni shitagae**) 'when in Rome do as the Romans do'.

## 7.4 Verb types: stative, dynamic, action and change

Verbs can be divided into two basic groups: stative and dynamic. Dynamic verbs can further be subdivided into action and change verbs.

### 7.4.1 Stative verbs

These indicate a state or quality. Examples include **aru** 'be there (inanimate)', **iru** 'be there (animate)', **iru** 'need', **wakaru** 'understand', **dekiru** 'be able to' (and other potential verbs).

The difference between **aru** and **iru** is that **iru** is used for animate subjects (i.e. humans and animals) and **aru** for inanimate ones (those that are not animate). However, **iru** can also be used for certain inanimate things such as vehicles (example d), and both **iru** and **aru** can be used in the sense of 'having siblings/family' (examples e–g) (see 2.1.10).

a 外に女性がいる。
**Soto ni josei ga iru.**
There's a woman outside.

b 夫人との間に一男三女がいる。
**Fujin to no aida ni ichinan sanjo ga iru.**
With his wife, he has one son and three daughters.

c 動物園や植物園あるいは水族館に行けば，数多くの形も機能も異なる動物、植物、魚がいる。

**Dōbutsuen ya shokubutsuen arui wa suizokukan ni ikeba, kazu ōku no katachi mo kinō mo kotonaru dōbutsu, shokubutsu, sakana ga iru.**

If you go to a zoo, botanical gardens or an aquarium, there are many animals, plants and fishes with different shapes and functions.

d 進学や就職で悩まない人は、ほとんどいない。

**Shingaku ya shūshoku de nayamanai hito wa, hotondo inai.**

There is almost nobody who doesn't agonize over choice of school and job.

e 東北出身の奥さんとの間に四人の子供がある。

**Tōhoku shusshin no okusan to no aida ni yo-nin no kodomo ga aru.**

With his wife, who is from northeast Japan, he has four children.

f 子、直系尊属または兄弟姉妹が数人あるときは、各自の相続分は相等しいものとする。

**Ko, chokkei sonzoku mata wa kyōdai shimai ga sūnin aru toki wa, kakuji no sōzokubun wa aihitoshii mono to suru.**

Where there is more than one child or lineal descendant, or brother and sister, each shall inherit equally.

g 妻子あるロッセリーニは、女優イングリッド・バーグマンと恋に落ち、彼女をハリウッドの映画界から奪った。

**Saishi aru Rosserīni wa, joyū Inguriddo Bāguman to koi ni ochi, kanojo o Hariuddo no eigakai kara ubatta.**

Rossellini, who was married with children, fell in love with Ingrid Bergman, the actress, and took her away from Hollywood's world of film.

Most stative V do not attach -te iru (but note **wakatte iru** and **tsumori de iru**); **dekiru** can also mean 'something will be ready' (see 7.4.2.2.3), in which use it can attach -te iru: **dekite iru** 'is ready'.

---

| 7.4.2 | *Dynamic verbs* |

These indicate an event, which can be an action or a change.

| 7.4.2.1 | Action verbs |

Action V include **taberu** 'eat', **nomu** 'drink', **yomu** 'read', **kaku** 'write', **warau** 'laugh', **naku** 'cry', **furu** 'fall (of rain, etc.)', **chiru** 'fall (of flowers)', **benkyō suru** 'study', **setsumei suru** 'explain'.

They also generally include the transitive member of transitive/intransitive V pairs, i.e. **hajimeru** 'begin something', **oeru/owaru** 'end something', **shimeru** 'close something', **kimeru** 'decide something', **akeru** 'open something', etc.

When an action V is attached to **-te iru** (see 8.4), the resulting meaning is often progressive ('is . . . ing' in English): **tabete iru** 'am/is eating', **benkyō shite iru** 'is studying'. However, with some verbs (V of motion/change) the same verb can be used in more than one way, i.e. **chiru** can also mean 'get scattered (across the ground etc.)', in which use it is a verb of change.

| 7.4.2.2 | Change verbs |

Whereas the action of action verbs can go on for some time, verbs of change indicate that their action brings about an instant change. For instance, **tatsu** 'stand up' brings about a change from sitting/lying to standing. Other V of change include those described in the next sections.

| 7.4.2.2.1 | Verbs of clothing |

These include **kiru** 'put on (whole-body garment like coat, pyjamas, kimono, etc., or an upper-body garment such as shirt, jacket, sweater)', **haku** 'put on (a lower-body garment, such as skirt, trousers, shoes)', **kaburu** 'put something on (one's head, e.g. hat, cap, etc.)', and others.

| 7.4.2.2.2 | Motion verbs |

Motion V include **hairu** 'enter', **deru** 'go/come out', **tomaru** 'come to a stop', etc. (but not **aruku** 'walk', **hashiru** 'run', which describe the manner of motion).

| 7.4.2.2.3 | Others |

'Others' include V that translate as 'become', or 'become/get + adv.', such as **naru** 'become', **dekiru** 'get ready, acquire', **naoru** 'get well', **kekkon suru** 'get married', etc.

Also included in 'others' are the intransitive members of transitive/intransitive V pairs: **hajimaru** 'begin', **owaru** 'come to an end', **shimaru** 'close', **kimaru** 'be decided', **aku** 'open', etc.

This also includes the V **shinu** 'die', **shiru** 'get to know'.

When V of change attach -**te iru** (see 8.4), the meaning is usually one of resulting state: **haitte iru** 'am/is/are inside' (as a result of **hairu**), **shinde iru** 'is/are dead', etc.

## 7.5 The copula and copular sentences

The copula is a grammatical word that is used in a similar way to English 'is' 'are', etc. It is always preceded by another word or word/particle combination, i.e. it functions like an inflectional ending. Forms of verbs and adjectives proper may complete a sentence with an inflectional ending, but **na-** and **no**-adjectives and nouns usually require the copula.

**Table 7.5** Forms of the copula

|  | Plain | Polite | Learned-plain | Learned-polite |
|---|---|---|---|---|
| 1 Non-past | **da**, 0 (zero), **na, no** | **desu** | **de aru** | **de arimasu** |
| 2 Past | **dat-ta** | **deshita** | **de atta** | **de arimashita** |
| 3 Negative | **dewa-nai** **ja-nai** | **dewa-arimasen** **ja-arimasen** | **de (wa) nai** | **de (wa) -arimasen** |
| 4 Negative-past | **dewa-nakatta** **ja-nakatta** | **dewa-arimasen-** **deshita** **de nakatta** **ja-arimasen-** **deshita** |  | **de (wa) -arimasen** **-deshita** |
| 5 Adverbial | **ni** | — | — | — |
| 6 Conjunctive | **de** | **deshi-te** | **de atte** | **de arimashite** |
| 7 Conditional | **nara** | — | **de areba** **de aru nara** | — |

### 7.5.1 Ways of saying 'is/am/are'

Compare different ways that 'is/am/are', etc. can be expressed in Japanese as follows (for more details, see 7.6).

| Adj | ✐ 大きい。 | **Ōkii.** | It/he/she's big. |
|------|------------|-----------|------------------|
| **na-Adj** | ✐ 静かだ。 | **Shizuka da/de aru.** | It's/they're quiet. |
| N | ✐ 日本人だ。 | **Nihonjin da/de aru.** | They're Japanese. |
| PLACE | ✐ 家にいる・ある。 | **Ie ni iru/aru.** | It/he/she's in the house. |

### 7.5.2 Plain non-past forms: da, 0 (zero), na, no

### 7.5.2.1 da/de aru

**da** is used clause- or sentence-finally, and is often replaced by 0 (zero) if nothing follows. It is *never* used before **ka** (and constructions using **ka** such as **kamoshirenai**) in the standard language, nor before modal endings such as **mitai, rashii, -sō, yō, hazu, tsumori**, etc.).

The 'learned' eqivalent **de aru** is used in written and/or formal language (example a and b). See 17.1.3 for negative use, and 25.5 for 'splitting' of copula by particles.

a 今こそ、チャンス到来である。
**Ima koso, chansu tōrai de aru.**
Now is the time for opportunity to present itself.

b 菊こそ日本の食用花である。
**Kiku koso Nihon no shokuyō-bana de aru.**
The chrysanthemum is truly the edible flower of Japan.

### 7.5.2.2 0 (zero)

Conversely, 0 is obligatory before **ka** (and constructions using **ka** such as **kamoshirenai**), **mitai, rashii, -sō**.

a 黄色いじゅうたんみたい。
**Kiiroi jūtan mitai.**
They [= wild flowers] are like a yellow carpet.

*Note* – whereas inflectional endings of verbs and adjectives can be used as predicates and to modify nouns, **na**-adjectives and nouns usually require the copula to be attached. However, the newspaper and other written styles tend to omit the copula (**da**, etc.), as example b illustrates.

b あらしの後の静かな朝。
**Arashi no ato no shizuka na asa.**
A quiet morning after the storm.

---

| 7.5.2.3 | **no** |

This is used as the noun-modifying form of **no**-Adj (see 6.4) and certain onomatope (see 28.3).

For nouns, **no** is also used before structural nouns like **yō**. Compare:

a インフレのようなもの (インフレ = N)
**infure <u>no</u> yō na mono (infure** = N)
It's (*lit.* "something") like inflation

b 特徴のある顔は得なようです。(得 = na-Adj)
**Tokuchō no aru kao wa toku <u>na</u> yō desu. (toku** = na-Adj)
It appears that [having] a distinctive face is an advantage.

*Note* – before the case particle **no** (incl. combinations like **no de, noni,** etc.), **no** is never found; instead, **na** is used (see 7.5.2.4).

---

| 7.5.2.4 | **na** |

**na** is used as a noun-modifying form before **no** (incl. the combinations **no da, no de, noni,** etc.); also *always* after **na**-adjectives before all nouns.

a ‘以心伝心’（言わなくても気持ちが通じること）、これが日本人の
　コミュニケーションの神髄なのだ。
**‘Ishin-denshin’ (iwanakute mo kimochi ga tsūjiru koto), kore
　ga Nihonjin no komyunikēshon no shinzui na no da.**
‘Ishin-denshin’ (understanding each other without saying anything), that is the essence of communication between Japanese.

b 山の上の静かな寺だ。
**Yama no ue no shizuka na tera da.**
It's a quiet temple on the top of the mountain.

| 7.5.2.5 | *Adverbial form of copula* |

Whereas **da** (and other forms of the copula) indicate a state, a change of state (including 'future' events like 'want to be' or 'intend to be') require not **da**, but the adverbial form of the copula, **ni**. This is most commonly found with the verb **suru** 'do' and **naru** 'become' (see 7.6.1.10).

a 今月三日、佐藤さんは三十歳になった。
  **Kongetsu mikka, Satō-san wa sanjus-sai ni natta.**
  On the 3rd of this month, Sato-san turned 30.

b 出す以上は地域で一番売れる店にしたい。
  **Dasu ijō wa chiiki de ichiban ureru mise ni shitai.**
  As long as I open it, I want to make it a shop that sells the best in the area.

| 7.5.2.6 | *Presumptive/-**tara**/-**tari** forms of copula* |

Although not given in Table 7.5, one can also distinguish a -**tara** form (**dat-tara, deshi-tara, de arimashi-tara**, see 26.1.2) and a -**tari** form (**dat-tari, de at-tari**, see 26.7).

## 7.6 Sentence types

Now that we have covered the main word classes that participate in making predicates, nouns (+ copula), adjectives (+ copula in case of **na**-adjectives) and verbs, as well as related issues such as the copula and valency, we can take a look at the types of sentence one can distinguish in Japanese.

Note that the types of sentence described in this section do not include negative sentences (see 17). Also not included here are hortative ('let's') sentences (see 9.1).

| 7.6.1 | *Minimal simple sentences* |

A simple sentence minimally consists of one predicate and one or more NP, as required by the valency of the predicate, except where the NP is ellipted/omitted (see 27.2).

A predicate can be a final form of V/Adj or **na**-Adj/N + copula, including the imperative form of verbs (see 7.1, 20.1). It can be plain or polite.

A NP consists of noun + case and/or focus particle. No NP is required with imperatives (see 20.1), nor with a small number of 'one place' verbs and adjectives (in some uses only; see 7.6.1.1 below).

7.6.1.1 *Predicate without 'obligatory' noun phrase*

Items like the verb **nomu** 'drink (alcohol)', the adjective **samui** 'cold' and the **na**-adjective **shizuka** 'quiet' can be used as predicates without any NP. A minimal sentence like **Shizuka da.** can be a complete sentence with the meaning of 'It's quiet'; when 'it' refers to something specific (i.e. a hotel), however, the same sentence would have an ellipted (or omitted) NP (one can tell the difference only from the context). Below are examples of predicates without NP.

a 四月からこれまでに四、五回飲んだかな。
 **Shigatsu kara kore made ni shi, go-kai nonda ka na.**
 Since April, I may have drunk [= had a drink] four or five times
  so far.

b 隊員らは「寒い、寒い」を連発。
 **Tai-in-ra wa 'samui, samui' o renpatsu.**
 The corps members kept saying, '(I'm) cold'.

c 蝉がしきりと鳴いている。音はそれだけだ。静かだ。
 **Semi ga shikiri to naite iru. Oto wa sore dake da. Shizuka da.**
 The cicadas are chirring incessantly. That's the only sound. [It's] quiet.

7.6.1.2 *Simple verb sentences*

In its simplest form, a verb sentence consists of a predicate and one NP + particle. However, in Japanese the verb can also be used by itself where the NP is understood, and this is considered a complete sentence. This also applies to adjective and **na**-adjective/noun + copula sentences.

a 涙が出た。
 **Namida ga deta.**
 Tears came [to my eyes].

b 見た。
 **Mita.**
 I saw [it/him/her, etc.].

*Converted verb sentences*

Verb sentences can be 'converted' into potential, causative and passive sentences, which often involves a change in valency (see 12–14).

*Simple adjective sentences*

Below are examples, one with a NP and the other with an ellipted (or omitted) NP.

a サービスが良い。
**Sābisu ga yoi.**
The service is good.

b 安い。
**Yasui.**
[It's] cheap.

*Simple **na**-adjective sentences*

The **na**-adjective predicate requires a form of the copula to complete the sentence; the NP is marked by the particle **wa**, to indicate that it is the topic about which the predicate is making a comment.

a スクワティ村は静かだった。
**Sukuwati-mura wa shizuka datta.**
Sukuwati village was quiet.

*Simple noun sentences*

Like **na**-adjective predicates, a noun predicate requires a form of the copula to complete the sentence.

a それが序曲だった。
**Sore ga jokyoku datta.**
That was [only] the overture [= the beginning].

### 7.6.1.7 | Equational sentences

Equational sentences are a kind of noun sentence, of the type [N/pronoun wa . . . N + copula] 'N is N', where N + copula serves to identify or equate the noun/pronoun. (see 11.3.7).

a これは誤解だ。
**Kore wa gokai da.**
That's a misunderstanding.

### 7.6.1.8 | Double-subject sentences

Double-subject sentences are thus called because they contain two NP that could both be subjects, typically marked NP1-**wa** NP2-**ga**.

As regards meaning, NP 1 is the more comprehensive (topic-like) part, with NP 2 being a more specific (predicate-like) comment on it (see 11.3.8).

a ✎酒はワインがいい。
**Sake wa wain ga ii.**
Of alcoholic drinks, I prefer wine.

### 7.6.1.9 | Existential/locational sentences

Existential or locational sentences consist of a NP **ni** indicating a place, a NP **ga** indicating who or what 'is there' and an existential verb such as **aru** or **iru** (see 7.4.1).

a 外に女性がいる。
**Soto ni josei ga iru.**
There's a woman outside.

### 7.6.1.10 | Adj-**ku**/**na**-adjective/noun **ni** → verb conversions (**suru**/**naru**)

Adjectives, and **na**-adjectives/nouns + copula can be converted into verbs by adding **suru** 'do' or **naru** 'become' to adjective-stem (incl. the negative ending –**naku**, see 25.6) and the adverbial form **ni** of **na**-Adjective/N + copula. (see 7.5).

In this use, the verbs **suru** 'do' and **naru** 'become' indicate a change of state. **suru** indicates that the change is brought about intentionally, whereas with **naru** it takes place naturally. Note also the irregular potential form of **suru**, dekiru (see 14).

| 7.6.1.10.1 | Adjectives |

a 空が暗くなった。
**Sora ga kuraku natta.**
The sky darkened.

b 賃下げは労使関係を悪くするだけ。
**Chinsage wa rōshi kankei o waruku suru dake.**
Lowering wages just worsens industrial relations.

| 7.6.1.10.2 | **na**-adjectives |

a タクシーがきれいになった。
**Takushī ga kirei ni natta.**
Taxis have become smart.

b 普通のせっけんを使って皮膚をきれいにする。
**Futsū no sekken o tsukatte hifu o kirei ni suru.**
You clean your skin using ordinary soap.

| 7.6.1.10.3 | Nouns |

a 一万人を目標にする。
**Ichiman-nin o mokuhyō ni suru.**
They aim for 10,000 people.

b ミンペイさんももう80歳になる。
**Shinpei-san mō hachijus-sai ni naru.**
Shinpei, too, will already be 80.

| 7.6.2 | *Expanded simple sentences* |

Simple sentences can be expanded. This can be effected by expanding the predicate (i.e. adding verb-modifying phrases), by expanding the NP (by adding noun-modifying phrases), or both. (A further addition can be an exclamation such as **ara** 'oh', but these can of course also be used by themselves.)

| 7.6.2.1 | *Predicate expansions* |

Predicates can be expanded (to the left) by verb-modifying phrases (one or several), which can be a modifying adverb (a) or adverbial phrase (b).

a 海はまだ静かだ。
**Umi wa <u>mada</u> shizuka da.**
The sea is still calm.

b 頭の中がぴかぴかと光った。
**Atama no naka ga <u>pikapika to</u> hikatta.**
There was a flash of light inside my head.

| 7.6.2.2 | *Noun phrase expansions* |

The noun phrase(s) can also be expanded by noun-modifying phrases. For instance, the verb **iru** 'be there' requires two NPs: 'where' (marked by **ni**) and 'who' (marked by **ga**). For an example see 7.6.1.9.

In the following examples, both NP are expanded by a noun-modifying phrase each, the first NP by [number + counter + **no**] , and the second NP by [number + **no**]).

a 一グラムの空気には百万の微生物がいる。
**<u>Ichi-guramu no</u> kūki ni wa <u>hyakuman no</u> bi-seibutsu ga iru.**
In one gram of air there are a million micro-organisms.

In the following example the intransitive verb **hajimaru** requires only NP **ga** (see 7.2), but the sentence is expanded with a time phrase + suffix (-**sugi** 'just after'), followed by a location NP + case particle **de**.

b 午前三時過ぎ機内で結婚式が始まった。
**<u>Gozen sanji-sugi</u> <u>kinai de</u> kekkonshiki ga hajimatta.**
Just after 3 a.m., the wedding ceremony began in the aeroplane.

| 7.6.3 | **Extended simple sentences (predicate extensions)** |

Predicates are typically extended, adding the speaker's opinion, intention, feelings, etc. regarding the content of the sentence after the predicate. Predicate extensions can be sentence-final particles or tense/aspect or modal endings.

*Sentence endings*

The modal ending yō indicates appearance, adding here to **jikan ga tomatta** the sense that this was the speaker/writer's impression of what happened (see 9.5.6).

a 時間が止まったようだった。
**Jikan ga tomatta yō datta.**
It was as if time had stopped.

7.6.3.2 *Extensions through sentence-final particles*

Sentence-final particles indicate various forms of the speaker's appeal to the listener. In the following, **wa** indicates emphasis, but also that the speaker is a woman (see 19.5).

a あら、ミーティングが始まるわ。
**Ara, mītingu ga hajimaru wa.**
Oh, a meeting is about to begin!

**7.6.4** **Complex sentences**

A complex sentence contains one (or more) subordinate clauses (underlined). In Japanese, a subordinate clause always precedes the main clause it modifies, but in English translation this order is often reversed.

7.6.4.1 *With subordinate clauses*

a 水を打ったように静かだった。
<u>**Mizu o utta yō ni**</u> **shizuka datta.**
[The meeting] was dead silent. (*lit.* "was silent as if water had been poured over")

b ···今じゃいても気付かないほど静かだ。
**...ima ja** <u>**ite mo kizukanai hodo**</u> **shizuka da.**
...now, they [= the nephews] are so quiet that even if they are there you don't notice [them].

c 私には「長期間留守につき、ゆっくり仕事できます。ゴッソリ持っていって」と聞こえてしまって…

**Watashi ni wa 'chōkikan rusu ni tsuki, yukkuri shigoto dekimasu. Gossori motte itte' to kikoete shimatte ...**

To me, [= the recorded message giving dates of absence from home] sounds like 'Owing to my extended absence from home, you [= the burglar] can work at your leisure. Take plenty' ...

d 襲われたらどうしよう……。

**Osowaretara dō shiyō**

What am I going to do if I get attacked ...?

| 7.6.4.2 | *With embedded subordinate clauses or sentences* |
|---|---|

An embedded sentence contains another sentence, such as a question, quotation, etc.

| 7.6.4.2.1 | Direct quotations and commands |
|---|---|

The main difference between direct and indirect quotations is the presence or absence of the Japanese quotation marks ( 「...」 ) . Also, in direct quotations polite forms (-**masu, desu,** etc.) can be used before the quotation particle **to** (examples a and b), whereas in indirect quotations plain forms are the rule.

a 「三日までゆっくり過ごそうと思います」と話していた。

**'Mikka made yukkuri sugosō to omoimasu' to hanashite ita.**

He was saying, 'I'm thinking of taking it easy until the 3rd'.

b 「一日二、三万円の収入が得られます」という広告が何枚も置かれている。

**'Ichinichi ni, sanman-en no shūnyū ga eraremasu' to iu kōkoku ga nanmai mo okarete iru.**

There are quite a few leaflets lying about saying 'You can earn 20 to 30 thousand yen a month'.

c 訓一は文子に「日本中で一番幸せな妻にしてやる」といった。

**Kun'ichi wa Fumiko ni 'Nihon-jū de ichiban shiawase na tsuma ni shite yaru' to itta.**

Kunichi said to Fumiko, 'I'll make you the happiest wife in Japan'.

d 「あの時、好きにさせてもらったのだから、妻にも思うように
　仕事をさせよう」と考えたという。

**'Ano toki suki ni sasete moratta no da kara, tsuma ni mo
omou yō ni shigoto o saseyō' to kangaeta to iu.**

He says that he thought, 'At that time, I was allowed to do as I liked,
so I'll let my wife work too as she likes to'.

---

| 7.6.4.2.2 | Indirect quotations and commands |
|---|---|

Below, quotations/commands are underlined. Note that imperative and
command forms like **kudasai** and **tsukuri-nasai** are 'reduced' to plain-form
equivalents such as **kure** and **tsukure** (see examples a–c below, 20, 15.3).
Example d has an implied imperative such as **kudasai** or **kure**.

a 全国から講演してくれという要請がたくさんきている。

**Zenkoku kara <u>kōen shite kure</u> to iu yōsei ga takusan kite iru.**

There are many requests from all over the country to come and give
a lecture.

b 社長になってくれと言われたのは今朝のこと。

**<u>Shachō ni natte kure</u> to iwareta no wa kesa no koto.**

It was [only] this morning that I was asked to be company president.

c 住民に聴けば道路をつくれという。

**Jūmin ni kikeba <u>dōro o tsukure</u> to iu.**

When I ask the residents, they tell me to build roads.

d 教師にこそ、もっと自由をと言いたい。

**Kyōshi ni koso, <u>motto jiyū o</u> to iitai.**

Especially to the teachers I'd like to say that they should give
themselves more freedom.

---

| 7.6.4.2.3 | Direct questions |
|---|---|

Depending on the presence or absence of Q-words, the question particle
**ka** and other factors, various kinds of direct question can be distinguished
(see 18, Table 5).

---

| 7.6.4.2.4 | Indirect questions |
|---|---|

Depending on the presence or absence of Q-words and other factors,
various kinds of indirect questions can be distinguished (see 18, Table 5).

### 7.6.4.3 *With noun-modifying (dependent) clauses*

Noun-modifying clauses include **to iu** clauses, complement clauses, cleft sentences and relative clauses (see 22, 21.2).

#### 7.6.4.3.1 **to iu** noun-modifying clauses

(See 21.2) The pattern [N1 **to iu** N2] means 'the N2 ("called") N1'.

a 家庭という言葉は家と庭からなっている。
   **Katei to iu kotoba wa ie to niwa kara natte iru.**
   The word *katei* (home) consists of *ka/ie* (house) amd *tei/niwa*
      (garden).

#### 7.6.4.3.2 Complement sentences

Here, a whole (nominalized) clause acts like a NP, marked by a case particle (see 22.2).

a 体を動かすのが好き。
   <u>**Karada o ugokasu no**</u> **ga suki.**
   I like moving my body.

#### 7.6.4.3.3 Cleft sentences

In a cleft sentence, a simple sentence split into two clauses and reversed for emphasis (see 22.2.2).

a 自宅でのんびりするのは正月三が日だけ。
   **Jitaku de nonbiri suru no wa shōgatsu sanganichi dake.**
   The only time I relax at home is the first three days of the
      new year.

#### 7.6.4.3.4 Relative clauses

In Japanese, relative clauses are one form of noun-modification (see 22.1).

a いつもと変わらない夕方だった。
   **Itsumo to kawaranai yūgata datta.**
   [It] was an evening [that was] no different from usual.

## 7.6.5 | Compound sentences

Compound sentences are sentences that consist of two or more clauses, joined by conjunctive forms of V/Adj and **na**-Adj/N + copula and their written-style variants (i.e. stem forms of V/Adj and **na**-Adj/N + copula, etc.) or conjunctive particles like **ga** 'and', 'but' (see 25, 26). In compound sentences, the English word order is usually the same as in Japanese.

### 7.6.5.1 | With conjunctive forms

a　部長に頭を下げて、部屋を出た。
**Buchō ni atama o sage<u>te</u>, heya o deta**
I bowed to the department head and left the room.

### 7.6.5.2 | With conjunctive particles

a　女性が多いが、ほとんど髪は肩ぐらいまでに短くしている。
**Josei ga ōi <u>ga</u>, hotondo kami wa kata gurai made ni mijikaku shite iru.**
There are many women, but most keep their hair short to about shoulder length.

# Chapter 8

# *Tense and aspect endings*

**Non-past verb forms**

Non-past forms of V/Adj and **na**-Adj/N + copula can be used as predicates, and to attach various endings.

Unlike Adjective and **na**-Adjective + copula sentences, which have adjectival meaning as predicates, and N + copula, which are equational in meaning, V-**ru** can express a variety of meanings as a predicate. (see 7.1.2).

V-**ru** can be used by itself as a predicate to complete a sentence in the present, habitual present, future, intention, or narrative present.

### 8.1.1 *Present*

8.1.1.1 *Present*

a 悔しくて涙が出る。
  **Kuyashikute namida ga deru.**
  I'm so annoyed that I feel like crying (*lit.* "tears come [to my eyes]").

8.1.1.2 *Habitual present*

a 今でも日曜日は近所に住む父といっしょに過ごす。
  **Ima demo nichiyōbi wa kinjo ni sumu chichi to issho ni sugosu.**
  Even now, he spends Sundays with his father, who lives nearby.

### 8.1.2 | Future

### 8.1.2.1 | Future

a　来年二月末までに会社を清算する。
**Rainen nigatsu-matsu made ni kaisha o seisan suru.**
They will liquidate the company by the end of next February.

### 8.1.2.2 | Intention

a　不要品、譲ります。
**Fuyōhin, yuzurimasu.**
I'll let you have things I no longer need.

b　絶対に日本には帰らない。
**Zettai ni Nihon ni wa kaeranai.**
No matter what, [I] won't go back to Japan.

### 8.1.3 | Narrative present

Non-past forms are often used at key points in a narrative to make them
more immediate or dramatic. In English, these are often translated into
the past tense.

a　話しているうちに忘れかけていた関西弁がポンポン飛び出して
　　くる。不思議ですね。
**Hanashite iru uchi ni wasurekakete ita kansaiben ga ponpon
tobidashite kuru. Fushigi desu ne.**
As I'm talking, the Kansai dialect that I'd almost forgotten pops out,
one word after another. Strange, isn't it?

b　30秒とたたないうちに電話がかかってくる。
**Sanjūbyō to tatanai uchi ni denwa ga kakatte kuru.**
Before 30 seconds had passed, the phone rang.

## 8.2　Past/perfective -ta

The past ending -**ta**, which can also indicate completion of action (= perfect), can be attached to V/Adj (see 7.1, 6.1) and **na**-Adj/N + copula (see

7.5), plus the V-conversion causative, passive endings, potential verb endings, and the polite ending **-masu** (see 7.1.2.4).

See also 26.2.5, 6.7.2.8.3, 26.2.1.2.3 for entries attaching always or mostly to **-ta**.

### 8.2.1 | Past tense, or completion of action

a 同僚たちがそろって「ハッピー・バースデー」を歌ってくれた。
**Dōryō-tachi ga sorotte 'Happī Bāsudē' o utatte kureta.**
My co-workers got together and sang 'Happy Birthday' to me.

b 日本は豊かになった。
**Nihon wa yutaka ni natta.**
Japan has become affluent.

### 8.2.2 | Realization of a present state

Here, there is no meaning of past; instead, **-ta** is used when the speaker realizes something.

a えっ、イギリスにもいじめはあったのか、日本だけのものかなと漠然と考えていたのは甘かった。
**E', Igirisu ni mo ijime wa atta no ka, Nihon dake no mono ka na to bakuzen to kangaete ita no wa amakatta.**
Eh? Bullying exists in Britain too? It was silly of me to vaguely think that it's unique to Japan.

b そういえばFさんは別姓夫婦だったね。
**Sō ieba F-san wa bessei fūfū datta ne.**
Come to think of it, you [= Mr and Mrs F] are a married couple with different surnames, right?

c ああ今日も外に出ずじまいだった。
**Aa kyō mo soto ni dezu-jimai datta.**
Ah well, today again I've ended up not going out of the house.

d だが、一年もたたぬうちに歯車が狂い始めた。「夫は一人では何もできない人だった」。
**Da ga, ichinen mo tatanu uchi ni haguruma ga kuruihajimeta. 'Otto wa hitori de wa nani mo dekinai hito datta'.**
However, before a year had passed [since marriage], the cogs began to slip. 'My husband turns out to be a person who can't do anything by himself.'

### 8.2.3.1 | State

Note the use of V-**ta** or VN-**shita** before a noun (in relative clauses etc.). Usually, -**ta** is used rather than -**te iru** if the meaning indicates a state (see 6.6.7.1, 22.1).

a 安定した生活 (cf., 生活が安定している)
  **antei shita seikatsu** (cf. **seikatsu ga antei shite iru**)
  a secure life          (cf. life is secure)

b 左右どちらかに偏った凝りは要注意だ。(cf., 凝りが偏っている)
  **Sayū dochira ka ni katayotta kori wa yōchūi da.** (cf. **kori ga katayotte iru**)
  [Shoulder] stiffness that is confined to either the left or right side requires care. (cf. stiffness is confined to one side)

### 8.2.3.2 | Completion of action

When the same combination has no adjectival meaning, however, (**shi**)-**ta** indicates completion.

a 沸騰した熱湯
  **futtō shita nettō**
  hot water that has come to the boil

## 8.3 -te aru

V-**te aru** consists of V-**te** + **aru** (as a lexical verb, **aru** means 'be there, have'). The combination indicates the state resulting from the action of the verb (V = volitional transitive V). No actor can be mentioned in a -**te aru** sentence, although clearly one is implied in the sense that someone must have performed the action of the verb (except for metaphorical uses such as **kao ni kaite aru yo** 'it's written in your face'); but phrasing something in a -**te aru** sentence in effect means that no responsibility is assigned to anyone for the action of the verb (see 7.3, 7.4).

The fact that no actor can be mentioned in a -**te aru** sentences contrasts sharply with -**te iru**, where an actor is typically present (see 8.4).

The object of V-**te aru** is marked by either **ga** or **o** (which in turn can be replaced by **wa**).

### 8.3.1 | *Object marked with ga*

a 工場内には三つのスローガンが掲げてある。
**Kōjō-nai ni wa mittsu no surōgan ga kakagete aru.**
Inside the factory, three slogans are displayed.

b トラックには計5,350キロのコメが積んであった。
**Torakku ni wa kei gosen sanbyaku gojuk-kiro no kome ga tsunde atta.**
On the truck, a total of 5,350kg of rice was piled up.

### 8.3.2 | *Object marked with o*

a テントの天井からはシャンデリアをつり下げてある。
**Tento no tenjō kara wa shanderia o tsurisagete aru.**
From the tent's ceiling a chandelier is hung.

### 8.3.3 | *Object marked with wa*

a 糸の表面は滑らかに加工してある。
**Ito no hyōmen wa nameraka ni kakō shite aru.**
The surface of the thread is processed to make it smooth.

b 朝食は食堂に用意してあります。
**Chōshoku wa shokudō ni yōi shite arimasu.**
Breakfast is laid out in the dining room.

c この件は弁護士に任せてあります。
**Kono ken wa bengoshi ni makasete arimasu.**
This matter is left to the lawyer.

### 8.3.4 | *Noun-modifying*

a 三人は止めてあった黒い乗用車で逃走した。
**San-nin wa tomete atta kuroi jōyōsha de tōsō shita.**
The three fled in a black car that had been parked.

## 8.4  -te iru/-teru

V-te iru consists of V-te + iru (as a lexical V, iru means 'be there'). The combination indicates action in progress (with action V), or the state resulting from the action of the verb (with state V). In either use the actor (the person responsible for the action of V) is usually mentioned (unless understood from the context), which contrasts sharply with -te aru, where no actor can be mentioned in the same sentence (see 8.3).

Colloquially, -te iru/-te inai/-te imasu, etc. are often contracted to -teru/-tenai/-temasu.

Note that certain verbs are used mostly in the -te iru form (sunde iru 'live', motte iru 'have', shitte iru 'know') except when there is clear future reference, when the -te iru form is almost never found (unless with a special nuance of non-change of the present situation), hence sumitai, sumu tsumori rather than sunde itai, sunde iru tsumori, etc. (see also 8.3, 8.5).

### 8.4.1 | Action in progress

a 大きなメイポールの下で人々が踊っている。
**Ōkina meipōru no shita de hitobito ga odotte iru.**
Under a big maypole people are dancing.

b 最近、写真集が売れている。
**Saikin, shashinshū ga urete iru.**
At the moment, collections of photographs are selling well.

### 8.4.2 | Resulting state

a お、メールが来てるぞ。
**O, mēru ga kiteru zo.**
Oh, a(n) (e-)mail has come!

b 知ってる知ってる。
**Shitteru shitteru.**
I know, I know.

c 遺書は見つかっていない。
**Isho wa mitsukatte inai.**
A will hasn't been found.

d 生徒のほとんどは教科書を持っていない。
   **Seito no hotondo wa kyōkasho o motte inai.**
   Most of the pupils don't have textbooks.

e 出版社の名も翻訳者の名も覚えてない。
   **Shuppansha no na mo hon'yakusha no na
   mo oboetenai.**
   I don't remember the name of the publisher or
   the translator.

f このところ自分の中で緊張感が欠けてるな、と感じてました。
   **Kono tokoro jibun no naka de kinchōkan ga kaketeru na,
   to kanjitemashita.**
   I was feeling that recently I was lacking internal motivation.

---

| 8.4.3 | *Both interpretations possible: verbs of motion/change* |

In isolation, both interpretations are possible, but the translation given has taken the context (not given here) into account (see also 8.5).

a 人件費は年々上がっている。
   **Jinkenhi wa nennen agatte iru.**
   Personnel costs are rising every year.

b 時代は変化している。
   **Jidai wa henka shite iru.**
   Times have changed.

c 競争が激しくなっている。
   **Kyōsō ga hageshiku natte iru.**
   Competition has become fierce.

---

| 8.4.4 | *In compound sentences (clause I-te ite, clause 2):
         implying a reason* |

In compound sentences -te ite, the conjunctive form of -te iru, is used to imply that S1 is a reason for S2. To indicate an explicit reason, particles like **kara** or **node** are used instead (see 26.5).

*Note* – in the written/formal spoken style, -te ori is used as the conjunctive form rather than -te i (which is not normally used) or -te ite (which is considered too colloquial for the written style). Compare:

217

a 「ちょっと変わっていて面白そう」と迷わずこのゼミを選んだ。
**'Chotto kawatte ite omoshirosō' to mayowazu kono zemi o eranda.**
I chose this seminar without hesitation, thinking 'This looks interesting, being a little unusual'.

b 「いじめは潜在化しており、まさに氷山の一角」と指摘している。
**'Ijime wa senzai-ka shite ori, masa ni hyōzan no ikkaku' to shiteki shite iru.**
He points out that 'bullying has become deeply entrenched, and is just the tip of the iceberg'.

## 8.5   -tsutsu aru

Attached to V-stem, -tsutsu aru is used as an alternative to -te iru, but with only the progressive interpretation 'in the process of' (see 8.4.1, 8.4.3).

a 「楽器を弾かないミュージシャン」として、日本でも認知されつつある。
**'Gakki o hikanai myūjishan' to shite, Nihon de mo ninchi sare-tsutsu aru.**
As a 'musician who doesn't play an instrument', he is in the process of becoming known in Japan too.

b 伝統方言は、今、急激に、確実に消滅しつつある。
**Dentō-hōgen wa, ima, kyūgeki ni, kakujitsu ni shōmetsu shi-tsutsu aru.**
Traditional dialects are now disappearing rapidly and steadily.

c 迷いつつも女子学生は、留年という「自由」を確実に手にしつつある。
**Mayoi-tsutsu mo joshi gakusei wa, ryūnen to iu 'jiyū' o kakujitsu ni te ni shi-tsutsu aru.**
Though hesitantly, women students are in the process of steadily acquiring the 'freedom' of studying an extra year.

## 8.6   -te iku/-teku

V-**te iku** consists of V-**te** + **iku** (as a lexical V, **iku** (行く) means 'go'). The combination has several uses related to movement of the action of the V (in place or time) *away* from the speaker, although in translation this is often not captured. This contrasts with V-**te kuru**, which indicates movement (in place or time) *towards* the speaker (see 8.7).

Note the contracted (colloquial) forms -**teku** for -**te iku**, -**tette** for -**te itte**, **tetta** for -**te itta**, etc.

### 8.6.1 | *Doing verb and then going*

a 皆がパンを手にすると、鴎が飛んできて器用に食べて行く。
  **Minna ga pan o te ni suru to, kamome ga tonde kite kiyō ni tabete iku.**
  When everyone picked up the bread [pieces], the seagulls came flying and took them away skillfully.

b 川床に座ると、ひんやりした風が頬をなでていく。
  **Kawadoko ni suwaru to, hin'yari shita kaze ga hoho o nadete iku.**
  When one sits down on the riverbed, a cool wind slowly blows past one's cheeks.

### 8.6.2 | *Action away from speaker*

a 所長が事務所を勇んで出ていった。
  **Shochō ga jimusho o isande dete itta.**
  The director left the office in high spirits.

b 今逃げていきました。
  **Ima nigete ikimashita.**
  They ran away just this moment.

### 8.6.3 | *Gradual action/development over time and space*

a この関係はぜひ維持していきたい。
  **Kono kankei wa zehi iji shite ikitai.**
  I very much want to keep up this relationship.

b 紫外線は、虫たちの生態にも影響を及ぼしていく。
  **Shigaisen wa, mushi-tachi no seitai ni mo eikyō o oyoboshite iku.**
  UV rays also have an influence on the ecology of insects.

c 「自分は仕事の能力を買われたのではない」。そんな疑いが日増し
に強くなっていった。

**'Jibun wa shigoto no nōryoku o kawareta no de wa nai.'**
**Sonna utagai ga himashi ni tsuyoku natte itta.**

'I wasn't employed because they valued my ability to do the job.'
That doubt grew stronger by the day.

d さらに歩くと、森はどんどん深まっていく。

**Sara ni aruku to, mori wa dondon fukamatte iku.**

When you walk further, the forest soon grows denser.

e 世界の果てに連れてって。

**Sekai no hate ni tsuretette.**

Take me to the end of the world.

f だんだん当り前のおかずに魚が食べられるようになってった。

**Dandan atarimae no okazu ni sakana ga taberareru yō ni**
**nattetta.**

I gradually became able to eat fish as an ordinary dish.

g これからも浅草独特のにおいを残してってほしいね。

**Kore kara mo Asakusa dokutoku no nioi o nokoshitette**
**hoshii ne.**

In future too I want [people] to leave intact the smells peculiar to
Asakusa.

### 8.6.4 | Lexical expressions

Some combinations have become lexical expressions: **yatte iku** 'get along',
**motte iku** 'take something', **tsurete iku** 'take someone', **tsuite iku** 'accompany someone'.

a 里帰りのたびに故郷の両親を温泉に連れていく。

**Satogaeri no tabi ni kokyō no ryōshin o onsen ni**
**tsurete iku.**

Whenever he goes back home he takes his parents to a hot spring.

### 8.6.5 | Honorific equivalents

The forms that are used in place of the lexical verb **iku** are also used in
place of iku in -te iku (see 16.3).

In humble usage (see 16), -te iku is replaced by -te mairu, and in honorific use, by -te irassharu.

a その推移を見守ってまいりたい。
**Sono suii o mimamotte mairitai.**
I'd like to watch these changes.

## 8.7 -te kuru

V-te kuru consists of V-te + kuru (as a lexical verb, kuru means 'come'). The combination has several uses related to movement of the action of the verb in place or time toward the speaker (see 8.6, which indicates movement of the action verb in place or time away from the speaker).

### 8.7.1 | Doing verb and then coming

The implication is that the speaker (or a second/third person) performs the action of the verb, and then comes to where the speaker is now, or was at the time 'go and do something'.

a 行ってくるよ。
**Itte kuru yo.**
I'm off/I'm going out.

b 原因を調べてこい」。
**Gen'in o shirabete koi.**
Go and check on the cause.

### 8.7.2 | Action of verb directed toward speaker

a 生あたたかい風が海から吹いてくる。
**Nama-atatakai kaze ga umi kara fuite kuru.**
An unpleasantly warm wind is blowing in from the sea.

b 二人の老人が中から出てきて話しかけてきた。
**Futari no rōjin ga naka kara dete kite hanashikakete kita.**
Two old men came out and addressed us.

c あの良き時代は永遠に返ってこない。
**Ano yoki jidai wa eien ni kaette konai.**
Those good times will never return [to us].

221

### 8.7.3 Gradual or sudden change/development

a にわか雨が降ってきた。
**Niwaka-ame ga futte kita.**
A sudden shower fell.

b 大学で中国語を勉強してきました。
**Daigaku de chūgokugo o benkyō shite kimashita.**
I studied Chinese at university.

c 何とかここまで生きてこられた。
**Nantoka koko made ikite korareta.**
Somehow I managed to live until now.

d 消費者意識も変わってきた。
**Shōhisha ishiki mo kawatte kita.**
Consumer consciousness has also changed.

e 神学校から東に進むと、テニスコートが見えてくる。
**Shingakkō kara higashi ni susumu to, tenisu kōto ga miete kuru.**
When one proceeds east from the divinity school, tennis courts come into view.

### 8.7.4 Lexical expressions

Note lexical expressions such as **yatte kuru** 'come, come along', **motte kuru** 'bring something', **tsurete kuru** 'bring someone', **tsuite kuru** 'accompany'.

a 今年もクリスマスがやってくる。
**Kotoshi mo kurisumasu ga yatte kuru.**
Christmas is almost here again this year.

### 8.7.5 Honorific/humble equivalents

In honorific usage (see 16), **kuru** is replaced by **oide ni naru** or **irassharu**. Instead of **oide ni natte kudasai**, **oide** alone can be used as the imperative (example a).

Humble equivalents of **kuru** are **mairu/mairimasu** (see 16).

a お菓子をあげるからついておいで。
**O-kashi o ageru kara tsuite oide.**
I'll give you some sweets, so please come with me.

b 町民の宇宙に対する興味も増えてまいりました。
**Chōmin no uchū ni taisuru kyōmi mo fuete mairimashita.**
The citizens' interest in space has increased too.

## 8.8 -te miru

V-**te miru** consists of V-**te** + **miru** (as a lexical verb, **miru** means 'see'). The combination indicates that the action of the verb (= volitional V) is performed to see what the result is, i.e. 'try', 'try and see' ('try' is often unneccessary in translation).

-**te miru** often attaches -**tai** (-**te mi-tai** 'want to try' and -**yō** (te-mi-yō 'let's try'). -**te miru** can also in turn attach to the lexical verb **miru** 'see': **mite miru** (見てみる) 'look at, examine' (see 9.1.1).

a 考えてみます。
**Kangaete mimasu.**
I'll think about it.

b 恐る恐る聞いてみた。
**Osoruosoru kiite mita.**
Timidly I asked.

c いつかまた、行ってみたい。
**Itsu ka mata itte mitai.**
Sometime, I'd like to go again.

d 米国の例を見てみよう。
**Beikoku no rei o mite miyō.**
Let's look at the example of the US.

e 今年はぜひスキューバダイビングをやってみたい。
**Kotoshi wa zehi sukyūba daibingu o yatte mitai.**
This year I'd very much like to try scuba diving.

f 昔のノートをチェックしてみると、間違いが結構多い。
**Mukashi no nōto o chekku shite miru to, machigai ga kekkō ōi.**
When I check old notebooks, there are quite a few mistakes.

223

**8.9** **-(y)ō to suru**

Attached to verbs (for formation of V-(y)ō, see 9.1.1), the ending -(y)ō to
suru (mostly used in the form **to shite iru** or **to shita**) indicates attempted
action, i.e. that an action is or was attempted in the sense of 'try'.

Unlike -te miru, which also often translates as 'try' and is typically used
of the first person, -(y)ō to suru is used of the third person, and cannot
be used of the first (see 8.8).

*Note* – with subjects that are impersonal, such as [computer] networks,
the implication is of course not one of 'trying to', but 'about to' do
something.

a 少しでも電気代を減らそうとしている。
**Sukoshi demo denkidai o herasō to shite iru.**
They are trying to reduce the electricity bill, if only by a little.

b 日本経済はどこに向かおうとしているのか。
**Nihon keizai wa doko ni mukaō to shite iru no ka.**
Where is the Japanese economy going?

c 突然、若い男がタクシーの前に飛び出し、後部座席のドアを開け
ようとした。
**Totsuzen, wakai otoko ga takushī no mae ni tobidashi,
kōbu-zaseki no doa o akeyō to shita.**
Suddenly, a young man hurled himself at the taxi, and tried to open
the rear door.

d ネットワークは企業自体のあり方すら変えようとしている。
**Nettowāku wa kigyō jitai no arikata sura kaeyō to shite iru.**
[Computer] networks are about to change the very nature of
business.

**8.10** **-te oku/-toku**

V-te oku consists of V-te + oku (as a lexical verb, oku (置く) means 'put').
The combination indicates that the action of the verb (= volitional V) is
performed in preparation or readiness. This often does not render itself to
explicit translation.

Note the combination **oite oku** (置いておく) 'put/place (in readiness)',
'leave (for further use)'.

In colloquial use, **-te oku** is often contracted to **-toku**, etc. (examples e and f).

*Note* – **-te oku** is often used in lectures or articles in the sense of 'let me (take the opportunity to) say/mention this', and such like (examples k and l).

a 覚悟しておいてください。
**Kakugo shite oite kudasai.**
Prepare yourself [for the worst].

b 社長室の扉は開けておく。
**Shachōshitsu no tobira wa akete oku.**
He leaves open the door to the president's office [so that people can walk in easily].

c 料金は一泊90ドルです。テーブルに置いておいてください。
**Ryōkin wa ippaku kyūjū-doru desu. Tēburu ni oite oite kudasai.**
The cost [of renting our house] is 90 dollars a night. Please leave it on the table.

d まかしておけ。
**Makashite oke.**
Leave it to me.

e 安いよ、まけとくよ。
**Yasui yo, maketoku yo.**
It's cheap. I'll take off some more money!

f これ名古屋の実家に送っといて。
**Kore Nagoya no jikka ni okuttoite.**
Send this to my home in Nagoya.

g 解熱剤とせき止めを出しておきましょう。
**Genetsu-zai to sekidome o dashite okimashō.**
I'll prescribe you an antifebrile and cough medicine.

h 事のついでに季節でもあり、生のキノコもご紹介しておこう。
**Koto no tsuide ni kisetsu de mo ari, nama no kinoko mo go-shōkai shite okō.**
At this opportunity, it being the season, I will also introduce raw mushrooms [= cookery programme].

i 生かしておくと犯罪を犯す危険がある。
**Ikashite oku to hanzai o okasu kiken ga aru.**
If you keep them alive, there is a danger they will commit crimes again.

j 欲しいものは予約しておいても買う。
**Hoshii mono wa yoyaku shite oite mo kau.**
I do buy things I want, even if it means placing an advance order.

k ここでは二つのポイントだけを指摘しておこう。
**Koko de wa futatsu no pointo dake o shiteki shite okō.**
Here, I will just point out two things.

l だが、スペースの関係でここでは詳細には触れないでおく。
**Da ga, supēsu no kankei de koko de wa shōsai ni wa furenai
de oku.**
However, for reasons of space I will not mention the details here.

## 8.11  -te shimau/-chau

V-**te shimau** consists of V-**te** + **shimau** (as a lexical V, **shimau** means 'put
away', 'finish'). The combination is usually said to have two meanings: (1)
the action of V is performed completely or with finality, and (2) the action
of V produces unexpected or inconvenient results. However, the two are
often difficult to distinguish (most examples have at least a shade of meaning 2). Here, no attempt is made to separate the two.

Note that the force of -**te shimau** can usually not be captured in translation.

Colloquially, -**te shimau** is often contracted to -**chau**, etc. (examples c, e,
h, i), and -**de shimau** to -**jau**, etc. (example a).

a 水ばかり飲んじゃった。
**Mizu bakari nonjatta.**
I drank just water.

b うっかり財布を落としてしまった。
**Ukkari saifu o otoshite shimatta.**
I absent-mindedly dropped my wallet.

c 前の髪形に飽きちゃっただけ。
**Mae no kamigata ni akichatta dake.**
I got bored with my previous hairstyle, that's all.

d 手に取ると壊れてしまいそうだ。
**Te ni toru to kowarete shimaisō da.**
It looks as if it'll break when you take it in your hand.

e 太っちゃってね。
**Futotchatte ne.**
I got fat, you know.

f 煮てしまえばさらにいい。
**Nite shimaeba sara ni ii.**
If you boil it, it's even better.

g 何とかしないとゴーストタウンになってしまう。
**Nantoka shinai to gōsuto taun ni natte shimau.**
Unless we do something, it'll end up becoming a ghost town.

h 定職に就くのはあきらめちゃいました。
**Teishoku ni tsuku no wa akiramechaimashita.**
I've given up hoping to find a permanent job.

i このリモコンカー、動かなくなっちゃった。
**Kono rimokon kā, ugokanaku natchatta.**
This remote-controlled car won't move any more.

j 日本はカラオケ民主主義になってしまった――。
**Nihon wa karaoke minshu shugi ni natte shimatta--.**
Japan has become a karaoke democracy.

k 気が付くと、一人で三人分を平らげてしまっていた。
**Ki ga tsuku to, hitori de sannin-bun o tairagete shimatte ita.**
Before I realized, I had wolfed down three portions by myself.

## 8.12 tokoro

tokoro is originally a noun meaning 'place' or 'situation'. Used after verb forms, it implies that something is taking place 'just at the time' indicated by the form of the verb.

In the case of action verbs, the combinations V-**ru**, V-**te iru** and V-**ta** plus tokoro + copula indicate that the action of the verb is 'about to' happen (V-**ru**), is in the process of happening (V-**te iru**), or has just been completed (V-**ta**), as shown in the made-up examples a–c.

In the media, -**ru** tokoro and related expressions often merely imply that something is taking place currently (examples f–g).

Note also that tokoro + copula in the form **tokoro datta** is also used after –**ba** clauses to indicate an unrealized occurrence in the sense of 'if not . . . would have' (see 9.1.2.5).

a ✐ご飯を食べるところです。
**Gohan o taberu tokoro desu.**
I'm about to eat.

b  ✐ご飯を食べているところです。

**Gohan o tabete iru tokoro desu.**

I'm just in the middle of eating.

c  ✐ご飯を食べたところです。

**Gohan o tabeta tokoro desu.**

I've just eaten.

d  被災地の1日も早い復旧・復興を祈っているところです。

**Hisaichi no ichinichi mo hayai fukkyū/fukkō o inotte iru tokoro desu.**

I'm praying for the earliest possible recovery and reconstruction of the areas struck by the disaster.

e  家具作りは修業が終わり、商品を作る第二段階に入ったところだ。

**Kagu-zukuri wa shūgyō ga owari, shōhin o tsukuru dai-nidankai ni haitta tokoro da.**

The apprenticeship for furniture making is over, and I've just entered the second stage of making things.

f  三人は避難を前に荷物を外へ出していたところだった。

**Sannin wa hinan o mae ni nimotsu o soto e dashite ita tokoro datta.**

The three people had just put out their luggage prior to evacuating (before their house was buried under a landslide).

g  新たな地震が各地で頻発し、今後の原発の状況も憂慮されるところです。

**Arata na jishin ga kakuchi de hinpatsu shi, kongo no genpatsu no jōkyō mo yūryo sareru tokoro desu.**

New earthquakes are occurring frequently everywhere, and the state of the nuclear power station from now on is also a concern.

h  完全自給主義がいかにもろいものであるかは、今回の凶作によるコメ不足が教えるところだ。

**Kanzen jikyūshugi ga ika ni moroi mono de aru ka wa, konkai no kyōsaku ni yoru kome-busoku ga oshieru tokoro da.**

The rice shortage due to the bad harvest demonstrates how fragile the total self-sufficiency doctrine is.

# Chapter 9

# Modal endings

## Hortative and presumptive

### 9.1.1 | *Verb-(y)ō: hortative use*

Hortative expresses proposed action 'shall I/we', or an invitation to do something together 'let's', and therefore can be attached only to verbs that express an action that can be controlled by the speaker.

For this purpose, the ending -(y)ō is used, attached to verbs. The combination V-(y)ō is the plain-form equivalent of V-**mashō** 'let's' etc.

Apart from the hortative meaning, -(y)ō can also be used in the presumptive sense, which is a supposition about what might happen or be the case (see 9.1.2).

The ending -(y)ō is attached to V as shown below:

| | |
|---|---|
| Group I: | change final -**u** to **ō** |
| Group II: | attach **yō** to V-stem |
| Group III: | **kuru** → **koyō** |
| | **suru** → **shiyō** |

*Note* – polite sentence ending: -**masu** → **mashō**.

### 9.1.1.1 | *Sentence-(y)ō in statements*

Apart from the speaker inviting others to join him or her in some action, -(y)ō is also commonly used in slogans, to offer one's services, and when suggesting to the public (or other groups of people) the correct rules of conduct (see 9.1.1.1.3).

9.1.1.1.1 | Invitation

This translates simply as 'let's'.

a どっか行こうよ。（どっか ＝ どこか）
**Dokka ikō yo. (dokka = doko ka)**
Let's go somewhere.

b さあ、いきましょう。
**Sā, ikimashō.**
Come on, let's go.

c 来年また会いましょう。
**Rainen mata aimashō.**
Let's meet again next year.

d 演題は「人生をどん欲に生きよう」。
**Endai wa 'jinsei o don'yoku ni ikiyō'.**
The subject of the lecture is 'Let's live our lives greedily'.

e 地域社会に子どもを帰そう。
**Chiiki shakai ni kodomo o kaesō.**
Let's return the children to local society.

f どんないじめもなくそう。
**Donna ijime mo nakusō.**
Let's get rid of any form of bullying.

9.1.1.1.2 | Offering one's services

This translates as 'I/we will', 'let me/us'. Note that **ga** or **kara** can be used to mark the person/s making the offer, but **wa** cannot be used (see 2.7, 11.3.2).

a お宅の犬の写真でカレンダーを作りましょう。
**Otaku no inu no shashin de karendā o tsukurimashō.**
We'll make [you] a calendar from photos of your dog.

b 足りない分は私が考えましょう。
**Tarinai bun wa watashi ga kangaemashō.**
I'll do something about the shortfall [in funds].

c 次の図でわかりやすく説明しましょう。
**Tsugi no zu de wakariyasuku setsumei shimashō.**
Let me explain things plainly with the following chart.

9.1.1.1.3 | Suggesting rules of conduct

This is used to tell others what they should do, couched in a way
that suggests that it should be done together 'one/you should' (see 9.4,
6.7.2.8.3).

a 蛇口はこまめに閉めましょう。
   **Jaguchi wa komame ni shimemashō.**
   The tap should be turned off diligently.

b マイカーの通勤は自粛しましょう。
   **Maikā no tsūkin wa jishuku shimashō.**
   People should refrain from commuting in private cars.

9.1.1.2 | *Verb-*(y)ō *in questions*

9.1.1.2.1 | Verb-(y)ō ka: offering

This translates as 'shall I/we?'.

a 何、話しましょうか・・・・・・。
   **Nani hanashimashō ka ...**
   What shall I talk about? ...

b テニスなんてやったことはないが、ひとつ挑戦してみよ
   うか。
   **Tenisu nante yatta koto wa nai ga, hitotsu chōsen
   shite miyō ka.**
   I've never played any tennis before, but maybe I'll give it a try.

c 秋の夜長をどう過ごそうか。
   **Aki no yonaga o dō sugosō ka.**
   How shall we spend the long autumn nights?

9.1.1.2.2 | Verb-(y)ō ka to/tte

Followed by a V of communication like **hanasu** 'discuss' or **omou** 'think'
etc., this indicates the meaning of (discuss, etc.) 'whether I/we should/
might'.

a クリスマス直前の週末には皆で横浜に行って、おいしいケーキで
も食べてブラブラする。イブの日は、友達の家に集まって、女
の子五人でなべパーティー。その翌日は、ディズニーランドに
行こうかって話しているんです……。

**Kurisumasu chokuzen no shūmatsu ni wa minna de Yokohama
ni itte, oishii kēki de mo tabete burabura suru. Ibu no hi
wa, tomodachi no ie ni atsumatte, onna no ko gonin de
nabe-pātī. Sono yokujitsu wa, Dizunīrando ni ikō ka tte
hanashite iru n desu ...**

On the weekend directly before Christmas, we'll go to Yokohama,
have some tasty cake and walk around. On the Eve, we'll gather at
a friend's place and have a hot-pot party among us five girls.
We're discussing whether we might go to Disneyland on the
following day ...

### 9.1.2 *Presumptive*

Presumptive forms of V/Adj and **na**-Adj/N + copula indicate a guess or
presumption on the part of the speaker. They can be attached to positive
predicates in the sense of 'should be', or negative ones in the sense of
'shouldn't'. There are also some other endings that do not use presumptive
verb forms as such, but have presumptive meaning.

*Note* – presumptives, including **darō**, *cannot* be used in relative clauses
(except by intermediating forms such as **to iu**).

### 9.1.2.1 *-(y)ō*

V/Adj-**(y)ō** is used as a formal/written style equivalent of V/Adj **darō**
'should', 'may'.

See 9.1.1 for how V-**(y)ō** forms are derived.

Adj-**(y)ō** (the presumptive form of adjectives, including the negative ending
**-nai**, which can be used instead of Adj-**i**/Adj-**ta darō** in both writing and
speech, as in examples b–d, 9.1.2.3.2 a, 9.1.2.3.4 a) is derived by replacing the final **-i** with **-karō**

| Non-past | **yasu-i** | → | **yasu-karō** |
|----------|------------|---|---------------|
| Past | **yasukat-ta** | → | **yasukatta-rō** |

9.1.2.1.1 | Verb/adjective-(y)ō: equivalent of verb/adjective **darō**

Note also the past-tense form -tarō, which is the equivalent to -ta darō, darō being the presumptive form of the copula (see 7.5).

a 史料として一級の価値があろう。(=あるだろう)
   **Shiryō to shite ikkyū no kachi ga arō.** (= **aru darō**)
   As a historical document, it should have first-rate importance.

b パチンコをしたことのないサラリーマンは少なかろう。
   (=少ないだろう)
   **Pachinko o shita koto no nai sararīman wa sukunakarō.**
   (= **sukunai darō**)
   There can't be many office workers who've never played pachinko.

c 米景気への過大な悪影響もなかろう。(=ないだろう)
   **Bei-keiki e no kadai na aku-eikyō mo nakarō.** (= **nai darō**)
   There shouldn't be an excessive negative influence on the US market.

d 「会社のためという理屈は、もう通らない」との思いを新たにした
   経営者は、少なくなかったろう。(=少なくなかっただろう)
   **'Kaisha no tame to iu rikutsu wa mō tōranai' to no omoi o
   arata ni shita keiei-sha wa, sukunakunakattarō.**
   (= **sukunaku nakatta darō**)
   There must have been quite a few managers who realized that the
   argument 'it's for the good of the company' is no longer acceptable.

e 近い将来、消極政策の反動時代が来よう。(=来るだろう)
   **Chikai shōrai, shōkyoku seisaku no handō jidai ga koyō.**
   (= **kuru darō**)
   In the near future, a time of reaction against passive policies should
   come.

9.1.2.2 | Sentence **darō/deshō/de arō**

darō, deshō, and de arō are the plain, polite and learned (or bookish) -(y)ō forms of the copula, but unlike the -(y)ō form itself, which can have hortative meaning (see 9.1.1), darō, deshō and de arō indicate only presumptive 'should', 'ought to'. Colloquially, deshō can be shortened to desho (example f).

Note that darō, etc. is attached directly to V/Adj-final (incl. (-)nai), even though da itself cannot be attached in the same way. darō, etc. is usually attached to plain forms, but in speech it is also occasionally found after -masu forms (see 1.6.1.5 e for an example). After plain past -ta, both **darō** and -**rō** can be used.

**darō**, etc. adds the meaning of 'should', 'ought to' to a sentence.

a 価格はどんどん下がるだろう。
   **Kakaku wa dondon sagaru darō.**
   The price should come down rapidly.

b 缶のお茶といえば、ウーロン茶を思いつく人が多いだろう。
   **Kan no o-cha to ieba, ūron-cha o omoitsuku hito ga ōi darō.**
   At the mention of tea in cans, many probably think of Oolong tea.

c それで十分なのだろう。
   **Sore de jūbun na no darō.**
   That ought to be sufficient.

d この内閣は二年くらい大丈夫だろう。
   **Kono naikaku wa ninen kurai daijōbu darō.**
   This Cabinet should last for two years or so.

e 第九偏重とはいえ、「文化貧国」は言い過ぎだろう。
   **Daiku henchō to wa ie, 'bunka hinkoku' wa iisugi darō.**
   Even though we have this fondness for [Beethoven's] Ninth,
   to call [us] a 'cultural desert' is an exaggeration.

f どうせわれわれは必要ないのだろう。
   **Dōse wareware wa hitsuyō nai no darō.**
   We are not needed anyway, I guess.

g 人と話すときも目を見ないと通じ合わないでしょう。
   **Hito to hanasu toki mo me o minai to tsūji-awanai deshō.**
   When you talk with someone, too, surely you don't understand each
   other unless you look at the eyes.

h 「あなたが本当のサンタさんならできるでしょ」とねだるシ
   ーン…
   **'Anata ga hontō no Santa-san nara dekiru desho' to nedaru
   shīn …**
   The scene where [the girl] asks [to be given a brother and father]
   with the words 'If you're the real Santa, you should be able to
   do it' …

9.1.2.3 *Other uses of presumptive forms*

9.1.2.3.1 Noun 1-presumptive **to** noun 2-presumptive **to** (**mo**)

With negative predicates indicating a difference or relation, this construction means 'whether . . . or', 'there is no difference/relation, whether N1 or N2'.

a 地元だろうと本土だろうと客に違いはない。

**Jimoto darō to hondo darō to kyaku ni chigai wa nai.**

Whether they are local or from the mainland, customers are customers.

b 親のコネであろうと何であろうと、使える手段はすべて利用しない手はない。

**Oya no kone de arō to nan de arō to, tsukaeru shudan wa subete riyō shinai te wa nai.**

All possible means should be employed, be it parents' connections or whatever.

9.1.2.3.2 Question word + presumptive **to** (**mo**)

This combination indicates the idea of 'no matter what/how'.

a いえ、どんなに速かろうと、ちゃんと歌詞が聞こえなきゃいけません。

**Ie, donna ni hayakarō to, chanto kashi ga kikoenakya ikemasen.**

No, you must be able to hear the words of the song, no matter how fast the tempo is.

b だれであろうと内部に入れないのが特色だ。

**Dare de arō to naibu ni hairenai no ga tokushoku da.**

The distinctive feature of [the protection system] is that absolutely no-one can gain access to the inner part.

c 自分としてできる限りのことをしたら、あとは何が起きようと対処できる状態にある。

**Jibun to shite dekiru kagiri no koto o shitara, ato wa nani ga okiyō to taisho dekiru jōtai ni aru.**

If one does everything in one's power, one is in a state of being able to deal with whatever might happen.

Clause 1-presumptive **ga** ... Clause 2-presumptive **ga**

Joining clauses with opposite or contrastive meanings, the combination expresses the idea of 'whether ... or not', 'regardless of whether ... or' (see 26.4.1).

a 制度があろうが無かろうが、男性だろうが女性だろうが、
　（仕事が）きちんとできる人はできるものです。
**Seido ga arō ga nakarō ga, dansei darō ga josei darō ga, (shigoto ga) kichinto dekiru hito wa dekiru mono desu.**
Whether there is a system (in place) or not, whether male or female, a good worker is a good worker (*lit.* "those who can do (a job) properly, can").

In a negative question

This is used in the sense of 'might it not be that?' (see 18.4.7)

a どうも男性より女性の方が外国に強いのではなかろうか。
　（=ではないだろうか）
**Dōmo dansei yori josei no hō ga gaikoku ni tsuyoi no de wa nakarō ka. (= de wa nai darō ka)**
Isn't it perhaps that women are better at [dealing with being in] foreign countries than men?

**kamoshirenai**

Made up of the question particle **ka**, the adverbial particle **mo** and the negative potential form of the verb **shiru**, this literally means 'one cannot know if', but is used as an ending indicating the idea of 'probably', 'possibly', or 'might' (see also 9.6.3).

**kamoshirenai** is attached to V/Adj-fin. After **na**-adjectives/N + copula, the forms are **na**-adjective/N + copula, except that **kamoshirenai** deletes a preceding **da**. **kamoshirenai** can also be attached to the ending **n(o) da**, where again it deletes a preceding **da** (example a).

a お寺や教会のようなものだったのかもしれない。
**Otera ya kyōkai no yō na mono datta no kamoshirenai.**
It may have been something like a temple or a church.

b 「話はわかった。ではいったい、どうすればいいんだ？」と思う人が少なくないかもしれない。

**'Hanashi wa wakatta. De wa ittai, dō sureba ii n da?' to omou hito ga sukunakunai kamoshirenai.**

There may be quite a few who think 'I understand the idea. What is it then that I need to do?'

c マラソンの場合、「二位キープ」という作戦は素人の想像以上に難しいようだ。企業についても、これと似たことが言えるかもしれない。

**Marason no baai, 'ni-i kīpu' to iu sakusen wa shirōto no sōzō ijō ni muzukashii yō da. Kigyō ni tsuite mo, kore to nita koto ga ieru kamoshirenai.**

In a marathon, the strategy to keep in second place seems harder than the layman would think. One could probably say similar things about business.

---

<h3>9.1.2.5   tokoro datta</h3>

**tokoro** is originally a noun meaning 'time' or 'situation', and is thus preceded by forms preceding nouns. Used mostly after a –**ba** clause, **tokoro datta** indicates an unrealized outcome 'if not . . . would have' This meaning can be reinforced by adverbs such as **ayauku** 'nearly', as in example c.

a 三基すべてが爆発すれば大惨事になるところだった。

**Sanki subete ga bakuhatsu sureba daisanji ni naru tokoro datta.**

Had all three [gas tanks] exploded, it would have been a great catastrophe.

b 口座を変えなければ、永久に他人の電話代を支払わされるところだった。

**Kōza o kaenakereba, eikyū ni tanin no denwadai o shiharawasareru tokoro datta.**

Had I not changed my bank account, I would have been made to pay some else's phone bill for ever after.

c あやうく手痛い1敗を喫するところだった。

**Ayauku teitai ippai o kissuru tokoro datta.**

They [= the team] nearly had a costly defeat.

| 9.2 | **Desiderative** |

Desiderative endings indicate what somebody wants to do, have, or wishes another to do. Endings like **-tai (to omou)** (see 9.2.1), **-(y)ō to omou/ kangaeru** (see 9.2.2) indicate what the speaker wants to do; the adjective **hoshii** (see 9.2.3) indicates what the speaker wants to have; and the performative ending **-te hoshii** (see 15.7) indicates what the speaker wants others to do for his/her benefit (see also 6.8.1).

*Note* – with **-tai** and **hoshii**, both the case particles **ga** and **o** can be used (see 2.1.5, 2.2.3).

| 9.2.1 | **-tai (to omou)** |

**-tai** indicates what the speaker (subject) wishes to do, 'want to', and is therefore used in the first person. The object of V-**tai** (where present) can be marked by either **ga** or **o** (see 9.2, 2.1.5, 2.2.3). For a more indirect way of expressing one's wishes, forms of **to omou** (the quotation particle **to** plus the verb of thinking **omou**) can be attached.

To indicate what second and third persons wish to do, **tai** (in its root-form) usually attaches the suffix **-garu** (see 6.8.1).

The past tense **-takatta** indicates what the subject wanted to do, for both realized or unrealized wishes.

| 9.2.1.1 | **-tai** |

a ピアノを習いたい。
　**Piano o narai-tai.**
　I want to learn the piano.

b 早く飛行機が見たい。
　**Hayaku hikōki ga mi-tai.**
　I want to see the aeroplane soon.

c できるだけ早く行きたいと思う。
　**Dekiru dake hayaku iki-tai to omou.**
　I'd like to go at the earliest opportunity.

d 仲良くしたいと思っている。
   **Nakayoku shi-tai to omotte iru.**
   We'd like to have a close relationship.

e 親しい仲間との囲碁やゴルフ、趣味の庭いじりなど悠々自適に暮
   らしたい気持ちもある。
   **Shitashii nakama to no igo ya gorufu, shumi no niwaijiri nado**
   **yūyū jiteki ni kurashi-tai kimochi mo aru.**
   I also feel that I'd like to live a life of leisure, playing Go and golf with
   close friends, and pursuing my hobbies such as gardening and so on.

### 9.2.1.2 -takatta

#### 9.2.1.2.1 Unrealized wish

a もっと生きたかった。
   **Motto iki-takatta.**
   I wanted to live longer [= suicide note].

b 大声で叫びたかったが、出来なかった。
   **ōgoe de sakebi-takatta ga, dekinakatta.**
   I wanted to shout at the top of my voice, but couldn't.

c 本当はハワイに行きたかったけど、休みが短いのでグアムで買い
   物と泳ぎを楽しんできます。
   **Hontō wa Hawai ni iki-takatta kedo, yasumi ga mijikai no de**
   **Guamu de kaimono to oyogi o tanoshinde kimasu.**
   Actually, I wanted to go to Hawaii, but because the holidays are short
   I'm going to Guam to enjoy shopping and swimming.

#### 9.2.1.2.2 Realized wish

a 「子供たちにはのびのびと教育を受けさせたかった」ので外国の大
   学に進学させた・・・
   **'Kodomo-tachi ni wa nobinobi to kyōiku o ukesase-takatta' no**
   **de gaikoku no daigaku ni shingaku saseta.**
   They enrolled them at a foreign university, because 'We wanted to
   give our children an unfettered education'.

b スキンヘッドにしたのは、「とにかく目立ちたかった」から。
   **Sukinheddo ni shita no wa, 'tonikaku medachi-takatta' kara.**
   The reason why he became a skinhead was because he 'just wanted to
   attract attention'.

239

## 9.2.2 -(y)ō to omou/kangaeru

The combination of V-(y)ō (see 9.1.1 for forms) + the verb of thinking **omou/kangaeru** (which use the quotation particle **to**) is similar in meaning to **–tai to omou**, having the sense of 'think of doing', 'want to'.

### 9.2.2.1 -(y)ō to omou/kangaeru

a 西欧文明の退廃や矛盾を感じとり、インディアンとして生きよう と考えた。
   **Seiō bunmei no taihai ya mujun o kanji-tori, Indian to shite ikiyō to kangaeta.**
   I felt the decadence and contradictions of Western and European civilization, and thought I'd live as an Indian.

b 人生の残りを考えた時、本当にやりたいことをやろうと考 えた。
   **Jinsei no nokori o kangaeta toki, hontō ni yaritai koto o yarō to kangaeta.**
   When I considered the rest of my life, I thought of doing the things I really want to do.

c 三日までゆっくり過ごそうと思います。
   **Mikka made yukkuri sugosō to omoimasu.**
   I'd like to take things easy until the 3rd.

d 同氏は自宅に風車を設置しようと考えている風力推進派。
   **Dōshi wa jitaku ni fūsha o setchi shiyō to kangaete iru fūryoku suishin-ha.**
   The aforementioned is a windpower advocate, who is considering installing a windmill at his home.

e いい会社として知られているのに、なぜ辞めようと思ったのです か。
   **Ii kaisha to shite shirarete iru noni, naze yameyō to omotta no desu ka.**
   Why did you think of quitting, even though it's known as a good company?

## 9.2.2.2 | -(y)ō to wa omou/omowanai, kangaeru/kangaenai

The adverbial particle **wa** can be inserted between **to** and the verb, mostly in the negative, but it can also be used with positive predicates for contrast or emphasis (example c).

a 短期間にもうけようとは考えていない。
**Tankikan ni mōkeyō to wa kangaete inai.**
We have no intention of making a quick buck.

b 結婚できないから子供はあきらめようとは考えなかった。
**Kekkon dekinai kara kodomo wa akirameyō to wa
    kangaenakatta.**
I didn't think of giving up [having] children because I can't get married.

c 「間違いのない演奏をしようとは思いましたよ」と話している。
**'Machigai no nai ensō o shiyō to wa omoimashita yo'
    to hanashite iru.**
'I [did] think that I wanted to perform flawlessly', he said.

d 私自身は監督になろうとは思わない。
**Watashi jishin wa kantoku ni narō to wa omowanai.**
I myself have no intention of becoming a coach.

## 9.2.3 | hoshii

The adjective **hoshii** indicates the object of the speaker's desire or wishes. 'Object' includes things, persons (children and other people that can belong to one or one's organization), time, money or other desirables. The object is usually marked by **ga**, but occasionally **o** is also found (see 2.1.5, 6.8.1, 2.2.3, 15.6).

Typically, **hoshii** is used of the first person in statements, and second person in questions, but examples of third-person use are also found, even though it is more usual to use **hoshi-garu** for third persons (see 6.8.1).

## 9.2.3.1 | Present

a ✐お金がほしい。
**Okane ga hoshii.**
I want money.

b ✐誕生日に何がほしい？

**Tanjōbi ni nani ga hoshii?**

What do you want for your birthday?

c テレビでも研究が紹介され、「出演者の一人がこのシステムをほ しいと話していた」。

**Terebi de mo kenkyū ga shōkai sare, 'Shutsuensha no hitori ga kono shisutemu o hoshii to hanashite ita'.**

[The virtual organism system] was shown on TV, too, and 'one of the people on the programme said he wanted this system'.

---

| 9.2.3.2 | *Past* |

Like **-te hoshikatta**, **hoshikatta** can indicate both desires that have been fulfilled and those that were left unfulfilled (see 15.7.1.2).

a 「自分の心の落ち着き場所がほしかった」ことが妊娠願望の原因 だったという。

**'Jibun no kokoro no ochitsuki-basho ga hoshikatta' koto ga ninshin ganbō no gen'in datta to iu.**

She says that the reason for her wish to become pregnant was that 'I wanted a place for my heart to settle down'.

b 話し相手がほしかった彼女は、時々親戚のシンプソン家を訪 ねた。

**Hanashi-aite ga hoshikatta kanojo wa, tokidoki shinseki no Shinpuson-ke o tazuneta.**

Wanting someone to talk to, she sometimes visited the Simpson family, who are relatives.

---

| 9.2.4 | **tsumori** |

As **tsumori** is a structural noun, it is attached to sentences ending in noun-modifying forms. Besides its use with the copula, it can also attach **wa/ga** (see 9.2.4.3). **tsumori** indicates intention.

Note how **tsumori** is mostly used in the first and third persons, whereas second-person use is generally restricted to questions. In practice, the referent is not usually mentioned in questions, however.

9.2.4.1 | *Clause-non-past* **tsumori**

9.2.4.1.1 | (First/second/third person) clause **tsumori** + copula

Used of the first or third person, this means 'I/we/he/she/they intend(s) to'.

a 新政権に働きかけるつもりだ。
**Shin-seiken ni hatarakikakeru tsumori da.**
I intend to make approaches to the new government.

b あらゆる機会をとらえて訴えていくつもりです。
**Arayuru kikai o toraete uttaete iku tsumori desu.**
I intend to appeal [to the public about this] at (*lit.* "making use of")
every possible opportunity.

c 今年は公務員試験を受けるつもりだ。
**Kotoshi wa kōmuin shiken o ukeru tsumori da.**
This year he intends to take the public service exams.

d 子供を産んだら仕事を辞めるつもりだ。
**Kodomo o undara shigoto o yameru tsumori da.**
When she has her baby, she intends to give up work.

e 三代目に訊いた。「跡目は、誰にするつもりですか」
**Sandaime ni kiita. 'Atome wa, dare ni suru tsumori desu ka'**
I asked the third-generation patriarch. 'Who are you intending to make
the next family head?'

f 「それに...お嬢様がアメリカへ発たれたら、その後、あなたと
奥様はどうなさるおつもりですか」
**'Sore ni ... ojōsama ga Amerika e tataretara, sono ato, anata
to okusama wa dō nasaru o-tsumori desu ka'**
'And ... once your daughter has departed for America, what are you
and your wife intending to do after that?'

9.2.4.1.2 | (Third person) clause **tsumori darō**

**tsumori darō** can only refer to a third person 'I think he/she/they intend(s)
to'.

a 選挙運動で連呼するつもりだろう。
**Senkyo undō de renko suru tsumori darō.**
He intends to call out his name repeatedly in the election campaign,
I think.

9.2.4.1.3 | (First/third person) clause-non-past **tsumori datta**

This is the same as 9.2.4.1.1, but in the past tense 'I/we/he/she/they intended to'.

a 学問の道に進むつもりだった。

**Gakumon no michi ni susumu tsumori datta.**

I had intended to go down the path of scholarship.

b しばらく一緒に暮らしてみて、結論を出すつもりだった。

**Shibaraku issho ni kurashite mite, ketsuron o dasu tsumori datta.**

We intended to live together for some time, and then reach a conclusion.

9.2.4.1.4 | (First/third person) clause **tsumori de** predicate

When **tsumori da** is used in the conjunctive form of the copula (i.e. the **tsumori**-clause modifies a following verb), the meaning is 'with the intention of'.

a 「いいものを歴史に残すつもりでつくった」といっている。

**'Ii mono o rekishi ni nokosu tsumori de tsukutta' to itte iru.**

He says, 'I made it with the intention of leaving something good for posterity'.

b 今国会中に補正が成立するつもりで準備してもらいたい。

**Kon-kokkai-chū ni hosei ga seiritsu suru tsumori de junbi shite moraitai.**

We'd like people to make preparations with the intent that the supplementary budget is effected during the current session of the Diet.

9.2.4.2 | *Clause-past* **tsumori**

9.2.4.2.1 | (First person) clause-past **tsumori da**

The speaker indicates that he hopes or flatters himself to have achieved something positive 'I hope that', 'I flatter myself that'.

a 僕は日本通ぶった視点は避けたつもりです。

**Boku wa Nihontsū-butta shiten wa saketa tsumori desu.**

I hope that I avoided a position of pretending to be a Japan expert.

b 私は長い間、女性の社会進出のための仕事をしてきたつも
りだ。

**Watashi wa nagai aida, josei no shakai shinshutsu no
tame no shigoto o shite kita tsumori da.**

I flatter myself that I've long worked for the social advancement of
women.

---

9.2.4.2.2 | (First/third person) clause-past **tsumori datta**

The speaker indicates that he thought or flattered himself that he had
achieved something positive, which subsequently turned out to be a negative result 'I thought that ... (but in fact) ...'. This can also be used in
commenting on third persons.

a 商売のコツは頭ではわかっていたつもりだったが、甘くはなか
った。

**Shōbai no kotsu wa atama de wa wakatte ita tsumori datta
ga, amaku wa nakatta.**

I thought that I'd understood the ways of business, but it wasn't
so easy.

b 大枚をはたいたつもりだったが、日本の知人の話を聞いてがく
然とした。

**Taimai o hataita tsumori datta ga, Nihon no chijin no hanashi
o kiite gakuzen to shita.**

I thought I had spent a large sum of money, but I was really shocked
when I heard what my Japanese friend told me.

---

9.2.4.3 | (First/third person) clause-NON-PAST **tsumori wa nai**

This means 'have no intention of'.

a 特に手の込んだ料理を作るつもりはない。

**Toku ni te no konda ryōri o tsukuru tsumori
wa nai.**

I have no intention of preparing any particularly
complicated dishes.

b 新しい歌を発表するつもりはなかった。

**Atarashii uta o happyō suru tsumori wa nakatta.**

I had no intention of publishing a new song.

*(First/third person) clause-non-past* **tsumori de iru**

This means 'have the intention of'; it is different from **tsumori da** in that the emphasis is on the intention a person has at a certain time, as the intention may of course change over time.

a 最低、あと七年は現役を続けるつもりでいる。
   **Saitei, ato shichinen wa gen'eki o tsuzukeru tsumori de iru.**
   His intention is to remain active [as a player] for at least another
   seven years.

b 最初は「この会社に骨を埋めるつもりでいた」という。
   **Saisho wa 'kono kaisha ni hone o umeru tsumori de ita' to iu.**
   He says that in the beginning 'I had the intention of staying in this
   company forever' (*lit.* "bury one's bones").

c 開発を手助けしたつもりでいたのが、「環境破壊に手を貸した」
   となじられる。
   **Kaihatsu o tedasuke shita tsumori de ita no ga, 'kankyō hakai
   ni te o kashita' to najirareru.**
   My intention was to assist development, but I'm being accused of
   'having assisted in destruction of the environment'.

## 9.3 Negative presumptive and desiderative: -mai

-**mai** is attached to V-ru. Exceptions are **dekiru, kuru/suru**, and the Group II-type verb causative ending -(s)**aseru**, where V-stem is used.

Note especially the combination -**neba/-nakereba narumai**, which is equivalent to the more colloquial -**nakereba naranai darō** (see 17.2).

-**mai** is used in two meanings: negative presumptive and negative desiderative. With the exception of V-**mai shi**, both have a formal/written language flavour.

The former is attached to predicates that indicate a state, the latter to predicates whose action is intentional, i.e. can be controlled by the subject (see 9.1.2, 9.2).

### 9.3.1 Negative presumptive

Instead of -**nai darō** (see 9.1.2.2), the somewhat archaic but concise ending -**mai** can be used.

---

## 9.3.1.1 Verb-mai

This is a written style equivalent of -nai darō 'oughtn't', 'no doubt'.

a ···国民も納得しまい。
   **...kokumin mo nattoku shimai.**
   ...the people are unlikely to be convinced, either.

b 知っておいても損ではあるまい。
   **Shitte oite mo son de wa arumai.**
   There shouldn't be any harm in knowing this.

c "戦争終結" の宣言もそう遠くはあるまい。
   **'Sensō shūketsu' no sengen mo sō tōku wa arumai.**
   A declaration of 'end of hostilities' oughtn't to be that far away.

---

## 9.3.1.2 Verb-mai ni

-mai ni is used in sentences with contrastive meaning (ni has the same
meaning as noni) (see 26.4.5).

a お前たち、昔はどんな暮らしだったか知りはすまい。知ってれば
   そんな言い方は出来まいに。
   **Omae-tachi, mukashi wa donna kurashi datta ka shiri wa
   sumai. Shittereba sonna iikata wa dekimai ni.**
   You girls don't know how we lived in the old days. If you did, you
   wouldn't make [critical] comments like that.

---

## 9.3.1.3 Verb-mai shi

This is used to make a point that the speaker thinks should be patently
obvious.

a そんな馬鹿な。未成年じゃあるまいし。銀行だけ特別に損をかぶ
   れという法律でもあるんですかね。
   **Sonna baka na. Miseinen ja arumai shi. Ginkō dake
   tokubetsu ni son o kabure to iu hōritsu demo aru n
   desu ka ne.**
   How ridiculous. They [= banks] are not minors [= devoid of
   responsibility], you know. Is there a law or something that states
   that only banks should make special losses?

*Sentence-***neba/-nakereba narumai**

Literally, this means 'unless I/we do . . . , it presumably won't do', i.e. 'must' (see 17.2).

a 大いに自戒せねばなるまい。
**Ōi ni jikai seneba narumai.**
No doubt we must take great care [not to repeat the same mistake].

b 慎重に判断しなければなるまい。
**Shinchō ni handan shinakereba narumai.**
We no doubt need to make a careful judgement.

**9.3.2** | *Negative desiderative*

**-mai** can also express a negative desiderative, i.e. what the speaker doesn't want to do (see 9.2, 9.2.4.3).

a 「気持ちだけは負けまいと思った」と投手。
**'Kimochi dake wa makemai to omotta' to tōshu.**
'I certainly didn't want to be defeated in spirit', said the [baseball] pitcher.

b 「過去を忘れさせまい」という中国当局の意思は明快だ。
**"Kako o wasuresasemai' to iu Chūgoku tōkyoku no ishi wa meikai da.**
The intention of the Chinese authorities of not wishing to allow the past to be forgotten is obvious.

c 自分は努めて目立つまいとの配慮からだ。
**Jibun wa tsutomete medatsumai to no hairyo kara da.**
[Not giving public lectures] is because of his wish to attract as little attention as possible.

**9.4** **Necessitative**

**9.4.1** | **-beki**

Suffix-like, **-beki** attaches to V-**ru**. However, after **suru**, or verbal nouns where **suru** gets voiced to VN-**zuru**, the classical forms **su-beki**/VN-**zu-beki** are still used (see examples 9.4.1.1 c, e and h).

-beki indicates obligation, 'must', 'ought to' (see 17.2.3, 9.6.2, 9.3, 9.6.4).

-beki is usually followed by forms of the copula, but note the classical negative form **bekarazu**, which is occasionally encountered (9.4.1.1 h) instead of -**beki de wa nai**. Also, the classical form -**beshi** is occasionally still found (see examples 9.4.1.1 c and d) instead of -**beki** + copula.

| 9.4.1.1 | *Clause-***beki** *copula* |

-beki is similar in meaning to -**ta hō ga ii** (-**nai hō ga ii** in the negative), meaning 'should', 'ought to' (see 6.7.2.8.3).

a  ✐その映画は一回見るべきだよ。
   **Sono eiga wa ikkai miru-beki da yo.**
   That film you should see once.

b  選挙で選ぶべきだ。
   **Senkyo de erabu-beki da.**
   [He [= party leader]] ought to be chosen by election.

c  未成年者の飲酒防止のため、酒の屋外自動販売機は撤廃す
   べし。
   **Miseinensha no inshu bōshi no tame, sake no okugai jidō hanbaiki wa teppai su-beshi.**
   In order to prevent minors from drinking alcohol, outdoor vending machines for alcoholic drinks should be abolished.

d  エイズに感染している時は相手にその事実を告げるべし。
   **Eizu ni kansen shite iru toki wa aite ni sono jijitsu o tsugeru-beshi.**
   If one's infected with AIDS, one should inform one's partner of that fact.

e  日本の外交をどのように改革すべきだろうか。
   **Nihon no gaikō o dono yō ni kaikaku su-beki darō ka.**
   In what way should Japan's diplomacy be reformed, I wonder.

f  死亡や障害を引き起こすことがあらかじめ予想される場合、
   実験は行うべきではない。
   **Shibō ya shōgai o hikiokosu koto ga arakajime yosō sareru baai, jikken wa okonau-beki de wa nai.**
   Experiments, where the possibility of their causing death or injury can be assumed beforehand, should not be carried out.

g 歴史的な公共建造物は公の利益のために使うべきで、金持ちが利
用する高級ホテルにすべきではない。

**Rekishi-teki na kōkyō kenzō-butsu wa ōyake no rieki no tame ni tsukau-beki de, kanemochi ga riyō suru kōkyū hoteru ni su-beki de wa nai.**

An historic public building should be used for the benefit of the public, and not be made into a hotel for use by the rich.

h 数字というものは、むしろ信ずべからず、ではないか。

**Sūji to iu mono wa mushiro shinzu-bekarazu dewa nai ka.**

Isn't it rather the case that numbers should not be trusted?

---

| 9.4.1.2 | *Clause-**beki** noun* |

When modifying a noun, the meaning is 'need to', 'must', and can be replaced by a double negative such as -**nakereba naranai**. Note that -**beki** here modifies N directly, without the copula (see 17.2).

a ✐ちょっと行くべきところがある。

**Chotto iku-beki tokoro ga aru.**

There's a place I need to go to.

b まだ研究を深めるべき課題が残っている。

**Mada kenkyū o fukameru-beki kadai ga nokotte iru.**

There are still problems on which we must do more research.

c 今後進むべき方向性ははっきりしてきた。

**Kongo susumu-beki hōkōsei wa hakkiri shite kita.**

The direction in which we need to go from now on has
    become clear.

## 9.5 Evidential

### 9.5.1 mitai

The ending **mitai** is used in informal language, in place of more formal **yō**, **sō** and **rashii**. It indicates appearance or simile (like other endings of appearance and simile, **mitai** can be 'reinforced' by adverbs like **maru de** 'just like' (see 10.2.4.7).

**mitai** can be followed by a form of the copula (e.g. **mitai da/desu**), but in line with its colloquial nature often ends a sentence by itself.

The forms **mitai** is attached to are plain forms (after **na-Adj** and N, without copula). **mitai** itself changes its endings like a **na-Adjective**.

**mitai** needs to be distinguished from **mitai** (the -**tai** form of -**te miru** that is attached to V-**te** (see 8.8, 9.2.1). Past tense forms can precede **mitai** 'like having . . . -ed', but can also follow it 'was like'.

Being a more colloquial variant of **yō**, **mitai** can be replaced (in uses 9.5.1.1 and 9.5.1.4 only) by **yō**, but **rashii** can only be used in those examples in 9.5.1.1 where **mitai** can be interpreted as indicating hearsay (9.5.1.1 c and g), where **sō** [hearsay] and **to iu** could also be used (see 9.5.4, 9.5.2, 9.5.1, 21.2).

---

9.5.1.1 | *Sentence* **mitai** *(copula/**na n da**)*

---

This means that some thing, situation or person, etc. 'seems like', 'is like' another.

a マグロのトロみたいでしょう。
**Maguro no toro mitai deshō.**
It's like fatty tuna, isn't it.

b 黄色いじゅうたんみたい。
**Kiiroi jūtan mitai.**
They [= wild flowers] are like a yellow carpet.

c 今回は違うみたいだ。
**Konkai wa chigau mitai da.**
This time it seems to be different.

d 外国に来たみたい。
**Gaikoku ni kita mitai.**
It's like having come to a foreign country.

e 「どう、似合うかしら」「うん、結構首が細く見えるみたい」。
**'Dō, niau kashira' 'Un, kekkō kubi ga hosoku mieru mitai'.**
'How does it look? Does it suit me?' 'Hm, it seems to make your neck look quite slender.'

f なんだか札幌では日の暮れるのが早いみたい。
**Nandaka Sapporo de wa hi no kureru no ga hayai mitai.**
Somehow in Sapporo it seems to get dark earlier.

g クッキングはストレス解消にも役立っているみたい。
**Kukkingu wa sutoresu kaishō ni mo yakudatte iru mitai.**
Cooking seems to help get rid of stress, too.

h 駅長さんの部屋みたいなんだよね。堅苦しいんですよ。

**Ekichōsan no heya mitai na n da yo ne. Katagurushii n desu yo.**

It's like a station master's office, isn't it. It's [too] stuffy.

<hr>

| 9.5.1.2 | *Clause1* **mitai de**, *clause 2* |
|---|---|

Besides being used in compound sentences, **mitai de** (**de** is the conjunctive form of the copula) can also be used to finish a sentence, leaving S2 to be understood from the context 'just like . . . , (and . . .)'.

a まるでスパイ映画みたいで面白かったね。

**Maru de supai eiga mitai de omoshirokatta ne.**

It was just like a spy movie, and very interesting.

b どうしても食欲に負けてしまうみたいで。

**Dōshite mo shokuyoku ni makete shimau mitai de.**

[Children] just seem to be unable to resist (*lit.* "get defeated by their appetite") [and end up eating between meals].

<hr>

| 9.5.1.3 | *Clause* **mitai ni** *predicate* |
|---|---|

**mitai ni** (**ni** is the adverbial form of the copula) is the adverbial form of **mitai da**, used to modify a predicate in the sense of 'like'.

a どれも短篇小説みたいにおもしろい。

**Dore mo tanpen shōsetsu mitai ni omoshiroi.**

All [= jottings on a postcard] are interesting, like short stories.

b 芸能プロダクションみたいに、電話がひっきりなしにかかってきます。

**Geinō purodakushon mitai ni, denwa ga hikkirinashi ni kakatte kimasu.**

The phone rings continuously, like in a showbiz office.

<hr>

| 9.5.1.4 | *Clause* **mitai na** *noun* |
|---|---|

This is used to make a simile 'like', 'such as', when comparing a situation to another situation, state or object.

a あれ以来、島の活動のすべてが止まってしまって······。
　　まるで、静止画像をみているみたいな毎日でした。

**Are irai, shima no katsudō no subete ga tomatte
shimatte ... Maru de, seishi gazō o mite iru mitai na
mainichi deshita.**

Since that time [of the earthquake], all activity on the island has come
to a standstill ... Every day was just like looking at movie stills.

b 洋服みたいなささいな理由で落とされちゃたまらない。

**Yōfuku mitai na sasai na riyū de otosarecha tamaranai.**

The last thing I want is to be rejected [in a job interview] for some
trifling reason such as the clothes [I'm wearing].

---

## 9.5.2 | sō

Attached to clauses (the forms preceding **sō** are plain final forms of V/
Adj/na-Adj/N, but **no da**, etc. can be inserted between the verb and **sō**),
the ending **sō** indicates that the sentence or clause it is attached to is not
the speaker's own opinion, but something which he or she has heard or
read 'apparently', 'I hear that ...'.

Note the difference from -**sō** [likelihood], which is attached to V/Adj-stem,
na-Adj/N minus the copula] (see 9.5.4).

As with **rashii** and **to iu**, the source of information can be indicated at the
beginning of the sentence with ... **ni yoru to/ni yoreba** ('according to ...')
or similar expressions.

**sō** itself is usually followed by a form of the copula (**da, de, desu, de aru**,
etc.), but informally can also be followed directly by the final particle **yo**
(9.5.2.2.4 a). Followed by the final particle **ne**, it is used to ask for another
person's reaction/comment, in interviews, etc. (9.5.2.1.1 d).

---

### 9.5.2.1 | *Clause-non-past* **sō da** *(and other forms of copula)*

#### 9.5.2.1.1 | Verb **sō da**

a エクササイズは、散歩と家事だけで足りるそうだ。

**Ekusasaizu wa, sanpo to kaji dake de tariru sō da.**

As far as exercise goes, just going for walks and doing the housework
are supposed to be enough.

b 猛暑の年は、冬の寒さが厳しくなるそうだ。
**Mōsho no toshi wa, fuyu no samusa ga kibishiku naru sō da.**
In years with very hot summers, the winters are said to get
    very cold.

c イタチやタヌキがよく顔を出すそうだ。
**Itachi ya tanuki ga yoku kao o dasu sō da.**
Apparently, weasels and badgers often show up.

d ネクタイを150本も持っているそうですね。
**Nekutai o hyaku gojup-pon mo motte iru sō desu ne.**
One hears that you own as many as 150 ties.

e その販売店では外国製乗用車を一台売ると、なんと約五十万円も
    うかるそうだ。
**Sono hanbaiten de wa gaikokusei jōyōsha o ichidai uru to,**
**nanto yaku gojūman-en mōkaru sō da.**
In that sales office they're said to earn a whopping 500,000 yen or so
    when they sell one foreign car.

---

9.5.2.1.2 | Adjective **sō da**

a 寿命はボルドーが圧倒的に長いそうだ。
**Jumyō wa Borudō ga attōteki ni nagai sō da.**
As for the [wines'] life, Bordeaux [wines] are supposed to last a great
    deal longer.

b 大学を卒業しても、すぐには就職できない人が少なくないそ
    うだ。
**Daigaku o sotsugyō shite mo, sugu ni wa shūshoku dekinai**
**hito ga sukunakunai sō da.**
There are supposed to be quite a few people who can't find a job
    straight away, even if they're university graduates.

c ことしは天候不順で山にはなお雪が多いそうだ。
**Kotoshi wa tenkō fujun de yama ni wa nao yuki ga ōi sō da.**
This year, owing to bad weather, they say that there is still a lot of
    snow in the mountains.

d 今年は例年に比べて雪の降る日が多いのだそうだ。
**Kotoshi wa reinen ni kurabete yuki no furu hi ga ōi no da**
**sō da.**
This year, apparently there were more days when it snowed than in
    average years.

| 9.5.2.1.3 | na-adjective **sō da** |

a 保存上、長期の展示は困難だそうだ。

**Hozon-jō, chōki no tenji wa konnan da sō da.**

Owing to their [poor] state of preservation, prolonged showing of [the prints] is said to be difficult.

b 鴨川などを散歩するのが好きだそうですね。

**Kamogawa nado o sanpo suru no ga suki da sō desu ne.**

I understand that you like walking along the Kamo river and such places.

| 9.5.2.1.4 | Noun **sō da** |

a 趣味は旅と山登りだそうだ。

**Shumi wa tabi to yamanobori da sō da.**

Apparently his hobbies are travelling and mountaineering.

b 諸外国と比べても、日本は女性が働きやすい国だそうだ。

**Sho-gaikoku to kurabete mo, Nihon wa josei ga hataraki-yasui kuni da sō da.**

Compared to most foreign countries, Japan is supposed to be a country where women find it easy to work.

| 9.5.2.1.5 | Verb **sō na** |

**sō na** is no different in meaning to **sō da,** but it presents some event as if told by a storyteller.

a 二十三歳の若さで店を切り盛りしているそうな。

**Nijūsan-sai no wakasa de mise o kirimori shite iru sō na.**

Apparently, she is running the shop at the tender age of 23.

| *9.5.2.2* | *Clause-past* **sō da** *(sō na)* |

This indicates hearsay about an event in the past.

| 9.5.2.2.1 | Verb **sō da** |

a この味を見つけるのに四年かかったそうだ。

**Kono aji o mitsukeru no ni yonen kakatta sō da.**

Apparently it took four years to discover this taste.

b 京都に住み始めたそうですね。
**Kyoto ni sumi-hajimeta sō desu ne.**
I understand that you have started living in Kyoto.

9.5.2.2.2 Adjective **sō da**

a 社風に合わなかったそうだ。
**Shafū ni awanakatta sō da.**
Apparently, you didn't fit the style of that company.

9.5.2.2.3 na-adjective **sō da**

a 歩道橋もなかったんで、東側の住民はずいぶん不便だったそうだ
よ。(んで ＝ ので)
**Hodōkyō mo nakatta n de, higashigawa no jūmin wa zuibun
fuben datta sō da yo. [n de = no de]**
As there wasn't even a footbridge, the people living on the east side
were quite inconvenienced, I understand.

9.5.2.2.4 Noun **sō da**

a 昔、相撲はその年の稲作を占う神事だったそうよ。
**Mukashi, sumō wa sono toshi no inasaku o uranau shinji datta
sō yo.**
In the old days, sumo was apparently a Shinto ceremony to divine
the rice harvest for that year.

b 当時は女性に名前を聞くのは求婚の意を表すことだったそうだ。
**Tōji wa josei ni namae o kiku no wa kyūkon no i o arawasu
koto datta sō da.**
At the time, asking a woman's name had the meaning of asking for her
hand in marriage, I understand.

9.5.2.2.5 **sō na**

For an explanation of the effect of **na** rather than **da**, see 9.5.2.1.5.

a そりゃあ百人から聴衆が集まって盛況だったそうな。
**Soryā hyakunin kara chōshū ga atsumatte seikyō datta
sō na.**
I understand that it [= the concert] was a great success, with more
than a hundred people in attendance.

9.5.2.3 *Source of information* **sō da**

The source of information is indicated by **N de wa, N ni yoru to**, or **N ni yoreba** 'according to'. (See also 9.5.3, 9.5.4)

*Note* – sentences with source of information can also end in forms other than **sō da** (see **ni yoru to**).

a ノンベーの友人によると、駅前の飲み屋で繁盛する三条件は
(1) 安い (2) うまい (3) 話を聞いてくれるおじさん、おばさ
んがいる―ことだそうだ。

**Nonbē no yūjin ni yoru to, ekimae no nomiya de hanjō suru
san-jōken wa (1) yasui (2) umai (3) hanashi o kiite kureru
ojisan, obasan ga iru --- koto da sō da.**

According to a drinker friend, the three conditions for a drinking joint
in front of the station to be popular are 1, to be cheap, 2, [food] to
be good, and the presence of a man or woman who can listen.

b 藤田氏によれば定信などは最初は神様のように、あがめられたそ
うだ。

**Fujita-shi ni yoreba Sadanobu nado wa saisho wa kamisama
no yō ni, agamerareta sō da.**

According to Mr Fujita, people like Sadanobu were at first adored like
gods.

c イギリスの現行法では、「たとえ、それが慈悲心から生じたもの
であっても、殺意はやはり殺意」なのだそうだ。

**Igirisu no genkōhō de wa, 'Tatoe, sore ga jihishin kara shōjita
mono de atte mo, satsui wa yahari satsui' na no da sō da.**

According to existing English law, 'The intention to kill is still intention
to kill, even if it comes from a feeling of mercy'.

9.5.3 **-tte**

**-tte** is a colloquial equivalent to **sō** [hearsay], often in the form **-tte
ne**. It can be attached to either the plain (example a) or polite form of the
copula (examples b and c). In this way, it differs from **sō**, which is added
to the plain form only (see 9.5.2, 9.5.5).

a 日本は何でも高いんだってね。
**Nihon wa nan demo takai n da-tte ne.**
I hear that everything's expensive in Japan.

b　ピアノが大変お上手なんですってね。
**Piano ga taihen o-jōzu nan desu-tte ne.**
I hear that you're very good at playing the piano.

c　ユニバーサル・スタジオ、楽しいんですってね。
**Yunibāsaru Sutajio, tanoshii n desu-tte ne.**
The Universal Studios are great fun, I hear.

d　王子様を好きだった人魚姫さんは、最後は空気の精になってお空
に飛んで行ってしまったんだって。
**Ōji-sama o suki datta ningyo hime-san wa, saigo wa kūki no
sei ni natte o-sora ni tonde itte shimatta n da-tte.**
The mermaid, who liked the prince, in the end turned into a sylph
and flew up into the sky, they say.

---

### 9.5.4 | -sō

The ending -sō 'likely to' is distinguished from sō (attached to V/Adj/na-
Adj-final form) by the forms that precede it: V-stem, Adj-ku, and na-Adj
without copula (-sō is not attached to N). V-stem includes the stem form
of the potential V **dekiru**, and also of potential endings. Note especially
the negative form -sō ni nai.

-sō (itself inflecting like a na-Adj) is usually followed by forms of copula
(**da/na/ni**), but colloquially and in newspaper style it can complete a sentence by itself, as in example 9.5.4.1.1 a (see 9.5.1, 9.5.4, 9.5.6, 21.2).

### 9.5.4.1 | Verb-stem-**sō da** *(and other forms of copula)*

### 9.5.4.1.1 | Verb-stem-**sō da**

a　混雑は十六日午後まで続きそう。
**Konzatsu wa jūroku-nichi gogo made tsuzukisō.**
The congestion is likely to continue until the 16th.

b　ミネラルウオーターは今後、身近な存在になっていきそうだ。
**Mineraruuōtā wa kongo mijika na sonzai ni natte ikisō da.**
Mineral water is likely to become a familiar presence from now on.

c　木枯らしはまだ吹きそうにない。
**Kogarashi wa mada fukisō ni nai.**
The winter winds are not likely to blow yet.

d 今後の環境教育に反映できそうなデータだ。

**Kongo no kankyō kyōiku ni han'ei dekisō na dēta da.**

They are data that we should be able to use for environmental
education in the future.

9.5.4.1.2 Verb-potential-stem-**sō da**

Being Group II verbs, the stem of potential verbs is the same as the vowel
root ending in -e (see Table 7.1).

*Note* – potential can also be expressed by **dekisō da**, as in 9.5.4.1.1 d.

a 十月下旬までぶどう狩りが楽しめそう。

**Jūgatsu gejun made budōgari ga tanoshimesō.**

It should be possible to enjoy picking grapes until late October.

b 今夜はおいしい酒が飲めそうです。

**Kon'ya wa oishii sake ga nomesō desu.**

Tonight, I should be able to enjoy my sake.

c 下期も需要回復は見込めそうにない。

**Shimoki mo juyō kaifuku wa mikomesō ni nai.**

Recovery of demand cannot be expected for the second half,
either.

d 時間を作り出そうという時に、簡単に思いつきそうなのが
「睡眠時間を削る」という方法だ。

**Jikan o tsukuridasō to iu toki, kantan ni omoitsukisō na no ga
'suimin jikan o kezuru' to iu hōhō da.**

When one tries to make more time, what one easily may think of is
the approach of 'cutting down on sleep'.

9.5.4.2 *Adjective-root-**sō da***

See Table 6.1 for the root form of adjectives. Note that **yoi** and **nai** (including the negative ending -**nai**) are irregular, taking the form **yosasō** and
**nasasō** (see 5.2.3.2.1 a for an example).

a うまそうだね。

**Umasō da ne.**

Looks delicious.

b 「みんなマイナス三十歳」と楽しそうだった。

**'Minna mainasu sanjus-sai' to tanoshisō datta.**

They seemed to enjoy themselves, saying, 'We're all in our fifties'
(= 80 minus 30).

c 訪れた子供たちは皆、珍しそうに石うすをのぞき込んでいた。

**Otozureta kodomo-tachi wa mina, mezurashisō ni ishiusu o
nozoki-konde ita.**

The visiting children all looked into the stone mortar with [apparent]
curiosity.

---

| 9.5.4.3 | **na**-*adjective minus copula*-**sō da** |

After **na**-Adj, -**sō da** is attached directly to the noun form of a **na**-Adj, i.e.
the form without the copula (**da**, **na**, **ni**, etc.).

a 思ったより元気そう。

**Omotta yori genkisō.**

You look better than expected.

b 雪像を作るために近くから雪を運んできたが、雪合戦は大丈夫そ
うだ。

**Setsuzō o tsukuru tame ni chikaku kara yuki o hakonde kita
ga, yukigassen wa daijōbusō da.**

The snow for making the snow sculptures was brought in from nearby,
but [snow for] snowballing seems to be OK.

c 小さな体だが元気そうで安心しました。

**Chiisa na karada da ga genkisō de anshin shimashita.**

[Father of quintuplets:] They're small ('bodies') but looked healthy, so
I'm relieved.

---

| 9.5.5 | **rashii** |

**rashii** expresses two basic meanings: appearance, on the basis of hearsay,
or visual information (see 9.5.1, 9.5.2, 9.5.3, 21.2, 9.5.6), and typicality,
i.e., that something/somebody is or isn't typical of its kind.

**rashii** attaches to the end of a sentence. The forms it is attached to are plain
forms (after non-past **na**-Adj and N, it is attached without copula, except
for **N de aru rashii**). **rashii** itself changes its endings like an adjective.

The past ending -ta usually precedes **rashii**, but occasionally also follows it. **rashikatta** is mostly used when the 'appearance' itself is considered to be in the past and no longer relevant to the present. In practice, **rashikatta** is mostly found in narrative fiction, -ta **rashii** being normal elsewhere. Compare examples 9.5.5.1.1 h and i for the use of -ta **rashii** and **rashikatta**.

*Note* – there are many lexical adjectives that end in -**rashii** (see 9.5.5.3 below) but have no hearsay or typicality meaning.

| 9.5.5.1 | *Clause/noun* **rashii** |

| 9.5.5.1.1 | Clause **rashii** |

**rashii** indicates appearance in two ways.

Firstly, 'seems to', 'apparently'. **mitai** and **yō** could also be used in the same way (see 9.5.1, 9.5.6).

With **rashii**, the appearance is based on hearsay. This is similar to **sō** and -**tte**, but **rashii** is vaguer. Whereas **sō** and -**tte** express explicitly that what precedes is something you have heard said or seen written, **rashii** simply suggests that what precedes is *based* on hearsay. It is possible to indicate the source of information (see 21.3, 9.5.2).

Secondly, based on observation, **mitai** and **yō** could also be used in a similar way. However, there is a difference. **mitai** and **yō** imply that 'S seems to be the case but definitely isn't' or 'S seems to be the case but I don't actually know whether it is or not'. **rashii** implies that 'S seems to be the case and definitely is' or 'to the best of my knowledge it is'. This explains the use of N1 **rashii** N2 in 9.5.5.2 (compare examples a and b below).

a ✎日本人らしい男
  **Nihonjin rashii otoko**
  A man who appears Japanese/A typical Japanese man

b ✎日本人みたいな男
  **Nihonjin mitai na otoko**
  A man who is like a Japanese

c 同容疑者はかなり酒を飲んでいたらしい。
  **Dō yōgisha wa kanari sake o nonde ita rashii.**
  It seems that the suspect had been drinking quite a lot.

d 言葉は分からないが、金をせびっているらしい。

**Kotoba wa wakaranai ga, kane o sebitte iru rashii.**

I can't understand the words, but he seems to be pestering for money.

e 女性が価格に敏感なのは、洋の東西を問わないらしい。

**Josei ga kakaku ni binkan na no wa, yō no tōzai o towanai rashii.**

Women's sensitivity to prices seems to be the same, East or West.

f 日本では、どうも若い女性がお金持ちで旅行好きらしい。

**Nihon de wa, dōmo wakai josei ga o-kanemochi de ryokō-zuki rashii.**

In Japan, it appears that young women are well off and like travelling.

g サルの世界も頼りは "女性" らしい。

**Saru no sekai mo tayori wa 'josei' rashii.**

It seems that in the monkey world, too, 'females' are the ones to be relied on.

h 彼の家族は最初、この結婚に反対だったらしい。

**Kare no kazoku wa saisho, kono kekkon ni hantai datta rashii.**

His family was apparently opposed to this marriage at first.

i なぜなのか調べたところ、節約ムードが広がり、それまで捨てて いた食べ残しを包装材に包んで冷蔵庫に保存し、翌日に食べる 家庭が多くなったのが原因らしかった。

**Naze na no ka shirabeta tokoro, setsuyaku mūdo ga hirogari, sore made sutete ita tabenokoshi o hōsō-zai ni tsutsunde reizōko ni hozon shi, yokujitsu ni taberu kazoku ga ōku natta no ga gen'in rashikatta.**

When they checked on why this happened, the cause was apparently that in the prevailing mood of frugality, more (*lit.* "there was an increase in the number of") families [who] wrapped up the leftover food, which they used to throw away, [in wrapping material,] kept it in the fridge and ate it the following day.

9.5.5.1.2 | Noun/clause **rashii** noun

When modifying N, the meaning of **rashii** is the same as in 9.5.5.1.1 'N who/which apparently', 'seems to'. N2 is given in [ ] where not immediately following **rashii**.

a そばに遺書らしいメモが残されていた。

**Soba ni isho rashii memo ga nokosarete ita.**

Next to [the body] a note which appears to be a suicide note had
been left.

b 遠くの方で看護婦さんらしい、懸命に励ます声が聞こえる。

**Tōku no hō de kangofu-san rashii, kenmei ni hagemasu [koe]
ga kikoeru.**

In the distance, a voice urging on strongly (*lit.* "hard") was heard, which
apparently belonged to a nurse.

c 大学から流出したらしいお産のフィルムまで映していました。

**Daigaku kara ryūshutsu shita rashii osan no [firumu] made
utsushite imashita.**

They were even showing a film of a birth, which apparently had been
leaked from a university.

### 9.5.5.1.3 | Noun **rashii**

This is used when a thing, place or person is typical of its kind or reputation: 'in keeping with', 'just like'.

a フグの本場らしくフグが泳ぐ水槽も設ける。

**Fugu no honba rashiku fugu ga oyogu suisō mo mōkeru.**

In keeping with a place famous for its *fugu* (blowfish), there are going
to be tanks where *fugu* swim about.

b フランス趣味のこの人らしく、酒はワインを好む。

**Furansu shumi no kono hito rashiku, sake wa wain o konomu.**

In keeping with this man's taste for things French, his favourite
drink is wine.

c 梨の渋みも消え、昨年よりワインらしくなった。

**Nashi no shibu-mi mo kie, sakunen yori wain rashiku natta.**

The astringent taste of [Japanese] pear has disappeared, and compared
to last year it has become more like wine.

### 9.5.5.2 | *Joining two nouns*

### 9.5.5.2.1 | Noun 1 **rashii/rashikunai** noun 2 (noun 1 = noun 2)

When joining identical nouns, the meaning is 'a N typical of its kind', 'a
real/proper N', 'a N worthy of that name'.

a 夏らしい夏がなかった。
**Natsu rashii natsu ga nakatta.**
There was no real summer.

b テレビなど刺激的文化の影響で、本らしい本の衰弱が目立つ。
**Terebi nado shigeki-teki bunka no eikyō de, hon rashii hon no suijaku ga medatsu.**
Under the influence of the stimulus culture such as TV, the decline of proper books is conspicuous.

c この半年、注意らしい注意を受けたことがない。
**Kono hantoshi, chūi rashii chūi o uketa koto ga nai.**
For these six months, I haven't received anything approaching a caution.

9.5.5.2.2 | Noun I **rashii/rashikunai** noun 2

Here, the implication is that the first noun is not something that is worthy of its name, or that it is different from what you might expect of a typical example of its kind 'a typical/atypical N1', 'like/unlike N1' (N2 in [ ] where not immediately following **rashii**).

a ゴルフをはじめ、運動らしいことは一切やらない。
**Gorufu o hajime, undō rashii koto wa issai yaranai.**
Including golf, he does not take any real exercise.

b 墨田は、古い家屋が残る下町らしい街である。
**Sumida wa furui kaoku ga nokoru shitamachi rashii machi de aru.**
Sumida is a typical *shitamachi* [= old part of Tokyo] area, where old houses are still found.

c 官僚出身らしくない柔軟な発想の持ち主と定評がある。
**Kanryō shusshin rashikunai jūnan na [hassō] no mochinushi to teihyō ga aru.**
Quite unlike a former administrator, he is renowned as a flexible thinker (*lit.* "the owner of flexible thinking").

9.5.5.3 | *Lexical adjective ending in* **-rashii**

These adjectives, which do not now have any meaning of **rashii** left (but see 9.5.5.3.2), are given below.

## 9.5.5.3.1 Adjectives without the meaning of **rashii**

**airashii** 'charming', **bakarashii** 'ridiculous', **hokorashii** 'proud', **ijirashii** 'sweet', 'touching', **iyarashii** 'disgusting', **kawairashii** 'cute', **mezurashii** 'unusual', **misuborashii** 'shabby', **mottomorashii** 'plausible', **nikurashii** 'odious', **otokorashii** 'masculine', **onnarashii** 'feminine', **shiorashii** 'gentle', **wazatorashii** 'affected'.

## 9.5.5.3.2 Adjectives which can have the meaning of **rashii**

Depending on the context, **bakarashii, otokorashii, onnarashii** and **iyarashii** *could* also be N/**na**-Adj + **rashii** (in speech these would however be pronounced with a different pitch accent).

# 9.5.6 yō

The ending **yō** indicates likeness, or the way something seems (see 9.5.4, 9.5.1, 6.9.2, 9.5.2, 21.2). Predicate-selecting adverbs (see 10.2.4) such as **maru de** 'just' can be used to emphasize the degree of likeness (examples 9.5.6.1.1.1 c and 9.5.6.1.1.4 a).

**yō** itself being a structural N, it attaches to the forms of V/Adj/**na**-Adj/N that precede N, i.e. N-modifying forms. Section 9.5.6.1.1 gives V/Adj/**na**-Adj/N separately to illustrate the way **yō** attaches to sentences that end in V/Adj/**na**-Adj/N respectively (Adj includes the negative ending -**nai**, example 9.5.6.1.1.2 b).

## 9.5.6.1 yō + copula

### 9.5.6.1.1 Clause **yō da/datta/de**

The meaning is 'seems (just like)', 'is just as if', 'appear to'. To recall situations where something 'was/appeared like' at the time, **yō datta** is attached to a sentence (example c), whereas with -**ta yō da**, i.e. when **yō da** is attached to a clause ending in the -**ta** form (example d), the implication is that it appears at the present moment that some action or development is completed.

9.5.6.1.1.1 *Verb* **yō**

a ぶらりと歩くと時がゆっくり流れていくようだ。
**Burari to aruku to toki ga yukkuri nagarete iku yō da.**
When one walks aimlessly, time seems to flow slowly.

b 不況は演劇にも次第にかげりを落としているようだ。
**Fukyō wa engeki ni mo shidai ni kageri o otoshite iru yō da.**
The recession slowly seems to cast dark clouds over the theatre, too.

c まるでもう一人の自分がそこにいるようだった。
**Maru de mō hitori no jibun ga soko ni iru yō datta.**
It was just as if another self were there.

d このごろは馬とも信頼関係ができてきたようで、うまく飛べるようになった。
**Kono goro wa uma to mo shinrai kankei ga dekite kita yō de, umaku toberu yō ni natta.**
Recently, it appears that I have developed a relationship of trust with the horse, so I can now jump well.

9.5.6.1.1.2 *Adjective* **yō**

a 未婚女性は「性格」「経済力」「価値観が同じ」といった点から結婚相手を選びたい人が多いようだ。
**Mikon josei wa 'seikaku' 'keizairyoku' 'kachikan ga onaji' to itta ten kara kekkon aite o erabitai hito ga ōi yō da.**
As for unmarried women, there appear to be many who would like to choose their partner from the angles of 'personality', 'economic power' and 'sharing the same values'.

b 私が見たところ、彼女の夫のほうはまったく英語ができないようだった。
**Watashi ga mita tokoro, kanojo no otto no hō wa mattaku eigo ga dekinai yō datta.**
According to my observation, her husband seemed to have no English ability at all.

9.5.6.1.1.3 **na-***adjective* **na yō**

a 男性の方がお金にはルーズなようだ。
**Dansei no hō ga okane ni wa rūzu na yō da.**
Men seem to be more careless with money.

b 特徴のある顔は得なようです。

**Tokuchō no aru kao wa toku na yō desu.**

[Type of doll that sells well] It appears that a distinctive face is
an advantage.

---

**9.5.6.1.1.4** *Noun* **no yō**

a まるでシュールレアリスムの絵画のようだ。

**Maru de shūrurearisumu no kaiga no yō da.**

It is just like a surrealist painting.

b テニスを通じて知り合った人たちと食べるバーベキューは最高の
味のようだ。

**Tenisu o tsūjite shiriatta hito-tachi to taberu bābekyū wa
saikō no aji no yō da.**

There's nothing better than eating a barbecue with friends one has
made over a game of tennis.

---

**9.5.6.1.2** Clause **yō da ga**

This is often used to ask questions at press conferences etc. 'it seems
that . . . (how do you explain the fact that . . . ?)'

a 問 各分野で米側の提案と日本の考え方に大きな隔たりがあるよ
うだが。

**Toi Kaku bunya de Bei-gawa no teian to Nihon no kangaekata
ni ōki na hedatari ga aru yō da ga.**

Q: It seems that in all areas there is a considerable gulf between
the US proposals and Japan's way of thinking.

---

**9.5.6.2** *Noun-modifying*

**9.5.6.2.1** Clause **yō na** N

In this use, **yō na** is used to link a N-modifying clause to the modified
noun in the sense of 'sort of'; **yō na** can often be omitted without much
change in meaning.

a なべ底をはうような景気の中では、まあまあの成績ではないか。

**Nabezoko o hau yō na keiki no naka de wa, māmā no seiseki
de wa nai ka.**

In an economy which is like scraping along the bottom (*lit.* "crawling
along the bottom of a pan"), that's not such a bad result.

b 夕食にラーメンしか食べられないような時期もあったけれど、今は経済的にも楽になった。

**Yūshoku ni rāmen shika taberarenai yō na jiki mo atta keredo, ima wa keizaiteki ni mo raku ni natta.**

There was a time when I could only afford **rāmen** [soup noodles] for dinner, but now I'm financially comfortable too.

c あのビル工事のせいで家が傾いたような気がする。

**Ano biru kōji no sei de ie ga katamuita yō na ki ga suru.**

I have a feeling that my house leans because of the construction of that building.

d まるで大雨のザァーザァーという音がきこえてくるような版画じゃないか。

**Maru de ōame no zāzā to iu oto ga kikoete kuru yō na hanga ja nai ka.**

Surely this is a woodblock print which is just as if the sound of heavy rain can be heard!

e 専業主婦でいることが、後ろめたいような風潮が強まっている。

**Sengyō shufu de iru koto ga, ushirometai yō na fūchō ga tsuyomatte iru.**

The sort of atmosphere where one feels guilty for being a housewife is getting more pronounced.

f 随所に織り込んだ一見、無駄なような会話のおかしさ。

**Zuisho ni orikonda ikken, muda na yō na kaiwa no okashisa.**

The comedy of the seemingly pointless conversation, which is woven [into the film] everywhere.

---

| 9.5.6.2.2 | Adjective 1 **yō na** adjective 2 **yō na** (noun) |
| --- | --- |
| | (adjectives of opposite meaning) |

Using adjectives of opposite meaning, the resulting meaning is 'not particularly Adj1'.

a 米国とEUの仲はいいような悪いような……。

**Beikoku to Īyū no naka wa ii yō na warui yō na ...**

Relations between the US and the EU are not particularly good.

| 9.5.6.2.3 | **atte nai yō na mono** |
|---|---|

This is a way of saying '(apparently so but) not really'.

a 株価の基準はあってないようなもの。
**Kabuka no kijun wa atte nai yō na mono.**
There isn't really a basis for share prices.

b ファドは楽譜があってないようなもの。
**Fado wa gakufu ga atte nai yō na mono.**
Fado is something that doesn't really have a score but
appears to.

| 9.5.6.2.4 | Noun **no yō na** noun |
|---|---|

This is used for making similes etc. 'something like N'.

a 駿河湾は巨大ないけすのようなものです。
**Suruga-wan wa kyodai na ikesu no yō na mono desu.**
Suruga Bay is like a giant fish tank [= full of fish farms].

b 地鳴りのような音がして地面がせり上がったようだった。
**Jinari no yō na oto ga shite jimen ga seriagatta yō datta.**
There was a sound like a ground rumble, and it was as if the ground
had lifted up.

c 消費不振が深刻になっていますが、回復の兆しのようなものはあ
りますか。
**Shōhi fushin ga shinkoku ni natte imasu ga, kaifuku no kizashi
no yō na mono wa arimasu ka.**
The slump in spending is severe, but is there anything like a sign of
recovery?

| 9.5.6.3 | *Adverbial use* |
|---|---|

| 9.5.6.3.1 | Clause **yō ni** |
|---|---|

Used adverbially, the **yō ni** clause indicates how something appears (but
actually isn't) in the sense of 'like', 'as if'. The likeness can again be reinforced with **maru de** 'just'.

a 手のひらの皮は「手袋をはめたように」厚くなった。
**Te no hira no kawa wa 'tebukuro o hameta yō ni' atsuku natta.**
The skin of his palms became thick 'as if wearing gloves'.

269

b きずは、まるで消しゴムで消すようにきれいになくなった。

**Kizu wa, maru de keshigomu de kesu yō ni kirei ni naku natta.**

The wound disappeared completely, just as if wiped out by an eraser.

c マラソンや駅伝が象徴するように、情報は人間が走って伝えることから始まった。

**Marason ya ekiden ga shōchō suru yō ni, jōhō wa ningen ga hashitte tsutaeru koto kara hajimatta.**

As the marathon and *ekiden* (relay race between stations) symbolize, information began as something that humans transmitted by running.

d 上の兄のように実家を継ぐことはできない。

**Ue no ani no yō ni jikka o tsugu koto wa dekinai.**

I cannot inherit the family home like my oldest brother.

e 企業も「リストラ、リストラ」とキズの入ったレコードのように繰り返す。

**Kigyō mo 'risutora, risutora' to kizu no haitta rekōdo no yō ni kurikaesu.**

Industry too repeats 'restructuring' like a broken record.

f 欧米人から見て日本人がどこか異質なように、東京軸の人間から見るとナゴヤニアンは異質に見える。

**Ōbeijin kara mite Nihonjin ga doko ka ishitsu na yō ni, Tōkyō-jiku no ningen kara miru to Nagoyanian wa ishitsu ni mieru.**

Just as the Japanese appear somehow strange to Westerners, Nagoyans appear strange in the eyes of people from around Tokyo.

---

| 9.5.6.3.2 | dono/ika-/onaji yō ni |

In these combinations, **yō ni** means 'how', 'in what way', 'in the same way'.

a 日本の外交をどのように改革すべきだろうか。

**Nihon no gaikō o dono yō ni kaikaku subeki darō ka.**

In what way should Japan's diplomacy be reformed, I wonder?

b 立派な言葉は実はいかようにも解釈できるものだということを、後になって悟った。

**Rippa na kotoba wa jitsu wa ikayō ni mo kaishaku dekiru mono da to iu koto o, ato ni natte satotta.**

Afterwards I realized that grand words can in fact be interpreted in any way.

c みな制服を着て、同じようにほほ笑むんだ。

**Mina seifuku o kite, onaji yō ni hohoemu n da.**

You will all wear uniforms, and smile in an identical way.

---

| 9.5.6.3.3 | Adverb **no yō ni** |
|---|---|

Attached to adverbs, **yō ni** means 'almost', 'practically'.

a 当然のように外国人騎手も日本市場に熱いまなざしを寄
せる。

**Tōzen no yō ni gaikokujin kishu mo Nihon shijō ni atsui manazashi o yoseru.**

Almost as a matter of course, foreign jockeys also eye the Japanese market expectantly.

b 高過ぎる服を普通のOLが毎月のようにカードで買う。

**Taka-sugiru fuku o futsū no ōeru ga maitsuki no yō ni kādo de kau.**

Ordinary female office workers buy overpriced [designer] clothes practically every month with [credit] cards.

---

| 9.5.6.3.4 | Clause **yō ni naru** |
|---|---|

This indicates that something takes place as the result of a development or effort over time 'get to the stage where', 'now'.

a 簡単な日常会話だけなら二、三カ月でできるようになる。

**Kantan na nichijō kaiwa dake nara, ni, sankagetsu de dekiru yō ni naru.**

If it's just basic daily conversation, you can master it in two to three months.

b 両ひざは無理がたたり、水がたまるようになった。

**Ryōhiza wa muri ga tatari, mizu ga tamaru yō ni natta.**

The strain on his knees has begun to tell, and [they] are now full of water.

c 仕事人間にとどまらず、柔軟に方向転換するようになった男性の
変化は注目に値する。

**Shigoto ningen ni todomarazu, jūnan ni hōkō tenkan suru yō ni natta dansei no henka wa chūmoku ni atai suru.**

The change in men, who have now smoothly changed course, ceasing to be workaholics, is worth noting.

d なぜ地球に生物が住めるようになったのか？

**Naze chikyū ni seibutsu ga sumeru yō ni natta no ka.**

Why has it become possible for living things to live on the earth?

e これまでタブー視されがちだった同性愛が、表舞台で語られるようになっている。

**Kore made tabūshi sare-gachi datta dōseiai ga, omote butai de katarareru yō ni natte iru.**

Homosexuality, which hitherto tended to be viewed as a taboo, is now being talked about openly (*lit.* "on the front stage").

---

| 9.5.6.3.5 | Clause **yō ni omou/mieru**, etc. |

Attached to a clause that indicates a state (using -**te iru**, -**te inai**, verbs that indicate a state by themselves, and adjectives) and followed by verbs that indicate an impression), the meaning is 'seems/appears to me that'.

a 家の寿命が短くなっているように思うのです。

**Ie no jumyō ga mijikaku natte iru yō ni omou no desu.**

I feel that the lifespan of a house has become shorter.

b 運転免許のない人が乗っているように思えた。

**Unten menkyo no nai hito ga notte iru yō ni omoeta.**

It seemed to me that a person without a driving licence was driving.

c 十一年ぶりの日本はあまり変わっていないように見えた。

**Jūichinen-buri no Nihon wa amari kawatte inai yō ni mieta.**

After 11 years, Japan appeared not to have changed much.

d 日本酒って多様化しているようにみえて、実はしてないんだ。

**Nihonshu tte tayōka shite iru yō ni miete, jitsu wa shite nai n da.**

Sake seems to have diversified, but in fact it hasn't.

---

| 9.5.6.3.6 | Clause **yō ni** |

This indicates that the predicate is carried out for a purpose 'that', 'so that'.

a 来年の開港まで無事故で工事が進むように祈願していた。

**Rainen no kaikō made mujiko de kōji ga susumu yō ni kigan shite ita.**

I was praying that the construction work would proceed without accident until next year's opening.

b　文化の違いを認め、お互いに理解し合えるように、雑誌で役に立ちたい。

**Bunka no chigai o mitome, otagai ni rikai shiaeru yō ni zasshi de yaku ni tachitai.**

I want to be useful through the magazine, so that we can realize the cultural differences and understand each other.

c　サラリーマンも通えるように、午後九時まで授業をする。

**Sararīman mo kayoeru yō ni, gogo kuji made jugyō o suru.**

They teach classes until 9 p.m. so that office workers can attend too.

---

9.5.6.3.7 | Clause **yō ni suru**, etc.

Followed by **suru** and some other verbs such as **kokorogakeru** 'try', the meaning is 'decide to', 'make a point of', 'try'.

a　そこで、父親に毎日手紙を書くようにした。

**Soko de, chichioya ni mainichi tegami o kaku yō ni shita.**

So I decided to write to my father every day.

b　週二度は映画館に通い、五本はビデオを見るように心掛けている。

**Shū ni-do wa eigakan ni kayoi, go-hon wa bideo o miru yō ni kokorogakete iru.**

I try to go to the movies at least twice a week, and watch at least five videos.

---

9.5.6.3.8 | Clause **yō ni**

Ending a sentence, **yō ni** indicates obligation 'should' (attached to an ending in a V form).

a　まず四月には店員ならだれでも包装できるように。それからだれでも店の中を案内できるように。

**Mazu shigatsu ni wa ten'in nara dare demo hōsō dekiru yō ni. Sore kara dare demo mise no naka o annai dekiru yō ni.**

First of all, by April every employee should be able to wrap things. Then, everyone should be able to show customers around the store.

| 9.5.6.4 | **ka no yō** |

This is similar in meaning to the equivalent sentence without **ka no**, but the addition of the question particle **ka** makes the S **no yō** sentences somewhat more tentative or hypothetical 'as if'.

| 9.5.6.4.1 | Clause **ka no yō da/data** |

a まるで群れに「見えざる力」が働いたかのようだ。

**Maru de mure ni 'miezaru chikara' ga hataraita ka no yō da.**

It is just as if an 'invisible force' worked in the herd.

b とつとつと説明する医者の声はどこか遠くから聞こえて来るかの
ようだった。

**Totsutotsu to setsumei suru isha no koe wa doko ka tōku
kara kikoete kuru ka no yō datta.**

The voice of the doctor, who was giving a faltering explanation,
seemed to come from a long way away.

| 9.5.6.4.2 | Clause **ka no yō na** N |

The meaning here is 'as if'.

a 人は、実際に体験していなくても、まるで自分が体験したかのよ
うな記憶を作り出してしまうことがある。

**Hito wa, jissai ni taiken shite inakute mo, maru de jibun ga
taiken shita ka no yō na kioku o tsukuridashite shimau koto
ga aru.**

Humans sometimes create a memory as if they had experienced
something, even if they actually haven't.

| 9.5.6.4.3 | Clause **ka no yō ni** |

This construction too means 'as if'.

a 日本の国際化と歩調を合わせるかのように、外国人観光客も秋葉
原を多く訪れるようになった。

**Nihon no kokusai-ka to hochō o awaseru ka no yō ni,
gaikokujin kankō-kyaku mo Akihabara o ōku otozureru yō
ni natta.**

As if keeping pace with Japan's internationalization, foreign tourists also
come to visit Akihabara in large numbers.

b 飲み屋でUFOの話をしていると、見知らぬ人が百年の知己に
   会ったかのように「私も見たんですよ」と話し掛けてく
   るという。

**Nomiya de yufo no hanashi o shite iru to, mishiranu hito ga
hyakunen no chiki ni atta ka no yō ni 'watashi mo mita n
desu yo' to hanashi-kakete kuru to iu.**

They say that if you mention UFOs in a drinking place, total
strangers will talk to you as if they were old friends, saying,
'I've seen them too'.

**9.5.7** | yō, mitai, sō, -sō, rashii, -tte *compared*

9.5.7.1 | *Forms with which they combine*

**Table 9.1** Forms to which **yō**, **mitai**, **sō**, **-sō**, **rashii**, **-tte** attach

| Form | Group | Pattern |
|------|-------|---------|
| **na**-Adj/N + | I Directly | na-Adj/N **mitai da** |
| | | na-Adj/N **rashii** |
| | | na-Adj-**sō da** |
| | II By means of **no/na** | na-Adj **na**/N **no yō da** |
| | III By means of **da** | na-Adj/N **da sō da** |
| | | na-Adj/N **da-tte** |
| + N | I Directly | **rashii** N |
| | II By means of **na** | **yō na** N |
| | | **mitai na** N |
| | | **sō na** N |
| | III NOT POSSIBLE | (**sō da**) |
| **-ta** form (non-narrative use) | | |
| | I Before | **-ta yō da** |
| | | **-ta mitai da** |
| | | **-ta rashii** |
| | | **-ta sō da** |
| | | **-ta-tte** |
| | II After | **-sō dat-ta** |

**Table 9.1** (cont'd)

| Form | Group | Pattern |
|---|---|---|
| **-ta** form (narrative use) | | |
| | | yō dat-ta |
| | | mitai dat-ta |
| | | rashikat-ta |
| | | sō na |
| **-nai** form | I Before | -nai yō da |
| | | -nai mitai da |
| | | -nai rashii |
| | | -nai sō da |
| | | -nai-tte |
| | | -na-sa-sō da |
| | II After | -sō ni nai |
| **desu/-masu** form | I Before | yō desu |
| | | mitai desu |
| | | sō desu |
| | | -sō desu |
| | | rashii desu |
| | II After | masu-tte |

---

**9.5.7.2** | *Core meaning*

| | | |
|---|---|---|
| Hearsay: | | **sō da, -tte, rashii** |
| Typicality: | | **rashii** |
| Visual: | imminent | |
| | (and quite certain) | **-sō da** |
| Other: | ...but isn't | **yō da, mitai da** |
| | ...but don't know | **yō da, mitai da** |
| | ...and is | **rashii** |
| | + Adj. (neutral) | **-sō da** |

---

**9.5.7.3** | *Special uses*

Illness: 'I think I've got a cold' is **Kaze o hiita yō da.**
(not **hiita to omou!**)

Imminent: 'I think I'm going to be sick' **Haki-sō da.**
(not **haku to omou!**)

## 9.5.8 | *gotoshi: written style variant of yō*

**gotoshi** is like a noun in that it is preceded by the case particle **no** (and occasionally still the classical genitive particle **ga**), but inflects like a classical adjective (see 28.4), ending in -**shi** (final form) and -**ki** (N-modifying form). It can nowadays also be followed by forms of the copula.

Like **yō**, **gotoshi** indicates a simile (likening two things or situations) in the sense of 'like', but has a written-language ring to it, with the exception of the pejorative 9.5.8.4 use.

### 9.5.8.1 | **gotoshi** *(+ copula)*

**gotoshi** can be attached to N + **no**, [S]-verb ending in V-**ru** + **ga**, or the Adj-i classical equivalent Adj-**ki** + **ga** in the set phrase **atte naki ga gotoshi** (example c), which is a written-style equivalent of **atte nai yō na mono** 'virtually non-existent' (see 9.5.6.2.3).

a 難しい政局だけど、心は鉄石のごとしだ。
   **Muzukashii seikyoku da kedo, kokoro wa tesseki no gotoshi da.**
   It's a difficult political situation, but my resolve is like steel.

b 「人生は重荷を負いて遠き道を行くがごとし、が今の心境」と言う。
   **'Jinsei wa omoni o oite tōki michi o yuku ga gotoshi ga ima no shinkyō' to iu.**
   He said, 'My feeling at the moment is that life is like going along a road with a heavy burden'.

c おれの田舎じゃ、誕生日やクリスマスなんてあってなきがごとしだけど。
   **Ore no inaka ja, tanjōbi ya Kurisumasu nante atte naki ga gotoshi da kedo.**
   In my part of the country, events like birthdays and Christmas are virtually non-existent.

### 9.5.8.2 | *Noun* **no gotoki** *noun*

This indicates the idea of 'like', making a simile in the same way as N **no yō na** N (see 9.5.6.2.4).

a いずれも過度の単純化による妄想、神話のごときものとされる。
   **Izure mo kado no tanjun-ka ni yoru mōsō, shinwa no gotoki mono to sareru.**
   Both ['supplysiders' and 'strategic traders'] are said to be something like a delusion or myth, caused by oversimplification.

b 読者は著者のとどまることを知らぬ発想にのせられ、ジェットコ
ースターのごとき快楽を味わうことになる。

**Dokusha wa chosha no todomaru koto o shiranu hassō ni noserare, jettokōsutā no gotoki kairaku o ajiwau koto ni naru.**

The reader is made to ride on the author's boundless [flow of] ideas, and ends up enjoying himself like being on a roller coaster.

---

| 9.5.8.3 | *Clause* **ka no gotoki** *noun* |

The combination S **ka no gotoki** N is equivalent to the more colloquial S **ka no yō na** N 'as if' (see 9.5.6.4.2). In example b, the N after the first **gotoki** is ellipted (omitted) because it is identical to the second one.

a 国会議員の名誉を傷付けるかのごとき質問は残念だ。

**Kokkai gi-in no meiyo o kizutsukeru ka no gotoki shitsumon wa zannen da.**

A question that looks as if [posed] to damage the reputation of an MP is regrettable.

b 政治家と官僚が対等であるかのごとき、争っているかのごとき
状態は自然ではない。

**Seijika to kanryō ga taitō de aru ka no gotoki, arasotte iru ka no gotoki jōtai wa shizen de wa nai.**

A state of affairs where politicians and administrators seem on an equal footing, and seem to compete, is unnatural.

---

| 9.5.8.4 | *Noun-***gotoki** + *particle* |

In this use, **gotoki** is used like a suffix, with a pejorative ring, in the sense of 'someone/something like'. The particle following **gotoki** is the one required by the valency of the V.

a 外国人ごときに何が分かるか。

**Gaikokujin-gotoki ni nani ga wakaru ka.**

How can a foreigner possibly understand [= my paintings]?

b メダカごときで人が呼べるのかね。

**Medaka-gotoki de hito ga yoberu no ka ne.**

Can we attract visitors with something [as lowly as] *medaka*?
[= a small freshwater fish]?

## 9.6 Evaluative

### 9.6.1 n(o) da

Adding **no da** (or the colloquial contraction **n da**) to the end of a sentence gives the sentence an explanatory force. In questions, it is typically used for eliciting/confirming information. However, the force of **n(o) da** is rarely captured in translation.

The forms preceding **n(o) da** are N-modifying forms, **except** that nouns insert **na** before **no**, just as na-Adj regularly do.

**n(o) da** itself changes in the same way as copula, i.e. polite **n(o) desu**, past **n(o) datta**, presumptive **n(o) darō**, etc. (see 7.5).

#### 9.6.1.1 n(o) da *in statements*

a 酷寒があるからこそ春の到来が待たれるのだ。
**Kokkan ga aru kara koso haru no tōrai ga matareru no da.**
Precisely because there is severe cold, one waits for the coming of spring (*lit.* "the advent of spring is awaited").

b 連絡がないが、彼女はどうしたのだろう。
**Renraku ga nai ga, kanojo wa dō shita no darō.**
There is no contact – I wonder what has happened to her.

c 若い世代はもはや政府の力など信用していないのだ。
**Wakai sedai wa mohaya seifu no chikara nado shin'yō shite inai no da.**
The young generation no longer believes in the power of the government.

d 新しいオペラ座がテレビで紹介されたんだぜ。
**Atarashii operaza ga terebi de shōkai sareta n da ze.**
The new opera house was introduced on TV, you know.

#### 9.6.1.2 n(o) desu ka *or* n(o) ka *in questions*

When used in questions, the form is **n(o) desu ka** or the plain form **no ka** (**no da ka** is not a standard form). This is used when asking for an explanation, in either direct or indirect questions (see 19.3, 18.1, 18.3).

a 私たちの生活はどうなるのですか。
**Watashi-tachi no seikatsu wa dō naru no desu ka.**
What's going to happen to our livelihood?

b インフラとは何を意味するのか。
**Infura to wa nani o imi suru no ka.**
What does 'infra' mean?

c どうして来なかったのか説明してほしい。
**Dōshite konakatta no ka setsumei shite hoshii.**
I want you to explain why you didn't come.

d 景気は本当によくなったんですか。
**Keiki wa hontō ni yoku natta n desu ka.**
Has business really picked up?

e 情報ハイウェーには光ファイバー網が必要なのですか。
**Jōhō haiuē ni wa hikari faibāmō ga hitsuyō na no desu ka.**
Is an optic fibre network necessary for the information superhighway?

---

| 9.6.2 | hazu |
|---|---|

**hazu** is originally a noun, and like other structural nouns is therefore preceded and followed by forms and particles that precede and follow nouns.

**hazu** expresses the speaker's conviction regarding the likelihood of an action or situation occurring, on the basis of some objective information, knowledge or common sense: 'is supposed to'. The speaker is not simply making a guess, as with the more subjective **darō** or **kamoshirenai** (see 9.1.2).

| 9.6.2.1 | *Clause* **hazu** |
|---|---|

| 9.6.2.1.1 | Clause **hazu da** |
|---|---|

Completing a sentence with a form of the copula, this means 'is/can be expected', 'should', 'ought to'. When applied to past-tense situations, **hazu da** is attached to the -ta form (example e).

a 外国産米が安ければ買うはずだ。
**Gaikoku-san-mai ga yasukereba kau hazu da.**
If foreign rice is cheap, people ought to buy it.

b　英文の論文誌なら世界中の科学者が目を通すはずだ。

　　**Eibun no ronbunshi nara sekai-jū no kagakusha ga me o tōsu hazu da.**

　　If it's [published] in an English-language journal, scientists throughout the world can be expected to look at it.

c　平和の嫌いな人間はいないはずだ。

　　**Heiwa no kirai na ningen wa inai hazu da.**

　　There are probably no human beings who dislike peace.

d　子供たちも転校はつらいはずだ。

　　**Kodomo-tachi mo tenkō wa tsurai hazu da.**

　　Changing schools must be hard for the children, too.

e　この現状を変えるのが政治改革の目的だったはずだ。

　　**Kono genjō o kaeru no ga seiji kaikaku no mokuteki datta hazu da.**

　　Changing this situation [of there being too many MPs] should have been the aim of political reform.

f　平和主義と国際主義は本来、コインの裏表のように一体のはずだ。

　　**Heiwa shugi to kokusai shugi wa honrai, koin no uraomote no yō ni ittai no hazu da.**

　　Pacifism and internationalism ought to have been one and the same thing from the beginning, like the two sides of a coin.

| 9.6.2.1.2 | Clause 1 **hazu da ga**, clause 2 |
|---|---|

In compound sentences joined by the conjunctive particle ga, S1 and S2 are contrastive in nature (see 26.4.1).

a　「光は直進する」はずだが、ブラックホールの周りでは光も曲がる。

　　**'Hikari wa chokushin suru' hazu da ga, burakku hōru no mawari de wa hikari mo magaru.**

　　Light is supposed to travel straight, but in the vicinity of a black hole, light also curves.

b　大阪が世界に誇れるのは"食"のはずだが、それを知っている外国人は少ない。

　　**Ōsaka ga sekai ni hokoreru no wa 'shoku' no hazu da ga, sore o shitte iru gaikokujin wa sukunai.**

　　What Osaka can boast about to the world is its food, but there aren't many foreigners who know this.

c 近代になって封建制はとっくに終わったはずだが、女性にはまだ
近代はない。

**Kindai ni natte hōkensei wa tokku ni owatta hazu da ga, josei
ni wa mada kindai wa nai.**

With the advent of the modern age the feudal system is supposed to
have long ended, but for women there is as yet no modern age.

---

9.6.2.1.3    Clause **hazu datta/datta ga/datta** Noun/**datta**

Here, the contrast is either implied, or made clear in the remainder of the
sentence 'was supposed to . . . (but actually)'.

a 地震さえなければ二人そろって学校に通っていたはずだった。

**Jishin sae nakereba futari sorotte gakkō ni kayotte ita hazu
datta.**

If there hadn't been the earthquake, the two were supposed to go to
school together.

b 彼女は幸せな結婚生活を送っているはずだったが ······。

**Kanojo wa shiawase na kekkon seikatsu o okutte iru hazu
datta ga ...**

She was supposed to have been leading a happy married life, but ...

c 父は仏壇屋の長男として家業を継ぐべきはずだったが、文学を
志し、東京に出てきた。

**Chichi wa butsudanya no chōnan to shite kagyō o tsugubeki
hazu datta ga, bungaku o kokorozashi, Tōkyō ni dete kita.**

As the oldest son of a Buddhist altar shop father was supposed to
take over the family business, but he aspired to be a writer and
came to Tokyo.

---

9.6.2.1.4    Clause **hazu ga/wa nai**

With the case particle **ga** or the adverbial particle **wa** + negative, the meaning is 'can't (possibly)'. As **hazu ga nai** carries a stronger conviction than
**hazu wa nai**, the difference can often be rendered in translation by adding
'possibly' for **hazu ga nai**.

a 法務局が不備な書類を受け付けるはずがない。

**Hōmukyoku ga fubi na shorui o uketsukeru hazu ga nai.**

The Legal Affairs Bureau can't possibly accept documents that are not
in order.

b 世界貿易拡大が悪いニュースであるはずはない。

**Sekai-bōeki kakudai ga warui nyūsu de aru hazu wa nai.**

An expansion of world trade can't be bad news.

c 一年足らずで四つの内閣ができるような国を世界が信用するはず
がない。

**Ichinen tarazu de yottsu no naikaku ga dekiru yō na kuni o
sekai ga shin'yō suru hazu ga nai.**

The world can't possibly be expected to trust a country that has had
four governments in less than a year.

d ⋯大量の資料が送られてきた。「ここの生産性は驚くほど高い。
日本も見習え」。「そんなはずはない」と最初は思ったが、
「資料を読むうちに、本当だと考え直した」。

**... tairyō no shiryō ga okurarete kita. 'Koko no seisan-sei wa
odoroku hodo takai. Nihon mo minarae.' 'Sonna hazu wa
nai' to saisho wa omotta ga, 'Shiryō o yomu uchi ni, hontō
da to kangaenaoshita'.**

I was sent a large amount of material. 'The productivity in this
company is amazingly high. Japan should learn from this.'
In the beginning I thought, 'That can't possibly be', but as I was
reading the material, I changed my mind.

---

| 9.6.2.1.5 | Verb-**nai hazu ga/wa nai** |

The combination V-neg and **hazu ga/wa nai** usually amounts to a positive
meaning 'must surely', 'can't but' (see 17.2).

a 政府がいつまでも約束を守らないはずはない。

**Seifu ga itsu made mo yakusoku o mamoranai
hazu wa nai.**

The government can't go on forever not keeping its promises.

b ニューファミリー、友達夫婦という言葉を生み出していった家庭
で育った子供たちがその影響を受けないはずがない。

**Nyū Famirī, tomodachi fūfu to iu kotoba o umidashite itta
katei de sodatta kodomo-tachi ga sono eikyō o ukenai hazu
ga nai.**

Children who were raised in a household that produced expressions
like New Family and Husband and Wife as Friends must surely be
influenced by that.

**9.6.3** | ni chigai nai

Attached to sentences, **ni chigai nai** indicates that the speaker is guessing with conviction, i.e. is convinced that his statement is true 'no doubt is', 'must be'. The forms to which **ni chigai nai** is attached are the forms used before nouns, except that **na-Adj/N** are used minus the copula.

The difference between this form and **hazu** (see 9.6.2) is that whereas **hazu** is used when the speaker bases the guess on some evidence (including common sense), **ni chigai nai** can be used with more subjective guesses that are not necessarily backed up by evidence.

a 西洋の陶磁器の歴史を多少なりともかじるか、もしくはギリシャ
の歴史に興味を持っている方なら、聞いたことがあるにちがい
ない。アンフォラ (amphora).
**Seiyō no tōjiki no rekishi o tashō nari tomo kajiru ka,
moshiku wa girisha no rekishi ni kyōmi o motte iru kata
nara, kiita koto ga aru ni chigai nai. Anfōra.**
Anyone who has read anything about the history of Western ceramics,
or has the slightest interest in the history of Greece, will have
heard this [word] before: 'amphora'.

b それは関西空港のハブ空港化にとって、ひとつの大きな障害とな
るにちがいない。
**Sore wa Kansai kūkō no habu kūkō-ka ni totte, hitotsu no ōki
na shōgai to naru ni chigai nai.**
That [= the expensive landing fees] will without doubt be a big
obstacle to Kansai becoming a hub airport.

c 地球からは衝突を直接観測できないといわれても、天文ファンの
目は夜空に注がれるにちがいない。
**Chikyū kara wa shōtotsu o chokusetsu kansoku dekinai to
iwarete mo, tenmon fan no me wa yozora ni sosogareru ni
chigai nai.**
Even if told that the collision cannot directly be observed from the
earth, amateur astronomers will no doubt have their eyes fixed on
the night sky.

d 世界遺産登録の観光効果は今後じわじわと出てくるにちがいない。
**Sekai isan tōroku no kankō kōka wa kongo jiwajiwa to dete
kuru ni chigai nai.**
The tourism effect of being registered as a World Heritage [site] will
no doubt appear gradually from now on.

e 「何かあったにちがいない」と社内では大騒ぎ。

**'Nani ka atta ni chigai nai' to shanai de wa ōsawagi.**

There was quite an uproar in the company '[with people saying] that
'something must have happened'.

---

| 9.6.4 | wake |

The ending **wake** is a structural noun, and as such is preceded/followed
by forms that precede or follow nouns. It is used when the speaker realizes
that there is an explanation or reason for some occurrence or phenomenon
(see also 9.6.2, 9.6.5).

---

| 9.6.4.1 | *Clause **wake** copula* |

| 9.6.4.1.1 | Clause **wake da** |

This indicates realization, based on information previously mentioned, 'so',
'then'.

a その意味では共に正しかったわけだ。

**Sono imi de wa tomo ni tadashikatta wake da.**

In that sense [those pointing out the pros and cons of the 1950s
conservative movement] were both right.

b ガムランは伝統的音楽の要素を持ちながら、現代音楽でもあるわ
けだ。

**Gamuran wa dentō-teki ongaku no yōso o mochinagara,
gendai ongaku de mo aru wake da.**

So gamelan, while having elements of traditional music, is also modern
music.

c 考えてみれば、国語辞典は日本人だけでなく外国人も利用し、
その人たちは、「日本語辞典」あるいは「日日辞典」として読
んでいるわけだ。

**Kangaete mireba, kokugo jiten wa Nihonjin dake de
naku gaikokujin mo riyō shi, sono hito-tachi wa,
'Nihongo jiten' arui wa 'Nichi-Nichi jiten' to shite yonde
iru wake da.**

When you think about it, not only Japanese but foreigners too, use
dictionaries of our language, and these people read them as
'Japanese language dictionaries' or 'Japanese–Japanese dictionaries'.

9.6.4.1.2 | Clause **wake da ga**,...

With the conjunctive particle **ga** attached, the meaning is 'so/then . . . , but' (see 26.4.1).

a 科学技術のおかげでめざましい経済成長ができたわけだが、
環境問題を引き起こしてしまった。

**Kagaku gijutsu no okage de mezamashii keizai seichō ga
dekita wake da ga, kankyō mondai o hikiokoshite
shimatta.**

So thanks to technology we have achieved phenomenal economic
growth, but ended up causing environmental problems.

b 「一人または数人」とあれば、二人でもいいわけだが、最大値は分
からない。

**'Hitori mata wa sūnin' to areba, futari de mo ii wake da ga,
saidaichi wa wakaranai.**

If it states 'one or several people', then two people are OK, but one
doesn't know the maximum figure [of people to be hired].

9.6.4.2 | *Clause* **wake ga/wa nai**

Being a structural noun, **wake** can attach the particle **wa** or **ga**, meaning
literally "there's no reason that". **wake ga/wa nai** can be used after positive
and negative forms. The latter is a case of double negative (see 17.2),
meaning 'there is no way that . . . not'.

9.6.4.2.1 | Clause **wake ga nai**

This is more emphatic than **wake wa nai** 'there is *no* way that'.

a 政府自身の改革を政府にできるわけがない。

**Seifu jishin no kaikaku o seifu ni dekiru wake ga nai.**

There is no way that the government itself can carry out a reform of
government.

b 市民に愛されない温泉が、観光客に愛されるわけがない。

**Shimin ni aisarenai onsen ga, kankōkyaku ni aisareru wake
ga nai.**

There is no way that a hot spring resort that is not loved by its
citizens will be loved by tourists.

c 最初は「なんてこと引き受けたんだろう」と思いましたけど、
　みんなとなら成功しないわけがないと思っています。

**Saisho wa 'Nante koto hikiuketa n darō' to omoimashita
kedo, minna to nara seikō shinai wake ga nai to omotte
imasu.**

In the beginning I thought 'What on earth have I taken on?'. But I feel
that if I do it together with everyone else there is no way we won't
be successful.

---

**9.6.4.2.2** | Clause **wake wa nai**

This is less emphatic than **wake ga nai** 'there is no way that . . .'.

a 上司が知らないわけはない。

**Jōshi ga shiranai wake wa nai.**

There's no way the superiors don't know [of their subordinates' illegal
doings].

b アルコールとストレスの複合効果が健康に良いわけはない。

**Arukōru to sutoresu no fukugō kōka ga kenkō ni yoi wake
wa nai.**

There's no way the combined effects of alcohol and stress are good
for one's health.

c 通報を受けた警察は「歩道を車が走るわけはない」と事故に関心
　を示さなかった。

**Tsūhō o uketa keisatsu wa 'Hodō o kuruma ga hashiru wake
wa nai' to jiko ni kanshin o shimesanakatta.**

The police who received the notification said, 'There's no way that
a car would drive on the pavement', and didn't show any interest
in the accident.

---

**9.6.4.3** | *Clause* **wake de wa nai**

This means 'it is not (the case) that'.

a 田舎に戻っても親しい友達がいるわけではない。

**Inaka ni modotte mo shitashii tomodachi ga iru wake de
wa nai.**

Even if I go back to my home town, it's not that I have [any] good
friends [there].

b ···何のための規制緩和か。規制といってもすべての規制が悪いわ
　けではない。

**...nan no tame no kisei kanwa ka. Kisei to itte mo subete no
kisei ga warui wake de wa nai.**

...[The question is,] relaxation of restrictions to what end? It's not
the case that all restrictions are bad.

c 第一、長く連れ添った女房殿との間にそんなに話題があるわけで
　はない。

**Daiichi, nagaku tsuresotta nyōbō-dono to no aida ni sonna ni
wadai ga aru wake de wa nai.**

To start with, it's not that there is all that much to talk about with
one's wife of many years.

---

9.6.4.4 | *Clause* **wake ni wa ikanai**

This indicates a social obligation 'it won't do to', 'I can't', 'it's not right
to'. (For other ways to say 'can't', see 14, 9.6.2.1.4).

a 投票は国民の義務だから、棄権するわけにはいかない。

**Tōhyō wa kokumin no gimu da kara, kiken suru wake ni wa
ikanai.**

Voting is the people's duty, so not exercising one's right won't do.

b タバコはやめられないけど、人に迷惑をかけるわけにはいか
　ないし ·······。

**Tabako wa yamerarenai kedo, hito ni meiwaku o kakeru wake
ni wa ikanai shi ...**

I can't stop smoking, but it isn't right to inconvenience others ...

c 暇な時にまとめて睡眠を取るというわけにはいかないんです。

**Hima na toki ni matomete suimin o toru to iu wake ni wa
ikanai n desu.**

One can't catch up on one's sleep all in one go when one has time.

---

9.6.5 | **wake** *and* **hazu:** *compared*

**hazu** is used in statements when the speaker's judgement is based on confirmed information, knowledge or simply good common sense. In contrast,
**wake** is used when the speaker realizes that some fact or occurrence is the
result of some other fact or occurrence.

a 外国産米が安ければ買うはずだ。

**Gaikoku-san-mai ga yasukereba kau hazu da.**

If foreign rice is cheap, people ought to buy it.

b その意味では共に正しかったわけだ。

**Sono imi de wa tomo ni tadashikatta wake da.**

In that sense both [those pointing out the pros and cons of the 1950s conservative movement] were right, then.

# Chapter 10

# *Adverbs*

## 10.1   **Adverbs: by derivation**

Adverbs are a class of words that modify verbs and other predicates, typically indicating when, how, where, by what means, to what degree, etc. the action or state of the verb takes place (see 10.2).

*Note* – in Japanese, adverbs always come before the predicates they modify.

Formally, adverbs can be divided into six main types, depending on what word class they are, or from what word class they are derived: adjective-stem, **na**-adjective-derived, **no**-adjective-derived, onomatope, verb-derived, and noun used as adjective.

### 10.1.1   *Adjective-stem*

Here, the stem form of an adjective is used as an adverb (see 6.1).

a 同じ部品を大量に購入すれば安く買える。
  **Onaji buhin o tairyō ni kōnyū sureba yasuku kaeru.**
  If you buy the same part in large numbers, you can buy it cheaply.

### 10.1.2   *na-adjective-derived adverb*

Adverbs derived from **na**-adjectives attach the adverbial form of the copula, ni (see 7.5).

a きれいに洗ってから二度漬けをする。
  **Kirei ni aratte kara nido-zuke o suru.**
  After you've washed it carefully, you pickle it a second time.

## 10.1.3 Adverb derived from no-adjective

no-adjectives attach the conjunctive form of the copula, **de**, to form adverbs (see 6.4, 7.5).

a 猛暑のせいか裸で寝るのが癖になった。

**Mōsho no sei ka hadaka de neru no ga kuse ni natta.**

Possibly because of the heatwave, I've developed the habit of sleeping naked.

## 10.1.4 Onomatope as adverbs

Many onomatope (= sound symbolism words) can be used as adverbs.

*Note* – onomatope are also used in a variety of other ways, with forms of the copula or **suru** as predicates, attaching **to shita**, etc. to modify N, etc. (see 6.6.7, 28.3).

Depending on the individual onomatope word, it can be used as an adverb unchanged, attach the adverbial particle **to** optionally or have it 'built in', i.e. end in **to**. Before **suru/naru**, the adverbial form **ni** of the copula is required (see 11.7, 7.6.1.10, 7.5).

| | |
|---|---|
| Unchanged: | **sukkari** 'completely', **wazawaza** 'purposely' |
| Ending in **to**: | **chanto** 'properly', **sotto** 'softly' |
| Optional **to**: | **yukkuri** (**to**) 'leisurely', **pikapika** (**to**) 'sparkling', 'flashing' |

### 10.1.4.1 Unchanged

a すっかり眠気が覚めてしまった。

**Sukkari nemuke ga samete shimatta.**

My sleepiness is totally gone.

### 10.1.4.2 Ending in **to**

a 日ごろ、ちゃんと悩みを聞いてやってるの？。

**Higoro, chanto nayami o kiite yatteru no?**

Do you always listen properly to his problems?

$\boxed{10.1.4.3}$ *With optional* **to**

a 頭の中がぴかぴかと光った。(Could also be: ぴかぴか光った。)
**Atama no naka ga pikapika to hikatta.** (Also: **pikapika hikatta.**)
There was a flash of light inside my head (*lit.* "The inside of my head
flashed like a spark").

$\boxed{10.1.4.4}$ *Before* **suru/naru**

Here, the adverbial form **ni** of the copula is required (see 7.6.1.10, 7.5).

a ゴルフをしないとよぼよぼになる。
**Gorufu o shinai to yoboyobo ni naru.**
If I don't play golf, I become decrepit.

$\boxed{10.1.5}$ **Verb-derived adverbs**

Verb-derived adverbs can be divided into two types: those ending in -**te**,
and reduplicated forms (i.e. formed by repeating the same verb).

$\boxed{10.1.5.1}$ *Those using the verb-**te** form*

These include **hajimete** 'for the first time', **kiwamete** 'extremely', **sugurete**
'exceedingly', etc.

a 百人一首ではじめて遊んだのは。
**Hyakunin isshu de hajimete asonda no wa.**
When did you first play *hyakunin-isshu* [= card game matching parts of
famous poems]?

b 石油会社の回答はきわめて明解だ。
**Sekiyu-gaisha no kaitō wa kiwamete meikai da.**
The reply from the oil company is extremely clear.

$\boxed{10.1.5.2}$ *Those formed by reduplicating verb*

Below are some examples of the very limited number of such formations.
Note that if the verb begins with a consonant that can be voiced (k, s, t,

etc.), voicing often occurs as part of the word-formation process (**kawaru-gawaru** is an example of this).

> **osoreru** 'fear'    **osoru-osoru** 'timidly' (cf., **osoru-beki** 'frightening')
> **kawaru** 'change'   **kawaru-gawaru** 'in turn'
> **miru** 'see'      **miru-miru** 'as you look on', 'fast'

a 二人の顔からみるみる血の気が引くのが分かる。

  **Futari no kao kara mirumiru chinoke ga hiku no ga wakaru.**

  You can see the colour ebbing fast from both their faces.

b 五十年前、外貨不足時代におそるおそるスタートした海外旅行自由化。

  **Gojūnen mae, gaika-busoku jidai ni osoru-osoru sutāto shita kaigai ryokō jiyūka.**

  The liberalization of foreign travel, which started timidly fifty years ago in the age when we were short of foreign currency.

### 10.1.6 | *Noun as adverb*

These are mainly nouns of time (as which they can attach case particles), but as adverbs of time they are used without case particles, except for **ni** with certain items (see 10.2.3).

## 10.2 Adverbs: by meaning

By meaning, adverbs can be divided into a number of groups (reduplicated forms – such as **osoru-osoru** – are hyphenated). Note that some adverbs can belong to more than one group.

### 10.2.1 | *Adverbs of manner*

These indicate the way some action is performed. They include **kirei ni** 'neatly', 'carefully', **sukkari** 'completely', **yukkuri** 'in a leisurely way', **osoru-osoru** 'timidly', etc. Many of these are onomatope by origin (see 28.3).

a 気になってゆっくり眠れない。

  **Ki ni natte yukkuri nemurenai.**

  I worry, and can't sleep well (*lit.* "in a leisurely way").

b 一人の生徒が教卓のまわりをきれいに掃除していた。

**Hitori no seito ga kyōtaku no mawari o kirei ni sōji shite ita.**

A pupil was cleaning the area around the teacher's desk carefully.

---

### 10.2.2 Adverbs of degree

As their name suggests, these indicate the degree to which the word they modify applies.

Note that some of these have other meanings and uses as well (e.g. **hotondo** can be used as a N 'the majority', and **taihen** 'great'/**kekkō** 'fine' as **na**-Adj).

Japanese has no comparative or superlative forms like the English 'longer, longest'; instead, adv. of degree like **motto** 'more' and **ichiban** 'most'/**mottomo** 'most' are used (see 6.7).

Common adv. of degree include the following: **daibu** 'plenty', 'pretty much', **hijō ni** 'very', **hotondo** 'almost', **ichiban** 'most', **issai** 'completely', **jitsu ni** 'very', **kanari/kekkō** 'quite', **kiwamete** 'extremely', **motto** 'more', **mottomo** 'most', **sukkari** 'totally', **taihen/totemo/sugoku** 'very', **takusan** 'a lot', **wazuka (ni)** 'by a whisker', **zuibun** 'quite', etc.

a とても軟らかい。

**Totemo yawarakai.**

[It's] very soft.

b 欧州の空港に行くと、ジャンボはほとんどいない。

**Ōshū no kūkō ni iku to, janbo wa hotondo inai.**

When you go to European airports, there are almost no jumbos.

---

### 10.2.3 Adverbs/nouns of time and frequency

#### 10.2.3.1 Adverbs (nouns) of time and frequency

Some of these adverbs can also be used as nouns, with case particles attached (e.g. **asa** 'morning', **hiru** 'noon', **yoru** 'night', **haru** 'spring', **natsu** 'summer', **aki** 'autumn', **fuyu** 'winter', **ima** 'now', **mukashi** 'olden times', and certain number + counter combinations such as **sanji(-goro)** '(about) 3 o'clock' (see 4.1, 4.2).

Here are the more common adverbs and N of time and frequency: **araka-jime** 'in advance', **hajime ni** 'first', **ima** 'now', 'currently', **ima ni mo** 'any time now', **kono aida** 'the other day', **kono hodo** 'recently', **kono tokoro** 'lately', **mada** 'not yet', **mamonaku** 'soon', **mare ni** 'rarely', **mata** 'again', **mō** 'already', **mukashi** 'in the past', **ōi ni** 'a lot', **saigo ni** 'last', **saikin** 'recently', **saisho (ni)** 'first of all', **saki(hodo)** 'earlier', **sakki** 'a little earlier', **shiba-shiba** 'frequently', **shotchū** 'all the time', **sude ni** 'already', **sugu (ni)**, 'straight away', **sukoshi** 'a little', **tabi-tabi** 'often', **tama ni** 'occasionally', **toki-doki** 'sometimes', **tsugi ni** 'next', **unto** 'lots', **yoku** 'often', **yagate** 'presently', **zutto** 'for a long time'.

a 彼は今、独学で中国語を勉強している。
**Kare wa ima, dokugaku de Chūgokugo o benkyō shite iru.**
He is currently learning Chinese through self-study.

b 企業家にはもう少し深い理解がほしい。
**Kigyōka ni wa mō sukoshi fukai rikai ga hoshii.**
One wants a little deeper understanding from an industrialist.

---

| 10.2.3.2 | *Time of day, days, months, years and use of* **ni**

Common adverbs/nouns include the following: **asa** 'in the morning', **hiru** 'during the day', 'at noon', **yūgata** 'in the evening', **yoru** 'at night', **gozen(chū)** 'a.m.', **gogo** 'p.m.', and num. + C combinations of time (**-ji** 'hour', **-fun** 'minute'). They also include the days of the week: **nichiyōbi** 'Sunday', **getsuyōbi** 'Monday', **kayōbi** 'Tuesday', **suiyōbi** 'Wednesday', **mokuyōbi** 'Thursday', **kin'yōbi** 'Friday', **doyōbi** 'Saturday', etc.) (see 10.2.3.3 for prefixes such as **mai-** 'every').

The particle **ni** can optionally be attached to items that indicate a fixed time, but *not* to those that indicate a relative (movable) time, such as **kyō** 'today', **kinō** 'yesterday', **maiasa** 'every morning', etc. (see 2.4.13).

a 毎朝、早起きですね。
**Maiasa, hayaoki desu ne.**
Every morning, you get up early, don't you?

b 会は毎週月曜日の朝に開かれる。
**Kai wa maishū getsuyōbi no asa ni hirakareru.**
The meeting is held every week on Monday morning.

c 朝、なんとか出かけても、夕方にはぐったり。
**Asa, nantoka dekakete mo, yūgata ni wa guttari.**
Even though he somehow manages to leave home in the morning, by the evening he [is] exhausted.

**Table 10.1** Adverbs/nouns of time with Native-Japanese and/or Sino-Japanese forms

|  |  | −2 | −1 | 0 | +1 | +2 |
|---|---|---|---|---|---|---|
| Days | (N-J) | ototoi | kinō | kyō | ashita | asatte |
|  | (S-J) | is-saku-jitsu | saku-jitsu | hon-jitsu | myō-nichi | myō-go-nichi |
| Months | (S-J) | sen-sen-getsu | sen-getsu | kon-getsu | rai-getsu | sa-rai-getsu |
| Years | (N-J) | ototoshi |  | kotoshi |  |  |
|  | (S-J) | is-saku-nen | kyo-nen<br>saku-nen | hon-nen | rai-nen | sa-rai-nen |

---

**10.2.3.3** *Adverbs/nouns of time with NJ and/or SJ forms*

Some Adv/N of time have either Native-Japanese or Sino-Japanese forms, or both (in SJ words, boundaries between morphemes (= *kanji*) are indicated by hyphens). Where both NJ and SJ forms exist, the latter are typically used in the written or formal spoken style (e.g. speeches).

Table 10.1 gives common items, centred on 0 (= the present day, month, year).

Note also **sen-jitsu** 'the other day' (colloquially, **kono aida**) and **sen-nen** 'the other year'. The SJ roots -**jitsu**/-**nichi** 'day', -**getsu** 'month' and -**nen** 'year' also combine with the prefixes **mai-** 'every', **yoku-** 'the following', and **kaku-** 'every second', e.g. **mai-nichi** 'every day', **yoku-jitsu** 'the following day', **kaku-jitsu** 'every second day'.

---

**10.2.3.4** *Other adverbs*

These include question words (**itsu** 'when' etc.), combinations of Q-words and the particle **demo** or **mo** (see 18), numeral + counter/time combinations (see 4), and adverbially used demonstrative words (see 5).

Example a shows an adverbially used demonstrative word.

a そんなに焦らなくても、まだ若いのだから。
   **Sonna ni aseranakute mo, mada wakai no da kara.**
   You needn't be so impatient; you're still young.

*Predicate-selecting adverbs*

Predicate-selecting adverbs are adverbs that tend to select (appear together with) certain types of predicate, or predicate extensions (i.e. negative predicates, presumptive predicates, etc.). Some do not always combine with such predicates, but when they do, they reinforce or emphasize the meaning of the predicate.

*Note* – some of these adverbs have more than one meaning, and are therefore found in more than one group.

Below are some of the more common predicate-selecting adverbs, grouped by the type of predicate they tend to select (i.e. combine with). In English translation, adverbs and predicates are, wherever possible, translated twice, even at the risk of making the translations somewhat unnatural.

10.2.4.1 *Presumptive predicates*

Adverbs selecting presumptive predicates include the following: **dōse** 'anyway', **hyotto shite/shitara** 'possibly', **kitto** 'doubtless', **moshi ka shitara/shite/suruto** 'perhaps', **nan demo** 'apparently', **sazo** 'certainly', **osoraku** 'probably', **tabun** 'in all likelihood' (see 9.1, 9.6.2, 9.6.3).

a きっと好奇心の強い魚なのだろう。
**Kitto kōkishin no tsuyoi sakana na no darō.**
Doubtless it is a fish with a strong sense of curiosity.

b これからきっと素敵な個性を発揮し始めるでしょう。
**Kore kara kitto suteki na kosei o hakki shi-hajimeru deshō.**
From now on, it [= the town] should exhibit some attractive
individuality.

c どうせ短命政権だろう。
**Dōse tanmei seiken darō.**
It should be a short-lived government anyway.

d どうも国際社会でお人よしなのは、日本人くらいなのかもしれ
ない。
**Dōmo kokusai shakai de o-hitoyoshi na no wa, Nihonjin kurai
na no kamoshirenai.**
It may well be that the Japanese are about the only ones in
the international society who are easy prey.

e きっと母は喜んだはずです。

**Kitto haha wa yorokonda hazu desu.**

No doubt mother must have felt happy.

f きっとイメージの違う自分を発見するに違いない。

**Kitto imēji no chigau jibun o hakken suru ni chigai nai.**

Doubtless you will discover a self with a different image.

---

| 10.2.4.2 | *Negative predicates*

Adverbs include the following (see 17): **amari** 'not much', **betsu ni** 'not particularly', **chittomo** 'not at all', **dōse** 'not ... anyway', **hotondo** 'almost no', **kanarazushimo** 'not necessarily', **kesshite** 'never', **masaka** 'never', **zenzen** 'not at all', **zettai ni** 'absolutely not'.

*Note* – **hotondo** can also be used as a noun, with case particle attached.

| 10.2.4.2.1 | With negative form present

a 自由な時間はあまりない。

**Jiyū na jikan wa amari nai.**

There isn't much free time.

b どうせ分かってくれない。

**Dōse wakatte kurenai.**

They won't understand anyway.

c 欧州の空港に行くと、ジャンボはほとんどいない。

**Ōshū no kūkō ni iku to, janbo wa hotondo inai.**

When you go to European airports, there are almost no jumbos.

d まさか近代都市の橋が落ちるとは思えない。

**Masaka kindai toshi no hashi ga ochiru to wa omoenai.**

One can't possibly imagine that a bridge in a modern city would fall down.

| 10.2.4.2.2 | With ellipted negative form

Here, the negative predicate is ellipted (omitted), because it is understood from the context (see 27.2.3).

a まさか取締役になるとは。(思わなかった **omowanakatta** 'didn't think' or similar is ellipted)

**Masaka torishimariyaku ni naru to wa.**

I never [thought] that I'd be executive president.

b 「ヨーロッパのブランドものはモノトーンで大人っぽく、私には
　どうも」と話す。(似合わない **niawanai** 'doesn't suit' or similar
　is ellipted)
**'Yōroppa no burando mono wa monotōn de otona-ppoku,
watashi ni wa dōmo' to hanasu.**
'European designer clothes are in plain colours and have a grown-up
feel about them, and are not quite [right] for me', she says.

---

| 10.2.4.3 | *Negative presumptive predicate*

Adverbs include **dōse** 'anyway', **masaka** 'hardly' (see 9.1).

a どうせわれわれは必要ないのだろう。
**Dōse wareware wa hitsuyō nai no darō.**
We are not needed anyway, I guess.

b 今年はまさか昨年のようなことはないでしょう。
**Kotoshi wa masaka sakunen no yō na koto wa
nai deshō.**
This year things couldn't possibly be like [= as bad as] last year.

---

| 10.2.4.4 | *Desiderative predicate*

Adverbs include **zehi/zehitomo** 'very much', 'by all means' (see 9.2).

a またぜひ働きに行きたい。
**Mata zehi hataraki ni ikitai.**
I very much want to go to work again.

---

| 10.2.4.5 | *Predicate of command*

Adverbs include **dōzo/dōka** 'please', **zehi** 'by all means' (see 20).

a A君もぜひ遊びに来て下さい。
**A-kun mo zehi asobi ni kite kudasai.**
You [= A-kun] too, please do come and visit.

b どうぞ、ご安心下さい。
**Dōzo, go-anshin kudasai.**
Please don't worry (*lit.* "feel at ease").

299

| 10.2.4.6 | *Conditional predicate* |

Conditional predicates are used in S1 in compound sentences, indicating a condition 'if' for S2 (see 26.1).

Adverbs include the following: **dōse** 'anyway', **moshi** 'if', **man'ichi** 'by any chance', **tatoe** 'even if'.

a どうせ買うなら新鮮でおいしい魚を選びたい。
   **Dōse kau nara shinsen de oishii sakana o erabitai.**
   If I buy (fish) anyway, I might as well choose fresh and good fish.

b もし金利が上昇したらどうなるか。
   **Moshi kinri ga jōshō shitara dō naru ka.**
   What will happen if the interest rate goes up?

c 私？ 私はどうせ生まれ変わるならクラゲがいいわ。
   **Watashi? Watashi wa dōse umare-kawaru nara kurage ga ii wa.**
   Me? If I am to be reborn anyway, I'd be a jellyfish.

d 万一、夫が死亡した場合、借金やその後の生活が心配です。
   **Man'ichi, otto ga shibō shita baai, shakkin ya sono go no seikatsu ga shinpai desu.**
   In the event that my husband should die, I'd be worried about debts and how to support myself afterwards.

| 10.2.4.7 | *Evidential predicate* |

These predicates use evidential endings (see 9.5).

Adverbs include **atakamo** 'just like', **dōmo** 'rather', **maru de** 'just as if'.

a あたかも審査員に圧力を掛けるかのようだ。
   **Atakamo shinsain ni atsuryoku o kakeru ka no yō da.**
   It's almost as if they [= the audience] are putting pressure on the jury members.

b あたかも一身にして二生を経るが如く。
   **Atakamo isshin ni shite nishō o furu ga gotoku.**
   It was just like living two lives in one body.

c まるでもう一人の自分がそこにいるようだった。
   **Maru de mō hitori no jibun ga soko ni iru yō datta.**
   It was just as if another self were there.

d 日本では、どうも若い女性がお金持ちで旅行好きらしい。

**Nihon-de wa, dōmo wakai josei ga o-kanemochi de
ryokō-zuki rashii.**

In Japan it rather appears that young women are well off and like
travelling.

e どうも上司と飲むのは苦手という人が多いようだ。

**Dōmo jōshi to nomu no wa nigate to iu hito ga ōi yo da.**

It would appear that there are many who find drinking with their
superiors quite trying.

## 10.2.4.8 *Non-past form predicates*

### 10.2.4.8.1 Intentional

**V-ru/V-masu** can, among other things, express intention (see 8.1.2.2). Adverbs
include **kitto** 'definitely'.

a 私はいつかきっと向田邦子になります。

**Watashi wa itsu ka kitto Mukōda Kuniko ni narimasu.**

One day, I'll definitely be [another] Mukōda Kuniko [= female novelist].

### 10.2.4.8.2 Other non-past predicates

Adverbs like **kitto, dōmo, dōse** also occur with other non-past forms (and
endings, such as **n(o) da** in example d) (see 9.6.1).

a きっとやりがいがあると思う。

**Kitto yarigai ga aru to omou.**

I think that without doubt it's worth doing.

b きっと、官僚の抵抗が壁になる。

**Kitto, kanryō no teikō ga kabe ni naru.**

No doubt the bureaucrats' resistance will stand in the way.

c たそがれどきになると、左党はどうも落ち着かない。

**Tasogaredoki ni naru to, satō wa dōmo ochitsukanai.**

When dusk comes, drinkers appear fidgety.

d 人生は、どうせ一幕のお芝居なんだから。

**Jinsei wa dōse hitomaku no o-shibai nan da kara.**

Life is a one-act play anyway.

# Chapter 11

# Adverbial particles

Adverbial particles are typically, but by no means exclusively, used to modify predicates in a variety of meanings, such as restrictive ('only', etc.), inclusive, de-focussing, emphasis, extent, exemplification, and manner.

## 11.1 Restrictive particles

These typically indicate the meaning of 'only'.

### 11.1.1 bakari

The adverbial particle **bakari** is attached to verbs, adjectives, and nouns as well as clauses in quite a variety of forms. The basic meaning is 'only', 'ever more', but depending on the grammatical pattern the resulting range of meanings is quite varied, as explained in the following sections.

#### 11.1.1.1 Verb-**ru bakari da**

Usually followed by a form of copula, **bakari** indicates that the action of a verb whose action is repeatable is taking place all the time, or with verbs whose action is (de-)intensifying (e.g. **takamaru** 'get higher', **fukamaru** 'get deeper', **tsuyomaru** 'get stronger', **yowamaru** 'get weaker'), that the action is (de-)intensifying 'ever more'.

##### 11.1.1.1.1 Repeatable verbs

With verbs whose action can be repeated, **bakari** means 'just keep doing'.

a 「警察にも何も言ってない」と繰り返すばかり。

**'Keisatsu ni mo nani mo itte nai' to kurikaesu bakari.**

He just keeps repeating, 'I didn't say anything to the police either'.

b 校長に直訴するが、「待ってくれ」というばかりで三年たった。

**Kōchō ni jikiso suru ga, 'Matte kure' to iu bakari de sannen
tatta.**

He appealed directly to the principal, but he just kept on saying,
'Wait', and three years passed.

c すでに一部が日本に到着済みで、あとは二月初めからの販売を待
つばかりだ。

**Sude ni ichibu ga Nihon ni tōchaku-zumi de, ato wa nigatsu
hajime kara no hanbai o matsu bakari da.**

A proportion has already arrived in Japan, and all that remains is to
wait for the sales from early February.

| 11.1.1.1.2 | Intensifying verbs

With (de-)intensifying verbs (usually formed by Adj-**ku naru**/na-Adj **ni
naru,** or Adj-root-**maru**), **bakari** indicates that the (de-)intensifying action
is 'ever more', 'increasingly' so.

a ✐なぞは深まるばかりだ。

**Nazo wa fukamaru bakari da.**

The mystery deepens ever more.

b 政治不信は高まるばかりだ。

**Seiji fushin wa takamaru bakari da.**

Distrust in politics is getting ever greater.

c 先行を許すと、あとは風が弱まるばかり。

**Senkō o yurusu to, ato wa kaze ga yowamaru bakari.**

If you allow [the other yacht] to go ahead, the wind gets increasingly
weaker.

d 近年、健康志向は強まるばかりだ。

**Kinnen, kenkō shikō wa tsuyomaru bakari da.**

In recent years, health-oriented thinking is getting ever stronger.

e コンビニ同士の競争は激しくなるばかり。

**Konbini dōshi no kyōsō wa hageshiku naru bakari.**

The competition between convenience stores is getting tougher
all the time.

| 11.1.1.2 | *Verb*-**ta bakari** |

After V-**ta**, **bakari** indicates that the action of the verb has 'only just' been completed. It can be used as a predicate, usually with the addition of the copula, or to modify a noun by means of **no** (see 8.2).

| 11.1.1.2.1 | *Verb*-**ta bakari** (+ copula, etc.) |

In newspaper style, the copula can be omitted.

a 合唱団は結成されたばかりですが、・・・、日々活動に取り組んでいます。

**Gasshōdan wa kessei sareta bakari desu ga, . . . , hibi katsudō ni torikunde imasu.**

The choir has only just been formed, . . . , but is active every day.

b 婚約したばかりだった。

**Kon'yaku shita bakari datta.**

He had only just got engaged.

| 11.1.1.2.2 | *Verb*-**ta bakari no** noun |

a 結婚したばかりの若い二人の写真

**Kekkon shita bakari no wakai futari no shashin.**

A photo of the young couple having just got married

b 新しい家は完成したばかりの社宅。

**Atarashii ie wa kansei shita bakari no shataku.**

Their new home is a newly built company house.

| 11.1.1.3 | *Verb*-**te bakari** (**wa/mo**) **iru** |

Sandwiched between V-**te** and a form of **iru**, **bakari** indicates that the action of V takes place all the time, at the expense of other things that could or should take place 'just . . . all the time', 'always' (see 25.5).

Where the negative potential form of **iru** (**irarenai**) is used (11.1.1.3.2), the meaning is 'can't just . . . all the time'.

| 11.1.1.3.1 | With non-potential predicates |

a ✐あの人は食べてばかりいます。

**Ano hito wa tabete bakari imasu.**

That person is eating all the time.

b お母さん、いつまでも泣いてばかりいちゃだめだ。
(いちゃ ＝ いては)

**Okāsan, itsu made mo naite bakari icha dame da.**
**(icha = ite wa)**

Mum, you mustn't just keep crying forever.

c 夫は家で将棋や囲碁のテレビ番組を見てばかりいる。

**Otto wa ie de shōgi ya igo no terebi bangumi o mite bakari
iru.**

At home, my husband just watches TV programmes of Shogi and
Go all the time.

| 11.1.1.3.2 | With negative potential predicates |

In the potential form, the meaning becomes 'can't just . . . all the time',
'can't afford to do nothing but'.

a しかし浮かれてばかりはいられない。

**Shikashi ukarete bakari wa irarenai.**

However, one can't just be in the clouds all the time.

b 悲嘆に暮れてばかりはいられなかった。

**Hitan ni kurete bakari wa irarenakatta.**

She couldn't spend all her time grieving [over her husband's illness].

| 11.1.1.4 | *Noun (+ particle)* **bakari** |

| 11.1.1.4.1 | Noun **bakari** + copula |

Followed by forms of the copula (in newspaper style, the copula is often
omitted at the end of a sentence), **bakari** means 'is all', 'was all', 'only',
etc. The implication with **bakari** is not 'only' in the exclusive sense (for
that, **dake/shika** are used), but that out of a choice of two or more entities,
one is much more represented that one would normally expect.

In examples a and b, for instance, there might well be the occasional
female (example a) or male (example b); the point is that where one

would normally expect a mixture of the two, one or the other group is predominant.

a 客も店員も男性ばかりだった。
**Kyaku mo ten'in mo dansei bakari datta.**
Both customers and sales personnel were all male.

b 百貨店の店頭でも元気なのは女性ばかり。
**Hyakkaten no tentō de mo genki na no wa josei bakari.**
At department store counters too, it's only the women who are
energetic.

c 悲観論ばかりでは生きていけない。
**Hikanron bakari de wa ikite ikenai.**
You can't live by pessimism alone.

d 地方の企業にとって不況は悪いことばかりではない。
**Chihō no kigyō ni totte fukyō wa warui koto bakari de wa nai.**
For businesses in the regions, the recession is not all bad.

**11.1.1.4.2** Noun (+ particle) **bakari** (+ particle)

Attached to nouns or [N + particle] that are subjects or objects, **bakari**
can replace **ga** and **o**, or alternatively attach them. **bakari** is added to all
other case particles, such as **ni, e, to**, etc. It indicates the idea of 'only' or
'all', in the sense that something is overwhelmingly so.

a 英語ばかりが外国語じゃない。
**Eigo bakari ga gaikokugo ja nai.**
English is not the only foreign language.

b 表面ばかり見ないで内面も見て欲しい。
**Hyōmen bakari minai de naimen mo mite hoshii.**
I want you to look not only at the surface, but also at the interior
[what's inside].

c 小物や陶芸作品ばかりを並べた店が、今人気を集めている。
**Komono ya tōgei sakuhin bakari o narabeta mise ga,
ima ninki o atsumete iru.**
Shops that display nothing but trinkets and items of pottery are
popular nowadays.

d 経営者が社員にばかり負担を強いているのはおかしい、···
**Keieisha ga shain ni bakari futan o shiite iru no wa okashii,...**
It's not right that managers are forcing contributions on employees only...

e 「交渉は永遠に続くかのようだ」というラーセンの言葉は、あなが
　ち誇張とばかりは言えない。
　**'Kōshō wa eien ni tsuzuku ka no yō da' to iu Rāsen no kotoba
　wa, anagachi kochō to bakari wa ienai.**
　The words of Larsen, 'Negotiations seem to continue forever', cannot
　necessarily be said to be all exaggeration.

11.1.1.4.3　Time noun **bakari**

With an amount of time, the meaning of **bakari** is 'about' (example a),
whereas with any other time N it serves to emphasize it in the sense of
'only', 'at least', etc. (example b).

a わずか数カ月ばかり前のことが、何年も前のことのように思える。
　**Wazuka sūkagetsu bakari mae no koto ga, nannen mo mae
　no koto no yō ni omoeru.**
　Something that took place just a few months ago seems like
　it happened years ago.

b 今度ばかりは降りない。
　**Kondo bakari wa orinai.**
　This time, at least, we're not going to quit.

11.1.1.5　Noun phrase 1 (+ particle) **bakari de (wa) naku, …** noun
　　　　　phrase 2 **(ni shite) mo …**

Used between NPs (and equivalent), this combination indicates the idea of
'not only, but also'. Note that a phrase ending in V-**te** can be used instead
of NP2 (example c) (see 11.1.2.7).

a ✐肉ばかりではなく、野菜も食べなさい。
　**Niku bakari de wa naku, yasai mo tabenasai.**
　Don't eat just meat, have some vegetables as well!

b 夫婦一緒の時間ばかりでなく自分の時間も持ちたい。
　**Fūfu issho no jikan bakari de naku jibun no jikan mo mochitai.**
　I want to have not only time together as a couple, but also time for myself.

c 鮮魚ばかりではなく冷凍でも輸入することにしている。
　**Sengyo bakari de wa naku reitō de mo yunyū suru koto ni
　shite iru.**
　We've decided to import them (= the fish) not only fresh, but also
　frozen.

307

*Noun/clause* **bakari ka,...(mo)**

In this use, **bakari ka** is attached to a noun or a clause (given below in [ ]), and signals an addition. S can either end in a positive or a negative form (or an expression that has negative meaning).

Instead of **mo, made** 'even' can also be used (see 11.2.4).

11.1.1.6.1 Noun/clause-positive **bakari ka,...(mo)**

Here, **bakari ka** is attached to a positive form, and thus signals a positive addition 'not only ... but also ...'.

a アドレスを間違うと、相手に届かないばかりか、誤送先のサーバ にも迷惑となります。

**Adoresu o machigau to, [aite ni todokanai] bakari ka, gosōsaki no sāba ni mo meiwaku to narimasu.**

If you get the email address wrong, not only will it not reach the [intended] addressee, it'll also inconvenience the server to which it has mistakenly been sent.

b 命が助かったばかりか、屋内で感じる恐怖を味わわずに済んだ。

**[Inochi ga tasukatta] bakari ka, okunai de kanjiru kyōfu o ajiwawazu ni sunda.**

Not only was his life saved, he managed not to experience the fright one feels when inside [during an earthquake].

11.1.1.6.2 Noun/clause-negative **bakari ka,...(mo)**

In this use, **bakari ka** is attached to an ending in a negative form (or an expression that has negative meaning).

**bakari ka** usually signals a negative addition 'not only not, but also', but it can be attached to what amounts to a double negative, in which case the negatives cancel each other out, indicating a positive addition (example b).

a 自分に合わないまくらを使えば疲れがとれにくいばかりか、肩凝 りの原因にもなる。

**Jibun ni awanai makura o tsukaeba [tsukare ga torenikui] bakari ka, katakori no gen'in ni mo naru.**

If you use a pillow that doesn't suit you, not only does it make it difficult to recover from fatigue, it also becomes the cause of a stiff neck.

b 中国の強大さは脅威にならないばかりか、世界各国の得に
なる。

**Chūgoku no kyōdaisa wa [kyōi ni naranai] bakari ka, sekai
kakkoku no toku ni naru.**

Not only is China's vastness not a menace, it will be an advantage for
the countries of the world.

11.1.1.7 *Noun* **bakari ka to iu to ... sō de wa/mo nai**
*(or similar negative)*

This means literally 'if you question if *X* is all *Y*, that is not so', and is
used as a rhetorical device or way of putting things in a somewhat dramatic
fashion 'you may think that . . . , but that's not so'.

If sō de *mo* nai (example b) is used rather than sō de *wa* nai (example a),
the meaning becomes 'not *necessarily* so'.

a 青森の冬は雪ばかりかというとそうではない。

**Aomori no fuyu wa yuki bakari ka to iu to
sō de wa nai.**

You may think that Aomori winters are nothing but snow,
but that's not so.

b 現代の若者の食生活が欠点ばかりかというと、そうでも
ない。

**Gendai no wakamono no shokuseikatsu ga ketten bakari
ka to iu to, sō de mo nai.**

You may think that the eating habits of today's young are all bad,
but that's not necessarily so.

11.1.1.8 *Adverb* **(to) bakari (ni)**

Attached to a clause (indicated below in [ ]), **bakari ni** makes that clause
into an adverbial phrase in the sense of 'as if', or 'almost', modifying a
following verb. This can also be attached to an adverb (example b) instead
of a clause.

a さらにこれでもかとばかりに、バラードが続く。

**Sara ni [kore demo ka to] bakari ni barādo ga tsuzuku**

And further, ballads continue with a vengeance (*lit.* "as if to say,
can you take more?").

309

b 初秋の日差しにまばゆいばかりに輝いていた調印当日のホワイト
ハウス。

**Shoshū no hizashi ni [mabayui] bakari ni kagayaite ita chōin
tōjitsu no Howaitohausu.**

The White House, on the day of the signing [of the treaty], had been
just dazzling as it glittered in the early autumn sunlight.

c それまではみな残業、交代勤務、出張が"男の道"とばかりに働
いてきた父親たちだった。

**Sore made wa mina [zangyō, kōtai kinmu, shutchō ga
'otoko no michi' to] bakari ni hataraite kita chichioya-tachi
datta.**

Until then, they were all fathers who had worked as if overtime,
shift work and business trips were 'the way of men'.

| 11.1.1.9 | Adjective **bakari no** noun

When adjective + **bakari** modifies a noun, **bakari** emphasizes the degree
to which the adjective applies, in the sense of 'almost'.

a 澄んだ水の流れと、まばゆいばかりの新緑が目に浮かぶ。

**Sunda mizu no nagare to, mabayui bakari no shinryoku ga
me ni ukabu.**

The clear stream of water and the almost blinding new leaves come
to my mind.

b 経営に対するすさまじいばかりの熱意に心打たれた。

**Keiei ni taisuru susamajii bakari no netsui ni
kokoro utareta.**

I was impressed by his almost frightening passion for management.

| 11.1.1.10 | Adjective **bakari de wa** ... negative

Followed by a negative, adjective + **bakari** indicates the idea of 'not
all', 'not ... just'. Note that the forms **bakari** attaches to are -**i** and **na**,
respectively.

a 安いばかりでは消費者も買わない。

**Yasui bakari de wa shōhisha mo kawanai.**

Consumers aren't going to buy [things] just because they're cheap.

b 決して地味なばかりではなかったのだ。

**Kesshite jimi na bakari de wa nakatta no da.**

He [= famous historial figure] was definitely not just conservative
(in his tastes).

## 11.1.2 dake

**dake** is an adverbial particle with the basic meaning of 'only' (see 11.1.1).
It is used in a variety of ways and with various meanings.

### 11.1.2.1 Noun dake (particle) predicate

In this use, **dake** is inserted between a noun and the case particle required
by the valency of the predicate. However, **o/ga** can be omitted.

Where no case particle is required in the first place, as after a N of time
(**yoru** 'night', etc.), **dake** is attached to N directly.

#### 11.1.2.1.1 Noun dake particle

##### 11.1.2.1.1.1 Replaceable by bakari

When used in the sense of 'just', or 'just...all the time', **dake** can be
replaced with **bakari**.

a 政府だけが悪いわけではない。

**Seifu dake ga warui wake de wa nai.**

It's not just the government that's at fault.

b 心は決まらないまま、時間だけが過ぎていく。

**Kokoro wa kimaranai mama, jikan dake ga sugite iku.**

While I remain unable to make up [my] mind, time just keeps passing.

c 形式だけをみていても本質は理解できない。

**Keishiki dake o mite ite mo honshitsu wa rikai dekinai.**

If you look at the form alone, you cannot grasp the substance.

##### 11.1.2.1.1.2 Not replaceable by bakari

In the more exclusive sense of 'just only', 'nothing but', **dake** cannot be
replaced by **bakari**.

a 自分のためだけに生きたい。

**Jibun no tame dake ni ikitai.**

I want to live only for myself.

b 昨年だけで約四十社が新設された。

**Sakunen dake de yaku yonjussha ga shinsetsu sare.**

About 40 companies were established just last year.

c ただ制度だけでは人は動かない。

**Tada seido dake de wa hito wa ugokanai.**

People don't take action when there is nothing but a system [in place].

| 11.1.2.1.2 | Noun/verbal noun **dake** (no particle)

In examples a and b, **o** is ellipted (omitted), whereas example c has a time
N, which takes no particle in the first place. **bakari** can replace **dake** after
verbal nouns (example b) only.

a 概要だけ聞けば、日米に違いはないようにも見える。

**Gaiyō dake kikeba, Nichibei ni chigai wa nai yō ni mo mieru.**

If you just listen to the outline, it looks as if there are no differences
between Japan and the US.

b 部下に指示だけして仕事したような気になっている管理者は要ら
ない。

**Buka ni shiji dake shite shigoto shita yō na ki ni natte iru
kanrisha wa iranai.**

We don't need administrators who think they've done a job just by
giving instructions to their subordinates.

c 会社に勤めるかたわら、週末や平日の夜だけ通ってくる。

**Kaisha ni tsutomeru katawara, shūmatsu ya heijitsu no yoru
dake kayotte kuru.**

He works in a company and comes only on weekends and weekday
nights [to the research institute].

| 11.1.2.2 | Noun **dake no** noun

In this use, **dake** cannot be replaced by **bakari**.

a 言葉だけの人間だ。

**Kotoba dake no ningen da.**

He is ["a person who is"] all talk.

b 再婚はお互いだけの問題ではない。
   **Saikon wa o-tagai dake no mondai de wa nai.**
   Remarrying is not a matter which concerns just the two of us.

c 待っているだけのスタンスの人はもう結構。
   **Matte iru dake no sutansu no hito wa mō kekkō.**
   [We've] had enough of people with just a 'wait-and-see' stance.

d 告別式は故人の遺志により近親者だけの密葬で行う。
   **Kokubetsu-shiki wa kojin no ishi ni yori kinshinsha dake no
   missō de okonau.**
   In accordance with the wish of the deceased, the funeral is held as
   a private ceremony for the next-of-kin only.

---

**11.1.2.3** | *Noun* **dake** *(+ copula)*

When used as a predicate, N **dake** attaches the copula, (although in practice
it is often omitted). This is commonly used with cleft sentences (see
22.2). **gurai** can also be used instead of **dake** here, although **dake** has a
more restrictive ring, i.e. 'only' as opposed to 'about the only' (see
11.5.1.1.3).

a 「それだけです」ときっぱり。
   **'Sore dake desu' to kippari**
   'That's all', [he] said flatly.

b 自宅でのんびりするのは正月三が日だけ。
   **Jitaku de nonbiri suru no wa shōgatsu sanganichi dake.**
   The only time I relax at home is the first three days of
   the new year.

---

**11.1.2.4** | *Clause* **bun dake**

**bun** is a noun meaning 'rate', and in combination with **dake** indicates that
a state (a clause ending in an adjectival expression) applies 'in proportion
to' or 'to the extent of S' of the clause to which it is attached.

a 人数が多い分だけ人間関係は複雑になる。
   **Ninzū ga ōi bun dake ningen kankei wa fukuzatsu ni naru.**
   As the number of persons [sharing accommodation] is large, human
   relationships become proportionally complex.

b 一緒にいる時間が少ない分だけ、真剣に息子と向き合えた。

**Issho ni iru jikan ga sukunai bun dake, shinken ni musuko to muki-aeta.**

It was because we had so little time together that I was able to face my son more seriously.

---

| 11.1.2.5 | *Verb* **(to iu) dake** *copula*

After V, **dake** (usually followed by a form of the copula) indicates that the action of a V is 'all one/it, etc. does/achieves'. **dake** can be reinforced by **tada**, as in example b.

Note also the combination V **dake de sumu** (see also 25.2 for similar uses of the copula).

a 「そうか。本当に行くのか」と簡単に答えただけ。

**'Sō ka. Hontō ni iku no ka' to kantan ni kotaeta dake.**

All [he] did was reply briefly, 'I see. Are you really going?'

b 大事な時に役に立たなくて ……。ただ謝るだけですよ。

**Daiji na toki ni yaku ni tatanakute ... Tada ayamaru dake desu yo.**

Having been useless when it matters ... all I can do is just apologize.

c 景観や生き物たちを眺めるだけでも楽しい。

**Keikan ya ikimono-tachi o nagameru dake de mo tanoshii.**

Just looking at the sights and the [wild]life is fun.

d カセット式にはめ込むだけで済む。

**Kasetto-shiki ni hamekomu dake de sumu.**

All you have to do is insert it [= the water filter] like a cassette.

---

| 11.1.2.6 | *Clause* **dake de (wa) nai**

With a following negative, the meaning is 'not only', 'not merely'.

a 創意工夫はメーカーだけではない。

**Sōi kufū wa mēkā dake de wa nai.**

It is not only the manufacturers who are creative and resourceful.

b 植林は緑を回復するだけではないのだ。

**Shokurin wa midori o kaifuku suru dake de wa nai no da.**

Reforestation does not merely restore the greenery.

| 11.1.2.7 | *Noun 1* **dake de** *(wa)* **naku** … *noun 2* **mo/ga** |

Attached to a N (or NP), this indicates the meaning of 'not only, but also'.
**bakari** can be used in exactly the same way (see 11.1.1.5).

a 量だけでなく質の面でも差異は大きい。
   **Ryō dake de naku shitsu no men de mo sai wa ōkii.**
   The difference is considerable, not only in quantity, but also in quality.

b 肉体だけでなく精神の若さを保つことが重要。
   **Nikutai dake de naku seishin no wakasa o tamotsu koto
   ga jūyō.**
   It is important to maintain youthfulness in spirit as well as in body.

c 音声だけではなく、鮮明な動画像も送り合うことができる。
   **Onsei dake de wa naku, senmei na dōgazō mo okuriau koto
   ga dekiru.**
   One can transmit not only sound, but also clear moving images.

d お年寄りは身の回りの世話だけでなく、話し相手も求めている。
   **O-toshiyori wa mi no mawari no sewa dake de naku, hanashi-
   aite mo motomete iru.**
   Elderly people are looking not only for someone to take care of them,
   but also for someone to talk to.

| 11.1.2.8 | *Clause 1* **dake** *clause 2* |

| 11.1.2.8.1 | Clause 1 **dake de** clause 2 -positive predicate |

**de** is the conjunctive form of the copula, making S1 a condition for S2 in
the sense of 'just by doing S1', 'doing S1 is all you need to do'. **bakari**
cannot be used in this way.

a 家庭のテレビに接続するだけで画像と音を同時に再生できる。
   **Katei no terebi ni setsuzoku suru dake de gazō to oto o dōji
   ni saisei dekiru.**
   All you do is hook it up to your television at home, and you can play
   back images and sound simultaneously.

b 女性はちょっと洋服を変えただけで気分が前向きになる。
   **Josei wa chotto yōfuku o kaeta dake de kibun ga maemuki
   ni naru.**
   Women get a positive feeling just from changing their clothes.

Clause 1 **dake de wa** clause 2 negative predicate

**de** is the conjunctive form of the copula, making S1 a condition for S2 in the sense that S1 is insufficient for S2 to happen: 'just by doing S1', 'if all you do is . . .'.

a 安いだけでは商品は売れない。
**Yasui dake de wa shōhin wa urenai.**
Products don't sell just by being cheap.

b 地理的に近いだけでは経済圏など成り立たない。
**Chiri-teki ni chikai dake de wa keizaiken nado naritatanai.**
Just because [certain countries] are in geographical proximity does not mean that an economic bloc is feasible.

*Clause* **dake ni**

This indicates an emphasized reason 'all the more so because', 'precisely because'.

a 前例がないだけに、どれだけ出したらいいのか見当がつかなかった。
**Zenrei ga nai dake ni, dore dake dashitara ii no ka kentō ga tsukanakatta.**
Because of the lack of precedent, we had no idea how much [severance money] we should pay.

b 大自然の中での競技だけに生傷が絶えない。
**Daishizen no naka de no kyōgi dake ni namakizu ga taenai.**
As might be expected from an outdoor contest [cycle racing], he's always bruised and raw.

c 育児休業をとれば、中小企業だけに現職復帰の保証はない。
**Ikuji kyūka o toreba, chūshō kigyō dake ni genshoku fukki no hoshō wa nai.**
As it's a small-sized business, if you take leave of absence for childcare, there is no guarantee of getting back your former post.

**shika**

**shika** is always used with negative predicates, the combination being equivalent in meaning to English 'only'. **shika** is more exclusive in meaning than **dake** and **bakari** (which also mean 'only' in some of their uses), having

the implication of 'nothing but', 'only . . . and nothing else' (see 11.1.1,
11.1.2).

| 11.1.3.1 | *Noun (+ particle)/number (+ counter)* **shika**

| 11.1.3.1.1 | Noun **shika**

**shika** replaces the case particles **ga** and **o**, imparting the meaning of 'only',
'no more than'.

a 必要なものしか買わなくなった。
   **Hitsuyō na mono shika kawanaku natta.**
   These days [people] buy no more than the necessities.

b 最近の若い者は決まりきった発想しかできない。
   **Saikin no wakai mono wa kimarikitta hassō shika dekinai.**
   Young people these days can only come up with ideas that are trite
   and conventional.

c 当時の人々は、自分の目でみたものしか描かなかった。
   **Tōji no hitobito wa, jibun no me de mita mono shika
   egakanakatta.**
   People of that time drew only things which they had seen with their
   own eyes.

d 絶頂を極めた後は下降しかない。
   **Zetchō o kiwameta ato wa kakō shika nai.**
   After you've reached the peak, it's downhill all the way.

| 11.1.3.1.2 | Noun + particle **shika**

The particle used depends on the valency of the verb, i.e. in example a
**omou** 'think' requires **to**.

a 拷問、脅迫としか思えない取り調べを受けた。
   **Gōmon, kyōhaku to shika omoenai torishirabe o uketa.**
   I underwent an investigation which was no less than torture and
   intimidation.

b ロッカーは住人が個別に携帯するIDカードでしか開けられない。
   **Rokkā wa jūnin ga kobetsu ni keitai suru aidī kādo de shika
   akerarenai.**
   The lockers can only be opened with ID cards that are carried by
   the individual residents.

c 幸枝さんを父の「新しい奥さん」としか見ることはできなかった。

**Yukie-san o chichi no 'Atarashii okusan' to shika miru koto
wa dekinakatta.**

I could see Yukie-san as nothing more than my father's 'new wife'.

d だが、この道路、歩道が途中までしかない。

**Da ga, kono dōro, hodō ga tochū made shika nai.**

However, there is only a pavement part of the way along this road.

11.1.3.1.3 | Number + counter **shika**

a 二つの棟は四メートルしか離れていない。

**Futatsu no tō wa yon-mētoru shika hanarete inai.**

The two houses are only 4 metres apart.

11.1.3.2 | Adjective/adverb **shika**

This also means 'only', 'nothing but'.

a オルガンのコンサートはまれにしか開かれない。

**Orugan no konsāto wa mare ni shika hirakarenai.**

Organ concerts are held only very rarely.

b 第三者にはこっけいにしか映らない省益の衝突である。

**Daisansha ni wa kokkei ni shika utsuranai shōeki no shōtotsu
de aru.**

It was a collision of ministerial interests which, to an outside observer,
looked nothing but comical.

11.1.3.3 | Verb/verbal noun **shika**

After verbs and verbal nouns, the meaning is 'all one can do is', 'there's
no choice but'.

a できるものなら、やるしかない。

**Dekiru mono nara, yaru shika nai.**

The only thing is to get on with it, if we can.

b 当面は事態を静観するしかない。

**Tōmen wa jitai o seikan suru shika nai.**

For the time being, all we can do is sit back and watch how
the situation develops.

c 内閣総辞職しかない。

**Naikaku sōjishoku shika nai.**

The only [option] is resignation of the Cabinet en masse.

11.1.3.4 *Noun copula-***de shika**

In this use (meaning 'is merely'), **shika** is sandwiched between the conjunctive form of the copula (**de**), and the negative form **nai** (or **arimasen**). Alternatively, one can analyse this form as **shika** replacing **wa** in the negative form of the copula **de wa nai** (see 7.5).

a 「塾が問題生徒のたまり場」という言い方はおごりでしかあり
　ません。

**'Juku ga mondai seito no tamariba' to iu iikata wa ogori de
shika arimasen.**

To say 'Crammers are just a haunt for problem children' is mere
arrogance.

b たしかに庭といっても、広さわずか七、八平方メートル、横浜の
　下町の家と家に挟まれた「すき間」のような空間でしかない。

**Tashika ni niwa to itte mo, hirosa wazuka shichi, hachi heihō
mētoru, Yokohama no shitamachi no ie to ie ni hasamareta
'sukima' no yō na kūkan de shika nai.**

It's true, the garden is just 7 or 8 square metres in size, and is no
more than a space that's like a gap between downtown Yokohama
houses.

11.1.4 **bakari, dake, shika** *compared*

These adverbial particles can all translate as 'only' in some of their uses. Formally, **shika** differs from **bakari** and **dake** in that it is used with negative forms. **dake** and **shika** are the only ones that can be used together, in the form **dake shika**.

a リゾートクラブ会員権を保有していても、これまでは同一クラブ
　の施設だけしか利用できなかった。

**Rizōto kurabu no kaiin-ken o hoyū shite ite mo, kore made
wa dōitsu kurabu no shisetsu dake shika riyō dekinakatta.**

Even if one holds membership of a resort club, so far one can only
use the facilities of that same club.

b あなたって、いつも用事のある時だけしか電話してこないのね。

**Anata tte, itsumo yōji no aru toki dake shika denwa shite konai no ne.**

You only ever ring when you want something, right?

In meaning, **shika** is the most 'exclusive', emphasizing the meaning of 'only' in the sense of 'nothing but'.

After amounts, **shika** + negative (see 11.1.3.1.3) and V/VN (see 11.1.3.3), **shika** can be replaced by **dake** (**da**), but the negative form needs to be changed to a positive one.

After N, **bakari** means 'only' or 'just' in the sense that something is 'overwhelmingly so' or 'all the time' (see 11.1.1.4.1 for examples), whereas **dake** and **shika** are used in the exclusive sense of 'only'.

**bakari** can be replaced by **dake** after a repeatable V (11.1.1.1.1) and in the uses shown in 11.1.1.4.1, 4.2 and 4.3 (but *not* with amounts of time (11.1.1.4.3 a), where the meaning of **bakari** is 'about'), 11.1.1.5 and 11.1.1.10.

After intensifying V (11.1.1.1.2), **dake** changes the meaning of the **bakari** sentence as shown below.

c 政治不信は高まるばかりだ。

**Seiji fushin wa takamaru bakari da.**

Distrust in politics is getting ever greater.

d ⊘政治不信は高まるだけだ。

**Seiji fushin wa takamaru dake da.**

Distrust in politics will only become greater.

The context that needs to be assumed for the **dake** version would be something like "If you were to do this, then the result would only/predictably be that...".

When compared to **dake** (see 11.1.2), **dake** can be replaced by **bakari** in uses shown in 11.1.2.1.1.1, 11.1.2.6 and 11.1.2.7. In use 11.1.1.2.2, **dake** can be replaced by **bakari** in example b only, i.e. when used after VN, but NOT other N.

## 11.2 Inclusive particles

Inclusive particles are particles such as **mo**, which typically have meanings like 'also' or 'too', i.e. the item they are attached to is included along with other items that have been mentioned or are understood from the context.

## 11.2.1 | mo

Like **wa**, **mo** replaces the case particle **ga** (but note **mo ga** after Q-words, see 11.2.1.6) and usually **o** (but **o mo** is also found), and is added to others. Like **wa**, **mo** can also be inserted between forms such as -**te iru**, Adj-**ku nai** and **de aru**.

Whereas **wa** (see 11.3) is separating or exclusive in nature, **mo** is inclusive. In its basic use, it translates as 'too' or 'also', but when used with negatives it serves to emphasize what is negated (see also 11.2.7).

### 11.2.1.1 | Noun (particle) **mo**

Here, **mo** means 'too', 'also'.

#### 11.2.1.1.1 | Noun (particle) **mo** predicate

a 値段も安い。

**Nedan mo yasui.**

The price is cheap, too.

b この冬も鍋の売れ行きが好調だ。

**Kono fuyu mo nabe no ureyuki ga kōchō da.**

This winter, too, casserole dishes are doing well.

c こうした犯罪グループは不法滞在者がほとんどで、取り締まりには困難が伴う。情報にも敏感だ。

**Kōshita hanzai gurūpu wa fuhō taizaisha ga hotondo de, torishimari ni wa konnan ga tomonau. Jōhō ni mo binkan da.**

This kind of crime syndicate consists almost entirely of people staying in the country illegally, and so they are difficult to control. They are sensitive to information, too.

#### 11.2.1.1.2 | With ellipted predicate

a 日本語のわからん日本人などというのが出てくる。—日本語のうまい米国人も。(わからん = わからない)

**Nihongo no wakaran Nihonjin nado to iu no ga dete kuru. --Nihongo no umai Beikokujin mo. [wakaran = wakaranai]**

[In a world without frontiers] There will be Japanese who don't understand the Japanese language. And Americans who are good at Japanese.

| 11.2.1.2 | *Noun* **mo**

| 11.2.1.2.1 | Noun = amount

After amounts, **mo** emphasizes the amount (with positive and negative predicates).

| 11.2.1.2.1.1 | With positive predicate

This is used to indicate an unexpectedly large amount 'as many as' etc.

a 途中、何十カ所もの橋を渡った。
   **Tochū, nanjukkasho mo no hashi o watatta.**
   On the way we crossed dozens of bridges.

| 11.2.1.2.1.2 | With negative predicate

With a negative predicate, the meaning is 'not even', or 'not either'.

a 今は一人も残っていない。
   **Ima wa hitori mo nokotte inai.**
   Now, there isn't even a single person left.

b 会員登録をしている人が百人弱、案内状を差し上げる人が三百人
   くらい。会則や会費もありません。
   **Kai-in tōroku o shite iru hito ga hyakunin-jaku, annaijō o
   sashiageru hito ga sanbyaku-nin kurai. Kaisoku ya kaihi mo
   arimasen.**
   The number of registered members is just under a hundred. People to
   whom we send information number about 300. There aren't any
   membership fees or statutes, either.

| 11.2.1.2.2 | After other nouns

After a noun not indicating an amount, **mo** can also impart the meaning of 'even'.

a 今度の不況期における財政の出動規模は第一次石油ショック時を
   もしのぐものだった。
   **Kondo no fukyōki ni okeru zaisei no shutsudō kibo wa
   dai-ichi-ji sekiyu shokku-ji o mo shinogu mono datta.**
   The magnitude of public finances marshalled in the present depression
   exceeded even those of the time of the first oil shock.

**11.2.1.3** *Verb-**te mo** negative predicate*

Note how **mo** can be sandwiched between -**te** (or V-stem, the conjunctive-form equivalent) and **iru, suru** (see 11.2.1.7, 25.5).

a 思ってもいなかった。
**Omotte mo inakatta.**
It never even occurred to me.

b まさか自分が優勝するなんて思いもしなかった。
**Masaka jibun ga yūshō suru nante omoi mo shinakatta.**
I never even imagined that I'd win.

**11.2.1.4** *With two or more items*

**11.2.1.4.1** With positive predicate

a 芸術家も科学者も同じ。
**Geijutsuka mo kagakusha mo onaji.**
Artists and scientists are the same sort.

b カネも出すが口も出す。
**Kane mo dasu ga kuchi mo dasu.**
They give money but also meddle [in our affairs].

**11.2.1.4.2** With negative predicate

This indicates the idea of 'neither . . . nor'.

**11.2.1.4.2.1** *After noun*

a ところが、部屋にはテレビもラジオも電話もない。
**Tokoro ga, heya ni wa terebi mo rajio mo denwa mo nai.**
However, in the room there is neither TV nor radio nor
telephone.

**11.2.1.4.2.2** *After adjective*

a 気候は暑くも寒くもない。
**Kikō wa atsuku mo samuku mo nai.**
The climate is neither hot nor cold.

11.2.1.5 *Time noun* **ni mo**

In journalistic writing, **mo** is often used to emphasize proximity of time: 'as soon as', 'as early as'.

a 二十八日にも発表する。

**Nijūhachi-nichi ni mo happyō suru.**

They are going to announce it as early as the 28th.

b 月内にも着工して、十月稼働を目指す。

**Getsunai ni mo chakkō shite, jūgatsu kadō o mezasu.**

They will start building within the month, and aim to have [the plant] running in October.

11.2.1.6 *After question words*

After question words, too, **mo** can be used with either positive or negative predicates; with positive predicates the combination means 'any' or 'every', with negative predicates 'no (one/thing, etc.)' (see 18).

11.2.1.6.1 After question words, with positive predicate

a だれもが一度は抱きそうな夢だ。

**Dare mo ga ichido wa idakisō na yume da.**

This is a dream that everyone is likely to entertain once.

11.2.1.6.2 After question words, with negative predicate

a 「私は芝居のうまい役者じゃありません」。「だれもそう思いませんよ」。

**'Watashi wa shibai no umai yakusha ja arimasen.'**
**'Dare mo sō omoimasen yo.'**

'I'm not an actor who's good on stage.' 'Nobody thinks that.'

b 死亡した五人はいずれも外傷などはなかった。

**Shibō shita gonin wa izure mo gaishō nado**
**wa nakatta.**

None of the five people who died had any external injuries.

### 11.2.1.7 Noun **de mo aru**

Here, **mo** is sandwiched between **de** (conjunctive form of the copula **da**) and **aru**; the combination also functions as a copula, with the added meaning of 'is *also*', 'is *at the same time*' (see also 11.2.1.3).

a 父親のかわりでもあった。
   **Chichioya no kawari de mo atta.**
   He was also a father-substitute.

b 着付けの教師でもある。
   **Kitsuke no kyōshi de mo aru.**
   She is also a teacher of how to dress [in kimono].

### 11.2.1.8 -te (de) mo

When **mo** is used instead of copula + **wa**, the implication is 'not necessarily', whereas after V/Adj-**te**, the meaning is 'even'. **mo** is also used in phrases like -te/de mo ii 'it's OK if' (see 25.2).

a そうでもない。(cf., そうではない。 **Sō de wa nai.** 'That's not so.')
   **Sō de mo nai.**
   That's not necessarily so.

b スターがいても勝てませんよ。(cf., いては勝てません。 **...ite wa
   katemasen** = If there's a star, we can't win.)
   **Sutā ga ite mo katemasen yo.**
   Even with a star [in the team] we can't win!

### 11.2.1.9 Idiomatic uses

a 一日も早く夫の声が聞きたい。
   **Ichinichi mo hayaku otto no koe ga kikitai.**
   I want to hear my husband's voice as soon as possible.

b 「経済界よ。お前もか」と思ってしまう。
   **'Keizaikai yo. Omae mo ka' to omotte shimau.**
   One feels 'You too, business world?' (Variation on Caesar's 'Et tu,
   Brute?' from Shakespeare's *Julius Caesar*)

c （予想より）一歩も二歩も後退した判決でショックだ。

**(Yosō yori) ippo mo niho mo kōtai shita hanketsu de shokku da.**

We are shocked by the verdict, which has reversed [what was expected] by several steps/degrees.

d いいも悪いもない。これが厳然とした事実なのだ。

**Ii mo warui mo nai. Kore ga genzen to shita jijitsu na no da.**

It's neither good nor bad. It's an indubitable fact.

## 11.2.2 datte

**datte** is attached to nouns and pronouns, as a more colloquial and emphatic equivalent to **mo** or **demo** (see also 26.3.1).

*Note* – there is also a conjunction **datte** (used on its own, at the beginning of a sentence, in the sense of 'but') (see 24.4).

a 私だって子供がほしい。

**Watashi datte kodomo ga hoshii.**

I too want children.

b 二万円台だってまだ高いくらいだ。

**Niman-en-dai datte mada takai kurai da.**

[A price in the] 20,000-yen range is still too high.

## 11.2.3 demo

**demo** must not be confused with **de mo** [case particle] + [adverbial particle]. In the latter case **mo** can be taken away without changing the logical meaning of the sentence. **demo**, on the other hand, is one (non-detachable) unit that indicates the idea of 'for instance', i.e. an item is specified that could be replaced by a similar one without changing the meaning (note, however, the use of **demo** with question words, where this test does not work (see 18). Examples a and b show instances where **mo** can be deleted.

a いずれ人間でも発見される可能性はある。(cf., 人間で発見される **ningen de hakken sareru**)

**Izure ningen de mo hakken sareru kanō-sei wa aru.**

There is a possibility that sooner or later it [= the body clock] will be discovered in humans, too.

b　もう少し小さければ二千五百万円でも建つ。(cf., 二千五百万円で
建つ **nisen gohyakuman-en de tatsu**)
**Mō sukoshi chiisakereba nisen gohyakuman-en demo tatsu.**
If it [= the house] were a little smaller, it could be built even for
25 million yen.

Another difference between **de mo** and **demo** is that the latter can attach
to other case particles, such as **kara, ni, to,** etc.:

c　良いものは日本だろうが欧州だろうが、どこからでも取り入れる。
**Yoi mono wa Nihon darō ga Ōshū darō ga doko kara demo
tori-ireru.**
We take good products from anywhere, whether it's Japan or Europe.

For a comparison with other particles used in the sense of 'even', see 11.2.7.

| 11.2.3.1 | *Noun (particle)* **demo**

| 11.2.3.1.1 | Noun **demo** + positive predicate

This indicates the idea of 'even', **mo** can also be used here, with less
emphasis on the idea of 'even'.

a　「こうした偏見は今でも残っている」と指摘する。
**'Kō shita henken wa ima demo nokotte iru' to shiteki suru.**
'This kind of prejudice remains even now', he points out.

b　五十万円を下回った場合でも、普通預金と同じ金利が適用される。
**Gojūman-en o shitamawatta baai demo, futsū yokin to onaji
kinri ga tekiyō sareru.**
Even when [the balance] falls below half a million yen, the same rate
of interest applies as for ordinary deposits.

| 11.2.3.1.2 | Noun **demo** + negative predicate

With a negative predicate, **demo** indicates the meaning of 'not even', **mo**,
**sae** and **sura** could all be used instead of **demo**; **mo** with less emphasis,
**sae/sura** with more.

a　昔の石原裕次郎とか美空ひばりでも百万枚は売れていない。
**Mukashi no Ishihara Yūjirō toka Misora Hibari demo
hyakuman-mai wa urete inai.**
Not even the old Yujiro Ishihara and Hibari Misora [albums] have sold
a million.

b テレビ好きの子供でもニュースやドキュメントはあまり見ないら
しい。

**Terebi-zuki no kodomo demo nyūsu ya dokyumento wa
amari minai rashii.**

It seems that not even children who like TV watch news and
documentaries much.

---

| 11.2.3.1.3 | Noun **to demo** + verb of communication

Sandwiched between N + quotation particle **to** and a verb of communication, this indicates a non-committal or unsure way of putting something
'for instance', 'perhaps'.

a 心のすき間を埋めるような本とでも呼べばよいだろうか。

**Kokoro no sukima o umeru yō na hon to demo yobeba yoi
darō ka.**

Couldn't one perhaps call it a book that heals a broken heart?

b 細身の体の線が強調されている。柳腰とでも言うのだろうか。

**Hosomi no karada no sen ga kyōchō sarete iru.
Yanagigoshi to demo iu no darō ka.**

The line of her slim body is emphasized. This is what one might call
'willow hips' (= a slim figure), I suppose.

---

| 11.2.3.2 | *Noun* **dake demo**

This expresses the idea of 'just', 'even just' (see 11.1.2).

a せめて交通費だけでも・・・

**Semete kōtsūhi dake demo ...**

If even just the transportation expenses (could be paid) ...

b この主要四業種だけでも三億円を超えたようだ。

**Kono shuyō yon-gyōshu dake demo san'oku-en o koeta yō da.**

It appears that [the donations by] just these four main types of
industry exceeded three hundred million yen.

---

| 11.2.3.3 | *Adverb clause-*te demo *predicate*

**demo** can be sandwiched between an adverbial clause and the predicate it
modifies, in the sense of 'even if it means doing', 'for instance' (see 25.5).

a 借金してでも返せばよかった。
**Shakkin shite demo kaeseba yokatta.**
I should have returned [the money], even if it meant borrowing.

b 「美術というものは、だましてでもいいから他人に作品をいかに
納得させるかで決まるもの」と言ってはばからない。
**'Bijutsu to iu mono wa, damashite demo ii kara tanin ni
sakuhin o ika ni nattoku saseru ka de kimaru mono'
to itte habakaranai.**
He doesn't hesitate to say 'Art [business] is decided by how you
convince others of the work, even if it means cheating them'.

| 11.2.3.4 | *Question word +* **demo**

| 11.2.3.4.1 | Question word (+ particle) **demo**

The combination of a question word and **demo** results in a variety of
meanings depending on the Q-word, including 'every', 'any', 'no matter'
(see Table 5.2, 5.2).

Note especially how particles like **ka** and **ni** are 'sandwiched' between the
question word and **demo** (examples d and e).

a 赤星さんは営業からふろ掃除まで何でもこなす。
**Akaboshi-san wa eigyō kara furo sōji made nan
demo konasu.**
Akaboshi-san handles everything [in the hotel], from operations to
cleaning the bath.

b 買ってくれるところがあれば、いつでも供給する。
**Katte kureru tokoro ga areba, itsu demo kyōkyū suru.**
If there are places that will buy from us, we'll supply any time.

c いつでも、どこでも、だれでも、酒やたばこなどを買うことがで
きる。
**Itsu demo, doko demo, dare demo, sake ya tabako nado
o kau koto ga dekiru.**
[In Japan,] anybody can buy alcohol and cigarettes any time,
any place.

d 何枚かでも絵を見せてごらん。
**Nanmai ka demo e o misete goran.**
Go ahead and show me even just a few pictures.

e 基地局をどこにでも設けられるため地下街でも通話できる。
**Kichikyoku o doko ni demo mōkerareru tame chikagai demo tsūwa dekiru.**
Because the base station can be set up anywhere, one can use the [mobile] telephone even in an underground mall.

| 11.2.3.4.2 | Noun-modifying question word + noun **demo** |

Question words used before N include **dono** and **donna**, with the combination meaning 'every' (see Table 5.2, 5.2). **mo** can also be used in the same sense.

a どの芝居でも前半に辛気臭いところがある。
**Dono shibai demo zenhan ni shinki-kusai tokoro ga aru.**
Every play has a tedious part in the first half.

| 11.2.3.4.3 | **donna ni … demo** |

Here the meaning is 'no matter how' or 'even'. Note that **demo** can be positioned quite a long distance away from the Q-word, as in example b (see 5.2.2.1.2).

a 制服はどんなにしゃれたデザインでも会社の物。
**Seifuku wa donna ni shareta dezain demo kaisha no mono.**
Uniforms, no matter how smart the design, belong to the company.

b どんなに預貯金をたくわえマンションを購入済みの独身貴族でも状況は同じ。
**Donna ni yochokin o takuwae manshon o kōnyūzumi no dokushin kizoku demo jōkyō wa onaji.**
The situation is the same, even with single people with large savings and an apartment already purchased.

| 11.2.3.5 | *Idiomatic uses* |

Idiomatic expressions with **demo** include **sukoshi demo** 'even a little' and **naka demo** 'of/among'.

a 少しでも電気代を減らそうとしている。
**Sukoshi demo denkidai o herasō to shite iru.**
We're trying to reduce our electricity bill, even by just a little.

b 見識、品格に少しでも近づきたいと思った。
**Kenshiki, hinkaku ni sukoshi demo chikazukitai to omotta.**
I thought that I wanted to come into contact with his discernment
and dignity, even in a minor way.

## 11.2.4 made

**made** attaches to nouns, N + particle, and adverbial clauses. It can in
turn be followed by case particles that are required by the valency of the
predicate.

**made** indicates the most unlikely item, or extent, that applies to a situation
or action 'even', 'so far as', 'as many as', etc.

### 11.2.4.1 Noun **made** (+ particle)

a このうち六巻までをゲーム化した。
**Kono uchi rokkan made o gēmuka shita.**
Of these [= volumes of a novel], they have turned as many as six
volumes into game software.

b 鉄を鍛えるためのふいごまでが自家製だ。
**Tetsu o kitaeru tame no fuigo made ga jikasei da.**
Even the bellows for forging the iron are self-made.

c 実際に製造部門では無人工場まであります。
**Jissai ni seizō bumon de wa mujin kōjō made arimasu.**
In fact, in the manufacturing division there is even an unmanned workshop.

### 11.2.4.2 Noun + particle **made**

a 病根は小学校にまで広がっている。
**Byōkon wa shōgakko ni made hirogatte iru.**
The roots of the disease extend all the way down to the elementary
schools.

b なぜ日本人は余暇にまでマニュアルを持ち込むのだろうか。
**Naze Nihonjin wa yoka ni made manyuaru o mochikomu no
darō ka.**
Why do the Japanese bring manuals even to leisure [activities]?

331

c 今年中に二店を新規出店、将来は十店程度にまで増やす考え。

**Kotoshi-jū ni niten o shinki shutten, shōrai wa jutten teido
ni made fuyasu kangae.**

They're planning to open two new restaurants in the course of this
year and increase [the number of restaurants] to as many as ten
or so in the future.

---

| 11.2.4.3 | *Adverbial clause-verb-***te made**

When **made** is attached to an adverbial clause ending in V-**te**, the combination means 'going to the extent of doing', 'even at the expense of doing'
(see also 11.2.3.3).

a 億単位の投資をしてまで農業をする人がいるだろうか。

**Okutan'i no tōshi o shite made nōgyō o suru hito ga iru
darō ka.**

Do you really think there are people who engage in farming even if
it means investing hundreds of millions of yen?

b ・・・たくさんのお金を使ってまでアピールすることはない。

**. . . takusan no o-kane o tsukatte made apīru suru koto
wa nai.**

. . . there is no point appealing [to the electorate] at great expense
(*lit.* "at the expense of using a lot of money").

c 肉は動物を殺してまで、と思うので、食べることが少なくなり
ました。

**Niku wa dōbutsu o koroshite made, to omou no de, taberu
koto ga sukunaku narimashita.**

I don't eat much meat now, because I feel that [I don't want to eat it]
if it means killing animals.

---

| 11.2.5 | **sae**

**sae** is attached to N, V-stem and VN, and clauses (direct or indirect quotations, usually ending in the quotation particle **to**), adding emphasis in
the sense of 'even' and, in combination with V/Adj-**ba**, 'as long as'. In use
11.2.5.1 (but with negative predicates only), it may be regarded as a more
emphatic equivalent of **mo**.

| 11.2.5.1 | *Noun/verb-stem* **sae**

The sense here is 'even'.

| 11.2.5.1.1 | Noun (particle) **sae**

**sae** replaces the case particles **ga** and **o**, but attaches to others such as **ni**, **kara** and **to**.

a 憤りさえ覚える。
  **Ikidōri sae oboeru.**
  One even feels rage.

b 資料に名さえ残っていない。
  **Shiryō ni na sae nokotte inai.**
  Not even his name appears in the [historical] documents.

c 最低限必要な施設さえなかった。
  **Saiteigen hitsuyō na shisetsu sae nakatta.**
  They didn't even have the minimum of facilities required.

d 日本では、今年度の予算さえ、まだ成立していない。
  **Nihon de wa, konnen-do no yosan sae, mada seiritsu shite inai.**
  In Japan, even the budget for this fiscal year hasn't been approved yet.

e 農畜産物は北海道の顔とさえ言っていいだろう。
  **Nōchikusan-butsu wa Hokkaidō no kao to sae itte ii darō.**
  It would probably even be all right to say that Hokkaido is best
    known for its farm (*lit.* "crops and livestock") products.

f 犬はテレパシーを持っているのかとさえ感じるそうだ。
  **Inu wa terepashī o motte iru no ka to sae kanjiru sō da.**
  He is even said to feel that dogs may have telepathic powers.

| 11.2.5.1.2 | (Noun **mo**) noun **sae mo**

In both positive and negative sentences, N **sae mo** is often used after other
N + **mo**, with emphasis on the N to which **sae mo** is attached.

a 農作業の分担も、水の配分さえも村単位で行われた。
  **Nōsagyō no buntan mo, mizu no bunpai sae mo mura tan'i
    de okonawareta.**
  The allotment of farm work and even the distribution of water were
    carried out at the village unit level.

b その家は窓ガラスもドアも床さえもないがらんどうだ。

**Sono ie wa mado-garasu mo doa mo yuka sae mo nai
garandō da.**

That house is completely bare, with no windowpanes, no doors,
and not even any floor.

c 驚くべきことに、腸内細菌の多寡さえもヒトの睡眠量を左右する
のだ。

**Odoroku-beki koto ni, chōnai saikin no taka sae mo hito no
suimin-ryō o sayū suru no da.**

Believe it or not, even the quantity of bacteria in the intestine affects
the amount of sleep a person gets.

11.2.5.1.3 Noun (particle) **de sae**

This is a more emphatic equivalent of N **demo** (see 11.2.3.1).

a 一国の中でさえその文化圏は異なる。

**Ikkoku no naka de sae sono bunka-ken wa kotonaru.**

Even within one country, the cultural area [= where garlic is eaten]
differs.

b 動物園にいる熱帯産の動物でさえむし暑さには参るらしい。

**Dōbutsu-en ni iru nettai-san no dōbutsu de sae mushiatsu-sa
ni wa mairu rashii.**

Even the zoo animals from the tropics seem unable to stand
the humidity.

c 今や子供でさえ、絵が動くだけでは喜ばない。

**Ima ya kodomo de sae, e ga ugoku dake de wa yorokobanai.**

Nowadays even children aren't impressed with pictures that do
nothing but move.

11.2.5.1.4 Verb-stem/verbal noun **sae suru**

In this use, **sae** can be attached to V-stem (example a) or sandwiched
between the verbal noun and a form of **suru** (example b) (see 1.9).

a 自分らしいバランスに気をつければ、モデルより素敵に見えさえ
する。

**Jibun rashii baransu ni ki o tsukereba, moderu yori suteki ni
mie sae suru.**

If you're careful to maintain a balance that suits you, you can look
even more attractive than a model.

b それどころか、積極的に相談に乗ってくれ、バックアップさえしてくれた。

**Sore dokoro ka, sekkyoku-teki ni sōdan ni notte kure, bakkuappu sae shite kureta.**

Not only that, they [= the government] actively gave us advice, and even backed us up.

| 11.2.5.2 | *Noun/verb-stem* **sae** ... *verb/adjective-***ba** |

As part of a conjunctional clause ending in -**ba**, the resulting meaning is 'as long as', 'provided that' (see 26.1.1).

a 実力さえあれば必ずチャンスがある。

**Jitsuryoku sae areba kanarazu chansu ga aru.**

As long as you have ability, your chance will come without fail.

b 品質さえ良ければタイヤは売れる。

**Hinshitsu sae yokereba taiya wa ureru.**

Tyres will sell as long as they're of good quality.

c ニミリのすき間さえあればゴキブリは入り込むという。

**Ni-miri no sukima sae areba gokiburi wa hairikomu to iu.**

As long as there is an opening of 2 mm., cockroaches will enter, they say.

d 早期発見さえできれば肺がんは怖くない。

**Sōki hakken sae dekireba haigan wa kowakunai.**

As long as it can be detected in the early stages, lung cancer isn't [a] frightening [thing].

e 地震さえなければ二人そろって学校に通っていたはずだった。

**Jishin sae nakereba futari sorotte gakkō ni kayotte ita hazu datta.**

Had it not been for the earthquake, the two of them would have gone to school together.

| 11.2.6 | **sura** |

The particle **sura** 'even' is like **sae** in meaning and, also like **sae**, it replaces the case particles **ga/o**, but attaches to others, such as **ni** and **de**. With the exception of the use explained in 11.2.6.2 (negative predicates only), **sura** can always be replaced by **sae**.

11.2.6.1 | *Noun (particle)* **sura**

11.2.6.1.1 | Noun **sura**

In this use, **sura** 'even' cannot usually be replaced by **mo** in the same sense, except with negative predicates.

11.2.6.1.1.1 | *Positive predicate*

a 著者の語りの旨さに感動すら覚える。
**Chosha no katari no umasa ni kandō sura oboeru.**
One even feels moved by the deftness of the author's narration.

b しかっても、殴っても言うことを聞かない娘に憎しみすら
覚えた。
**Shikatte mo, nagutte mo iu koto o kikanai musume ni
nikushimi sura oboeta.**
I even felt hatred towards my daughter, who wouldn't listen to me
even if I scolded her or hit her.

c 演奏には円熟味が増し、余裕すら感じられる。
**Ensō ni wa enjukumi ga mashi, yoyū sura kanjirareru.**
There is an increased mellowness in her [musical] performance,
and one even feels that she still has something in reserve.

d ネットワークは企業自体のあり方すら変えようとしている。
**Nettowāku wa kigyō jitai no arikata sura kaeyō to shite iru.**
[Computer] networks are about to change even the very nature of
business.

11.2.6.1.1.2 | *Negative predicate*

Here, **mo** can be used in the same sense, but with less emphasis.

a 都心では一等星すら見られない。
**Toshin de wa ittōsei sura mirarenai.**
In the heart of the city, one can't even see stars of the first
magnitude.

b 住宅が密集し、子供が遊ぶ空き地すらなかった。
**Jūtaku ga misshū shi, kodomo ga asobu akichi
sura nakatta.**
The houses were close together and there wasn't even any open
space for the children to play.

c 世界の飢えの問題解決に、薄明かりすら見えない。

**Sekai no ue no mondai kaiketsu ni, usuakari sura mienai.**

We don't see even a glimmer [of hope] for a solution to the problem of world hunger.

| 11.2.6.1.2 | Noun + particle **sura** |

Here, **sura** can be replaced by **mo** in a similar sense, but **sura** is more emphatic.

a 税制をあずかる主税局にすら伝えていない構想だった。

**Zeisei o azukaru shuzeikyoku ni sura tsutaete inai kōsō datta.**

It [= lowering taxes backdated by 15 months] was an idea that they hadn't even communicated to the revenue department, which is in charge of the taxation system.

b 子どもというのは長いこと接している教師ですら信じられないような力を出すことがある。

**Kodomo to iu no wa nagai koto sesshite iru kyōshi de sura shinjirarenai yō na chikara o dasu koto ga aru.**

Children can sometimes display a strength that even their teachers, who have been in daily contact for a long time, cannot believe.

c 本社ですらつくっていないので、現地でもつくらせない。

**Honsha de sura tsukutte inai no de, genchi de mo tsukurasenai.**

We're not even making [that product] at our headquarters, so we aren't going to let them make it overseas either.

| 11.2.6.1.3 | Noun **sura mo** |

Combining **sura** and **mo** makes for an even more emphatic effect.

a 一極集中は東京すらも苦しめている。

**Ikkyoku shūchū wa Tōkyō sura mo kurushimete iru.**

Unipolar centralization is even hurting Tokyo, too.

| 11.2.6.2 | **de sura aru/nai**: *sandwiched between parts of the copula* |

This means 'is (not) even'. The parts of the copula are **de aru** (positive) and **de nai** (negative), and variations (see 7.5).

Inclusive particles

337

If **mo** is used instead of **sura**, the translations 'not either' in negative sentences (example a), and 'also' in positive ones (example b) are more appropriate. In example b only, **sura** can be replaced by **sae**.

a 鬼頭さんは役職者でもなく、正社員ですらない。
   **Kitō-san wa yakushokusha de mo naku, seishain
   de sura nai.**
   Kitō-san isn't in a managerial position; he's not even a full-time
   employee.

b 現在の課題に挑戦し続ける今村の姿勢は、ある種感動的ですら
   ある。
   **Genzai no kadai ni chōsen shi-tsuzukeru Imamura no shisei
   wa, aru shu kandō-teki de sura aru.**
   The stance taken by Imamura, who continues to face the challenge of
   the tasks at hand, is even, in a way, touching.

---

| 11.2.6.3 | *Clause* **sura**: *attached to indirect quotations*

In this use, **sura** can be replaced by the weaker **mo**.

a 本当にいくらお金がかかるかすら発表されない。
   **Hontō ni ikura o-kane ga kakaru ka sura happyō sarenai.**
   How much money it will actually cost is not even being
   made public.

b これでは、規制が撤廃の方向に向かうのかどうかすら明確
   でない。
   **Kore de wa, kisei ga teppai no hōkō ni mukau no ka dō ka
   sura meikaku de nai.**
   With this, it is not even clear whether restrictions will move in
   the direction of being abolished or not.

---

| **11.2.7** | mo, demo, made, sae, sura *compared*

These particles can all mean 'even'. However, **mo** is used in this sense only in certain uses (see 11.2.1.2, 11.2.1.3 and 11.2.1.8 (after V/A-**te**)). In several uses (see 11.2.1.2.2, 11.2.1.2.1.2 and 11.2.1.3), **sae/sura** can be used instead of **mo**. In 11.2.1.6.1, **mo** can be replaced with **demo**. In 11.2.1.7, **sae/sura** could be used instead of **mo**, but with the meaning of 'even', not 'also'.

demo can be replaced with the weaker **mo** in uses 11.2.3.1.1 and 11.2.3.1.2, and by **sae** and **sura** in 11.2.3.1.2.

made can be replaced by **sae** and **sura** in uses 11.2.4.2 a and b (**mo** is also possible, but only in the sense of 'also'), but *not* after amounts (see 11.2.4.2 c).

sae can be replaced by the weaker **mo** in uses 11.2.5.1.1 (negative sentences only; with positive sentences **mo** means 'also', not 'even') and 11.2.5.1.3. sae can be replaced by **sura** in all its uses, except in uses sae 11.2.5.1.4 (but *only* with N-**suru** V) and 11.2.5.2.

sura can be replaced by **sae** in all uses, and by **mo** in uses 11.2.6.1 and 11.2.6.2 (negative sentences only; in positive sentences the meaning of **mo** would be 'also'), 11.2.6.1.2 and 11.2.6.3. In 11.2.6.1.1.1, **made** can also be used instead of **sura**, and in 11.2.6.1.3 **sura mo** can be replaced with **sae mo** and **made mo**.

## 11.3   **The defocussing or topic particle** wa

The widely used particle **wa** has a focussing function, but unlike **mo** (see 11.2.1), which focusses the noun, etc. it is attached to, the basic function of **wa** is to move the focus away from the item it attaches to. Thus it focusses on what follows, i.e. the predicate. Traditionally, **wa** has been called a 'separating' or 'isolating' particle, a name that also explains its defocussing effect, and is perhaps most typically seen in the way **wa** is inserted, wedge-like, between forms that are normally used without **wa** (see 11.3.5.3.2).

This basic function explains the various labels that have been used to describe this particle, which is particularly difficult for English speakers because it usually has no translation equivalent (the exception is illustrated in 11.3.3) in English. **wa** is often called a topic particle, because it typically marks the topic of a topic–comment type sentence. The focus in these sentences is on the comment (or predicate). In this respect **wa** contrasts with **ga**, which can place emphasis on the noun preceding it (see 2.1, 11.3.12, 7.6).

However, emphasis or focus is something that is inherent in the different nature of **wa** and **ga**, relating to their basic meaning, which is said to be considered or categorial judgement (**wa**) versus perceptual judgement (**ga**). For more details, see 11.3.1.1 and 11.3.2.

11.3.1 *Replacing case particles ga/o*

When attached to subjects and objects, **wa** replaces the case particles **ga** and **o** (in other words, combinations like **ga wa** or **o wa** do not exist). Case particles other than **ga/o**, on the other hand, combine with **wa** by attaching it (11.3.2).

11.3.1.1 *Replacing* **ga**

In considered statements, **wa** is used rather than **ga**. In example a, a general statement is made about black tea, which implies at the same time that black tea is also contrasted implicitly with other foods or drinks that may be not so good for you. That is the source of the 'contrast' meaning of **wa** (see 11.3.5).

If the same sentence is formed with **ga**, instead of considered judgement a sudden realization or perception is implied.

a 紅茶は体にいい。
**Kōcha wa karada ni ii.**
Black tea is good for you (*lit.* "your body").

b 日本は豊かになった。
**Nihon wa yutaka ni natta.**
Japan has become affluent.

c 「お客さんは賢いです」と話していた。
**'O-kyaku-san wa kashikoi desu' to hanashite ita.**
'The customers are clever', he said.

d 日本の裁判は長い。
**Nihon no saiban wa nagai.**
Japanese trials are long.

11.3.1.2 *Replacing* **o**

With **o**, the most common word order for example a would be a'. The object of the verb in this sentence is in the basic Japanese word order [subject-**ga** object-**o** verb]. In example a, the object is moved to the beginning of the sentence now marked by **wa**. The effect of **wa** is to make the wa-marked NP into the topic, which is usually placed at the beginning of the sentence, i.e. a″ is not possible. Notice the English translation, which uses the definite article. Generally speaking, **wa** attaches to given information, whereas **ga** introduces new information.

a 献金は秘書が取り仕切っていた。
**Kenkin wa hisho ga torishikitte ita.**
The donations were managed by the secretary (*lit.* "as for the donations, the secretary managed [them]").

a′ ✎秘書が献金を取り仕切っていた。
**Hisho ga kenkin o torishikitte ita.**
The secretary managed donations/the donations.

a″ ✎×秘書が献金は取り仕切っていた。
**Hisho ga kenkin wa torishikitte ita.**

## 11.3.2 Added to case particles (other than ga/o)

With other cases, **wa** is added after the case particle required by the valency of V. The examples that follow (in 11.3.2.1–5) are not exhaustive, i.e. there are other combinations too. Note that **wa** is especially common in sentences with negative predicates, but can be used in positive sentences too, where it has a contrastive or emphasizing effect (see 11.3.5.3). Inserting **wa** between particles and their predicate is in line with its separating nature. All these combinations imply a weak contrast. For instance, example a implies that skill is needed for packing a rucksack, but not necessarily other items.

## 11.3.2.1 ni wa

a ザックの詰め方にはコツがいる。
**Zakku no tsumekata ni wa kotsu ga iru.**
Packing a rucksack requires skill.

b 外国人に的を絞った警察の取り締まりには批判もある。
**Gaikokujin ni mato o shibotta keisatsu no torishimari ni wa hihan mo aru.**
There are also voices critical of police control aimed at foreigners.

The defocussing or topic particle wa

341

## 11.3.2.2 de wa

a 情報はカネでは買えない。
**Jōhō wa kane de wa kaenai.**
You can't buy information with money.

b もう暑いところでは研究ができない。
**Mō atsui tokoro de wa kenkyū ga dekinai.**
I can't do research in hot climates (*lit.* "places") any more.

## 11.3.2.3 e wa

a 関西空港へは週五便が就航している。
**Kansai kūkō e wa shū gobin ga shūkō shite iru.**
To Kansai airport, five flights per week have entered service.

## 11.3.2.4 to wa

a 米国とは政治、経済的にぜひ仲良くしたいと思っている。
**Beikoku to wa seiji, keizai-teki ni zehi nakayoku shitai to omotte iru.**
With the US, we'd very much like to establish good political and economic relations.

## 11.3.2.5 kara wa

a 庄山常務は「守りのリストラは終わった。これからは攻める」。
**Shōyama-jōmu wa 'mamori no risutora wa owatta. Kore kara wa semeru'.**
Managing director Shōyama [said], 'Defensive restructuring is over. From now on, we're going on the attack'.

## 11.3.3 Not replacing any case particle

Here, **wa** is a genuine topic particle 'as for . . .'. Again, note the use of the definite article in the English translation ('Christmas' in example a is of course also a given that doesn't require the definite article).

a クリスマスはどんな過ごし方をしたっていい。
   **Kurisumasu wa donna sugoshikata o shi-tatte ii.**
   Christmas you can spend any way you like.

b 旅客ターミナルは現在のビルを東側に拡張する。
   **Ryokyaku tāminaru wa genzai no biru o higashigawa ni kakuchō suru**
   As for the passenger terminal, we will extend the present building eastwards.

## 11.3.4 Marking known information

### 11.3.4.1 In considered statements

#### 11.3.4.1.1 With **wa** present

One function of **wa**, which is in keeping with its predicate-focussing effect, is to attach to information that is already known or understood. In this use, **wa** has an effect similar to the English definite article (and other cases where a noun refers to something known or previously mentioned).

a 写真撮影は厳しく禁じられた。
   **Shashin satsuei wa kibishiku kinjirareta.**
   The taking of photographs was strictly forbidden.

b 「多少経営の怪しい金融機関でも、一千万円までなら大丈夫」と、目先の金利を優先する向きがある。しかし、これは誤解だ。預金保険の保証は元本だけで、利子分は含まない。
   **'Tashō keiei no ayashii kin'yū kikan de mo, issenman'en made nara daijōbu' to mesaki no kinri o yūsen suru muki ga aru. Shikashi kore wa gokai da. Yokin hoken no hoshō wa ganpon dake de, rishi-bun wa fukumanai.**
   People tend to give preference to [higher-] interest [institutions], because they think that 10 million yen is guaranteed even though the financial institution may be a little shaky. However, that is a misunderstanding. The savings insurance guarantees only the capital, not the interest.

c 同水族館では、二匹のウナギが水中に放電した電気をアンプで
増幅して点灯に成功した。ツリーは年明けまで展示される。

**Dō-suizokukan de wa, nihiki no unagi ga suichū no hōden
shita denki o anpu de zōfuku shite tentō ni seikō shita.
Tsurī wa toshiake made tenji sareru.**

At the aquarium, they have succeeded in lighting up [a Christmas tree]
by amplifying the electricity discharged into the water by two
[electric] eels. The tree will be displayed until the beginning of
the new year.

| 11.3.4.1.2 | With ellipted **wa** |

In colloquial usage, **wa** can be omitted. This is usually accompanied by
comma intonation (and a comma in writing) (see also 27.2).

a ユニバーサル・スタジオ、楽しいんですってね。
**Yunibāsaru sutajio, tanoshii n desu-tte ne.**
The Universal Studios are great fun, I hear.

b このケーキ、私が作ったのよ。
**Kono kēki, watashi ga tsukutta no yo.**
I've made this cake!

| 11.3.4.2 | *In questions* |

| 11.3.4.2.1 | *In questions with question word (+ copula)* |

In information-seeking questions (questions containing a question word
that asks for the information sought), the focus can only be on the part
of the sentence containing the Q-word, which is again the predicate (see
11.3.2). Example a, for instance, establishes first a topic about which
something is to be asked, followed by the question word and question
particle. Literally, this can be mimicked in English as follows: 'the secret
of their success – what is it?'.

a その成功の秘密は何か。
**Sono seikō no himitsu wa nani ka.**
What's the secret of their [= convenience stores'] success?

b インフラとは何を意味するのか。
**Infura to wa nani o imi suru no ka.**
What does 'infra' mean? (*lit.* "'infra', what does it mean?")

11.3.4.2.2  In questions with ellipted question word (+ copula)

In information-seeking questions, the part that is most obvious (i.e. the predicate containing the Q-word + copula, etc.) is frequently ellipted (omitted).

a 今後のスケジュールは。
**Kongo no sukejūru wa.**
[What is] the future schedule?

b 今の気持ちは。
**Ima no kimochi wa.**
[What are] your feelings now?

## 11.3.5  Indicating contrast

Linked to its basic meaning of considered judgement, **wa** naturally implies a constrast. Such contrast is naturally more explicit when it is used more than once in a sentence; in this case, at least the rightmost **wa** indicates a contrast (where there are three **wa,** the rightmost two indicate contrast, as in example b). As the leftmost **wa** (indicating the subject or topic) is often omitted, in sentences with two **wa** both can be contrastive.

### 11.3.5.1  Used twice: explicit contrast in considered statements

Where **wa** is used twice in a sentence, it serves to indicate a contrast between the two **wa**-marked N/NP. The leftmost **wa** in example b indicates the subject/topic.

a 「男は仕事、女は家庭」という考え方。
**'Otoko wa shigoto, onna wa katei' to iu kangae-kata.**
The proposition 'Men should work, and women stay at home'.

b 札幌は日の出は早く、日没は遅い。
**Sapporo wa hinode wa hayaku, nichibotsu wa osoi.**
In Sapporo/As for Sapporo, the sunrise is early, and the sunset is late.

c 絵を見ない日はあっても建築を見ない日はない。
**E o minai hi wa atte mo kenchiku o minai hi wa nai.**
Even though there are days when I don't look at a painting, there are no days when I don't look at architecture.

In such statements, a comment is made on the N (or NP). This implies that the comment may not apply to other N (or NP), i.e. a contrast is implied.

a 紅茶は体にいい。
   **Kōcha wa karada ni ii**
   Black tea is good for you.

b WASPは少子化傾向にある。
   **WASP wa shōshika keikō ni aru.**
   WASPs [= White Anglo-Saxon Protestants] have a tendency to have
   few[er] children.

To be noted in this context are also common daily greetings such as **konnichi wa** 'good day' and **konban wa** 'good evening'. In fact, the 'good' part has been abbreviated, from something like, 'today is a good day', originally a considered statement.

**wa** is used in negative sentences to indicate the scope or range of what is being negated, essentially in implied contrast to a positive situation. **wa** and the negative form following it negate the item they are attached to. This is done in two ways, as set out below.

a 今年は帰るつもりはなかったのだが ‥‥‥。(cf., 帰るつもりがな
   かった kaeru tsumori ga nakatta)
   **Kotoshi wa kaeru tsumori wa nakatta no da ga . . .**
   This year I had no intention of going back, but . . .

b 大阪市では大阪駅に近い立地には有力酒類DS、徳岡（大阪市、
   徳岡豊裕社長）が来春出店する。売り場面積は約七十平方メ
   ートル。駐車場はない。
   **Ōsaka-shi de wa Ōsaka eki ni chikai ritchi ni wa yūryoku
   sakerui DS, Tokuoka (Ōsaka-shi Tokuoka Toyohiro shachō)
   ga raishun shutten suru. Uriba menseki wa yaku nanajū
   heihō mētoru. Chūshajō wa nai.**
   In Osaka, the large drinks discount shop Tokuoka ([based in] Osaka;
   President Tokuoka Toyohiro) will open a store in a location near

Osaka station. The shop floor space will be about 70 square metres. There will be no parking. (cf., 駐車場がない。**Chūshajō ga nai.**)

c フランスで買える日本のマンガの90％以上が日本語版だが、在仏日本人向けの日本の本専門書店にも、わざわざマンガを求めてフランス人の若者が買いにくるという。彼らは、もちろん日本語はできない。(cf., 日本語ができない。**Nihongo ga dekinai.**)

**Furansu de kaeru nihon no manga no kyūjup-pāsento ga
nihongo-ban da ga, zaifutsu Nihonjin-muke no Nihon no
hon senmon shoten ni mo, wazawaza manga o motomete
furansu-jin no wakamono ga kai ni kuru to iu. Karera wa
mochiron Nihongo wa dekinai.**

Over 90 per cent of comics one can buy in France are in Japanese, yet young French people are said even to visit specialist bookshops catering for Japanese residents in France to buy comics. Of course, they don't understand Japanese [= language].

d 「松坂屋銀座店」の中二階にある女性用トイレに中年の男がナイフを持って侵入し、中にいた横浜市のOL (27) のハンドバッグを奪って店の外に逃げた。・・・ハンドバッグに現金は入っていなかった。(cf., 現金が入っていなかった。**genkin ga haitte inakatta.**)

**'Matsuzakaya Ginza-ten' no chūnikai ni aru josei-yō toire ni
chūnen no otoko ga naifu o motte shinnyū shi, naka ni ita
Yokohama-shi no ōeru (27) no handobaggu o ubatte mise
no soto ni nigeta.... handobaggu ni genkin wa haitte inakatta.**

A middle-aged man with a knife entered the ladies' toilet on the level 2 mezzanine at the 'Ginza Matsuzakaya', and fled outside having taken the handbag of an office worker (27) from Yokohama.... There wasn't any cash in the handbag.

| 11.3.5.3.2 | Sandwiched before a negative form

Typical of the 'separating' nature of **wa** is the way it can be inserted between forms such as **-te iku**, **-te kureru**, etc. (examples c and d), the quotation particle **to** and a V of communication (example g), or a V and its negative form (examples a and b), or an adjective and its negative form (examples e and f). See also examples under 11.3.6 for instances where **wa** intervenes between a V and the particle it takes.

The effect of inserting **wa** is one of emphasizing the negative. Recall also that the negative form of the copula is **de wa nai**, which is another instance of an inserted **wa**, except that this one has become fossilized.

With a V and its negative form, depending on the type of V, there are two formations: 1) with VN (N that attach **suru**), **wa** is inserted between the N and **suru**, but 2) any other V needs first to be converted to its N form (V-stem), to which **suru** can then be added. **wa** is then inserted between the two.

Colloquially, the V-stem endings + **wa** can be contracted as follows. After the -e or -i of Group II verbs, including potential endings, **wa** is changed regularly to **ya**, as with the Group III verbs **ki-** and **shi-**). for Group I verbs, see Table 11.1.

**Table 11.1** Group I verbs + **wa**

| V-stem ending | Replacement pattern | | | |
|---|---|---|---|---|
| **-i** | wa | shinai* | → | **-iya shinai*** |
| **-ki** | wa | shinai | → | **-kiya/kya shinai** |
| **-gi** | wa | shinai | → | **-giya shinai** |
| **-shi** | wa | shinai | → | **-shiya/sha shinai** |
| **-chi** | wa | shinai | → | **-chiya/cha** ** shinai** |
| **-ni** | wa | shinai | → | **-niya shinai** |
| **-bi** | wa | shinai | → | **-biya shinai** |
| **-mi** | wa | shinai | → | **-miya shinai** |
| **-ri** | wa | shinai | → | **-riya/rya shinai** |

*Note* * and other neg. forms
** **-te wa** can also be contracted to **-cha**

a 隠している山のような作品がある。死ぬまで公開はしない。
   (cf., 公開しない **kōkai shinai**)
   **Kakushite iru yama no yō na sakuhin ga aru. Shinu made kōkai wa shinai.**
   There is an extensive (*lit.* "mountain-like") work I'm hiding. I will not make it public until I die.

b 人間の力なんてそんなに変わりゃしません。
   **Ningen no chikara nante sonna ni kawarya shimasen.**
   People's abilities don't vary that much.

c ✐日本ではくつをはいたまま、家に上がってはいけない。
   **Nihon de wa kutsu o haita mama, ie ni agatte wa ikenai.**
   In Japan, you must not enter a home with your shoes on.

d　愚痴を繰り返していても、だれもあなたを救い出しては
　　くれない。

**Guchi o kurikaeshite ite mo, dare mo anata o sukui-dashite
wa kurenai.**

If you just keep complaining, no one is going to help you.

e　ご夫婦でやっている小さくて明るい気取らないレストランで、
　　地下鉄南阿佐ケ谷駅から歩いて六、七分と、よそから訪れる
　　にはやや交通が不便だけれど、値段も含めてその価値は十分
　　ある。料理の品数は多くはない。(cf., 多くない)

**Go-fūfu de yatte iru chiisakute akarui kidoranai resutoran de,
chikatetsu Minami-Asagaya eki kara aruite roku, shichi-fun
to, yoso kara otozureru ni wa yaya kōtsū ga fuben da
keredo, nedan mo fukumete sono kachi wa jūbun aru.
Ryōri no shinakazu wa ōku wa nai.**

It's a small, bright and unpretentious restaurant run by a husband and
wife. Being six or seven minutes on foot from Minami-Asagaya tube
station, it is a little out of the way for those coming from further
afield, but it is well worth it, including the price. The number of
dishes is not large.

f　一人でカラボクに行って歌っている若者も珍しくはない。
　　(cf., 珍しくない **mezurashikunai**)

**Hitori de karaboku ni itte utatte iru wakamono mo
mezurashiku wa nai.**

Young people who go to a karaoke box and sing alone aren't
unusual either.

g　悪いけど、蛍池には行きたいとは思わない。

**Warui kedo, Hotarugaike ni wa ikitai to wa omowanai.**

I'm sorry, I don't feel like going to Hotarugaike.

h　従来型のホテルをつくろうとは考えていない。

**Jūrai-gata no hoteru o tsukurō to wa kangaete inai.**

I'm not thinking of building a hotel in the traditional mould.

| 11.3.5.3.3 | Sandwiched before a positive form

Less frequently than with negatives (see 11.3.5.3.2), **wa** also gets sandwiched between items such as VN and **suru** (example b), or parts of the
copula, i.e., between the **de aru** variant (example a). The effect is one of
emphasizing the contrast expressed by **keredo** 'but' (example a), and of
**kaizen sareta** in example b.

349

a 離婚が少しずつではあるけれど増えていること。
**Rikon ga sukoshi-zutsu de wa aru keredo fuete iru koto.**
The fact is that divorce is on the increase, albeit little by little.

b いくらか改善はされた。
**Ikura ka kaizen wa sareta.**
[Things] *have* been improved somewhat.

### 11.3.6 Attached to time noun/number (+ counter)

After time N, number (+ counter) (including time and frequency) combinations, **wa** serves to emphasize the time/amount etc., in the sense of 'at least'. Note that with time N, **wa** can also be attached to particles such as **kara/made** (example b) (see also 2.4.14).

a あと二十年は漫画を描き続けたい。
**Ato nijūnen wa manga o kaki-tsuzuketai.**
I want to keep creating comics for at least another 20 years.

b 政局不安も二月までは残る。
**Seikyoku fuan mo nigatsu made wa nokoru.**
The political instability will remain until February at least.

c 人は生涯に一回は家を建てる。
**Hito wa shōgai ni ikkai wa ie o tateru.**
A person builds a house at least once in his lifetime.

### 11.3.7 In equational sentences

Equational sentences can be statements (example a) or questions (example b). Both have the basic structure N/pronoun **wa** N copula/**ka** (N/pronoun **wa** can be omitted where clear from the context, as in example a, where the reply omits pronoun-**wa** because it is mentioned in the equational question) (see 7.6.1.7, 18.1.10).

a 「それは反乱か」という王に、公爵は答えた。「いえ陛下、革命で
ございます」。
**'Sore wa hanran ka' to iu ō ni, kōshaku wa kotaeta. 'Ie heika, kakumei de gozaimasu'.**
To the king's question, 'Is this an uprising?', the duke replied, 'No, Your Majesty, it's a revolution'.

b あれは何だい。[だい ＝ だ ＋ male intimate Q particle かい]
**Are wa nan dai. [dai** = **da** + male intimate Q particle **kai]**
What's that?

---

### 11.3.8 In double-subject sentences

For an explanation of double-subject sentences, see 2.1.11, 7.6.1.8.

a 私は人気がない。
**Watashi wa ninki ga nai.**
I am not popular (*lit.* "As far as I am concerned, there is no popularity").

b 今年のプレゼントは、パパがカシミヤのマフラー。
**Kotoshi no purezento wa, papa ga kashimiya no mafurā.**
For this year's [Christmas] present, hubby [gets] a cashmere muffler.

---

### 11.3.9 Marking the subject of a compound sentence

In line with its focus on what follows, the force of **wa** extends all the way to the predicate. Therefore **wa** is used where the subject of a compound sentence is identical in both clauses (re compound sentences, see 7.6.5). This is another important difference to **ga**, which does not extend beyond the clause it is part of.

In the example, **otoko** is the subject of both **abareru** 'struggle' and the passive verb **taiho sareru** 'be arrested'.

a 男は暴れることもなく、その場で逮捕された。
**Otoko wa abareru koto mo naku, sono ba de taiho sareta.**
The man didn't put up a struggle and was arrested on the spot.

---

### 11.3.10 Marking the subject of a complex sentence

As the force of **wa** extends all the way to the predicate just as in 11.3.9 above, **wa** (never **ga**) is used where the subject of a complex sentence is identical in both the main and the subordinate clauses (re complex sentences, see 7.6.4). In example a, for instance, **dorobō** is the subject of both the subordinate clause verb **miru** 'see' and the main clause verb **nigeru** 'flee'.

a どろぼうは警察を見ると、逃げていった。

**Dorobō wa keisatsu o miru to, nigete itta.**

The burglar fled when he saw the police.

b Kさんは出勤するときに自転車に乗る。

**K-san wa shukkin suru toki ni jitensha ni noru.**

When he goes to work, K-san rides a bicycle.

## 11.3.11 In cleft sentences

Typically, **wa** is used in cleft sentences, which again is very much in line with its 'separating' function. Note that if **kara** is used in S2, **no wa** can also translate as 'the reason why', as in example c (see 22.2).

a 技術を伝えるのは難しい。

**Gijutsu o tsutaeru no wa muzukashii.**

Passing on technology is difficult.

b 暑さに音を上げたのは人間だけでない。

**Atsusa ni ne o ageta no wa ningen dake de nai.**

It wasn't only humans that got defeated by the heat.

c 親が子供にやさしすぎるのは、自分に自信がないからである。

**Oya ga kodomo ni yasashi-sugiru no wa, jibun ni jishin ga nai kara de aru.**

The reason why parents are too kind to their children is because they have no confidence in themselves.

## 11.3.12 wa and ga compared

When comparing the differences between **wa** and **ga**, we first need to examine the basic meaning or nature of the two particles, and then go on to see how this is reflected in a variety of uses and sentence types.

## 11.3.12.1 Basic meaning and use in simple sentences and questions

In simple sentences, **ga** is used when something is noticed or described (example a); **wa**, on the other hand, when a considered judgement or statement is made (example b). In other words, **wa** splits a sentence in two. First, the object of judgement is given to the left of **wa**, then the judgement itself is made to the right of **wa**. Hence one of the labels used to describe **wa**: a separating particle.

With **ga**, no such separation obtains; instead, the sentence perceives things as an unanalyzed whole.

a 空を見上げると真っ暗。たたきつけるように雨が降り始めた。
**Sora o miageru to makkura. Tatakitsukeru yō ni ame ga furihajimeta**
When I looked up at the sky, it was pitch black. Heavy rain started pounding down.

b インドにも雪は降る。
**Indo ni mo yuki <u>wa</u> furu**
Even in India it snows.

When attached to the subject, **ga** is often explained as emphasizing what precedes, whereas **wa** focusses on what follows (in English, this difference is sometimes explained by different placement of intonational stress). While the latter is true and is clearly related to the basic nature of **wa**, the former is not, i.e. it only appears that way when compared to sentences using **wa**. The following pair of sentences has often been used to explain the so-called difference in emphasis, as indicated by the underlining.

c ✎これがいい。
**Kore <u>ga</u> ii.**
<u>This</u> is good (i.e. I'll take <u>this</u> one).

d ✎これはいい。
**Kore <u>wa</u> ii.**
This is <u>good</u>.

Example c typically is the result of a choice posed by an earlier question, example e.

e ✎どれがいい？
**Dore <u>ga</u> ii?**
Which one do you like/prefer?

Therefore, question words such as **dore**, as well as the words occupying the same slot in response to question words in a sentence, such as **kore** in example c above), as a rule attach **ga**. This also applies to **dochira, dore** and **hō** etc. as used in comparison (see 6.7), as well as indeterminates such as **nani ka** 'something', etc.

f 何が問題なのか。

**Nani ga mondai na no ka.**

What is the problem?

g カネはだれが出すのか。

**Kane wa dare ga dasu no ka.**

Who's going to put up the money?

h 心の中で、何かが変わった気がした。

**Kokoro no naka de, nani ka ga kawatta ki ga shita.**

I felt that in my heart something had changed.

i 写った天体の中で、どれが銀河でどれが恒星かも自動的に識
別できる。

**Utsutta tentai no naka de, dore ga ginga de dore ga kōsei ka
mo jidō-teki ni shikibetsu dekiru.**

It can also automatically distinguish which among the heavenly bodies
on screen are galactic and which are fixed stars.

Whereas **ga** attaches to question words (what?, which?, who?, etc.), **wa** is
typically used in information-seeking questions. Being of the structure [N/
pronoun-**wa** Q-word (copula) Q-particle], these sentences naturally focus
on the Q-word, which is in line with the basic nature of **wa**.

j あれは何だい。—フェミカジ君ですね。[だい = だ + male
intimate Q-particle かい]

**Are <u>wa</u> nan dai. --Femikaji-kun desu ne. [dai = da + male
intimate Q-particle kai]**

What is that? – It's a boy wearing ladies' casuals.

k その成功の秘密は何か。

**Sono seikō no himitsu <u>wa</u> nani ka.**

What is the secret of this success?

<u>11.3.12.2</u> *Use in various sentence types*

<u>11.3.12.2.1</u> **ga**

It has often been pointed out that verbs like **aru/iru, dekiru** as well as
desiderative predicates are almost always used with **ga**. Therefore, **ga** is
typically used to mark the subject in existential/locational sentences (see
7.6.1.9), and what in English translation is the object of a potential verb
in potential sentences (see 2.1.4, 14) and the object of a verb/adjective of
desire in desiderative sentences (see 2.1.5, 9.2.1), except when there is a
contrast involved, in which case **wa** is used. From what we saw above

about **ga** attaching to Q-words and their slots in their replies, **ga** is also used to indicate the preferred item in comparative/superlative sentences (see 6.7).

**ga** also marks the subject in noun-modifying clauses (shown in [ ]), i.e. relative and complement clauses (see 2.1.13, 22.3.1.3). In these sentences, **wa** cannot be used istead of **ga**.

a 外国人犯罪が増える最大の背景は日本の豊かさだ。

   **[Gaikokujin hanzai ga fueru] saidai no haikei wa Nihon no yutakasa da.**

   The biggest reason why crimes by foreigners are on the increase is Japan's affluence.

b 平和が続くことを祈りたい。

   **[Heiwa ga tsuzuku koto] o inoritai.**

   I wish to pray that the peace will last.

| 11.3.12.2.2 | **wa**

Whereas **ga** marks the subject within clauses like noun-modifying clauses, the force of **wa** extends beyond clauses to the main predicate. It is therefore used to mark the sentence subject in compound and complex sentences (see 7.6.4 and 7.6.5).

Equational sentences (see 7.6.1.7) are also the domain of **wa** in that they conform to the [N/pronoun **wa** predicate] pattern that is characteristic of basic **wa** sentences.

a これは誤解だ。

   **Kore wa gokai da.**

   That's a misunderstanding.

If one inserts a nominalized clause into the slot before **wa** in example a, it results in a cleft sentence (22.3.1.1), which is another typical sentence where **wa** tends to be used.

b かわいそうなのは選手だ。

   **Kawaisō na no wa senshu da.**

   It's the athletes who are to be pitied.

Compare this to the following example, which uses **ga**. The structure is very similar to b, except that **ga** is used. The difference, which is captured in the translation, is that **ga** in c is marking the subject of a nominalized clauses (in [ ]), which could be replaced by **kore** 'this', which would mean 'this is my job'. A cleft sentence, on the other hand, has **wa** separating the nominalized clause from the predicate, thus providing it with emphasis.

c いい演奏をするのが私の仕事だ。
**[Ii ensō o suru no ga] watashi no shigoto da.**
Giving a good performance is my job.

The separating function of **wa** is also very much in evidence (see 11.3.6) in its use after time nouns and number/counter combinations.

d あと二十年は漫画を描き続けたい。
**Ato nijūnen wa manga o kaki-tsuzuketai.**
I want to keep creating comics for at least another 20 years.

This sentence is perfectly possible without **wa**, in which case the meaning would be' I want to keep creating comics for another 20 years.' The insertion of **wa** thus adds to the meaning. The 'meat of the sandwich' insertion of **wa** in 11.3.5.3 is another example of its separating use.

| 11.3.12.2.3 | **wa** and **ga** used together |

Both particles are used together in double-subject sentences (7.6.1.8, 2.1.11). The basic structure is always [N-**wa** N-**ga** Predicate], with [N-**ga** Predicate] constituting the comment on the topic N-**wa**.

a イタリアとギリシャは統計がない。
**Itaria to Girisha wa tōkei ga nai.**
For Italy and Greece, there are no statistics.

## 11.4 Emphatic particles

### 11.4.1 koso

**koso** attaches to a variety of items: noun (+ particle), nominalized clauses, the nominalizers **koto** and **no**, conjunctive particles such as -**ba/nara/kara/-te**, and conjunctions like **da kara** and **sore de**.

**koso** adds emphasis to the noun phrase, conjunction or conjunctive clause it is attached to (but note that it is not used for everyday situations). English translations for **koso** vary, from 'indeed' (11.4.1.1.1 a, c), 'exactly' (11.4.1.1.1 b), a cleft sentence 'is . . . that' (11.4.1.1.1 e, f), to nothing (11.4.1.1.1 d).

| 11.4.1.1 | *Noun* **koso**: *emphasizing noun (or noun phrase)* |

| 11.4.1.1.1 | Noun **koso** (+ particle) |

**koso** usually replaces case particles like **ga/o**, and adverbial particles like **wa**, but occasionally these are retained after **koso**.

a 妻こそ最良のパートナー。
**Tsuma koso sairyō no pātonā.**
My wife is indeed [my] best partner.

b 女性の能力発揮こそ、これからの企業の盛衰を決める。
**Josei no nōryoku hakki koso, kore kara no kigyō no seisui o kimeru.**
How women exercise their abilities is exactly what will determine the rise and fall of future businesses.

c 菊こそ日本の食用花である。
**Kiku koso Nihon no shokuyō-bana de aru.**
The chrysanthemum is truly the edible flower of Japan.

d 自然とスポーツこそ成長のビタミン剤。
**Shizen to supōtsu koso seichō no bitaminzai.**
Nature and sports are the vitamins for growth.

e 相互の信頼こそが我々を平和に導く。
**Sōgo no shinrai koso ga wareware o heiwa ni michibiku.**
Mutual trust is the thing that will lead us to peace.

f 「秋こそは勝負です」と力が入る。
**'Aki koso wa shōbu desu' to chikara ga hairu.**
'It is autumn that will tell the tale', she stresses.

| 11.4.1.1.2 | Noun + particle **koso** |

Case particles other than **ga/o** are retained before **koso**.

a この作品にこそ真のリアリティーがある。
**Kono sakuhin ni koso shin no riaritī ga aru.**
In this work [of art] lies true reality.

b 「精かんな顔にこそひげは似合う」。
**'Seikan na kao ni koso hige wa niau'.**
'A fearless face is just the kind that a beard suits.'

c 情報通信は首都圏などと距離的なハンディのある過疎地でこそ、
その機能が生かせる。

**Jōhō tsūshin wa shutoken nado to kyori-teki na handi no aru
kasochi de koso, sono kinō ga ikaseru.**

Information communications can be put to best use precisely in
remote areas, which have the ["distance"] disadvantage of being
away from the capital area.

d 「安くてもけっこうぜいたくに暮らす」知恵。あるいは「安い
からこそぜいたくに暮らせる」という合理的精神。それさえ
あれば、日本人はこんどこそ本物の豊かさに近づけるはずで
ある。

**'Yasukute mo kekkō zeitaku ni kurasu' chie. Arui wa 'yasui
kara koso zeitaku ni kuraseru' to iu gōriteki seishin. Sore
sae areba, Nihonjin wa kondo koso honmono no yutakasa
ni chikazukeru hazu de aru.**

Knowing how to live in relative luxury even though one doesn't spend
much money, the rational spirit of [knowing that] one can live in
luxury precisely because one doesn't spend much money – as long
as the Japanese have that [ability], they ought eventually to come
close to [living in] real comfort this time round.

---

| 11.4.1.1.3 | Time noun + **koso** (+ particle): emphasizing the time noun or clause

Attached to N of time, **koso** emphasizes the time noun, or the whole time
clause. When comparing examples e and b, it can be seen that in b the
predicate is ellipted.

a 今こそ、チャンス到来である。

**Ima koso, chansu tōrai de aru.**

Now is the time for opportunity to present itself.

b 来年こそは。

**Rainen koso wa.**

Next year [or never]!

c 不況の時こそ革新的な創造が必要だ。

**Fukyō no toki koso kakushin-teki na sōzō ga hitsuyō da.**

A recession is the very time that innovative creation is needed.

d 今度こそは必ず完成させます。

**Kondo koso wa kanarazu kansei sasemasu.**

This time I will finish it, without fail.

e 昨年は不況にやられっぱなしだった。今年こそはよい年になって
欲しいですね。

**Sakunen wa fukyō ni yarare-ppanashi datta. Kotoshi koso wa
yoi toshi ni natte hoshii desu ne.**

All of last year, I was hit by the recession. This year I want to be
a good year, right?

| 11.4.1.1.4 | Nominalized clause **koso**: emphasizing the nominalized clause |

a 地味でも長く続けることこそ大切だ。

**Jimi demo nagaku tsuzukeru koto koso taisetsu da.**

Even if [one's way of doing things is] quiet and unpretentious,
it's keeping at it for a long time that's important.

b 何もしないことこそ責められるべきだ。

**Nani mo shinai koto koso semerareru-beki da.**

It's taking no action at all that must be criticized.

| 11.4.1.2 | *Conjunctional clause* **koso**: *emphasizing a condition* |

| 11.4.1.2.1 | Conjunctional clause-**ba koso** |

a 周りの理解があったればこそですけどね。（あったれば ＝
あれば）

**Mawari no rikai ga attareba koso desu kedo ne.
[attareba = areba]**

It was only because I had the understanding of the people
around me.

b 確かにファンの支援があればこそだろう。

**Tashika ni fan no shien ga areba koso darō.**

No doubt this [= charity activities] is [possible] because of
the support of the [horse-racing] enthusiasts.

c 虚心なればこそ、目は曇らない。(なれば **nareba** is the -ba
form of the classical copula **nari**)

**Kyoshin nareba koso, me wa kumoranai.**

It's precisely because he's open-minded that he can see [things]
clearly.

| 11.4.1.2.2 | Conjunctional clause-**te koso** |

After a clause ending in V-**te**, **koso** emphasizes the state or condition indicated by S-**te**, in the sense of 'only if', 'only when'.

a 釣りは、やはり釣れてこそ楽しめるもの。
  **Tsuri wa yahari tsurete koso tanoshimeru mono.**
  Fishing is, after all, something that can only be enjoyed if you actually
    catch something.

b タンゴは二人の息が合ってこそ成り立つものだから。
  **Tango wa futari no iki ga atte koso naritatsu mono da kara.**
  It's because the tango only works when both people are perfectly
    co-ordinated.

c 「同じ時間を過ごしてこそ夫婦」が持論で夫人同伴の赴任。
  **'Onaji jikan o sugoshite koso fūfu' ga jiron de fujin dōhan
  no funin.**
  Their philosophy being 'Married couples only qualify as such if they
    spend time together', when the husband is transferred to a new
    post, the wife goes along.

d 花火は夜空をバックに花開いてこそ美しい。
  **Hanabi wa yozora o bakku ni hana-hiraite koso utsukushii.**
  Fireworks are beautiful only if they blossom against the background of
    the night sky.

| 11.4.1.2.3 | Conjunctional clause-**kara koso** |

Here, **koso** is used to emphasize a reason 'precisely because'.

a 古いからこそ新しい。
  **Furui kara koso atarashii.**
  They [= antiques] are novel precisely because they're old.

b 酷寒があるからこそ春の到来が待たれるのだ。
  **Kokkan ga aru kara koso haru no tōrai ga matareru no da.**
  It's because there is a time of bitter cold that we look forward to
    the arrival of spring.

c 自分で見つけたテーマだからこそ、研究者は熱中する。
  **Jibun de mitsuketa tēma da kara koso, kenkyūsha wa
  netchū suru.**
  It is because they themselves came up with their subjects of research
    that scholars get absorbed [in their work].

d むしろ女だからこそ新しい体験ができる時代だ。

**Mushiro onna da kara koso atarashii taiken ga dekiru jidai da.**

If anything, this is an era in which you can undergo new experiences for the very reason that you are a woman.

---

11.4.1.3 *Conjunction +* **koso**: *emphasizing the conjunction*

a 第九は平和への希求と人間愛に満ちた作品といわれる。だから こそ、この曲が選ばれたのだろう。

**Daiku wa heiwa e no kikyū to ningen-ai ni michita sakuhin to iwareru. Dakara koso, kono kyoku ga erabareta no darō.**

[Beethoven's] Ninth is said to be a work full of desire for peace and love of humanity. I suppose that's the very reason this piece [of music] was chosen.

b それでこそ、協力の意味がある。

**Sore de koso, kyōryoku no imi ga aru.**

That's just why there is meaning in co-operation.

---

11.4.1.4 *Noun/verbal noun* **koso sure**, *noun* **koso are**, *noun/verbal noun* **koso**, *verb/adjective* **ga/mono no**: *emphasizing a contrast*

The forms **sure/are** are classical forms expressing a contrast; in combination with **koso** only, these forms are still found in the modern language. **ga/mono no** are conjunctions of contrast 'but', 'although' (26.4.1, 26.4.7).

Note how with N-**suru** verbs such as **kansha suru** 'be thankful' (example 11.4.1.4.1 a) and **funayoi o suru** 'get seasick' (example 11.4.1.4.3 b), **koso** is 'sandwiched' between N and **suru** (replacing the case particle **o**).

---

11.4.1.4.1 Noun/verbal noun **koso sure**

a 金さんは財布を隠した女房に感謝こそすれ怒りは感じない。

**Kin-san wa saifu o kakushita nyōbō ni kansha koso sure ikari wa kanjinai.**

[In the *rakugo* story, a fisherman finds a wallet full of money, but his wife hides it and tells him it was a dream to save him from turning into a drunkard:] Kin-san may feel grateful towards his wife, who hid the wallet; he certainly feels no anger.

Noun **koso are**

a 程度の差こそあれ、だれの耳も目からの情報を参考にしている。
   **Teido no sa koso are, dare no mimi mo me kara no jōhō o
   sankō ni shite iru.**
   There may be differences in degree, but everyone's ears refer to
   information coming from the eyes.

Noun/verbal noun **koso** verb/adjective **ga/mono no**

a 車こそ多いが、歩道はガラガラだ。
   **Kuruma koso ōi ga, hodō wa garagara da.**
   As many cars as there are, there are very few people on
   the pavements.

b 船酔いこそしなかったが、体中が塩まみれになった。
   **Funayoi koso shinakatta ga, karadajū ga shio-mamire ni natta.**
   Though I didn't get seasick, my whole body got covered in salt.

## 11.4.2 nanka

**nanka** is very similar in use to **nante** (see 11.4.3). Like **nante**, it places
emphasis on the noun or verb etc. preceding it, with either a positive or
negative implication 'such a thing/place as'. Often there is no need to
translate it, its force being clear from the context.

The difference from **nante** is that **nante** attaches mainly to N that are
subjects and objects (replacing the case particle **ga/o**), whereas **nanka** can
also attach to other cases. **nanka** can attach case particles like **de, ni, yori**;
can be sandwiched between **ni** (adverbial form of the copula) and **naru**,
and between an adjective and its negative ending. **nanka** is also used before
a predicate in the sense of 'somehow'.

## 11.4.2.1 Noun **nanka** + negative

This indicates that the N to which **nanka** is attached is belittled, slighted
or emphasized 'and such like', 'any such', etc.

a 別に秘密なんかない。
   **Betsu ni himitsu nanka nai.**
   There aren't any particular secrets or anything.

b こちらの意見なんか聞きませんよ。

**Kochira no iken nanka kikimasen yo.**

They won't listen to the likes of our opinions, I tell you!

c スポーツに学歴なんか関係ない。

**Supōtsu ni gakureki nanka kankei nai.**

In sports, academic background and all that doesn't matter.

d 僕は金なんか稼ぎたくもないし、先生だなんて呼ばれたくも
ない。

**Boku wa kane nanka kasegitaku mo nai shi, sensei da nante
yobaretaku mo nai.**

I have no desire to make money or anything like that, and I don't want
to be called a teacher either.

e 日本ではサラリーマンはだれ一人豪邸なんか建てることはで
きない。

**Nihon de wa sararīman wa dare hitori gōtei nanka tateru
koto wa dekinai.**

In Japan, no white-collar worker can build a great big fancy house.

| 11.4.2.2 | *Noun* **nanka** + *rhetorical question*

The meaning imparted by **nanka** is the same as in 11.4.2.1.

a 絵なんかで食っていけるか。

**E nanka de kutte ikeru ka.**

Do you expect one can make a living from painting!

| 11.4.2.3 | *Noun* **nanka** + *positive*

With positive predicates, **nanka** is also used in a belittling or emphasizing
sense; after first-person pronouns, the implication is usually one of modesty
'such a person/thing/place/time as'.

a 私なんかおとなしい方よ。

**Watashi nanka otonashii hō yo.**

I'm on the quiet side, you know.

b 公募なんかうそばっかり。

**Kōbo nanka uso bakkari.**

Public advertisements for posts are a total fake.

c テレビなんかけとばせるよう、足元に置けばいい。

**Terebi nanka ketobaseru yō, ashimoto ni okeba ii.**

Something like TV should put be on the floor, so that one
can kick it.

d 誰かが言っていた。「悩みのない人生なんか退屈だぞ〜」

**Dare ka ga itte ita. 'Nayami no nai jinsei nanka taikutsu
da zo--'**

Somebody has said, "A trouble-free life, that's really boring—"

e 「洋服なんか何でもいい」と言いたいのだ。

**'Yōfuku nanka nan demo ii' to iitai no da.**

I want to state [= by the way I dress] 'Clothes are of no concern
to me'.

f 魚市場の活気に触れ、「銀座なんかよりニッポンを実感できた
よ」と笑う。

**Uoichiba no kakki ni fure, 'Ginza nanka yori Nippon o jikkan
dekita yo' to warau.**

Mentioning the energy of the fish market, 'I've got a much more real
feel about Japan than [having gone somewhere] like Ginza', he laughs.

g 口の悪いKさんは「オリンピックなんか全く関心がない」と言った。

**Kuchi no warui K-san wa 'Orinpikku nanka mattaku kanshin
ga nai' to itta.**

The foul-mouthed K-san said, 'I haven't the faintest interest in the
Olympics'.

---

11.4.2.4 | *Verb/adjective* **nanka** *(negative)*

Sandwiched between conjunctive forms (-te forms and conjunctive-form
equivalents) of V/Adj and **iru, nai**, etc., **nanka** emphasizes the meaning of
V/Adj + **iru/nai**, etc.

a 私は別に外見にこだわってなんかいないの。

**Watashi wa betsu ni gaiken ni kodawatte nanka inai no.**

I'm not particularly concerned about my appearance.

b どうか、私の主張に賛同された方は、清くなんかない
一票を・・・。

**Dōka, watashi no shuchō ni sandō sareta kata wa, kiyoku
nanka nai ippyō o . . .**

Those who agree with my position, please [give me] your tarnished
(*lit.* "far-from-clean") vote . . .

| 11.4.2.5 | **nanka** + *predicate* |

When modifying a predicate, **nanka** indicates the idea of 'somehow'.

a お父さん! 僕が腕相撲で勝ってしまったとき、なんか寂しかった。
   **Otōsan! Boku ga udezumō de katte shimatta toki, nanka
   sabishikatta.**
   Dad! When I defeated you at arm-wrestling, I felt somehow lonely.

b 「この人、なんかものすごくシロウトだなあ」という印象を持って
   しまう。
   **'Kono hito, nanka monosugoku shirōto da nā' to iu inshō o
   motte shimau.**
   One gets the impression that this person is somehow unbelievably
   amateurish.

| 11.4.3 | **nante** |

**nante** places emphasis on the noun or verb etc. preceding it, with either a
positive or negative implication 'such a thing as'. Often there is no need
to translate it, its force being clear from the context (see 11.4.2, 11.6).

| 11.4.3.1 | Noun **nante** + *negative* |

With a negative predicate, **nante** emphasizes that the proposition of the
sentence is out of the question or ridiculous for the speaker, or that he/she
never even considered it before 'no such person/thing/place/time'.

a 年齢なんて数えたこともない。
   **Nenrei nante kazoeta koto mo nai.**
   I've never done anything like count my age.

b 世界中どこに行っても豚肉が牛肉より高い所なんてない。
   **Sekai-jū doko ni itte mo butaniku ga gyūniku yori takai
   tokoro nante nai.**
   No matter where you go in the world, there is no place where pork
   is more expensive than beef.

c 人間の力なんてそんなに変わりゃしません。(変わりゃしません
   = 変わりはしません)
   **Ningen no chikara nante sonna ni kawarya shimasen.
   (kawarya shimasen = kawari wa shimasen)**
   [Don't be ridiculous,] people's abilities don't vary that much.

11.4.3.2 *Noun* **nante** + *positive*

With positive predicates, **nante** singles out (or emphasizes) the N (or NP) it is attached to as something specially attractive or frightening etc. 'such a person/thing/place/time as'.

a とくに星降る夜なんて最高よ！
   **Toku ni hoshi furu yoru nante saikō yo!**
   In particular, nights with shooting stars are great, you know!

b 「まあ、赤ちゃんの声なんて何年ぶり」と老夫婦が感動した面持ち。
   **'Mā, akachan no koe nante nan-nen-buri' to rōfūfu ga kandō
   shita omomochi.**
   'Oh my, how many years has it been since we've heard a baby's voice',
   said the elderly couple, with an emotional look on their faces.

c 無言の生活なんて恐怖ですよね。
   **Mugon no seikatsu nante kyōfu desu yo ne.**
   How dreadful a life without words would be, wouldn't it?

11.4.3.3 **nante** + *(iu)* **mono/koto/no**/*noun* **wa** + *predicate*

Here, **nante** often imparts a belittling nuance 'such a thing as'.

a 昔は偏差値なんてものはなかった。
   **Mukashi wa hensachi nante mono wa nakatta.**
   Formerly there was no such thing as 'deviation value' [in the exam system].

b 教科書なんていうものは永らくつまらないのが当たり前だった。
   **Kyōkasho nante iu mono wa nagaraku tsumaranai no ga
   atarimae datta.**
   It was long taken for granted that a textbook was something that was
   tedious.

11.4.3.4 *Clause* **nante**

Depending on whether the predicate is positive or negative, the meaning is 'something like' or 'anything like', but is often best not translated.

a 学校に行ってこんなにうれしいなんて初めて。
   **Gakkō ni itte konna ni ureshii nante hajimete.**
   It's the first time I've been so happy to be at school.

b 初めは、芸術だなんてとても思えなかった。

**Hajime wa, geijutsu da nante totemo omoenakatta.**

At first, it just didn't feel like art.

c お父さん、もう勉強しなさいなんていわないで。

**Otōsan, mō benkyō shinasai nante iwanai de.**

Daddy, please don't tell me to study any more.

d 「まさか、こんなことになるなんて」と驚いた表情だった。

**'Masaka, konna koto ni naru nante' to odoroita
hyōjō datta.**

'I never thought it would come to this', [the relatives of the hostage]
said with a shocked look.

e 大学をドロップアウトするなんてとんでもない。

**Daigaku o doroppuauto suru nante tonde mo nai.**

Dropping out of university is out of the question.

---

| 11.4.3.5 | *Quoted speech or thought* **nante** |

This gives emphasis to the quoted speech or thought (direct or indirect)
'saying/thinking things like'.

a 「会社に一生尽くす気はない」なんていう新人もいた。

**'Kaisha ni isshō tsukusu ki wa nai' nante iu shinjin
mo ita.**

There were even some new employees who had the nerve
to say, 'I have no intention of devoting my whole life to the
company'.

b 別々に住むなんて考えられない。

**Betsubetsu ni sumu nante kangaerarenai.**

Living apart is unthinkable.

c 昔はどこの大学かなんて関係なかった。ところが会社が大きくな
るると一流大学の学生が来て、つい採用してしまう。

**Mukashi wa doko no daigaku ka nante kankei nakatta.
Tokoro ga kaisha ga ōkiku naru to ichiryū daigaku no
gakusei ga kite, tsui saiyō shite shimau.**

In the old days, it didn't make any difference which university
[applicants came from]. But as the company gets bigger, students
from first-rate universities come [to apply], and you end up
employing them.

11.4.3.6 **nante** *with ellipted predicate*

The meaning of the predicate being clear from the context, this indicates the meaning of 'fancy (that)', 'can you believe it?', 'how can they'.

a こんな不況の時期に値上げするなんて。

**Konna fukyō no jiki ni neage suru nante**

How can they raise prices during this [terrible] recession?

b 「女性が泊まりで旅行だなんて。危ないからやめなさい」「だって もう二十六歳よ。少しは自由にさせて」

**'Josei ga tomari de ryokō da nante. Abunai kara yamenasai'**
**'Datte mō nijūroku-sai yo. Sukoshi wa jiyū ni sasete'**

'A woman going on an overnight trip? Cancel, it's too dangerous.'
'But, I'm 26 already! Give me a bit of freedom.'

c 「こんな所で発砲事件があるなんて」と声を震わせた。

**'Konna tokoro de happō jiken ga aru nante' to koe o**
**furuwaseta.**

'How could there be a shooting incident in a place like this?' she said, with a tremor in her voice.

## 11.5 Particles of extent

### 11.5.1 gurai/kurai

**gurai** (or **kurai**) is an adverbial particle that is attached directly to nouns (including N of amount, amount + counter, and N of time), and to N-modifying forms of verbs and adjectives. It indicates an approximate amount, or an extent (see 11.5.2, 1.7.3).

Comparing **gurai/kurai** and **goro**, **gurai/kurai** is much wider in use than **goro**. After time N, **goro** indicates an approximate point in time, whereas **gurai** indicates an approximate period of time. The difference between **kurai** and **gurai** is that **kurai** has a slightly more formal ring.

### 11.5.1.1 *Noun (amount, etc.)* **gurai/kurai** *(wa)*

11.5.1.1.1 Number (+ counter) **gurai/kurai**

Attached to amounts [number (+ counter)] including time, **gurai/kurai** indicates that the amount or period of time is approximate 'approximately', 'about'. Note the combination **gurai wa**, which has the implication of 'at least' that amount.

a 母よ！一分ぐらいだまっとれ。（だまっとれ ＝ だまっておれ）
**Haha yo! Ippun gurai damattore. [damattore = damatte ore]**
Mother! Shut up for a minute or so.

b この内閣は二年くらい大丈夫だろう。
**Kono naikaku wa ninen kurai daijōbu darō.**
I suppose this Cabinet will be all right for about two years.

c 月収は「十万円ぐらい」という。
**Gesshū wa 'jūman-en gurai' to iu.**
She says that her monthly income is 'about 100,000 yen'.

d 今の七十歳は明治時代の五十六歳ぐらい。
**Ima no nanajus-sai wa Meiji-jidai no gojūroku-sai gurai.**
Being 70 now is equivalent to being about 56 during the Meiji era.

e 「企業のリストラや銀行の不良債権の償却などにどのくらいの時間がかかるとみますか」。「二年ぐらいはかかるだろう」。
**'Kigyō no risutora ya ginkō no furyōsaiken no shōkyaku nado ni dono kurai no jikan ga kakaru to mimasu ka'. 'Ninen gurai wa kakaru darō'.**
'How long do you think it'll take for companies to restructure and banks to sell off their bad debts?' 'It will probably take at least two years.'

---

11.5.1.1.2 **gurai/kurai shika** negative

In combination with **shika . . . neg.** 'only', **gurai/kurai** indicates that the N is 'about the only N' (see 11.1.3).

a 名古屋というと金のしゃちほこぐらいしか思い浮かばない。
**Nagoya to iu to kin no shachihoko gurai shika omoi-ukabanai.**
At the mention of Nagoya, about the only thing that comes to mind are the gold dolphins [on top of the castle roof].

b 観光くらいしか産業がなく、それで私もホテルマンになったのです。
**Kankō kurai shika sangyō ga naku, sore de watashi mo hoteruman ni natta no desu.**
Tourism is about the only industry [here], and so I too became a hotel keeper.

c 夜間は、トイレの時ぐらいしか水を使わないので、ほとんど困っ
ていない。

**Yakan wa, toire no toki gurai shika mizu o tsukawanai no de,
hotondo komatte inai.**

[Water restrictions] During the night, I have almost no problems as
about the only time I use water is for the toilet.

11.5.1.1.3 Cleft sentence **no wa** noun **gurai/kurai** (copula)

Here, **gurai/kurai** indicates that the noun (item/s) it is attached to is/are
'about all' there is to it, 'only' (see 22.2).

a ほかに必要なのは送料、箱代、氷代ぐらい。

**Hoka ni hitsuyō na no wa, sōryō, hakodai, kōridai gurai.**

The only other things required are money for postage, the charge for
the box and the charge for ice.

b 買えるのは一部の駅の新幹線ホームぐらいだ。

**Kaeru no wa ichibu no eki no shinkansen hōmu gurai da.**

About the only place you can buy it [= the magazine] is on the bullet-
train platform of some stations.

11.5.1.1.4 (semete) noun **gurai/kurai wa**

**wa** adds the idea of 'at least' (see 11.3.6), which is often reinforced by the
adverb of degree **semete** 'at (the very) least'. This is used in situations
where the speaker wants to emphasize that surely he or she is not asking
too much.

a せめて電車の中くらいはゆっくりしたいものだ。

**Semete densha no naka kurai wa yukkuri shitai mono da.**

I want to take it easy, at least on the train.

b トイレの水くらいは雨水を使えないものか。

**Toire no mizu kurai wa amamizu o tsukaenai mono ka.**

Why can't rainwater be used, at least for water in the toilet?

11.5.1.1.5 Noun phrase **gurai/kurai**

This gives the noun phrase to which **gurai/kurai** is attached a belittling
ring 'doesn't amount to much'.

a やってみれば調理タオルの洗濯くらいたいしたことではない。

**Yatte mireba chōri taoru no sentaku kurai taishita koto de
wa nai**

When you try doing it, laundering the kitchen towels doesn't amount
to much.

### 11.5.1.2 Clause **gurai/kurai**: *indicating an extent or degree*

#### 11.5.1.2.1 Clause **gurai/kurai** predicate

This indicates that the predicate applies 'to a . . . extent/degree', 'so . . . that'
(see 11.5.2).

a 見事なくらい何もない。

**Migoto na kurai nani mo nai.**

[The place] is so empty that it's spectacular.

b 間近に定年が迫っているとは思えないくらい健康である。

**Majika ni teinen ga sematte iru to wa omoenai kurai kenkō
de aru.**

He is in such good health that it's hard to believe his retirement is
close at hand.

#### 11.5.1.2.2 Clause **gurai/kurai da**

Attached to clauses or sentences that express insufficiency or comparison,
**gurai/kurai** emphasizes this insufficiency or the comparison 'if anything'
(see 11.5.2).

a まだ足りないくらいだ。

**Mada tarinai kurai da.**

It's not quite enough yet.

b 対策は遅すぎたくらいだ。

**Taisaku wa oso-sugita kurai da.**

The countermeasures were practically too late.

c 周りの道路などの音の方がうるさいくらいだつた。

**Mawari no dōro nado no oto no hō ga urusai kurai datta.**

The noise from the nearby roads were just about louder
  [than the sound of planes landing at the airport].

Clause-imperative **to gurai/kurai**

After a quoted sentence ending in the imperative, the meaning is 'say at least'.

a 「覚えておけ」とぐらい言ってやれ、松井クン。
**'Oboete oke' to gurai itte yare, Matsui-kun.**
Matsui-kun, tell them at least 'Remember this!'

Clause **gurai/kurai no** noun

When used to modify N, the implication is that the modifying section is the minimum that is required for the N 'akin to', 'no less than'.

a 安全には十分すぎるくらいの用意と注意を心がけること。
**Anzen ni wa jūbun-sugiru kurai no yōi to chūi o kokorogakeru koto.**
For safety, it is necessary to aim for more than adequate preparation and attention.

b 君は一年間謹慎するくらいの反省が必要だろう。
**Kimi wa ichinenkan kinshin suru kurai no hansei ga hitsuyō darō.**
You probably need as much reflection on your past conduct as confinement at home for a year [would give you].

c 失業率が三%というのは奇跡に近いぐらいのことです。
**Shitsugyōritsu ga san-pāsento to iu no wa kiseki ni chikai gurai no koto desu.**
The fact that the unemployment rate is [no more than] 3 per cent amounts to a miracle.

Clause **gurai/kurai de**

With **de** (the conjunctive form of the copula), attached, the combination means 'just because' (see 7.5).

a 眠いくらいで死にはしない。
**Nemui kurai de shini wa shinai.**
No one dies just of sleepiness.

b 子供たちと海遊館や遊園地に行ったくらいで、のんびりできました。
**Kodomo-tachi to kaiyūkan ya yūenchi ni itta kurai de, nonbiri dekimashita.**
I had a relaxed time. Just about all I did was go to the aquarium and the amusement park with my children.

11.5.1.2.6 | Clause **gurai/kurai ga (chōdo) ii**

This indicates that the situation or state mentioned is the least that one would expect 'just about right'.

a　子供は少しケガをするくらいがいい。

**Kodomo wa sukoshi kega o suru kurai ga ii.**

It's just about right for a child [to be active enough] to get a few cuts.

b　男は生意気ぐらいがちょうどいい。（歌）

**Otoko wa namaiki gurai ga chōdo ii. (Uta)**

Men who are cocky and brash – no more, no less –
   are just right. (song)

11.5.1.2.7 | Verb **gurai/kurai nara**

The combination means 'If it means doing . . . , I'd rather' (see 26.1.4).

a　「温厚」は周囲の一致した人物評。ケンカは絶対にしない。
   するくらいなら降りる。

**'Onkō' wa shūi no itchi shita jinbutsu-hyō. 'Kenka wa zettai ni
   shinai. Suru kurai nara oriru.**

The people around him judge his personality to be 'affable'. 'He never
   gets into fights. He'd sooner give in [than fight].'

b　毛皮を着るぐらいなら裸の方がまし。

**Kegawa o kiru gurai nara hadaka no hō ga mashi.**

I would rather go naked than wear a fur.

## 11.5.2 | hodo

**hodo** is attached directly to nouns, and to the forms of verbs and adjectives that precede nouns.

**hodo** and the word it is attached to together form an adverbial phrase, i.e. modify a following V/Adj or the copula, indicating the degree to which the following V/Adj (or copula) applies 'about' (see 11.5.1).

11.5.2.1 | *Number + counter* **hodo**

Attached to number + counter, **hodo**, like **gurai**, indicates an approximate amount 'about' (see 11.5.1, 4).

a 高さ五メートルほどはあるだろうか。

**Takasa go-mētoru hodo wa aru darō ka.**

The height [of the building replica] might be about five metres.

b 研究会は十人ほどで構成する。

**Kenkyūkai wa jūnin hodo de kōsei suru.**

The research society will consist of about ten people.

c 五キロのコースを一時間半ほどかけてゆっくり歩く。

**Go-kiro no kōsu o ichi-jikan-han hodo kakete yukkuri aruku.**

They walk the 5-km course slowly, taking about an hour and a half.

| 11.5.2.1.2 | Noun (or noun phrase) **wa** ... number + counter **hodo** (**da**)

In equational sentences, the meaning is 'A is about B'. The N can be a simple noun, a noun phrase (N **no** N, etc.), or a nominalized noun (V + **no**, etc.).

a 現在の会員は二百五十人ほどだ。

**Genzai no kai-in wa nihyakugojū-nin hodo da.**

There are currently about 250 members.

b 一日の乗降客は現在一万人ほどだ。

**Ichinichi no jōkōkyaku wa genzai ichiman-nin hodo da.**

At present, the number of passengers getting on and off in a day is about 10,000.

c 働くのは一カ月のうち半月ほどだ。

**Hataraku no wa ikkagetsu no uchi hantsuki hodo da.**

He works about two weeks out of every month.

| 11.5.2.1.3 | Number + counter **hodo no** noun (noun-modifying)

When modifying a noun, the meaning is 'of about', 'or so'.

a 二十年ほどの間に何が変わったのだろう。

**Nijū-nen hodo no aida ni nani ga kawatta no darō.**

I wonder what has changed over the past 20 years or so.

b 九月に休みをもらって二泊ほどの旅行を考えている。

**Kugatsu ni yasumi o moratte nihaku hodo no ryokō o kangaete iru.**

I'm thinking of taking some time off in September and going on a trip of about [three days and] two nights.

c 開館日には一日十組ほどの客が訪れる。

**Kaikanbi ni wa ichinichi juk-kumi hodo no kyaku ga otozureru.**

On the days when the museum is open, about ten groups of visitors come per day.

### 11.5.2.2 Noun **hodo** noun (indicating an extent)

#### 11.5.2.2.1 Noun **hodo** (. . . noun) (negative predicate)

This indicates the meaning of 'not as . . . as'. The predicate is either negative, or has negative meaning.

a これほど多国籍な銀行もまれです。

**Kore hodo ta-kokuseki na ginkō mo mare desu.**

There are very few banks that are as multinational as this.

b 日本人からみれば中国人ほど手ごわい相手はいない。

**Nihonjin kara mireba Chūgokujin hodo tegowai aite wa inai.**

From the point of view of the Japanese, there are few [negotiating] partners who are as tough as the Chinese.

c そんな中、これほど大きくて目立つ時計も珍しい。

**Sonna naka, kore hodo ōkikute medatsu tokei mo mezurashii.**

Among such [clocks at well-known meeting points], there are few clocks that are so large and noticeable.

d どんな動物でも犬ほどバラエティーに富む例は見当たらない。

**Donna dōbutsu demo inu hodo baraetī ni tomu rei wa miataranai.**

There is no other kind of animal as rich in variety as the dog.

#### 11.5.2.2.2 Noun **hodo** noun (positive predicate)

With positive predicates, the meaning is 'more than', 'to the extent that'.

a 苦しい時ほど愛する対象が欲しいんです。

**Kurushii toki hodo aisuru taishō ga hoshii n desu.**

One never wants something to love [= a pet] as much as in hard times.

b 母の居ない人ほど母への思いは強くなる。

**Haha no inai hito hodo haha e no omoi wa tsuyoku naru.**

No one has stronger feelings towards his mother than someone who doesn't have one.

| 11.5.2.2.3 | Idiomatic use of noun **hodo** predicate |

Idiomatic uses include expressions like **yama hodo** 'lots', sayings, etc.

a　したいことは山ほどある。
**Shitai koto wa yama hodo aru.**
There are heaps of things I want to do.

b　わからないことは山ほどある。
**Wakaranai koto wa yama hodo aru.**
There are lots of things I don't understand.

| 11.5.2.3 | *Verb/adjective* **hodo** |

| 11.5.2.3.1 | Verb/adjective **hodo** (positive predicate) |

Here, **hodo** is modified by a N-modifying clause ending in the same forms that are used before N (note the classical negative form -**nu** instead of -**nai**, example e). Together with **hodo**, this forms an adverbial clause in the sense of 'so . . . that' (with positive predicates).

a　安すぎるほど安い。
**Yasusugiru hodo yasui.**
It's so cheap that it's almost too cheap.

b　驚くほど甘い。
**Odoroku hodo amai.**
It's amazingly sweet.

c　腰を抜かすほど驚いた。
**Koshi o nukasu hodo odoroita.**
I was so surprised that I could hardly move.

d　泣けてきそうなほど、感激した。
**Nakete kisō na hodo kandō shita.**
I was moved so deeply that I almost cried.

e　人間の体は数えきれぬほど多くの細胞でできている。
**Ningen no karada wa kazoekirenu hodo ōku no saibō**
**de dekite iru.**
The human body is made up of innumerable cells.

| 11.5.2.3.2 | Verb/adjective **hodo no** noun

When modifying a noun, the meaning is 'a N that is so . . . that'.

a まぶしいほどの笑顔だった。
  **Mabushii hodo no egao datta.**
  It was a smile that was virtually dazzling.

b 会場の大教室は立ち見が出るほどの盛況ぶりだった。
  **Kaijō no daikyōshitsu wa tachimi ga deru hodo no
  seikyōburi datta.**
  The [event in the] large auditorium (*lit.* "at the venue") was so well
  attended that there was standing room only.

c はたから見れば恋人と見間違えるほどの親密な交際ぶりだ。
  **Hata kara mireba koibito to mimachigaeru hodo no
  shinmitsu na kōsaiburi da.**
  To the innocent bystander, their friendship looks so intimate that
  they might be mistaken for sweethearts.

| 11.5.2.3.3 | Verb/adjective **hodo da**

As the predicate of an equational sentence, V/Adj **hodo da** means '*A is B*
to the extent that'.

a 技術力の進歩は驚くほどだ。
  **Gijutsuryoku no shinpo wa odoroku hodo da.**
  The advances made in technical skill are amazing.

b 街を歩くサラリーマンの姿は数えるほどだ。
  **Machi o aruku sararīman no sugata wa kazoeru
  hodo da.**
  There are so [few] white-collar workers walking around town that
  you could count them.

c 外は猛暑でもここの気温は十三度で寒いほどだ。
  **Soto wa mōsho demo koko no kion wa jūsando de samui
  hodo da.**
  Even if there's a heatwave outside, the temperature in here, at thirteen
  degrees, still feels cold.

| 11.5.2.3.4 | Verb/adjective **hodo** (negative predicate) |

With negative predicates, the meaning is 'not as . . . as'.

a しかし、それは口で言うほど簡単なことではない。

**Shikashi, sore wa kuchi de iu hodo kantan na koto de wa nai.**

[Making clothes that customers buy regardless of price] However, that's easier said than done.

b 道は広いし、交通マナーも言われているほど悪くない。

**Michi wa hiroi shi, kōtsū manā mo iwarete iru hodo waruku nai.**

The streets are wide and people's driving manners are not as bad as they are said to be.

c 女性は本当に意外なほど、男性の「好きなモノ」を知らない。

**Josei wa hontō ni igai na hodo, dansei no 'sukina mono' o shiranai.**

It's quite incredible how little women know about the things men like.

| 11.5.2.4 | *(Verb/adjective-***ba***) verb/adjective* **hodo** |

| 11.5.2.4.1 | Verb/adjective-**ba** verb/adjective **hodo** (with repeated verb or adjective) |

Here, a verb or adjective is repeated, first in the -**ba** form, then in the N-modifying form, in the sense of 'the more . . . , the . . . -er' (see 26.1.1).

a まちづくりをすればするほど、まちが悪くなる。

**Machizukuri o sureba suru hodo, machi ga waruku naru.**

The more you 'engineer' a town, the worse it gets.

b 組織が大きければ大きいほど決定は遅い。

**Soshiki ga ōkikereba ōkii hodo kettei wa osoi.**

The larger an organization is, the longer it takes to make decisions.

c 計画達成は早ければ早いほど良い。

**Keikaku tassei wa hayakereba hayai hodo yoi.**

The sooner we achieve the plan the better.

d 日本政府の態度を知れば知るほど、怒りが高まった。

**Nihon seifu no taido o shireba shiru hodo, ikari ga takamatta.**

The more I got to know the attitude of the Japanese government, the angrier I became.

e 住宅は、建築後年数がたてばたつほど、維持費用がかさむ。

**Jūtaku wa, kenchiku-go nensū ga tateba tatsu hodo, iji-hiyō ga kasamu.**

The older a house gets, the greater the cost of maintaining it.

11.5.2.4.2 Verb/adjective **hodo**

Without repeated verb/adjective, the meaning also works out as 'the more . . . , the -er'.

a 高齢化が進むほど医療費は膨らみます。

**Kōrei-ka ga susumu hodo iryōhi wa fukuramimasu.**

The further the ageing of society progresses, the bigger the medical bills get.

b コメは気温が高いほど消費量が減る傾向にある。

**Kome wa kion ga takai hodo shōhiryo ga heru keikō ni aru.**

Higher temperatures make for less consumption of rice.

11.5.2.4.3 Verb **hodo ni** predicate

This may be regarded as a variant of 11.5.2.4.1 and 11.5.2.4.2, 'the more . . . , the more . . .'.

a かむほどにうまみが出てくる。

**Kamu hodo ni umami ga dete kuru.**

The longer one chews the better it tastes.

## 11.5.2.5 Noun **hodo . . . mono/koto wa nai**

### 11.5.2.5.1 **hodo . . . mono wa nai**

**hodo . . . mono wa nai** expresses the meaning of 'nothing better than' (see 19.1).

a 絹製品ほど体に良いものはない。

**Kinu seihin hodo karada ni yoi mono wa nai.**

There is nothing better for the body than silk products.

b 一方通行の会議ほど退屈なものはない。

**Ippō tsūkō no kaigi hodo taikutsuna mono wa nai.**

There is nothing as dull as a one-way meeting (= where all the communication is from one direction only).

Particles of extent

11.5.2.5.2 **hodo . . . koto wa nai**

Here, the meaning is 'never . . . more than . . .'.

a 今年ほど、夏休みが待ち遠しかったことはない。
**Kotoshi hodo, natsuyasumi ga machidōshikatta koto wa nai.**
I've never looked forward to the summer holidays as much as I did
this year.

## 11.6 Exemplifying particle: nado

**nado** is basically used as an adverbial particle, but can also be used to
modify a noun by means of **no** or **to iu** (see also 23.2.3).

### 11.6.1 *Noun* nado

Attached to nouns, **nado** indicates that the item(s) mentioned is/are representative samples, with further ones being implied 'for example', 'among
others', 'and so on'.

### 11.6.1.1 *Noun* nado *particle . . . predicate*

**nado** is sandwiched between the noun and the case (or other) particle
required by the valency of the verb. Note that the predicate can be a
sentence-final predicate, or the predicate of a subordinate (example c) or
co-ordinate (example d) clause.

a 代表作に「桜川」「花軍」「雨月物語」などがある。
**Daihyōsaku ni 'Sakuragawa' 'Hanaikusa' 'Ugetsu Monogatari'
nado ga aru.**
Representative works include among others *Sakuragawa, Hanaikusa* and
*Ugetsu Monogatari.*

b 契約者には腕時計などを贈る。
**Keiyakusha ni wa udedokei nado o okuru.**
They give wristwatches and so on to the contracting parties.

c 周りは大掃除などに大忙しだけど、ボクらの年越し準備は快適だ。
**Mawari wa ōsōji nado ni ōisogashi da kedo, bokura no
toshikoshi junbi wa kaiteki da.**
[Everyone else in] the neighbourhood is very busy with general housecleaning
and whatnot, but our year-end preparations are quite pleasant.

d 八戸市内などでは断水が続き、市民生活に影響が出ている。

**Hachinohe shinai nado de wa dansui ga tsuzuki, shimin seikatsu ni eikyō ga dete iru.**

In the city of Hachinohe, for instance, the water supply remains shut off, and the living conditions of the townspeople are being affected.

### 11.6.2 Noun nado ... noun

### 11.6.2.1 Noun **nado** noun/noun phrase

Modifying a noun or noun phrase, **nado** serves to give concrete examples of the content of that noun or noun phrase.

a ハモ、カキ料理など季節メニューも増やすことを検討中だ。

**Hamo, kaki ryōri nado kisetsu menyū mo fuyasu koto o kentō-chū da.**

We are presently looking into the possibility of adding seasonal menus offering, for example, sea eel and oyster dishes.

b すでに十月から宮城、福島など四県で販売している。

**Sude ni jūgatsu kara Miyagi, Fukushima nado yonken de hanbai shite iru.**

Since October, we have already been marketing [our product] in four prefectures, including Miyagi and Fukushima.

c 今後はボランティアの育成など、ソフト面の準備が課題になるだろう。

**Kongo wa borantia no ikusei nado, sofutomen no junbi ga kadai ni naru darō.**

In the future, the task at hand will probably be to set up the 'soft' side – for instance, training volunteers etc.

### 11.6.2.2 Noun **nado** no/to iu noun

Similar to 11.6.2.1, the noun **nado** is attached to serves as one or several example/s of the content of the modified noun.

a トウモロコシは品種改良、栽培技術の改善などの努力が続いている。

**Tōmorokoshi wa hinshu kairyō, saibai gijutsu no kaizen nado no doryoku ga tsuzuite iru.**

With respect to corn, efforts continue to be made in areas like improving strains and cultivation techniques.

b　ヌエは顔がサル、胴はタヌキ、尻尾はヘビなどという怪物である。

**Nue wa kao ga saru, dō wa tanuki, shippo wa hebi nado to iu
kaibutsu de aru.**

The Japanese chimera is a creature with [features] like the face
of a monkey, the body of a *tanuki* [raccoon dog], and the tail
of a snake.

### 11.6.3 *Verb* **nado**

Here, **nado** is attached to examples of actions taken and means 'such as
doing', as a more formal/written equivalent of -**tari** (see 26.7).

Note how the verb can attach an 'extra' **shite** (**ori**) after **nado** (examples
a and b).

a　PRチラシを作成するなどして地元の協力を求めていく。

**PR chirashi o sakusei suru nado shite jimoto no kyōryoku o
motomete iku.**

We'll draw up PR flyers and do other such things to request
co-operation at the local level.

b　優輝ちゃんは病院に運ばれたが頭の骨を折るなどしており、
　約二時間半後に死亡した。

**Yūki-chan wa byōin ni hakobareta ga atama no hone o oru
nado shite ori, yaku ni-jikan-han-go ni shibō shita.**

Yūki-chan was taken to hospital but had a broken skull, and died two
and a half hours later.

c　スーパーが営業時間を延長するなど、業態間競争も起きている。

**Sūpā ga eigyō jikan o enchō suru nado, gyōtai-kan kyōsō mo
okite iru.**

Competition in business conditions is also taking place – for instance,
grocery stores are extending their hours of business and so on.

### 11.7　Particle of manner: to

The adverbial particle **to** is used to describe the manner in which the
preceding word or clause takes place (see also 28.3).

*Note* – this is also possible with negative predicates (example d, *lit.* "doesn't
require a matter of five minutes.").

a 頭の中がぴかぴかと光った。
**Atama no naka ga pikapika to hikatta.**
There was a flash of light inside my head.

b サクっとあがった天ぷらがおいしい季節になってきた。
**Sakutto agatta tempura ga oishii kisetsu ni natte kita.**
It's the season now when crisply fried tempura tastes good.

c 小説、随筆、旅行記、童話、詩と何でもこなした。
**Shōsetsu, zuihitsu, ryokōki, dōwa, shi to nan demo konashita.**
He could write anything [= any genre], novels, essays, travelogues, fairy
   tales, poems.

d パソコン通信に慣れた人なら、5分とかからない。
**Pasokon tsūshin ni nareta hito nara, gofun to kakaranai.**
Someone who is used to communicating by computer can do it
   [= order through the Internet] in less than five minutes.

# Chapter 12

# Passive sentences

Passive sentences can be explained as conversions from active sentences, although often only one of the two (the active or the passive sentence) is idiomatic.

Compare the pair of sentences below, based on 12.1.1.1.1 a (the passive sentence is the idiomatic one, whereas the active sentence is artificial or unnatural).

a ✍ 試験官が/は私を笑った。ACTIVE
**Shikenkan ga/wa watashi o waratta.**
The invigilator laughed at me.

b 私が/は試験官に笑われた。PASSIVE
**Watashi ga/wa shikenkan ni warawareta.**
I was laughed at by the invigilator.

In the construction *X* **ga/wa** *Y* **ni V-pass.**, *Y* is the 'agent' (the person carrying out the action of the verb), whereas *X* is the 'patient' (the person influenced or affected by the action). A passive sentence is used when the interest focusses on what happens to *X*, whereas an active sentence in concerned with what *Y* does.

Note that the agent (and/or other NP) is frequently omitted, thus instead of b the same meaning could also be expressed by **shikenkan ni warawareta**, or just **warawareta**. The notion of a 'complete sentence' as taught in English-speaking schools is almost totally absent in Japanese, where a verb is often sufficient. Of course, the identity of agent and patient has to be clear from the context.

Apart from the particle **ni**, the agent can also be marked by the particle **kara** in some patterns, or the phrasal particle **ni yotte**.

Passive verb formation (possible with both transitive and intransitive verbs) is as shown below.

Group I verbs: attach **reru** to the negative base

| | | |
|---|---|---|
| **tora-(nai)** | → | **tora-reru** |
| **tanoma-(nai)** | → | **tanoma-reru** |
| **shina-(nai)** | → | **shina-reru** |

Group II verbs: attach **rareru** to the negative base

| | | |
|---|---|---|
| **tabe-(nai)** | → | **tabe-rareru** |
| **mi-(nai)** | → | **mi-rareru** |

Group III verbs: replace the final form with the passive form

| | | |
|---|---|---|
| **suru** | → | **sareru** |
| **kuru** | → | **korareru** |

Note that the resulting passive verb forms (ending in -(ra)reru) behave like Group II verbs, i.e. they can attach other endings (such as past/perfective -ta, or polite -masu, etc.) like any other Group II verb.

| | | |
|---|---|---|
| **-(ra)re-ru** | → | **-(ra)re-ta**, **-(ra)re-masu**, etc. |

Passive sentence types are shown below. They can be broadly divided into passives proper and passive forms with non-passive meaning (= spontanous and honorific uses). Passives proper can be subdivided into passives using transitive verbs, and passives using intransitive verbs. Transitive passives can be further divided into those with an object (marked by **o**), without an object, and without an agent.

## 12.1 Passive sentences proper

### 12.1.1 *With transitive verbs*

#### 12.1.1.1 *Passives without an object present or implied*

##### 12.1.1.1.1 *X*-**ga** *Y* (person)-**ni/kara** verb-passive

With animate agents, both **ni** (example a) and **kara** (example c) can mark the agent, although the agent is mostly ellipted as seen in the remaining examples.

a 最終の口述試験では試験官に笑われた。
**Saishū no kōjutsu shiken de wa shiken-kan <u>ni</u> warawareta.**
I was laughed at by the invigilator in the final interview test.

b 男は暴れることもなく、その場で逮捕された。
   **Otoko wa abareru koto mo naku, sono ba de taiho sareta.**
   The man was arrested on the spot, without a struggle.

c 同級生からいじめられた。
   **Dokyūsei <u>kara</u> ijimerarete ita.**
   He was being bullied by his classmates.

d 学生時代に一度だけ好きな男の子に告白したが、ふられてしまった。
   **Gakusei jidai ni ichi-do dake suki na otoko no ko ni kokuhaku shita ga, furarete shimatta.**
   When I was a student, I once declared my love to a boy, but I was rejected.

e お母さんかわいくないから飽きられちゃったのか。
   **Okāsan kawaikunai kara akirarechatta no ka.**
   Has [your father/my husband] lost interest in me because I'm not cute?

---

| 12.1.1.1.2 | *X*-**ga** *Y* (thing)-**ni** verb-passive |

When the same pattern is used with inanimate agents, only **ni** can mark the agent.

a 台風に見舞われて、交通機関がまひしてしまった。
   **Taifū <u>ni</u> mimawarete, kōtsū kikan ga mahi shite shimatta.**
   Struck by a typhoon, the transport system was paralysed.

b K町の会社員Aさんが乗用車にはねられ、頭を強く打って即死した。
   **K-chō no kaisha-in A-san ga jōyō-sha <u>ni</u> hanerare, atama o tsuyoku utte sokushi shita.**
   The company employee A of town K was hit by a car and died instantly from the heavy blow to his head.

---

| 12.1.1.1.3 | *X*-**ga** *Y*-**ni yotte** verb-passive |

This type of passive is similar to the English passive. It is mostly used in written-style language. Again, the agent is omitted where obvious from the context, or unnecessary to specify.

a 7ヵ国の代表によって話し合いが再開される。
   **Nanakakoku no daihyō <u>ni yotte</u> hanashiai ga saikai sareru.**
   Talks will be resumed by the delegates from the seven countries.

b ヤミ米は専門の業者によって密輸入されている。

**Yamigome wa senmon no gyōsha <u>ni yotte</u> yunyū sarete iru.**

The illegal rice is being imported by specialized companies.

c 夏休みには子供たちを対象とした科学教室が各地で開催された。

**Natsuyasumi ni wa kodomo-tachi o taishō to shita kagaku
kyōshitsu ga kakuchi de kaisai sareta.**

In the summer vacation science classes aimed at children were held in
many places.

d 手帳には、鉛筆で故郷の家の絵が書かれていた。

**Techō ni wa, enpitsu de furusato no ie no e ga
kakarete ita.**

In the diary, a picture of his birthplace was drawn in pencil.

12.1.1.2 *Passives with an object present or implied*

12.1.1.2.1 *X-ga Y-ni Z-o verb-passive: indirect passive*

Here, Z (some entity belonging to X, such as a thing, part of body, family
member, etc.) is affected by the action of Y, and as a result, X is affected
indirectly. Therefore this type of passive is often called 'indirect passive'.
The implication is usually one of adversity, i.e. something unfortunate
happening to X.

a 泥棒に財布をとられた。

**Dorobō ni saifu <u>o</u> torareta.**

(I) had my wallet taken by a thief.

b 電気を止められたことも何度もある。

**Denki <u>o</u> tomerareta koto mo nando mo aru.**

I've had the electricity cut off many times.

12.1.1.2.2 *X-ga Y-ni Z-o verb-passive: direct passive*

Although the sentence pattern is identical, the difference to 12.1.1.3.1 is
that here the object (Z) is not part of the subject (X), but the object of
the verb. Therefore this is called a direct passive, with an object present
or implied in the sentence.

a その猫はガソリンか灯油をかけられていた。

**Sono neko wa <u>gasorin ka tōyu o</u> kakerarete ita.**

That cat had petrol or kerosene poured over it.

387

b 今の仕事はきついけれど店を任せられているという充実感
　がある。

**Ima no shigoto wa kitsui keredo <u>mise o</u> makaserarete iru to
iu jūjitsu-kan ga aru.**

My current work is tough, but there is the satisfaction of being
entrusted with the shop.

---

12.1.1.3 *Passives without agent*

12.1.1.3.1 *X* **ga** verb-passive

This type of passive lacks an agent (and therefore has no active counterpart). It is typically used in the media, academic papers, etc. Apart from
**ga**, the subject/patient can be marked by particles replacing **ga**, such as
**wa**, and **mo**, or is omitted (example a).

a 誠実な人柄で知られる。

**Seijitsu na hitogara de shirareru.**

[He] is known for his sincere personality.

b 最近、公共の場での禁煙の問題がクローズアップされている。

**Saikin, kōkyō no ba de no kin'en no mondai <u>ga</u> kurōzuappu
sarete iru.**

Recently, the problem of outlawing smoking in public places is
receiving attention.

c 地球温暖化の穀物生産への影響はまだ解明されていない。

**Chikyū ondanka no kokumotsu seisan e no eikyō <u>wa</u> mada
kaimei sarete inai.**

The effects of global warming on grain production have not yet been
clarified.

d 心の安らぎを得るものとして宗教音楽も注目されている。

**Kokoro no yasuragi o eru mono to shite shūkyō ongaku <u>mo</u>
chūmoku sarete iru.**

As a means of achieving peace of mind religious music too is
attracting attention.

e 将来、化粧品の価格<u>は</u>下落することが予想される。

**Shōrai, keshōhin no kakaku <u>wa</u> geraku suru koto ga yosō
sareru.**

In the future, it is expected that the price of cosmetics will drop.

*With intransitive verbs*

12.1.2.1 *X-ga Y-ni verb-passive*

The existence of intransitive passives has been pointed out as a characteristic of Japanese passive sentences. Here, X is directly affected (not just in part, as in 12.1.1.2.1) by the action of Y, usually adversely.

a 妻に先立たれた。
**Tsuma ni sakidatareta.**
[His] wife died (*lit.* "went on") before [him].

b 七十五歳のおばあちゃんが息子に突然死なれた。
**Nanajūgosai no obāchan ga musuko ni totsuzen
shinareta.**
The 75-year old woman's son suddenly died on her.

## 12.2 Sentences using passive forms with non-passive meanings

12.2.1 *Spontaneous passive (with verbs of feeling,
expectation, etc.)*

This indicates a feeling that occurs spontaneously or naturally, which the subject cannot help feeling, which translates as 'seems to me', 'is felt', 'feel attracted to', etc. (see 14.2).

a これまでは政治改革の意義を無視しているとしか思われない。
**Kore made wa seiji kaikaku no igi o mushi shite iru to shika
omowarenai.**
I can only think that until now they have been ignoring the meaning of
political reform.

b 幼いころから乗馬の優雅なイメージにひかれていた。
**Osanai koro kara jōba no yūga na imēji ni hikarete ita.**
From an early age, she was attracted to the elegant image of
horseriding.

c その言葉にはかつてない切実さが感じられる。
**Sono kotoba ni wa katsute nai setsujitsu-sa ga kanjirareru.**
In his words one feels an urgency that wasn't there before.

| 12.2.2 | *X wa/ga verb-passive (X = person): passive honorific*

Passive honorifics are less polite than other honorific forms, but are popular with the younger generation and in professional situations (see 16.1.3).

a 負傷された方々には心からのお見舞いを申しあげたい。

**Fushō sareta katagata ni wa kokoro kara no o-mimai o mōshiagetai.**

I wish to express my heartfelt sympathy to those who got injured.

b 自然を壊すなと、反対派の方は主張されているようです。

**Shizen o kowasu na to, hantaiha no kata wa shuchō sarete iru yō desu.**

Those against [the project] appear to advocate that nature should not be destroyed.

# Chapter 13

# Causative and causative passive sentences

## 13.1 Causative sentences

Causative sentences can be seen as a kind of sentence conversion, in that an extra NP (and the meaning of causation or permission) is added to a non-causative sentence. Compare:

- **Kodomo ga gakkō ni iku.** The child goes to school.

- **Oya ga kodomo o/ni gakkō ni ikaseru.** The parents make/let the child go to school.

In the basic sentence, the verb **iku** requires the NP + **ga** to indicate the person carrying out the action of the verb. By contrast, the causative sentence involves an extra NP (**oya ga**, the causer) who influences the actor (or causee) to carry out the action of the verb. Also, the valency is changed (the actor is now marked by **o** or **ni**). Of course, not all these NPs are usually present in a given sentence (those understood from the context are often omitted).

Causative sentences can express three meanings or functions: 'make someone do something' (coercion), 'let someone do something' (permission) or substituting for a transitive verb by using an intransitive verb in the causative form. This last function is shown below.

a 関係者を驚かせる
**kankeisha o odorokaseru**
amaze the persons concerned

instead of

b 関係者が驚いている
**kankeisha ga odoroite iru**
the persons concerned are amazed

The distinction between a and b is, however, not always clear-cut, even when the context is taken into consideration.

Causative verbs are formed from V-**ru** as in Table 13.1. The resulting causative verbs behave like Group II verbs, i.e. **nomaseru, tabesaseru, misaseru, saseru** etc., and have the conjunctional forms **nomase-te, tabesase-te, misase-te, sase-te.**

**Table 13.1** Causative verb formation

| Verb type | Replacement pattern | | |
|-----------|------|---|--------|
| Group I | **_-u_** | → | **_-aseru_** |
| | **ik-u** | → | **ik-aseru** |
| | **nom-u** | → | **nom-aseru** |
| | **ka(w)-u** | → | **kaw-aseru** |
| Group II | **_-ru_** | → | **_-saseru_** |
| | **tabe-ru** | → | **tabe-saseru** |
| | **mi-ru** | → | **mi-saseru** |
| Group III | **kuru** | → | **kosaseru** |
| | **suru** | → | **saseru** |

---

**13.1.1** *X (person) ga/wa Y (person) o/ni\**
*(verb-intransitive-causative)*

Person *X* (usually ellipted, being understood from the context) exerts influence to allow or force person *Y* (also often ellipted) to do the action of the intransitive verb.

*Note\** – with verbs expressing emotion (**odoroku** 'be surprised', **warau** 'laugh', etc.), only **o** is used.

a ✐ 先生は学生を帰らせた。
**Sensei wa gakusei o kaeraseta.**
The teacher sent the students home.

b 学生を一年間企業で働かせる。
**Gakusei o ichinenkan kigyō de hatarakaseru.**
They place [= make work/allow to work] the students for one year in a firm.

c　かわいい子には旅させろ。
   **Kawaii ko ni wa tabi sasero.**
   Children one cares about, one should send [= make go/allow to go]
   on journeys (= spare the rod and spoil the child).

d　家族を食わせないといけないし。
   **Kazoku o kuwasenai to ikenai shi.**
   I also need to feed (*lit.* "let eat") my family.

e　小さいころから人を笑わせることが好きだった。
   **Chiisai koro kara hito o warawaseru koto ga suki datta.**
   From the time he was small, he liked making people laugh.

f　予想以上の活躍に関係者を驚かせている。
   **Yosō ijō no katsuyaku ni kankeisha o odorokasete iru.**
   Their [= foreign jockeys'] unexpected success amazes the people
   concerned.

### 13.1.2　*X (person) ga/wa Y (person) ni Z (thing) o (verb-transitive-causative)*

Person X exerts influence to allow or force person Y to do the action of
[transitive verb + object].

a　✐ 先生は学生に作文を書かせた。
   **Sensei wa gakusei ni sakubun o kakaseta.**
   The teacher made/had the students write a composition.

b　この絵は神を感じさせる。
   **Kono e wa kami o kanjisaseru.**
   This painting makes [you/one] feel God.

c　息子に資産を相続させたい。
   **Musuko ni shisan o sōzoku sasetai.**
   I want my son to inherit my property.

### 13.1.3　*X (person/thing) ga/wa Y (thing) o/wa (verb-intransitive-causative)*

Here, NP **o** + the causative equivalent of NP **ga** + intransitive verb is used to
indicate what a person or thing/matter does. The NP **o** + intransitive causative verb often translates as a transitive V in English, or sometimes idiomatically.

393

13.1.3.1 X = *person*

a ちらっと本音をのぞかせた。(cf., 本音がのぞく **honne ga
nozoku**)
**Chiratto honne o nozokaseta.**
Momentarily, [he] showed (*lit.* "allowed to appear") his real
concern.

b 想像力を働かせて聴いてください。(cf., 想像力が働く **sōzōryoku
ga hataraku**)
**Sōzōryoku o hatarakasete kiite kudasai.**
Please listen using your imagination.

c 関係者は夢を膨らませている。(cf., 夢が膨らむ **yume ga
fukuramu**)
**Kankeisha wa yume o fukuramasete iru.**
The people concerned are full of expectation (*lit.* "they make their
dreams swell").

d キャンプに行ってくみ置いた生水は沸騰させて使う方が安全
だ。(cf., 生水が沸騰する **namamizu ga futtō suru**)
**Kyanpu ni itte kumioita namamizu wa futtō sasete tsukau hō
ga anzen da.**
It is safer to use the water one has drawn at the camp after boiling it.
(*lit.* "making it boil")

13.1.3.2 X = *thing*

a 過去のしがらみが改革を遅らせているという。(cf., 改革が遅れる
**kaikaku ga okureru**)
**Kako no shigarami ga kaikaku o okurasete iru to iu.**
They say that the fetters of the past delay reform.

b 戦後の日本経済は他の資本主義国のどこよりも自由と平等を調和
させて発展してきた。(cf., 自由と平等が調和する **jiyū to byōdō
ga chōwa suru**)
**Sengo no Nihon keizai wa hoka no shihon shugi-koku no
doko yori mo jiyū to byōdō o chōwa sasete hatten shite
kita.**
The postwar Japanese economy has developed by blending freedom
and equality more than any other capitalist country.

## 13.1.4 Verb-intransitive/verb-transitive-causative-te + performative verb

When the speaker indicates that he has his action condoned by others (or wants it that way), the patterns [(first person) V-causative-**te morau/itadaku**] or [(second/third person) V-causative-**te kureru/kudasaru**] are used.

These patterns can also be used in question form to request permission politely, in the form V-causative-**te moraemasen ka/itadakemasen ka** 'may I?', 'am I allowed to?'/**kuremasen ka/kudasaimasen ka** 'would you?' (note that **morau** and **itadaku** are used only in the potential form here). See 15.3.3.5.

### 13.1.4.1 (First person) verb-causative-**te morau/itadaku**

The combination means 'may I', 'be allowed to'.

a 自己紹介させていただきます・・・
 **Jiko shōkai sase-te itadakimasu ...**
 Please allow me to introduce myself ...

b 今はのんびりさせてもらっている。
 **Ima wa nonbiri sase-te moratte iru.**
 At present I'm taking a breather [= after stepping down from
   a government post].

c はっきり言わせてもらえば、誤解に基づく批判である。
 **Hakkiri iwase-te moraeba, gokai ni motozuku hihan de aru.**
 If I may say things straight, it's a criticism that is based on a
   misunderstanding.

### 13.1.4.2 (Second/third person) verb-causative-**te kureru/kudasaru**

The combination means 'let me' 'allow me to'.

a 一晩考えさせてくれ。
 **Hitoban kangaesase-te kure.**
 Let me sleep on it (lit. "think about it overnight").

b 何でこんなことしか、やらせてくれないのよ。
 **Nande konna koto shika, yarase-te kurenai no yo.**
 Why do they allow me to do only such [boring] work?

*Idiomatic uses*

A number of verbs (or noun-verb combinations) use the causative form idiomatically.

a 酒を飲んでは仕事の話に花を咲かせたという。

**Sake o nonde wa shigoto no hanashi ni hana o sakaseta to iu.**

He says that each time they had a drink they had a lively conversation about work.

(**hanashi ni hana o sakaseru** 'have an animated conversation', *lit.* "make blossoms bloom in talk")

b 母親のみさ子さん（47）も「ありがとうございました」と言葉を詰まらせた。

**Hahaoya no Misako-san (47) mo 'arigatō gozaimashita' to kotoba o tsumaraseta.**

Misako-san (47), the mother, too, could only say 'thank you very much'. (**kotoba o tsumaraseru**, *lit.* "make one's words choke")

c 地図を見るには磁石が欠かせない。

**Chizu o miru ni wa jishaku ga kakasenai.**

To consult a map, a compass is a must.

(**kakasenai** = negative of the causative form of **kaku** 'to be lacking')

## 13.2 Causative passive sentences

Causative passives are causative sentences (see 13.1) with added passive (see 12). The causative sentence a below can be converted into b by attaching the passive ending, making **gakusei** into the patient, and **sensei** into the agent of the passive sentence. The causative sentence 'make someone do something' thus has the added meaning of passive 'be made to do something (by someone)'.

a ✐ 先生が学生を立たせた。

**Sensei ga gakusei o tataseta.**

The teacher made the pupil stand up.

b ✐ 学生が先生に立たせられた。

**Gakusei ga sensei ni tataserareta.**

The student was made to stand up by the teacher.

**Table 13.2** Causative-passive verb formation

| Verb type | Verb | Causative | Causative-passive |
|-----------|------|-----------|-------------------|
| Group I | ik-u | ik-ase-ru | ik-ase-rareru |
| | | | ik-as-areru |
| | nom-u | nom-ase-ru | nom-ase-rareru |
| | | | nom-as-areru |
| Group II | tabe-ru | tabe-saseru | tabe-sase-rareru |
| | mi-ru | mi-saseru | mi-sase-rareru |
| Group III | suru | sase-ru | sase-rareru |
| | kuru | kosase-ru | kosase-rareru |

The difference between the two is that the causative sentence is concerned with what the teacher has done to the pupil (from the point of view of the teacher), whereas the causative-passive sentence is concerned with how the pupil was influenced by the teacher (from the point of view of the pupil).

The basic meaning of a causative-passive sentence is 'be made to do something (against one's will)', but there are also examples where the implication is a positive one 'be given the opportunity to feel/discover something'.

Causative-passive verb forms are formed as given in Table 13.2 (see 13.1, 12).

c 交通渋滞のひどさには閉口させられた。
  **Kōtsū jūtai no hidosa ni wa heikō saserareta.**
  I was dumbfounded by how bad the traffic jams were.

d まず著者が驚かされたのは大学の公開性だった。
  **Mazu chosha ga odorokasareta no wa daigaku no kōkaisei datta.**
  What surprised the author first of all was the openness of universities.

e 運用責任者の「暴走」のツケは、これから住民が払わされること
  になる。
  **Un'yō sekininsha no 'bōsō' no tsuke wa, kore kara jūmin ga
  harawasareru koto ni naru.**
  The citizens will now be made to pay the bill run up through the
  'recklessness' of those responsible for running it [= local government].

f 同氏の証言次第では、大統領が窮地に立たされることもありそうだ。
  **Dōshi no shōgen shidai de wa, daitōryō ga kyūchi ni
  tatasareru koto mo arisō da.**
  Depending on his testimony, the president may be put into a critical
  position.

# Chapter 14

# *Potential and spontaneous sentences*

## 14.1   **Potential sentences**

Potential sentences basically express the idea of 'can', 'be able to' do something.

Potential verbs forms are derived from V-**ru** as shown below.

*Note* – the *forms (and note that apart from the Group III **koreru**, only selected Group II verbs have such formations) are as yet regarded as 'incorrect', but are in fact widely used in the spoken language.

**Table 14.1** Potential verb formation

| Verb type | Replacement Pattern | | |
|---|---|---|---|
| Group I | *-u* | → | *-eru* |
| | **ik-u** | → | **ik-eru** |
| | **nom-u** | → | **nom-eru** |
| | **ka(w)-u** | → | **ka(w)-eru** |
| Group II | *-ru* | → | *-rareru/reru* |
| | **tabe-ru** | → | **tabe-rareru/\*tabe-reru** |
| | **mi-ru** | → | **mi-rareru/\*mireru** |
| Group III | **suru** | → | **dekiru** |
| | **kuru** | → | **korareru/\*koreru** |

The -**ru** ending of these potential forms (all groups) itself works like a Group II ending, i.e. ik-e-ru → ik-e-masu, ik-e-nai, mi-rare-ru, etc. → mi-rare-masu, mi-rare-nai, etc., korare-ru → korare-masu, korare-nai, etc.

There are several types of potential sentences, which can be broadly divided into those where an agent (a person etc. who 'can') is mentioned (or

implied), and those without a mentioned or implied agent. The former can
be subdivided according to whether the potential verb is transitive or
intransitive, and which case particles are used to mark the person (or other
entity) who 'can' and, where applicable, the object of that ability.

### 14.1.1 Agent (person, etc.) mentioned or implied

#### 14.1.1.1 Intransitive verb-potential

##### 14.1.1.1.1 (Person ga/wa/mo) verb-intransitive-potential

Where V-potential is intransitive, there can of course be no object. This
construction indicates (in)ability to perform the action of the verb, but the
agent or person NP is often omitted (understood from the context).

a 働けなくなるまで働きたい。
**Hatarakenaku naru made hatarakitai.**
[I] want to work until I can't manage any more.

b 声も出ないし、動けないし、大変だった。
**Koe mo denai shi, ugokenai shi, taihen datta.**
[I] couldn't project my voice, and couldn't move well, so it
    [= my first time on stage] was hard.

c 主婦やOLも気軽に来れるような雰囲気づくりに努めたい。
**Shufu ya ōeru mo kigaru ni koreru yō na fun'iki-zukuri ni
tsutometai.**
We'd like to try and create an atmosphere where housewives and
    female office workers can come readily.

#### 14.1.1.2 Transitive verb-potential

##### 14.1.1.2.1 (Person wa) (object ga/o) verb-transitive-potential

The object of V-pot can be marked by either **o** or **ga**, or by adverbial
particles such as **wa** replacing these (see 2.2.2, 2.1.4). Person **wa**, and/or
object **ga/o**, are often omitted (understood from the context).

a 渡辺氏は政権へのラストチャンスの芽を見いだせないでいる。
**Watanabe-shi wa seiken e no rasutochansu no me o
miidasenai de iru.**
Mr Watanabe is unable to find his last chance to be PM.

b もう暑いところでは研究ができない。
**Mō atsui tokoro de wa kenkyū ga dekinai.**
I can't do research in hot climates (*lit.* "places") any more.

c コメントは出せない。
**Komento wa dasenai.**
We can't make any comments.

d みんなを助けたかったけれどどうにもできなかった。
**Minna o tasuke-takatta keredo dō ni mo dekinakatta.**
I wanted to rescue them all, but just couldn't.

e 「特別な例では」と、いまだに驚きを隠せないでいた。
**'Tokubetsu na rei de wa' to, imada ni odoroki o kakusenai
de ita.**
'Isn't it a special case?' he said, even now unable to conceal his
surprise.

f 賃上げができても単純に喜べない事情がある。
**Chin'age ga dekite mo tanjun ni yorokobenai jijō ga aru.**
Even if [the company] can raise wages, there are reasons why [the
union] cannot simply rejoice.

g ウエートトレーニングなど練習方法も研究して自分に自信が持て
るようになりました。
**Uētotorēningu nado renshū hōhō mo kenkyū shite jibun ni
jishin ga moteru yō ni narimashita.**
He has worked out ways of practising such as weight training,
and is now able to have confidence in himself.

h 海洋調査について一人でも多くの人に理解、協力をいただけるよ
う努力を続けたい。
**Kaiyō chōsa ni tsuite hitori demo ōku no hito ni rikai,
kyōryoku o itadakeru yō doryoku o tsuzuketai.**
We'd like to keep making efforts to have as many people as possible
understand and co-operate in the ocean survey.

i 登山経験は皆無に近かったが、食虫植物や自然のランを見れると
聞いて参加した。
**Tozan keiken wa kaimu ni chikakatta ga, shokuchū
shokubutsu ya shizen no ran o mireru to kiite sanka shita.**
I've had practically no experience of mountaineering, but
took part because I heard that one can see insectivorous plants
and wild orchids.

In relative clauses and cleft sentences, the object is not mentioned, as it is
identical with the modified noun (relative clauses), or the noun in S2 in
cleft sentences.

(i)  Relative clauses and cleft sentences:

  a  只で見れるものに金と時間を費す者はない。
     **Tada de mireru mono ni kane to jikan o tsuiyasu <u>mono</u>
     wa nai.**
     There's nobody who'll spend money and time on something one
       can see for free.

  b  頼れるのは自分だけだ。
     **Tayoreru no wa <u>jibun</u> dake da.**
     It's only myself I can rely on.

(ii) Other noun-modification: pseudo-relative clauses are sentences that are
     constructed like relative clauses, except that the modified (or head) N
     is a relational N, time N or N of amount (see 22.1.2).

  a  とても全部は食べれない量だ。
     **Totemo zenbu wa taberenai <u>ryō</u> da.**
     It's far too much to eat.

  b  考えてみれば、家族一緒に過ごせる日などそうはない。
     **Kangaete mireba, kazoku issho ni sugoseru <u>hi</u> nado sō
     wa nai.**
     When you think about it, there aren't that many days that one can
       spend with the family.

### 14.1.1.3  *Person (etc.)* **ni** *(object* **ga/wa***) verb-potential*

This also indicates what the person (or other entity that can control its
actions) can or cannot do. Where present, the object of the potential verb
can be marked by **ga** or **wa**, but not by **o**. The order of N **ni** and N **ga/wa**
can be reversed (see 2.4.7).

  a  本当に自分に仕事ができるのか。
     **Hontō ni jibun <u>ni</u> shigoto ga dekiru no ka.**
     Can I really do work [properly]?

b 自分たちに何ができるか考えたいのです。

**Jibun-tachi <u>ni</u> nani ga dekiru ka kangae-tai no desu.**

We want to think about what we can do.

c それがなぜ京都にはできないのか。

**Sore ga naze Kyōto <u>ni</u> wa dekinai no ka.**

Why can't Kyoto do this [= control the height of buildings]?

d 祖国から追い立てるようなことは、私には受け入れられない。

**Sokoku kara oitateru yō na koto wa, watashi <u>ni</u> wa ukeirerarenai.**

I can't accept an action that amounts to expelling people from their country.

e ・・・私には片道二時間以上かかる通勤は耐えられない。

**. . . watashi <u>ni</u> wa katamichi ni-jikan ijō kakaru tsūkin wa taerarenai.**

I can't put up with a commuting [time] that takes over two hours one way.

Example f shows a sentence where person + **ni** (**watashi ni**, etc.) is omitted.

f なるほど、その方が自然に思えた。

**Naruhodo, sono hō ga shizen ni omoeta.**

Fair enough, that [= posing with a towel rather than nude] seemed more natural.

---

| 14.1.1.4 | *Clause* **koto ga dekiru**

The phrase **koto ga dekiru** can be attached to clauses ending in V-**ru** only. Where an object is present, it can be marked by **o** (or adverbial particles like **wa/mo/datte** etc.) only (see 22.3.2.3.1).

a 一度株を植えておけば毎年花を楽しむことができる。

**Ichi-do kabu o uete okeba maitoshi hana o tanoshimu koto ga dekiru.**

Once [you] plant the rootstock, [you] can enjoy the flowers every year.

b 男性がスカートをはくわけにはいかないが、女性は三つぞろいのビジネススーツだって着ることができる。

**Dansei ga sukāto o haku wake ni wa ikanai ga, josei wa mitsu-zoroi no bijinesu-sūtsu datte kiru koto ga dekiru.**

A man can't wear a skirt, but a woman can wear a three-piece business suit.

## 14.1.2 *No agent (person, etc.) mentioned or implied*

### 14.1.2.1 *(0 ga/wa) verb-potential*

Here, no human agent (person-**ga/wa**) can be mentioned (or implied). In other words, this construction is concerned with the ability or inability of the object of the verb, and in English it often translates as a passive.

a 官僚に任せてはおけない。
   **Kanryō ni makasete wa okenai.**
   [It] can't be left to the bureaucrats.

b 軽いうえ、家庭の洗濯機で洗える。
   **Karui ue, katei no sentakuki de araeru.**
   [They = clothes] are light, and moreover can be machine washed at home.

c 毎日の掃除は欠かせない。
   **Mainichi no sōji wa kakasenai.**
   Daily house cleaning is a must (*lit.* "cannot be done without").

### 14.1.2.2 *(0 ga/wa) verb-potential: with verbs of seeing*

Here, no person can be mentioned (or implied). Only **ga** is used to mark the object in these sentences, which typically use verbs of seeing.

a 窓からは草原が見渡せる。
   **Mado kara wa sōgen ga miwataseru.**
   The window affords a view of the prairie.

b 事態の深刻さがうかがえる。
   **Jitai no shinkoku-sa ga ukagaeru.**
   One can see the seriousness of the situation.

c 最近、社長交代をにおわせるような行動が見受けられる。
   **Saikin, shachō kōtai o niowaseru yō na kōdō ga miukerareru.**
   Recently, one can see actions that hint at a change of company president.

### 14.1.2.3 *Intransitive use of transitive verb-potential*

There are some verbs that look like potential verbs but function more like intransitive verbs, such as **ureru** 'sell well', **kireru** 'cut well' and **kakeru** 'write well'.

Note, however, that some of these V, such as **kakeru** (which otherwise appear identical), can also be transitives in their potential form, in which use an agent or person *can* be mentioned (example c) (see also 14.2).

a エアコン、夏物飲料などが爆発的に売れている。
**Eakon, natsumono-inryō nado ga bakuhatsu-teki ni urete iru.**
Things like air conditioners and summer drinks are selling really fast.

b インクの粘度を下げ、滑らかに書けるようにした。
**Inku no nendo o sage, yawaraka ni kakeru yō ni shita.**
We've made the ink less sticky and smooth[er] to write with.

c 社員は全員原稿を書けることが採用条件。
**Shain wa zen'in genkō o kakeru koto ga saiyō jōken.**
The condition for being given a job at the company is that everyone must be able to write [creatively].

## 14.2 Spontaneous sentences

'Spontaneous' refers to a number of constructions which indicate that the person having the experience is overcome by a mental state involuntarily or without being able to control it. With spontaneous potentials (example b), the meaning is that some object sells, writes, etc. 'by itself' (see 12.2.1, 14.1.2.3).

a これでは政治改革の意義を無視しているとしか思われない。
**Kore de wa seiji kaikaku no igi o mushi shite iru to shika omowarenai.**
I can only think that they are ignoring the meaning of political reform.

b 泣けてきそうなほど、感激した。
**Nakete kisō na hodo kangeki shita.**
I was moved so deeply that I almost cried.

c 二位に甘んじているうちに、モラールが落ちてしまった。そんな感じがしてならない。
**Nii ni amanjite iru uchi ni, morāru ga ochite shimatta. Sonna kanji ga shite naranai.**
While [Japan] was content to be number two in the world, her morale hit rock bottom. I can't help feeling that.

# Chapter 15

# *Performative sentences*

Performative sentences use performative verbs (**ageru, kureru** etc.) or the performative adjective **hoshii**, attached to V-te. The resulting combination has the force of "want someone to do/not do something for someone else's benefit", i.e. the action of the verb is typically performed for someone's benefit. The social status of the recipient of the action in relation to the speaker conditions the choice of the performative verb.

## 15.1    -te ageru

When the performative verb **ageru** (see 28.5.4.1) 'give to someone else' is attached to V-te, the implication is that someone does the action of the V for someone else's benefit. V-**te ageru** is used when the receiver of the action is of equal or lower social status than the giver; there is an object-honorific equivalent, **sashiageru**, that is used for receivers of higher status (see 16.3 e).

-**te ageru** needs to be used with care, as it explicitly indicates that something is done as a favour, so depending on the situation it may be more appropriate to use the V without -**te ageru**.

### 15.1.1  *Verb-te ageru*

In principle -**te ageru** indicates that the action of the verb is performed for the benefit of second or third persons (or animals) 'do for someone else', but it is possible to perform the action of V for one's own benefit (first person), by making it look as if it's done for someone else, as in 15.1.1.3.

15.1.1.1 *Second person*

a 「困った時にはいつでも相談に乗ってあげるから」と言って下さったのです。
 **'Komatta toki ni wa itsu demo sōdan ni not-te ageru kara' to itte kudasatta no desu.**
 He was kind enough to say to me, 'If you run into trouble, I'd be happy to help you out any time'.

b 盛川容疑者はAちゃんに対し、「お菓子を買ってあげる」などと言って近付き、···
 **Morikawa-yōgisha wa A-chan ni taishi, 'okashi o kat-te ageru' nado to itte chikazuki ...**
 Morikawa, the suspect, said things like, 'I'll buy you some sweets' to A-chan and approached her ...

c マフィアはまず「あなたの企業を守ってあげよう」と申し出てくる。
 **Mafia wa mazu 'anata no kigyō o mamot-te ageyō' to mōshidete kuru.**
 At first, the Mafia come to suggest, 'We'll protect your business for you'.

d 「おうちまで乗せてってあげようか」などと声をかけて誘拐。
 　(てって=ていって **tette = te itte**)
 **'O-uchi made nosetet-te ageyō ka nado to koe o kakete yūkai.**
 He said things like, 'Shall I give you a ride home?' and then kidnapped her.

15.1.1.2 *Third person*

a 皆さんにこの地球を見せてあげたいなと思います。
 **Mina-san ni kono chikyū o mise-te agetai na to omoimasu.**
 I really want to show everyone this earth [= astronaut].

b 子供たちに自然と触れ合う機会をたくさん作ってあげたい。
 **Kodomo-tachi ni shizen to fureau kikai o takusan tsukut-te agetai.**
 We want to provide our children with many opportunities to come into contact with nature.

c 事件でお手柄の警察犬には、ご褒美として夕食に卵をつけてあげる。

**Jiken de o-tegara no keisatsu-ken ni wa, go-hōbi to shite yūshoku ni tamago o tsuke-te ageru.**

To reward police dogs which perform well in incidents, we give them an egg with their supper.

d 来日したものの、日本での生活に戸惑う外国人に何かしてあげたかった。

**Rainichi shita mono no, Nihon de no seikatsu ni tomadou gaikokujin ni nani ka shite agetakatta.**

I wanted to do something for foreigners who had come to Japan [to live] but were experiencing difficulties with their lives here.

e 相手の食事代を出してあげることが愛している証（あかし）になるとは思わない。

**Aite no shokujidai o dashite ageru koto ga aishite iru akashi ni naru to wa omowanai.**

I don't think that paying for the other person's meal serves as proof that you love her.

f 学生時代に何をしたか、社会に出て何をしたいのかを気づかせてあげるのが講師の仕事。

**Gakusei jidai ni nani o shita ka, shakai ni dete nani o shitai no ka o kizukase-te ageru no ga kōshi no shigoto.**

The instructor's task is to help them become aware of what they did when they were students and what they want to do when they get out into the world.

### 15.1.1.3 *First person*

a だれも評価してくれないから、せめて自分で自分をほめてあげたい。

**Dare mo hyōka shite kurenai kara, semete jibun de jibun o home-te agetai.**

Since no one else values what I've done, I'd like at least to give myself a pat on the back.

### 15.1.2 *Verb-te agete kudasai/hoshii*

In this combination the meaning is 'please do (for others)', 'I/we want you to do (for others)'.

-te ageru

407

This is a combination of two performatives, -te ageru indicating that the action of the V is performed by the listener (or a third person) for someone else, and -te kudasai/hoshii indicating that this is done at the command or request of the speaker (see 20.2).

a でもねえ、たまにはおじいちゃんとおばあちゃんの話し相手もし
　　てあげてほしい。
　　**Demo nē, tama ni wa ojii-chan to obā-chan no hanashiaite
　　mo shite age-te hoshii.**
　　But I'd like him to talk to Grandpa and Grandma once in a while.

b 「自分の家は狭いし汚いなどといわず、ケーキ一つで構わないか
　　ら隣の外国人を自宅に招いてあげて下さい」と語る。
　　**'Jibun no ie wa semai shi kitanai nado to iwazu, kēki hitotsu
　　de kamawanai kara tonari no gaikokujin o jitaku ni maneite
　　agete kudasai' to kataru.**
　　'Don't say that your house is small and messy and so on; invite
　　the foreigner next door into your home, even if it's only for a piece
　　of cake,' he says.

### 15.1.3 Verb-te age-rare-ru (=potential)

This combination means 'able to do for someone else'. It is used in the sense of a potential, not as a passive. (see 14.1).

a 自分には、途上国とよばれるこの国の人たちに、教えてあげられ
　　ることがたくさんあるだろう。
　　**Jibun ni wa, tojōkoku to yobareru kono kuni no hito-tachi ni,
　　oshie-te agerareru koto ga takusan aru darō.**
　　There are probably a lot of things that I could teach the people of
　　this country, which is referred to as a developing nation [, and
　　thereby help them].

b 中国語や手話などができたら、もっと相手のことを分かってあげ
　　られたと思うと、ちょっぴり残念。
　　**Chūgokugo ya shuwa nado ga dekitara, motto aite no koto o
　　wakat-te agerareta to omou to, choppiri zannen.**
　　When I think that I could have understood more about them [and
　　thereby benefited them] if I'd been able to speak Chinese and do
　　sign language, I am a little bit disappointed.

## 15.1.4 Verb-causative-te ageru

Using a causative verb, this means '(doing someone a favour by) letting someone do something'.

In line with the meaning of -te ageru 'doing someone a favour', causative V usually have the permissive reading 'let' in this combination (see 13.1).

a こんな山の楽しさをほかの人にも体験させてあげたい。

**Konna yama no tanoshisa o hoka no hito ni mo taiken sase-te agetai.**

I would like to have other people experience this kind of enjoyment of the mountains too.

b なるべく多くの選手に試合を経験させてあげよう。

**Narubeku ōku no senshu ni shiai o keiken sasete ageyō.**

We want to have as many of the players as possible experience matchplay.

c 宇宙での生活の様子を日本の人たちに、今すぐにでも話して聞かせてあげたい。

**Uchū de no seikatsu no yōsu o Nihon no hitotachi ni, ima sugu ni demo hanashite kikase-te agetai.**

I'd like to let people in Japan know, right now, what life in space is like.

d 帰ってきたら、夫が好きなスシを食べさせてあげたい。

**Kaette kitara, otto ga suki na sushi o tabesase-te agetai.**

When he gets home, I want to give my husband his favourite [food] sushi to eat.

## 15.1.5 Verb-te ageru in subordinate clauses

(Re subordinate clauses, see 7.6.4.1).

a お客さんの県の石を探してあげればきっと喜ばれます。

**O-kyaku-san no ken no ishi o sagashi-te agereba kitto yorokobaremasu.**

I'm sure your client would be happy if you found a stone from his prefecture for him.

b 外国のトッププレーヤーと話をしたり、家に泊めてあげた
りするうちに、友人の輪もずいぶん広がりました。

**Gaikoku no toppu-purēyā to hanashi o shitari, ie ni
tome-te agetari suru uchi ni, yūjin no wa mo zuibun
hirogarimashita.**

In the course of talking with the top foreign players and letting them
stay at my house, my circle of friends also expanded greatly.

c 男子の中には、雑用をすぐいいつけたり、何かをやってあげても
感謝の気持ちを表さない人がいる。

**Danshi no naka ni wa, zatsuyō o sugu iitsuketari, nani ka o
yat-te agete mo kansha no kimochi o arawasanai hito ga
iru.**

Among the boys, there are some who don't hesitate to order us
[= the girls] to do odd jobs, and some who don't show any
appreciation even if you do something for them.

## 15.2 -te yaru

When the performative verb **yaru** (see 28.5.4.1) is attached to V-**te**, the
implication is that someone does the action of the V for someone else's
benefit. V-**te yaru** is used when the receiver of the action is of lower social
status than the giver, i.e. the giver's own junior family members, animals,
plants, etc., otherwise -**te ageru** (or the superpolite -**te sashiageru**) is used
in the same way (excepting use 15.2.2).

Note that in English translation the force of -**te yaru** ('do for your/his, etc.
benefit' etc.) is usually lost, being left to the context.

### 15.2.1 Verb-te yaru 'do (a favour by doing) something for
someone else'

a 家に帰ってやれ。
**Ie ni kaet-te yare.**
Go home [to your family].

b 子供が望めば大学まで出してやりたい。
**Kodomo ga nozomeba daigaku made dashi-te yaritai.**
I'd like to send my children to university, if that's what
they want.

c 父よ！母よ！あと三年もしたら出ていってやる。

**Chichi yo! Haha yo! Ato sannen mo shitara dete it-te yaru.**

Father! Mother! I'll get out [= of home] in three years – just wait and see!

d 訓一は文子に「日本中で一番幸せな妻にしてやる」といった。

**Kun'ichi wa Fumiko ni 'Nihon-jū de ichiban shiawase na tsuma ni shi-te yaru' to itta.**

Kun'ichi said to Fumiko, 'I'll make you the happiest wife in Japan'.

e 教えてやる、という態度では相手のプライドを傷つける。

**Oshie-te yaru, to iu taido de wa aite no puraido o kizutsukeru.**

With an 'I'll teach you as a favour' attitude, you will hurt people's pride.

f 今は難しい年ごろの中学生がいる。そばにいてやりたい。

**Ima wa muzukashii toshigoro no chūgakusei ga iru. Soba ni i-te yaritai.**

I have [children] at a difficult age, who are in junior high school now. I want to be near them [for their sake].

g よくやったね、と自分に言ってやりたい部分がある。

**Yoku yatta ne, to jibun ni it-te yaritai bubun ga aru.**

There's a part of me that wants to say to myself, 'You did a good job'.

h 庭に植える場合も苗を高めに植えてやることがポイント。

**Niwa ni ueru baai mo nae o takame ni ue-te yaru koto ga pointo.**

When you plant seedlings in the garden, too, the important thing is to plant them high.

## 15.2.2 Verb-te yaru: 'doing something as a threat to the listener'

Apart from making a threat, this is also used when you want to prove yourself for others to see.

a 殺してやる。

**Koroshi-te yaru.**

I'll kill you!

b どうせだめなら暴れてやろう。

**Dōse dame nara abare-te yarō.**

If it's no use anyway, let's put up a good fight.

411

c 次の大会では学生世界一になってやろうと誓ったんです。

**Tsugi no taikai de wa gakusei sekai ichi ni nat-te yarō to chikatta n desu.**

I swore that at the next tournament I would become the best student in the world – let them just wait and see!

---

### 15.2.3 Verb-causative-te yaru 'make/allow someone (to) do something'

Apart from the form -te yaru, -te yaritai is often used (see also 9.2.1).

a 編集科なら受験させてやる。

**Henshūka nara juken sase-te yaru.**

If it's for the editorial section, we'll allow you to take the entrance exam.

b 最高齢を目指していたのですが ……。孫を見せてやりたかった。

**Saikōrei o mezashite ita no desu ga … Mago o mise-te yaritakatta.**

We were aiming at [breaking the record of a captive panda's] longevity … We did want to show him his grandchildren.

c 百三十人の社員に夢を持たせてやりたい。

**Hyakusanjū-nin no shain ni yume o motase-te yaritai.**

I want to give the 130 company employees a dream for the future.

---

### 15.3 -te kureru

When the performative V **kureru** (a less formal equivalent of **kudasaru**, see 28.5.4.2) is attached to V-**te**, the implication is that someone does the action of the V for the benefit of the speaker, or a member of the speaker's group (such as his family members, colleague, etc.).

When third persons are concerned, the choice between -te **kureru** and -te **ageru** depends on which side the speaker (or writer) sympathizes or identifies with: if he takes the third party's side, -te **kureru** is used, otherwise -te **ageru** (see 15.2).

In a story about a 'career woman', the reporter goes home to have dinner with her and her husband, and therefore he identifies with the woman.

a 自宅近くの駅には夫が車で迎えにきてくれていた。

**Jitaku chikaku no eki ni wa otto ga kuruma de mukae ni kite kure-te ita.**

Her husband had come by car to pick her up at the station near[est] to their home.

V-**te kureru** is used when the performer of the action of the V is of equal or lower social status than the receiver (see 15.4).

### 15.3.1 | Verb-te kureru

V-**te kureru** can be used for second or third persons, or personified non-human entities (non-human items treated the same as if they were human – 15.3.12 examples) 'you/someone else/it gives me/us'.

### 15.3.1.1 | Subject = human

*Note* – the effect of -**te kureru** is often difficult to capture in translation; as in example c, there are even cases where a passive is the most appropriate translation.

a よく来てくれました。

**Yoku ki-te kuremashita.**

Thank you for coming.

b みんなが応援してくれました。

**Minna ga ōen shi-te kuremashita.**

[Father of Olympic gold medallist:] Everyone cheered him on.

c 館内では解説のため係の人が案内してくれる。

**Kannai de wa kaisetsu no tame kakari no hito ga annai shi-te kureru.**

Inside the building, one is shown around by the clerk in charge to explain things.

d 食事は母親が毎日作ってくれるし、平日は洗濯もしてくれる。

**Shokuji wa hahaoya ga mainichi tsukutte kureru shi, heijitsu wa sentaku mo shi-te kureru.**

The mother makes the meals for them [= children] every day, and on weekdays she also does the laundry.

e 大人は分かってくれない。

**Otona wa wakat-te kurenai.**

Adults don't understand me.

413

f 中学生から吸っている。どうして、もっと早く教えてくれなかっ
　　たろう。

**Chūgakusei kara sutte iru. Dōshite, motto hayaku oshie-te
kurenakattarō.**

I've been smoking from the time I was in junior high. Why didn't
[people] tell me sooner [about the dangers of smoking], I wonder.

g 同僚たちがそろって「ハッピー・バースデー」を歌ってくれた。

**Dōryō-tachi ga sorotte 'Happī Bāsudē' o utat-te kureta.**

My co-workers sang 'Happy Birthday' to me together.

h 二千万出してくれれば一億にはなる。

**Nisenman dashi-te kurereba ichioku ni wa naru.**

If you give us twenty million, we'll turn it (*lit.* "it'll turn") into
a hundred million at least.

---

15.3.1.2  *Subject = non-human*

These non-human subjects are treated linguistically as if they were human,
e.g. the lottery tickets in example b (if they win), are seen to do the speaker
a favour!

a 答えは時間が出してくれる ···

**Kotae wa jikan ga dashi-te kureru ...**

Time will give us the answer ...

b 当たってくれたら、仕事はやめちゃうよ。

**Atat-te kuretara, shigoto wa yamechau yo.**

If [the lottery tickets] win, I'm going to quit my job, you know.

c とにかく雨さえ降ってくれれば。

**Tonikaku ame sae fut-te kurereba.**

Anyway, if it would only rain.

d 会話だけでは伝えられない事を文章は伝えてくれる。

**Kaiwa dake de wa tsutaerarenai koto o bunshō wa tsutae-te
kureru.**

The written word conveys to us things which cannot be
communicated by conversation alone.

e 女性を大切にしてくれる会社がいい。

**Josei o taisetsu ni shi-te kureru kaisha ga ii.**

I'd prefer a company that values women.

f　植物も愛情を与えれば与えるほど報いてくれる。
**Shokubutsu mo aijō o ataereba ataeru hodo mukui-te kureru.**
With plants too, the more affection you give them, the more they reward you.

## 15.3.2 | Verb-te kurete + evaluatory predicate

Depending on the meaning of the predicate this combination means 'it's good that you/he, etc. are/were . . .' 'I/we are happy that you/he/she do/did something (for me/us) . . .'.

a　あなたがいてくれて助かったわ。
**Anata ga ite kure-te tasukatta wa.**
It really helped that you were here [for me].

b　あなたのような日本人がいてくれてうれしい。
**Anata no yō na Nihonjin ga ite kure-te ureshii.**
[Apology for war atrocities to Korean school, reply:] We're glad there are Japanese people like you.

c　最初はビビったが、今では来てくれて良かったと思う。
**Saisho wa bibitta ga, ima de wa ki-te kurete yokatta to omou.**
At first we were afraid, but now we're happy that it [= new computing magazine] entered the fray.

## 15.3.3 | Verb-te kure (direct and indirect commands)

(See also 20.2, 7.6.4.2.1, 7.6.4.2.2.)

### 15.3.3.1 | Direct commands

a　ドアを開けてくれ。
**Doa o ake-te kure.**
Open the door [for me].

b　わかってくれ。
**Wakat-te kure.**
Do understand.

415

c これを見てくれ。

**Kore o mi-te kure.**

Look at this.

d 今日は寝ないで起きていてくれ。

**Kyō wa nenai de okite i-te kure.**

Today, don't go to sleep; stay awake.

e さっさと出て行ってくれえっ。

**Sassa to dete it-te kure'.**

Just get out!

f ちょっと待ってくれ。

**Chotto mat-te kure.**

Wait a minute.

---

| 15.3.3.2 | *Indirect commands*

Indirect commands are a kind of embedded sentence (see 7.6.4.2), and follow the same rule, i.e. that the form of the actual command is reduced to its simplest form, that is, without any polite endings such as -**masu**, and using the least honorific of the relevant set of performative V (where the original command may have ended in -**te kudasai**, the indirect command uses -**te kure**, for example).

a 全国から講演してくれという要請がたくさんきている。

**Zenkoku kara kōen shi-te kure to iu yōsei ga takusan
   kite iru.**

There are lots of requests from all over the country asking me to
   give a lecture.

---

| 15.3.3.3 | *Verb-**te kureru na***: *negative commands*

This is used to tell someone off for doing something out of line (see 20.1.7).

a 余計なことをしてくれるなと、文句を言われた。

**Yokei na koto o shite kureru na, to monku o iwareta.**

He complained that I shouldn't give him help he didn't ask for.

| 15.3.3.4 | Verb-**nai de kure**: *negative commands* |

This is a less polite version of -**nai de kudasai**, and compared to 15.3.3.3, the more usual way of making a negative command (see also 25.6.4.4).

a 待ってくれ。置いていかないでくれ。
   **Matte kure. Oite ika-nai de kure.**
   Wait! Don't leave me here!

b これ以上出費の機会を増やさないでくれー。
   **Kore ijō shuppi no kikai o fuyasa-nai de kurē--.**
   Please don't create even more occasions for spending money [on presents]!

| 15.3.3.5 | Verb-**te kure-nai/-masen ka**: *requests in negative question form* |

Being less direct, requests in negative question form are more polite than V-**te kure** commands. They are roughly equivalent to English 'can you', 'will you' in the plain form, and 'could you' or 'would you' in the -**masu** form (see 18.4, 20.2.2).

a 仕事を手伝ってくれないか。
   **Shigoto o tetsudat-te kurenai ka.**
   How about giving us a hand with our work?

b ちょっと話があるから来てくれないか。
   **Chotto hanashi ga aru kara ki-te kurenai ka.**
   I want to speak to you a moment, so could you come here.

c ちょっと上の会議室まで来てくれませんか。
   **Chotto ue no kaigishitsu made ki-te kuremasen ka.**
   Could you come to the conference room upstairs for a moment.

| 15.3.4 | Verb-*causative*-**te kureru** |

The causative has permissive meaning in this use 'let me/us do' (see 13.1).

a 一晩考えさせてくれ。
   **Hitoban kangaesasete kure.**
   Let me think about it overnight.

b 何でこんなことしか、やらせてくれないのよ。
   **Nan de konna koto shika, yarasete kurenai no yo.**
   Why do they only let me do [boring] things like this?

417

## 15.4 -te kudasaru

When the performative V **kudasaru** (a formal equivalent of **kureru**, see 28.3.4.2) is attached to V-**te**, the implication is that someone does the action of V for the benefit of the speaker or a member of the speaker's group (such as his family members, colleagues, etc.). V-**te kudasaru** is used when the subject (or performer) of the action of V is of higher social status than the receiver (see 15.3, 16).

The Group II V **kudasaru** is somewhat irregular in that the imperative form (used for polite requests) is **kudasai**, which is also the form to which -**masu** attaches.

### 15.4.1 Verb-**te kudasaru**

#### 15.4.1.1 Verb-**te kudasaru**, etc.

This is used of the second or third person.

a 今決めてくだされば××をサービスします。
**Ima kimete kudasareba xx o sābisu shimasu.**
If you would oblige us by deciding now, we will throw in such-and-such free of charge.

b みなさん一生懸命にしてくださってますよ。(てます = ています
**temasu = te imasu)**
**Minasan isshōkenmei ni shite kudasat-temasu yo.**
They [= assistant staff] are all helping as much as they can, you know.

c まだ無名だった私の表装に合わせて、自分の作品を塗り直してくだ さった。
**Mada mumei datta watashi no hyōsō ni awasete, jibun no sakuhin o nurinaoshi-te kudasatta.**
He was kind enough to re-paint one of his own pieces to go with the mount that I, who was still an unknown, had made.

d 温かく見守り、応援してくださった皆様に感謝の気持ちでいっぱ いです。
**Atatakaku mimamori, ōen shi-te kudasatta mina-sama ni kansha no kimochi de ippai desu.**
I am filled with thanks for all the people who so kindly watched over and supported me.

| 15.4.1.2 | *Verb*-**te kudasai**

Being the imperative form of **kudasaru**, **kudasai** expresses a command to someone else to do (or not to do) something 'please do'. In tone, it is less blunt than **kure** (see 15.3).

The addition of the final particle **ne** (example h) to **kudasai** makes the command more intimate (see also 20.2.2).

a メニューを見せてください。
  **Menyū o mise-te kudasai.**
  Please show me a menu.

b 待ってください。
  **Mat-te kudasai.**
  Please wait.

c わかってください。
  **Wakat-te kudasai.**
  Please understand.

d 落ち着いてください。
  **Ochitsui-te kudasai.**
  Please calm down.

e もちろん、飲み過ぎには注意してください。
  **Mochiron, nomisugi ni wa chūi shi-te kudasai.**
  Of course, be careful not to drink too much, please.

f 早く元気になってください。
  **Hayaku genki ni nat-te kudasai.**
  Please get well soon.

g 虫歯になるので、娘にはアメをあげないでください。
  **Mushiba ni naru no de, musume ni wa ame o agenai
    de kudasai.**
  Please don't give my daughter any sweets as she'll get tooth decay.

h じゃ、しばらく我慢してくださいね。
  **Ja, shibaraku gaman shi-te kudasai ne.**
  Now, please put up with [this = medical examination] for a bit.

419

*Verb-causative*-te kudasai

The causative expressing here the permissive, this means 'please let/allow me to' (see 13).

a もっと聞かせてください。
**Motto kikase-te kudasai.**
Please let me hear more.

b 一日だけ考えさせてください。
**Ichinichi dake kangaesase-te kudasai.**
Please let me think it over for just one day.

c 家族と相談させてください。
**Kazoku to sōdan sase-te kudasai.**
Please let me discuss it with my family.

d 発売するワックスの宣伝に、あなたの車を使わせてください。
**Hatsubai suru wakkusu no senden ni, anata no kuruma o tsukawase-te kudasai.**
Please let us use your car for an advertisement for a wax we're putting on the market.

## 15.5 -te morau

When the performative verb **morau** (a less-formal equivalent of **itadaku**, see 15.6) is attached to V-**te**, the implication is that the subject/speaker has the action of the V done by someone else for his/her benefit. V-**te morau** is used when the subject (= recipient of the favour/action) is of equal or lower social status than the giver. -**te morau** often implies that the subject (who is often the speaker) is getting the performer to do the action by asking or persuasion.

*Note* – like -**te itadaku**, -**te morau** can be used for second or third persons.

15.5.1 *Verb*-te morau

a 東京に行ってもらうよ。
**Tōkyō ni it-te morau yo.**
I'm transferring you to Tokyo.

b 皆さんによくお話をして、理解してもらう。
**Mina-san ni yoku o-hanashi o shite, rikai shi-te morau.**
I'll talk it over thoroughly with everyone and get them to understand.

c 早朝四時、松村さんに市場に連れて行ってもらった。
**Sōchō yoji, Matsumura-san ni ichiba ni tsurete it-te moratta.**
At 4 o'clock in the morning, I had Matsumura-san take me to the market.

d 家の掃除は月に二度ハウスクリーニングに来てもらう。
**Ie no sōji wa tsuki ni nido hausu kurīningu ni ki-te morau.**
For cleaning the house, I have someone from a maid service come in
twice a month.

e 借りる人には住所、氏名、電話番号を書いてもらう。
**Kariru hito ni wa jūsho, shimei, denwa bangō o kai-te morau.**
Those who borrow [= an umbrella] we get to write down their name,
address and phone number.

f 管理職にはポストにふさわしい活躍をしてもらう。
**Kanrishoku ni wa posuto ni fusawashii katsuyaku o shi-te morau.**
We expect our managerial officers to take an active part
[in the company] in keeping with their position.

g さらに胃や体のあちこちが痛むため近所の医者に診てもらった。
**Sara ni i ya karada no achikochi ga itamu tame kinjo no isha ni mi-te moratta.**
On top of that, since my stomach and various other parts of my body
hurt, I had a doctor in the neighbourhood examine me.

## 15.5.2 Verb-te moraō

Using the -(y)ō form, the meaning is 'I/we'll have you/them', etc. (see 9.1.1).

a これを見てもらおう。
**Kore o mi-te moraō.**
Let's get him to look at this [painting].

b あなたは社風に合わないようだ。"試用期間"でもあるし、やめてもらおうか。
**Anata wa shafū ni awanai yō da. 'Shiyō kikan' de mo aru shi, yame-te moraō ka.**
You seem unfit for the style of our company. It's only a 'trial period',
so we'll have you quit, shall we?

c 新製品から紹介してもらいましょう。

**Shinseihin kara shōkai shi-te moraimashō.**

Will you introduce the new products first?

d ホタテの消費量が少ない九州で、もっと食べてもらおうとの
狙いだ。

**Hotate no shōhiryō ga sukunai Kyūshū de, motto tabe-te**
**moraō to no nerai da.**

The aim is to get people in Kyushu, where the level of consumption
of scallops is low, to eat more.

e すぐ家族に面倒をみてもらおうとする発想はおかしい。

**Sugu kazoku ni mendō o mi-te moraō to suru hassō wa**
**okashii.**

The idea of trying to get your family to look after you right away
[= without trying anything else] is odd.

---

| 15.5.3 | *Verb*-te moraeru

With the potential form, the literal meaning is "can get others to do" ( in
the negative "can't get others to do").

---

| 15.5.3.1 | *Verb*-te moraeru

a だれにも理解してもらえない。独りぼっちだ。

**Dare ni mo rikai shi-te moraenai. Hitori-botchi da.**

No one understands me. I'm all alone.

b 子供が病気で保育所では預かってもらえない。

**Kodomo ga byōki de hoikusho de wa azukat-te**
**moraenai.**

My child is ill, so the nursery school won't look after him
(*lit.* "I can't get the nursery school to look after him").

c 半年間は太鼓をたたかせてもらえず、縄を巻いた丸太相手の練習
が続いた。

**Hantoshi-kan wa taiko o tatakase-te moraezu, nawa o maita**
**maruta aite no renshū ga tsuzuita.**

For six months I wasn't allowed to beat the drum, and practising using
a log with string around it continued.

d 同僚の男性は研修に行かせてもらえるのに女性の私には声がかか
　らない。

**Dōryō no dansei wa kenshū ni ikase-te moraeru noni josei no
watashi ni wa koe ga kakaranai.**

Male colleagues get to be sent on courses, but I, a woman, don't get
asked.

e 東京製作所が移転することになった。室蘭に行ってもらえるだ
　ろうか。

**Tōkyō seisakusho ga iten suru koto ni natta. Muroran ni it-te
moraeru darō ka.**

It's been decided that the Tokyo factory will move. Will you go to
Muroran [for us]?

f 国際的に納得してもらえる政権でないと円高が進む。

**Kokusai-teki ni nattoku shi-te moraeru seiken de nai to
endaka ga susumu.**

If we do not have a government in office which can gain acceptance
internationally, the yen exchange rate will continue to rise.

---

| 15.5.3.2 | *Verb*-**te moraenai ka** *(na)*

In question form, -**te moraeru** is used to make a polite request 'can we ask
you to', 'could we get you to', 'would you'. With **ka na** rather than **ka**,
the meaning is 'I wonder', 'perhaps' (see 18, 18.3.1.2.4).

a 一緒に応援してもらえないか。

**Issho ni ōen shi-te moraenai ka.**

Would you join in supporting us?

b あの人に地元の建設会社を紹介してもらえないかな。

**Ano hito ni jimoto no kensetsu-gaisha o shōkai shi-te
moraenai ka na.**

Could I get this man to introduce me to a local construction company,
I wonder.

c うちは最近新しい雑誌を出したんです。付き合ってもらえませ
　んか。

**Uchi wa saikin atarashii zasshi o dashita n desu. Tsukiat-te
moraemasen ka.**

We have recently launched a new magazine. Can we ask you to
participate?

| 15.5.4 | *Verb*-te moraitai |

In line with the meaning of -**tai** 'want to', V-**te moraitai** indicates what the speaker wants a second or third person(s) to do (see 9.2.1).

a 水の大切さを知ってもらいたい。
**Mizu no taisetsusa o shit-te moraitai.**
I want people to realize how precious water is.

b 多くの人に博物館を好きになってもらいたい。
**Ōku no hito ni hakubutsukan o suki ni nat-te moraitai.**
We want lots of people to develop a liking for the museum.

c できたら、息子にも野球選手になってもらいたい。
**Dekitara, musuko ni mo yakyū senshu ni nat-te moraitai.**
If it's possible, I'd like my son to become a baseball player too.

d 男・女でなく、仕事ができる・できないで分けてもらい
たいわね。
**Otoko, onna de naku, shigoto ga dekiru, dekinai de wake-te moraitai wa ne.**
I wish they'd classify us according to whether or not we can do the work, not according to whether we're men or women.

e 立派な強い子になってもらいたい。
**Rippa na tsuyoi ko ni nat-te moraitai.**
I want them [= the babies] to grow up to be fine, strong boys.

| 15.5.5 | *Verb-causative*-te morau |

V-causative-**te morau** is a less polite version of V-causative-**te itadaku**, indicating that the speaker or a third person is allowed to do something as a privilege 'thanks to the listener, or a third person' (see 15.6.3).

Note also example e, where the potential form of **morau** is used.

a 昨晩は楽しませてもらいました。
**Sakuban wa tanoshimase-te moraimashita**
I had a good time last night, thanks to you.

b 今はのんびりさせてもらっている。
**Ima wa nonbiri sasete morat-te iru.**
Right now I'm taking it easy (*lit.* "I have the pleasure of being allowed to take it easy").

c 今晩はしみじみと飲ませてもらうよ。

**Konban wa shimijimi to nomase-te morau yo.**

Tonight I'm going to (*lit.* "get you to let me") do some serious drinking!

d 「産ませてもらうんじゃなくて、自分で産む」というのが基本姿勢。

**'Umase-te morau n ja nakute, jibun de umu' to iu no ga kihon shisei.**

The basic stance [in the exercise programme] is not to be allowed [by the doctor] to have the baby, but to have it by yourself.

e はっきり言わせてもらえれば、誤解に基づく批判である。

**Hakkiri iwase-te moraereba, gokai ni motozuku hihan de aru.**

If I may speak frankly, it's a criticism that's based on a misunderstanding.

## 15.6 -te itadaku

When the performative V **itadaku** (a formal equivalent of **morau**, see 28.5.4.3) is attached to V-**te**, the implication is that the subject has the action of the V performed by someone else for his/her benefit. V-**te itadaku** is used when the subject (= recipient of the favour) is of lower social status than the giver. -**te itadaku** often implies that the subject (who is often the speaker) is getting the performer to do a favour by asking or persuading him/her (see 16).

### 15.6.1 Verb-te itadaku

#### 15.6.1.1 Verb-te itadaku

Usually, V-**te itadaku** implies that you get others to do something for you 'I/we get you/others to do something for me/us', but as in example c, -**te itadaku** can be used as if it were the passive form (**kudasareru** does not exist) of -**te kudasaru**, 'kindly do(es) for me/us'.

a 成績表はちゃんと提出していただきます。

**Seisekihyō wa chanto teishutsu shi-te itadakimasu.**

We get them to submit their transcripts properly.

b 委員会ができればそこで具体的な作業をやっていただく。

**Iinkai ga dekireba soko de gutai-teki na sagyō o yat-te itadaku.**

After the committee is formed, we'll have it do the actual work.

c その時かけていただいた言葉は、今でも私の宝物のようになって
いる。

**Sono toki kake-te itadaita kotoba wa, ima demo watashi no
takaramono no yō ni natte iru.**

The words they [= the people who helped me] spoke to me at that
time are like a treasure to me even now.

<hr/>

| 15.6.1.2 | *Verb-***te itadakitai**

In line with the meaning of **-tai**, this means 'I/we'd like you to do (for me/
us) . . .' (see 9.2.1).

a 理解していただきたい。
**Rikai shi-te itadakitai.**
I'd like you to understand.

b 今後も協力していただきたい。
**Kongo mo kyōryoku shi-te itadakitai.**
We hope to have your continued co-operation in the future.

c 最終日は確定していませんから。もう少し後にしていただきたい。
**Saishūbi wa kakutei shite imasen kara. Mō sukoshi ato ni
shi-te itadakitai.**
[My] last day [in office] hasn't been set yet. I'd like you to put [that
question about how I look back on my time in the Cabinet] off
a little longer.

d グラフをみていただきたい。
**Gurafu o mi-te itadakitai.**
Please look at the graph (*lit.* "I'd like you to look at the graph").

<hr/>

| 15.6.1.3 | *Clause 1-verb-***te itadai-te**/**itadaki** *clause 2* (**arigatō**, *etc.*)

Compound sentences where S1 ends in the conjunctive form (or conjunctive form equivalent) of **-te itadaku**, followed in S2 by an expression of
thanks, express the meaning 'thank you for doing' (see 25.3.4).

a こんなに暑い中に来ていただいてみなさんありがとう。
**Konna ni atsui naka ni ki-te itadaite mina-san arigatō.**
Thank you all for taking the trouble to come when it [the weather]
is so hot.

b 私だけでなく光を温かく迎えていただき感謝している。

**Watashi dake de naku Hikaru o atatakaku mukae-te itadaki kansha shite iru.**

Thank you for giving a warm welcome not only to me but also to Hikaru.

### 15.6.2 Verb-te itadaku (=potential form)

### 15.6.2.1 Verb-te itadake-ru ka/-nai ka

This signals a polite request in question form, positive or negative, in the sense of 'could you please'.

a 返事はちょっと待っていただけますか。

**Henji wa chotto mat-te itadakemasu ka.**

Could I ask you to wait a little while for my answer?

b ほかにはない目玉商品として扱っていただけませんか。

**Hoka ni wa nai medama shōhin to shite atsukat-te itadakemasen ka.**

Can't we get you to handle it as a loss leader that nobody else has?

### 15.6.2.2 Verb-te itadakeru + conjunctive particle to/-ba/-tara + evaluatory predicate

-te **itadakeru** in subordinate clauses ending in **to/-ba/-tara** followed by an evaluatory pred. such as **ii** 'good', **ureshii** 'happy', etc. indicates the idea of 'it would be nice if . . .', 'I/we'd be happy if . . .'.

*Note* – the evaluatory predicate can be omitted (example c).

a 気に入っていただけたらいいのですが。

**Ki ni it-te itadaketara ii no desu ga.**

I hope you'll like it.

b 鈴木さんは「同世代に聴いていただけるとうれしい」とニッコリ。

**Suzuki-san wa 'dōsedai ni ki-ite itadakeru to ureshii' to nikkori.**

Suzuki-san, with a smile, said, 'I'll be happy if my generation listens to it'.

c 本人は固辞しているそうだが、やっていただければと思う。

**Honnin wa koji shite iru sō da ga, yat-te itadakereba to omou.**

I hear that he himself has firmly declined, but I hope he'll take it
   [= the chairmanship] on.

427

## 15.6.3 | Verb-*causative*-te itadaku

The causative here is used in the permissive meaning 'allow', 'let' (see 13.1), with the combination literally meaning "I receive the favour of being allowed to do something".

### 15.6.3.1 | Verb-*causative*-te **itadaku**

This means 'allow me to do', or 'have the pleasure of doing'.

a はい、やらせていただきます。
**Hai, yarase-te itadakimasu.**
OK, I'll do it (= allow me to do it).

b 大変興味深く読ませていただきました。
**Taihen kyōmi-bukaku yomase-te itadakimashita.**
I had the privilege of reading it with great interest.

c 祝い金十万円を贈らせていただきます。
**Iwaikin jūman-en o okurase-te itadakimasu.**
I take the liberty of sending you a congratulatory gift of one hundred thousand yen.

d 公私にわたり親しくお付き合いさせていただいた。
**Kōshi ni watari shitashiku o-tsukiai sase-te itadaita.**
I had the pleasure of close association with him in both official and private life.

### 15.6.3.2 | Verb-*causative*-te **itadakitai**

This combination means 'please let/allow me to'.

a 考えさせていただきたい。
**Kangaesase-te itadakitai.**
Please let me think it over.

b 二人で合意書に署名させていただきたい。
**Futari de gōisho ni shomei sase-te itadakitai.**
Please let both of us sign the letter of agreement.

c そういう状況が生まれれば、喜んでやらせていただきたい。
**Sō iu jōkyō ga umarereba, yorokonde yarase-te itadakitai.**
If it came to that situation [= having a top-level talk], I'd be happy to do so.

## 15.7  -te hoshii

Whereas the adjective of desire **hoshii** indicates what things or persons etc. the speaker wants (see 9.2.3), **-te hoshii/–nai de hoshii** indicates what the speaker(s) wish(es) second or third persons to do/not to do. These second/ third persons are often omitted, but can be marked in the same sentence by **ni**, or by other particles (see also 6.8.1).

### 15.7.1  *Without mention of second/third person*

#### 15.7.1.1  *Present*

a　ビデオを分けてほしい。
  **Bideo o wake-te hoshii.**
  Would you spare me [a copy of] the videotape?

b　最後に、今後の望ましい企業像について考えを聞かせてほしい。
  **Saigo ni, kongo no nozomashii kigyōzō ni tsuite kangae o kikase-te hoshii.**
  Finally, I'd like you [= the panellists] to give us your thoughts on the desirable company image of the future.

c　地元の酒をもっと愛してほしい。
  **Jimoto no sake o motto aishi-te hoshii.**
  We want [people] to love the local rice wine more.

d　私と父とを混同しないでほしい。
  **Watashi to chichi to o kondō shi-nai de hoshii.**
  I don't want you to confuse me with my father.

e　中日関係を簡単に壊さないでほしい。
  **Chū-nichi kankei o kantan ni kowasa-nai de hoshii.**
  I don't want you to destroy China–Japan relations
    at one stroke.

f　子供の本だと軽く見ないでほしい。
  **Kodomo no hon da to karuku mi-nai de hoshii.**
  I don't want people to take it lightly, thinking it's
    a children's book.

| 15.7.1.2 | *Past* |

In the past tense, **-te hoshikatta** indicates what the speaker(s) wanted people to do (or things to happen), both for actions that were realized and those that weren't.

a もう少し長く生きてほしかった。
   **Mō sukoshi nagaku iki-te hoshikatta.**
   I wanted [him] to have lived a little longer.

b もっと売れてほしかった。
   **Motto ure-te hoshikatta.**
   We wanted it [= our beer] to sell more.

c 輸入米をもっと安くしてほしかった。
   **Yunyū-mai o motto yasuku shi-te hoshikatta.**
   I wanted them [= the government] to sell imported rice
   more cheaply.

| 15.7.2 | *With mention of second/third person* |

| 15.7.2.1 | *Marked by* **ni** |

**ni** (often in the form **ni wa**) specifically marks the person who the speaker wants to perform the verb to which **-te hoshii** is attached.

a 米国人自身に銃を持つことの誤りに気づいてほしい。
   **Beikokujin jishin <u>ni</u> jū o motsu koto no ayamari ni kizui-te
   hoshii.**
   We want the Americans themselves to realize the 'wrongness' of
   carrying guns.

b 地元の人には自分たちの住む地域の良さを認識してほしい。
   **Jimoto no hito <u>ni wa</u> jibun-tachi no sumu chiiki no yosa o
   ninshiki shi-te hoshii.**
   We want the local people to be aware of the merits of the area they
   live in.

c 裁判所には真実を理解してほしい。
   **Saibansho <u>ni wa</u> shinjitsu o rikai shi-te hoshii.**
   I want the court to understand the truth.

| 15.7.2.2 | *Marked by particles other than* **ni**

a 消費者も、水田が環境を守っていることを理解してほしい。

**Shōhisha <u>mo</u>, suiden ga kankyō o mamotte iru koto o rikai shi-te hoshii.**

We want the consumers, too, to understand that paddy fields protect the environment.

b 女性は運動によってではなく、研究実績で地位を上げてほしい。

**Josei <u>wa</u> undō ni yotte de wa naku, kenkyū jisseki de chii o age-te hoshii.**

We want women to raise their position not through movements but through the results of their research.

c 聖夜のひととき、家族連れやカップルでプラネタリウムを楽しんでほしい。

**Seiya no hitotoki, kazoku-zure ya kappuru <u>de</u> puranetariumu o tanoshin-de hoshii.**

During the short period of Christmas Eve, we want [people] to enjoy the planetarium in groups such as families and couples.

# Chapter 16

# Honorific and humble forms (subject- and object-honorifics)

In comparison to 'ordinary' or unmarked forms expressing the same cognitive meaning, honorific and humble forms both elevate the listener or referent in relation to the speaker. The assumption behind this is that persons senior to or of higher social status than the speaker are linguistically treated as superiors.

Honorific forms are distinct from the polite ending -**masu**, but in practice often combine, especially when used as predicates (i.e. many forms given below are often used in their -**masu** form (see 7.1.2.4, 1.8).

## 16.1 Regular honorific forms

There are two regular honorific formations, **o/go** V-stem **ni naru** and passive-form honorifics (see 12.2.2). Verbs that have special (irregular) forms do not usually have regular equivalents (see 16.3).

### 16.1.1 *o/go-verb-stem* ni naru

In this structure, V-stem is sandwiched between **o/go** and **ni naru**. In the case of VN (see 1.9), **ni naru** replaces **suru**.

The choice between the honorific prefixes **o-** and **go-** basically depends on whether the item they attach to are NJ (**o-**) or SJ (**go-**) nouns (see 1.1), but there are some exceptions, such as **o-denwa** ('telephone'), which is SJ.

By replacing **ni naru** with **kudasai**, i.e. in the form **o/go**-V-stem **kudasai**, a polite imperative or command is formed, which is commonly used (see 20.1.5).

a お辞めになったのはもったいない。(cf., 辞める **yameru** 'quit')
**O-yame ni natta no wa mottainai.**
It's a waste that he quit.

b やりたい方がいればおやりになればいい。(cf., やる **yaru** 'do')
**Yaritai kata ga ireba o-yari ni nareba ii.**
If there's anyone who'd like to give it a try, let them.

In the media, **o/go**-V-stem **ni naru** (but also passive honorifics) is often used with reference to members of the Imperial family, although some newspapers have largely abandoned the practice.

Note also that in super-honorific usage, (**o/go**-V-stem **ni**) **naru** can be used in the passive honorific form (**o/go**-V-stem **ni**) **narareru** to make it even more polite (example d).

c 昭和天皇もお泊まりになったことがあるという。(cf., 泊まる
**tomaru** 'stay')
**Shōwa tennō mo o-tomari ni natta koto ga aru to iu.**
They say that the Showa emperor too has stayed there.

d 両陛下は参加者とともに苗木をお手植えになられます。(cf., 手植
えする **teue suru** 'plant in person')
**Ryōheika wa sankasha to tomo ni naegi o o-teue ni
nararemasu.**
Their Majesties will personally plant the saplings together with
the participants.

Note that there are some fixed expressions that look like **o/go** V-stem **ni
naru**, but are in fact not (example e). Also note example f, where the expression **sankō ni naru** 'be useful' (*not* **sankō suru!**) is made honorific by attaching the prefix **go-**.

e いろいろな人にお世話になった。(**o-sewa ni naru** 'be taken
care of')
**Iroiro na hito ni o-sewa ni natta.**
I was looked after by all sorts of people.

f 観光関係者の方々、ご参考になっただろうか。
**Kankō kankeisha no katagata, go-sankō ni natta darō ka.**
[Advice on how to advertise a local area for sightseeing] Has [our
advice] been useful for you people in the sightseeing business?

### 16.1.2 Clause-te (de) irassharu

In honorific use, -te/-de iru is regularly changed to te/de irassharu, and da/desu to de irassharu (see 8.4, 7.5).

On irregular -masu and imperative forms, see 16.3.

a あなた大変困っていらっしゃいましたよね。

**Anata taihen komatte irasshaimashita yo ne.**

You were greatly embarrassed [at the time], weren't you.

b 先月お見舞いに行ったときには元気に笑っていらっしゃって、
必ず帰ってくると信じていたのに。

**Sengetsu o-mimai ni itta toki ni wa genki ni waratte
irasshatte, kanarazu kaette kuru to shinjite ita noni.**

When I visited him last month, he was laughing and in good spirits,
and I believed that he'd definitely come back.

c お志高く、行動力にあふれるお二人でいらっしゃいますので、
必ずや素晴らしいご家庭をお築きになられることと確信してお
ります。

**O-kokorozashi takaku, kōdōryoku ni afureru o-futari de
irasshaimasu no de, kanarazuya subarashii go-katei o
o-kizuki ni narareru koto to kakushin shite orimasu.**

As both are of noble mind and brimming with vitality, I'm convinced
that they will surely build a wonderful family.

### 16.1.3 Passive honorifics

Passive forms (for the forms, see 12) can be used as slightly less polite honorifics; this is particularly popular with the younger generation.

However, in combination with o/go-ni naru, -te orimasu in the passive honorific form makes for a super-honorific form (see 16.2.2 re -te orimasu).

a 28日は音楽をきいたり、読書をして過ごされた。

**Nijūhachinichi wa ongaku o kiitari, dokusho o shite
sugosareta.**

The 28th she [= a member of the Imperial family] spent [doing things
like] listening to music and reading.

b ご自身に対する警備が厳しすぎると感想をもらされたこともある。

**Go-jishin ni taisuru keibi ga kibishi-sugiru to kansō o morasareta koto mo aru.**

He [= a member of the Imperial family] once commented that he felt that he was being guarded too strictly.

c 「どちらからいらっしゃいましたか」「どの程度入院されていますか」などと声をかけられた。

**'Dochira kara irasshaimashita ka' 'Dono teido nyūin sarete imasu ka' nado to koe o kakerareta.**

She addressed people with questions like 'Where do you come from?' and 'How long have you been in hospital?'

*Note* – compare the above honorific uses to the following example of passive use (see 12).

d おばあさんに席を譲ったら、何度もお礼を言われ、降りる際には最敬礼されて、とまどってしまった。

**Obāsan ni seki o yuzuttara, nando mo orei o iware, oriru sai ni wa saikeirei sarete, tomadotte shimatta.**

After I'd given my seat to the old woman, she thanked me many times, and I was really embarassed when she bowed deeply as she got off the train.

## 16.2 Regular humble forms

### 16.2.1 o/go-verb-stem suru

The regular humble formation takes the form of **o/go**-V-stem **suru** (for an extra humble expression, **suru** can be changed to **itasu**, see 16.3 below).

The choice between **o-** and **go-** is conditioned by the same factors as mentioned above under 16.1. V that have special (irregular) forms do not usually have regular formations (see 16.3).

a 時には「しばらくお会いしていないので、ごあいさつということで ……」という訳のわからない名目もある。

**Toki ni wa 'Shibaraku o-ai shite inai no de, go-aisatsu to iu koto de ...' to iu wake no wakaranai meimoku mo aru.**

On occasion, people come under the flimsy pretext of 'I haven't seen you for a while, so [I'd like to see you] to extend my greetings ...'.

b 副党首をお願いしたらすぐになってくれた。
**Fukutōshu o o-negai shitara sugu ni natte kureta.**
When I asked [him to be] deputy party chairman, he took it on
right away.

c お客様には、表示と適合しない製品をお届けし、多大な迷惑をか
けたことをおわびしたい。
**O-kyaku-sama ni wa, hyōji to tekigō shinai seihin o o-todoke
shi, tadai na meiwaku o kaketa koto o o-wabi shitai.**
I want to apologize for having delivered to our customers a product
that does not match the labelling, and for having inconvenienced
them greatly.

## 16.2.2 Clause (-te/de) gozaimasu and (-te/de) orimasu

**gozaimasu** is humble for **aru**, and **orimasu** for **iru**. Similarly, -te (-de)
**gozaimasu** is used instead of -te aru (see 8.3), -te gozaimasu and -te orimasu
for -te iru (see 8.4), and de gozaimasu instead of da/desu (see 7.5).

For irregular -masu and imperative forms see 16.3.

### 16.2.2.1 gozaimasu and adjective-u gozaimasu/mashita

**gozaimasu** is the humble equivalent of **aru/arimasu**. Note also the somewhat
archaic combination Adj-**u** (o + u = ō) **gozaimasu** (the adjective ending -**u**
is a variant of -**ku**), which is still used, especially by elderly ladies, but
also in greetings such as **arigatō gozaimasu, o-hayō gozaimasu, o-medetō
gozaimasu**, etc.

*Note* – when referring to events that are completed, -**mashita** is used rather
than -**masu**.

a 「白寿」を迎えた感想をきかれると「とくにございません。」
**'Hakuju' o mukaeta kansō o kikareru to 'Toku ni gozaimasen.'**
When asked about his thoughts on having reached the age of 99,
[he replied] 'I don't really have any'.

b ・・・に失敗したという話があるが。「全くございません。」
**... shippai shita to iu hanashi ga aru ga. 'Mattaku
gozaimasen.'**
...there's talk that you made a mistake ...'That's not at all so'.

c 「今日は何から始まるんじゃ？」「まず最初は閣議の前に閣僚
　会議がございまして、そこでの主なテーマは ……」

**'Kyō wa nani kara hajimaru n ja?' 'Mazu saisho wa kakugi no
mae ni kakuryōkaigi ga gozaimashite, soko de no omo na
tēma wa …'**

(PM) 'What's on first today?' (Secretary) 'First, before the Cabinet
meeting there is a Ministerial conference; the main topic there
is …'

d 悪うございました。

**Warū gozaimashita.**

I'm sorry (*lit.* "It was bad of me").

e 第三子誕生おめでとうございました。

**Daisanshi tanjō omedetō gozaimashita.**

Congratulations on the birth of your third child.

f 「本日は私の葬儀にご出席頂き、ありがとうございます」と故人
　がスクリーンに登場し、会葬者に別れのあいさつをする。

**'Honjitsu wa watakushi no sōgi ni go-shusseki itadaki,
arigatō gozaimasu' to kojin ga sukurīn ni tōjō shi,
kaisōsha ni wakare no aisatsu o suru.**

With the words 'Thank you for attending my funeral today',
the deceased appears on the screen, and gives a farewell speech
to the funeral guests.

---

| 16.2.2.2 | *Noun/**na**-adjective/clause* **de gozaimasu**

**de gozaimasu** is humble for **da/desu** (strictly speaking, **de aru/arimasu** is
converted into **de gozaimasu**, which is used in place of **da/desu**).

Note that **wa** can be 'sandwiched' between **de** and **gozaimasu** for contrast/
emphasis (example d) in the same way as between **de** and forms of the
copula. (see 11.3.5.3.3).

In fairy tales and some other forms of literature, **no de gozaimasu** is also
used instead of endings such as **n/no da/desu**.

For irregular -**masu** and imperative forms, see 16.3.

a 右手に見えますのは、二条城でございます。

**Migite ni miemasu no wa, Nijōjō de gozaimasu.**

What can be seen on the right is Nijō Castle.

437

b 「それは反乱か」という王に、公爵は答えた「いえ陛下、革命で
ございます」。

**'Sore wa hanran ka' to iu ō ni, kōshaku wa kotaeta. 'Ie heika,
kakumei de gozaimasu'.**

To the king's question 'Is this an uprising?' the duke replied, 'No, Your
Majesty, it's a revolution'.

c 三世代同居時代には嫁は姑（しゅうとめ）に「お食事でございま
す」と告げたが、核家族では「ご飯よ」でも済んでしまう。

**Sansedai dōkyo jidai ni wa yome wa shūtome ni 'O-shokuji de
gozaimasu' to tsugeta ga, kakukazoku de wa 'go-han yo' de
mo sunde shimau.**

In the times when three generations lived under one roof, the wife
would say to the mother-in-law 'Your dinner is served', but in the
nuclear family 'Dinner!' is sufficient.

d はなはだせんえつではございますが、自己紹介させていただきま
す ……。

**Hanahada sen'etsu de wa gozaimasu ga, jikoshōkai sasete
itadakimasu ...**

Please permit me (*lit.* "It is totally out of order of me to do so, but
allow me") to introduce myself ...

e 男は、それまでにそんな美しい女の肌を見たことがなかったので
ございます。

**Otoko wa, sore made ni sonna utsukushii onna no hada o
mita koto ga nakatta no de gozaimasu.**

The man had never before seen the body of such a beautiful woman.

---

| 16.2.2.3 | **-te/de oru/orimasu** *and* **orimasu**

**-te/de orimasu** is the humble equivalent to **V-te/de iru/imasu**. Note how
**nado** causes the insertion of an 'extra' **shite ori** in example f; the non-
honorific, non-formal equivalent would be **hone o ottari shite ite**, i.e.
**orimasu** is used instead of **iru**.

*Note* – the imperative plain form **-te ore** (example a) is used as an imperative form of **-te iru** (**-te iro** being not a standard form), and does not have
any honorific meaning.

a 母よ！一分ぐらいだまっとれ。（だまっとれ＝だまっておれ）

**Haha yo! Ippun gurai damattore. [damattore = damatte ore]**

Mother! Shut up for a minute or so.

b 釣り銭が不足しております。
**Tsurisen ga fusoku shite orimasu.**
We are short of change.

c 冷えたドリンクを販売いたしております。
**Hieta dorinku o hanbai shite orimasu.**
We're selling cold drinks.

d まったく存じておりません。
**Mattaku zonjite orimasen.**
I know absolutely nothing [about it].

e 電話や消火器も床に転がっており、手が付けられない状態だった。
**Denwa ya shōkaki mo yuka ni korogatte ori, te ga
tsukerarenai jōtai datta.**
Telephones and fire extinguishers too were lying on the floor, and
[the place] was in a state where we couldn't do anything.

f 優輝ちゃんは病院に運ばれたが頭の骨を折るなどしており、
約二時間半後に死亡した。
**Yūki-chan wa byōin ni hakobareta ga atama no hone o oru
nado shite ori, yaku ni-jikan-han-go ni shibō shita.**
Yūki-chan was taken to hospital but had a fractured skull and died
two and a half hours later.

## 16.3 Irregular honorific and humble verb forms

A number of commonly used verbs that refer to a person's action are
not used in their regular honorific form; instead, a different 'specialized'
honorific V is used (some honorific V can be used for more than one
action: **meshiagaru** is used for both eating and drinking, and **irassharu** is
used for coming, going, and being there).

Table 16.1 shows the more common of these irregular V (for slots where
no irregular verb exists, regular formations are given in brackets).

Note also that the following among the verbs below are irregular in forming their -**masu** form and imperative form. This also applies when they are
used with V-**te** (see 16.1.2 and 16.2.2 above).

| honorific verb | -masu form | imperative form |
| --- | --- | --- |
| **gozaru** | **gozai-masu** | — |
| **irassharu** | **irasshai-masu** | **irasshai** |
| **kudasaru** | **kudasai-masu** | **kudasai** |
| **nasaru** | **nasai-masu** | **nasai** |
| **ossharu** | **osshai-masu** | **osshai** |

439

As seen already above (16.1.2 and 16.2.2), many of the above forms can
in turn be used to replace the second V in [V-te + V] combinations, such as
-te iru into -te irasshaimasu/-te orimasu, and -te kuru into -te irasshaimasu/
-te mairimasu, etc.

a ご覧になりましたか。
  **Go-ran ni narimashita ka.**
  Have you seen [it]?

b 続いて陛下は別館の標本館に移動し、魚類標本をご覧になった。
  **Tsuzuite heika wa bekkan no hyōhonkan ni idō shi, gyorui
  hyōhon o go-ran ni natta.**
  Thereafter, His Majesty moved to the Specimen Hall, which is
  a separate building, and looked at fish specimens.

c 負傷された方々には心からのお見舞いを申し上げたい。
  **Fushō sareta katagata ni wa kokoro kara no o-mimai o
  mōshiagetai.**
  To those wounded, I'd like to extend my heartfelt wishes for their
  recuperation.

d ···歌舞伎にも時々おいでいただいております。
  **...Kabuki ni mo tokidoki o-ide itadaite orimasu.**
  ...occasionally he [= Imperial Family member] honours us with a visit
  to the kabuki.

e 着物のお客様にナプキンを差し上げたり、女性らしい気配りにも
  気を使います。
  **Kimono no o-kyaku-sama ni napukin o sashiagetari, josei
  rashii kikubari ni mo ki o tsukaimasu.**
  I provide napkins for people in kimonos, and try to pay attention to
  things in a feminine sort of way.

f 焼き物を始めて四十八年、土との闘いをずっと続けてまいりました。
  **Yakimono o hajimete yonjūhachi-nen, tsuchi to no tatakai o
  zutto tsuzukete mairimashita.**
  [It's] 48 years since I've taken up pottery, and I've continued
  the struggle with the clay all the way.

**Table 16.1** Major irregular honorific and humble verbs

| Ordinary | Honorific | Humble |
|---|---|---|
| **ageru**<br>'give' | **kudasaru** | **sashiageru** |
| **aru**<br>'be', 'have' | **o-ari da** | **gozaru** |
| **au**<br>'meet' | **(o-ai ni naru)** | **o-me ni kakaru**<br>**(o-ai suru)** |
| **deru**<br>'attend' | **(o-de ni naru)** | — |
| **iku**<br>'go' | **irassharu**<br>**o-ide ni naru** | **mairu** |
| **iru**<br>'be' | **irassharu**<br>**o-ide ni naru**<br>**orareru** | **oru**<br>**iru** |
| **iu**<br>'say' | **ossharu** | **mōsu**<br>**mōshiageru** |
| **kariru**<br>'borrow' | **(o-kari ni naru)** | **haishaku suru**<br>**(o-kari suru)** |
| **kiku** 'ask' | **(o-kiki ni naru)** | **ukagau** |
| **kiku** 'hear' | | **uketamawaru**<br>**(o-kiki suru)** |
| **kiru**<br>'wear' | **o-meshi ni naru** | |
| **kuru**<br>'come' | **irassharu**<br>**o-ide ni naru**<br>**o-ide itadaku**<br>**o-koshi ni naru**<br>**mieru**<br>**o-mie ni naru** | **mairu** |
| **miru**<br>'see' | **go-ran ni naru** | **haiken suru** |
| **miseru**<br>'show' | **(o-mise ni naru)** | **o-me ni kakeru** |
| **morau**<br>'receive' | **(o-morai ni naru)** | **itadaku**<br>**chōdai suru** |
| **motsu**<br>'have' | **o-mochi da**<br>**motte irassharu** | **(o-mochi suru)**<br>**motte oru** |
| **neru**<br>'go to bed',<br>'sleep' | **o-yasumi ni naru** | — |

**Table 16.1** (cont'd)

| Ordinary | Honorific | Humble |
|---|---|---|
| **nomu** 'drink' | **o-agari ni naru** **meshiagaru** | **itadaku** |
| **omou** 'think' | **(o-omoi ni naru)** | **zonjiru** |
| **shinu** 'die' | **o-nakunari ni naru** | **naku naru** |
| **shiru** 'know' | **go-zonji da** **go-shōchi da** | **zonjiru** **zonjite oru** |
| **shiru** 'know s.o.' | **go-zonji da** | **zonjiageru** |
| **suru** 'do' | **nasaru** **sareru** **o-yari ni naru** | **itasu** |
| **taberu** 'eat' | **o-agari ni naru** **meshiagaru** | **itadaku** |
| **tazuneru** 'ask', 'visit' | **o-tazune ni naru** | **ukagau** **o-tazune suru** |

## 16.4 Pejorative verbs

Just as there are verbs that show respect to the subject of the action, Japanese also has pejorative verbs that express disrespect (see 16 and also 9.5.8.4).

The basic construction is V-stem-**yagaru**, a Group I verb. When used to someone's face, it often results in a fight, which is why most of the time it is used when talking to oneself. It is often encountered in Japanese comics (*manga*), from which the examples below are taken. In example b, **yagaru** follows the –te form, replacing the more neutral imperative form **oboete iro**.

a へえーあのやろうけっこうしぶとくなりやがったな。
   **Hē-- ano yarō kekkō shibutoku nari-yagatta na.**
   Well, that guy's got quite tough!

b ち…畜生あとでおぼえてやがれ。
   **Chi … chikushō ato de oboete yagare.**
   D … damn, you just remember for later!

# Chapter 17

# Negation and negative sentences

Negation is formally expressed by the negative forms of V (see 7.1), Adj (see 6.1) and na-Adj/N (see 7.5) which end in -nai or de wa/ja nai in the plain form.

For variants of -nai (-n, nu, zu, . . .), see 17.1.2.

Like V-ru, V-nai can also indicate intention or future (example a).

a 絶対に日本には帰らない。
**Zettai ni nihon ni wa kaeranai.**
No matter what, [I] will not go back to Japan.

There is also a negative adjective **nai** 'there isn't', 'haven't' (see 6.1.2).

Both the negative ending -nai (and its variants -nu, -n) and the adjective **nai** can be used as predicates and before N and structural N (see 17.1.2).

## 17.1 Simple negative sentences

### 17.1.1 Negative existential/possessive sentences

#### 17.1.1.1 Noun + case and/or defocussing particle **nai**

The meaning here is 'there isn't'.

a 私は人気がない。
**Watashi wa ninki ga nai.**
I am not popular (*lit.* "I have no popularity").

b 駐車場はない。
**Chūshajō wa nai.**
There is no parking space.

| 17.1.1.2 | *Noun + case and/or defocussing particle* **nashi** |

The meaning is again 'there isn't'.

**nashi** is a written-style equivalent of **nai**, and is often used without the case particle **ga**, in line with the compressed nature of this style. Note especially that in the form N **nashi de** and **nashi no**, no particle can be used before **nashi**.

a 入会金なし。
   **Nyūkaikin nashi.**
   No joining fee.

b テレビも新聞もなし。
   **Terebi mo shinbun mo nashi.**
   No TV or newspapers.

c 読経はなし、お焼香はなし、香典もなし。
   **Dokyō wa nashi, o-shōkō wa nashi, kōden mo nashi.**
   [Funeral] There's no sutra-chanting, no incense-burning and no condolence money either.

d 「肉声コンサート」というのを手がけたことがある。マイクなしで
   歌うのである。
   **'Nikusei konsāto' to iu no o tegaketa koto ga aru.**
   **Maiku nashi de utau no de aru.**
   We've done some 'natural-voice [pop] concerts'. One sings without a microphone.

| 17.1.1.3 | **wa** *in negative sentences* |

(See 11.3.)

Note also how **wa** can colloquially be shortened to **ya**, attached to the consonant of the preceding syllable (i.e. **ri wa → rya**), etc. (example b).

a 系列の問題が足かせになっているのか。「そんなことはない」。
   **Keiretsu no mondai ga ashikase ni natte iru no ka.**
   **'Sonna koto wa nai'.**
   Is the *keiretsu* [affiliation of companies] hampering [developments]?
   'That's not so'.

*Note* – **wa** can also be sandwiched between VN and some other forms (see example b; see also 11.3.5.3.2).

b 人間の力なんてそんなに変わりゃしません。
   **Ningen no chikara nante sonna ni kawarya shimasen.**
   People's abilities don't vary that much.

### 17.1.2 *Variants of the negative ending -nai (-nu, -n, -zu, ...)*

### 17.1.2.1 -nu

-nu is a written-style variant of -nai (but note that some idiomatic expressions such as [omowanu N] 'unexpected' cannot be changed into
omowanai N).

a 眠れぬ夜が続いている。
   **Nemurenu yoru ga tsuzuite iru.**
   Nights when one can't sleep [because of the heat] continue.

b 秋の訪れは存外はやいかもしれぬ。
   **Aki no otozure wa zongai hayai ka mo shirenu.**
   (= **kamoshirenai**, see 9.1.2.3)
   The coming of autumn can be surprisingly sudden.

### 17.1.2.2 -n

-n is a spoken variant of -nai, used by men and in some regional dialects.
Note especially the form **sen** instead of **shinai**.

a おれは何にも知らん。
   **Ore wa nanni mo shiran. [nanni = emphatic variant
   of nani]**
   I don't know anything.

b 正直に白状せんか。
   **Shōjiki ni hakujō sen ka.**
   Just make a frank confession, won't you.

### 17.1.2.3 -zu

-zu is mostly used as the written-style negative conjunctive form, but can
also be used to end a negative sentence, especially in newspaper headlines
and sayings etc.

445

Group I/II verbs attach **-zu** to the same forms as **-nai** (note especially the form **arazu** for colloquial **nai**); for the Group III verbs **kuru** and **suru**, the forms are **kozu** and **sezu**.

a インテルの優位は動かず。
**Interu no yūi wa ugokazu.**
The predominance of Intel is unshaken.

b ロシア機墜落、邦人遺体発見できず。(headline)
**Roshia-ki tsuiraku, hōjin itai hakken dekizu.**
Russian plane crashes, no Japanese bodies (*lit.* "can be") discovered.

c 輸入米、2月はブレンドせず。(headline)
**Yunyū-mai, nigatsu wa burendo sezu.**
Imported rice – no blending in February.

d 百聞は一見にしかず。
**Hyakubun wa ikken ni shikazu.**
Seeing is believing (*lit.* "100 hearings do not rival one viewing").

| 17.1.3 | *Negative equational sentences* |

(See 7.6.1.7)

| 17.1.3.1 | **de wa nai**, *etc.* |

(See also 11.3.2)

a 電子メールそのものは決して新しい技術ではない。
**Denshi mēru sono mono wa kesshite atarashii gijutsu de wa nai.**
Electronic mail per se is not a new technology at all.

b システムの見直しは必要だが、ことはそう簡単ではない。
**Shisutemu no minaoshi wa hitsuyō da ga, koto wa sō kantan de wa nai.**
A reconsideration of the system is needed, but things aren't that simple.

c 冗談ではない。
**Jōdan de wa nai.**
[It]'s no joke.

| 17.1.3.2 | ni arazu *(= de wa nai)* |

**ni arazu** can be used as a written-style equivalent of **de wa nai** (**ni** here is the conjunctive form of the copula).

a 自分は任にあらず。
  **Jibun wa nin ni arazu.**
  I'm not the person for the job.

b 若いカップルや女にあらずんば、人にあらず。
  **Wakai kappuru ya onna ni arazunba, hito ni arazu.**
  **(ni arazunba = de nakereba)**
  If you're not a young couple or a female, you don't count
  (*lit.* "you're not human").

c 一見ただのヤクザ映画だが、さにあらず。（さ=そう）
  **Ikken tada no yakuza eiga da ga, sa ni arazu.**
  **[sa = sō]**
  At first glance it's just an ordinary *yakuza* film, but that's
  not so.

| 17.1.4 | *Negative questions* |

Negative questions are questions ending in **-nai** (**ka/no**) (see 18.4).

| 17.1.5 | *Noun-modifying uses* |

| 17.1.5.1 | **-nai/-nu** *noun* |

Like its more colloquial equivalent **-nai**, **-nu** can also be used to modify nouns.

a とても全部は食べれない量だ。
  **Totemo zenbu wa taberenai ryō da.**
  It's [such a large] amount that one can't possibly eat it all up.

b そして女性とは思えぬほど発達した筋肉。
  **Soshite josei to wa omoenu hodo hattatsu shita**
  **kinniku.**
  And their [= female swimmers'] muscles are developed to a degree
  where you'd hardly believe they're women.

| 17.1.5.2 | A **naranu** B |

A **naranu** B ('B rather than/as opposed to A', 'not A, but B') is used to compare what is often a newly coined expression that is created by twisting a familiar one.

a 蝶（ちょう）の中にも渡り鳥ならぬ渡り蝶がいる。
   **Chō no naka ni mo wataridori naranu wataricho
   ga iru.**
   Amongst butterflies, there are migrating butterflies, as opposed to migrating birds.

b 日本的ならぬアメリカ的経営とは何なのかを手際よく教えてくれる。
   **Nihon-teki naranu Amerika-teki keiei to wa nan na no ka o
   tegiwayoku oshiete kureru.**
   It informs us efficiently what American management, as opposed to Japanese, is.

| 17.1.5.3 | *Idiomatic use:* **omowanu** *noun* |

This phrase means 'unexpected N'. Note that **omowanai** cannot be used in the same context.

a 思わぬハプニングに場内が沸いた。
   **Omowanu hapuningu ni jōnai ga waita.**
   The audience got excited at the unexpected happening.

| 17.1.5.4 | **-zaru** *noun* |

**-zaru** is a classical noun-modifying form of **-zu**. Apart from the common phrase V-**zaru o enai** 'must', it is used occasionally in the written style and more commonly in titles of books, films, headlines, slogans etc.

Note example g, where **-zaru** attaches **-beki**, with the combination functioning like a double negative 'must' (see 9.4.1.2, 17.2).

a 「帰らざる河」 (film title)
   **'Kaerazaru Kawa'**
   *River of No Return*

b 「許されざる者」 (film title)
   **'Yurusarezaru Mono'**
   *The Unforgiven*

c 「責任ある政治、たゆまざる改革」 (slogan)
   **'Sekinin aru seiji, tayumazaru kaikaku'**
   'Responsible politics, relentless reform'

d 過ぎたるは及ばざるが如し
   **Sugitaru wa oyobazaru ga gotoshi**
   Too much is the same as too little (Too much water drowned
   the miller).

e 我が社に欠くべからざる人なんていない。
   **Wa ga sha ni kaku-bekarazaru hito nante inai.**
   In our company, there's no such thing as an indispensable person.

f 好むと好まざるとにかかわらず、それに見合った責任を担わねば
   ならない。
   **Konomu to konomazaru to ni kakawarazu, sore ni miatta
   sekinin o ninawaneba naranai.**
   Like it or not, it [= Japan] needs to assume the responsibility that is
   commensurate [with its position].

g 「やらざるべきことはやらなかった」と述べ、日銀の独立性・
   中立性の維持に努めてきたことを強調した。
   **'Yarazaru-beki koto wa yaranakatta' to nobe, Nichigin no
   dokuritsu-sei, chūritsu-sei no iji ni tsutomete kita koto o
   kyōchō shita.**
   He stated, 'We didn't do anything we shouldn't have done', emphasizing
   that he had worked to maintain the independence and neutrality of
   the Bank of Japan.

## 17.2 Double negative sentences

Double negatives are widely used in Japanese. There are three types:
double negatives proper, which are a rhetorical device (e.g. 'it's not that
I don't . . .'), negative conditionals ('must', etc.), and the phrase V-**zu ni wa
irarenai** 'can't help doing'.

As negatives cancel each other out, resulting in a positive meaning, they
can be seen as an alternative way of expressing things, which in meaning
ranges from tentative to emphatic.

Double negatives can consist of two negative forms (incl. the negative adjective **nai** 'there isn't'), or a negative form following a lexical word that has negative meaning, such as **chiisai** 'little', **sukunai** 'few', **yasui** 'cheap', etc.

## 17.2.1 Double negatives proper

(See also 18.4.8)

### 17.2.1.1 Negative noun **wa nai**

This is an emphatic way of expressing positive states such as 'always', 'everyone' by using two negatives.

a 絵を見ない日はあっても建築を見ない日はない。
  **E o minai hi wa atte mo kenchiku o minai hi wa nai.**
  Even though there are days when I don't look at a painting, there are no days when I don't look at architecture.

b 目を細めぬ方はない。
  **Me o hosomenu kata wa nai.**
  There is no one who doesn't narrow their eyes [with delight].

### 17.2.1.2 nai/*verb*-nai de wa/mo nai

*Lit.* "it's not the case that . . . doesn't", etc.: this is a tentative way of expressing a positive state of affairs 'a bit', 'some'.

a 中小側の気持ちもわからないではない。
  **Chūshō-gawa no kimochi mo wakaranai de wa nai.**
  We do have some sympathy for the feelings of small and medium businesses.

b 股さきのシーンには、ちょっとゾクゾクしないでもない。
  **Matasaki no shīn ni wa chotto zokuzoku shinai de mo nai.**
  The scene [in the film] where the legs are torn apart feels a bit creepy.

c 開会前にはさめた声が聞こえないではなかった。
  **Kaikai-mae ni wa sameta koe ga kikoenai de wa nakatta.**
  Before the congress, some sensible opinions were heard.

## 17.2.1.3 -nai de wa nai ka

In question form, double negatives are a way of making a point forcefully or aggressively (see 18.4.7).

a 日本でもほとんど普及していないではないか。
   **Nihon de mo hotondo fukyū shite inai de wa nai ka.**
   Even in Japan, it [= high-definition TV] has practically no popular support, has it?

b 「それが守られないではないですか」と怒りをあらわにする。
   **'Sore ga mamorarenai de wa nai desu ka' to ikari o arawa ni suru.**
   'That [promise that the performances will be strictly local] will not be kept, right?' he said, making his anger clear.

## 17.2.1.4 Adjective-**ku (wa) nai**

An Adj with negative meaning plus negative makes for a somewhat emphatic way of expressing a positive content, in the sense of *lit.* "*not* few", i.e. '*quite* a few', etc.

a 売却に際し、地価下落に泣かされたところも少なくない。
   **Baikyaku ni saishi, chika geraku ni nakasareta tokoro mo sukunakunai.**
   At the time of selling, quite a few places suffered from the drop in land prices.

## 17.2.2 Negative conditionals

These are found in many combinations between *A* and *B* below; literally, they all mean "it won't do"/"it's no good (= B) if not (= A)", i.e. 'must'.

**Table 17.1** Negative conditional combinations

| A Neg. condition/informal variant | | B Second neg. (often omitted) |
|---|---|---|
| -nakereba | /-nakya* | naranai |
| -nakute wa | /-nakucha | ikenai |
| -nai to | | ikan |
| -neba | /-nya | dame |

*Note* * Can be lengthened to **nakyā**, etc.

17.2.2.1 *Negative conditionals + negative*

a パパと話してはダメ。
**Papa to hanashite wa dame.**
You mustn't talk with daddy.

b 本を読まなくてはならない。
**Hon o yomanakute wa naranai.**
We need to read the book.

c 言わなければならないことは申し上げた。
**Iwanakereba naranai koto wa mōshiageta.**
I've told him the things that needed saying.

d 企業の社会的責任からいっても続けなきゃいかん。
**Kigyō no shakai-teki sekinin kara itte mo tsuzukenakya ikan.**
We must continue, also from the point of view of the company's
responsibility towards society.

e その志は僕らが引き継いで、行革はやらねばならない。
**Sono kokorozashi wa bokura ga hikitsuide, gyōkaku wa
yaraneba naranai.**
We need to carry on his [= late MP] intentions, and carry out
administrative reform.

f しかし、ほかの可能性も考えなくてはならなかった。
**Shikashi, hoka no kanōsei mo kangaenakute wa naranakatta.**
However, we had to consider other possibilities, too.

g コンパニオンはずっと笑顔で立ってなくちゃいけないから疲れる。
**Konpanion wa zutto egao de tatte nakucha ikenai kara
tsukareru.**
[Being a] companion is tiring as you need to be standing all the time
with a smile on your face.

h （プレゼントを）「やらなくちゃいかんな、そりゃ」とニヤリ。
（そりゃ＝それは）
**(purezento o) 'yaranakucha ikan na, sorya' to niyari.
(sorya = sore wa)**
'I'll have to give her a [birthday] present, won't I', he smirked.

i とにかく新しいことをやらにゃいかん、…
**Tonikaku atarashii koto o yaranya ikan,…**
At any rate, we must do something new…

| 17.2.2.2 | *Negative conditionals (with ellipted negative)*

The second negative (B) is frequently omitted in speech and when indicating the content of one's thoughts.

a 今やらねば。
**Ima yaraneba.**
We must do [it] now.

b 納得してもらわにゃ。
**Nattoku shite morawanya.**
We must get people convinced.

c 記者団に対し「どうするかって？決めにゃーなー」
**Kishadan ni taishi 'Dō suru ka tte? Kimenyā nā'**
To the press corps [he said] 'What are we going to do? We've
   got to decide'

d 今さら変えるわけには行かないでしょ。誇りを持ってや
   らないと。
**Imasara kaeru wake ni wa ikanai desho. Hokori o motte
   yaranai to.**
We can't change things now. We must do it [= forming a cabinet]
   with pride.

e 勉強しなくては。
**Benkyō shinakute wa.**
We must study it [= the proposal].

f まず教習所に行かなくちゃ。
**Mazu kyōshūjo ni ikanakucha.**
First of all, I need to go to driving school.

g たばこ、やめなきゃ。
**Tabako, yamenakya.**
I must stop smoking.

h 大脳のように創造的であらねば。
**Dainō no yō ni sōzō-teki de araneba.**
It [= the Council] must be creative like the brain proper
   [= not mechanical like the cerebellum].

**17.2.2.3** *Negative conditionals followed by other negative expressions*

a とりまとめは早くやらないと意味がない。
**Torimatome wa hayaku yaranai to imi ga nai.**
There's no point unless we settle matters quickly.

**17.2.2.4** *Negative conditionals + -mai (negative presumptive)*

-**mai** is a negative presumptive ending, which has the same meaning as
**nai darō** (ex. b) (see 9.1.2.2, 9.3).

a 大いに自戒せねばなるまい。
**Ōi ni jikai seneba narumai.**
No doubt we must take great care [not to repeat the same mistake].

b 日本の経済システムを変えていかねばならないだろう。
**Nihon no keizai shisutemu o kaete ikaneba naranai darō.**
We'll probably need to change Japan's economic system.

**17.2.2.5** *Negative conditionals: verb-zaru o enai*

V-**zaru** is a classical negative, and the combination V-**zaru o enai** literally
means "cannot not", i.e. 'must', 'have to'. It has a more written/formal
ring than combinations like **nakereba naranai** (see 17.2.2.1).

a お客様がいるならやらざるをえない。
**O-kyaku-sama ga iru nara yarazaru o enai.**
If there are customers, we have to [provide it = the service].

b サービスのあり方も変わってこざるを得ない。
**Sābisu no arikata mo kawatte kozaru o enai.**
The way service is [provided] must change too.

c 介護のために仕事を辞めざるを得なかった。
**Kaigo no tame ni shigoto o yamezaru o enakatta.**
She had to quit working to look after her bedridden parent.

| 17.2.3 | *Verb*-zu ni (wa) irarenai |

Attached to the negative V-base, this combination consists of the written/
formal style negative conjunctive ending -**zu ni** (equivalent to colloquial
-**nai de**) + the negative potential form of **iru**, together meaning literally
"cannot exist without doing", i.e. 'can't help doing' (see 14.2).

a 「ただ、なぜか酒を飲まずにいられなかった」と振り返る。
   **'Tada, naze ka sake o nomazu ni irarenakatta' to furikaeru.**
   'But for some reason I couldn't help drinking', he recalls.

b 「物は十分すぎるぐらい持っているが、何か物足りない。小さな花
   でも育てずにはいられなくなった」と話す。
   **'Mono wa jūbun sugiru gurai motte iru ga, nani ka
   monotarinai. Chiisana hana demo sodatezu ni wa irarenaku
   natta' to hanasu.**
   'I have plenty of material things, but don't feel fulfilled. I can't help but
   feel like growing [something like] a small flower now', she says.

# Chapter 18

# *Questions*

## 18.1 Direct questions

Unlike English, Japanese questions use the same word order as statements.

Any statement (including equational sentences (see 7.6) can therefore be made into a question by changing the intonation and/or attaching the question particle **ka**, and/or inserting a question word (see 5.2). These three elements can be called question markers.

In this section, questions are grouped mainly by the presence or absence of such question markers.

### 18.1.1 *Questions by intonation only*

Usually, the formal mark of a question is the presence of a question word and/or the question particle **ka**, but intonation alone (indicated in writing often by '?') can be sufficient.

a 上がります？ビールでいいですか。
  **Agarimasu? Bīru de ii desu ka.**
  Will you have something [to drink]? Is beer OK?

b あなた、ドレス買ってもいい？
  **Anata, doresu katte mo ii?**
  Darling, is it OK if I buy a dress?

c やっぱり夫婦そろってが一番？
  **Yappari fūfu sorotte ga ichiban?**
  After all, husband and wife [going to the movies] together is best?

### 18.1.2 *Questions without question words, ending in (final form verb) no*

This form of question belongs to the informal or intimate style, and is used by both women and men. Note that the final particle **no** used here cannot attach **da** (i.e. **no da ka** is not possible), whereas it can attach the polite form of the copula, **desu**, i.e. **no desu ka** is OK (see 19.3).

a 自由に出歩けるの？
   **Jiyū ni dearukeru no?**
   Can you walk around freely?

b 「ねえ、どんな所に住んでるの？」と彼。
   **'Nē, donna tokoro ni sunderu no?' to kare.**
   'Say, what sort of place do you live in?' [said] he.

c 日ごろ、ちゃんと悩みを聞いてやってるの？
   **Higoro, chanto nayami o kiite yatteru no?**
   Do you regularly listen to his problems?

### 18.1.3 *Questions without question words, ending in* ka/no ka

a ビールでいいですか。
   **Bīru de ii desu ka.**
   Is beer OK?

b 高くないですか。
   **Takakunai desu ka.**
   Isn't it expensive?

c 空洞化は進んでいるか。
   **Kūdō-ka wa susunde iru ka.**
   Is hollowing out deindustrialization (*lit.* "hollowing out") progressing?

d 飽きちゃったのか。
   **Akichatta no ka.**
   Has he lost interest in me?

e 日本の素材はほんとうに高いのか。
   **Nihon no sozai wa hontō ni takai no ka.**
   Are Japanese ingredients really expensive?

f 若者にとって恋愛とは何なのか。

**Wakamono ni totte ren'ai to wa nan na no ka.**

What does love mean to the young?

g 冷戦後の米国とアジアの関係はどうなっていくのか。

**Reisen-go no beikoku to ajia no kankei wa dō natte iku no ka.**

How will relations between the US and Asia be after the end of the Cold War?

### 18.1.4 Questions with question words

(See 5.2.)

a あれは何だい。[だい = だ + male intimate Q-particle かい]

**Are wa nan dai. [dai = da + male intimate Q-particle kai]**

What's that?

b 「ねえ、どんな所に住んでるの？」と彼。

**'Nē, donna tokoro ni sunderu no?' to kare.**

'Say, what sort of place do you live in?' [says] he.

c 「ではいったい、どうすればいいんだ？」と思う人が少なくないかもしれない。

**'Dewa ittai, dō sureba ii n da?' to omou hito ga sukunakunai kamoshirenai.**

There may be quite a few people who think 'What is it I need to do?'

### 18.1.5 Questions with question words and the question particle ka/no ka

(See 5.2, 19.3.)

a いまいくつですか。

**Ima ikutsu desu ka?**

How old are you [now]?

b 何が問題なのか。

**Nani ga mondai na no ka.**

What's the problem?

c どう痛むのか。

**Dō itamu no ka.**

In what way does it hurt?

d なぜ、女たちは子供を産まなくなったのか。
**Naze, onna-tachi wa kodomo o umanaku natta no ka.**
Why are women not giving birth any more?

e どこに大画面テレビを置くのか。
**Doko ni dai-gamen terebi o oku no ka.**
Where does one put a large-screen TV [in a Japanese home]?

f カネはだれが出すのか。
**Kane wa dare ga dasu no ka.**
Who's going to put up the money?

g 住宅購入時には、なぜ"頭金"が必要なのですか。
**Jūtaku kōnyū-ji ni wa, naze atamakin ga hitsuyō na no desu ka.**
Why is a deposit needed when buying a home?

**18.1.6** *Questions with question words, ending in* **ka tte**

(See 21.2, 21.3)

The meaning is 'you ask why . . .'.

a なぜ入ったかって？弟が銃で殺されてね。
**Naze haitta ka tte? Otōto ga jū de korosarete ne.**
Why did I join [Hell's Angels], you ask? My brother was shot dead (*lit.* "killed with a gun"), you see.

**18.1.7** *Ellipted questions*

**18.1.7.1** *Ellipted questions: with ellipted question word and/or predicate*

This can take the form [N/NP/nominalized sentence **wa.**], with omitted Q-word + copula, or [Q-word N/NP **ga.**] with omitted predicate. (see 11.3.4.2.2, 2.1.3).

The media also uses a form of a question to invite a comment, in the form [Sentence **da ga.**] (see 18.1.7.1.3)

| 18.1.7.1.1 | Noun/noun phrase **wa** |

a 今の気持ちは。[= 何ですか、etc.]
**Ima no kimochi wa.** [= **nan desu ka**, etc.]
[What are your] feelings now?

b 経済活性化の条件は。[= 何ですか、etc.]
**Keizai kassei-ka no jōken wa.** [= **nan desu ka**, etc.]
[What are] the conditions for revitalizing the economy?

| 18.1.7.1.2 | Question word noun/noun phrase **ga** |

a 天国のベートーベンもなぜ日本人が、と首をかしげているに
違いない。
**Tengoku no Bētōben mo naze Nihonjin ga, to kubi o
kashigete iru ni chigai nai.**
Beethoven in heaven is no doubt wondering why the Japanese
[do this]. [= Re the popularity of the Ninth Symphony in Japan
at the end of the year]

| 18.1.7.1.3 | Sentence **da ga** |

This is often used in the media, when asking people to make a comment.

a 問：当日は担当部長と会っているはずだが。
**Toi: Tōjitsu wa tantō buchō to atte iru hazu da ga.**
Q: On the day, you're supposed to have met with the department
head in charge [= please comment].

| 18.1.7.2 | Ellipted questions ending in -**te wa** |

Here, expressions like **dō/ikaga desu ka** 'how about' are omitted. The
resulting meaning is one of suggesting a course of action (see 26.1.7.5,
26.1.2.4).

a あなたの会社も試してみては。
**Anata no kaisha mo tameshite mite wa.**
How about your company giving [it] a try too?

**18.1.7.3** *Ellipted negative questions ending in* **no de wa**

Here, expressions like **nai darō ka, nai deshō ka** 'might not?' are omitted
(see 18.4, 9.1).

a ますます雇用は減るのでは。
**Masumasu koyō wa heru no de wa.**
Might employment not decrease even further?

b ドイツ国内の生産、雇用が空洞化するのでは。
**Doitsu kokunai no seisan, koyō ga kūdō-ka suru no de wa.**
Might not Germany's domestic production and employment be
hollowed out? (= deindustrialization process)

**18.1.8** *Inverted questions*

These are questions with reversed word order (and usually omitted **wa**),
which tend to be used when being emotional (angry, excited, etc.).

a きゃー、何なのこれ。
**Kyā--, nan na no kore.**
Eek, what is [it] this?

b 何、これ？
**Nani, kore?**
What's this?

c 日本になじんだ？外国たばこ。
**Nihon ni najinda? Gaikoku tabako.**
Foreign cigarettes – have they acclimatized to [= been accepted in] Japan?

**18.1.9** *Questions in cleft-sentence form*

(See 22.2.)

a ブームが起きるのはなぜなのかね。
**Būmu ga okiru no wa naze na no ka ne.**
Why is it that booms arise?

| | |

## 18.1.10  Equational questions (wa – copula) using tte instead of wa

tte gives the question a more colloquial/informal ring than **wa** (see 21.3, 11.3.7).

a　大分市ってどんなまち？
**Ōita-shi tte donna machi?**
What sort of town is Oita?

## 18.1.11  Alternative questions

These consist of repeated questions with different content, i.e. questions which present a choice of alternatives 'is it *A*, or *B*?'. They can be joined by conjunctions such as **arui wa** or **sore tomo** 'or', and they generally follow the pattern [S1 **ka**, S2 **ka**.]

a　果たしてこれは一時的なものか、あるいは定着するのか。
**Hatashite kore wa ichiji-teki na mono ka, arui wa teichaku suru no ka.**
Is this [rented accommodation without 'key money'] a temporary thing or is it going to be permanent?

b　うれしさなのか、寂しさなのか。感慨が胸に込み上げた。
**Ureshi-sa na no ka, sabishi-sa na no ka. Kangai ga mune ni komiageta.**
Was it happiness, or sadness? I was overcome with emotion.

## 18.2  Formal questions with non-question meanings

These are questions in form, but not in meaning.

## 18.2.1  Rhetorical questions

Rhetorical questions can be expressed with the ending **mono/mon ka**, and in some other ways as shown below.

## 18.2.1.1  Sentence **mon(o) ka**

The meaning of this type of rhetorical question is 'definitely not!' A similar effect is conveyed by English 'Me lose? (You must be joking!)' (see 19.1.1.7).

a 負けるもんか。
**Makeru mon ka.**
I'm *not* going to lose!

b 負けてなるものか。
**Makete naru mono ka.**
I'm *not* going to lose!

c 特例が二度もあるものか。
**Tokurei ga nido mo aru mono ka.**
A special case can't possibly take place twice (*lit.* "How could a special case take place twice?")

| 18.2.1.2 | *Sentence* **no ka**

a 中古部品をだれが買うのか。
**Chūko buhin o dare ga kau no ka.**
Who is going to buy second-hand parts!?

| 18.2.1.3 | *Sentence* **ka yo/yō**

This is a rather colloquial way of forming a rhetorical question, used by men only.

a おいおい、美少女っていう年かよぉ。
**Oioi, bishōjo tte iu toshi ka yō.**
Come on, you're hardly the age of [being called] a beautiful maiden!

| 18.2.1.4 | *Question word verb-***te(i)ru n da**

Apart from rhetorical questions (example a), this is used to scold someone for doing things wrong: 'What (the hell) are you doing!' (example b).

a 一体だれがカネを払ってると思ってるんだー。
**Ittai dare ga kane o haratteru to omotteru n da--.**
Who the hell do they think is paying! [= we are!]

b 何をやってるんだ。
**Nani o yatteru n da.**
What [do you think you] are doing!

| 18.2.1.5 | *In inverted question form*

This is used when the speaker is angry: 'What's this supposed to be!' (see 18.1.8).

a 何だその言い方は。
**Nan da sono iikata wa.**
Mind your words! (*lit.* "This way of speaking – what is it?")

| 18.2.1.6 | *In the form* **dō ka to omou, ikaga na mono ka** *(to omou)*

This is a kind of rhetorical question, but used with **omou** (although this can be omitted) in the literal sense of "I wonder if this is a good idea", i.e. 'I don't think it's right/wise'. It is used to voice criticism diplomatically.

a 行政庁の人事に政党が介入するのはいかがなものか。
**Gyōsei-chō no jinji ni seitō ga kainyū suru no wa ikaga na mono ka.**
I don't think it's right for a political party to intervene in a staffing matter of the Administrative Management Agency.

b 勝つために四年生を外すのもどうかと思うんですよ。
**Katsu tame ni yonen-sei o hazusu no mo dō ka to omou n desu yo.**
I don't think it's right to leave out the fourth graders in order to win.

| 18.2.2 | *Questions ending in* **ka na/nā**

This form is used to indicate the speaker's wondering about something or making a guess when (or as if) talking to self 'I wonder', 'may have'. After -**ta**, it indicates that the speaker is trying to recall something (see 19.2, 18.3.1.2.4).

a 人生、こんなもんかなあ。
**Jinsei, konna mon ka nā.**
That's (*lit.* "this is") life, I suppose.

b うーん、どの色がいいかなあ。
**Ūn, dono iro ga ii ka nā.**
Hm, I wonder which colour is best ...

c 四月からこれまでに四、五回飲んだかな。

**Shigatsu kara kore made ni shi, go-kai nonda ka na.**

Since April I've been drinking maybe four or five times so far.

d 君はダービーに勝ったことがあったかな。

**Kimi wa dābī ni katta koto ga atta ka na.**

Have you really won the derby before?

e 今、大阪弁を代表しているのは、お笑いと食べ物かな。

**Ima, Ōsaka-ben o daihyō shite iru no wa, o-warai to
tabemono ka na.**

[Advertising executives:] What people think of in connection with
the Osaka dialect right now is comedy and food, I suppose.

*Questions ending in* **darō ka/deshō ka**

Like 18.2.2, this also indicates that the speaker is wondering or guessing 'I wonder', but in this case he or she is addressing the question to a listener.

a 「これで十分でしょうか」と逆に問い返した。

**'Kore de jūbun deshō ka' to gyaku ni toikaeshita.**

'Do you think this is sufficient?' He turned the tables, answering
the question with a question

*Questions ending in* **ka dō ka/ka ina ka**

This means '(The question is) if/whether'. **ka ina ka** is a written-style equivalent of **ka dō ka**.

a だが、空洞化の歯止め効果を発揮するかどうか。

**Daga, kūdōka no hadome kōka o hakki suru ka dō ka.**

However, the question is whether it will have a curbing effect on
deindustrialization.

b メキシコは先進国か否か。

**Mekishiko wa senshinkoku ka ina ka.**

Is Mexico an advanced country or not?

**Indirect questions**

An indirect question is a sentence that contains another sentence which is a question. The question ends in **ka** or **ka dō ka** (after **na-Adj/N** and **no**, copula-non-past is deleted before **ka**) and is followed by a predicate. The question part functions like a noun or NP, in that case/adverbial/phrasal particles can be attached to it (see 18.1).

Two types of indirect question can be distinguished by the presence or absence of a Q-word.

In the examples, indirect questions and their translation equivalents are shown in [ ].

18.3.1  *Indirect positive questions*

18.3.1.1  *With question word*

With a Q-word, the sentence takes the form [Q-word . . . (**no**) **ka**] (+ case/ adverbial particle)] + Pred.

a 「なぜ自殺したのか分からない」と話した。
   **'[Naze jisatsu shita no ka] wakaranai' to hanashita.**
   'I don't know [why he killed himself]', he said.

b どんなものか一度食べておきたい。
   **[Donna mono ka] ichi-do tabete oki-tai.**
   I'd like to eat it once [to see what it's like].

c どこに行ったかも思い出せない。ただ練習がきつかったというこ
   とははっきり覚えている。
   **[Doko ni itta ka] mo omoidasenai. Tada renshū ga kitsukatta
   to iu koto wa hakkiri oboete iru.**
   I can't recall [where we went], either. I just remember clearly that
   practising was tough.

d 写った天体の中で、どれが銀河でどれが恒星かも自動的に識別で
   きる。
   **Utsutta tentai no naka de, [dore ga ginga de dore ga kōsei
   ka] mo jidō-teki ni shikibetsu dekiru.**
   It can also automatically discriminate [which among the heavenly
   bodies on screen are galactic and which are fixed stars].

e これ何だかわかりますか。
**[Kore nan da ka] wakarimasu ka.**
Do you know [what this is]?

f 何のことかお分かりだろうか。
**[Nan no koto ka] o-wakari darō ka.**
Do you [= the reader] understand [what these words refer to], I wonder.

| 18.3.1.2 | *Without question word* |

Without a Q-word, the sentence usually takes the form of [. . . **ka** (**dō ka**)]
(+ case/adverbial/phrasal particle) + predicate. **ka** alone translates as 'might',
whereas **ka dō ka** becomes 'if/whether . . . (or not)'.

| 18.3.1.2.1 | **ka to** + predicate |

This translates as 'might'.

a 銃を見て本物かと思った。
**Jū o mite [honmono ka] to omotta.**
Seeing the gun, I thought [it might be real].

b 「これが幸せというものか」と思う。
**[Kore ga shiawase to iu mono ka] to omou.**
I feel that [this might be what's called happiness].

| 18.3.1.2.2 | **ka dō ka** + predicate |

This combination indicates the meaning of 'if', 'whether'.

a 作戦が成功したかどうかはまだ不明だ。
**[Sakusen ga seikō shita ka dō ka] wa mada fumei da.**
It's still unclear [whether the strategy worked (*lit.* "or not")].

b 日本で有名かどうかは関係ない。
**[Nihon de yūmei ka dō ka] wa kankei nai.**
[Whether they [fashion labels] are famous in Japan] doesn't matter.

c 死者の中に外国人がいるかどうかは確認されていない。
**[Shisha no naka ni gaikoku-jin ga iru ka dō ka] wa kakunin
  sarete inai.**
It hasn't been confirmed [whether there are any foreigners among
  the dead].

d いじめがあったかどうかはもう考えたくない。
**[Ijime ga atta ka dō ka] wa mō kangae-takunai.**
I don't want to think any more about [whether bullying took place].

e 部長や係長という役職が本当に必要かどうか考えさせられた。
**[Buchō ya kakarichō to iu yakushoku ga hontō ni hitsuyō ka
dō ka] kangaesaserareta.**
One was made to reconsider [whether managerial posts such as
department chief and section head are really necessary].

f 現在、この遺伝子が体内時計遺伝子そのものかどうかを調
べている。
**Genzai, [kono idenshi ga tainai dokei idenshi sono mono ka
dō ka] o shirabete iru.**
Currently, we are investigating [whether these genes are the body
clock genes themselves].

g いじめがあったかどうかについては、「今のところ思い当たる事
は全くない」。
**[Ijime ga atta ka dō ka] ni tsuite wa, 'ima no tokoro
omoiataru koto wa mattaku nai'.**
About [whether bullying took place], 'At this stage, nothing at all
comes to mind'.

---

18.3.1.2.3 | **ka ina ka** + predicate

This is a written-style equivalent of **ka dō ka** + predicate.

a 参加するか否かを判断する。
**[Sanka suru ka ina ka] o handan suru.**
They will decide [whether to participate].

b 映画はヒットするか否かがカケのようなビジネス。
**Eiga wa [hitto suru ka ina ka] ga kake no yō na bijinesu.**
[Deciding] Whether a film [will be a hit] is a business like betting.

c リストラも、結局はこの天下りに手を着けることができるか否か
にかかっている。
**Risutora mo, kekkyoku wa [kono amakudari ni te o tsukeru
koto ga dekiru ka ina ka] ni kakatte iru.**
Restructuring in the end depends on [whether something can be done
about this (system of) 'descending from heaven'] [= employing
former government officials].

18.3.1.2.4 **ka na** + predicate

This indicates wondering or supposing 'I guess', 'might be', etc. (see 18.2.2).

a こう言われてしまうと、そういうものかな、と一瞬、納得してし
  まう。
  **Kō iwarete shimau to, [sō iu mono ka na], to isshun, nattoku
  shite shimau.**
  When told this [= why not use dirty money for a clean purpose],
  you are persuaded for a moment, thinking [it might be right].

18.3.1.2.5 **ka ... ka**: alternative questions

These are indirect alternative questions (see 18.1.11).

a 要はヤル気があるかないかだ。
  **Yō wa [yaru ki ga aru ka nai ka] da.**
  The question is, [do they have the willingness (*lit.* "or not")].

b 従来、選挙に際して「党」か「人」かがよく問題になった。
  **Jūrai, senkyo ni saishite ['tō' ka 'hito' ka] ga yoku mondai ni
  natta.**
  In the past, a problem in elections has often been [whether (to
  choose) 'party' or 'person'].

c 誰（だれ）が犯人なのか誰が正しいのか、はっきりしない。
  **[Dare ga hannin na no ka dare ga tadashii no ka], hakkiri shinai.**
  It is unclear [who the culprit is [and] who is in the right].

## 18.3.2 *Indirect negative questions*

(See also 18.4.)

18.3.2.1 *(no)* **de wa nai ka** + *predicate*

The combination indicates the meaning of 'might' (see also 18.4.7).

a 中央アジアから輸入された馬ではないかとの説もある。
  **[Chūō ajia kara yunyū sareta uma de wa nai ka] to no setsu
  mo aru.**
  There is also a theory that [it may be a horse that was brought in
  from Central Asia].

b くさりにつながれたままではストレスがたまるのではないかと心
配だ。

**Kusari ni tsunagareta mama de wa [sutoresu ga tamaru no
de wa nai ka] to shinpai da.**

If one leaves it [= the dog] chained up, the worry is [that it might get
stressed].

---

| 18.3.2.2 | *Potential-**nai mono ka** + predicate* |

This asks 'whether it mightn't be possible'.

a その一方で、この大雪をなんとか村おこしに利用できないもの
かと、思案してきた。

**Sono ippō de, [kono ōyuki o nantoka muraokoshi ni riyō
dekinai mono ka] to, shian shite kita.**

On the other hand, we racked our brains as to [whether we mightn't
be able to use this heavy snow to revitalize the village].

---

| 18.3.3 | **nanto . . . mono ka** *predicate* |

Although formally a question, this is a way of making an emphatic statement, **nanto** being an emphatic adverb 'how very . . .', which is reinforced
by the final particle **mono ka** (see 19.1.1.7).

a そう思った瞬間、Y子さんは自分の悩みがなんとちっぽけなもの
かと思った。

**Sō omotta shunkan, Y-ko-san wa [jibun no nayami ga nanto
chippoke na mono ka] to omotta.**

The moment she realized this [= how large the universe is], Y-ko felt
[how ridiculously insignificant her problems were].

---

## 18.4  Negative questions

Negative questions are questions that end with a negative form, such as
**nai (ka), nai no (ka), -masen (ka)**, etc. (see elsewhere in 18).

## 18.4.1 By intonation only

a 味に変わりはありません？
  **Aji ni kawari wa arimasen?**
  The taste hasn't changed?

b 「ちょっと見てみない」「これって、浅井慎平の写真じゃん。」
  **'Chotto mite minai' 'Kore tte, Asai Shinpei no shashin jan.**
    [**jan** = equivalent of **da** used by the young]
  'Won't you take a look [over here]?' 'That's a photo by Asai Shinpei,
  isn't it!'

## 18.4.2 Ending in no (+ intonation)

a 買わないの？新しい車。(see 19.3, 28.1)
  **Kawanai no? Atarashii kuruma**
  Aren't you going to buy one? A new car, I mean.

b パパ、歴史は夜つくられるって言葉知らないの。
  **Papa, rekishi wa yoru tsukurareru tte kotoba shiranai no.**
  Daddy, don't you know the saying 'History is made at night'?

## 18.4.3 Ending in question word + no

a ぼくにはどうしてお父さんがいないの。
  **Boku ni wa dōshite otōsan ga inai no.**
  Why don't I have a father?

## 18.4.4 Ending in question particle ka

Note that with verbs that express an action, the meaning is usually one
of invitation to do something 'how about' (example b).

a 高くないですか。
  **Takakunai desu ka.**
  Isn't it expensive?

b 一緒に農業ネットワークを作りませんか！
  **Issho ni nōgyō nettowāku o tsukurimasen ka!**
  How about joining with us to form an agricultural network!

c 仕事、ありませんか。

**Shigoto, arimasen ka.**

Got any work?

*Ending in* -nai ka na/nā/ne

**ka na** is a combination of the question particle **ka** and **na**, a variant of the final particle **ne**. The combination expresses wondering or guessing, in the fashion of thinking out loud. Although **ka na** by itself doesn't usually ask for a reaction, with **moraenai** it does (example d). **na** can be lengthened to **nā** (example d) (see 18.4.7, 15.5.3.2).

*Note* – **ka ne** is mostly used in a different way, for extracting a reaction from someone else (example e).

a 解散は再来年以降じゃないかな。

**Kaisan wa sarainen ikō ja nai ka na.**

The dissolution [of the Diet] should be the year after next or beyond.

b 来年はやっと回復を実感できる年になるんじゃないかな。

**Rainen wa yatto kaifuku o jikkan dekiru toshi ni naru n ja nai ka na.**

Next year might be the year when we can finally feel the [economic] recovery.

c 小遣いの半分は社員との飲み代に消えているんじゃないかな。

**Kozukai no hanbun wa shain to no nomidai ni kiete iru n ja nai ka na.**

About half of my pocket money goes on drinking with the employees.

d 「わたしの写真もこんなきれいなところに飾ってもらえないかなぁ」「だめだめ、このギャラリーはけやきがメーンテーマなんだから」

**'Watashi no shashin mo konna kirei na tokoro ni kazatte moraenai ka nā' 'Damedame, kono gyararī wa keyaki ga mēn tēma na n da kara'**

'I wish I could have my photo displayed in such a beautiful place, too.' 'No way, the main theme of this gallery is Zelkova trees.'

e そうじゃないかね、寅さん。

**Sō ja nai ka ne, Tora-san.**

Isn't that right, Tora-san?

**18.4.6** *Ending in -nai mono ka*

This means 'is there not some way' (see 19.1.1.6).

a トイレの水くらいは雨水を使えないものか。
**Toire no mizu kurai wa amamizu o tsukaenai mono ka.**
Why can't rainwater be used at least for water in the toilet?

b 安全でおいしい養殖魚はつくれないものか。
**Anzen de oishii yōshokugyo wa tsukurenai mono ka.**
Isn't there some way to breed fish that are safe to eat and taste good?

**18.4.7** *Questions ending in (positive/negative)* **de wa/ja nai**
*(ka/no/kashira)*

These are a kind of rhetorical device similar to so-called tag questions
('won't it', 'will you', etc.) in English. These are used after positive (18.4.7.1)
and negative (18.4.7.2 and 18.4.7.3) forms. Of the last two, the 18.4.7.3
forms have a more formal ring.

**18.4.7.1** *Questions ending in* **de wa/ja nai** *(ka/no/kashira)*

a いっそCMをやめても良いのではないか。
**Isso shīemu o yamete mo yoi no de wa nai ka.**
We might as well stop advertising it [our product on TV],
  mightn't we?

**18.4.7.2** *Questions ending in* **-nai (n) ja nai** *(ka/no/kashira)*

a けど、やってみないとどんなもんか分かんないじゃない。
  （分かんない = 分からない）
**Kedo, yatte minai to donna mon ka wakannai ja nai.**
  **[wakannai = wakaranai]**
But, unless I try, I won't know what it's like, right?

b 劇作だけで食べている人はいないんじゃないか。
**Gekisaku dake de tabete iru hito wa inai n ja nai ka.**
There is no one who can make a living just from writing plays,
  is there?

c 自分はこうなんだ、という価値観が全く確立されていないんじゃ
ないの？

**Jibun wa kō nan da, to iu kachikan ga mattaku kakuritsu
sarete inai n ja nai no.**

They don't have any values about what they're on about,
don't you agree?

d 子孫のための小額な負担を嫌う人はいないんじゃないかしら。

**Shison no tame no shōgaku na futan o kirau hito wa inai n ja
nai kashira.**

I wouldn't think that there's anyone who'd object to footing a small
bill for his descendants.

18.4.7.3 *Questions ending in* **-nai de wa nai ka**

a そうすると、株価はかえって下がるかも知れないではないか。

**Sō suru to, kabuka wa kaette sagaru kamoshirenai de
wa nai ka.**

In that case, the share price might rather drop, mightn't it?

b 日本でもほとんど普及していないではないか。

**Nihon de mo hotondo fukyū shite inai de wa nai ka.**

Even in Japan, it [= high-definition TV] has practically no popular
support, has it?

18.4.8 *Negative questions: how to answer*

Negative questions and how to answer them are an oft-discussed characteristic of the Japanese language (as in example a).

The rule given in textbooks, etc. is that in reply to a negative question you
answer in the negative (introduced with **hai** = yes!) if the predicate matches
the negative ('yes, what you're suggesting is quite right, I didn't'), whereas
if the predicate is positive (and therefore disagrees with the negative form
used in the question, you begin your reply with no (**iie**) ('no, what you're
suggesting is wrong, I did').

a 日本語と英語の表現で「はい」と「いいえ」が逆になる場合が
  ある。日本人に「映画を見ませんでしたか」と否定疑問文で
  聞いたら、答えは「いいえ、見ました」「はい、見ませんで
  した」。

  **Nihongo to eigo no hyōgen de, 'hai' to 'iie' ga gyaku ni naru
  baai ga aru. Nihonjin ni 'eiga o mimasen deshita ka' to
  hitei gimonbun de kiitara, kotae wa 'iie, mimashita' 'hai,
  mimasen deshita'.**

  In Japanese and English expressions, there are cases where 'Yes' and
  'No' are reversed. If you ask a Japanese using a negative question
  'Didn't you see the movie?', the answer is 'No, I did', 'Yes, I didn't'.

b 「(ミッキーには)代役はいないんですか。同じ人がやっているわ
  けじゃないんでしょ」という知事の突飛な質問にも、「いい
  え、ミッキーは世界でただ一人です」ときっぱり。

  **'(Mikkī ni wa) daiyaku wa inai n desu ka. Onaji hito ga
  yatte iru wake ja nai n desho' to iu chiji no toppi na
  shitsumon ni mo, 'Iie, Mikkī wa sekai de tada hitori desu'
  to kippari.**

  In reply to the governor's eccentric question 'Is there no understudy
  [for Mickey]? It's not always the same person who performs him,
  is it?', she said firmly, 'No, there's only one Mickey [Mouse] in
  the world'.

However, reality doesn't always conform to the textbook explanations
(examples c and d).

c 中部電力三重支店が六月、主要新聞六紙の三重県版に出した
  「原子力発電所って、爆発せーへんの!?はい、大丈夫です」
  との新聞広告について、…

  **Chūbu Denryoku Mie-shiten ga rokugatsu, shuyō shinbun
  rokushi no Mie-ken-ban ni dashita 'Genshiryoku
  hatsudensho tte bakuhatsu sēhen no!? Hai, daijōbu desu' to
  no shinbun kōkoku ni tsuite,... (sēhen no: Kansai dialect for
  shinai no).**

  About the newspaper ad that Chūbu Electricity placed in June in the
  Mie prefecture versions of the six major dailies 'Don't atomic
  power stations explode!?' 'No (*lit.* "yes"), it's OK',...

d 「よほど遠くでないと、乗り物は使いません」「こんな人込みの
開会式に一人で来て、家族の方は心配しませんか」「いいえ、
全然」。

**'Yohodo tōku de nai to, norimono wa tsukaimasen' 'Konna
hitogomi no kaikaishiki ni hitori de kite, kazoku no kata wa
shinpai shimasen ka' 'Iie, zenzen'.**

'I don't use transport unless I have to go a really long way.' 'Don't
your people worry [about you], coming by yourself to an opening
ceremony this crowded?' 'No, not a bit.'

*Note* – Rhetorical negative questions such as **no de wa** (**nai ka**), etc. (see
18.4.7) are answered like positive questions (see examples e and f).

e ・・・売上税、消費税に反対の立場だったのでは？「はい、道義的
に許せなかったんです」。

**...uriage-zei, shōhi-zei ni hantai no tachiba datta no de wa?
'Hai, dōgiteki ni yurusenakatta n desu'.**

'...weren't you opposed to sales tax and consumption tax?'
'Yes, I couldn't approve of it morally.'

f 「そんなに大事なものなら、生物にあまねく存在するのではない
か」「はい、微生物から人間まで、この酵素を持たない生物は
ありません」。

**'Sonna ni daiji na mono nara, seibutsu ni amaneku sonzai
suru no de wa nai ka' 'Hai, biseibutsu kara ningen made,
kono kōso o motanai seibutsu wa arimasen'.**

'If it's such an important element, wouldn't it exist in all living things?'
'Yes, from micro-organisms to humans, there's no organism that
hasn't got this enzyme.'

# Chapter 19

# Sentence-final particles

Sentence-final particles are used at or towards the end of a sentence or clause, and indicate the speaker's attitude towards the listener. 'Speaker's attitude' includes, among others, agreement, assertion, explanation, emphasis, questioning and understanding. Most of these particles are used mostly in conversation, but some, such as some uses of **mono**, are used in writing too.

Despite their designation 'sentence-final', some can also be used in S1 of a compound/complex sentence.

## 19.1 mon(o)

As a final particle, **mon(o)** is basically used in two ways, sentence-finally and at the end of S1 in complex sentences.

### 19.1.1 *Sentence-final use*

### 19.1.1.1 *mon(o) (da)*

Attached to statements, **mon (da)** emphasizes the statement in the sense of 'you see'. **mon** tends to be used by women, and **mon da** by men.

a この仕事、"風俗" とは思ってないもん。(思ってない = 思ってい
　ない)
  **Kono shigoto, 'fūzoku' to wa omottenai mon.**
  **(omottenai = omotte inai)**
  I don't think of this job [= working in a massage parlour] as 'immoral',
  you know.

b 想像以上に難しいもんだ。

**Sōzō ijō ni muzukashii mon da.**

[The work] is a lot more difficult than I imagined.

c ボランティアなんて、ヒマな人がするもんだ。

**Borantia nante, hima na hito ga suru mon da.**

Volunteer [work] is something that people with time on their hands do.

19.1.1.2 **gurai no mon(o) (da)**

This is used in the sense of 'that's about it' (see 11.5.1).

a ・・・もう何日も、家族以外の者と顔を合わせていない。お医者さんぐらいのもんだ。

**...mō nannichi mo, kazoku igai no mono to kao o awasete inai. Oishasan gurai no mon da.**

...for many days now, [the sick child] hasn't seen anyone outside the family. The doctor is about the only exception.

19.1.1.3 **da mon(o)**

Often used in combination with **datte** 'but', **da mon/mono** (usually preceded by **n**, i.e. in the form **n da mon/mono**) is typically used by children and teenagers when complaining. It is not really translatable, but perhaps '. . . . ! (+ context)' comes close.

a だって、もう家にいるのあきちゃったんだもん。

**Datte, mō ie ni iru no akichatta n da mon.**

But, I've got bored with being in the house ...!

b だってえ、港の近くには見たり遊んだりする所がないんだもん。

**Dattē, minato no chikaku ni wa mitari asondari suru tokoro ga nai n da mon.**

But, near the port there is nowhere to see or have fun ...!

c 不審に思って一人の子に問いただしたところ、「だって、学校のトイレじゃ、おしりが洗えないんだもの」。

**Fushin ni omotte hitori no ko ni toitadashita tokoro, 'Datte, gakkō no toire ja, oshiri ga araenai n da mono'.**

The teacher thought it strange [that some pupils had soiled their trousers] and asked one of the children. The reply was 'But I can't wash my bottom in the school toilet [unlike at home]!'

### 19.1.1.4 -tai mon(o) da

This is used for general statements about the way one ideally would like things to be 'would really like to' (see 9.2).

a やはり子供には元気に外で遊んでもらいたいものだ。
**Yahari kodomo ni wa genki ni soto de asonde morai-tai mono da.**
After all, one does want one's children to play energetically outside.

b もう一度、日常の生活を見直したいものである。
**Mō ichido, nichijō no seikatsu o minaoshi-tai mono de aru.**
I really want to take another good look at our daily life.

### 19.1.1.5 -ta mon(o) da

This is used when recalling the past with a feeling of nostalgia 'used to', often together with **mukashi wa** 'in the old days'.

a 昔は春と秋だけ、商売したもんだ。
**Mukashi wa haru to aki dake, shōbai shita mon da.**
In the old days, we used to do business only in spring and autumn.

b 小さい子どもは、年上の子から遊びを教わったものだ。
**Chiisai kodomo wa, toshiue no ko kara asobi o osowatta mono da.**
The small children used to be taught games by the older children.

### 19.1.1.6 nai mon(o) darō ka

In negative question form, this is used as a rhetorical device 'might there not' (see 18.4.7, 9.1.2.3.4).

a 何か新しい、別の人生はないものだろうか。
**Nani ka atarashii, betsu no jinsei wa nai mono darō ka.**
Might there not be a new and different life, I wonder.

19.1.1.7 *Verb-***ru mon(o) ka**

This indicates a rhetorical question 'certainly not' (see 18.2.1.1).

a 負けてなるものか。
**Makete naru mono ka.**
I'm *not* going to lose! (*lit.* "Losing will do? No way!")

19.1.2 **In compound and complex sentences**

In compound and complex sentences, **mon(o)** is used at the end of S1, including sentences where S2 is ellipted (understood from the context).

19.1.2.1 *Clause 1* **mon(o) de** ... *(clause 2 ellipted)*

Being an unfinished sentence, this is often used to make unenthusiastic or non-committal statements. The phrase itself is equivalent to 'you see ...'.

a 私、ゲームやらないもんで⋯⋯
**Watashi, gēmu yaranai mon de ...**
I don't play games, you see ...

b 「攻撃するのはいやなもんでしてね」と ⋯
**'Kōgeki suru no wa iya na mon deshite ne' to ...**
[He] said 'Going on the attack is something I don't like,
    you see'

19.1.2.2 *Clause 1* **hayai mon(o) de,** *clause 2*

Often used in combination with **mō**, this idiomatic combination emphasizes the rapid passage of time 'already'.

a 早いもので、入社してもう7年目に入っていた。
**Hayai mono de, nyūsha shite mō shichinen-me
    ni haitte ita.**
Time passing so fast, it was already the seventh year since I had
    entered the company.

19.1.2.3 *Clause 1* **mon(o) da kara,** *clause 2*

Like the conjunctive particle **kara,** this combination indicates a reason; **mono** serves to emphasize the reason 'you see ..., because' (see 26.5.2).

a 呼吸困難で言葉が出ないものだから、手と目で必死に「アリガトウ」と伝えようとしてくれたんですね。

   **Kokyū konnan de kotoba ga denai mono da kara, te to me de hisshi ni 'arigatō' to tsutaeyō to shite kureta n desu ne.**

   You see, as he could not talk due to breathing difficulties, he tried his hardest to convey 'thank you' with his hands and eyes.

b 久しぶりに熱出して一人で寝たもんだから、子供のころ、カゼで熱出した時を思い出した。

   **Hisashiburi ni netsu dashite hitori de neta mon da kara, kodomo no koro, kaze de netsu dashita toki o omoidashita.**

   Because I had a fever, something I hadn't had for a long time, and went to bed alone, I remembered the times when I had had a fever because of a cold.

19.1.2.4 *Clause 1-(verb-potential)* **mon(o) nara** *clause 2*

Used with the same potential verb (or a potential verb with similar meaning) repeated, **mono** emphasizes the condition indicated by **nara** '*if* you can' (see 26.1.4).

a やれるものなら、やってみろ。自社なれあいが天下に明らかになる。

   **Yareru mono nara, yatte miro. Jisha nareai ga tenka ni akiraka ni naru.**

   Go ahead and try (*lit.* "if you can do it, give it a try") [but] the conspiracy between the LPD and the Socialist Party will be obvious to all.

b 短くできるものなら、短くすべく努力してほしいと思う。

   **Mijikaku dekiru mono nara, mijikaku su-beku doryoku shite hoshii to omou.**

   If they can speed things up (*lit.* "shorten them"), I'd like them to try.

| 19.1.2.5 | *Clause 1-(y)ō mon(o) nara, clause 2* |

This indicates a hypothetical condition 'if you were to do anything like . . .'
(see 26.1.6).

a 悠長に酒など飲んでいようものなら、まったく取材にならない。

   **Yūchō ni sake nado nonde i-yō mono nara, mattaku shuzai ni
   naranai.**

   [Foreign correspondent:] If you were to hang around idly having
   drinks etc., you wouldn't be able to collect any news.

| 19.1.2.6 | *Clause 1-ba* + **ii to iu/tte mon/mono ja/dewa nai** |

This means 'not necessarily'.

a 休みだって長けりゃいいってもんじゃないらしい。

   **Yasumi datte nagakerya ii tte mon ja nai rashii.**
   [**nagakerya** = contraction of **nagakere-ba**]
   Holidays, it seems, are not necessarily the longer the better.

| 19.1.2.7 | *Clause 1-te/***sore kara to iu mono** *clause 2* |

Here, **to iu mono** is used to emphasize **kara** 'since', in the sense of 'ever
since' (see 26.5.2).

a 小説『帝都物語』のヒットで脚光を浴びてからというもの、ほと
   んど休む間もなかった。

   **Shōsetsu 'Teito Monogatari' no hitto de kyakkō o abite kara
   to iu mono, hotondo yasumu ma mo nakatta.**

   Ever since he was thrown into the limelight through the popularity of
   the novel *Teito Mononogatari*, he's hardly had time to rest.

b ・・・温泉施設をオープンしてからというもの人気はうなぎ登り。

   **. . . onsen shisetsu o ōpun shite kara to iu mono ninki wa
   unagi-nobori.**

   . . . ever since they opened a hot spring facility, their popularity has
   been rising fast.

c それからというもの、妻やその両親を説得するために頻繁に九州
   に足を運んだ。

   **Sore kara to iu mono, tsuma ya sono ryōshin o settoku suru
   tame ni hinpan ni Kyūshū ni ashi o hakonda.**

   Ever since [his divorce], he has visited Kyushu frequently in order to
   convince his wife and her parents [to allow him access to his son].

## 19.2 ne (also nē/nā/na)

Attached to sentences that are statements (also exclamations, etc.), **ne** (and its variants **nē** and **na/nā**, the former emphatic, the latter mostly male usage) are basically used for soliciting agreement from the listener, but in the form ねっ **ne'** (example 19.2.1 c) can also express anger or frustration.

**ne**, etc. can also be used for talking to oneself, especially in the form **nā**.

### 19.2.1 Statement ne

Depending on the type of sentence, statements end variously in final forms of V/Adj, **na**-Adj/N + copula, or with the modal ending (**na**) **n(o) da**, the sentence-final particles **no** and/or **yo**, or the conjunctive form of the copula -**te** used in the sense of 'you see' (see 25.6.3.5, 19.3, 9.6.1, 19.6).

a うまそうだね。
**Umasō da ne.**
Looks delicious, doesn't it.

b 忙しそうだね。
**Isogashisō da ne.**
You look busy.

c 娘を全然信用しないのねっ。
**Musume o zenzen shin'yō shinai no ne'.**
You don't trust your daughter [=me] at all, do you!

d マンションなんて、ただでも住む気ないな。
**Manshon nante, tada de mo sumu ki nai na.**
An apartment building? I don't feel like living there even for free.

e そう聞いて皆から「いいなあ」と感想が漏れた。
**Sō kiite mina kara 'ii nā' to kansō ga moreta.**
Hearing this, all gave vent to their feelings, saying 'How nice'.

f やけに重いなあ。
**Yake ni omoi nā.**
It's bloody heavy!

g 「大きいなあ」「きれいな空港だね」。
**'Ōkii nā' 'Kirei na kūkō da ne'.**
'How big!' 'It's a beautiful airport.'

h マルチメディアも分かったような分からないような言葉だな。
**Maruchimedia mo wakatta yō na wakaranai yō na kotoba
da na.**
Multimedia too is a term that one thinks one understands but
doesn't really.

i だれにも話せなくてね。
**Dare ni mo hanasenakute ne.**
I can't tell anyone, you see.

### 19.2.2 | Question na/nā/ne

Attached to a question (positive or negative) ending in the question particle **ka**, the resulting meaning is one of wondering or supposing. For more
examples, see 18.4.5, 18.2.

a 収穫は七月末かなあ。
**Shūkaku wa shichigatsu-matsu ka nā.**
The harvest will be at the end of July, I suppose.

## 19.3 no

**no** is an informal variant of the modal ending **n(o) desu** or **no desu ka**,
depending on whether the intonation is falling or rising (see 9.6.1). The
forms preceding **no** are noun-modifying forms.

### 19.3.1 | Indicates a question (rising intonation)

Questions ending in **no** have an intimate or familiar tone (see 18.1.2).

a どこへ行くの。
**Doko e iku no.**
Where are you going?

b 怒っていらっしゃるの。
**Okotte irassharu no.**
Are you angry?

c お父さん、社長になるの。
**Otōsan, shachō ni naru no.**
Daddy, are you going to be company president?

d どうしたの。
**Dō shita no.**
What's the matter?

e パパ、歴史は夜つくられるって言葉知らないの。
**Papa, rekishi wa yoru tsukurareru tte kotoba shiranai no.**
Daddy, don't you know the saying 'History is made at night'?

### 19.3.2 *Shows understanding (falling intonation)*

This indicates the speaker's understanding of some situation, or of something said by someone else.

a 「このリンゴ、一つ100円だって。」「そんなに高いの。」
**'Kono ringo, hitotsu hyakuen datte.' 'Sonna ni takai no.'**
'These apples are ¥100 a piece, it seems.' 'That expensive,
   are they?'

b ああ、そうなの。
**Ā, sō na no.**
Oh, I see.

### 19.3.3 *Gives or requests an explanation*
### *(falling/rising intonation)*

This is used mainly by women, sometimes with **yo** added.

a 痛いの!?
**Itai no!?**
Does it hurt!?

b このケーキ、私が作ったのよ。
**Kono kēki, watashi ga tsukutta no yo.**
I've made this cake!

c またA子さん遅刻なの。
**Mata A-ko-san chikoku na no.**
Is A-ko late again?

d 今夜はお父さん帰ってこないの。ウフフ。
**Kon'ya wa otōsan kaette konai no. Ufufu.**
Tonight, hubby's not coming home. Hee hee.

**19.3.4** *Verb/adjective no, verb/adjective no*

In this use, **no** is attached to pairs of V/Adj of opposite meaning, including using the positive and negative forms of the same word. The effect of this colloquial use is placing emphasis on the first member of the pair.

a 彼女はいつも死ぬの生きるのと、大騒ぎをする。

 **Kanojo wa itsumo shinu no ikiru no to, ōsawagi o suru.**

 She's always making a racket, saying she's gonna die.

b 柱に頭をぶつけてしまった。痛いの痛くないの、すっかり眠気が
 覚めてしまった。

 **Hashira ni atama o butsukete shimatta. Itai no itakunai no, sukkari nemuke ga samete shimatta.**

 I hit my head on a pole. It was so painful, I am wide awake (*lit.* "my sleepiness is totally gone").

**19.4** **sa**

**sa** attaches to noun-modifying forms of V/Adj, but replaces the copula after **na**-Adj/N. It can also attach to other forms (such as unfinished sentences, and appear in non-final position in the sentence, marking the end of a clause, as in example g) and particles. **sa** has a ring of assertion, pointing out the obvious to the listener. It is not usually translated, but the implication is often one of 'don't you see?', 'that should be obvious', etc. For this reason it is also often attached to the conjunctive particle **kara**, which means 'because', but can also be used simply to indicate the obvious.

a 小学校はずっと休みさ。

 **Shōgakkō wa zutto yasumi sa.**

 The primary school will be closed for some time.

b 払わなくても違法ではなかったからさ。

 **Harawanakute mo ihō de wa nakatta kara sa.**

 It wasn't against the law if one didn't pay [alimony], you see.

c 確かに日本は核兵器を持つ能力はあるさ。

 **Tashika ni Nihon wa kakuheiki o motsu nōryoku wa aru sa.**

 Japan has the ability to have nuclear weapons all right.

d 師は「俳諧師」、俳人さ。

 **Shi wa 'haikai-shi', haijin sa.**

 *Shi* ("teacher") means 'Haiku teacher', a Haiku poet, you know.

e 適当なゴールを探していたら、体育館の物置にピーチ（桃）の籠
　があったのでそれを利用したのさ。

**Tekitō na gōru o sagashite itara, taiikukan no monooki ni
pīchi (momo) no kago ga atta node sore o riyō shita no sa.**

When we were looking for something to use as a goal, there was a peach
crate in the storeroom of the gym, and so we used that, you see.

f 「ご隠居、ビールなんてものは、余計なうんちくを傾けず、
　ぐーっと飲みほすもんだ」「まあ、そう言わずにさ」。

**'Go-inkyo, bīru nante mono wa, yokei na unchiku o
katamukezu, gūtto nomihosu mon da' 'Mā, sō iwazu ni sa'.**

'Old man, beer is not something you lecture about, you just drink up
in one draught.' 'Come on, don't say that.'

g 四、五人で取り巻いて、寂しいところへ連れてってさ、でかいシ
　ャベルを持たして、テメェでテメェの穴を掘れっつうわけ。
　（掘れっつうわけ＝掘れというわけ）

**Shi, go-nin de torimaite, sabishii tokoro e tsuretette sa, dekai
shaberu o motashite, temē de temē no ana o hore-ttsū
wake. [hore-ttsū wake = hore to iu wake]**

You see, four or five [of us] surround him, take him to a deserted
spot, hand him a big shovel and tell him to dig his own grave.

## 19.5 wa

The sentence-final particle **wa** (attached to statements) is used for slight
emphasis or assertion. It is generally restricted to female usage in Standard
Japanese, but is widely used by males in Western Japan (Kansai).

It is also often combined with the final particle **yo**, and its lengthened
variant **yō**.

a あら、ミーティングが始まるわ。
**Ara, mītingu ga hajimaru wa.**
Oh, the meeting is about to begin!

b 姓なんていらないわよ。
**Sei nante iranai wa yo.**
I don't need (*lit.* "any such thing as") a surname.

c 私そんなもの見たことないわよー。
**Watashi sonna mono mita koto nai wa yō.**
I've never seen any such thing! [= mosquito eyeball soup]

487

## 19.6 yo

The particle **yo** serves to make a statement (examples a–e) or invitation (example h, see also 9.1.1.1.1). It can be lengthened to **yō** for emphasis (example 19.5 c).

After imperatives (example i), it serves to soften the impact of the imperative form (see 20.1.2).

Apart from verbs, adjectives, **no**-adjectives and nouns (plain or polite, positive or negative), **yo** can also attach to modal endings (example f), and the sentence-final particle **no** (example d) (see 19.3).

In statements and after modal endings (**n(o) da**, **sō da** and many others), **yo** can be attached to the copula (i.e. **na**-Adj/N + copula), but in female use (and for a familiar effect in general), it can also *replace* the copula (examples e and f).

Note also the use seen in example g, where N **yo** cannot be replaced by N **da**, this being a way of addressing a person (or personalized entity by name), in a variation of the Latin 'Et tu, Brute?'

a まだ硬いと思いつつ、気になるので、指先で押してみる。
「昨日より軟らかいよ」と言っては、家人にむいてもらう。
**Mada katai to omoi-tsutsu, ki ni naru node, yubisaki de oshite miru. 'Kinō yori yawarakai yo' to itte wa, kajin ni muite morau.**
While thinking that [the pears] are still hard, I can't take my mind off them and poke them with my fingertip. 'They are softer than yesterday', I say, and get the family to peel [them] one at a time for me.

b 中学に入ったら···別々の学校になっちゃうんだよ。さびしいよ。
**Chūgaku ni haittara . . . betsubetsu no gakkō ni natchau n da yo. Sabishii yo.**
When we enter junior high school . . . will be going to different schools. I'll be lonely.

c 本当のことだから怒りませんよ。
**Hontō no koto da kara okorimasen yo.**
It's the truth, so I'm not getting upset.

d このケーキ、私が作ったのよ。
**Kono kēki, watashi ga tsukutta no yo.**
I've made this cake!

e ワイエスさんってとてもすばらしい方よ。

**Waiesu-san tte totemo subarashii kata yo.**

Wyeth is a wonderful person, you know.

f 昔、相撲はその年の稲作を占う神事だったそうよ。

**Mukashi, sumō wa sono toshi no inasaku o uranau shinji datta sō yo.**

In the old days, sumo was apparently a Shinto ceremony to divine the rice harvest for that year.

g 「経済界よ。お前もか」と思ってしまう。

**'Keizaikai yo. Omae mo ka' to omotte shimau.**

One feels 'You too, business world?' (Variation on Caesar's 'Et tu, Brute?' from Shakespeare's *Julius Caesar*)

h どっか行こうよ。

**Dokka ikō yo.**

Let's go somewhere.

i おれにも撮らせろよ。(PM to cameramen)

**Ore ni mo torasero yo.**

Let me take one [= a picture] too.

## 19.7 ze

ze is used chiefly by men, mostly in informal language, to call the listener's attention to something, in the sense of 'you know', 'I tell you', etc.

Note example e, where ze is used after a -masu form.

a ナイターの照明があたるともっときれいだぜ。

**Naitā no shōmei ga ataru to motto kirei da ze.**

In the floodlight (*lit.* "when the lights for the night match shine on it"), it [= the stadium] looks even nicer, I tell you.

b 新しいオペラ座がテレビで紹介されたんだぜ。

**Atarashii opera-za ga terebi de shōkai sareta n da ze.**

The new opera house was introduced on TV, you know.

c この順番を待つ通路、壁にも床にもテレビのモニターがはまってるぜ。

**Kono junban o matsu tsūro, kabe ni mo yuka ni mo terebi no monitā ga hamatteru ze.**

This passage where you wait for your turn has TV monitors fitted in both the wall and the floor, you know!

d まったく、お兄ちゃんの影響力の大きさにはまいるぜ。
**Mattaku, oniichan no eikyōryoku no ōkisa ni wa mairu ze.**
The influence of the older brother [on the younger one] is really
amazing, you know.

e ご尽力ありがとうございます。しかしこれじゃいけませんぜ。
土地取引は動きません。
**Go-jinryoku arigatō gozaimasu. Shikashi kore ja ikemasen ze.**
**Tochi torihiki wa ugokimasen.**
Thank you for your effort. But this is not good enough. Land deals
aren't moving [at all].

## 19.8  zo

zo is a stronger variant of **yo** (see 19.6), used chiefly by men.

As **zo** is used to alert the listener, it can also be used to threaten others.
However, it is also common for people to use **zo** when talking to them-
selves/thinking aloud.

a 撃つぞ。
**Utsu zo.**
I'll shoot!

b おかしいぞ。
**Okashii zo.**
This is strange!

c 「手土産じゃすまないぞ」などと脅した疑い。
**'Temiyage ja sumanai zo' nado to odoshita utagai.**
He is suspected of having threatened him, saying, 'A present ain't
good enough!'

d 上司から家に火をつけるぞ、犬を殺すぞと脅された。
**Jōshi kara ie ni hi o tsukeru zo, inu o korosu zo to**
**odosareta.**
He was threatened by his superior, saying he'd set his house
on fire and kill his dog.

e この分では胴上げでなくお手上げになってしまうぞ。
**Kono bun de wa dōage de naku o-teage ni natte shimau zo.**
If we go on like this, it's not going to be 'dōage' [being lifted in
triumph] but 'o-teage' [throwing up hands in despair]!

f 「お父さん、競争だよ」「よし、負けないぞ」。
  **'Otōsan, kyōsō da yo' 'Yoshi, makenai zo'.**
  'Daddy, it's a race!' 'OK, I'm not going to lose!'

g 「お、メールが来てるぞ」。小学校から帰った春樹君 (11) はコンピ
  ューターの画面をのぞいた。
  **'O, mēru ga kiteru zo'. Shōgakkō kara kaetta Haruki-kun**
  **(jūichi) wa konpyūtā no gamen o nozoita.**
  'Oh, a(n) (e-)mail has come!' Haruki-kun (11), who had got back from
  primary school, looked at the computer screen.

# Chapter 20

# *Imperative sentences, commands and requests*

## 20.1   Imperative sentences

Imperative sentences typically use the imperative form of V (see 7.1) for plain imperatives. Plain imperatives are used on some traffic signs (止まれ **tomare** 'stop!'), by robbers, for yelling slogans in demonstrations, etc., but also to an extent in informal communication between males.

For 'softened' imperatives, the sentence-final particle **yo** is attached. 'Familiar' imperatives involve adding final particles such as **na (yo)** to V-stem (see 20.1.3). Negative imperatives used the form **V-ru na** (see 20.1.7).

*Note* – In Japanese imperatives and commands the subject of the sentence can be included. However, since this is not possible in English imperatives, they cannot be translated as imperatives in English.

a 学生はコピーをとらないで下さい [= written notice on copier]
  **Gakusei wa kopī o toranai de kudasai**
  Students must not take copies

b 「ここの生産性は驚くほど高い。日本も見習え」。
  **'Koko no seisan-sei wa odoroku hodo takai. Nihon mo minarae'.**
  'The productivity in this company is amazingly high. Japan should learn from this.'

c 官僚は株に手を出すな。
  **Kanryō wa kabu ni te o dasu na.**
  Bureaucrats shouldn't dabble in shares!

Polite imperatives or commands attach performatives such as **kudasai** to V-**te**, but informally V-**te** is also used by itself, especially by women (see 25.3.1).

## 20.1.1 Plain imperatives (imperative forms)

Imperative forms are derived from V-(r)u as given in Table 20.1.

**Table 20.1** Imperative verb formation

| Verb type | Replacement pattern | | |
|---|---|---|---|
| Group I | _-u_ | → | _-e_ |
| | ik-u | → | ik-e |
| | nom-u | → | nom-e |
| | ka(w)-u | → | ka(w)-e |
| Group II | _-ru_ | → | _-ro_ |
| | tabe-ru | → | tabe-ro |
| | mi-ru | → | mi-ro |
| Group III | kuru | → | koi |
| | suru | → | shiro |
| | kureru | → | kure |

a 手を挙げろ。
**Te o agero.**
Hands up!

b 一億円払え。
**Ichioku-en harae.**
Pay one hundred million yen!

c 静かな空を返せ。
**Shizuka na sora o kaese.**
Give us back a quiet sky!

d 身代金を用意しろ。
**Minoshirokin o yōi shiro.**
Bring a ransom!

## 20.1.2 'Softened' plain imperatives (imperative form + yo)

For the softer form of plain imperatives, the final particle **yo** is added (see 19.6).

a きてみろよ。
**Kite miro yo.**
Try it on.

b いいから早く買いに行けよ。
**Ii kara hayaku kai ni ike yo.**
Never mind, just go and buy it.

c 元気出せよ。
**Genki dase yo.**
Cheer up.

d がんばれよ。
**Ganbare yo.**
Keep going.

*'Familiar' imperatives (verb-stem + na/na yo)*

Plain imperatives with an intimate or familiar ring are formed by using the combination V-stem + **na** (**yo**). These are used (mostly by males) towards younger members of family, between schoolfriends, etc.

a なあオヤジ、早く隠居しなよ。
**Nā oyaji, hayaku inkyo shi na yo.**
Come on, Dad, retire soon, will you.

b 「孝行をしたい時にジジババなし」とは、言わないけど、そうなんだよ、早く気がつきなよ。
**'Kōkō o shitai toki ni jiji baba nashi' to wa, iwanai kedo, sō na n da yo, hayaku ki ga tsuki na yo.**
There is no saying 'When you want to be filial, your parents are already gone', but that's the way it is, come on, wake up to it!

20.1.4 *Classical form imperatives*

Imperative forms from the classical language are still used in the written language, or formal spoken style. Such forms exist only for Group II verbs and the irregular verb **suru**. For Group II verbs, the final -ro is replaced with -yo. For **suru**, the form is **seyo**.

a 県名を全部、あげよ。
**Kenmei o zenbu, ageyo.**
Give the names of all the prefectures.

b マフィアに法律はいらない。その場で射殺せよ。
**Mafia ni hōritsu wa iranai. Sono ba de shasatsu seyo.**
No laws are needed for the Mafia. Shoot [them] on the spot.

c その思い込みをまず捨てよ。
**Sono omoikomi o mazu suteyo.**
Discard that preconception first of all.

20.1.5 *Polite imperatives and commands: -nasai, -te kudasai, o/go-verb-stem kudasai*

Polite imperatives are formed by attaching the polite ending -**nasai** to V-stem, and commands by adding **kudasai** to V-**te**, or using **o/go**-V-stem kudasai (examples c and d). The rules for attaching o/go- are set out in 16.1.1 (see also 15.4.1.2).

a 「泣いてないで、部屋の掃除でもしなさい」「マラソンでもなさい」。（泣いてない＝泣いていない）
  **'Naitenai de, heya no sōji demo shinasai' 'Marason demo shinasai'. [naitenai = naite inai]**
  'Don't cry, clean up your room or something.' 'Go for a run or something.'

b A君もぜひ遊びに来て下さい。
  **A-kun mo zehi asobi ni kite kudasai.**
  You [= A-kun] too please do come and visit.

c どうぞ、ご安心下さい。
  **Dōzo, go-anshin kudasai.**
  Please don't worry (*lit.* "feel at ease").

d どうぞ、安らかにお眠りください。
  **Dōzo, yasuraka ni o-nemuri kudasai.**
  Please rest in peace.

## 20.1.6 Indirect imperatives or commands

Indirect (or quoted) commands are usually given in their communicative content only, by 'reducing' any polite forms to plain ones. That means that a command in the form -te kudasai 'please' is reduced to a plain imperative. (see 15.3.3.2).

a 以前のように早く嫁にいけといった周囲からのプレッシャーも弱くなり、女性も納得できる生き方をしたいと考えるようになった証拠。
  **Izen no yō ni hayaku yome ni <u>ike</u> to itta shūi kara no puresshā mo yowaku nari, josei mo nattoku dekiru ikikata o shitai to kangaeru yō ni natta shōko.**
  This is proof that the pressure from the family to get married quickly has weakened, and women too now want a way of life they find acceptable.

## 20.1.7 Negative imperatives

Negative imperatives ('don't . . .') can be formed by attaching **na** to V-**ru**. Used by itself, this is quite rude, and is therefore limited to such situations as the army and other mostly male bastions, and irate remarks to strangers. The combination **na yo**, on the other hand, gives the imperative a familiar or friendly ring. Note also the informal contraction V-**ru na** → V-**nna** (20.1.7.2 c).

In the media, the written-style form **nakare** is also used.

$\boxed{20.1.7.1}$ **na**

a 押すな。
**Osu na.**
Don't push!

b 電車の中でいちゃいちゃするな。
**Densha no naka de ichaicha suru na.**
Don't fondle [each other] on the train!

c 官僚は株に手を出すな。
**Kanryō wa kabu ni te o dasu na.**
Bureaucrats shouldn't dabble in shares!

d 心配なさるな。
**Shinpai nasaru na.**
Don't worry, please!

$\boxed{20.1.7.2}$ **na yo**

a おふくろ、死ぬなよ。
**Ofukuro, shinu na yo.**
Mother, don't die!

b いいと言うまで死ぬなよ。
**Ii to iu made shinu na yo.**
Don't die until I say so!

c …無理すんなよ。(すんな = するな)
**…muri sun na yo. (sun na = suru na)**
…don't overexert yourself!

d いきなり変なものを送るなよ。
**Ikinari hen na mono o okuru na yo.**
Don't just send something strange all of a sudden.

| 20.1.7.3 | **nakare** |

Apart from the usual way of forming negative imperatives, there is a written-style form, **nakare**, that is used as below.

| 20.1.7.3.1 | **nakare** |

| 20.1.7.3.1.1 | *V-*ru **nakare** |

**nakare** is a classical imperative form of **nai** that is often used in the media, etc. when addressing the reader. It is attached to V-**ru** and has the general meaning of 'don't'.

a 「これがパジャマ！？」と驚くなかれ。

**'Kore ga pajama!?' to odoroku nakare.**

You may not believe it, but these are pyjamas. (*lit.* "Don't be taken aback, saying, 'Are these pyjamas!'")

b おセンチ、と笑うなかれ。

**O-senchi, to warau nakare.**

Don't laugh, calling me sentimental.

## 20.2 Commands and requests

| 20.2.1 | *Commands* |

Commands (which can be positive or negative) can use imperative forms as such, but commonly the imperative forms of the performative verb **kureru** (**kure**) and its more formal equivalent **kudasaru** (**kudasai**) are used.

Commands with these performative verbs can be divided into those that ask others for something (N **o kure/kudasai**) and those that tell others to do (or not to do) something on their behalf, in which case V-**te kure/kudasai** is used.

| 20.2.1.1 | **kudasai/kure** |

| 20.2.1.1.1 | Noun **o kudasai/kure** |

This can only be used with positive commands, in the sense of 'give' (**kure**) and 'please give' (**kudasai**).

497

a 配当をくれ。
**Haitō o kure.**
Give us a dividend!

b 少し時間を下さい。
**Sukoshi jikan o kudasai.**
Please give me some time.

---

20.2.1.1.2 Verb-**te kudasai/kure**

Parallel to the difference between -**te kure** and -**te kudasai**, **kure** is more informal than **kudasai**, and is used between male friends or by senior men to their subordinates: 'please do'. The final particle **ne** can be attached to commands for a softer ring.

This can also be used for negative commands (examples c and d) (see 25.6.4.4, 15.3.3.3, 15.3.3.4).

a その時に二カ月分の家賃を払うから待ってくれ。
**Sono toki ni nikagetsu-bun no yachin o harau kara matte kure.**
I'll pay two months' rent at that time [= when I get money], so wait.

b きのう買ったのを見せて下さい。
**Kinō katta no o misete kudasai.**
Please show me the one you bought yesterday.

c 息は止めないで下さいねー。
**Iki wa tomenai de kudasai nē.**
Don't hold your breath, please.

d 余計なことをしてくれるなと、文句を言われた。
**Yokei na koto o shite kureru na to, monku o iwareta.**
He complained that I shouldn't give him help he didn't ask for.

---

20.2.1.2 Verb-**te (ne)**

V-**te (ne)** can be regarded as an informal abbreviation of -**te kudasai (ne)**, which is used by both men and women to friends, family, children and other intimate relations that are of equal or lower status or age (see 15.4).

For negative commands, -**nai de (ne)** (examples c and d) is used (see 25.6.4.4).

a 友達連れてきてね。
**Tomodachi tsurete kite ne.**
Bring some friends, will you.

b 会社つぶさないように頑張ってね。

**Kaisha tsubusanai yō ni ganbatte ne.**

Try your best so you won't make the company go bust.

c 先生には言わないで。

**Sensei ni wa iwanai de.**

Don't tell the teacher.

d お父さん、試合のチケットを忘れないでね。

**Otōsan, shiai no chiketto o wasurenai de ne.**

Daddy, don't forget the tickets for the match.

## 20.2.2 Requests

There are two basic types of request, one requesting an item and the other requesting an action (or service) to be performed.

For the former, **onegai shimasu** is used, whereas for the latter, **itadakitai/moraitai** and **hoshii** are attached to V-**te**, while **yō (ni) onegai shimasu** is attached to verbs or potential verbs.

Requests can also be made in question form.

Requesting an action can be positive or negative (i.e. requesting the listener to do, or *not* to do, something).

## 20.2.2.1 Noun/verbal noun (o) onegai shimasu

This is used to request items (things or persons) and also actions (in the case of verbal nouns). It usually translates as 'please', but note that the polite command (-**te**) **kudasai** also translates as 'please'.

*Note* – This can only be used with positive requests 'May I/we please have a/your N/VN', 'please'.

a 弁護士をお願いします。

**Bengoshi o onegai shimasu.**

May I have a lawyer, please.

b ご協力お願いします。

**Go-kyōryoku onegai shimasu.**

May I have your co-operation, please.

c それでは白石さん、支払いをお願いします。
**Sore de wa Shiraishi-san, shiharai o onegai shimasu.**
Well then, Mrs Shiraishi, please pay up.

20.2.2.2 *Verb-***te** *(+ performative verb/adjective)*

20.2.2.2.1 Verb-**te itadaki-tai/morai-tai**

Using a performative verb with the desiderative ending -**tai** (see 9.2), this can be attached to positive or negative verbs, in the meaning of 'I/we want you to (do/not do something for my/our benefit)' (see 15.6.1.2, 15.5.4).

a もう少し後にしていただきたい。
**Mō sukoshi ato ni shite itadakitai.**
I'd like to request you to put it off a little longer.

b 慎重に検討してもらいたい。
**Shinchō ni kentō shite moraitai.**
We'd like you to review it carefully.

c 決して腰くだけにならないでもらいたい。
**Kesshite koshikudake ni naranai de moraitai.**
We'd want them [= securities firms] to carry it [= restructuring] out
    decisively (*lit.* "want them not to give way").

d 首都圏の農地には手をつけないでいただきたい。
**Shuto-ken no nōchi ni wa te o tsukenai de itadakitai.**
We want you not to touch the farmland in the metropolitan area
    [= for land development].

20.2.2.2.2 Verb-**te hoshii**

This means 'I want you to (do/not do something for my/others' benefit)'. For negative requests, -**nai de hoshii** is used (for **hoshii**, see 9.2.3).

a ビデオを分けてほしい。
**Bideo o wakete hoshii.**
Would you spare me the videotape.

b 元気なので心配しないでほしい。
**Genki na node shinpai shinai de hoshii.**
I'm OK, so don't worry.

## 20.2.2.3 | Sentence **yō** (ni) onegai shimasu

yō is formally a noun, and is therefore preceded by forms that modify nouns, i.e. plain forms of verbs (see 9.5.6).

a 誤解のないようにお願いします。
   **Gokai no nai yō ni onegai shimasu.**
   Please do not misunderstand.

b 今後とも道徳教育の推進のため、特段の努力を図られるようお願いします。
   **Kongo tomo dōtoku kyōiku no suishin no tame, tokudan no doryoku o hakarareru yō onegai shimasu.**
   Please make a special effort to further moral education from now on, too.

## 20.2.2.4 | Requests in neg./pos./potential question form

### 20.2.2.4.1 | Verb-**te kure-nai/-masen ka**

Requests in negative question form 'will you' (plain form), 'would you' (-**masu** form) are more polite than V-**te kure** commands (see 15.3.3.1).

a 今度会ってくれませんか。
   **Kondo atte kuremasen ka.**
   Would you meet me sometime?

### 20.2.2.4.2 | Verb-**te moraenai ka (na)**

In potential negative question form, -**te moraeru** is used to make a polite request 'can we ask you to', 'could we get you to', 'would you'. With **ka na** rather than **ka**, the meaning is 'I wonder' (see 15.5.3.2).

a 一緒に応援してもらえないか。
   **Issho ni ōen shite moraenai ka.**
   Would you join in supporting us?

b あの人に地元の建設会社を紹介してもらえないかな。
   **Ano hito ni jimoto no kensetsu-gaisha o shōkai shite moraenai ka na.**
   Could I get this man to introduce me to a local construction company, I wonder.

20.2.2.4.3 | Verb-**te itadake-ru/-masu ka/-nai/-masen ka**

In positive or negative potential question form, this indicates a very polite request 'could you please' (**itadaku** being more polite than **morau**) (see 15.6.2.1).

a 返事はちょっと待っていただけますか。
**Henji wa chotto matte itadakemasu ka.**
Could I ask you to wait a little while for my answer?

# Chapter 21

# *Quotation:* to, to iu, tte *and* ni yoru to

## 21.1 to

The quotation particle **to**, which is distinct from the case particle **to**, is used for quoting the content of a communication (with a verb of communication, such as **iu** 'say', **hanasu** 'speak', 'tell' etc.) or thought (with a verb of thinking, such as **omou** 'feel', 'think', **kangaeru** 'think'), etc., in both direct and indirect quotations (see 7.6.4.2.1, 7.6.4.2.2).

The verb of thought can be omitted, which gives a sense of 'with the intention of' (example 21.1.1a).

In the media especially, the phrase **to no koto** (+ copula) is commonly used instead of **to iu**, etc.

The particle **to** is also used in the phrase **to iu**, which is used in a variety of ways, from quotation to modification of nouns.

### 21.1.1 Clause to (ellipted verb)

a 新しい展開を図ろうと、名称変更に踏み切った。
  **Atarashii tenkai o hakarō to, meishō henkō ni fumikitta.**
  They took the step of changing the name, with the intention of
    opening up about new developments.

21
Quotation:
to, to iu, tte
and ni yoru to

| 21.1.2 | *Clause* to no koto da

a この日は結婚式の二次会とのことで、なかなかのにぎわい。

**Kono hi wa kekkonshiki no nijikai to no koto de, nakanaka no
nigiwai.**

On that day [the bar] had a party from a wedding, they said, so it
[= the bar] was quite lively.

b 礼を言ったら、ドイツでは男が家事をするのは当たり前とのこと。

**Rei o ittara, Doitsu de wa otoko ga kaji o suru no wa
atarimae to no koto.**

When we thanked him, he said that in Germany it was normal for
a man to do housework.

c 先日、アナウンサーなしの野球中継放送があった。見た人の話
では、静かでなかなかよかったとのこと。

**Senjitsu, anaunsā nashi no yakyū chūkei hōsō ga atta. Mita hito
no hanashi de wa, shizuka de nakanaka yokatta to no koto.**

The other day, there was a live baseball broadcast without a commentator.
According to those who watched it, it was nice and quiet.

d 「当面はソロ活動に専念する」とのことだ。

**'Tōmen wa soro katsudō ni sennen suru' to no koto da.**

He says 'For the time being, I will concentrate on solo performances'.

## 21.2　to iu

**to iu** consists of the quotation particle **to** and the verb **iu** 'say'. It has a
wide range of functions, ranging from direct and indirect quotation to
indicating that something is based on hearsay.

**to iu** is preceded by plain forms of V/Adj/**na**-Adj/N (in some usages, **da** or
**to iu** can follow N).

| 21.2.1 | *Noun* to iu

This combination has the meaning 'is called'.

a 子供の名前を慎二という。

**Kodomo no namae o Shinji to iu.**

The (*lit.* "name of the") child is called Shinji.

## 21.2.2 Sentence **to iu**

This indicates a direct or indirect quotation (see 7.6.4.2).

### 21.2.2.1 Sentence (**da**) **to iu**

With a quotation, the meaning is 's/he said "..."', etc. After an indirect quotation, it translates as 'they say', 'it is said', 's/he says that . . .'.

a 「父は解剖学の偉大な先生だった」という。
 **'Chichi wa kaibōgaku no idai na sensei datta' to iu.**
 He says, 'Father was an eminent professor of anatomy'.

b 最も高い部屋は一億円を超えるという。
 **Mottomo takai heya wa ichioku-en o koeru to iu.**
 They say that the most expensive room is over ¥100 million.

c 警笛を鳴らし、急ブレーキをかけたが間に合わなかったという。
 **Keiteki o narashi, kyūburēki o kaketa ga ma ni awanakatta
 to iu.**
 He says that he blew the horn and applied the emergency brakes
 but didn't make it.

### 21.2.2.2 Clause (**da**) **tte iu**

**tte** is an informal variant of **to** (see 21.1).

a 天気予報であさっては雨だって言ってたから。(てた = ていた)
 **Tenki yohō de asatte wa ame da tte itteta kara.**
 **[teta = te ita]**
 Because the weather forecast said that the day after tomorrow
 it'll rain.

b 「飛んでいる飛行機を見ながら、『あの飛行機のエンジンはオレが
 つくったんだ』って言ってみたいんですよ」。
 **'Tonde iru hikōki o minagara, "Ano hikōki no enjin wa ore
 ga tsukutta n da" tte itte mitai n desu yo'.**
 Looking at a flying aircraft, I'd like to say, 'I built the engine of that
 aircraft'.

**21**
Quotation:
to, to iu, tte
and ni yoru to

| 21.2.2.3 | *Clause* (**da**) **to iwarete iru** |

**iwarete iru** is the passive **-te iru** form of **iu**, expressing a passive state 'it's (being) said' (see 12, 8.4).

a 大型動物は普通、一つの地域で百頭を切ると絶滅すると言われている。

**Ōgata dōbutsu wa futsū, hitotsu no chiiki de hyakutō o kiru to zetsumetsu suru to iwarete iru.**

It is said that large animals usually become extinct when they fall to under 100 head per area.

b 不況、不況と言われているが、企業にとっては今がチャンス。

**Fukyō, fukyō to iwarete iru ga, kigyō ni totte wa ima ga chansu.**

It's said that it's a bad recession, but for business now is a time of opportunity.

c 米国などでは、脱税は非常に恥ずかしい犯罪だと言われている。

**Beikoku nado de wa, datsuzei wa hijō ni hazukashii hanzai da to iwarete iru.**

It is said that in the US, tax fraud is a crime to be very ashamed of.

| 21.2.3 | *Noun/clause* **to iu/tte** *N* |

| 21.2.3.1 | *Noun 1* **to iu** *noun 2* |

N1 explains the content of N2 by name 'N2 (named) N1', 'N2 (of/that is) N1' (see also 1.2).

a アップル、IBMという情報機器メーカー

**Appuru, IBM to iu jōhō kiki mēkā**

The information appliance makers Apple and IBM ('and' = indicated by comma)

b 世界中がJリーグという新しいマーケットに注目している。

**Sekai-jū ga Jei-rīgu to iu atarashii māketto ni chūmoku shite iru.**

The world is watching the new market that is the J-League.

### 21.2.3.2 | Clause **to iu/tte** noun

**to iu** (and its informal variant **tte**, example d) explains the content of N 'the N which says', 'the N of'.

a 犬の嗅覚は人間の百万倍以上、十億倍という説もある。

 **Inu no kyūkaku wa ningen no hyakuman-bai ijō, jūoku-bai to iu setsu mo aru.**

 There is also a theory saying that a dog's sense of smell is a million times, 100 million times that of a human being.

b 三十年後には四人に一人が高齢者という社会が確実にやってくる。

 **Sanjūnen-go ni wa yonin ni hitori ga kōreisha to iu shakai ga kakujitsu ni yatte kuru.**

 In 30 years, the sort of society where one in four people is elderly, will come without fail.

c 本社をどこに置くのがいいかという問題もある。

 **Honsha o doko ni oku no ga ii ka to iu mondai mo aru.**

 There is also the problem of where best to position the main firm.

d 「小学校でも早寝早起きと教わっただろ」「パパ、歴史は夜つくら れるって言葉知らないの」

 **'Shōgakkō de mo hayane hayaoki to osowatta daro'. 'Papa, rekishi wa yoru tsukurareru tte kotoba shiranai no'**

 'At primary school too, no doubt you were taught [the maxim of] going to bed early and rising early.' 'Papa, don't you know the saying "History is made at night"?'

### 21.2.4 | Noun/clause **to iu no wa**

### 21.2.4.1 | Noun/clause **to iu no wa**, . . . predicate

This is used to explain the nature or essence of something 'is' (see 22.3.1).

a 高齢化社会というのは、労働力が不足する社会でもある。

 **Kōrei-ka shakai to iu no wa, rōdō-ryoku ga fusoku suru shakai de mo aru.**

 An ageing society is also a society lacking manpower.

b 言葉というのは、あんまり安っぽく使うと値打ちが下がります。

 **Kotoba to iu no wa, anmari yasuppoku tsukau to neuchi ga sagarimasu.**

 Words depreciate in value if you use them too cheaply.

507

21
Quotation:
to, to iu, tte
and ni yoru to

*Noun/clause* **to iu no wa...kara**

This is used to explain the nature or essence of something, by giving a reason (see 26.5.2).

a 植物というのは手をかければこたえてくれるからうれしい。

**Shokubutsu to iu no wa te o kakereba kotaete kureru kara ureshii.**

Plants give joy because they respond if you look after them.

b 猫が顔を洗うと雨になるというのは、湿度が上がると、ノミの活動が活発になるからといわれている。

**Neko ga kao o arau to ame ni naru to iu no wa, shitsudo ga agaru to, nomi no katsudō ga kappatsu ni naru kara to iwarete iru.**

The reason why they say that when cats wash their faces it's going to rain is supposed to be because fleas become active when humidity rises.

21.2.5 *Clause* **to iu koto wa**

21.2.5.1 *Clause* **(da) to iu koto wa ...**

Like **koto** by itself, **to iu koto** nominalizes the sentence it is attached to, to form a complement clause 'the fact that' (see 22.2, 22.3.2).

a 国際協調を崩してはならないということは、明らかである。

**Kokusai kyōchō o kuzushite wa naranai to iu koto wa, akiraka de aru.**

It is obvious that we mustn't damage international co-operation.

b 人が人の肉を食うなどということは、自由な流通システムがあれば起こりませんよ。

**Hito ga hito no niku o kuu nado to iu koto wa, jiyū na ryūtsū shisutemu ga areba okorimasen yo.**

Things like cannibalism do not happen if there is a system of free distribution.

21.2.5.2 *Clause* **(da) to iu koto wa (...) nai**

This means 'it's not (the case) that', 'it doesn't happen' (see 21.2.9.2).

a 消費者は価格に敏感になっているが、安ければなんでもいいということはない。

**Shōhisha wa kakaku ni binkan ni natte iru ga, yasukereba nan demo ii to iu koto wa nai.**

The consumers have become sensitive to price, but it's not the case that everything goes as long as it's cheap.

b アジアと米国との対立ということは全くなかった。

**Ajia to Beikoku to no tairitsu to iu koto wa mattaku nakatta.**

A confrontation between Asia and the US didn't happen.

## 21.2.6 Clause to iu koto ni naru

Like **koto ni naru**, this indicates the meaning of 'it comes about', 'end up doing/being' (see 22.3.2.3.7).

a だからいつも宵張りの朝寝坊ということになる。

**Da kara itsu mo yoippari no asa-nebō to iu koto ni naru.**

Therefore [= body clock running late] one always ends up having late nights and sleeping in the next day.

b 砂漠の真ん中に乗り継ぎ専用のドデカイ空港を開発する。
···これこそ究極の国際スーパーハブ空港ということになる。

**Sabaku no mannaka ni noritsugi senyō no dodekai kūkō o kaihatsu suru. Kore koso kyūkyoku no kokusai sūpāhabu kūkō to iu koto ni naru.**

They will develop an enormous airport specializing in changing planes in the middle of the desert.... This will be the ultimate super-hub airport.

## 21.2.7 to iu koto wa

This construction (meaning 'that is to say') is used like a conjunction (see 24.6).

a ということは、私はオーストラリアで「ヨシオ・スギモト」を名乗るかわりに、ヒラリー・クリントンは日本語表記では、「クリントン・ヒラリー」と表記すればいいということだ。

**To iu koto wa, watashi wa Ōsutoraria de 'Yoshio Sugimoto' o nanoru kawari ni, Hirarī Kurinton wa Nihongo hyōki de wa 'Kurinton Hirarī' to hyōki sureba ii to iu koto da.**

[The order of people's names should follow the rules of the language in which they're used:] That is to say, as I call myself 'Yoshio Sugimoto' in Australia, so Hillary Clinton in Japanese order should be written 'Clinton Hillary'.

**21**

Quotation:
to, to iu, tte
and ni yoru to

*Noun/clause* **to iu mono**

21.2.8.1 *Noun* **to iu mono wa**...*predicate*

Similar **to iu no wa**, this also explains the nature of something 'is' (see 21.2.4).

a 「カネというものは恐ろしい」と思う時もあった。
   **'Kane to iu mono wa osoroshii' to omou toki mo atta.**
   There were times when I thought that money was frightening.
   [= Retrieving debts]

b 博物館というものは、永遠に未完成な存在。
   **Hakubutsukan to iu mono wa, eien ni mikansei na sonzai.**
   Museums are forever incomplete entities.

c 風俗や習慣は違っても、人情というものはどこへいっても同じですね。
   **Fūzoku ya shūkan wa chigatte mo, ninjō to iu mono wa doko e itte mo onaji desu ne.**
   Even if manners and customs differ, human feelings are the same wherever you go, right?

21.2.8.2 *Noun/clause/***to iu mono**

Unlike **kara** by itself, which only indicates the idea of time passed 'since', the implication with **to iu mono** is that is has been an inordinately long time 'ever since', 'over (the period that)' (see 26.5.2).

a 母はこちらに来てからというもの、テレビだけが友人の状態です。
   **haha wa kochira ni kite kara to iu mono terebi dake ga yūjin no jōtai desu.**
   Ever since Mother came here, she has been in a state where her only friend is the TV.

b A子さんが入社して十三年間というもの、新たな女性の管理職登用はなかった。
   **A-ko-san ga nyūsha shite jūsannen-kan to iu mono, aratana josei no kanrishoku tōyō wa nakatta.**
   Throughout the whole 13-year period since A-ko-san joined the company, there has been no new appointment of a woman to a management post.

### 21.2.9 Clause to iu wake

### 21.2.9.1 Clause to iu wake da

This is used when drawing a conclusion from what has been said earlier 'so, what you are saying is' (see 9.6.4).

a 同じ犬でも人気が出て手に入りにくくなると値段が上がるという わけだ。

**Onaji inu demo ninki ga dete te ni hairi-nikuku naru to nedan ga agaru to iu wake da.**

So, what you're saying is that once it gets popular and difficult to get, the same [kind of] dog rises in price.

b 「香港に投資することは、中国全体に投資すること」という わけだ。

**'Honkon ni tōshi suru koto wa, chūgoku zentai ni tōshi suru koto' to iu wake da.**

So, what you're saying is 'investing in Hong Kong amounts to investing in China as a whole'.

### 21.2.9.2 Clause to iu wake de wa nai

In the negative, the meaning is 'it's not the case that'.

a 安いから車が売れるというわけではない。

**Yasui kara kuruma ga ureru to iu wake de wa nai.**

It's not the case that cars sell [just] because they are cheap.

b 大卒女性を本格的に採用し始めてから十年たつが、処遇は男性と 同じというわけではない。

**Daisotsu josei o honkaku-teki ni saiyō shi-hajimete kara jūnen tatsu ga, shogū wa dansei to onaji to iu wake dewa nai.**

It's been ten years since they started to employ female graduates in earnest, but it's not the case that their treatment is the same as the men's.

21
Quotation:
to, to iu, tte
and ni yoru to

### 21.2.10 | Noun to iu yori (mo/wa)

Like the comparative particle **yori** by itself, this indicates comparison 'rather than' (see 2.9.2, 6.7).

a 見てくれはリンゴというより、ナシに近い。
   **Mitekure wa ringo to iu yori nashi ni chikai.**
   The appearance is closer to a [Japanese] pear than an apple.

b バイタリティーあふれる語り口は、聖職者というよりはビジネス
   マンのようだ。
   **Baitaritī afureru katarikuchi wa, seishokusha to iu yori wa
   bijinesuman no yō da.**
   His way of telling a story, which is brimming with vitality, is more
   reminiscent of a businessman than a priest.

### 21.2.11 | Noun to iu to, ... ga, ...

N **to iu to** is similar to N **(to) wa**, which is used to comment on some entity
or activity X generically 'N is . . . , but', followed by a qualifying statement.

a 乗馬というと、はた目には何でもないように見えるが、両足に常
   に力を込め、体を安定させていなければならない。
   **Jōba to iu to, hatame ni wa nan demo nai yō ni mieru ga,
   ryōashi ni tsune ni chikara o kome, karada o antei sasete
   inakereba naranai.**
   Riding looks dead easy to the onlooker, but one needs to keep both
   legs tense and one's body stable.

b 美術館というと作品になかなか近付けないが、この美術館は触っ
   ても大丈夫。
   **Bijutsukan to iu to sakuhin ni nakanaka chikazukenai ga, kono
   bijutsukan wa sawatte mo daijōbu.**
   Art galleries don't usually let you get close to the works, but in this
   art gallery it's OK to touch [them].

### 21.2.12 | Verb/adjective/na-adjective/noun to iu ka,
   verb/adjective/na-adjective/noun to iu ka

This is used when searching for an appropriate way of describing something
'how shall one describe it – A or B?'. It is often followed by some conclusion (examples b and c).

a はっきりした顔というか、シンプルな顔というか。

**Hakkiri shita kao to iu ka, shinpuru na kao to iu ka.**

How shall I describe it – a distinct face, or a simple face?

b 痛快というか、不遜（ふそん）というか、勇ましい役だ。

**Tsūkai to iu ka, fuson to iu ka, isamashii yaku da.**

It's thrilling or perhaps haughty – anyhow, it's a dashing part.

c 私は、どちらかというと、ピュアというか白というか、どんな役にも染まることができると思います。

**Watashi wa, dochira ka to iu to, pyua to iu ka shiro to iu ka, donna yaku ni mo somaru koto ga dekiru to omoimasu.**

I think that if anything, I'm pure or maybe white, so I can be coloured by any part [= actress].

### 21.2.13 | Clause **to wa ie**

The form **ie** is a classical form of the verb **iu**, that expresses a contrastive conjunction 'but'. The combination means literally "although one says", i.e. 'may be . . . but', 'it may be A, but in fact it's no more than B' (see 24.4).

a 一種のコンピューターとは言え、ゲーム機器もしょせんは玩具。

**Isshu no konpyūtā to wa ie, gēmu kiki mo shosen wa gangu.**

It may be a kind of computer, but game appliances are after all [no more than] toys.

b 大型連休とは言え、不景気も手伝ってやはり主流はミニ旅行。

**Ōgata renkyū to wa ie, fukeiki mo tetsudatte yahari shuryū wa mini ryokō.**

It may be a long string of holidays, but partly through the effects of the recession the trend is for short trips.

### 21.2.14 | **to ieba, sō ieba**

(See 26.1.1.3.3, 26.1.1.3.4.)

## 21.3 **tte/te**

**tte/te** is a common colloquial equivalent of **to**, **to iu** or (**to iu no**) **wa** (see 21.1, 21.2, 21.2.4).

*Note* – after 何 (**nan**), **tte** becomes **te**, resulting in **nante**.

21
Quotation:
to, to iu, tte
and ni yoru to

### 21.3.1 Equivalent of *to*

In example a, **nante** is an equivalent of **nan to**, i.e. **nan** + quotation particle. In example c, **nante**, preceding an evaluatory adjective, is emphatic, expressing astonishment.

a 僕の名字にちゃんと変えてもらわないと、田舎の両親に何て言われるか……。

**Boku no myōji ni chanto kaete morawanai to, inaka no ryōshin ni nan te iwareru ka....**

Unless you change your surname to mine, God knows what my traditional-minded parents will say to me...

b 今年のクリスマスは家でホームパーティーしようって言ったのは君だぜ。

**Kotoshi no kurisumasu wa ie de hōmu pātī shiyo tte itta no wa kimi da ze.**

It was you who said that this Christmas we should have a house party.

c 人間って何て美しいんでしょう。まあ、すばらしい新世界。

**Ningen tte nante utsukushii n deshō. Mā, subarashii shin-sekai.**

How beauteous mankind is! O brave new world [that has such people in it]! (From Shakespeare's *The Tempest*) [Re. the first **tte**, see 21.3.3 c below]

### 21.3.2 Equivalent of *to iu*

As in 21.3.1 c, **nante** combines here with an evaluatory adjective, emphasizing its meaning. Unlike 21.3.1 c, however, these adjectives are followed by a noun (hence the equivalent **to iu** . . . N).

Note also **te koto wa** (= **to iu koto wa**) in example c, which is used like a conjunction (see 21.2.7, 24.6).

a 恐れ入りましたって感じ。

**Osore irimashita tte kanji.**

One's staggered (*lit.* "The feeling's one of being staggered").

b 役者が役者をやるってのは難しいです。

**Yakusha ga yakusha o yaru tte no wa muzukashii desu.**

An actor playing an actor – that's difficult.

c てことは、私もあと何年かしたらああなるってことなのかしら？
(てことは＝ということは)

**Te koto wa, watashi mo ato nannen ka shitara ā naru tte
koto na no kashira.**

Does that mean that in a few years I'll end up like that [= **o-tsubone-
san**, a grumbling middle-aged female office worker disliked by all]
too?

d 悲しみの両親、「何てむごいこと・・・」―三重バラバラ事件。

**Kanashimi no ryōshin, 'Nante mugoi koto …' —
Mie barabara jiken.**

The saddened parents [said], 'What a cruel thing …' –
the dismembered body case in Mie [prefecture].

---

## 21.3.3 Equivalent of (to iu no) wa

After a noun (examples c, e), the equivalent can be thought of as either
wa or to iu no wa.

a 出生率が1.5を下回るって本当ですか。

**Shussei-ritsu ga ittengo o shitamawaru tte
hontō desu ka.**

Is it true that the birth rate will drop below 1.5?

b 人々に感動や夢を与えるってスゴイ。

**Hitobito ni kandō ya yume o ataeru tte sugoi.**

Touching people's hearts and giving them dreams,
that's wonderful.

c エプロン姿のお父さんって「かっこいい」。

**Epuron sugata no otōsan tte 'kakko ii'.**

Daddy wearing an apron – that's 'cool'.

d 記者団に対し「どうするかって？決めにゃーなー」
(にゃーなー ＝ なければならないなぁ)

**Kishadan ni taishi 'Dō suru ka tte? Kimenyā nā.'
[nyā nā = nakereba naranai nā]**

To the press corps [he said] 'What are we going to do?
We've got to decide.'

e 「私って何？」「何ができるの？」

**'Watashi tte nani?' 'Nani ga dekiru no?'**

'What am I?' 'What can I achieve?'

**21**
Quotation:
to, to iu, tte
and ni yoru to

## 21.4 ni yoru to **and** de wa: **source of information**

### 21.4.1 ni yoru to

**ni yoru to** (less commonly **ni yoreba**) is added directly to nouns to indicate the source of information 'according to'. Because such situations, by their nature, express hearsay, it is normal to complete the sentence with **sō** (examples a, d and e) or **rashii** (examples b and c); in English, this use of **sō** and **rashii** does not normally require translation.

Synonymous is the combination **de wa** (for restrictions on its use in comparison to **ni yoru to** and **ni yoreba**, see 21.4.2).

Rather than **sō** or **rashii**, ordinary verb forms are also used (example f), which is similar to English usage.

Note also the combination **tokoro ni yoru to** (example g), which is also used widely in the media, attached to verbs of communication.

*Note 1* – -**tte** is too informal to be used in source of information sentences.

*Note 2* – **ni yoru to** and **ni yotte** are often confused by English speakers because they sound similar, and both are translated as 'according to'. They are *not* interchangeable. **ni yoru to** expresses source of information, while **ni yotte** expresses basis of difference.

a 田村さんによれば、「ある流通業者が安売りすると、他の業者も
　その値段で売りたいと要望してくる」そうだ。
   **Tamura-san ni yoreba, 'Aru ryūtsū gyōsha ga yasuuri suru to,
   hoka no gyōsha mo sono nedan de uri-tai to yōbō shite
   kuru' sō da.**
   According to Tamura-san, 'When one distributor sells [something]
   cheaper, the others also ask to sell it at that price'.

b 伊予署の調べでは、双方の安全不確認が原因らしい。
   **Iyo-sho no shirabe de wa, sōhō no anzen fu-kakunin ga
   gen'in rashii.**
   According to the Iyo Police Station enquiry, the cause appears to be
   both parties' failure to check that it was safe to proceed.

c 前橋署によると、米田さんは一人でアユ釣りに来て川に入って転
  倒、流されたらしい。

  **Maebashi-sho ni yoru to, Yoneda-san wa hitori de ayutsuri ni
  kite kawa ni haitte tentō, nagasareta rashii.**

  According to Maebashi Police Station, Mr Yoneda apparently came
  alone and got into the river to fish for sweetfish; [he then] fell
  over and got washed away.

d 武田さんによると、「よく運動するため、筋繊維がしまって脂肪
  の質が良く、歯触りもいい」そうだ。

  **Takeda-san ni yoru to, 'Yoku undō suru tame, kinsen'i ga
  shimatte shibō no shitsu ga yoku, hazawari mo ii' sō da.**

  According to Mr Takeda 'Because they [= pigs] move around a lot,
  the muscle fibres are tight, the fat's good quality, and the texture's
  good too'.

e 都教育庁によると、今後十年間に進学する生徒数は約三割減りそ
  うだ。

  **To-kyōiku-chō ni yoru to, kongo jūnen-kan ni shingaku suru
  seito-sū wa yaku sanwari herisō da.**

  According to the Metropolitan Education Agency, the number of pupils
  who will go on to high school during the coming ten years is likely
  to decrease by 30 per cent.

f 愛知県警安城署の調べによると、二人組は小池さんらの前に飛び
  出し、前を走っていた妻の自転車のカゴから袋をひったくった。

  **Aichi-ken-kei Anjō-sho no shirabe ni yoru to, futari-gumi wa
  Koike-san-ra no mae ni tobidashi, mae o hashitte ita tsuma
  no jitensha no kago kara fukuro o hittakutta.**

  According to the Aki station of the Aichi Prefectural Police, the two
  jumped in front of the Koikes, and snatched the bag from
  the bicycle basket of the wife, who was riding in front.

g ここカタールの首都ドーハの新空港ですが、昨年末から色々なプ
  レス発表で報道されているところによると、2012年12月には開
  港するとの情報です。

  **Koko Katāru no shuto Dōha no shin-kūkō desu ga, sakunen-
  matsu kara iroiro na puresu-happyō de hōdō sarete iru
  tokoro ni yoru to, nisenjūni-nen jūnigatsu ni wa kaikō
  suru to no jōhō desu.**

  Regarding the new airport of the capital Doha here in Qatar, according
  to what has been reported in various press releases since the end
  of last year, the information is that it will open in December 2012.

ni yoru to
and de wa:
source of
information

21

Quotation:
to, to iu, tte
and ni yoru to

**21.4.2** de wa

Other than being simply a regular combination of **de** [case particle or copula] + **wa** [adverbial particle], **de wa** also has the specialized use of indicating source of information (see 9.5.2.3). In this use it is synonymous with **ni yoru to** and **ni yoreba**, but can only be added to non-human sources (see 21.4.1).

a ✐テレビでは     **terebi de wa**     according to the TV

But *not*

b ✐ Suzuki-san     **de wa**

With human sources, **hanashi** or an other appropriate noun (**shirabe**, etc.) must be inserted.

c 天野技官の話では、アパレルなどは「JISを厳密に守った服は売れない」とまで主張しているそうだ。
**Amano gikan no hanashi de wa, apareru nado wa 'JIS o genmitsu ni mamotta fuku wa urenai' to made shuchō shite iru sō da.**
According to what technical officer Amano says, garment
     [maufacturers] even claim that clothing that follows the JIS [= Japan
     Industrial Standard] to the letter doesn't sell.

# Chapter 22

# *Nominalizations*

## 22.1   Noun modification and relative clauses

Formally, there is no distinction between noun modification by verbs and adjectives, and relative clauses.

For the various way of modifying a noun, see 6.6. In Japanese, the modifying always precedes the modified, so in case of modified nouns, a verb, adjective, **na-** or **no-**adjective, or a clause ending in a verb, adjective or **na-**adjective in normal word order is simply placed before a following noun.

Unlike relative clauses in English, Japanese relative clauses are a variant of noun modification, and therefore Japanese has no relative pronouns, or changes in word order. Compare the English relative clause with its Japanese equivalent (based on example 22.1.1 a).

a   Iguchi, who has come from Tokyo.
a′  **Tokyo kara kita Iguchi.**

The English sentence has a head noun ('Iguchi', a name in this case), which is followed by a relative pronoun ('who'), and the remaining relative clause ('has come from Tokyo'). In Japanese, the order is reversed in that **Iguchi** comes last, and the relative clause without the relative pronoun is simply placed ahead of the head noun.

As there are no relative pronouns (or any other indication of the case relation between the modifying clause and the noun it modifies), it is sometimes only from the context (or knowledge of the world) that this relationship can be determined.

In the following example, for instance, the modifying section (given in [ ]), modifies the 'head noun' (= modified noun) **dokusha** (which in turn is modified by **aru** 'a certain'). In this sentence, **tegami ga todoita aru dokusha** could mean 'A certain reader, <u>who</u> received a letter recently, . . .', but in the context of a newspaper column, the interpretation below is the correct one.

b　最近手紙が届いたある読者は「・・・」と喝破している。
　　**[Saikin tegami ga todoita] aru dokusha wa '...' to kappa shite iru. [aru N = a certain N]**
　　A certain reader, <u>from whom I/we</u> received a letter recently, claims '...'

There is also no formal distinction between 'restrictive' and 'non-restrictive' relative clauses (in English, non-restrictive relative clauses are set off by comma intonation, and written between commas). In 22.1.1 below, examples b, e, f are restrictive, whereas examples a, d, g are non-restrictive (in their translation equivalents only!).

When the noun-modifying clause ends in -**ta**, the meaning differs depending on whether -**ta** indicates a state, or completion of action. In 22.1.1 a, -**ta** indicates completion, but in 22.1.1 b it indicates a state, i.e. describes *what sort of* burglars they are. In a finite (i.e. non-noun-modifying) sentence this would be expressed with -**te iru** (**takuhaibin o yosōtte iru** 'they are dressed as a delivery service') (see 8.2.3, 1.7).

There is also a variant called pseudo-relatives (see 22.1.2).

| 22.1.1 | *Relative clauses* |

A look at the examples a–g below show that the English translation of Japanese relative clauses can range from rendering with relative pronouns (who, etc.) to cases where the modifying section (again given in [ ]) is translated by just a participle (example c).

Note example g, where the noun **josei** is modified by two modifying sections, **heya kara deyō to shinakatta** and **karui chihōshō no**.

a　東京から来た井口です。
　　**[Tōkyō kara kita] Iguchi desu.**
　　I'm Iguchi, [who has come from Tokyo].

b　最近、宅配便を装った強盗が出るそうだ。
　　**Saikin, [takuhaibin o yosōtta] gōtō ga deru sō da.**
　　Recently, there are supposed to be burglars [who are dressed as a home delivery service].

c 勝つゴルフが出来ない。

**[Katsu] gorufu ga dekinai.**

I can't play [winning] golf.

d 怖くなった主婦は、ほぼ全額を支払った。

**[Kowaku natta] shufu wa, hobo zengaku o shiharatta.**

The housewife, [who got frightened], paid more or less
the whole amount.

e ビルの揺れで船酔いを起こす人もいるそうだ。

**[Biru no yure de funayoi o okosu] hito mo iru sō da.**

There are supposed to be people [who get seasick from the swaying
of the building].

f 新幹線の座席で靴を脱いで素足を足台に乗せている婦人を見ると
西欧人はギョッとするそうだ。

**[Shinkansen no zaseki de kutsu o nuide suashi o ashidai
ni nosete iru] fujin o miru to seiō-jin wa gyotto suru
sō da.**

Western Europeans are said to be flabbergasted when they see ladies
[who take their shoes off on the bullet train and rest their bare
feet up on the footrest].

g 部屋から出ようとしなかった軽い痴ほう症の女性が車いすで食堂
に出てきて食事をするようになった。

**[Heya kara deyō to shinakatta] [karui chihōshō no] josei
ga kurumaisu de shokudō ni dete kite shokuji o suru
yō ni natta.**

A woman [with slight dementia], [who had made no attempt to
come out of her room], now began to appear in her wheelchair
in the refectory to eat.

## 22.1.2 Pseudo-relative clauses

Pseudo-relative clauses are sentences that are constructed like relative
clauses, but where the modified (or head) noun is a relational noun, time
noun or noun of amount (see 14.1.1.2.2).

a 眠れぬ夜が続いている。

**[Nemurenu] yoru ga tsuzuite iru.**

Nights [when one can't sleep] are continuing.

b だから今度は、そうじゃなくなる始まりではないでしょうか。
**Da kara kondo wa, [sō ja naku naru] hajimari de wa nai
deshō ka.**
So, I wonder if this mightn't be the start [of things no longer being
the way they were] (= citizens being expected to be passive).

c [西洋人がベルと言い、日本人が鐘という時、それぞれの頭の中で
鳴る鐘の音は違う。
**[Seiōjin ga beru to ii, Nihonjin ga kane to iu] toki, sorezore
no atama no naka de naru kane no oto wa chigau.**
When [= **toki**] [Western Europeans say 'bell', and Japanese say *kane* ('bell')],
the sound of the bell ringing in their respective heads is different.

Pseudo-relative clauses are especially common with the time noun **toki**
'time'. As a noun, it is usually written with the *kanji* 時 or in *hiragana*
(とき), whereas as a conjunctive particle (26.2) it nowadays tends to be
written in *hiragana* only. However, the distinction is not always clear, there
being examples of **toki** that are translated as 'when' or 'the time when'.
Being formally a noun, when **toki** is modified by a clause in such sentences
(examples f–i), it acts as a relative clause head noun, just like any other
noun (see 22.1.1).

d こんな時に歌なんて……。
**Konna toki ni uta nante ...**
Singing at a [difficult] time like this? [That's hard to believe.]

e 何であの時、入院なんかしたんだろう。
**Nande ano toki, nyūin nanka shita n darō.**
Why did I get myself hospitalized that time, I wonder.

f とうとうユニホームを脱ぐときが来た。
**Tōtō [unihōmu o nugu] toki ga kita.**
Finally the time has come to take off the uniform [= retire].

g 借金は15年前に家を新築したときのローンの残り。
**Shakkin wa [jūgonen mae ni ie o shinchiku shita] toki no rōn
no nokori.**
The debt is the remainder of the loan [taken out] when we rebuilt
our house 15 years ago.

h 人間生きていればつらい目にあうときも落ち込むときもある。
**Ningen ikite ireba [tsurai me ni au] toki mo [ochikomu] toki
mo aru.**
As long as one is alive, there are times when things are hard and
times when one feels down.

i 学生と接しているときが一番楽しいという教員はいっぱいいる。

**[Gakusei to sesshite iru] toki ga ichiban tanoshii to iu kyōin wa ippai iru.**

There are many teachers who feel that the time when they are in contact with the students is the most enjoyable of all.

j 赤ん坊の時に抱かれた記憶もなく、父の愛情を実感できずにいた。

**[Akanbō no toki ni dakareta] kioku mo naku, chichi no aijō o jikkan dekizu ni ita.**

I have no memories of being cuddled when I was a baby, and was unable to realize my father's love.

---

22.1.3 *Noun modification/relative clauses in question form*

In written language only, it is possible to modify a noun or noun phrase by a relative clause etc. that ends with a question mark, in the sense of 'which may be N'.

a 官僚主義が生んだ？「現代版ちょんまげ」

**[Kanryō shugi ga unda?] 'Gendai-ban chonmage'.**

[The male company worker's uniform hairstyle is a] 'Present-day topknot', which may have been produced by the bureaucratic system.

---

## 22.2 Complement and cleft sentences

### 22.2.1 *Complement sentences*

Where a simple sentence has just a NP consisting of noun + particle, a *complement sentence* contains instead a whole clause which has been converted (nominalized) into a NP by **no** or **koto**, for example with the na-Adj **suki** in example a. The valency (see 7.2) of **suki** requires the case particle **ga** to mark the object of one's liking. In the first sentence, that object (in [ ]) is a noun (**sora** 'the sky'), but the two following sentences have one complement clause each (**karada o ugokasu no**, 'moving the body'), (**hito to hanasu no**, 'talking with people'), occupying the same slot as **sora**. Both are made into a noun equivalent by the nominalizer **no**, as shown in the list beneath example a. All three N/NPs in this case are marked by the same case particle, **ga**.

a 空が好き。体を動かすのが好き。人と話すのがもっと好き。

**[Sora] ga suki. [Karada o ugokasu no] ga suki. [Hito to hanasu no] ga motto suki.**

I like the sky. I like moving [my] body. Talking with people I like [even] more.

| **Sora** | 'the sky' | **ga suki.** |
|---|---|---|
| **Karada o ugokasu no** | 'moving the body' | **ga suki.** |
| **Hito to hanasu no** | 'talking with people' | **ga (motto** 'more') **suki.** |

Depending on the valency of the V/Adj constituting the predicate, various other case (and/or adverbial) particles are used. (For differences between the nominalizers **koto** and **no**, see 22.3).

b ✐ビルがビールを飲むのを見た。

**[Biru ga bīru o nomu no] o mita.**

I saw Bill drink beer.

c ✐今日試験があることを忘れていた。

**[Kyō shiken ga aru koto] o wasurete ita.**

I'd forgotten that there's an exam today.

d 平和が続くことを祈りたい。

**[Heiwa ga tsuzuku koto] o inori-tai.**

I [wish to] pray that the peace will last.

e 猛暑のせいか裸で寝るのが癖になった。

**Mōsho no sei ka [hadaka de neru no] ga kuse ni natta.**

Possibly because of the heatwave, sleeping naked has become a habit.

f 新鮮なのが一目で分かる。

**[Shinsen na no] ga hitome de wakaru.**

You can see it's fresh at a glance.

## 22.2.2 Cleft sentences

A *cleft sentence*, by comparison, is a sentence that is equivalent to a simple sentence in meaning. Example a is a simple sentence (locational phrase **basu no naka de**, adverbial phrase **hajimete**, indirect object **kanojo ni**, verb **atta**). By attaching the nominalizer **no** to the section in [ ] in example a, this part of the sentence is converted into a noun-equivalent (= noun phrase or NP). That part is then brought to the front and marked by the adverbial particle **wa**, which has a 'separating' function (see 11.3).

A cleft sentence is thus the result of splitting a sentence into two parts and reversing the order for emphasis.

a ✐バスのなかではじめて彼女に会った。

**Basu no naka de [hajimete kanojo ni atta].**

I met her for the first time on a bus.

b ✐はじめて彼女に会ったのはバスの中だった。

**[Hajimete kanojo ni atta no] wa basu no naka datta.**

It was inside a bus that I met her for the first time. (*lit.* "That I met her for the first time, was inside a bus")

## 22.3 Nominalizers

### 22.3.1 no

#### 22.3.1.1 Sentence **no wa** … copula: cleft sentence

In English, the noun phrase moved to the front is emphasized: 'It is/ was … who/that …', but in Japanese, it is the second part (the part after **wa**) that is emphasized. This is in line with the de-focussing function of **wa** (see 11.3).

a ✐彼が来なかったのは病気だったからだ。

**Kare ga konakatta no wa byōki datta kara da.**

It was because he was ill that he didn't come.

b かわいそうなのは選手だ。

**Kawaisō na no wa senshu da.**

It's the athletes who are to be pitied.

(cf., 選手が/はかわいそうだ。**Senshu ga/wa kawaisō da.**

The athletes are to be pitied.)

c 信用できるのは自分だけ。

**Shin'yō dekiru no wa jibun dake.**

It's only myself that I can trust.

(cf., 自分だけが/は信用できる。**Jibun dake ga/wa shin'yō dekiru.**

I can trust only myself.)

d 確かなのは、危機は去っていないということだ。

**Tashika na no wa, kiki wa satte inai to iu koto da.**

What is certain is that the crisis is not over.

525

e レフェリーに向けられるファンの目が冷ややかなのは、どのスポ
ーツでも一緒だ。

**Referī ni mukerareru fan no me ga hiyayaka na no wa,
dono supōtsu de mo issho da.**

That the fans' attitude towards the umpire is frosty applies to
any sport.

| 22.3.1.2 | *Noun* **to iu no wa** |
|---|---|

This is often used for definitions, or definition-like comments (see 21.2).

a 人生というのは面白くて悲しいものだ。

**Jinsei to iu no wa omoshirokute kanashii mono da.**

Life (*lit.* "this thing called life") is a fascinating and sad thing.

| 22.3.1.3 | *Sentence* **no***: complement clause* |
|---|---|

| 22.3.1.3.1 | *Sentence* **no** + verb of perception |
|---|---|

Here, the object of the verb of perception is made into a complement
clause. It indicates that some happening or state is seen/heard/felt.

The particle attached to the nominalized clause depends on the valency of
the verb: **miru** 'see', **kiku** 'hear', etc. take **o**; **mieru** 'be seen', **kikoeru** 'be
heard' take **ga**; and **ki ga tsuku** 'notice' takes **ni**.

a ✐彼女がレストランに入るのを見た。

**Kanojo ga resutoran ni hairu no o mita.**

I saw her enter the restaurant.

b ✐飛行機が飛んでいるのが見える。

**Hikōki ga tonde iru no ga mieru.**

One can see the aeroplanes fly.

c ✐小鳥が鳴いているのが聞こえる。

**Kotori ga naite iru no ga kikoeru.**

The singing/song of the birds is/can be heard.

d ✐子供の体が少し熱いのに気がついた。

**Kodomo no karada ga sukoshi atsui no ni ki ga tsuita.**

I noticed that the body of the child was a little hot.

e 打球が右中間を破るのが見えた。
**Dakyū ga uchūkan o yaburu no ga mieta.**
I could see the [base] ball break through the middle right
   [defending] space.

f 官僚たちがほくそ笑むのが見えるようである。
**Kanryō-tachi ga hokuso-emu no ga mieru yō de aru.**
You can almost see the bureaucrats chuckling to themselves
   [with delight].

g 私には成長した子供たちがこんな話をしているのが聞こ
   えます。
**Watashi ni wa seichō shita kodomo-tachi ga konna
   hanashi o shite iru no ga kikoemasu.**
I hear [my] grown-up children talking as follows.

22.3.1.3.2 Sentence **no** + other predicate

a ✐映画を見るのが好きだ。
**Eiga o miru no ga suki da.**
He likes watching films.

b ✐漢字を覚えるのはちょっと大変だ。
**Kanji o oboeru no wa chotto taihen da.**
It is a little hard remembering (the) *kanji*.

c ✐きのう地震があったのを知らなかった。
**Kinō jishin ga atta no o shiranakatta.**
I didn't know there was an earthquake yesterday.

d 子供が泣くのは仕方のないことだ。
**Kodomo ga naku no wa shikata no nai koto da.**
That children cry can't be helped.

22.3.2 koto

koto is a basically a lexical noun 'thing/fact', which is also used as a
nominalizer. Like no, it is preceded and followed by the forms that precede
and follow nouns.

22.3.2.1 *Lexical noun 'thing(s)'*

In Japanese, no distinction can be made between noun modification and relative clauses (see 22.1), as both take the form of a modifying clause (given below in [ ]) + noun (example a doesn't have a modifying clause).

a システムの見直しは必要だが、ことはそう簡単ではない。
**Shisutemu no minaoshi wa hitsuyō da ga, koto wa sō kantan de wa nai**
A reconsideration of the system is needed, but things are not so simple.

b 今しかやれないことを一生懸命やりたい。
**[Ima shika yarenai] koto o isshōkenmei yaritai.**
I want to do things I can only do now as much as I can.

c 会社に無理して勤めるより、好きなことで生活したい。
**Kaisha ni muri shite tsutomeru yori, [suki na] koto de seikatsu shitai.**
Rather than force myself to work for a company, I'd like to earn my living doing things I like.

d これほどうれしいことはありません。
**[Kore hodo ureshii] koto wa arimasen.**
Nothing could make me happier (*lit.* "there is no thing that's as joyful as this").

22.3.2.2 *Nominalizer*

22.3.2.2.1 With number of times

a これまでに現地に渡ること七回。
**Kore made-ni [genchi ni wataru] koto nanakai.**
So far he has gone to the country seven times.

22.3.2.2.2 With other predicates

In this use, **koto** indicates the meaning of 'that', or 'doing'.

a あれこれ一人で悩んでいたことがばかばかしくなった。
**[Arekore hitori de nayande ita] koto ga bakabakashiku natta.**
I feel stupid now having worried by myself about all sorts of things.

b もう少し安くしないと売れないことがわかった。

**[Mō sukoshi yasuku shinai to urenai] koto ga wakatta.**

We've realized that it won't sell unless we make it a bit cheaper.

c ハイテクの力を借りることで，自然の知恵も生きてくる。

**[Haiteku no chikara o kariru] koto de, shizen no chie mo ikite kuru.**

Through using the power of advanced technology, one's natural resourcefulness gets activated too.

d モウレツに働くことの意味を見いだしにくくなっている。

**[Mōretsu ni hataraku] koto no imi o miidashinikuku natte iru.**

It has become difficult to find a meaning in working like a Trojan (*lit.* "furiously").

22.3.2.3 *Idiomatic uses*

Note that instead of **ga**, **wa/mo** can also be used.

22.3.2.3.1 Clause-verb-**ru koto ga dekiru**

After clauses ending in V-**ru**, **koto ga dekiru** indicates potential 'can', 'be able to'. This is one of several ways of forming a potential sentence (see 14.1).

a 動物や自然物はなぜか人の心に入り込むことができる。

**Dōbutsu ya shizenbutsu wa naze ka hito no kokoro ni hairikomu koto ga dekiru.**

Animals and [other] things in nature can somehow work their way into people's hearts.

b 生まれたばかりの子は自分ではどうすることもできない。

**Umareta bakari no ko wa jibun de wa dō suru koto mo dekinai.**

A newborn child is incapable of doing anything by itself.

22.3.2.3.2 Clause-verb-**ta koto ga aru/nai**

After V-**ta**, **koto ga aru/nai** means 'have the experience of', 'have not/never'.

a マルチメディア？耳にしたことはあるけど、いったい何？。

**Maruchimedia? Mimi ni shita koto wa aru kedo, ittai nani?**

Multimedia? I've heard it before, but what on earth is it?

b ぼくはまだ留学生とじっくり話したことがない。

**Boku wa mada ryūgakusei to jikkuri hanashita koto ga nai.**

I haven't as yet had a proper chat with a foreign student.

c 小学生のころ、クラスの新聞委員を買って出たことがあった。

**Shōgakusei no koro, kurasu no shinbun-iin o katte deta koto ga atta.**

When I was a primary school pupil, I once volunteered to be a member of the newspaper committee.

---

| 22.3.2.3.3 | Clause-verb-**ru koto ga aru/nai** |

After a clause ending in V-**ru,** this indicates that something happens, or can happen, 'occasionally', 'sometimes' or, in the negative, 'never'.

a 雨が降ったときは一時的に気温が下がることがある。

**Ame ga futta toki wa ichijiteki ni kion ga sagaru koto ga aru.**

After it has rained, the temperature can drop temporarily.

b ハワイやカリフォルニアの海岸まで足を伸ばすこともある。

**Hawai ya Kariforunia no kaigan made ashi o nobasu koto mo aru.**

Sometimes he goes as far as Hawaii or the Californian coast [to surf].

c この事件はほぼ終息したし、二度と起こることはない。

**Kono jiken wa hobo shūsoku shita shi, nido to okoru koto wa nai.**

This incident has more or less ended, and will never happen again.

---

| 22.3.2.3.4 | Clause-verb-**ru koto naku**,... |

After a clause ending in V-**ru, koto naku** (a negative conjunctive equivalent of **koto ga nai**) means 'without doing'.

a 彩子ちゃんは移植手術を受けることなく、この世を去った。

**Ayako-chan wa ishoku shujutsu o ukeru koto naku, kono yo o satta.**

Ayako-chan left this world without receiving a transplant operation.

b 互いに言葉を交すこともなく、押し黙ったままだった。

**Tagai ni kotoba o kawasu koto mo naku, oshidamatta mama datta.**

[The families of the victims] kept silent, not saying anything to each other.

| 22.3.2.3.5 | Clause **koto de**, **koto kara**, **koto mo atte** |

**koto de** 'due to' and **koto kara** 'from the fact that' are combinations of **koto** and case particles indicating a reason. V-**te** can also indicate a reason, and in combination with the adverbial particle **mo**, **koto mo atte** means 'partly because'.

a 年少者が減り，老年者が増えたことで，高齢化は確実に進んだ。

**Nenshōsha ga heri, rōnensha ga fueta koto de, kōrei-ka wa kakujitsu ni susunda.**

Due to the decrease in the young and the increase in the old, the ageing [of society] has definitely advanced.

b （捨て子）へその緒がついていたことから、生後間もないと見られる。

**(Sutego) Heso no o ga tsuite ita koto kara, seigo ma mo nai to mirareru.**

(Abandoned baby) From the fact that it still had [part of] its umbilical cord, it is thought to have been [abandoned] soon after birth.

c 晴天が続いていることもあって、プールや海水浴場は大盛況だ。

**Seiten ga tsuzuite iru koto mo atte, pūru ya kaisuiyoku-jō wa daiseikyō da.**

Due in part to the continued good weather, swimming pools and seaside resorts are doing great business.

| 22.3.2.3.6 | Clause **koto ni suru** |

This combinations means 'decide to', 'make a point of' (see 7.6.1.10).

a そこで、平日の夜は出来る限り全員で夕食をとることにした。

**Soko de, heijitsu no yoru wa dekiru kagiri zen'in de yūshoku o toru koto ni shita.**

Therefore, we decided to have dinner together on weekday nights as often as possible.

b 妻に何も言わないことにしたのは当然だった。

**Tsuma ni nani mo iwanai koto ni shita no wa tōzen datta.**

That I decided to say nothing to my wife was natural.

c 他人ごととは思わずに、日ごろの運転を省みることにしよう。

**Taningoto to wa omowazu ni, higoro no unten o kaerimiru koto ni shiyō.**

Let's not think that this is something that concerns only others, and make a point of rethinking our everyday driving.

Clause **koto ni naru**

**naru** means 'happen naturally' or 'come about', and the combination means 'be decided', 'come about' (see 7.6.1.10).

a　2年半を過ごした浜松を離れることになった。

**Ni-nenhan o sugoshita Hamamatsu o hanareru koto ni natta.**

It came about that we left Hamamatsu, where we had spent two and a half years.

b　十代の娘二人と私が、その間、家事を分担することになった。

**Jūdai no musume futari to watashi ga, sono aida, kaji o buntan suru koto ni natta.**

It was decided that during this time my two teenage daughters and I should share the household chores.

22.3.2.3.8 **koto ni** (adverbial phrase)

Used after Adj or **na**-Adj indicating positive or negative feelings, this is used as an adverbial phrase in the sense of 'to (my/our delight etc.)'.

a　嬉しいことにその大ホールが満員になるほど人が来た。

**Ureshii koto ni sono daihōru ga man'in ni naru hodo hito ga kita.**

To my delight, so many people came that that big hall was full.

22.3.2.3.9 Question word **koto ka**

Question word + **koto ka** indicates emotion, positive or negative.

a　病院でコンサートを聞ければどんなに素晴しいことか。

**Byōin de konsāto o kikereba donna ni subarashii koto ka.**

How wonderful it would be to be able to listen to a concert in hospital!

b　それがどんなに難しいことかをわかるのにしばらく時間がかかった。

**Sore ga donna ni muzukashii koto ka o wakaru no ni shibaraku jikan ga kakatta.**

It took me some time to realize how difficult that is.

(= foregoing the first drink)

Sentence **koto**

This is used in oral orders and written notices, in the sense of 'you should', 'you must'.

a 氏名，職業，住所，電話番号を明記のこと。
   **Shimei, shokugyō, jūsho, denwabangō o meiki no koto.**
   Write clearly your family and given name, occupation, address and telephone number.

b 「まずはしっかり守ること」と守備の整備に余念がない。
   **'Mazu wa shikkari mamoru koto' to shubi no seibi ni yonen ga nai.**
   He is busy reorganizing the defence, saying 'The first thing is to defend properly'.

22.3.2.3.11 Sentence **koto da**

This is used for giving advice 'you/he etc. should', 'you/they etc. must'.

a とにかくメーカー自身がコスト競争力を強めることだ。
   **Tonikaku mēkā jishin ga kosuto kyōsōryoku o tsuyomeru koto da.**
   At any rate the manufacturers themselves must raise their cost competitiveness.

b この政権を長持ちさせるコツは選挙の話をしないことだよ。
   **Kono seiken o nagamochi saseru kotsu wa senkyo no hanashi o shinai koto da yo.**
   The secret of making this government last is not to mention elections.

22.3.2.3.12 Clause **wa** … clause **koto da**

**koto da** is used to complete a cleft or equational sentence. After the verb, **to iu** can optionally be inserted before **koto** (see 21.2.2).

a 何より大事なことは話し合いで解決するということだ。
   **Nani yori daiji na koto wa hanashiai de kaiketsu suru to iu koto da.**
   The most important thing is to find a solution through talks.

b 一番困るのは祖父が「田舎に帰りたい」と言うことだ。
   **Ichiban komaru no wa sofu ga 'inaka ni kaeri-tai' to iu koto da.**
   The most troublesome thing is that grandfather says, 'I want to go back to the country'.

c 最初にその島に行ったのは1982年のことだ。

**Saisho ni sono shima ni itta no wa senkyūhyaku hachijūni-nen no koto da.**

It was in 1982 that I first visited that island.

After clauses ending in V-**ru**, **koto (wa) nai** indicates the meaning of 'there is no need to'.

a 慣れないことを無理してまでやることはない。

**Narenai koto o muri shite made yaru koto wa nai.**

There is no need to force oneself to do things one isn't used to.

b 今さら結婚して，わざわざ苦労することもないのに。

**Ima sara kekkon shite, wazawaza kurō suru koto mo nai noni.**

After all these years, what's the point of getting married and making a hard time for herself?

This is used in the sense of 'about', usually with verbs of communication such as **hanasu** 'talk', etc. and verbs of knowing such as **shiru** 'get to know', etc.

a 将来のことを話し合った。

**Shōrai no koto o hanashiatta.**

We talked about the future.

b 人間の方も犬のことをよく知ってから飼う必要がありそうだ。

**Ningen no hō mo inu no koto o yoku shitte kara kau hitsuyō ga arisō da.**

It seems that humans need to keep dogs once they've got to know them.

The use of **koto** and **no** overlaps to some degree, but the following tendencies can be stated.

### 22.3.3.1 In cleft and equational sentences

If a cleft or equational sentence takes the form [S koto/no wa . . . S2], then S2 can only use **koto da** (see 22.3.2.3.12).

### 22.3.3.2 In complement clauses

In complement clauses, either **no** or **koto** can be used. When the predicate following the nominalizer expresses perception (i.e. **miru** 'see', **mieru** 'be seen', **kiku** 'hear', **kikoeru** 'be heard', **kanjiru** 'feel', etc.), **no** is used, except when **kiku** is used in the hearsay meaning, in which case **koto** is used. As a general tendency, **no** indicates that the complement clause is immediate or concrete, whereas with **koto** it is more abstract, as for instance 'the fact that' (see 22.2, 22.3).

Compare the following.

a ✐花子がピアノを弾くのを聞いた。
   **[Hanako ga piano o hiku no] o kiita.**
   I heard Hanako play the piano.

b ✐花子がピアノを弾くことを聞いた。
   **[Hanako ga piano o hiku koto] o kiita.**
   I heard that Hanako plays the piano.

# Chapter 23

# Conjoining

## 23.1 Conjoining by comma

A comma can conjoin numbers, items or clauses in the sense of 'or' or 'and'.

### 23.1.1 Numbers

With numbers, approximate numbers are formed by lining up two successive numbers, usually SJ, with a comma between them, in the sense of 'four or five', etc. Note that in combinations like 'eight or nine' the consonant of the second number is doubled, i.e. **hak-ku**, and for 'four', **shi** is used rather than **yon** (as in example a).

Depending on what's being counted, appropriate counters are attached (see 4.2).

The two numbers form one unit, and no other conjoining particles can be used.

a 賢人会議のメンバーは四、五人でいいでしょう。
   **Kenjin kaigi no menbā wa shi, go-nin de ii deshō.**
   As for the members of the wise men's committee, four or five should be sufficient.

### 23.1.2 Items

With items lined up in sequence in the sense of 'and' or 'or'.

Note, however, that in example b, although the comma translates as 'or', the [A **to** B **to dochira**] construction means (see 6.7.2.6) that this is in fact also an instance of 'and'.

**ka, ya** and **toka** can also be used instead of a comma (for examples, see 23.2.2–23.2.4).

a ほかに必要なのは送料、箱代、氷代ぐらい。
**Hoka ni hitsuyō na no wa sōryō, hakodai, kōridai gurai.**
The only other things required are money for postage, the charge for the box and the charge for ice.

b 往復ともJR、航空機のどちらでも選択できる。
**Ōfuku tomo Jeiāru, kōkū-ki no dochira demo sentaku dekiru.**
For both the outward and inward journeys, you can select either Japan Rail or aeroplane.

### 23.1.3 *Phrases*

This is seen with pairs of opposites 'or'; **toka** could also be used instead of a comma (see 23.2.2, 23.2.4).

a 写真がうまい、へたは関係ない。
**Shashin ga umai, heta wa kankei nai.**
Being good or bad at photography doesn't matter.

## 23.2 Conjoining particles

Conjoining particles are used mostly between and/or after nouns to indicate the idea of 'and' or 'or'. They include **to, toka, ya** and **ka**.

### 23.2.1 to

Unlike **ya, to** must be used after each item but the last; optionally, it may be repeated after the last item as well. The resulting string (shown in [ ]) functions as one NP, i.e. case particles are attached to the end of the string in the same way as to single nouns (see 23.2.3).

### 23.2.1.1 *Noun **to** noun*

a 周りにいすとテーブルが並ぶ。
**Mawari ni [isu to tēburu] ga narabu.**
Chairs and tables are lined up in the vicinity.

b ヘアとメーク担当でペアを組む。
**[Hea to mēku tantō] de pea o kumu.**
They form pairs consisting of a hair and a make-up specialist.

c ロシアと西欧の長い対立の歴史を忘れてはならない。
**[Roshia to Seiō] no nagai tairitsu no rekishi o wasurete wa naranai.**
We mustn't forget the long history of opposition between Russia and Western Europe.

d （本文と写真は関係ありません）
**([Honbun to shashin] wa kankei arimasen)**
(No relation between the text and the photo)

23.2.1.2 *Noun* **to** *noun* **to**

a 国際化と「アメリカ化」との差別化を。
**[Kokusai-ka to Amerika-ka to] no sabetsu-ka o.**
[We need] differentiation between internationalization and Americanization.

b もう一つ、出発前と今とで変わったことがある。
**Mō hitsotsu, [shuppatsu-mae to ima to] de kawatta koto ga aru.**
There is one more thing that has changed since the time before departure and the present day.

**23.2.2** **toka**

**toka**, a combination of the quotation particle **to** and the question particle **ka**, can join nouns (and phrases, example e) in the same way that **ya** does in the sense of 'and', 'or' (see 23.2.3), but unlike **ya** it can be used more than once in a sentence. It is also wider in use in that it can also be used in the sense of **nado** (see 11.6.1, 23.1.2).

23.2.2.1 *'and (the like)', 'or'*

a 中国の「県」は日本の「市」とか「郡」に近い。
**Chūgoku no 'ken' wa Nihon no 'shi' toka 'gun' ni chikai.**
Chinese *ken* [districts] are approximate to Japan's *shi* [cities] or *gun* [districts].

b 当時はイヤホンとか字幕などなかったですしね。

**Tōji wa iyahon toka jimaku nado nakatta desu shi ne.**

At the time there weren't any earphones or subtitles, etc.

c 論旨が明快かどうか、途中ではさんだジョークは適切かなどはもちろん、話すスピード、マナーも対象になる。アーとかウーとかの乱発など論外である。

**Ronshi ga meikai ka dō ka, tochū de hasanda jōku wa
tekisetsu ka nado wa mochiron, hanasu spīdo, manā mo
taishō ni naru. Ā toka ū toka no ranpatsu nado rongai de
aru.**

[Speeches] are judged not only by clarity of argument and whether
the occasional joke is appropriate, but also [on] speed and manner
of delivery. Excessive use of 'ahs' and 'uhs' and suchlike is out of
the question.

d 低所得者とか高齢者とかに与える影響が大きいですから。

**Tei-shotokusha toka kōreisha toka ni ataeru eikyō ga ōkii
desu kara.**

The influence it [= tax on essentials] has on people like low earners
and the aged is considerable, you see.

e 生意気だとか態度が悪いとか言われ、傷ついた。

**Namaiki da toka taido ga warui toka iware, kizutsuita.**

My feelings were hurt, being told things like [I was] being impertinent
and had a bad attitude.

23.2.2.2 *Colloquial equivalent of* **nado**

a 「日本の新聞とか読むの」「うーん。あんまり」「ことばはどうやって覚えるの」「マンガ！クレヨンしんちゃんとか」。

**'Nihon no shinbun toka yomu no'. 'Ūn. Anmari'. 'Kotoba wa
dō yatte oboeru no'. 'Manga! Kureyon Shin-chan toka'.**

'Do you read Japanese newspapers and the like?' 'No. Not much.'
'How do you learn the language?' 'Comics! Things like *Crayon
Shin-chan*.'

b そのバッグ、アメ横とかで売っている安物っぽいですね。

**Sono baggu, Ameyoko toka de utte iru yasumono-ppoi
desu ne.**

That bag is one of those cheap and nasty ones they sell in places like
Ameyoko, right?

## 23.2.3 ya

**ya** joins items in the sense of 'and (among others)' or 'or'. It is used (once) between items only. As it is used for listing representative items, it is often together with **nado** 'among others', 'etc.' (see 11.6.1, 23.2.2).

### 23.2.3.1 'and (among others)'

a 自動車や家電などの部品に使われる。

**Jidōsha ya kaden nado no buhin ni tsukawareru.**

[The resin pellets] are used in parts for cars and home electrical appliances.

b 地域紛争は欧州やアフリカで続く。

**Chiiki funsō wa Ōshū ya Afurika de tsuzuku.**

Regional conflicts continue in places like Europe and Africa.

*Note* – in writing, **ya** is also often used in combination with punctuation marks, as in examples c and d (see also 23.2).

c 歯形や指輪、持ち物などから四人の身元が分かった。

**Hagata ya yubiwa, mochimono nado kara yonin no mimoto ga wakatta.**

From [things] like the shape of their teeth and rings, belongings, etc., the identities of the four came to light.

d オフィス・住宅の価格や人件費の上昇が理由だ。

**Ofisu, jūtaku no kakaku ya jinkenhi no jōshō ga riyū da.**

The reason is the rise in office and house prices and personnel costs [= US companies withdrawing from Hong Kong].

### 23.2.3.2 'or'

a お寺や教会のようなものだったのかもしれない。

**O-tera ya kyōkai no yō na mono datta no kamoshirenai.**

[The building on the excavated site] may have been something like a temple or a church.

b ゴムやプラスチックの焼けるようなにおいがした、という。

**Gomu ya purasuchikku no yakeru yō na nioi ga shita, to iu.**

He says there was a smell like burning rubber or plastic.

## 23.2.4 ka

ka conjoins **na**-adjectives and nouns in the sense of 'or' (see 23.1.2).

ka can optionally be repeated after the second item. The resulting (conjoined) NP (shown in [ ]) can attach case particles like any other NP.

a プレゼントは花束か陶磁器を用意している。
**Purezento wa [hanataba ka tōjiki] o yōi shite iru.**
For presents, they use flowers or pottery.

b 気温は平年並みか平年より高い所が多い。
**Kion wa [heinen-nami ka heinen yori takai] tokoro ga ōi.**
There are many places where temperatures are average or above for
the time of year.

c 前菜とパスタかピザ、手作りデザートで二千七百円のコース。
**Zensai to [pasuta ka piza], tezukuri dezāto de nisen nana
hyaku-en no kōsu.**
A ¥2,700 set menu consisting of an entrée and pasta or pizza, and a
homemade dessert.

*Note* – examples such as d appear to consist of N **ka,** but this is in fact
the question particle **ka** (replacing the copula), indicating an indirect question
'whether . . . or' (see 18.1.11, 18.3.1.2.5).

d 今の時点で一概に有利か不利かを判断するのは難しい。
**Ima no jiten de ichigai ni [yūri ka furi ka] o handan suru no
wa muzukashii.**
At this point in time it is difficult to make an unconditional judgement
as to advantage or disadvantage.

# Chapter 24

# *Conjunctions*

These are normally used to connect clauses or sentences, i.e. they're typically found at the beginning of a clause or sentence.

Conjunctions connect clauses in a variety of meanings. Some conjunctions of addition (24.1), conjunctions of choice (24.8), etc., can also be used between nouns or phrases.

## 24.1  Addition

In the sense of 'and', 'besides', 'moreover', these include **soshite, mata, shikamo, sono ue, sore ni, sara ni, oyobi**.

a 料理は味つけが大事です。そして、旬のものを使い、素材の持ち
  味を生かしてこそ健康な料理が作れます。
  **Ryōri wa ajitsuke ga daiji desu. Soshite, shun no mono o
  tsukai, sozai no mochiaji o ikashite koso kenkō na ryōri ga
  tsukuremasu.**
  In cooking, seasoning is important. And, if you use things that are in
  season and bring out the taste of the ingredients, then you can
  make healthy dishes.

b 蛤の殻は一つとして同じ模様のものがない。また、もとの片割れで
  なければ噛み合わせが合わない。
  **Hamaguri no kara wa hitotsu to shite onaji moyō no mono
  ga nai. Mata, moto no kataware de nakereba kamiawase ga
  awanai.**
  There is not one shell of the cherrystone clam that has the same
  pattern as another. Moreover, the shell fits only its original
  counterpart.

c パイユート族は遊牧民で、絶えず、しかも長距離を移動しましたか
　ら、常に身軽でした。

**Paiyūto-zoku wa yūbokumin de, taezu, shikamo chōkyori o
idō shimashita kara, tsune ni migaru deshita.**

The Paiutes were nomads, and because they constantly moved, and
over large distances at that, they always travelled light.

d コンパクトボディなのに、大きなモニターだから、ベストアング
　ルが探しやすい。そのうえ、長時間撮影もラク。

**Konpakuto bodi na noni, ōki na monitā da kara, besuto
anguru ga sagashiyasui. Sono ue, chōjikan satsuei mo raku.**

Although it has a compact body, because it has a large monitor
the best angle is easy to find. Moreover, extended filming
is easy too.

e その後妻が近所で捨てられていた小猫を拾ってきた。大部分まっ
　黒でそれに少しの白を交えた雌猫であった。

**Sono go tsuma ga kinjo de suterarete ita koneko o hirotte
kita. Daibubun makkuro de sore ni sukoshi shiro o majieta
mesuneko de atta.**

Subsequently, my wife picked up a kitten that had been abandoned
nearby. It was a predominantly black female with a little white
mixed in.

f なかには日の丸交通のように250メートル、百円に引き下げたい
　という積極派もいる。さらに年内にはタクシー業界のディスカ
　ウンター、エムケイ・タクシーが東京に進出する。

**Naka ni wa hinomaru kōtsū no yō ni nihyaku gojū mētoru,
hyaku-en ni hikisage-tai to iu sekkyokuha mo iru. Sara ni
nennai ni wa takushī gyōkai no disukauntā, emukei takushī
ga Tōkyō ni shinshutsu suru.**

There are also some aggressive companies such as Hinomaru
Transport, who want to lower [the fare] to one hundred yen per
250 metres. Furthermore, before the end of the year the discounter
of the taxi world, MK Taxi, is going to extend its operations to
Tokyo.

## 24.2　Consequence

Indicating the meaning of 'consequently', 'therefore', these include **da kara**,
**sore de, soko de, shitagatte, sono tame**.

a 寒さに弱い熱帯産の植物だが、温室で育てれば真冬にも花が
　咲く。だから、冬から春にかけては洋ランの季節で、園芸店に
　も華麗な色どりの花があふれている。

**Samusa ni yowai nettai-san no shokubutsu da ga, onshitsu de
sodatereba mafuyu ni mo hana ga saku. Da kara, fuyu kara
haru ni kakete wa yōran no kisetsu de, engeiten ni mo
karei na irodori no hana ga afurete iru.**

It's a plant from the tropics which is easily affected by the cold, but if
raised in a hothouse it flowers even in the middle of winter.
Therefore, [the time] from winter to spring is the season for
Western orchids, and gardening shops too are full of [their]
gorgeous many-coloured flowers.

b 大学の公開講座は回数が少ない上に、担当教員も毎回変わる講座
　が多い。そこで、通常の講義のように16回とおしで、上級レベ
　ルの講座を開いた。

**Daigaku no kōkai kōza wa kaisū ga sukunai ue ni, tantō kyōin
mo maikai kawaru kōza ga ōi. Soko de, tsūjō no kōgi no yō
ni jūrokkai tōshi de, jōkyū reberu no kōza o hiraita.**

University courses for the general public are short and often have
different lecturers each time. Therefore, we have established an
advanced-level course that runs continuously for 16 classes, just like
a regular course.

c 今年は猛暑だったせいもあり、北海道のトマトがことさら上等。
　したがってジュースもたいへん美味だ。

**Kotoshi wa mōsho datta sei mo ari, Hokkaidō no tomato ga
kotosara jōtō. Shitagatte jūsu mo taihen bimi da.**

Partly because [this summer] was a very hot one, this year's
Hokkaido tomatoes are especially good. Consequently, the juice is
very tasty too.

d インフルエンザワクチンはインフルエンザ以外の風邪に効果がな
　い。そのため、「ワクチンを接種しても、風邪にかかった。き
　かなかったのではないか」と感じる人が多い。

**Infuruenza wakuchin wa infuruenza igai no kaze ni kōka
ga nai. Sono tame, 'Wakuchin o sesshu shite mo, kaze ni
kakatta. Kikanakatta no de wa nai ka' to kanjiru hito
ga ōi.**

Influenza vaccine has no effect on colds, only on flu. Therefore, many
feel that even though they had a vaccination, they [still] caught
a cold, [and] it didn't work.

## 24.3 Immediate consequence

The sense of 'just then', 'thereupon' is indicated by **suru to**.

a するとその日の夜のうちに、東京へ逃げて帰った。するとすぐさま父親が飛んで来て、連れ戻された。

**Suru to sono hi no yoru no uchi ni, Tōkyō e nigete kaetta.**
**Suru to sugusama chichioya ga tonde kite, tsure-modosareta.**

Thereupon, they fled back to Tokyo that night. Then their father rushed over, and they were taken back.

## 24.4 Contrast

In the meaning of 'however', 'but', 'on the contrary', the following are used: shikashi, keredomo, da ga, datte, sore demo, demo, tokoro ga, to wa ie, etc.

a 子どもを可愛がりなさいということは正しいが、しかし三歳までに規則正しい生活習慣をつけさせることも大切である。

**Kodomo o kawaigari-nasai to iu koto wa tadashii ga, shikashi sansai made-ni kisoku tadashii seikatsu shūkan o tsukesaseru koto mo taisetsu de aru.**

It's right to tell people to dote on their children, but it's also important to make them acquire regular living habits by the age of 3.

b 豪華なシャンデリアもなければ赤い絨毯が敷かれたエントランスホールもない。けれども、私には、この簡素な場所が東京でもっとも贅沢な劇の場であるように思える。

**Gōka na shanderia mo nakereba akai jūtan ga shikareta entoransu hōru mo nai. Keredomo, watashi ni wa kono kanso na basho ga Tōkyō de mottomo zeitaku na geki no ba de aru yō ni omoeru.**

There is no luxurious chandelier, nor an entrance hall with red carpet. However, for me this simple place feels like the most luxurious spot for [staging] plays.

c ビルはケンブリッジ大学教授、労働法の権威である。だが彼と会っても話はすべて野球がらみである。

**Biru wa Kenburijji daigaku kyōju, rōdōhō no ken'i de aru. Da ga kare to atte mo hanashi wa subete yakyū-garami de aru.**

Bill is a Cambridge University professor, and an authority on labour law. But when you meet him, everything he says has to do with baseball.

d 「どっか行こうよ」「今年のクリスマスは家でホームパーテ
ィーしようって言ったのは君だぜ」「だって、もう家にいる
のあきちゃったんだもん」「じゃあ、原宿の表参道にでも行
くか。」

**'Dokka ikō yo'. 'Kotoshi no Kurisumasu wa ie de hōmu-pātī
shiyo tte itta no wa kimi da ze' 'Datte, mō ie ni iru no
akichatta n da mon'. 'Jā, Harajuku no Omotesandō ni de
mo iku ka.'**

'Let's go somewhere.' 'It was you who said that this Christmas we
should have a house party.' 'All right then, let's go to Omotesandō
in Harajuku or somewhere.'

e 真冬で雪がちらつく夜中の二時ごろ、凍えながら馬を引き、こち
らが倒れそうになったこともあった。でも、こうして一生懸命
に世話をしても、馬が死んじゃうことはよくある。

**Mafuyu de yuki ga chiratsuku yonaka no niji-goro,
kogoe-nagara uma o hiki, kochira ga taoresō ni natta koto
mo atta. De mo, kōshite isshōkenmei ni sewa o shite mo,
uma ga shinjau koto wa yoku aru.**

There've been times when I pulled the horse around at 2 a.m.
in the middle of winter with snow falling, numb with cold, and
on the verge of breaking down from exhaustion. But even
when I looked after the horse with great devotion like that, it
often died.

f 六万円前後のボードのほか、ブーツ、ウエアなど一通りそろえる
と、十五万—二十万円はかかる。それでも週末ともなると、
店は二十歳前後の若者でごった返す。

**Rokuman-en zengo no bōdo no hoka, būtsu, uea nado hitotōri
soroeru to, jūgoman kara nijūman-en wa kakaru. Sore
demo shūmatsu to mo naru to, mise wa nijussai zengo no
wakamono de gottagaesu.**

If one gets a complete outfit comprising boots and gear besides a
snowboard [costing] around 60,000 yen, it sets you back at least
150,000 to 200,000 yen. And yet, at weekends the shop is bustling
with young people around 20 years old.

g 決して手間を惜しむことなく、丹念に作り上げていった。それが
職人の誇りであり自慢でもあった。ところが、今、職人という
言葉さえ死語になりつつあり、その作品は消えていく。

**Kesshite tema o oshimu koto naku, tannen ni tsukuri-agete
itta. Sore ga shokunin no hokori de ari jiman de mo atta.**

**Tokoro ga, ima, shokunin to iu kotoba sae shigo ni naritsutsu ari, sono sakuhin wa kiete iku.**

They used to make things scrupulously, sparing no trouble. That was the craftsman's pride, and something he would boast of. But now, even the word craftsman is going out of use, and their products are disappearing.

## 24.5　Qualification

**tadashi, tada, mottomo,** etc. indicate the sense of 'mind you', 'though', 'however'.

a　県内の生産関連指標は、改善傾向を示している。ただし、設備投資は年間を通じて動きが乏しかった。

**Ken-nai no seisan kanren shihyō wa, kaizen keikō o shimeshite iru. Tadashi, setsubi tōshi wa nenkan o tsūjite ugoki ga toboshikatta.**

The productivity-related indices in the prefecture are showing an upward trend, but investment in equipment showed poor movement throughout the year.

b　若いんだし、別にカタにはまることはないし、カッコつけて生きたっていいと思う。ただ、いじめは、最低だ。恥ずかしい。

**Wakai n da shi, betsu ni kata ni hamaru koto wa nai shi, kakko tsukete ikitatte ii to omou. Tada, ijime wa saitei da. Hazukashii.**

They are young, there's no need for them to conform, and I think it's OK to make themselves look smart. However, bullying is the pits. It makes you feel ashamed.

c　英国から入った子ども半額が、官製料金として広まり、常識になったというわけだ。もっとも、官製の常識は万能ではない。

**Eikoku kara haitta kodomo hangaku ga, kansei ryōkin to shite hiromari, jōshiki ni natta to iu wake da. Mottomo, kansei no jōshiki wa bannō de wa nai.**

So half-price for children, which came in from England, spread through government-controlled prices, and became common sense. The common sense of government control is not universal, though.

**Reason**

The meaning of 'because', 'the reason for', etc. is indicated by **naze nara**, **naze ka to iu to, to iu no wa, to iu koto wa,** etc.

a ただ、パジェロミニはジムニーよりワゴンRの対抗車だ。なぜな らパジェロミニは本当のRV志向というよりも乗用車志向の車だ からだ。

**Tada, Pajero Mini wa Jimunī yori Wagon R no taikōsha da. Naze nara Pajero Mini ni wa hontō no RV shikō to iu yori mo jōyōsha shikō no kuruma da kara da.**

Mind you, the Pajero Mini is a rival car for Wagon R rather than Jimny. That is because the Pajero Mini is more of a passenger car than a real RV car.

b バブル時代には「企業メセナ」という言葉が流行したが、バブル 崩壊とともに消滅してしまった。なぜかというと、メセナの名 の下に企業は単に「モノを売る」ための広告をしていたに過ぎ なかったからだ。

**Baburu jidai ni wa 'kigyō mesena' to iu kotoba ga ryūkō shita ga, baburu hōkai to tomo ni shōmetsu shite shimatta. Naze ka to iu to, mesena no na no moto ni kigyō wa tan ni 'mono o uru' tame no kōkoku o shite ita ni suginakatta kara da.**

During the bubble years, the expression 'business *mécénat* (= sponsorship of the arts)' was popular, but disappeared with the bursting of the bubble. The reason is that businesses were simply advertising to sell things under the name of *mécénat*.

c 昔の人は御不浄へいったらかならず咳払いしなさい、と言っ たものである。というのは、そのころチミモウリョウが出 て災いをもたらすからなので、咳払いはその魔除けなの である。

**Mukashi no hito wa gofujō e ittara kanarazu sekibarai shinasai, to itta mono de aru. To iu no wa, sono koro chimimōryō ga dete wazawai o motarasu kara na node, sekibarai wa sono mayoke na no de aru.**

In the old days, people used to say that when you went to the toilet you must clear your throat. The reason is that because around that time of day the evil spirits of mountains and rivers came out and made trouble, and clearing your throat would protect you from them.

## 24.7 Sequence

This indicates the sense of 'first *X*, then *Y*', 'thereafter', which includes mazu, hajime ni, sore kara, daiichi/ni/san ni (see also 4.3).

a 会社に入ってからは、まずレンズの技術を、次にレンズ以外のことを極めるのが夢となった。

**Kaisha ni haitte kara wa, mazu renzu no gijutsu o, tsugi ni renzu igai no koto o kiwameru no ga yume to natta.**

After I entered the company, my dream was first to master lens technology, and then things other than lenses.

b いかのつぎは、白身の魚を食べることができた。鯛と比良目である。赤貝の身や、さよりなども食べられるようになった。それから、だんだん当り前のおかずに魚が食べられるようになってった。

**Ika no tsugi wa, shiromi no sakana o taberu koto ga dekita. Tai to hirame de aru. Akagai no mi ya, sayori nado mo taberareru yō ni natta. Sore kara, dandan atarimae no okazu ni sakana ga taberareru yō ni natta.**

After squid, I was able to eat white-fleshed fish. That is, snapper and flounder. I also became able to eat the flesh of ark shell and halfbeak. After that, I gradually became able to eat fish as an ordinary part of a meal.

c 三島由起夫が、「小説家の休暇」というエッセイの中で書いている。「私が太宰治の文学に対して抱いている嫌悪は一種猛烈なものだ。第一私はこの人の顔がきらいだ。第二にこの人の田舎者のハイカラ趣味がきらいだ。第三にこの人が自分に適しない役を演じたのがきらいだ。」

**Mishima Yukio ga, 'Shōsetsuka no kyūka' to iu essē no naka de kaite iru. 'Watashi ga Dazai Osamu no bungaku ni taishite idaite iru ken'o wa isshu mōretsu na mono da. Dai-ichi watashi wa kono hito no kao ga kirai da. Dai-ni ni kono hito no inakamono no haikara shumi ga kirai da. Dai-san ni kono hito ga jibun ni tekishinai yaku o enjita no ga kirai da.'**

Mishima Yukio writes in an essay titled 'The Novelist's Vacation': 'The aversion I have to Dazai Osamu's works is quite strong. Firstly, I dislike his face. Secondly, I dislike his country-bumpkin sense of stylishness. Thirdly, I dislike the fact that he played a part for which he was unsuited.'

## 24.8 Choice

The meaning of 'or' is expressed by **mata wa, arui wa, moshiku wa, naishi (wa), sore tomo**, etc. Note that these are exceptional in that they commonly occur in mid-sentence, unlike most other forms classed here as 'conjunctions'.

a 契約期間中は、時価または「買取価格」でいつでも換金できます。
**Keiyaku kikan-chū wa, jika mata wa 'kaitori kakaku' de itsu demo kankin dekimasu.**
During the contract period, you can change them into money any time, at the current market price or at the 'purchase price'.

b 私はこの40年を、開発技術者として、あるいは経営者として仕事に没頭してきた。
**Watashi wa kono yonjūnen o, kaihatsu gijutsusha to shite, arui wa keieisha to shite shigoto ni bottō shite kita.**
I have devoted the past 40 years to my work, as technical developer or as manager.

c マンションを借りる？買う？それとも持家にする？このご時世に最もすぐれた選択肢とは
**Manshon o kariru? Kau? Sore tomo mochiie ni suru? Kono go-jisei ni mottomo sugureta sentakushi to wa**
Rent an apartment? Buy it? Or deciding on owning a house? [What] is the choice best suited to our time? [= headline]

## 24.9 Alternative

These include **ippō de, ippō, tahō**, etc., in the sense of 'on the one hand', 'on the other hand'.

a 現代では、高級品だった洋ランもスーパーマーケットで売られるほどになった。一方で、切り花として売買され、花が終われば捨ててしまうようになったのは残念である。
**Gendai de wa, kōkyūhin datta yōran mo sūpāmāketto de urareru hodo ni natta. Ippō de, kiribana to shite baibai sare, hana ga owareba sutete shimau yō ni natta no wa zannen de aru.**
In our times, the Western orchid, which used to be a luxury item, is sold even in supermarkets. On the other hand, it's a pity that they are now sold as cut flowers and people throw them away when the flowers are finished.

b 「表現して伝達されるべき思想」が目標であり、一方「言語」
　がその目標を達成すべき手段であるということになり
　ます。

**'Hyōgen shite dentatsu sareru-beki shisō' ga mokuhyō de ari, ippō 'gengo' ga sono mokuhyō o tassei su-beki shudan de aru to iu koto ni narimasu.**

The goal is 'an idea that needs to be expressed and communicated', but on the other hand 'language' is the means to achieve that goal.

## 24.10 Paraphrasing

In the sense of 'in other words', 'in short', 'that is', 'for example', this includes tsumari, sunawachi, yōsuru ni, tatoeba, iwaba.

a 館内には月替わりの展示ギャラリーもあり、広い庭園では定期的
　に文化の祭典も開かれている。つまりこの博物館は、民族や地
　域、あるいはコミュニティの百科事典なのだ。

**Kannai ni wa tsukigawari no tenji gyararī mo ari, hiroi teien de wa teiki-teki ni bunka no saiten mo hirakarete iru. Tsumari kono hakubutsukan wa, minzoku ya chiiki, arui wa komyuniti no hyakkajiten na no da.**

Inside, there is a display gallery with monthly changing exhibits, and in the large garden periodic cultural festivals are held. In short, this museum is an encyclopedia of peoples and regions, or the community.

b 行政には規定に先立つ常識、すなわち良識が欠かせない。

**Gyōsei ni wa kitei ni sakidatsu jōshiki, sunawachi ryōshiki ga kakasenai.**

Administration cannot work without the common sense that comes before regulations, in other words, sensibility.

c それぞれの組織や団体は政府から独立しており、要するに民間の
　もので、企業と違って営利活動が目的ではない。

**Sorezore no soshiki ya dantai wa seifu kara dokuritsu shite ori, yōsuru ni minkan no mono de, kigyō to chigatte eiri katsudō ga mokuteki de wa nai.**

The various organizations and bodies are independent of the government, in short they are private, but unlike businesses their purpose is not to make a profit.

d 日本の社会には無用の音が多いという。例えば、バスの中。

**Nihon no shakai ni wa muyō no oto ga ōi to iu. Tatoeba, basu no naka.**

He says that in Japanese society there are many unnecessary noises. For instance, inside a bus.

e 我々のような重工業は、いわば高級便利屋。必ず世の中に必要とされる。

**Wareware no yō na jūkōgyō wa, iwaba kōkyū benriya. Kanarazu yo no naka ni hitsuyō to sareru.**

Our kind of heavy industry is in a manner of speaking a high-class Jack-of-all-trades. Society will definitely have a need for us.

## 24.11 Change of topic/coming to the point

In the meaning of 'well', 'by the way', sate, tokoro de, de wa, ja, etc. are used.

a 「···うまい酒を飲みたかっただけ。そうしたら思いもかけず盛り上がってしまった。」と、太田さんと鈴木さんは顔を見合わせ笑う。--さて冒頭の貝原益軒の言葉には続きがある。ほどよく飲めば体にいいが、「多く飲むとひとを害する。酒ほどひとを害するものはないのである」というくだりだ。

'...**umai sake o nomitakatta dake. Sō shitara omoi mo kakezu moriagatte shimatta.' to, Ōta-san to Suzuki-san wa kao o miawase warau. --Sate bōtō no Kaibara Ekiken no kotoba ni wa tsuzuki ga aru. Hodo yoku nomeba karada ni ii ga, 'Ōku nomu to hito o gaisuru. Sake hodo hito o gaisuru mono wa nai no de aru' to iu kudari da.**

'...we just wanted to drink good sake. And, unexpectedly, it ended up becoming quite a party.' Mr Ōta and Mr Suzuki looked at each other and laughed. – Well, the words of Ekiken Kaibara quoted in the beginning have a sequel to them. It's the passage that says that drinking in moderation is good for you, but 'When you drink lots, it harms you. Nothing harms people more than alcohol.'

b 生まれつきカッコいい男なんてものは、存在しない。普段の努力でおのれに磨きをかけることで、ようやくそうなれるのだ。では、どうやって磨くのか。

**Umaretsuki kakko ii otoko nante mono wa, sonzai shinai. Fudan no doryoku de onore ni migaki o kakeru**

koto de, yōyaku sō nareru no da. De wa, dō yatte migaku no ka.

There's no such thing as an elegant man by birth. By making constant efforts to polish oneself one finally gets there. OK then – how does one do the polishing?

Change of topic/coming to the point

c 「よい水とよい米さえあればよい酒ができる。酒は正直だから」とか。

じゃ、おれたちがよい米をつくるからおまえやってみろってけしかけたんだ。

**'Yoi mizu to yoi kome sae areba yoi sake ga dekiru. Sake wa shōjiki da kara' to ka. Ja, ore-tachi ga yoi kome o tsukuru kara, omae yatte miro tte keshikaketa n da.**

He said things like, 'As long as you have good water and good rice you can make good sake. Sake doesn't lie, you see.' 'Well then,' we spurred him on, 'we'll make the rice, and you try [making the sake]'.

d 元文部大臣井上毅は、間違いを指摘されて自分の無学を深く恥じ、その後、国文のほうに打ち込んだだけではなく、文部大臣になると、大いに国語教育を充実させた。これはこれなりに立派な態度だと思うが、どうだろうか。ところで、こういう話を聞いたとき、中年以上の読者は、一つ思い当たることがありませんか。

**Moto Monbu-daijin Inoue Tsuyoshi wa, machigai o shiteki sarete jibun no mugaku o fukaku haji, sono ato, kokubun no hō ni uchikonda dake de wa naku, Monbu-daijin ni naru to, ōi ni kokugo kyōiku o jūjitsu saseta. Kore wa kore nari ni rippa na taido da to omou ga, dō darō ka. Tokoro de, kō iu hanashi o kiita toki, chūnen ijō no dokusha wa, hitotsu omoiataru koto ga arimasen ka.**

Tsuyoshi Inoue, the former Minister of Education, had a mistake pointed out to him and felt deeply ashamed about his ignorance; thereafter, he not only devoted himself to Japanese literature, but when he became Minister of Culture he also greatly improved the teaching of Japanese in the schools. I think that that in its own way is a laudable attitude – what do you [= the reader] think? Incidentally, when you hear a story like this, aren't those of you readers who are middle-aged or older reminded of something?

# Chapter 25

# *Conjunctive forms*

The conjunctive form of V/Adj (-**te**/-**de**) and **na**-Adj/N + copula (**de**) has several important functions:

To connect or attach various verbs to the main verb, in order to form performative sentences, aspectual sentence endings, and the conjunctive particle -**te kara**;

To attach the adverbial particles **wa** and **mo** to form a variety of combinations with following items;

To form compound sentences;

To act as a NP-equivalent (sometimes called 'gerund') that can attach certain case and other particles such as **ga, no, demo, bakari.**

There is also a conjunctive-form equivalent, formed by V/Adj-stem, used in the written style; of the above four meanings; this is used in the first meaning only, but has some further uses, too (see 7.6.5, 7.1.2.3, 6.1.1).

## 25.1 With verb/adjective-te and na-adjective/noun + copula-de: forming compound sentences

Compound sentences could also be expressed by two separate sentences. The meaning of a and b in 25.1.1 below can alternatively be expressed in the following way:

a ✐ふたをする。赤くなるまで蒸す。
**Futa o suru. Akaku naru made musu.**
You put on the lid. You steam it until it turns red.

With verb/
adjective-te and
na-adjective/
noun +
copula-de:
forming
compound
sentences

b ✐二人組は車で逃走した。夫婦にけがはなかった。

**Futari-gumi wa kuruma de tōsō shita. Fūfu ni kega wa
nakatta.**

The gang of two took flight. The couple were not injured.

Note how the tense of the compound sentence is indicated only by the
second predicate. For this reason, the **-te** form is also sometimes called
'suspensive' form.

With V/Adj, this function can also be carried out by the stem forms, in
the written and formal spoken style (speeches, etc.), and 'zero forms' with
verbal nouns.

Compound sentences where the two halves are joined by stem forms indicate an addition 'and', whereas with **-te** the meaning is wider (see 25.1.3
below).

---

**25.1.1** *Compound sentences with stem forms of verb/adjective*

a ふたをし、赤くなるまで蒸す。

**Futa o shi, akaku naru made musu.**

You put on the lid, and steam it [= crab] until it turns red.

b 二人組は車で逃走し、夫婦にけがはなかった。

**Futari-gumi wa kuruma de tōsō shi, fūfu ni kega wa nakatta.**

The gang of two took flight, and the couple were not injured.

c 札幌は日の出は早く、日没は遅い。

**Sapporo wa hinode wa hayaku, nichibotsu wa osoi.**

In Sapporo, the sunrise is early, and the sunset late.

---

**25.1.2** *With verbal noun: 'zero conjunctive form'*

With verbal nouns, V-stem (**shi**) can be omitted, as the verbal noun itself
implicates an action. This is found only in the written language, i.e. newspapers (see 1.9).

a 車はそのまま逃走、女性にけがはなかった。

**Kuruma wa sono mama tōsō, josei ni kega wa nakatta.**

The car drove off without stopping, and the woman was not hurt.

**25.1.3** *Compound sentences using verb/adjective-te and na-adjective/noun + copula-de*

-te/-de indicates a variety of meanings, ranging from addition 'and', reason or consequence 'and therefore', and sequence of time 'since'. However, these are meanings that result from the relationship between the two parts of the sentence, and can be expressed more explicitly (see 26.5.2).

a せつなくて、つらい事件だ。
**Setsunakute, tsurai jiken da.**
It's a distressing and cruel incident.

b スポーツ好きで、とりわけ「素潜り」が得意。
**Supōtsu-zuki de, toriwake 'sumoguri' ga tokui.**
He likes sports, and is especially good at skin diving.

c ドラフト3位の山田広は長打力があって、足も速い。
**Dorafuto san'i no Yamada Hiroshi wa chōdaryoku ga atte, ashi mo hayai.**
Hiroshi Yamada, who was third in the draft, has long hitting power, and fast legs, too.

d 実験やスライド映写を多用して、分かりやすい。
**Jikken ya suraido eisha o tayō shite, wakariyasui.**
It [= the course] is easy to follow, using a lot of experiments and slide projections.

e それも生まれてはじめての体験だった。
**Sore mo umarete hajimete no taiken datta.**
Also, it [= cutting glass] was a first for me (*lit.* "first time since I was born").

**25.1.4** *Colour words: modification and addition*

Note that although colour words use their -te form to modify another adjective, when joining colours in the sense of 'and', -te cannot be used. Instead, their noun form is used, joined by the conjoining particle **to**. Compare examples a and b.

Modifying another adjective:

a 一メートルくらい掘ると、赤くて固い土の層にぶつかった。
**Ichimētoru kurai horu to, akakute katai tsuchi no sō ni butsukatta.**
When we had dug [to the depth of] about a metre, we came upon a layer of red, hard soil.

Colours *A* and *B*:

b 色は青とエンジの二色。
**Iro wa ao to enji no nishoku.**
It comes in two colours, blue and dark red.

## 25.2 Uses of clause-te (de) + wa/mo

### 25.2.1 *Verb/adjective/na-adjective/noun-te (de) yoi/ii/jūbun*

With evaluatory predicates like **yoi/ii** 'good', **jūbun** 'sufficient', the combination indicates sufficiency (that the state indicated by Adj/na-Adj/N 'is OK', 'is sufficient'), or recommendation, i.e. that the course of action indicated by V-**te** is/isn't recommendable.

a 判を押すだけでいい。
**Han o osu dake de ii.**
All you need to do is put your seal on it.

b コメが予想以上の大豊作でよかった。
**Kome ga yosō ijō no daihōsaku de yokatta.**
Thankfully, the rice harvest was a bumper harvest beyond expectation.

### 25.2.2 *Verb/adjective/na-adjective/noun-te (de) mo ii/-tatte ii*

-**te mo ii**, etc. is used to give (or ask for) permission to carry out the action of the verb it is attached to ('it's OK if . . .', 'you may . . .' and in questions, 'is it OK if . . . ?').

Instead of V-**te/de mo ii** only (but not in questions!), an even more colloquial variant -**tatte/-datte ii** can be used.

a ✐ここは泳いでもいいですか。
**Koko wa oyoide mo ii desu ka.**
Can one swim here?

b ドレス買ってもいい？
**Doresu katte mo ii?**
Is it OK if I buy a dress?

c クリスマスはどんな過ごし方をしたっていい。
**Kurisumasu wa donna sugoshikata o shitatte ii.**
You can spend Christmas any way you like.

25.2.3 *Verb/adjective/na-adjective/noun-te (de) wa/chā (jā) +*
*negative form/expression*

Here, -te wa (or its variant -chā) or -de wa (variant -jā) is followed by a
negative expression such as naranai, ikenai, dame, etc. The combination
expresses the idea of 'must', 'have to'.

It can be attached to either positive (examples a and c) or negative forms
(example b) (see 26.1.7.3, 26.1.7.4, 17.2.2).

a 趣味は仕事になってはならない。
  **Shumi wa shigoto ni natte wa naranai.**
  [One's] hobby must not turn into one's job.

b 「おもしろくなくちゃだめだ」という。
  **'Omoshirokunakucha dame da' to iu.**
  'It has to be interesting', he says.

c 机上の勉強だけではだめ。
  **Kijō no benkyō dake de wa dame.**
  Learning about things just from books (*lit.* "on the desk") is no good.

25.2.4 *na-adjective/noun de wa nai/ja nai*

de wa nai/ja nai is the negative form of the copula (see 7.5, 17.1.3.1).

a 安くなければ、おしゃれじゃない。
  **Yasukunakereba, oshare ja nai.**
  If it isn't cheap, it's not fashionable.

25.2.5 *Verb-te (de) wa*

V-te (de) wa joins two different V to indicate repeated action, i.e. that the
combined action occurs over and over again (see 26.1.7).

a ✐波が寄せては返す。
  **Nami ga yosete wa kaesu.**
  The constant motion of the surf (*lit.* "The waves keep coming in and
    going out").

b ちょっと口にしては次々と灰皿へ。
  **Chotto kuchi ni shite wa tsugitsugi to haizara e.**
  He smokes them briefly [each time], and then one after the other
    [stubs them out] in the ashtray.

## 25.3 Uses of verb-te (de)

### 25.3.1 *Verb-te ageru, etc.*

With the addition of performative verbs like **ageru,** V-te forms performatives like -**te ageru** (see 15.1)/**hoshii/kudasaru/kureru/morau** (see 15.3–15.6), although with informal commands, **kudasai,** etc. can also be omitted (see also 20.2.2).

a お菓子を買ってあげる。
   **Okashi o kat-te ageru.**
   I'll buy you sweets.

### 25.3.2 *Verb-te iru, etc.*

V-te forms aspectual endings like -**te aru/-te iku/-te iru/-te kuru/-te miru,** -**te oku/-te shimau** (see 8.3–8.10).

a いつかまた、行ってみたい。
   **Itsu ka mata, it-te mitai.**
   Sometime, I'd like to go again.

### 25.3.3 *Verb-te kara*

This combination indicates the idea of 'after', 'once' (see 26.2.4).

a 年をとってからは町の方が暮らしやすい…
   **Toshi o tot-te kara wa machi no hō ga kurashiyasui . . .**
   Once you're old, it's easier to live in town . . . [than the country]

### 25.3.4 *Clause-te sumimasen/gomen nasai/warui, etc.*

Followed by an expression of apology, the combination means 'sorry for . . .'. To apologize about something that took place in the past, apologies with past forms are used. This use is also found with conjunctive forms of Adj, and **na-**Adj/N + copula.

a 返事が遅れてすみません。
   **Henji ga okure-te sumimasen.**
   Sorry for the late reply (*lit.* "reply being late")

b 汗臭くてすみません。

**Ase-kusaku-te sumimasen.**

Sorry I smell of sweat.

---

**25.3.5** *Verb-te naranai*

**25.3.5.1** *After verbs of feeling*

After verbs of feeling (**kanji/ki ga suru** 'have a feeling', **oshimareru** 'to be regretted', **omoeru** 'be felt', **-te naranai** indicates that one 'can't help having that feeling' (see 14.2).

a 大江健三郎氏がノーベル文学賞受賞者に決まり、にわかに著作が
売れ出したというが、日本人の文化享受の在り方を端的に示す
皮肉な現象と思えてならない。

**Ōe Kenzaburo-shi ga Nōberu Bungakushō jushōsha ni kimari,
niwaka ni chosaku ga uredashita to iu ga, Nihonjin no
bunka kyōju no arikata o tanteki ni shimesu hiniku na
genshō to omoe-te naranai.**

It is said that when Kenzaburō Ōe was given the Nobel prize his
works suddenly began to sell; I can't help feeling that this is a
phenomenon that epitomizes the way the Japanese import culture.

b 何か順序が違っているような気がしてならない。

**Nani ka junjo ga chigatte iru yō na ki ga shi-te naranai**

I can't help feeling that somehow the order of things is wrong.

c 関西財界にとって惜しまれてならない。

**Kansai zaikai ni totte oshimare-te naranai.**

For the Kansai economic world, [his death] is a great loss
(*lit.* "one cannot but regret [his death]").

---

**25.3.5.2** *After other verbs*

After other V, **-te (wa) naranai** indicates prohibition 'must not'.

a 俳人は毎年原爆忌の名で、忘れてならない日のことを確かめる。

**Haijin wa mainen genbaku-ki no na de, wasure-te naranai hi
no koto o tashikameru.**

Every year the haiku poet confirms the day not to be forgotten,
in the name of the anniversary of the atomic bomb.

## 25.4 [Verb-te no] noun

When V-te no modifies a following noun, it functions like a noun phrase.

### 25.4.1 Verb-te no noun (verb-te modifying noun)

For details and examples, see 6.6.3.3, 2.3.1.13, also 2.1.8.2.

## 25.5 Splitting of predicate/copula by a 'sandwiched' particle

The forms that get split include -te/de aru/iru, and the copula variant de aru, as da itself cannot be split any further.

Splitting particles include mo and wa (see 11.1.1.3, 11.2.3.3, 11.2.1.3, 11.2.1.7, 11.2.1.8 and 11.3.5.3.2, 11.3.5.3.3).

Example a is an instance of de aru being split by the particle mo, which adds the sense of 'also'.

a 父親のかわりでもあった。
**Chichioya no kawari de mo atta.**
He was also a father-substitute.

## 25.6 Negative conjunctive forms

The negative adjective **nai** and the negative ending -**nai** have both **nakute** (and the stem form **naku** as written-form equivalent) and -**nai de** as their conjunctive forms. Instead of -**nai de**, -**zu** is also used in written language (see 6.1.2).

The use of these forms to add other verbs or clauses is shown in the following sections.

### 25.6.1 Noun/sō de wa/ja naku naru

-**naku** is used to attach the verb **naru** 'become', or the adverb **sō** 'this way', 'so', with the combined meaning being 'cease to be', 'be no longer'.

a がんは不治の病ではなくなった。
**Gan wa fuji no yamai de wa naku natta.**
Cancer is no longer an incurable disease.

b だから今度は、そうじゃなくなる始まりではないでしょうか。
**Da kara kondo wa, sō ja naku naru hajimari de wa nai
  deshō ka.**
So, I wonder if this time might be the beginning of things no longer
  being the way they were [= citizens being expected to be passive].

### 25.6.2 *Noun + particle* **naku(te)**

**nakute** is the negative conjunctive form of the negative adjective **nai** 'there
isn't' (in the written style, **naku** is often used instead). The meaning is
'without', 'free from', 'not . . . and'.

a 癖がなくて予想以上に飲みやすい。
**Kuse ga nakute yosō ijō ni nomiyasui.**
It's free from peculiar tastes, and easier to drink than expected.

b けが人はなく、大きな混乱もなかった。
**Keganin wa naku, ōki na konran mo nakatta**
Nobody was injured, and there wasn't any major disturbance.

c 事故当時、海上は波がなく静かだった。
**Jiko tōji, kaijō wa nami ga naku shizuka datta.**
At the time of the accident, the ocean was calm (*lit.* "free of waves")
  and smooth.

### 25.6.2.1 *A* **de wa/ja naku(te)**, *B*

This indicates the sense of 'not *A*, but *B*'.

a 丈夫なだけではなくて美しい歯を。
**Jōbu na dake de wa nakute utsukushii ha o.**
[One should have] teeth that are not only strong, but [also] beautiful.

b ピアニストの命は、手や指だけじゃなくて、心なんです。
**Pianisuto no inochi wa, te ya yubi dake ja nakute, kokoro
  nan desu.**
The life of a pianist is not only in the hands or fingers, but [also] in
  the heart.

c 「ドル安ではなく、円高だ」と強調した。
**'Doruyasu de wa naku, endaka da' to kyōchō shita**
'It's not that the dollar is low, but the yen is high', he emphasized.

d 「ハーフって何」 ・・・ 「ハーフじゃなくてダブルよ」
**'Hāfu tte nani' ... 'Hāfu ja nakute daburu yo'**
'What's half[-breed]?' 'You're not "half", you know, you're "double"!'
[= by having parents from two different cultures]

**25.6.2.2** *Noun* **de wa/ja naku(te),** ...

As a negative equivalent of **de, . . .** , this means 'not N, and'.

a 私は政治家ではなく、特別なイデオロギーを持っていない。
**Watashi wa seijika de wa naku, tokubetsu na ideorogī o
motte inai.**
I'm not a politician, and don't have any particular ideology.

**25.6.2.3** *Adjective/noun-***dokoro de wa naku,** ...

This expresses that some state is of a surprising degree 'you must be joking', 'far from it'.

a 暗いどころではなく、もう真っ暗。
**Kurai dokoro de wa naku, mō makkura.**
Dark? You must be joking, it was pitch-black!

b 紅葉どころではなく、冬山になっている。
**Kōyō dokoro de wa naku, fuyuyama ni natte iru.**
Far from [having] coloured leaves, the mountains are covered in snow.

**25.6.3** *Verb-***nakute**

**25.6.3.1** *Verb-***nakute** *(mo)* **yoi/ii/daijōbu**

This indicates permission not to do something: 'it's OK if you don't', 'you needn't' (see 25.2.2).

a 「明日から来なくていい」と言われた。
**'Ashita kara konakute' ii to iwareta.**
I was told 'You needn't come from tomorrow'.

563

b お米は買いだめしなくても大丈夫です。
**Okome wa kaidame shinakute mo daijōbu desu.**
There is no need to hoard rice.

c そんなに焦らなくても、まだ若いのだから。
**Sonna ni aseranakute mo, mada wakai no da kara.**
You needn't be so impatient; you're still young.

d ふろを沸かす熱も少なくてすむ。
**Furo o wakasu netsu mo sukunakute sumu.**
One also needs less heat to warm the water for a bath [= using waste energy].

25.6.3.2 *Verb-**nakute gomen/sumanai**, etc.*

Like its counterpart using the positive conjunctive form (see 25.3.4), this is used for apologies: 'sorry for not having done'.

a 就職しなくてごめんね。
**Shūshoku shinakute gomen ne.**
Sorry I haven't found a job.

b ご期待に沿えなくてすみません。
**Go-kitai ni soenakute sumimasen.**
I'm sorry not to have met your expectations.

25.6.3.3 *Noun + particle/clause **nakute wa** (negative)*

With ellipted second negative, the meaning is usually 'must' or 'without' (see 17.2.2.1).

a 人間は酸素がなくては生きていけない。
**Ningen wa sanso ga nakute wa ikite ikenai.**
Man cannot live without oxygen.

b でも、産んだからには子供を幸せにしなくては。
**Demo, unda kara ni wa kodomo o shiawase ni shinakute wa.**
But, now that you've had a child you have to make him happy.

c 映画館は学校ではない。まず、見る人が楽しめなくては。
**Eigakan wa gakkō de wa nai. Mazu, miru hito ga tanoshimenakute wa.**
A movie theatre is not a school. Above all, the viewers have to be able to enjoy themselves.

## 25.6.3.4 | Noun **narade wa**

**narade wa** is a classical equivalent to modern **de (wa) nai to** 'unless is'; it is used in the sense of 'not possible unless', 'the hallmark of'.

a はらわたの苦みは新鮮なアユならでは。
**Harawata no nigami wa shinsen na ayu narade wa.**
The bitter [and delicious] taste of the entrails is the hallmark of fresh sweetfish [= is what you get only with fresh sweetfish].

## 25.6.3.5 | Noun + particle/clause **nakute ne**

In the form **nakute**, **ne** is used to complete a sentence in the explanatory sense of 'you see'. The second half of the sentence, which is ellipted or 'understood', implies something like **komatte iru** 'I'm in trouble' (see 19.2).

a 肉が買えなくてね。
**Niku ga kaenakute ne.**
We can't buy any meat, you see.

b 集中力がなくてね。
**Shūchūryoku ga nakute ne.**
He has no ability to concentrate, you see.

c 料亭が悪いと言ったわけじゃなくてね。
**Ryōtei ga warui to itta wake ja nakute ne.**
I didn't say that Japanese restaurants are to blame.

## 25.6.4 | Verb-**nai de**

-**nai de** is the other negative conjunctive form of the negative V ending -**nai**. It has four uses, as shown below (compare with the uses of -**nakute** in 25.6.3).

## 25.6.4.1 | In compound sentences

When joining two clauses in a compound sentence (which could easily be expressed in two separate sentences – see also 25.1) the meaning is 'not . . . and'.

a 「心配しないで強気で行ってくれ」と進言したほどだ。
**'Shinpai shinai de tsuyoki de itte kure' to shingen shita hodo da.**
We went so far as to suggest, 'Don't worry; just take the bull by the horns'.

b 日系人にはすぐ帰らないでもっといなさいと言いたい。
**Nikkeijin ni wa sugu kaeranai de motto inasai to iitai.**
To [foreigners] of Japanese descent I want to say, don't go back home so soon, stay longer.

c 「泣いてないで、部屋の掃除でもしなさい」「マラソンでもしなさい」。（泣いてない ＝ 泣いていない）
**'Naite nai de, heya no sōji demo shinasai' 'Marason demo shinasai'). [naitenai = naite inai]**
'Don't cry; clean up your room or something.' 'Go for a run or something.'

---

| 25.6.4.2 | *Modifying predicate* |

This expresses the idea of 'without (doing)'.

a あんたが決断しないでどうする。
**Anta ga ketsudan shinai de dō suru.**
If you don't decide, who will? (*lit.* "What are we going to do without your deciding?")

b 役者が面白いと思えるようになったのは50すぎてから。それまでは人生、分からないでやってたから。
**Yakusha ga omoshiroi to omoeru yō ni natta no wa gojū sugite kara. Sore made wa jinsei, wakaranai de yatteta kara.**
It was after 50 that I was able to begin to think that acting was fun. Until then, I had led my life without understanding things, you see.

---

| 25.6.4.3 | *Verb-potential-**nai de iru*** |

The potential verb gives it a literal meaning of "be in a state without being able to", i.e. 'be unable to'.

a 「特別な例では」と、いまだに驚きを隠せないでいた。
**'Tokubetsu na rei de wa' to, imada ni odoroki o kakusenai de ita.**
'Isn't it a special case?' he said, even now unable to conceal his surprise.

b 約束はまだ果たせないでいる。
**Yakusoku wa mada hatasenai de iru.**
He is still unable to fulfil his promise.

*Verb-**nai de** (**kudasai/kure/hoshii/moraitai**)*

The pattern V-**nai de** can be followed by a request (**kure/kudasai/hoshii/ moraitai**), although these forms are often ellipted.

**kudasai/kure** is used for negative commands, but as **kudasai/kure** is often ellipted (or 'understood'), the command frequently ends in **-te** (**ne**) or **-te** (**nē**). Without **kudasai/kure**, the command has a more informal and intimate ring 'don't' (see 20.2, 19.2).

With **hoshii** and **moraitai**, the meaning is one of request (see 9.2.3, 15.5).

a 息は止めないで下さいねー。
**Iki wa tomenai de kudasai ne--.**
Please don't hold your breath.

b マミー行かないで。
**Mamī ikanai de.**
Mummy, don't go.

c その子が「先生には言わないで」と私に手を合わせる。
**Sono ko ga 'Sensei ni wa iwanai de' to watashi ni te o awaseru.**
The child said beseechingly (*lit.* "clasped her hands towards me"),
    'Don't tell the teacher'.

d 会合には出ないで欲しい。
**Kaigō ni wa denai de hoshii.**
I don't want you to attend the meeting.

e 決して腰くだけにならないでもらいたい。
**Kesshite koshikudake ni naranai de moraitai.**
I don't want you to lose your nerve on any account.

*Verb-**zu** (**ni**): written-style negative conjunctive form*

This is the written-style equivalent of -**nai de** (see 25.6.5.2). The difference between -**zu** and -**zu ni** is that -**zu** joins two clauses in the sense of 'not . . . , but' or 'not . . . , and', whereas -**zu ni** modifies a predicate in the sense of 'without'.

25.6.5.1 -zu, . . .

-zu joins two clauses in the sense of 'not . . . , but . . .' or 'not . . . , and . . .'

a 中華麺を油で揚げず、ゆでて袋詰めした。(= 揚げないで)
**Chūkamen o abura de agezu, yudete fukurozume shita.
(= agenai de)**
We have packaged Chinese noodles boiled, not deep-fried in oil.

b 熱帯雨林の内部は光が届かず、意外に静かなのだ。
(= 届かなくて)
**Nettai urin no naibu wa hikari ga todokazu, igai ni shizuka na
no da. (= todokanakute)**
Light doesn't penetrate the inside of a tropical rainforest, and it's
surprisingly quiet.

c 名前を知らず、話したことがなくてもあいさつをする。
(= 知らないで)
**Namae o shirazu, hanashita koto ga nakute mo aisatsu o
suru. (= shiranai de)**
He says hello even if he doesn't know the person's name, and hasn't
talked [to the person] before.

25.6.5.2 Verb-**zu ni** (= -nai de)

Here, V-**zu** modifies a following predicate in the sense of 'without (doing)'.

a 男は何も取らずに逃走した。
**Otoko wa nani mo torazu ni tōsō shita.**
The man fled without taking anything.

b つまらないことを考えずに勉強しなさい。
**Tsumaranai koto o kangaezu ni benkyō shinasai.**
Don't think silly thoughts, and get on with your studies.

c メモも見ずにすらすら数字が出る。
**Memo mo mizu ni surasura sūji ga deru.**
Without even consulting his notes, figures flow smoothly [from his mouth].

d 売り込むことはせずに、自然にということらしい。
**Urikomu koto wa sezu ni, shizen ni to iu koto rashii.**
The intention seems to leave things [= selling sake in India] to
the market, without pushing it.

After time expressions, **-zu ni** can mean the equivalent of **-nai uchi ni** 'before' (see 26.2.8).

e 半年たたずに先輩四人を飛び越し社長に。

**Hantoshi tatazu ni senpai yonin o tobikoshi shachō ni.**

Before six months had elapsed, he rose over the heads of four of his superiors to become company president.

## 25.6.5.3 Verb-**zu ni iru** (= -**nai de iru**)

This is the equivalent of -**nai de iru** 'unable to' (see 25.6.4.3).

a 赤ん坊の時に抱かれた記憶もなく、父の愛情を実感できず
   にいた。

**Akanbō no toki ni dakareta kioku mo naku, chichi no aijō o jikkan dekizu ni ita.**

I didn't even have any recollection of being held when I was a baby, and I was unable to feel my father's love.

## 25.6.5.4 Verb-**zu-jimai da**

This consists of the negative ending -**zu** and the stem form of the verb **shimau** (voiced), a combination that means 'end up' (see 8.11). It indicates that one ends up not doing something one was going to do or wanted to do.

a 結局はおふろに入れずじまい。

**Kekkyoku wa o-furo ni hairezu-jimai.**

In the end I was unable to take a bath.

b ああ今日も外に出ずじまいだった。

**Aa kyō mo soto ni dezu-jimai datta.**

Ah, I ended up not going outside again today.

# Chapter 26

# *Conjunctive particles*

Conjunctive particles are used to conjoin clauses in a variety of meanings, which include condition, time, concession, contrast, purpose/reason, addition, and range of activities.

## 26.1 Condition

### 26.1.1 -ba

S1-**ba** basically indicates the condition which is necessary for S2 to become possible 'if . . . then . . .'; typically, this can be 'turned around' and interpreted as 'if not . . . , then not . . .'. In -**ba** sentences, the action or state of S1 or S2, or both, is *not* controllable by the speaker (see 26.1.2).

For -**ba** forms of V, Adj, (**na**-Adj/N) + copula, see conditional forms listed under 7.1, 6.1, 7.5.

-**ba** tends to be used in the written (or formal spoken) language rather than in the spoken style, although there are colloquial contractions that are used in the spoken style, such as -**kerya** instead of -**kereba** (see also 17.2.2).

With N and **na**-Adj, **nara** is often used instead of -**ba** (see 26.1.4).

#### 26.1.1.1 *Clause 1-**ba** clause 2 (clause 2 = non-past)*

##### 26.1.1.1.1 Necessary condition 'if'

-**ba** implies that if the condition of S1 is not fulfilled, S2 cannot take place.

**tara** can also be used in these sentences, but **to** can only be used in examples a and b (but with a different implication, i.e. in the habitual sense of 'always').

**Seiseki ga yokereba, gōkakusho ga dete kuru.**
If the results are good, a certificate is issued.

b だだをこねれば、無理が通る。
**Dada o konereba, muri ga tōru.**
If they throw a tantrum, they get their own way.

c 安くなければおしゃれじゃない。
**Yasukunakereba oshare ja nai.**
If it's not cheap it's not fashionable.

d いい土地があればすぐにも移る。
**Ii tochi ga areba sugu ni mo utsuru.**
If there's a good plot of land, we'll move right away.

e がんばれば、いつかはチャンスがある。
**Ganbareba, itsu ka wa chansu ga aru.**
If you try your best, your chance will come sometime.

| 26.1.1.1.2 | General condition 'when'

Instead of -**ba**, both -**tara** and **to** can also be used in these sentences.

a 障害とは人が歳をとれば必ず持つようになるものだ。
**Shōgai to wa hito ga toshi o toreba kanarazu motsu yō ni
naru mono da.**
A disability is something that everyone inevitably gets when
getting old.

b 会えば話がはずむ。
**Aeba hanashi ga hazumu.**
When they meet, their conversation is lively.

| 26.1.1.2 | *Clause 1-**ba** clause 2 (clause 2 = past): hypothetical condition*

Here, S2 uses the past/perfect ending -**ta** (often in the form -**te ita**), often
with an expression of conjecture or guessing. The combination indicates
a hypothetical (i.e. unrealized) condition 'if . . . would have . . .'. -**tara** can
also be used in the same sense.

a シートベルトをしていれば、助かった。
**Shītoberuto o shite ireba, tasukatta.**
If he had been wearing a seatbelt, he would have lived.

b これからも、あのときああすればよかったと後悔することはした
くない。

**Kore kara mo, ano toki ā sureba yokatta to kōkai suru koto
wa shitakunai.**

From now on, too, I don't want to regret things, thinking that I should
have done things differently that time.

### 26.1.1.3 | *Idiomatic uses*

### 26.1.1.3.1 | -ba ii

-**ba ii** (*lit.* "is good if") indicates the idea of 'should', 'would be good if'
or, in the past tense, 'would have been good if', 'was OK if'. -**reba ii** can
colloquially be contracted to -**rya ii** (example d).

*Note* – **ii** (+ copula), etc. can be omitted (examples g–i), in which case the
meaning can be a statement (= -**ba ii desu**), or with question intonation a
recommendation 'how about . . .' (see 25.2.1, 26.4.5.2.2, 26.1.2.4.1).

a では、どうすればいいだろう。

**Dewa, dō sureba ii darō.**

What should we do then, I wonder.

b 年末で修理業者は休みだし、どうやって正月を迎えればいいのか
と嘆息した。

**Nenmatsu de shūri-gyōsha wa yasumi da shi, dō yatte
shōgatsu o mukaereba ii no ka to tansoku shita.**

Repair shops being closed at the end of the year, I just wonder
how we can make it to the New Year, he sighed.

c いっしょに過ごすボーイフレンドがいればいいんですけど。

**Issho ni sugosu bōifurendo ga ireba ii n desu kedo.**

It's OK if one has a boyfriend to spend [Christmas] with.

d 休みだって長けりゃいいってもんじゃないらしい。

**Yasumi datte nagakerya ii tte mon ja nai rashii.**

Holidays, it seems, are not necessarily the longer the better.

e 私に似ればよかったのだが、残念ながら子供たちのツメは切
りにくい。

**Watashi ni nireba yokatta no da ga, zannen-nagara
kodomo-tachi no tsume wa kiri-nikui**

It would have been OK if they'd taken after me, but unfortunately
the children's nails are hard to cut.

f 四年生になると、大学は週一回授業に通えばよかった。

**Yonen-sei ni naru to, daigaku wa shū ikkai jugyō ni kayoeba yokatta.**

Once you got to the fourth year, you just needed to go to university once a week for classes.

g 微力ながら町のお手伝いができれば。

**Biryoku-nagara machi no o-tetsudai ga dekireba.**

It would be good (= I'd be happy) if I could use my limited abilities to help the town.

h 空港さえなければ。

**Kūkō sae nakereba.**

If only there wasn't the airport [= Itami, after opening of Kansai].

i 献体をなされば？お葬式は不要。

**Kentai o nasareba? O-sōshiki wa fuyō.**

How about donating your body? No funeral needed.

---

26.1.1.3.2 | Negative-**ba** + negative

The combination indicates the meaning of 'must', 'have to' (for more examples and variations of form, see 17.2.2).

a 言わなければならないことは申し上げた。

**Iwanakereba naranai koto wa mōshiageta.**

I've told him the things that needed saying.

---

26.1.1.3.3 | **to ieba**

to ieba is used when one thinks of something or when two things are automatically associated with each other (see also 21).

a 缶のお茶といえば、ウーロン茶を思いつく人が多いだろう。

**Kan no o-cha to ieba, ūron-cha o omoitsuku hito ga ōi darō.**

At the mention of tea in cans, many probably think of Oolong tea.

b 鳥といえば、近くにはスズメかハトくらいしかいない。

**Tori to ieba, chikaku ni wa suzume ka hato kurai shika inai.**

Birds? Around here there are only sparrows and pigeons.

---

26.1.1.3.4 | **sō ieba**

This is used when the speaker indicates that he or she has just recalled some fact (by association from the preceding context or otherwise) 'come to think of it'.

573

a 送電の故障はこの10年で40%減少したという。そういえば、ちか
　ごろは停電でろうそくの世話になることも少なくなった。

**Sōden no koshō wa kono jūnen de yonjup-pāsento genshō
shita to iu. Sō ieba, chikagoro wa teiden de rōsoku no sewa
ni naru koto mo sukunaku natta.**

Breakdowns in electricity transmission are said to have decreased by
40 per cent over the past 10 years. Come to think of it, having to
rely on candles because of power failure doesn't happen much
these days.

b そういえば、Fさんは別性夫婦だったね。

**Sō ieba, F-san wa bessei fūfū datta ne.**

Come to think of it, you [= Mr and Mrs F] are a couple using
different surnames, right?

26.1.1.3.5 | Verb-**ru to sureba**

This is a way of emphasizing the condition 'if (at all)'.

a 問題があるとすれば大学の工学部離れが進んでいることという
　関係者もいる。

**Mondai ga aru to sureba daigaku no kōgakubu-banare ga
susunde iru koto to iu kankeisha mo iru.**

Some of those concerned say that if there is a problem, it's the trend
away from engineering departments in the university.

26.1.1.3.6 | **iikaereba, kurabereba, nazoraereba**, etc.

These expressions mean 'in other words' (**iikaereba**) and 'compared to'
(**kurabereba** and **nazoraereba**). The difference between the last two is that
whereas **kurabereba** is a straightforward comparison between *A* and *B*,
**nazoraereba** involves 'likening' *B* to *A*, or using *A* to explain *B*.

a 言い換えれば、今の教育現場はいじめの温床づくりをしている
　のだ。

**Iikaereba, ima no kyōiku genba wa ijime no onshō-zukuri o
shite iru no da.**

In other words, the classrooms are now hotbeds of bullying.

b 10月の地震に比べれば、軽くてよかった。

**Jūgatsu no jishin ni kurabereba, karukute yokatta.**

It was a relief that it was mild compared to the October
earthquake.

c 柔道になぞらえれば、いじめにも"受け身"がある。
**Jūdō ni nazoraereba, ijime ni mo 'ukemi' ga aru.**
If you compare it to judo, there are safe ways of being thrown in
bullying, too.

## 26.1.2 -tara

-tara links two clauses (S1-**tara** S2) in the sense of 'when' or 'if'. The basic
meaning of -**tara** is temporal, i.e. it is concerned with a sequence of time.

-tara forms of V, Adj, **na**-Adj and N + copula are formed by attaching -**ra**
to their respective plain past form, -**ta**.

S1-**tara** S2 indicates a condition that is used in the spoken language rather
than in the formal written style. S2 can use non-factual forms such as
request or hortative (-**te kudasai**, -**y(ō)**, etc.). The condition indicated by
-tara tends to be a specific or individual condition rather than a general
one (see 26.1.5).

### 26.1.2.1 *Clause1-**tara** clause 2 (clause 2 = non-past)*

#### 26.1.2.1.1 Clause 1-**tara** clause 2 'when'

This means 'when . . . , then . . .' in the sense that when S1 happens (which
is a matter of certainty), then S2 will happen. The implication is that S1
will occur inevitably.

a 花が終わったら、こまめに摘み取る。
**Hana ga owattara, komame ni tsumitoru.**
When the flowers are finished, you pick them carefully.

b 大きくなったら、絵かきさんになりたい。
**Ōkiku nattara, ekaki-san ni naritai.**
When I grow up, I want to be a painter.

c 中学に入ったら、ヨッちゃんともナッくんとも別々の学校になっ
ちゃうんだよ。さびしいよ。
**Chūgaku ni haittara, Yot-chan to mo Nak-kun to mo**
**betsubetsu no gakkō ni natchau n da yo. Sabishii yo.**
When we enter junior high school, both Yot-chan and Nak-kun will be
going to different schools. I'll be lonely.

26.1.2.1.2
Clause I-**tara** clause 2 'if'

In this case, there is nothing inevitable about S1. Instead, the implication is that if the action of S1 is carried out, then the action or state of S2 will happen or apply. In this use, -**tara** has the same sense as -**ba** 'if ..., then ...', but with a more colloquial ring.

a こんな領収書を税務署に出したら、すぐに突っ返される。
**Konna ryōshusho o zeimusho ni dashitara, sugu ni tsukkaesareru.**
If you show this sort of receipt to the tax office, they'll throw it right back at you.

b この機会を逃したら、永遠にチャンスは来ないのではないか。
**Kono kikai o nogashitara, eien ni chansu wa konai no de wa nai ka.**
If we miss this opportunity, we'll never get another chance!

c 漁師の仕事は好きじゃなかったら、できないからね。
**Ryōshi no shigoto wa suki ja nakattara, dekinai kara ne.**
If you don't like the work of a fisherman, you can't do it, you see.

26.1.2.2
*Clause I-**tara** clause 2 (clause 2 = past)*

26.1.2.2.1
Clause I-**tara** clause 2: 'when'

Here, S2 cannot be controlled by the speaker, being a realization or discovery on the part of the speaker, in the sense of 'when ..., then ...'.

a 電話で話したら、息子が泣いて困ったよ。
**Denwa de hanashitara, musuko ga naite komatta yo.**
When we spoke on the phone, my son was crying, and I didn't know what to do.

b 困って即興でソロ演奏したら、これが意外に受けた。
**Komatte sokkyō de soro ensō shitara, kore ga igai ni uketa.**
Not knowing what to do, I improvised a solo number, and unexpectedly that was a success.

c 人間ドックに入ったら、肝臓に問題ありと注意された。
**Ningen dokku ni haittara, kanzō ni mondai ari to chūi sareta.**
When I had a medical check-up, I was warned that I had a liver problem.

d 4月になったら、とたんに売り注文がこなくなった。
**Shigatsu ni nattara, totan ni urichūmon ga konaku natta.**
Once April came, requests for selling [shares] suddenly stopped.

**26.1.2.2.2** Clause 1 **-tara/dattara** clause 2: 'if/had' (hypothetical condition)

Here, S2 uses an expression of conjecture or guessing in combinations with the past/perfect ending **-ta** (often in the form **-te ita**). The combination indicates a hypothetical (i.e. unrealized) condition 'if . . . , would have . . .'.

a 操業停止がなかったら、営業利益は増えたはずだった。
**Sōgyō teishi ga nakattara, eigyō rieki wa fueta hazu datta.**
Had there not been a halt in operations, the operating profit would be expected to have increased.

b 湿度の高い気候だったら、金属器はさび，木製品は腐っていただ ろう。
**Shitsudo no takai kikō dattara, kinzokuki wa sabi, mokuseihin wa kusatte ita darō.**
Had it been a climate with high humidity, the iron vessels would have rusted, and the wooden items rotted.

c 留学先が米国だったら、父はうんといわなかったでしょうね。
**Ryūgakusaki ga beikoku dattara, chichi wa un to iwanakatta deshō ne.**
Had I wanted to study in the US, Father would probably not have allowed it.

**26.1.2.3** *Clause 1* **dattara** *clause 2*

Like **nara**, its somewhat less colloquial variant, **dattara** (which may be thought of as the **-tara** form of the copula) is attached to V/A and **na**-Adj/N as follows (see 26.1.4):

V-ru/Adj-**i** (n(o)) **dattara**
**na**-Adj/N **dattara**

**26.1.2.3.1** (n) **dattara**

(n) **dattara** is used in the same way as (n) **nara**.

a やるんだったら情熱をもってやりたい。
**Yaru n dattara jōnetsu o motte yaritai.**
If I do it [= voluntary work], I want to do it with dedication.

b 結婚を控えているのに申し訳ない。嫌だったらそう言ってくれ。
**Kekkon o hikaete iru noni mōshiwake nai. Iya dattara sō itte kure.**
I'm sorry [to transfer you] even though you're about to get married. If you don't want to go, say so.

c　永住者が自分の生活に不満があるんだったら、日本よりも豪州の
　選挙権を取得するのが筋ではないですか。

**Eijūsha ga jibun no seikatsu ni fuman ga aru n dattara, Nihon yori mo Gōshū no senkyoken o shutoku suru no ga suji de wa nai desu ka.**

If the permanent residents are unhappy with their lot, surely what they should be doing is acquiring the right to vote in Australia rather than Japan.

d　もし二〇度以下だったら死んでいたかもしれない。

**Moshi nijū-do ika dattara shinde ita kamoshirenai.**

If the water temperature had been below 20 degrees, I could have died.

e　ホリデーだったら、フェリーがやっぱりお薦めだね。

**Horidē dattara, ferī ga yappari o-susume da ne.**

If you're going on holiday (*lit.* "if it's a holiday"), then I recommend using the ferry.

f　日本だったら大学に行けない。

**Nihon dattara daigaku ni ikenai.**

In Japan, you wouldn't be able to get into university [= with these qualifications].

26.1.2.3.2 | Clause I **dattara** clause 2 (clause 2 = past)

This indicates a hypothetical condition (see 26.1.4.5, 26.1.2.2.2).

a　あのままだったら、コンパックはどこにでもある会社になってい
　たでしょう。

**Ano mama dattara, Konpakku wa doko ni demo aru kaisha ni natte ita deshō.**

Had things remained that way, Compaq would have ended up a company like any other.

26.1.2.3.3 | Noun **dattara**

In this use, **dattara** functions like **wa** (see 26.1.4.7).

a　昔だったら自宅から最寄り駅まで車で十五分だったが今は倍以上
　かかる。

**Mukashi dattara jitaku kara moyori eki made kuruma de jūgofun datta ga ima wa bai ijō kakaru.**

In the old days, it took about 15 minutes by car from home to the nearest station, but now it takes twice that time.

## 26.1.2.4  -tara *to make recommendations/suggestions*

Recommendations use the form V-**tara** + evaluatory adjective, most typically **ii** 'good'. The combination literally means "is good if", i.e. 'would be nice if', or 'you should' in statements, and 'should I?' in questions.

Suggestions use the form -**tara dō** copula **ka**.

## 26.1.2.4.1  -tara ii, etc.

The non-past -**tara ii** means 'should', whereas in the past -**ta** form, the meaning becomes hypothetical, 'should have' (with or without **noni** attached). However, attaching a form like **noni** to -**tara ii** also makes a non-past sentence hypothetical (see 26.4.5).

For similar uses of conditional particles, see 26.1.1.3.1, 26.1.3.6 and also 15.6.2.2.

a 「遊びと勉強の両方がやれたらいい」とパソコン効果に期待している。

**'Asobi to benkyō no ryōhō ga yaretara ii' to pasokon kōka o kitai shite iru.**

He expresses his expectations for [the children's] use of personal computers with the words 'It would be nice if they could use them for both play and study'.

b スーツケースには何を詰めたらいいだろうか。朝はちゃんと起きられるだろうか……。

**Sūtsukēsu ni wa nani o tsumetara ii darō ka. Asa wa chanto okirareru darō ka...**

What should I pack in the suitcase? Will I be able to get up in the mornings? [= stewardess training].

c こんなコンピューターがあったらいいのに。

**Konna konpyūtā ga attara ii noni.**

It would be nice to have this kind of computer [= brainstorming].

d 「男だったらよかったのに」と言われて落とされたといったケースも報告され、…

**'Otoko dattara yokatta noni' to iwarete otosareta to itta kēsu mo hōkoku sare,...**

There were even reports of cases where [female applicants] were turned down with the words 'It would have been OK had you been male...' [= tight job market]

26.1.2.4.2 **-tara/dattara (dō)**, etc.

Note that **dō** (**desu**) **ka** etc. can be omitted, as in example c (see also 26.1.7.5).

a 静岡県に引っ越したらどうですか。
**Shizuoka-ken ni hikkoshitara dō desu ka.**
How about moving to Shizuoka prefecture?

b もっと頻繁に来られたらどうですか。
**Motto hinpan ni koraretara dō desu ka.**
How about coming more often?

c それほど興味があった訳ではないが、「やってみたら」と誘われ、参加を決めた。
**Sore hodo kyōmi ga atta wake de wa nai ga, 'Yatte mitara' to sasoware, sanka o kimeta.**
I wasn't that interested in the debate, but someone asked me to give it a try, so I decided to join in.

26.1.2.5 *Verb-***tara** *verb-***ta de**

Here, the same verb is repeated, once with **-tara** and the second time with **-ta de**. The combination indicates that 'once the action of the verb is completed, some new perspective or problem appears'.

a 知名度はすでに高いため、「いっそCMをやめても良いのではないか」との指摘もあるが、やめたらやめたで「会社が危ないのか」と疑われかねません。
**Chimeido wa sude ni takai tame, 'Isso shīemu o yamete mo yoi no de wa nai ka' to no shiteki mo aru ga, yametara yameta de 'kaisha ga abunai no ka' to utagaware-kanemasen.**
As it [our product] is already well known, some point out that we could stop advertising it [on TV], but once we stop it, people might think the company is in danger of going bust.

b そういえば散歩に出る時は何となく浮き浮きした気分になるし、出たら出たであっちの路地こっちの路地と"探検"したくなる。
**Sō ieba sanpo ni deru toki wa nantonaku ukiuki shita kibun ni naru shi, detara deta de atchi no roji kotchi no roji to 'tanken' shitaku naru.**
Come to think of it, when you go out for a walk you somehow feel cheerful, and once you've gone out, you feel like exploring this or that side street.

### 26.1.2.6 *Idiomatic expressions*

Idiomatic expressions include **to shitara** 'if one assumes', **moshi ka shitara** 'perchance', 'possibly', **dattara** 'in that case', **dō yattara** 'how', **-ttara** (an equivalent of **to ittara**, or the adverbial particle **wa**).

a 日本のメディアがご飯だとしたら、我々はしょうゆ。つまり風味づけが仕事なのです。
**Nihon no media ga gohan da to shitara, wareware wa shōyu. Tsumari fūmizuke ga shigoto na no desu.**
If one compares the Japanese media to rice, then we [foreign TV] are the soy sauce. In other words, our job is [to provide] the seasoning.

b もしかしたら努力が一生報われないかもしれない。
**Moshi ka shitara doryoku ga isshō mukuwarenai kamoshirenai.**
My efforts may not be rewarded in my lifetime [in this job].

c アクセサリーや小物だと、趣味に合うかどうかわからないし、予算が五、六千円だから中途半端なものしか買えない。だったら一ランク上の日用品がいいかな。
**Akusesarī ya komono da to, shumi ni au ka dō ka wakaranai shi, yosan ga go, rokusen-en da kara chūto hanpa na mono shika kaenai. Dattara ichiranku ue no nichiyōhin ga ii ka na.**
With accessories and trinkets, you don't know whether they'll suit [the recipient's] taste, and with a budget of five or six thousand yen you can't buy anything decent. In that case, an everyday item of better quality is preferable [as a present], I guess.

d どうやったらもっと売り上げを伸ばせるか、固定客を増やせるか。
**Dō yattara motto uriage o nobaseru ka, koteikyaku o fuyaseru ka.**
How can we increase sales and increase [the number of] regular customers?

e A子ったら、彼氏ができたとたんに、つきあいが悪くなって。
**A-ko-ttara kareshi ga dekita totan ni, tsukiai ga waruku natte.**
The moment A-ko got herself a boyfriend she became less chummy.

### 26.1.3 to

**to** is a conjunctive particle that indicates a condition for S2, the main predicate. The condition indicated by **to** is essentially habitual or immediate (when S1 occurs, S2 always, or immediately occurs) (see 26.1.2).

*Clause 1 non-past* **to**, *clause 2 non-past*

This indicates a habitual condition, i.e. when the action of S1 happens, the action or state of S2 regularly or habitually occurs 'when/if S1, something habitually does'.

a  ✑春になると花が咲く。
   **Haru ni naru to hana ga saku.**
   In spring/When spring comes, the blossoms bloom.

b  寒くなると、フグがおいしくなる。
   **Samuku naru to, fugu ga oishiku naru.**
   When it gets cold, blowfish becomes tasty.

c  雨上がりに探すと、採取しやすい。
   **Ameagari ni sagasu to, saishu shiyasui.**
   When you look for them after it's been raining, they [= mushrooms] are easy to collect.

d  政治と経済は同時に改革できない。一方で誤ると、結局両方とも失敗する。
   **Seiji to keizai wa dōji ni kaikaku dekinai. Ippō de ayamaru to, kekkyoku ryōhō tomo shippai suru.**
   You can't reform politics and the economy at the same time. If you make a mistake with one, in the end you go wrong with both.

e  一つ問題が片付くと、次の問題が起こる。
   **Hitotsu mondai ga katazuku to, tsugi no mondai ga okoru.**
   When one problem is taken care of, invariably the next problem arises.

*Clause 1 non-past* **to**, *clause 2 non-past/past*

Here, S2 takes place as a result of the action of S1 in the sense of 'when S1, something becomes apparent/is noticed'.

a  玄関を入ると、まず「大広間」。
   **Genkan o hairu to, mazu 'ōhiroma'.**
   When you enter the entrance hall, the first [thing you see] is 'the grand hall'.

b  玄関を入ると、元気のいい声が掛かる。
   **Genkan o hairu to, genki no ii koe ga kakaru.**
   When one enters the entrance hall, one is greeted by a cheery voice.

| 26.1.3.3 | *Clause 1 non-past* **to**, *clause 2 past* |
| --- | --- |

With past S2, the meaning is that the action of S2 'happened immediately' as a result of S1.

a 事務所に電話すると、所長が出た。
**Jimusho ni denwa suru to, shochō ga deta.**
When I rang the office, the director answered.

b どろぼうは警察を見ると、逃げていった。
**Dorobō wa keisatsu o miru to, nigete itta.**
When he saw the police, the burglar fled.

c 思い出すと、自然と元気が出た。
**Omoidasu to, shizen to genki ga deta.**
Whenever I remembered [the bustle of Hong Kong], I automatically cheered up.

| 26.1.3.4 | *Clause 1 non-past* **to**, *clause 2 past* **mono da** |
| --- | --- |

This is used to recall the past with nostalgia 'when S1, someone/something used to do' (19.1.1.5).

a 昔は、合戦の日になると、母親がささだんごを作ってくれたものです。
**Mukashi wa kassen no hi ni naru to, hahaoya ga sasadango o tsukutte kureta mono desu.**
In the old days, when the day of the battle came, the mothers would make bamboograss dumplings.

| 26.1.3.5 | *Clause 1 non-past* **to**, *clause 2* |
| --- | --- |

This construction means 'for example', 'generally speaking'.

a 新幹線から乗り継ぐと、特急料金が半額。
**Shinkansen kara noritsugu to, tokkyū ryōkin ga hangaku.**
If you change from the bullet train, the express train surcharge is half price.

b 結論的にいうと、筆者はそうは考えない。
**Ketsuron-teki ni iu to, hissha wa sō wa kangaenai.**
[Said] in conclusion, the author doesn't think so.

26.1.3.6 *Sentence* **to ii/yoi**

This expresses a recommendation 'should', in the same way as **-ba ii** and **-tara ii** (see 26.1.1.3.1, 26.1.2.4.1).

a 「手当て」という言葉があるように、自分で自分の体を触ってみ
   るといい。その部分が疲れていると感じたら、マッサージし
   たり、伸ばしてやる。

   **'Teate' to iu kotoba ga aru yō ni, jibun de jibun no karada o
   sawatte miru to ii. Sono bubun ga tsukarete iru to
   kanjitara, massāji shitari, nobashite yaru.**

   Just as there's a word '*teate*' ('care', *lit.* "placing hands"), one should
   touch one's own body. If one feels that part is tired, one should
   massage it, or stretch it.

b カリウムが豊富な果物や梅干しも十分に食べるとよい。

   **Kariumu ga hōfu na kudamono ya umeboshi mo jūbun ni
   taberu to yoi.**

   You should also eat plenty of fruit and dried plums, which contain
   lots of potassium.

c 事前に予約をしておくとよいだろう。

   **Jizen ni yoyaku o shite oku to yoi darō.**

   One should probably make a reservation in advance.

26.1.3.7 *Clause 1* **to**, *clause 2: idiomatic uses*

a 言い換えると、効率を悪くしています。

   **Iikaeru to, kōritsu o waruku shite imasu.**

   In other words, it [= the high phone rate] lowers the efficiency.

b 全通貨で見ると、ドルは安定している。

   **Zentsūka de miru to, doru wa antei shite iru.**

   Seen against all currencies, the dollar is stable.

c パリと比べると、ずっと素朴でわびしい。

   **Pari to kuraberu to, zutto soboku de wabishii.**

   Compared with Paris, it [Pont-Aven in Brittany] is much more
   unsophisticated and remote.

## 26.1.4 nara

Like -ba, dattara, -tara and to, nara indicates a condition, and often translates as 'if'. Note especially use 26.1.4.1, which is particular to nara and dattara (i.e. -ba, -tara and to cannot be used in this way).

nara (like its more colloquial variants (n) nara and (n) dattara) is attached to V/A, and na-A/N as follows.

V-ru/A-i (n(o)) nara    (Past: -ta (n(o)) nara)
na-A/N nara    (Past: noun datta (no) nara)

### 26.1.4.1 Taking up what someone else has said

a 会社に文句があるなら、自分で変えてみたら。
  **Kaisha ni monku ga aru nara, jibun de kaete mitara.**
  If you have complaints about the company, how about changing it
  yourself?

b 出るというなら、どうしてもいたくないと言うのなら、
  仕方がない。
  **Deru to iu nara, dōshite mo itakunai to iu no nara,
  shikata ga nai.**
  If he says he'll leave [the Party], and doesn't want to stay
  under any circumstances – that can't be helped.

c ワイエスさんなら今朝この店に来たわよ。
  **Waiesu-san nara kesa kono mise ni kita wa yo.**
  If you're looking for Wyeth, he came to my shop this morning.

d そんなに高いなら、おたくで買わないからいいですよ、
  という態度···
  **Sonna ni takai nara, otaku de kawanai kara ii desu yo,
  to iu taido ...**
  [The attitude of:] if it's that price, no thanks, I won't buy it at
  your shop ...

### 26.1.4.2 Clause 1 nara(-ba) clause 2: replaceable by -tara

Here, the hypothetical nature of S1 is weak, being more like an established fact.

a これ以上水不足が続くなら、ここらの稲が駄目になるのも時間の
問題だ。

**Kore ijō mizu busoku ga tsuzuku nara, kokora no ine ga
dame ni naru no mo jikan no mondai da.**

If the water shortage continues any longer, it's only a matter of time
before the rice plants around here are ruined.

b 直接あったなら、ありがとうと言いたい。

**Chokusetsu atta nara, arigatō to iitai.**

Once I've met her in person, I want to say thanks.

c 百万円預けたなら、三年後の受取額は百十万二千円。

**Hyakuman-en azuketa nara, sannen-go no uketori-gaku wa
hyakujūman nisen-en.**

If one has invested one million yen, the amount one receives after
three years is 1,102,000 yen.

d しかし、せっかく自然を求めて野外に来たならば、日帰りハイキ
ングのような気持ちで、車から降り自分の足で散策することを
勧めたい。

**Shikashi, sekkaku shizen o motomete yagai ni kita naraba,
higaeri haikingu no yō na kimochi de, kuruma kara ori
jibun no ashi de sansaku suru koto o susumetai.**

However, if people have come all the way in search of nature, I would
recommend they get out of the car and travel on foot, like on
a one-day hiking trip.

e 最初、冷水であら熱をとったなら、たっぷり氷を入れた水に移し
入れ、キューっと冷やす。

**Saisho, reisui de aranetsu o totta nara, tappuri kōri o ireta
mizu ni utsushiire, kyūtto hiyasu.**

After you've cooled off the first heat [of the dumplings] in cold water,
you put them in water with plenty of ice, and make them really
cold.

f ブランド品や有名店で買ったのならすぐ分かりますよ。

**Burandohin ya yūmeiten de katta no nara sugu wakarimasu
yo.**

If it's a well-known brand or one [= a diamond] that was bought in
a reputable shop, you check [the price] easily.

g …金融機関は「ダブルAなら安心」と油断していた。

**…kin'yū kikan wa 'daburu ē nara anshin' to yudan shite ita.**

…monetary institutions were off their guard, thinking that if they
were [rated] double A, there was nothing to worry about.

26.1.4.3 *Clause 1 = condition for clause 2 to take place*

Usually, S2 (if it takes place) precedes S1 in time.

a 三つの願いがかなうなら、何を望むか。
   **Mittsu no negai ga kanau nara, nani o nozomu ka.**
   If you could have three wishes fulfilled, what would you ask for?

b 君が喜ぶなら、ダイヤの指輪だって買ってあげよう。
   **Kimi ga yorokobu nara, daiya no yubiwa datte katte ageyō.**
   If it makes you happy, I'll even buy you a diamond ring.

c 女性があんないい人生を送れるなら、今度は断然女性に生まれ変わりたいですね。
   **Josei ga anna ii jinsei o okureru nara, kondo wa danzen josei ni umare-kawaritai desu ne.**
   If women can have such good lives, I definitely want to be reborn as a woman next time.

d フルタイムで働くなら、子供は産んでも一人。
   **Furutaimu de hataraku nara, kodomo wa unde mo hitori.**
   If I was to work full time, I'd have one child at most.

e ねえ、入るんならこっちのホテルがいいな。
   **Nē, hairu n nara kotchi no hoteru ga ii na.**
   Look, if we go [to a love hotel], then I'd like this one.

f 「あなたが本当のサンタさんならできるでしょ」とねだるシーン…(でしょ=でしょう)
   **'Anata ga hontō no Santa-san nara dekiru desho' to nedaru shīn … [desho = deshō]**
   The scene where [the girl] asks [to be given a brother and father] with the words 'If you're the real Santa, you should be able to do it' …

26.1.4.4 *Clause 1 and clause 2 expressing a contrast*

'If on the one hand . . . , then on the other'.

a 東京が欧米を向くなら、関西はアジアへの玄関口となるべきだ。
   **Tōkyō ga Ōbei o muku nara, Kansai wa Ajia e no genkanguchi to narubeki da.**
   If Tokyo looks to the West, then Kansai should became the gateway to Asia.

b 理事長が辞めるなら、私も辞める。

**Rijichō ga yameru nara, watashi mo yameru.**

If the chairman is going to quit, then I will too.

c 相手がタックル練習を百回やるなら、こっちは二百回
やったんだ。

**Aite ga takkuru renshū o hyakkai yaru nara, kotchi wa
nihyakkai yatta n da.**

If the rival team practised a tackle 100 times, we'd do it 200 times.

26.1.4.5 | *Clause 1-***ta nara** *(clause 2 = past)*

This indicates a hypothetical condition, although S2 can be left unsaid
(example a).

Note the combination **kari ni . . . nara** 'supposing that', 'assuming that'.

a 君がここにいてくれたなら。

**Kimi ga koko ni ite kureta nara.**

If you'd only stayed here.

b 仮に、いじめと認識できていたなら、学校側はどんな対応ができ
たのか。

**Kari ni, ijime to ninshiki dekite ita nara, gakkō-gawa wa
donna taiō ga dekita no ka.**

Supposing that they'd perceived things as bullying, what would
the school have been able to do about it?

c コンピューターよりパイロットの操縦を優先させるボーイング社
の航空機だったなら、今回のような事故は起きなかったという
意見はある。

**Konpyūtā yori pairotto no sōjū o yūsen saseru Bōingu-sha no
kōkūki datta nara, konkai no yō na jiko wa okinakatta to iu
iken wa aru.**

There are some who feel that had it been a Boeing plane, which gives
priority to the pilot's control rather than the computer, this
accident wouldn't have happened.

26.1.4.6 | *Idiomatic expressions*

26.1.4.6.1 | **onaji/dōse** verb-**ru nara**

This has the meaning 'if . . . anyway'.

a 同じもめるなら、今もめた方がいい。

**Onaji momeru nara, ima mometa hō ga ii.**

If we're going to have a dispute anyway, we might as well have it now.

b 同じ払うなら、ローンを払った方が資産が残っていい。

**Onaji harau nara, rōn o haratta hō ga shisan ga nokotte ii.**

If one pays anyway, it's better to pay off a loan, in which case property remains.

c 同じ働くなら、自分の好きなことを仕事にした方がやりがいがあるし、楽しい。

**Onaji hataraku nara, jibun no suki na koto o shigoto ni shita hō ga yarigai ga aru shi, tanoshii.**

If one works anyway, doing a job one likes is more rewarding and enjoyable.

| 26.1.4.6.2 | With same verb repeated |

| 26.1.4.6.2.1 | *Verb-***ru nara** *verb-***te miro** |

This involves a repetition of the same verb, flanked by **nara** and **-te miro**, literally meaning "if you do, then just try", i.e. 'I'll be ready for you!'

a 大型店進出に対する危機感を「来るなら来てみろ」と迎え撃つ気概に変える地元商店が増えることが結局は商店街の活性化につながるのではないか。

**Ōgata-ten shinshutsu ni taisuru kikikan o 'kuru nara kite miro' to mukae-utsu kigai ni kaeru jimoto shōten ga fueru koto ga kekkyoku wa shōtengai no kassei-ka ni tsunagaru no de wa nai ka.**

I think that the emergence of more local shops which stop panicking about the arrival of large retailers and adopt an attitude of defiance such as 'You come and we'll be ready for you' will in the end revitalize the shopping streets.

| 26.1.4.6.2.2 | *Verb-***ru mono nara** *verb-***tai** |

This is one way of emphasizing the condition, with a repeated V (see 19.1.2.4).

a 信組の監督は好きでやっているんじゃない。こんな権限、返せるものなら返したい。

**Shinkumi no kantoku wa suki de yatte iru n ja nai. Konna kengen, kaeseru mono nara kaeshitai.**

Supervising the credit associations is not something we enjoy doing. We'd rather give up this power if we could.

26.1.4.6.2.3 *Verb-(y)ō mono nara*

This indicates a hypothetical condition 'if you were to do anything like' (see 19.1.2.5, 26.1.6).

a うかつに手を出そうものなら、大けがしかねない。

**Ukatsu ni te o dasō mono nara, ōkega shi-kanenai.**

If you were to dabble [in the stock market], you might get your fingers badly burned.

26.1.4.7 *Noun* **nara**, *where* **nara** *functions like* **wa**

Here, **nara** can be replaced with the adverbial particle **wa**, except when **nara** is used twice (**wa** in the sense of topic can be used only once in a sentence).

a 震度5までの地震なら慣れっこだが、今回の揺れは過去と比べものにならないほど激しかった。

**Shindo go made no jishin nara narekko da ga, konkai no yure wa kako to kurabemono ni naranai hodo hageshikatta.**

An earthquake up to an intensity of 5 is something one's used to, but this tremor was so violent that it defies all comparisons with the past.

b パソコン通信に慣れた人なら、5分とかからない。

**Pasokon tsūshin ni nareta hito nara, gofun to kakaranai.**

Someone who is used to communicating by computer can do it [= order through the Internet] in less than five minutes.

c 観光客相手なら、ギフト用なら、高く売れる。

**Kankōkyaku aite nara, gifuto-yō nara, takaku ureru.**

If the buyers are tourists, and it's [bought] as a present, it'll sell for a good price.

26.1.5 **-ba, dattara, nara, -tara, to** *compared*

-ba, nara (dattara), to and -tara are all conjunctive particles indicating a condition. The fact that comparison of their uses is a favourite research topic shows that their differences cannot be explained easily.

Things are complicated by both the fact that classical usage, which was different from modern spoken usage, affects formal written modern

Japanese, and the fact that there is considerable overlap between the forms. Furthermore, there are combinations of these particles, such as -**tara-ba** and (-**ta**) **nara-ba**.

Below is a brief comparison of these particles, centring chiefly on their meanings. *All examples in this section are made-up examples* (the ✎ sign is omitted).

26.1.5.1 *Comparison of forms*

**Table 26.1** Forms used with conjunctional particles: comparison

| to | -tara | -ba | nara | |
|---|---|---|---|---|
| [V-**ru**] **to** | [V-**ta**] **ra** | [V-conditional] | [V-**ru**] **nara** | [V-**ta**] **nara** |
| [Adj-**i**] **to** | [Adj-**katta**] **ra** | [Adj-conditional] | [Adj-**i**] **nara** | [Adj-**katta**] **nara** |
| [N/**na-A**] **da to** | [N/**na-A**] **dattara** | [copula-conditional] | [N/**na-A**] **nara** | [N/**na-A datta**] **nara** |

26.1.5.2 *Comparison of use*

In English translation, these particles mostly translate as 'when' or 'if'. The equivalents without () are typical meanings, but the ones in () are also found.

| | |
|---|---|
| **to** | when (if) |
| **-tara** | when (if) |
| **-ba** | if (when) |
| **nara**/**-dattara** | if |

26.1.5.2.1 Used in the sense of 'if'

26.1.5.2.1.1 -**ba**

The speaker/writer makes a presumption in S1, and states the expected outcome in S2 (in this respect -**ba** differs from **nara**).

Basically, S1-**ba** S2 operates with the restriction that the actor (subject) cannot control the action of the V or state in either S1 and S2, or both. Below, the + sign expresses 'control', and the − sign, 'no control'.

× Indicates that this is not a possible sentence.

| SI-ba | S2 | |
|-------|-----|---|
| – | – | ✎安ければ売れる。<br>**Yasukereba ureru.**<br>If it's cheap, it'll sell. |
| + | – | ✎話せば分かる。<br>**Hanaseba wakaru.**<br>If I talk to him, he'll understand. |
| – | + | ✎高ければ買わない。<br>**Takakereba kawanai.**<br>If it's expensive, I won't buy it. |
| – | + | ✎安ければ買う。<br>**Yasukereba kau.**<br>If it's cheap, I'll buy it. |
| – | + | ✎あなたが行けば私も行く。<br>**Anata ga ikeba watashi mo iku.**<br>If you go*, I'll go too. |
| + | + | ✎×カメラを買えば貸してあげる。<br>×**Kamera o kaeba kashite ageru.**<br>If I buy a camera I'll lend it to you. |

*Note* – * From the subject/actor's point of view, the action of the second person (you) cannot be controlled.

When S2 is in the past, the condition becomes hypothetical 'if . . . had'.

---

| 26.1.5.2.1.2 | **nara/dattara** |

With **nara/dattara**, the presumption of S1 does not state the speaker's judgement, as with **-ba**. Instead, it takes up something from the previous context or some other, already established, fact, and expresses the meaning of 'I don't really know, but if the assumption is correct/if what you're saying is right'. In other words, S1 is an assumption that is based on something/somebody other than the speaker, and S2 is the speaker's evaluation or judgement based on that assumption.

Normally, S1 concerns something outside the speaker, and even if it concerns the speaker, it sounds as if it concerned someone else.

a 不満があるなら、直接言え。

**Fuman ga aru nara, chokusetsu ie.**

[To someone who seems to be muttering some complaint:] If you have something to complain about, tell me directly!

**nara/dattara** do not express a succession in time 'when' (except in the combination **-ta nara**, which is similar in meaning to **-tara**), and therefore there is no fixed time order of S1 and S2; often, S2 actually precedes S1:

b あした返してくれるなら、この本を貸してあげる。

**Ashita kaeshite kureru nara, kono hon o kashite ageru.**

If you'll return it tomorrow, I'll lend you this book.

Noun + **nara** can indicate the topic of a sentence, and can be replaced by N **wa**. The difference can been explained as a topic raised by someone else (**nara**), and by the speaker himself (**wa**).

| 26.1.5.2.1.3 | **-tara** |

When **-tara** translates as 'when', it can basically be replaced by **-ba**. However, this is not always possible due to the restrictions on controllability of the verb in the case of **-ba** (see 26.1.5.2.1.1).

In **-tara** sentences, S2 can freely indicate the speaker's intention (requests, hortative, etc.). Also, when S2 is in the past, it can express a hypothetical condition.

**-tara** has a colloquial ring, and therefore in expository and academic prose, etc. **-ba** is used instead.

| 26.1.5.2.1.4 | **to** |

With **to**, the conditional meaning of 'if . . . then . . .', 'if not . . . then not . . .' is weak, being more like 'when' or 'whenever', with the result of S1 becoming apparent (in S2).

a そこを曲がると、駅はすぐです。

**Soko o magaru to, eki wa sugu desu.**

When you turn that corner, it's just a short distance to the station.

With **to**, the speaker's intention (expressions of request, hortative, etc.) cannot be used.

b ×そこを曲がると、駅に行ってください。

**×Soko o magaru to, eki ni itte kudasai.**

| 26.1.5.2.2.1 | **to**

Essentially, **to** means 'when', expressing habitual or natural (commonsense) occurrences in the present or past.

a 学校から帰ると毎日泳いだ。
   **Gakkō kara kaeru to mainichi oyoida.**
   When I got back from school, I used to swim every day.

**to** is typically used in the sense that S2 is noticed or discovered as a result of the realization of S1. In this use, the predicate of S2 cannot express intention, i.e. S2 has a different subject than that of S1, or expresses a state, usually in the past.

b 家に帰ると／帰ったら手紙が来ていた。
   **Ie ni kaeru to/kaettara, tegami ga kite ita.**
   When I got back home, there was a letter.

The difference between **to** and **-tara** here is that **-tara** is colloquial, everyday language, whereas the effect of **to** is more dramatic, i.e. it is typically used to tell some gripping tale, or in written stories.

| 26.1.5.2.2.2 | **-tara**

**-tara** can be used freely in the sense of both 'when' and 'if', with a colloquial ring. With **-tara**, S2 can express the speaker's intention (request, hortative, etc.), as in example a.

a 3時になったら、お茶にしましょう。
   **Sanji ni nattara, o-cha ni shimashō.**
   At 3 o'clock, let's have some tea.

**-tara** cannot be used for a time sequence in the past (example b), but it's OK in the present tense. Note that example d has a narrative (story) ring to it.

A simple sequence of actions, in the sense of 'and' rather than 'when' is expressed by **-te** (example e, see 25.1.3).

b ×彼は家に帰ったら電話をかけた。
   ×**Kare wa ie ni kaettara denwa o kaketa.**

c 朝起きたら新聞を取りにいく。
   **Asa okitara shinbun o tori ni iku.**
   When I get up in the morning, I'll go and fetch the paper.

d 彼は家に帰ると電話をかけた。
**Kare wa ie ni kaeru to denwa o kaketa.**
When he got back home, he made a phone call.

e 彼は家に帰って、電話をかけた。
**Kare wa ie ni kaette, denwa o kaketa.**
He went home, and made a phone call.

26.1.5.2.2.3 **-ba**

In generalizing statements, -ba can be used in the sense of 'when', but only in the present, *not* the past.

a 歳をとれば、見えにくくなる。
**Toshi o toreba, mienikuku naru.**
When/as one gets older, one's eyesight deteriorates.

26.1.5.2.2.4 **nara**

**nara** cannot be used in the sense of 'when'.

# 26.1.6 -(y)ō mono nara

This is a combination of the presumptive V-(y)ō and **nara**, meaning 'if you do anything like', 'if anything like . . . should happen' (see 19.1.2.4, 26.1.4, 9.1.2).

a 板を無理に回したり、体をひねったりしようものなら、
間違いなく転ぶ。
**Ita o muri ni mawashitari, karada o hinettari shiyō mono nara, machigainaku korobu.**
If you turn the board forcefully, or twist your body, you'll fall over without fail.

b そしていまや、規制緩和ないし撤廃論を批判しようものなら、
たちまち「世論の圧制」に言論の自由を阻まれる。
**Soshite ima ya, kisei kanwa naishi teppairon o hihan shiyō mono nara, tachimachi 'yoron no assei' ni genron no jiyū o habamareru.**
And now, if you were to criticise the arguments for relaxing or abolishing restrictions, your freedom of speech would quickly be obstructed by 'the tyranny of public opinion'.

595

| 26.1.7 | -te wa |
|---|---|

-te wa consists of the conjunctive form (-te/(-)de) plus the adverbial particle wa. It basically indicates a condition 'if', but between two actions also indicates repeated actions (see 25).

Colloquially, -te wa/de wa are often contracted to -cha/ja/jā (example 26.1.7.2 c).

| 26.1.7.1 | Clause I-te wa, clause 2 (positive predicate): repeated actions |
|---|---|

Joining two actions, this indicates that the actions take place repeatedly 'keep doing' (see 25.2.5).

a 繰り返し見たミフネの顔が浮かんでは消えた。
  **Kurikaeshi mita Mifune no kao ga ukande wa kieta.**
  Mifune's face, which I'd looked at over and over again, kept appearing and disappearing [in my mind].

b 今では園芸は生活の一部になっており、暇を見つけては、丹念に
  手入れをしてやる。
  **Ima de wa engei wa seikatsu no ichibu to natte ori, hima o mitsukete wa, tannen ni teire o shite yaru.**
  By now, gardening has become a part of his life, and he keeps finding time to tend to [the garden] with care.

c 講演など機会をとらえてはボランティアの支援制度の導入を呼び
  かけている。
  **Kōen nado kikai o toraete wa borantia no shien seido no dōnyū o yobikakete iru.**
  Using every occasion such as lectures etc., he keeps calling for the introduction of a volunteer support system.

| 26.1.7.2 | Clause I-te wa, clause 2 (negative predicate) |
|---|---|

The predicate can be a negative form, or an expression with negative meaning 'if . . . , then' (negative outcome).

a ✐こんなに高くては買えない。
  **Konna ni takakute wa kaenai.**
  If it's this expensive, I can't buy it.

b ✐病気では働けないだろう。
  **Byōki de wa hatarakenai darō.**
  If you're ill, then surely you can't work.

c そんなに言っちゃかわいそうよ。
**Sonna ni itcha kawaisō yo.**
It's cruel if you say that much.

d すべての企業が好き勝手をやっていてはやがて人類が滅びるのは
必然。
**Subete no kigyō ga sukikatte o yatte ite wa yagate jinrui ga horobiru no wa hitsuzen.**
If all businesses do as they like, the end of mankind is inevitable.

e 言葉も必要だが、言葉では抽象化されてしまう。
**Kotoba mo hitsuyō da ga, kotoba de wa chūshō-ka sarete shimau.**
Words are necessary as well, but words make things abstract.

26.1.7.3 *Sentence-**te wa** (**naranai/ikenai/dame da**): negative obligation*

This indicates an obligation that is negative. Literally the meaning is "it won't do if", i.e. 'mustn't' (see 25.2.3).

a 趣味は仕事になってはならない。
**Shumi wa shigoto ni natte wa naranai.**
[One's] hobby mustn't turn into one's job.

b リストラの火を絶やしてはならない。
**Risutora no hi o tayashite wa naranai.**
We mustn't extinguish the flame of restructuring.

26.1.7.4 *Sentence-**nakute wa** (**naranai/ikenai/dame da**): obligation*

This is a double negative expressing obligation. Literally the meaning is "it won't do if not", i.e. 'must', 'must/have to do' (see 25.2.3, 17.2.2).

a 水は工業にとってなくてはならないもの。
**Mizu wa kōgyō ni totte nakute wa naranai mono.**
Water is indispensable for industry.

b 財政のさらなる悪化は避けなくてはいけない。
**Zaisei no sara naru akka wa sakenakute wa ikenai.**
A further worsening of finances must be avoided.

c 難しいことはやさしく書かなくては。
**Muzukashii koto wa yasashiku kakanakute wa.**
One must write simply about complicated matters.

26.1.7.5 *Sentence-**te wa** (**dō ka**): suggestion*

This is used for suggesting a course of action in the sense of 'how about', 'should'. Instead of -te wa, -tara can also be used (see 26.1.2.4.2).

Colloquially, the question word + copula (dō da, etc.) part can be omitted (see 18.1.7.2).

a 老舗の店員も、たまには量販店を回ってはどうだろうか。

**Shinise no ten'in mo, tama ni wa ryōhanten o mawatte wa dō darō ka.**

Those working in smart shops should sometimes go and look at places selling things for the mass market.

b 今年5月に理容師と相談したら、縛ってみてはと勧められてやってみた。

**Kotoshi gogatsu ni riyōshi to sōdan shitara. shibatte mite wa to susumerarete yatte mita.**

When I consulted with my barber in May this year, he suggested that I might tie back [my hair], so I gave it a try.

## 26.2 Time

### 26.2.1 toki

toki is formally a noun. Like any other noun it can attach the copula, particles, etc., but is also used like a conjunctive particle in complex sentences in the pattern S1 toki S2, in the sense of '(the time) when'.

Note that even when S2 (the main clause) is in the past tense, Adj, na-Adj and N modifying toki in S1 are often in the non-past, i.e. Adj-i toki, na-Adj na toki and N no toki.

The past tense is used with these in S1 when events in the past are contrasted with those in the present. Compare the following examples:

a ✐暇なときはよく散歩した。

**Hima na toki wa yoku sanpo shita.**

I often went for walks when I wasn't busy.

b ✐暇だったときはよく散歩した。

**Hima datta toki wa yoku sanpo shita.**

In the times when I wasn't busy, I often went for walks.

As evident from the translation, the S1 past-tense example contrasts the present (busy) state with a (not busy) state in the past, whereas the non-past sentence has no such implication.

With V **toki,** there is a three-way distinction, which is independent of the tense of S2:

**V-ru toki:** the action of V is not yet realized or completed (see 26.2.1.2.1)
**V-te iru toki:** the action of V is in the process of being realized or completed (see 26.2.1.2.2)
**V-ta toki:** the action of V is realized or completed (see 26.2.1.2.3)

Compare examples c–f:

c ✐外国旅行に出るとき、鞄を買う。
**Gaikoku ryokō ni deru toki, kaban o kau.**
I'll buy a bag (at home) when I go abroad.

d ✐外国旅行に出るとき、鞄を買った。
**Gaikoku ryokō ni deru toki, kaban o katta.**
I bought a bag (at home) when I went abroad.

e ✐外国旅行に出たとき、鞄を買う。
**Gaikoku ryokō ni deta toki, kaban o kau.**
I'll buy a bag (abroad) when I go abroad.

f ✐外国旅行に出たとき、鞄を買った。
**Gaikoku ryokō ni deta toki, kaban o katta.**
I bought a bag (abroad) when I went abroad

The forms to which **toki** is attached are the same as those before other N:

V/Adj: N-modifying form + **toki**
na-Adj/N-copula: N-modifying form + **toki**

26.2.1.1 | *Adjective/**na**-adjective/noun* **toki**

a 毎日、好きなときに、好きな人と会える自由さは、非常に大きい
ですね。
**Mainichi, suki na toki ni, suki na hito to aeru jiyū-sa wa,
hijō ni ōkii desu ne.**
The freedom to see daily, at a time one wants to, the people one
wants to, is extremely important.

b つらいとき、悲しいとき、いつも心に浮かんだのは、大好きな香
港の情景だった。

**Tsurai toki, kanashii toki, itsu mo kokoro ni ukanda no wa, daisuki na Honkon no jōkei datta.**

In times of hardship and times of sadness, it was always the sight of my beloved Hong Kong that came to mind.

c 定期検診のとき医者から注意を受けると焦ってしまう。

**Teiki kenshin no toki isha kara chūi o ukeru to asette shimau.**

One gets nervous when the doctor at the time of the regular check-up warns one about things.

d 二十一歳のときからフランス料理一筋で腕を振るい続けた。

**Nijūissai no toki kara furansu ryōri hitosuji de ude o furui-tsuzuketa.**

From the time he was 21 he has devoted his talents purely to French cuisine.

e 写真はその発表のときのもの。

**Shashin wa sono happyō no toki no mono.**

The photograph [is] from the time of the announcement of it [= the creation of a female baseball team].

f 最も多かったときで年七百本という記録を持っている。

**Mottomo ōkatta toki de nen nanahyap-pon to iu kiroku o motte iru.**

When he was at his most productive, he held the record for [having watched] 700 films per year.

| 26.2.1.2 | *Verb* **toki** |

| 26.2.1.2.1 | Verb-**ru toki** |

As explained in the previous section (recall examples c and d), with V-**ru toki** the action of V is not yet realized or completed.

a 子どもの靴を選ぶとき、何を基準に選びますか。

**Kodomo no kutsu o erabu toki, nani o kijun ni erabimasu ka.**

On what basis do you make your choice when choosing children's shoes?

b 空港に着陸するときに眺めた美しい景色は印象的だった。

**Kūkō ni chakuriku suru toki ni nagameta utsukushii keshiki wa inshō-teki datta.**

The beautiful scenery I saw when landing at the airport was memorable.

c 会えないときは手紙でやり取りした。

**Aenai toki wa tegami de yaritori shita.**

At times when they couldn't meet they communicated by letter.

d プレゼントの包みを開けるときの子供の輝くような笑顔が自分の
喜びにもなるという。

**Purezento no tsutsumi o akeru toki no kodomo no kagayaku
yō na egao ga jibun no yorokobi ni mo naru to iu.**

He says that the radiant smiles of the children when they open their
presents is a pleasure for him, too.

e 外国旅行に出るとき、空港で出国手続きを済ませる。

**Gaikoku ryokō ni deru toki, kūkō de shukkoku tetsuzuki o
sumaseru.**

When he goes overseas on business, he undergoes the departure
formalities at the airport.

---

26.2.1.2.2 | Verb-**te iru toki**

The meaning of -**te iru** in these sentences is progressive, i.e. it is used with
action verbs only.

a だれでも仕事をしているときに感動の瞬間というものがある。

**Dare de mo shigoto o shite iru toki ni kandō no shunkan to
iu mono ga aru.**

Everybody has moments of excitement when working.

b 絵を描いているときはいつも、頭の中で音や言葉のフレーズが流
れている。

**E o kaite iru toki wa itsu mo, atama no naka de oto ya
kotoba no furēzu ga nagarete iru.**

When I paint pictures, there's always a flow of sounds and language
phrases inside my head.

---

26.2.1.2.3 | Verb-**ta toki**

As explained above (recall examples e and f), with V-**ta toki** the action of
the verb is already realized or completed.

a 店に商品を置いたときにいかに客の目を引くか。

**Mise ni shōhin o oita toki ni ika ni kyaku no me o hiku ka.**

When you've introduced a product to the shop, [the question is] how
best to catch the eyes of the customers.

b 群集心理というのは、「多数が一カ所に密集したときに生ずる心
　理状態」をいう。

**Gunshū shinri to iu no wa, 'tasū ga ikkasho ni misshū shita
toki ni shōzuru shinri jōtai' o iu.**

Mass psychology is 'the psychological state that arises when many
congregate in one place'.

c 十五年ぶりに帰国したとき、家の周辺の変わりように驚き
　ました。

**Jūgonen-buri ni kikoku shita toki, ie no shūhen no kawariyō
ni odorokimashita.**

When I went back to my country for the first time in 15 years,
I was amazed at the changes in my neighbourhood.

d PSは実験に関して深い知識が要求されます。実験装置が故障した
　ときには修理もしなければなりません。

**Pīesu wa jikken ni kanshite fukai chishiki ga yōkyū saremasu.
Jikken sōchi ga koshō shita toki ni wa shūri mo shinakereba
narimasen.**

A PS [= payload specialist on space probe] needs to be very
knowledgeable about experiments. When the experimental
apparatus breaks down s/he needs to repair it, too.

---

| 26.2.1.3 | *Sentence ending* + **toki** |

**toki** can also be attached to modal endings, such as **-tai**, **-sō** and others,
again in the N-modifying form.

a 利用者は、遊びたいときに好みのソフトを選択してゲームを楽
　しむ。

**Riyōsha wa, asobitai toki ni konomi no sofuto o sentaku shite
gēmu o tanoshimu.**

The users enjoy the game by selecting software of their choice when
they want to play.

b 冷夏が来そうなとき、早めに花を咲かせて実をつくってしまうこ
　ともできる。

**Reika ga kisō na toki, hayame ni hana o sakasete mi o
tsukutte shimau koto mo dekiru.**

[If the agent that makes a flower bloom is discovered] We will be able
to do things like getting them to flower and fruit early when there
are indications that a cold summer is in store.

*Idiomatic uses*

Phrases like **aru toki** 'one time', **iza to iu toki** 'in case of emergency', **masaka no toki** 'if the worst comes to the worst', 'in case of trouble' are idiomatic or lexical expressions.

a あるとき、大学で実験中の装置が突然壊れたという。

**Aru toki, daigaku de jikken-chū no sōchi ga totsuzen kowareta to iu.**

One time, the experimental apparatus suddenly broke down during an experiment at the university, he says.

b いざというときのために、着衣泳体験でサバイバル・テクニックを心得ておきたい。

**Iza to iu toki no tame ni, chakuiei taiken de sabaibaru tekunikku o kokoroete okitai.**

In case of emergency, one wants to familiarize oneself with survival techniques by experiencing swimming with clothes on.

c ・・・安いところから買おうとすると、儲からん仕入れ先は離れていく。まさかのときには助けてくれない。

**...yasui tokoro kara kaō to suru to, mōkaran shiiresaki wa hanarete iku. Masaka no toki ni wa tasukete kurenai.**

...if we try to buy only from cheap places, suppliers who don't make a profit will steer clear of us. In case of trouble, they won't help.

**baai**

Apart from its use as a conjunctive particle, **baai** can be used as a regular noun in the sense of 'case' or 'circumstances':

a しかし、総務庁は「場合によっては早期退職の勧奨もしなくては」という。

**Shikashi, Sōmu-chō wa 'baai ni yotte wa sōki taishoku no kanshō mo shinakute wa' to iu.**

However, the General Affairs Bureau says 'Depending on the circumstances, we also have to recommend early retirement'.

However, **baai** is mostly used like a conjunctive particle in the sense of 'in case of', 'when', or 'if'. Formally being a structural noun, **baai** is preceded by noun-modifying forms of V, Adj, **na**-Adj and N, and attaches case and adverbial particles etc. like other N. **baai** has a written or formal ring to it and therefore tends to be used in legal and other written documents (examples 26.2.2.1 c and 26.2.2.2 b).

*Non-past form* **baai**

As in the case of **toki**, a verb/adjective preceding **baai** generally uses the non-past form when the action has not been completed.

a 休業日に使用する場合は手数料百三円がかかる。

**Kyūgyōbi ni shiyō suru baai wa tesūryō hyakusan-en ga kakaru.**

When you use it [= teller machine] on a bank holiday, a handling fee of 103 yen applies.

b 世界史を見る場合、近代化はすなわち西洋化とする考えが日本では長く続いた。

**Sekai-shi o miru baai, kindai-ka wa sunawachi Seiyō-ka to suru kangae ga Nihon de wa nagaku tsuzuita.**

When looking at world history, the view that holds that modernization is Westernization has continued in Japan for a long time.

c 日本で生まれ、父母がともに知れない場合は日本国籍を認める。

**Nihon de umare, fubo ga tomo ni shirenai baai wa nihon kokuseki o mitomeru.**

If [the child] is born in Japan, and both parents are unknown, it is granted Japanese citizenship.

d 他店より価格が高い場合は店員にお申し付けください

**Taten yori kakaku ga takai baai wa ten'in ni o-mōshitsuke kudasai**

If the price is higher than elsewhere, please inform our staff.

**-ta baai**

When the action has been completed, a verb/adjective preceding **baai** generally uses the -ta form. However, the effect of -ta can also be to make the **baai** clause more hypothetical, as in example d.

a　一日二十四時間運転した場合、一カ月当たりの電気料金は最も小型のもので二百—三百円という。

**Ichinichi nijūyo-jikan unten shita baai, ikkagetsu atari no denki ryōkin wa mottomo kogata no mono de nihyaku kara sanbyaku-en to iu.**

They say that when run for 24 hours a day, the electricity charge per month is 200–300 yen for the smallest type [of refuse converter].

b　父の医療費を私が支払った場合、医療費について私は医療費控除を受けることができますか。

**Chichi no iryōhi o watashi ga shiharatta baai, iryōhi ni tsuite watashi wa iryōhi kōjo o ukeru koto ga dekimasu ka.**

If I have paid my father's medical fees, can I have tax deducted for medical expenses?

c　番号を間違えた場合の訂正なども音声応答システムに従ってできる。

**Bangō o machigaeta baai no teisei nado mo onsei ōtō shisutemu ni shitagatte dekiru.**

Making a correction after having dialled a wrong number can also be done via the voice-activated system.

d　・・・男同士の会話で盛り上がっちゃう。・・・でもさ、男の人数が多かった場合に一人の女のためにみんながサービスする必要があるのかどうか。

**...otoko dōshi no kaiwa de moriagatchau ...demo sa, otoko no ninzū ga ōkatta baai ni hitori no onna no tame ni minna ga sābisu suru hitsuyō ga aru no ka dō ka.**

...the conversation [at after-hours business entertainment] gets animated between the men.... But, when there is a large number of men, do they all need to entertain one woman, I wonder.

e　不祥事が無かった場合と同じには進まないだろう。

**Fushōji ga nakatta baai to onaji ni wa susumanai darō.**

[cases where there has been dishonesty] cannot be dealt with in the same way as where there hasn't.

| 26.2.2.3 | na-*adjective/noun* **na/no baai** |

na-adjectives and nouns use the noun-modifying **na/no** before **baai**.

a 中国への直航便がない国内の地方空港の客はソウル経由の方が
便利な場合もある。

**Chūgoku e no chokkōbin ga nai kokunai no chihō kūkō no
kyaku wa Sōru keiyu no hō ga benri na baai mo aru.**

For customers from local domestic airports, where there are no
direct flights to China, there are instances where travelling via Seoul
is more convenient.

b 当日が日曜・祝日の場合は翌日に順延する。

**Tōjitsu ga nichiyō, shukujitsu no baai wa yokujitsu ni jun'en
suru.**

When the day falls on a Sunday or holiday, the session is held on
the following day.

| 26.2.3 | **baai, toki** *compared* |

When **toki** is made into a topic in the form of **toki (wa)** or **toki (ni) wa**,
**toki** indicates a general or habitual condition 'if' or 'always'. **baai** can be
used in the same way, although **baai wa**, etc. has a much more formal ring
than **toki wa**, as seen in examples a and b. For this reason, **baai** is often
in legal and other forms of 'officialese' (cf. 26.2.2.1 a, c and 26.2.2.2 c).

In example c, **toki ni** cannot be replaced by **baai ni**, as the content is too
personal, lacking the officialese tone typical of **baai**.

a ✐火事のときはエレベーターを使用しないでください。

**Kaji no toki wa erebētā o shiyō shinai de kudasai.**

Please don't use the lift when there's a fire.

b ✐火災の場合はエレベーターを使用しないこと。 [= written notice]

**Kasai no baai wa erebētā o shiyō shinai koto.**

Do not use lift in case of fire.

c ✐火事のときに私の大切なアルバムが焼けてしまった。

**Kaji no toki ni watashi no taisetsu na arubamu ga yakete
shimatta.**

My treasured album was destroyed in the fire (*lit.* "at the time of
the fire").

## 26.2.4 -te kara

V-**te kara** is a conjunctive particle that basically joins two clauses in the sense of 'after', but has some other uses too.

The relational noun **ato** (see 1.6.1.2) can also be used in the sense of 'after' (see 26.2.5 and 26.2.6).

### 26.2.4.1 Clause 1-**te kara** clause 2

In this use, -**te kara** means 'after'.

*Note* – With time expressions the suffix -**go** 'after (amount of time)' can be added, resulting in the idea of 'after' being expressed twice (examples c and f).

a きちんと調べてからにしてほしい。
**Kichinto shirabete kara ni shite hoshii.**
We want them to [put things on the market] after they've checked them out properly.

b ただいまお取り扱いできません。申し訳ございませんが、しばら
くしてから再度アクセスしてください。
**Tadaima o-toriatsukai dekimasen. Mōshiwake gozaimasen ga, shibaraku shite kara saido akusesu shite kudasai.**
**[= Internet travel agency]**
We can not serve [you] at the moment. We are sorry, but please access [us] again after a while.

c 最初の死亡例が日本商事に報告されてから二十二日後だった。
**Saisho no shibōrei ga Nippon Shōji ni hōkoku sarete kara nijūninichi-go datta.**
It was (*lit.* "after") 22 days after the first death [case] was reported to Nippon Shōji.

d ミッション系の学校で学んだ人でも、卒業してから教会へ何度足
を運んだか。
**Misshon-kei no gakkō de mananda hito demo, sotsugyō shite kara kyōkai e nando ashi o hakonda ka.**
One wonders how often even those who went to a mission school have been to church after graduating.

e 旧聖堂はフランシスコ・ザビエルが日本初のキリスト教会を山口
に建ててから四百年を記念し、一九五二年に造られた。

**Kyūseidō wa Furanshisuko Zabieru ga Nihon-hatsu no
Kirisuto kyōkai o Yamaguchi ni tatete kara yonhyaku-nen
o kinen shi, senkyūhyaku gojūni-nen ni tsukurareta.**

The old church had been built in 1952 in commemoration of
the 400th anniversary of Francis Xavier's building of Japan's first
Christian church in Yamaguchi.

f 地震が起きてから約十分後に駆けつけた本田彰駅長は「これまで
に経験したこともない大きな地震で立っていられなかった」。

**Jishin ga okite kara yaku juppun-go ni kaketsuketa Honda
Akira ekichō wa 'kore made ni keiken shita koto mo nai
ōki na jishin de tatte irarenakatta'.**

Akira Honda, the stationmaster, who rushed to the scene (*lit.* "after")
10 minutes after the earthquake struck, [said], 'It was a quake of
a magnitude I haven't experienced before; I was unable to remain
standing'.

---

26.2.4.2 *Clause 1*-**te kara** *clause 2* **made** *(ni) clause 3*

This expresses a range of actions in time, 'from . . . to/until', with S3 indicating a time (see also 2.7, 2.10, 2.11).

a 一瞬の出来事で異常を感じてから転覆するまで一分間ぐらいだっ
たという。

**Isshun no dekigoto de ijō o kanjite kara tenpuku suru made
ippun-kan gurai datta to iu.**

He says that it happened very quickly, taking only about one minute
from the time they felt something amiss to the boat's capsizing.

b 初めは一日あたり百人台だった。それが三百人になり、五百人に
なり、千人を超えてから三千人を突破するまでにはわずか三日
しかかからなかった。

**Hajime wa ichinichi atari hyaku-nin-dai datta. Sore ga
sanbyaku-nin ni nari, gohyaku-nin ni nari, sennin o koete
kara sanzen-nin o toppa suru made ni wa wazuka mikka
shika kakaranakatta.**

At first [the number of refugees] was in the range of 100 per day.
That became 300, 500, and from the time it exceeded 1,000 till
it reached the 3,000 mark took only three days.

| 26.2.4.3 | *Noun phrase* **wa** *clause-***te kara** *(+ copula)* |

a 「私たちの正月休みは三が日が過ぎてからです」という。

**'Watashi-tachi no shōgatsu yasumi wa sanganichi ga sugite kara desu' to iu.**

'Our New Year vacation begins after the three official holidays', he says.

| 26.2.4.4 | *Cleft sentence-***te kara** *(+ copula)* |

a しかし、その笠智衆でも、味が本当に出せるようになったのは、『八十すぎてからですよ』と、自ら語っていたそうだ。

**Shikashi, sono Ryū Chishu demo, aji ga hontō ni daseru yō ni natta no wa 'hachijū sugite kara desu yo' to mizukara katatte ita sō da.**

But even that [formidable actor] Chishu Ryu apparently said himself that it was 'from his eighties' that he could really give meaning [to a part].

## 26.2.5 -ta ato

| 26.2.5.1 | *Clause 1-***ta ato** *clause 2* |

After a sentence or clause ending in **V-ta** (never **V-ru**), **ato** is used like a conjunctive particle linking two clauses in the sense of 'after' (see also 26.2.4). However, grammatically it behaves like a structural noun in that it can attach a variety of case and adverbial particles.

For differences between S1-**ta ato** S2 and S1-**te kara** S2, see 26.2.6.

a 会社で働いた後、スイートホームで一家だんらん。

**Kaisha de hataraita ato, suīto hōmu de ikka danran.**

After you've worked in the company, you relax with the family back (*lit.* "sweet") home.

b 司法修習を終えた後は、両親の待つ福井で弁護士を目指すという。

**Shihō shūshū o oeta ato wa, ryōshin no matsu Fukui de bengoshi o mezasu to iu.**

After finishing his legal training, he aims to work as an attorney in Fukui, where his parents await his return.

c 周辺には火が消えた後もゴムが焼けた刺激臭が漂った。

**Shūhen ni wa hi ga kieta ato mo gomu ga yaketa shigeki-shū
ga tadayotta.**

Even after the fire had been put out, a strong smell of burnt rubber
remained in the vicinity.

d パソコン研修をした後で各店に配置する。

**Pasokon kenshū o shita ato de kaku-ten ni haichi suru.**

After training them [= new employees] in the use of personal
computers, they assign them to the various branch offices.

e ひと通り、買い物した後で、花を買い求める消費者がほとんどと
いう。

**Hitotōri, kaimono shita ato de, hana o kai-motomeru
shōhisha ga hotondo to iu.**

They say that almost all customers buy flowers after having done
their basic shopping.

f 書棚が折り重なるように倒れ、本が散らばる様は、まるで爆発事
故か、砲撃を受けた後のよう。

**Shodana ga orikasanaru yō ni taore, hon ga chirabaru
sama wa, maru de bakuhatsu jiko ka, hōgeki o uketa ato
no yō.**

[After earthquake:] The way the bookshelves had fallen on top of each
other and books were scattered everywhere was just like the
aftermath of an explosion or mortar attack.

## 26.2.6 -ta ato *and* -te kara *compared*

S1-**ta ato** S2 and S1-**te kara** S2 both express the idea of 'after'. The main
difference between the two is as follows.

S1-**ta ato** S2 is concerned with the simple sequence of events (example a).

S1-**te kara** S2, on the other hand, emphasizes the sequence, more like a
temporal condition for S2. Thus, in example b the implication is that
manufacturers should check out their goods *first* [to make sure there are
no faults] before releasing them to the market.

S1-**te kara** S2, but *not* S1-**ta ato** S2, is used to indicate the idea of 'it
was such-and-such a length of time after something happened'. Similarly,
S1-**te kara** S2 can also be used in cleft sentences (see 26.2.4.4).

a 女性は近くの銀行で現金を引き出した後、息子の家まで歩いて行 くところだったという。

**Josei wa chikaku no ginkō de genkin o hikidashita ato, musuko no ie made aruite iku tokoro datta to iu.**

The woman says that she was about to walk to her son's house after having withdrawn some cash from a nearby bank.

b きちんと調べてからにしてほしい。

**Kichinto shirabete kara ni shite hoshii.**

We want them to [put things on the market] after they've checked them out properly.

**26.2.7** aida

Although used to form a conjunctive clause, **aida** is formally a noun (see 1.6.1), and is therefore modified by forms that precede nouns. As a conjunctive particle, **aida** is used for time only, in the sense of 'while', 'during', 'throughout', etc. (see 26.2.6).

Even when the main clause is in the past, the conjunctive clause uses non-past forms, especially -**te iru aida** with verbs.

**aida** is often followed by the case particle **ni** or the adverbial particle **wa**, but can also be used without any particle (example e). Note also the combination **aida-jū** 'throughout' (example g).

**26.2.7.1** *Clause 1-positive* **aida**

a 働ける間は働きたい。

**Hatarakeru aida wa hatarakitai.**

I want to work while I am able to.

b 眠っている間に体に異変が起きていた。

**Nemutte iru aida ni karada ni ihen ga okite ita.**

While he had been asleep, an unexpected change had taken place in his body.

c こうした空気が強い間は、農地の集約化は難しい。

**Kōshita kūki ga tsuyoi aida wa, nōchi no shūyaku-ka wa muzukashii.**

While this kind of atmosphere prevails, it is difficult to make more intensive use of the farmland.

d わずかな間に部門の第一人者になってしまった。

**Wazuka na aida ni bumon no daiichi-ninsha ni natte shimatta.**

In a very short time he had become the leading figure of his section.

e 冬のあいだ落ち込んでいた気分は春先から高揚しはじめる。

**Fuyu no aida ochikonde ita kibun wa harusaki kara kōyō shihajimeru.**

The feeling of depression [one has had] during the winter begins to lift in early spring.

f 月刊誌が1回出る間に番組は4回放送される。

**Gekkanshi ga ikkai deru aida ni bangumi wa yonkai hōsō sareru.**

During the period [in which] the monthly magazine appears once, the programme is broadcast four times.

g 式のあいだ中，来賓のあいさつもうわの空のようだった。

**Shiki no aida-jū, raihin no aisatsu mo uwanosora no yō datta.**

Throughout the ceremony, he paid little attention to the guests' speeches.

26.2.7.2 *Clause 1-negative* **aida**

After a negative S1, **aida** also means 'while', whereas **uchi ni** after negative S1 means 'before' (see 26.2.8.1.2).

a わからない間にプルトニウムがどんどん作られてしまう。

**Wakaranai aida ni purutoniumu ga dondon tsukurarete shimau.**

While people are unaware, plutonium gets produced in large quantities.

b 心配なのは、政治が動かない間に官僚主導が強くなっているようにみえることだ。

**Shinpai na no wa, seiji ga ugokanai aida ni kanryō shudō ga tsuyoku natte iru yō ni mieru koto da.**

What's worrying is that it appears that while politics is stagnant bureaucratic leadership is getting stronger.

26.2.8 **uchi**

Although it functions as a conjunctive particle, **uchi** is formally a noun, and therefore attaches forms that precede and follow nouns.

The basic meaning of **uchi** is 'within a certain limit' in terms of both time and space. Note that regardless of tense, **uchi** is attached to V-**ru** (see 26.2.9).

Time

| 26.2.8.1 | *Clause 1* **uchi** *clause 2* |
|---|---|

S1 indicates a state. The implication in **uchi** sentences is that as the state (positive or negative) indicated in S1 is liable to change, the action of S2 takes place 'while' that state still remains.

It is mostly used in the form **uchi ni**, but **uchi wa** is also found. For example (in 26.2.8.1.1 b), **uchi wa** emphasizes the idea of 'while', whereas in example 26.2.8.1.1 d, where there is a contrast between the two clauses, the effect is one of emphasizing the contrast.

| 26.2.8.1.1 | Clause 1-positive **uchi** clause 2 |
|---|---|

a 条件の良いうちに判を押した方がいい。
**Jōken ga yoi uchi ni han o oshita hō ga ii.**
You should seal [the agreement] while the conditions are good.

b 元気なうちは人のために働きたい。
**Genki na uchi wa hito no tame ni hatarakitai.**
While I'm healthy I want to work for [the benefit of] others.

c 貯蓄が潤沢なうちに、来るべき高齢化社会に備えて社会資本の整備を急ぐべきだ。
**Chochiku ga juntaku na uchi ni, kitaru-beki kōrei-ka shakai ni sonaete shakai shihon no seibi o isogu-beki da.**
While savings are plentiful, we must hurry and prepare social funds in preparation for the coming aged society.

d もうけられるうちにもうけておこうという姿勢は慎んでほしい。
**Mōkerareru uchi ni mōkete okō to iu shisei wa tsutsushinde hoshii.**
I want them to restrain their attitude of 'Let's make money while we can'.

e 「校舎が残っているうちはまだ実感が無いが、いざ無くなってしまうと寂しくなるかも」と語る。
**'Kōsha ga nokotte iru uchi wa mada jikkan ga nai ga, iza naku natte shimau to sabishiku naru ka mo' to kataru.**
'While the school building is still there, it doesn't hit you, but once it's gone, I might feel lonely', he says.

613

26.2.8.1.2 | Clause 1-negative **uchi ni** clause 2

After S1 ending in a negative form (-**nai**, -**nu**), **uchi ni** is used. The meaning is literally "while still not", i.e. 'before something happens', or with expression of time 'before (time) has passed'.

a 電車がなくならないうちに帰ります。
   **Densha ga naku naranai uchi ni kaerimasu.**
   I'm going home before the trains stop running.

b 知らないうちに山林が開発されていた。
   **Shiranai uchi ni sanrin ga kaihatsu sarete ita.**
   Before we knew it, the mountain forest had been developed.

c 30秒とたたないうちに電話がかかってくる。
   **Sanjūbyō to tatanai uchi ni denwa ga kakatte kuru.**
   Before 30 seconds had passed, the phone rang.

d ほとんどの人は5分もしないうちに手足が重くなり、眠りに近い
   めい想状態に入る。
   **Hotondo no hito wa gofun mo shinai uchi ni teashi ga omoku
   nari, nemuri ni chikai meisōjōtai ni hairu.**
   [Traditional Indian sesame oil massage] Before five minutes have
   passed, most people feel their limbs become heavy and enter
   a meditative state akin to sleep.

e カビに占領されないうちに早く処理したい。
   **Kabi ni senryō sarenai uchi ni hayaku shori shitai.**
   [Dried foods] should be used promptly, before they go mouldy.

f 「知らないうちに逃げ道を用意していたのかもしれない」と打ち
   明ける。
   **'Shiranai uchi ni nigemichi o yōi shite ita no kamoshirenai' to
   uchiakeru.**
   'They may have prepared an escape route without our knowledge',
   he reveals.

g だが、一年もたたぬうちに歯車が狂い始めた。「夫は一人では何
   もできない人だった」。
   **Da ga, ichinen mo tatanu uchi ni haguruma ga kurui-hajimeta.
   'Otto wa hitori de wa nani mo dekinai hito datta'.**
   However, before a year had passed [since marriage], the cogs
   began to slip.
   'My husband turned out to be a person who can't do anything by
   himself.'

*Clause 1 (verb-ru/verb-te iru) uchi ni clause 2*

After V-**ru** and V-**te iru**, **uchi ni** indicates a gradual change that occurs 'as' or 'while' the action of S1 takes place, or 'in the course of' it.

a 電話の声は相談するうちにだいぶ明るくなってきた。

**Denwa no koe wa sōdan suru uchi ni daibu akaruku natte kita.**

In the course of talking [with me], the voice on the other end of the phone became quite cheerful.

b 議論しているうちに時間ばかりがたっている。

**Giron shite iru uchi ni jikan bakari ga tatte iru.**

While we're arguing, time is slipping rapidly away [= all we're doing is wasting time].

c 何度も聴くうちに耳に残るメロディー。

**Nando mo kiku uchi ni mimi ni nokoru merodī.**

[It's] a melody that sticks in your head (*lit.* "ears") as you listen to it over and over again.

d 何回も会ううちに自然に話しができるようになるんですけどね。

**Nankai mo au uchi ni shizen ni hanashi ga dekiru yō ni naru n desu kedo ne.**

In the course of seeing [the other person] many times, one comes to be able to talk naturally [to him], you know.

e 話しているうちに忘れかけていた関西弁がポンポン飛び出してくる。

**Hanashite iru uchi ni wasure-kakete ita Kansai-ben ga ponpon tobidashite kuru.**

As I'm talking, the Kansai dialect that I'd begun to forget pops out, one word after another.

f 本を書いているうちに、船を動かす人、船をつくった人に対する興味も募った。

**Hon o kaite iru uchi ni, fune o ugokasu hito, fune o tsukutta hito ni taisuru kyōmi mo tsunotta.**

While he was writing the book [= history of ships], he also developed an interest in the people who man ships and the people who built the ships.

g 失敗を重ねるうちに、コツは手を放すタイミングにあることに
　気付く。

**Shippai o kasaneru uchi ni, kotsu wa te o hanasu taimingu ni
aru koto ni kizuku.**

As they fail repeatedly [to fly *take-tonbo*, a propeller-like bamboo toy],
they realize that the trick is in the timing of when to let go.

26.2.8.3 *Adjective/***na-***adjective/noun* **uchi ni**

Here, the structure is not S1 **uchi** S2, but Adj/**na-**A/N **uchi ni** modifying a
following verb in the sense of 'while'. In this use, **uchi ni** cannot be replaced
by **uchi wa**.

a 熱いうちにどうぞ。

**Atsui uchi ni dōzo.**

Please, go ahead [and eat] while it's hot.

b そこで、健康なうちに宣言しておくことが必要だという。

**Soko de, kenkō na uchi ni sengen shite oku koto ga hitsuyō
da to iu.**

[You might fall into a coma and no longer be able to express your
wishes] Therefore, it's necessary to declare [your wishes re life
support machines] while you're healthy.

c 会わせたい人がいたら、今のうちに会わせておいてください。

**Awasetai hito ga itara, ima no uchi ni awasete
oite kudasai.**

If there's someone you want to see him, please let them see him now
[while he's still conscious].

26.2.8.4 *Idiomatic uses*

26.2.8.4.1 Near future

In this use, **uchi ni** has the meaning 'soon', 'before long'.

a 近いうちに必ず値上がりする。

**Chikai uchi ni kanarazu ne-agari suru.**

The price will go up without fail in the near future.

b ここ数年のうちに概要を詰める。

**Koko sūnen no uchi ni gaiyō o tsumeru.**

They will firm up the outline sometime within the next few years.

26.2.8.4.2 | Short time

This meaning is 'in a flash', 'instantly', etc.

a みるみるうちに顔が青ざめる。
   **Mirumiru uchi ni kao ga aozameru.**
   His face went pale in an instant.

b 12月の声を聞くか聞かないうちに街は早くもクリスマス一色だ。
   **Jūnigatsu no koe o kiku ka kikanai uchi ni machi wa hayaku
   mo kurisumasu isshoku da.**
   December having barely arrived, the town has swiftly taken on
   an atmosphere of Christmas.

c 両親が寝たきりになったら、ボケてしまったらどうしよう。おし
   めをしてあげられるだろうか。おふろに入れてあげられるだろ
   うか。食事は。着替えは。そんな思いが一瞬のうちに脳裏を駆
   け巡った。
   **Ryōshin ga netakiri ni nattara, bokete shimattara dō shiyō.
   Oshime o shite agerareru darō ka. Ofuro ni irete agerareru
   darō ka. Shokuji wa. Kigae wa. Sonna omoi ga isshun no
   uchi ni nōri o kakemegutta.**
   What am I going to do if my parents become bedridden and senile?
   Will I manage to change their nappies for them? Will I be able to
   bathe them? What about meals? Dressing and undressing? Those
   kinds of ideas raced through my head in a flash.

26.2.8.4.3 | Others: **muishiki no uchi ni**

This phrase means 'subconsciously'.

a 人間の耳は無意識のうちに聞きたい音と聞きたくない音を区別し
   ている。
   **Ningen no mimi wa muishiki no uchi ni kikitai oto to
   kikitakunai oto o kubetsu shite iru.**
   The human ear subconsciously distinguishes between sounds it wants
   to hear and sounds it doesn't want to hear.

26.2.9 | aida, mae, -nagara, -tsutsu, uchi *compared*

All of the above can link two clauses in the sense of 'while' (excepting
**mae**) and 'before' (excepting **aida**, **-nagara** and **-tsutsu**); **-nagara** and **-tsutsu**
are additionally used in the sense of 'even though'. The following sections
give a comparison.

aida and uchi ni can both be used in the sense of 'while'; with uchi ni (and occasionally also aida, as in example b) the implication is usually 'before a change for the worse occurs'.

a 眠っている間に体に異変が起きていた。
**Nemutte iru aida ni karada ni ihen ga okite ita.**
While he had been asleep, an unexpected change had taken place in his body.

b 働ける間は働きたい。
**Hatarakeru aida wa hatarakitai.**
I want to work while I am able to.

c もうけられるうちにもうけておこうという姿勢は慎んでほしい。
**Mōkerareru uchi ni mōkete okō to iu shisei wa tsutsushinde hoshii.**
I want them to restrain their attitude of 'Let's make money while we can'.

d 条件の良いうちに判を押した方がいい。
**Jōken no yoi uchi ni han o oshita hō ga ii.**
You should seal [the agreement] while the conditions are good.

Unlike uchi, aida can indicate a period of time 'while', objectively (example a above). With uchi, on the other hand, the implication is that S2 is a negative outcome or development.

e 議論しているうちに時間ばかりがたっている。
**Giron shite iru uchi ni jikan bakari ga tatte iru.**
While we're arguing, time is slipping away rapidly.

After a negative form in S1, aida can also be used in the sense of 'while' (but uchi in the sense of 'before' is far more common (see next section (26.2.9.2)).

f ファンが知らない間にトレードされてしまったのだろうか。
**Fan ga shiranai aida ni torēdo sarete shimatta no darō ka.**
Has he been sold [to another team] while the fans were unaware, I wonder.

-nagara and -tsutsu are limited to use in sentences where the subject is the same for S1 and S2 (= actions). The main action being that of S2, the implication is that it is carried out while performing (constantly or occasionally) a secondary action.

g 眠い目をこすりながら、空港へ急ぐ。

**Nemui me o kosuri-nagara kūkō e isogu.**

I rush to the airport, rubbing my sleepy eyes.

h 冗談を交えつつ、沖縄音楽の近況を語った。

**Jōdan o majie-tsutsu, Okinawa ongaku no kinkyō o katatta.**

He talked about the current state of Okinawan music, mixing in jokes.

### 26.2.9.2 *'Before'*

Unlike **aida** and **mae**, **uchi** can follow negative forms in the sense of 'before' (something adverse happens).

a 電車がなくならないうちに帰ります。

**Densha ga naku naranai uchi ni kaerimasu.**

I'm going home before the trains stop running.

b 知らないうちに山林が開発されていた。

**Shiranai uchi ni sanrin ga kaihatsu sarete ita.**

Before we knew it, the mountain forest had been developed.

**mae**, on the other hand, is objectively concerned with the order of actions.

c なぜ死を選ぶ前に、救いを求めなかったのか。

**Naze shi o erabu mae ni, sukui o motomenakatta no ka.**

Why didn't he seek help before choosing death?

### 26.2.9.3 *'Even Though'*

Both -**nagara** (**mo**) and -**tsutsu** (**mo**) can be used in the sense of a contrast 'even though'. When **mo** is present, the meaning is always contrastive. Note that unlike -**nagara** (**mo**), which can be attached to Adj., na-Adj. and N, -**tsutsu** (**mo**) attaches only to forms of V (see 26.4.3).

a 彼等は悲しみや苦しみがありながら誇りをもって生きている。

**Karera wa kanashimi ya kurushimi ga ari-nagara hokori o motte ikite iru.**

Even though they have sorrows and pain, they live with pride.

b 最終的には自分で考えろと言いつつも、退職を促すようなアドバ
イスを繰り返した。

**Saishū-teki ni wa jibun de kangaero to ii-tsutsu mo, taishoku
o unagasu yō na adobaisu o kurikaeshita.**

While telling me to make the final decision myself, he repeatedly gave
advice that urged me to resign.

### 26.2.10 tokoro

Used like a conjunctive particle, **tokoro**, which is originally a noun meaning 'place' and by extension means 'situation', 'time', preceded by forms
that modify nouns, indicates the idea of 'as', 'just when'. It can be used
without a following particle, or followed by the case particles **ga, o, e/ni**,
and the conjunctive form of the copula **de**.

Followed by the phrase **ni yoru to**, **tokoro** is frequently used in the media
to indicate the source of information (see 21.4.1).

### 26.2.10.1 -ta tokoro

This indicates that something happens or becomes apparent as a result of
S1 (the **tokoro** clause).

a 乗用車に乗ろうとしたところ、男がナイフを突きつけ乗り込んで
きた。

**Jōyōsha ni norō to shita tokoro, otoko ga naifu o tsukitsuke
norikonde kita.**

As she was getting into her car, a man entered, pointing a knife
at her.

b カネボウ化粧品本部が三十代から五十代の既婚の男女計三百人を
対象に、白髪に関するアンケートを実施したところ、白髪に対
する印象は、男女に差があることが分かった。

**Kanebō keshōhin honbu ga sanjū-dai kara gojū-dai no kikon
no danjo kei sanbyaku-nin o taishō ni, hakuhatsu ni kansuru
ankēto o jisshi shita tokoro, shiraga ni taisuru inshō wa,
danjo ni sa ga aru koto ga wakatta.**

The head office of Kanebo cosmetics surveyed a total of 300 men
and women in their 30s to 50s. They showed that there were
differences in attitudes between men and women towards white
hair. (*lit.* "when they conducted a survey, it became clear...")

## 26.2.10.2 -ta tokoro ga

This combination often indicates a contrast, but can also indicate a cue for what follows (example c).

a 「さあ、勝った」と思ったところが、レフリーの笛が鳴らない。
**'Sā, katta' to omotta tokoro ga, refurī no fue ga naranai.**
Just when you thought 'now, we've won', the referee's whistle won't sound. [=soccer stoppage time]

b ここに着陸し始めたところが、どうしてもいつもの調子が
出ない。
**Koko ni chakuriku shihajimeta tokoro ga, dōshite mo itsumo no chōshi ga denai.**
I started to land [the aeroplane] at this airport, but just couldn't get the usual feel.

c 現地の皆さんにいろいろお尋ねをいたしましたところが、
二通りの答えが返ってきたわけです。
**Genchi no minasan ni iroiro otazune o itashi mashita tokoro ga, futatōri no kotae ga kaette kita wake desu.**
When I asked the locals all sorts of questions, two kinds of replies came back.

d ...酒元の従業員が主人に恨みをいだき、腹いせに竈の灰を酒樽
の中に投げ入れて出奔したところが、灰によって濁り酒が清酒
になっていた、とか。
**...sakamoto no jūgyōin ga shujin ni urami o idaki, haraise ni kamado no hai o sakadaru no naka ni nageirete shuppon shita tokoro ga, hai ni yotte nigorizake ga seishu ni natte ita, to ka.**
...it is said that an employee of the sake brewery held a grudge against the boss, threw ash from the oven into the sake barrel and ran away; it turned out that the cloudy sake had changed to clear sake because of the ash.

## 26.2.10.3 -ta tokoro de

The meaning is one of point of time 'once', 'the moment something happens', but followed by a comment negative in form or meaning, can also indicate a contrast 'even if'.

a 煙が出たところで、火から外し、やや冷めたところで再び油を塗
って加熱。

**Kemuri ga deta tokoro de, hi kara hazushi, yaya same
ta tokoro de futatabi abura o nutte kanetsu.**

Once it starts smoking, you take it off the heat, and brush it
with oil again once it has cooled a little, and reheat it.
[= preparing Dutch oven for use]

b ある程度、アウトラインが出来たところでレポートを書く。

**Aru teido, autorain ga dekita tokoro de repōto o kaku.**

Once the outline is done to a certain extent, you start writing the report.

c バターはアッという間にとろけ、かすかに茶色に変わったところ
で、一気に溶いた卵を流し込む。

**Batā wa atto iu ma ni toroke, kasuka ni chairo ni kawatta
tokoro de, ikki ni toita tamago o nagashikomu.**

The butter melts almost instantaneously, and the moment it has gone
ever so slightly brown, you pour in the beaten egg in one go.

d 早くから教えたところで何も進歩はないと思います。

**Hayaku kara oshieta tokoro de nani mo shinpo wa nai to
omoimasu.**

Even if they start teaching [English] from an early age, I don't think
there will be any improvement.

e たとえ事件が解決したところで、内田さんはここの席に戻ってこ
ない。

**Tatoe jiken ga kaiketsu shita tokoro de, Uchida-san wa koko
no seki ni modotte konai.**

Even if the crime is solved, Mr Uchida will not be coming back to his
seat here.

26.2.10.4 **-ta tokoro ni/e**

The meaning here is again in accordance with the basic use of **tokoro** as
a conjunctive particle, 'just when' or 'as'.

a 4ヶ月前に一時停止していたところに前から脇見運転の車が正面
衝突してきました。

**Yonkagetsu mae ni ichijiteishi shite itatokoro ni mae kara
wakimi-unten no kuruma ga shōmen-shōtotsu shite kimashita.**

Four months ago, a car whose driver wasn't looking bashed into the
front of my car as I was stationary.

b 眠くなったところへメールが（笑）。

**Nemuku natta tokoro e mēru ga (warai).**

Just as I got sleepy an email [came] (laughter).

c 信長が手と顔を洗い終わって手拭いを使っていたところへ、明智
の兵が背に矢を放った。

**Nobunaga ga te to kao o arai-owatte tenugui o tsukatte ita
tokoro e, Akechi no hei ga se ni ya o hanatta.**

Just as Nobunaga had finished washing his face and hands and was
using a towel, Akechi's soldiers shot their arrows at his back.

d カツオのブロック（さく）に塩、コショウを少々かけたとこ
ろへ、このハーブ粉末をまぶす。

**Katsuo no burokku (saku) ni shio, koshō o shōshō  kaketa
tokoro e, kono hābu-funmatsu o mabusu.**

Once you've put a little salt and pepper on a piece (or cut) of bonito,
you sprinkle it with this herb powder.

26.2.10.5 | **tokoro o**

Apart from expressing a contrast (example a), this mostly indicates the idea
of 'just as'. In the media it is frequently used in the sense of being seen as you
are doing something, or being found in a certain state. It is also used in set
phrases when thanking people for attending despite being busy (example g).

a 通常はパソコンで作っているところを、今回は敢えて手書きのチ
ラシを用意するのである。

**Tsūjō  wa pasokon de tsukutte iru tokoro o, konkai wa aete
tegaki no chirashi o yōi suru no de aru.**

Normally they make them on a PC, but this time they made a point
of preparing handwritten pamphlets.

b 演題を修正するところを誤って削除してしまいました。

**Endai o shūsei suru tokoro o ayamatte sakujo shite
shimaimashita.**

I mistakenly erased the title of my lecture as I was editing it.

c 女子生徒は今年六月二十六日、JR駅の階段で、男子生徒と二人で
たばこを吸っているところを見つかった。

**Joshi seito wa kotoshi rokugatsu nijūrokunichi, JR eki no
kaidan de, danshi seito to futari de tabako o sutte iru
tokoro o mitsukatta.**

The female pupil was caught on the 26th of June this year smoking
with a male pupil on the steps of the JR station.

623

d 友一朗ちゃんは岸近くの川底でおぼれているところを発見
された

**Yūichiro-chan wa kishi chikaku no kawazoku de oborete iru
tokoro o hakken sareta.**

Yuichiro was found lying drowned on the bottom on the river near
the bank.

e 海中に沈め、魚が入ったところを引き上げる。

**Kaichū ni shizume, sakana ga haitta tokoro o hikiageru.**

They let it [= net] sink into the sea, and pull it up just as fish have
swum into it.

f 目撃者の話では、遮断機が下り始めたところを乗用車が無理に横
断したらしい。

**Mokugekisha no hanashi de wa, shadanki ga orihajimeta
tokoro o jōyōsha ga muri ni ōdan shita rashii.**

According to witnesses, a passenger car appears to have squeezed
across just as the barrier had begun to come down.

Idiomatic use

g 忙しいところをお集まりいただきまして、ありがとうござ
います。

**Isogashii tokoro o o-atsumari itadakimashite, arigatō
gozaimasu.**

Thank you for gathering despite being busy.

## 26.3 Concession

### 26.3.1 -te mo

The conjunctive particle -te/de mo consists of the conjunctive -te/de form
and the adverbial particle **mo**, and basically means 'even if'. It can attach
to V, Adj, **na**-Adj and N.

*Note* – there is an informal variant -tatte for -te mo (see example a and
the second sentence of example b), -**datte** for -**de mo**, and **datte** for **de mo**
or **mo** (example b), see also 11.2.2).

a クリスマスはどんな過ごし方をしたっていい。

**Kurisumasu wa donna sugoshikata o shi-tatte ii.**

As for Christmas, you can [it] spend any way you like.

b 男性がスカートをはくわけにはいかないが、女性は三つぞろいの ***Concession***
  ビジネススーツだって着ることができる。
  **Dansei ga sukāto o haku wake ni wa ikanai ga,**
  **josei wa mitsu-zoroi no bijinesu-sūtsu datte kiru**
  **koto ga dekiru.**
  A man can't wear a skirt, but a woman can wear a three-piece
  business suit.

---

| 26.3.1.1 | *Clause 1-***te**/***-de mo** *clause 2*

This means 'even if', 'even though'. Note also that –**te mo** can also be
attached to -**te iru** when a state is being referred to, as in example d.

a 船賃を加えても関西から運んだ方がまだ10%安い。
  **Funachin o kuwaete mo Kansai kara hakonda hō ga mada**
  **jup-pāsento yasui.**
  Even if shipping charges are added, it's still 10 per cent cheaper to
  transport from the Kansai area.

b あなたが抗議しても、彼女たちは鼻で笑いながら言うだろう。
  「触られたって減るもんじゃなし」「冗談も通じないなんて」。
  **Anata ga kōgi shite mo, kanojo-tachi wa hana de warainagara**
  **iu darō. 'Sawarare-tatte heru mon ja nashi' 'Jōdan mo**
  **tsūjinai nante'.**
  [Sexual harassment:] Even if you protest, they [= the female bosses]
  will probably say, laughing ironically, 'You're not going to wear out by
  being touched', [or] 'My god, you can't even take a joke'.

c 地味でも長く続けることこそ大切だ。
  **Jimi de mo nagaku tsuzukeru koto koso taisetsu da.**
  It's important to carry on doing things, even if it's in
  a modest way.

d リゾートクラブ会員権を保有していても、これまでは同一クラブ
  の施設だけしか利用できなかった。
  **Rizōto kurabu no kaiinken o hoyū shite ite mo, kore**
  **made wa dōitsu kurabu no shisetsu dake shika riyō**
  **dekinakatta.**
  Even if one held membership of a resort club, as yet one could only
  use the facilities of that same club.

26.3.1.2 *Clause 1-***nakute mo** *clause 2*

In the negative, the meaning is 'even if not'.

a 名前を知らず、話したことがなくてもあいさつをする。
**namae o shirazu, hanashita koto ga nakute mo aisatsu o suru**
Even if he doesn't know their names and has never spoken to them
before, he greets them [= employees].

b 「事件があってもなくても田中先生は日中友好関係の大功労者」
と述べた。
**'Jiken ga atte mo nakute mo Tanaka-sensei wa nitchū yūkō
kankei no daikōrōsha' to nobeta.**
'Regardless of whether or not he was involved in an incident,
Mr Tanaka has made a great contribution to friendly relations
between Japan and China', he stated.

26.3.1.3 *Clause 1-***te/-de mo**,... *clause 2-negative*

Followed by a negative, the meaning of **-te/-de mo** is 'even if', 'even'.

a テレビ好きの子供でもニュースやドキュメントはあまり見ないら
しい。
**Terebi-zuki no kodomo demo nyūsu ya dokyumento wa
amari minai rashii.**
It seems that even children who like TV don't watch news and
documentaries much.

b 輸入米が日本人の味覚に合わず、安くても売れない状況になる可
能性もある。
**Yunyū-mai ga Nihonjin no mikaku ni awazu, yasukute mo
urenai jōkyō ni naru kanōsei mo aru.**
Imported rice doesn't suit the Japanese palate, so it's possible that we
end up with a situation where it won't sell even if it's cheap.

c 「ブラジルに帰っても仕事があるかどうかわからない」
とうつむく。
**'Burajiru ni kaette mo shigoto ga aru ka dō ka wakaranai' to
utsumuku.**
'Even if I went back to Brazil, I don't know whether or not I could get
work', he says, with downcast eyes.

d ここではドロップアウト（中途退学）の比率が60%近くもある
　高校が珍しくない。卒業してもいい仕事につける望みはな
　いからだ。

**Koko de wa doroppu-auto (chūto taigaku) no hiritsu ga 60%
chikaku mo aru kōkō ga mezurashikunai. Sotsugyō shite
mo ii shigoto ni tsukeru nozomi wa nai kara da.**

In this area there are quite a few high schools where the dropout rate
is almost 60 per cent. That's because even when one graduates,
there's no hope of getting a good job.

e 勉強したいと思っても、なかなか時間がとれずイライラすること
　もある。

**Benkyō shitai to omotte mo, nakanaka jikan ga torezu iraira
suru koto mo aru.**

There are times when, even if you want to study, it's rather difficult to
find the time, so you get irritated.

### 26.3.1.4 *Clause-***te/de mo ii**

Followed by an evaluatory adjective. such as **ii/yoi** 'good', the combination
means 'it's OK if', 'you could', 'you can/may'.

a 文明は民族と置き換えてもいい。
**Bunmei wa minzoku to okikaete mo ii.**
For 'civilization', you could substitute 'race'.

b 必要なら町が買い取ってもいいと思っている。
**Hitsuyō nara machi ga kaitotte mo ii to omotte iru.**
I think it would be all right for the town to purchase it
[= government-owned forest], if necessary.

c 食品、動物、薬以外なら大抵の商品を販売してもいい。
**Shokuhin, dōbutsu, kusuri igai nara taitei no shōhin o hanbai
shite mo ii.**
[Flea market:] Apart from food, animals, and medicine, one is allowed
to sell almost anything.

### 26.3.1.5 *Question word (+ counter)-***te mo**

Depending on the question word, the combination has a variety of meanings, such as 'no matter how/when', etc. (see 5.2, 4.2, Table 5.2).

a ところが、生徒たちは「どうしても歌いたい」とステージを離れ
　　ようとしない。
　**Tokoro ga, seito-tachi wa 'Dōshite mo utaitai' to sutēji o
　hanareyō to shinai.**
　However, the pupils said, 'We want to sing no matter what', and made
　no move to leave the stage.

b どちらにしても店を維持するのは難しい。
　**Dochira ni shite mo mise o iji suru no wa muzukashii.**
　Either way, it will be difficult to keep the store going.

c 現在、いつ停電してもおかしくない状態にある模様だ。
　**Genzai, itsu teiden shite mo okashikunai jōtai ni aru
　moyō da.**
　At present, they seem to be in a situation where the power could go
　out at any time.

d だれの目から見ても分かりやすい条件設定が可能となる。
　**Dare no me kara mite mo wakari-yasui jōken settei ga kanō
　ni naru.**
　It will be possible to stipulate terms [for corporate bond issues] in
　a way that is easy for anyone to understand.

e どんなに変形させても、温めると元の形にもどる不思議な素材、
　形状記憶合金。
　**Donna ni henkei sasete mo, atatameru to moto no katachi ni
　modoru fushigi na sozai, keijō kioku gōkin.**
　It's a form-retention alloy, an amazing material which returns to its
　original shape when you heat it up, no matter how you've modified
　it.

f 「ダメな自分をいくら分析してもダメな自分しか出てこない」。
　**'Dame na jibun o ikura bunseki shite mo dame na jibun shika
　dete konai'.** [= advice on what not to do in a job interview]
　"No matter how much you analyse the useless side of yourself, all
　that comes out is your useless side".

g しかし、こんな状態を続けていてはいつまでたっても自立した
　証券会社は育たない。
　**Shikashi, konna jōtai o tsuzukete ite wa itsu made tatte mo
　jiritsu shita shōken-gaisha wa sodatanai.**
　However, as long as they continue with this kind of situation,
　a securities company which stands on its own won't develop,
　no matter how much time passes.

| 26.3.1.6 | *(hitokuchi ni) clause 1* **to it-te mo** *clause 2*

This is used in the sense of '(even though/if . . . but) actually' (see 21.2).

a 「一口にレースと言っても、それは手法のこと」と話すのは近沢
　弘明社長。
　**'Hitokuchi ni rēsu to itte mo, sore wa shuhō no koto' to
　hanasu no wa Chikazawa Hiroaki shachō.**
　It is President Hiroaki Chikazawa who states, 'Even if you say
　[in general terms] "lace", what is being referred to is
　a technique'.

b 「不況といってもツアー料金が安いので影響は特にありません」
　とニッコリ。
　**'Fukyō to itte mo tsuā ryōkin ga yasui node eikyō wa toku ni
　arimasen' to nikkori.**
　'Even if business is bad, [our] tour prices are low, so [we] don't feel
　any particular effects', she said with a smile.

c なべ物メニューといっても、大半が千円以下の商品であるこ
　とも、共通の特色だ。
　**Nabemono menyū to itte mo, taihan ga sen-en ika no shōhin
　de aru koto mo, kyōtsū no tokushoku da.**
　Even if the menu is *nabemono* (hotpot dishes), the fact that the great
　majority of items are under a thousand yen is also a common
　feature [of the chain restaurants].

d 日本ではJリーグ人気がすごいといっても、ほとんどはチームあ
　るいは選手のファン。
　**Nihon de wa Jei-rīgu ninki ga sugoi to itte mo, hotondo wa
　chīmu arui wa senshu no fan.**
　In Japan, the popularity of the J-League is tremendous, but in fact it's
　only among fans of [certain] teams or players.

e 日本の歌曲を歌う、といっても、ドイツ語に訳されたもの
　を歌う。
　**Nihon no kakyoku o utau, to itte mo, Doitsugo ni yakusareta
　mono o utau.**
　She sings Japanese songs, but actually what she sings are [songs that
　have been] translated into German.

26.3.1.7 **sō wa itte mo**

This is used like a conjunction, in the sense of 'even so'.

a そうはいっても、リストラの成果が表れた企業を評価しようとい
う動きは出ている。

**Sō wa itte mo, risutora no seika ga arawareta kigyō o hyōka
shiyō to iu ugoki wa dete iru.**

Even so, a trend is emerging of giving positive evaluations to
businesses which have shown the fruits of restructuring.

26.3.1.8 *Clause 1* **tatoe ...-te mo** ... *clause 2-negative*

**tatoe** (and some other adverbs) can reinforce the meaning of **-te mo** 'even
if', 'even assuming that' (10.2.4.6).

a たとえ景気が回復しても、日本の石油化学業界は回復しないので
はないか。

**Tatoe keiki ga kaifuku shite mo, Nihon no sekiyu kagaku
gyōkai wa kaifuku shinai no de wa nai ka.**

Even if the market were to recover, the Japanese petrochemical
industry wouldn't recover, would it?

26.3.1.9 *Idiomatic use:* **hayaku/osoku-te mo**

This use means 'at the earliest/latest'.

a 消費は早くても来年後半から緩やかに回復するという程度
だろう。

**Shōhi wa hayakute mo rainen kōhan kara yuruyaka ni kaifuku
suru to iu teido darō.**

Probably all that can be expected is that consumption will recover
slowly, starting in the latter half of next year at the earliest.

b 着陸料をめぐる交渉が再開されるのは早くても来年一月中旬の
見通しだ。

**Chakurikuryō o meguru kōshō ga saikai sareru no wa
hayakute mo rainen ichigatsu chūjun no mitōshi da.**

The outlook is for negotiations concerning landing charges to be
resumed in mid-January of next year, at the earliest.

## 26.4 Contrast

### 26.4.1 ga

**ga** basically expresses a weak contrast between S1 and S2 'but' (see 26.4.2, 26.4.5, 26.4.6).

#### 26.4.1.1 *Clause 1* **ga**, *clause 2 noun + copula 'but'*

This is a noun-modifying sequence (indicated in [ ]) where two clauses are linked by **ga** in the sense of 'N (which is/was) *A* but *B*'. In writing, this use is usually distinguished from that shown in 26.4.1.2 below by the presence of a comma in the latter.

a 忙しかったがいい一年だった。
**[Isogashikatta ga ii ichinen] datta.**
It was a busy but good year.

#### 26.4.1.2 *Clause 1* **ga**, *clause 2*

Unlike 26.4.1.1, in this use **ga** 'but' links are two clauses with separate predicates (i.e. the content of these sentences could equally be expressed in two separate sentences). A comma is usually present in writing.

a 約一時間かかるが、ドライブは快適だ。
**Yaku ichi-jikan kakaru ga, doraibu wa kaiteki da.**
It takes about one hour, but it's a pleasant drive.

b 料理はちょっと辛いが、なかなかの味だ。
**Ryōri wa chotto karai ga, nakanaka no aji da.**
The dishes are a little spicy, but quite tasty.

c 参加は無料だが、事前申し込みが必要。
**Sanka wa muryō da ga, jizen mōshikomi ga hitsuyō.**
Attendance is free, but one needs to apply in advance.

d 技術的には難しい歌ですが、みな熱心でした。
**Gijutsu-teki ni wa muzukashii uta desu ga, mina nesshin deshita.**
Technically it's a difficult song, but everyone was enthusiastic.

*Clause 1* **ga**, *clause 2 expressing 'and' or ';'*

In some contexts, the force of **ga** is so weak that it is more appropriate to translate it as 'and', or use a semicolon.

a 四七年に米国に渡ったが、彼の才能をいち早く認めたのはベニー・グッドマンだったという。

**Yonjūnana-nen ni Beikoku ni watatta ga, kare no sainō o ichihayaku mitometa no wa Benī Guddoman datta to iu.**

In '47 he went to the US, and it was Benny Goodman who was the first to discover his talent, it is said.

b 今年の自動車業界は低価格車ブームにわいたが、この傾向はまだ続くのか。

**Kotoshi no jidōsha gyōkai wa teikakakusha būmu ni waita ga, kono keikō wa mada tsuzuku no ka.**

In this year's car business low-priced models were all the rage; is this trend going to continue?

26.4.1.4 *Clause1* **ga**. (...) *in unfinished sentences*

Sentences where S2 is left unsaid (implied) are commonly used, especially for introducing requests, to test the listener's reaction, but also to imply that realization of S2 is not possible or realistic.

a ちょっとすみませんが……。

**Chotto sumimasen ga ...**

Excuse me.

b ちょっとお伺いしたいんですが。

**Chotto o-ukagai shitai n desu ga.**

Could I ask you something?

c 覚えていないんですが……。

**Oboete inai n desu ga ...**

I don't remember.

26.4.1.5 *Clause 1-presumptive* **ga** *clause 2-presumptive* **ga**: *adverbial clauses*

Here we see **ga** repeated twice (or three times, as in example h) after positive, or positive and negative hortative or presumptive forms, the combination forming adverbial clauses in the sense of 'whether . . . or', 'regardless of' (see 9.1.2, 28.2.2).

a 彼がいようがいまいが、大した違いはなかった。

**Kare ga iyō ga imai ga, taishita chigai wa nakatta.**

Whether he was there or not didn't make [or wouldn't have made] much difference.

b 足をくじこうが転倒しようが何が何でも完走する。

**Ashi o kujikō ga tentō shiyō ga nani ga nan demo kansō suru.**

Whether I sprain my foot or fall, I'll complete [the marathon], no matter what.

c 外に着ようが内に着ようが着る人次第といったところ。

**Soto ni kiyō ga uchi ni kiyō ga kiru hito shidai to itta tokoro.**

Whether one wears [clothes] inside or out is up to the person wearing them, I guess.

d この二十二年間、元日だろうが外国に居ようが毎朝欠かさず六キ
　ロメートル歩いてきた。

**Kono nijūni-nenkan, ganjitsu darō ga gaikoku ni iyō ga maiasa kakasazu rok-kiromētoru aruite kita.**

For the past 22 years, I've walked 6 km every morning without fail, be it New Year's Day, [at home] or abroad.

e 良いものは日本だろうが欧州だろうが、どこからでも取り入
　れる。

**Yoi mono wa Nihon darō ga Ōshū darō ga, doko kara demo tori-ireru.**

We take good products from anywhere, whether it's Japan or Europe.

f すこし前までビールはどこの店でも、大量に買おうが少量だろう
　が価格はメーカー希望価格だった。

**Sukoshi mae made bīru wa doko no mise de mo, tairyō ni kaō ga shōryō darō ga kakaku wa mēkā kibō kakaku datta.**

Until a short time ago, in every shop the price of beer was the price recommended by the manufacturer, regardless of whether you bought large or small quantities.

g 二人の間に愛がなくなり争いが激しくなれば、結婚していようが
　いまいが別れるし、別れるべきだ。

**Futari no aida ni ai ga naku nari arasoi ga hageshiku nareba, kekkon shite iyō ga imai ga wakareru shi, wakareru-beki da.**

If love's gone and the fighting gets worse, a couple will split, and ought to do so, whether they are married or not.

h ・・・料亭などには旬（しゅん）のタケノコだろうが山菜の珍味だ
　ろうが高価な魚だろうが、おいしいものをドーンと出して、
　お客さんからは高いお金をバーンと取る。

...**ryōtei nado ni wa shun no takenoko darō ga sansai no
chinmi darō ga kōka na sakana darō ga, oishii mono o
dōn to dashite, o-kyaku-san kara wa takai okane o bān
to toru.**

...they deliver lots of delicious things to places like Japanese
restaurants, whether seasonal bamboo shoots, prized wild
vegetables or expensive fish, and charge them plenty of money.

### 26.4.2 keredomo (kedo/kedomo/keredo)

**keredomo** is a conjunctive particle that joins two clauses in a sense of
contrast 'but', 'however'. **kedo**, **keredo** and **kedomo** are colloquial variants.

### 26.4.2.1 Clause 1 ke(re)do(mo) clause 2

This indicates 'but', 'however', 'although' (see 26.4.1, 26.4.5).

#### 26.4.2.1.1 Clause 1 ke(re)do(mo), clause 2: with comma

When there is a comma between S1 and S2, S1 can usually be understood
to indicate a qualification for S2.

a 仕事は厳しいけれど、やりがいがある。
**Shigoto wa kibishii keredo, yarigai ga aru.**
The work is hard, but it's rewarding.

b 父さんを嫌いではないけれど、離婚するしかないよ。
**Tōsan o kirai de wa nai keredo, rikon suru shika nai yo.**
I don't dislike daddy, but divorce is the only choice.

c 長い旅で疲れたけど、行って良かった。
**Nagai tabi de tsukareta kedo, itte yokatta.**
I'm tired from the long trip, but I'm glad I went.

d 怖いけれども、それが魅力でもある。
**Kowai keredomo, sore ga miryoku de mo aru.**
It's [a] frightening [town], but that's also its attraction.

26.4.2.1.2 | Clause 1 **ke(re)do(mo)** clause 2: without comma

Without a comma, the implication is usually one of contrast.

a 愛しているけど結婚はしたくない。
**Aishite iru kedo kekkon wa shitakunai.**
I love you, but I don't want to marry you.

b デパートは高いけれど便利。
**Depāto wa takai keredo benri.**
Department stores are expensive but convenient.

c 日本で言うプロというのは鋭いけれど狭いんですね。
**Nihon de iu puro to iu no wa surudoi keredo semai n desu ne.**
Those called professional [researchers] in Japan are sharp but narrow [in specialization].

26.4.2.2 | *Introducing a comment or request*

In English, this often indicates a preamble for S2. It often translates as two sentences.

a 顔色悪いけど、大丈夫かね。
**Kaoiro warui kedo, daijōbu ka ne.**
You look pale – are you OK?

b 「みんなは来春卒業するけれど、自分も早く学校に通って立派な技術を身に着けたい」と胸を膨らませていた。
**'Minna wa raishun sotsugyō suru keredo, jibun mo hayaku gakkō ni kayotte rippa na gijutsu o minitsuketai' to mune o fukuramasete ita.**
'Everyone's going to graduate next spring; I, too, want to go to school and learn proper skills', he said expectantly.

c 悪いけど、蛍池には行きたいとは思わない。
**Warui kedo, Hotarugaike ni wa ikitai to wa omowanai.**
I'm sorry, I don't feel like going to Hotarugaike.

26.4.2.3 | *Clause 1* **ke(re)do(mo)** *(...) in unfinished sentences*

In unfinished sentences, **ke(re)do(mo)** conveys a nuance of interacting with the listener. Depending on the context, this ranges from 'you see', 'mind you', etc. to an implied S2. After **-ba ii**, it indicates a hypothetical condition 'would be good if'. Here, **ga** can also be used, but **noni** cannot be used in the same meaning (see 26.1.1.3.1, 26.4.1.4, 26.4.5).

a ダメだ、ダメだと、いつも思ってますけれどね。
   **Dame da, dame da to, itsumo omotte imasu keredo ne.**
   I always think I'm no good, you see.

b 今年で四年目なんですけれど。主人は赴任先に女ができてしまっ
   たから帰ってくる様子は全くありません。来年になると自動的
   に離婚されてしまうんでしょうか。
   **Kotoshi de yonenme nan desu keredo. Shujin wa funinsaki ni
   onna ga dekite shimatta kara kaette kuru yōsu wa mattaku
   arimasen. Rainen ni naru to jidōteki ni rikon sarete shimau
   n deshō ka.**
   [Introduction of five-year separation clause.] It's the fourth year this
   year, you see. My husband has found a woman during his posting
   and shows no signs of returning. Will I automatically get divorced
   next year?

c 同じようにしてくれとは言わないけれども‥‥‥。
   **Onaji yō ni shite kure to wa iwanai keredomo ...**
   It's not that we're asking to be treated in the same way [as other war
   victims], but ... [something should be done].

d 一緒に過ごすボーイフレンドがいればいいんですけど。
   **Issho ni sugosu bōifurendo ga ireba ii n desu kedo.**
   It'd be nice to have a boyfriend to spend [Christmas] with.

e スキンヘッドにしたのは、「とにかく目立ちたかった」から。
   「冬は寒くて大変ですけど」と笑う。
   **Sukinheddo ni shita no wa, 'tonikaku medachi-takatta' kara.
   'Fuyu wa samukute taihen desu kedo' to warau.**
   The reason why he became a skinhead was because he 'just wanted
   to attract attention'. 'Mind you, in winter you feel terribly cold',
   he laughed.

f 「お母さん。友達の誕生パーティーに呼ばれているんだけど、
   行っていいかな」「いいけど。いつ」
   **'Okāsan. Tomodachi no tanjō pātī ni yobarete iru n da kedo,
   itte ii ka na' 'Ii kedo. Itsu'**
   'Mum, I'm invited to a friend's birthday party – is it OK to go?'
   'Sure. When [is it]?'

## 26.4.3 -nagara

-nagara has two major uses, linking simultaneous actions 'while', and actions that are contrastive in nature 'even though'. In the second use only -nagara can attach **mo**.

### 26.4.3.1 Clause 1-verb-stem-**nagara** clause 2

-nagara indicates that two concurrent or simultaneous actions are performed by the same person (or subject) in the sense of 'while'. V1 can be a durative (i.e. action or state is lasting for some time – see 7.4.2.2) or repeatable V, but not an instant V, i.e. in example a -nagara cannot be used.

a  ✐×私たちはすわりながら話した。
**×Watashitachi wa suwari-nagara hanashita.**
Instead, this would be expressed by V1-**te**, V2 (see 25.1):

b  ✐私たちはすわって話した。
**Watashitachi wa suwatte hanashita.**
We talked while sitting down.

Other conjunctive particles that translate as 'while' are **aida**, **-tsutsu**, and **uchi** (see 26.2.9).

Japanese being a verb-final language, the main verb or verb-phrase is S2. Note that in English the word order is usually reversed, with the main verb coming first.

c  眠い目をこすりながら、空港へ急ぐ。
**Nemui me o kosuri-nagara, kūkō e isogu.**
I rush to the airport, rubbing my sleepy eyes.

d  小学校の教師をしながら地元紙に連載小説を書いたこともある。
**Shōgakkō no kyōshi o shi-nagara jimotoshi ni rensai shōsetsu o kaita koto mo aru.**
Once he wrote serial novels for a local newspaper while working as a primary school teacher.

### 26.4.3.2 Clause 1-verb-stem/adjective-noun-modifying/**na**-adjective/ noun-**nagara** (**mo**) clause 2

This indicates a contrast 'even though' (see 26.4.5, 26.4.1, 26.4.2, 26.4.6).

The actions or events before and after -**nagara** are contrastive in meaning.

a 彼等は悲しみや苦しみがありながら誇りをもって生きて
　 いる。
**Kare-ra wa kanashimi ya kurushimi ga ari-nagara hokori
o motte ikite iru.**
Even though they have sorrows and hardship, they live with pride.

b あふれる情報の刺激を受けながらも退屈している。
**Afureru jōhō no shigeki o uke-nagara mo taikutsu
shite iru.**
Even though [modern man] is exposed to the stimulus of abundant
information, he is bored.

c 若いながら、次期社長との呼び声も高かった。
**Wakai-nagara, jiki shachō to no yobigoe mo takakatta.**
Though he was young, there were many calls for him to be the next
company president.

d 家計の消費支出が穏やかながらも着実に上向いてきた。
**Kakei no shōhi shishutsu ga odayaka-nagara mo chakujitsu ni
uwamuite kita.**
The household outgoings were steadily improving, albeit slowly.

e 80歳の高齢ながらかくしゃくとしている。
**Hachijus-sai no kōrei-nagara kakushaku to shite iru.**
Despite her advanced age of 80 she is full of vigour.

---

| 26.4.3.3 | *Idiomatic uses* |

As part of a lexical expression, -**nagara** forms an adverbial expression
(some expressions require **ni/ni shite** after -**nagara**). When used to modify
a noun, the particle **no** is attached. Translations are idiomatic.

Note example d, where the verb **iru** is used in the somewhat archaic sense
of 'to sit'. In example e, too, -**nagara** is attached to the classical adverb **sa**
'so'; the combination is best seen as a lexical item.

a 「微力ながら町のお手伝いができれば」と抱負を語った。
**'Biryoku-nagara machi no o-tetsudai ga dekireba' to hōfu o
katatta.**
He talked about his aspirations, saying '[I'd be glad] to be of help to
the town with my limited abilities'.

b 残念ながらこの病気の原因はまだ分からない。

**Zannen-nagara kono byōki no gen'in wa mada wakaranai.**

Unfortunately, the cause of this disease is still unknown.

c 社長が涙ながらに謝罪したが，会場は重苦しいムードが支配していた。

**Shachō ga namida-nagara ni shazai shita ga, kaijō wa omokurushii mūdo ga shihai shite ita.**

The company president apologized in tears, but in the hall a strained atmosphere prevailed.

d 居ながらにしてアフリカを体験できる番組になりそうだ。

**I-nagara ni shite Afurika o taiken dekiru bangumi ni narisō da.**

It should be a programme where you can experience Africa from your armchair.

e 負傷者の救出訓練が本番さながらに繰り広げられた。

**Fushōsha no kyūshutsu kunren ga honban sa-nagara ni kurihirogerareta.**

The practice for rescuing the injured took place as if real.

f 昔ながらの簡素なパッケージも人気がある。

**Mukashi-nagara no kanso na pakkēji mo ninki ga aru.**

Simple packaging as of old is popular, too.

g 生まれながらの悲観主義者（ペシミスト）もオプティミストに変身できる。

**Umare-nagara no hikan shugisha (peshimisuto) mo oputimisuto ni henshin dekiru.**

Even born pessimists can change to optimists.

## 26.4.4 -tsutsu

Attached to V-stem, -tsutsu expresses the idea of 'while' (see 26.4.3). Like -nagara (mo), -tsutsu can also imply a contrast.

Note that like -nagara, -tsutsu requires that the subject (or actor) of the verb be the same in S1 and S2.

### 26.4.4.1 Clause 1-tsutsu clause 2: simultaneous actions

-tsutsu expresses simultaneous actions performed by the same agent or subject 'while' (see 26.4.3).

*Note* – 'simultaneous actions' does not necessarily mean that both actions are carried out at the same time; one of them can be intermittent (e.g. example b).

a 楽しみつつ、生き方を充実させたい。
**Tanoshimi-tsutsu, ikikata o jūjitsu sasetai.**
I want to make the most of my life while [also] having fun.

b 冗談を交えつつ、沖縄音楽の近況を語った。
**Jōdan o majie-tsutsu, Okinawa ongaku no kinkyō o katatta.**
He told about the current state of Okinawan music, mixing in jokes.

c 各民族の特徴を生かしつつ、国家を形成しようというわけだ。
**Kaku-minzoku no tokuchō o ikashi-tsutsu, kokka o keisei shiyō to iu wake da.**
What they're saying is that they want to form a nation while making the most of the characteristics of each ethnic group.

d 自己を大切にしつつ、いかにチームに溶け込むか。
**Jiko o taisetsu ni shi-tsutsu, ika ni chīmu ni tokekomu ka.**
How does one blend into the team while keeping one's own interest in mind?

---

26.4.4.2 | *Clause 1-**tsutsu** (**mo**) clause 2: contrasted actions*

-**tsutsu** (**mo**) expresses a contrast 'while', 'even though' (see 26.4.1, 26.4.2, 26.4.3, 26.4.5, 21.2.13).

a このような理念は当時の人々が持ちつつ、実行に移さなかった。
**Kono yō na rinen wa tōji no hitobito ga mochi-tsutsu, jikkō ni utsusanakatta.**
While the people at the time had this kind of ideal, they didn't put it into practice.

b 野球を続けたいと思いつつ、やむなく断念した選手も多い。
**Yakyū o tsuzuketai to omoi-tsutsu, yamunaku dannen shita senshu mo ōi.**
While wanting to go on with baseball, there are many players who had to give it up.

c 最終的には自分で考えろと言いつつも、退職を促すようなアドバイスを繰り返した。
**Saishū-teki ni wa jibun de kangaero to ii-tsutsu mo, taishoku o unagasu yō na adobaisu o kurikaeshita.**
While telling me to make the final decision myself, he repeatedly gave me advice urging me to resign.

## 26.4.5 | noni

This **noni** is a conjunctive particle, which attaches to V/Adj/**na**-Adj/N in the forms that modify nouns. It is distinct from **noni** indicating purpose, which is attached to V-**ru** (see 26.5.1).

**noni** expresses a strong contrast between two clauses, S1 and S2 'despite' (26.4.1–26.4.3, 26.4.6).

**noni** shows emotional involvement on the part of the speaker, which can range from amazement to disappointment or anger.

### 26.4.5.1 | *Clause I* **noni**, *clause 2*

**noni** joins S1 and S2 in a variety of ways, in the sense of 'even though', 'despite'.

#### 26.4.5.1.1 | Followed by a statement

Neither **ga** nor **keredomo** can be used in the same meaning.

a 冬間近だというのに、連日、暖かい日が続いている。
   **Fuyu majika da to iu noni, renjitsu, atatakai hi ga tsuzuite iru.**
   Even though winter is just around the corner, the warm weather continues.

b ウィークデーなのに家族連れなどで、かなりにぎわっていた。
   **Uīkudē na noni kazoku-zure nado de, kanari nigiwatte ita.**
   Despite it being a weekday, it was quite busy, with family customers etc.

c 外は真っ暗なのに、サンディはちゃんと起きているんですよ。
   **Soto wa makkura na noni, Sandi wa chanto okite iru n desu yo.**
   Even though it's pitch-dark outside, Sandy [= the dog] is awake.

#### 26.4.5.1.2 | Followed by a question

Neither **ga** nor **keredomo** can be used in this way.

a せっかく来たのに、今日はおしまいなの。
   **Sekkaku kita noni, kyō wa oshimai na no.**
   Are you closing today, even though we've gone to the trouble of coming?

b おれがこんなに働いてるのに、なんでお前は遊んでるんだ。
**Ore ga konna ni hataraite iru noni, nande omae wa asonderu
n da.**
How come you're loafing, even though I'm working so hard?

26.4.5.1.3 | Joining contrasting noun-modifying clauses

Two N-modifying clauses of a contrasting nature are joined by **noni**, forming a unit (indicated in [ ]). Neither **ga** nor **keredomo** can be used in this
way.

a 婚約したわけでもないのに、あまり高価なものをもらうのは心配
です。
**[Kon'yaku shita wake de mo nai noni, amari kōka na mono o
morau] no wa shinpai desu.**
It's worrying to be given overly expensive things even though we're
not engaged.

b 外観は二階建てに見えるのに、実は五階建てという不思議な造り。
**[Gaikan wa nikai-date ni mieru noni, jitsu wa gokai-date] to
iu fushigi na tsukuri.**
It's a mysterious structure that actually has five storeys even though
it looks like two storeys from the outside.

26.4.5.2 | *Clause 1* **noni** *(...) in unfinished sentences*

26.4.5.2.1 | With non-conditional clause 1

This expresses regret or disappointment, although the expression of regret
etc. is not mentioned here, but implied in the unfinished part. It is therefore
often used when commenting on people who have died or committed
suicide (examples a and b). The meaning of **noni** can be reinforced with
**nani mo**, as in example c. Again, neither **ga** nor **keredomo** can be used in
this way.

a （A君は）友達も多かったのに。
**(A-kun wa) tomodachi mo ōkatta noni.**
What a pity, he (= A-kun) had so many friends, too.

b 良きライバルであり、相談相手でもあったのに……。
**Yoki raibaru de ari, sōdan aite de mo atta noni.**
[It's so sad,] he was a good rival, and also someone I could talk things
over with.

c 何も、辞めなくてもいいのに。
**Nani mo, yamenakute mo ii noni.**
What a pity, there was no need to quit.

d 私たちから見れば全然カッコよくないのに。
**Watashi-tachi kara mireba zenzen kakko yokunai noni.**
From our perspective, they aren't stylish at all.

26.4.5.2.2 | With conditional form + **ii/yokatta noni**

**ii/yokatta noni** can be attached to positive and negative conditional forms, such as **-ba**. This forms a hypothetical sentence 'would be . . . if', or, where referring to an established fact, 'shouldn't' (see 26.1.1.3). Neither **ga** nor **keredomo** can be used in this meaning.

a 会社に託児所があればいいのに。
**Kaisha ni takuji-sho ga areba ii noni.**
It would be nice if the company had a daycare centre.

b それなら就職しなければいいのに。
**Sore nara shūshoku shinakereba ii noni.**
In that case [= already thinking of quitting] he shouldn't have taken the job.

## 26.4.6 | *Contrast expressions compared*

A contrast can occur between nouns or NPs, or between clauses.

### 26.4.6.1 | *Contrast between nouns or noun phrases*

This is effected by **wa** (see 11.3.5), including combinations with conjunctive particles.

### 26.4.6.2 | *Contrast between clauses*

Contrast between clauses can be indicated by the conjunctive particles **ga**, **keredomo**, **-nagara (mo)** (see **-tsutsu (mo)**), and **noni** (see 26.4.1–26.4.5). See also 26.4.6).

**ga** and **keredomo**

26.4.6.2.1.1 *Weak contrast*

Both express a weak contrast between two clauses (often in the form [N **wa** ga/keredomo, N **wa**], 'but'.

a 恋人に別れはあるけど、友達に別れはありません。

**Koibito ni wakare wa aru kedo, tomodachi ni wakare wa arimasen.**

Lovers can split up, but not friends.

26.4.6.2.1.2 *Weak contrast in noun-modifying clauses*

Both can be used in noun-modifying sequences (in [], i.e. *both* Adj/V connected by **ga/keredomo** modify the final N), usually without a comma (and accompanying comma intonation in speech). Note example b, where the modified noun **mono** 'person' in **hataraki-mono** 'hardworking person' is also modified by S1.

a 忙しかったがいい一年だった。

**[Isogashikatta ga ii] ichinen datta.**

It was a busy but good year.

b 貧しいけれども村一番の働き者。

**[Mazushii keredomo mura ichiban no hataraki] mono.**

She's poor but the hardest worker in the village.

26.4.6.2.1.3 *Introducing a comment or request*

Both can be used to introduce a comment or request. Both can be used in unfinished sentences.

a 「特に予定はないけれど」「じゃあ、朝十時に来てください」。

**'Toku ni yotei wa nai keredo'. 'Jā, asa jūji ni kite kudasai'.**

'I don't have anything particular to do.' 'In that case, come at 10 a.m.'

b 「今の字名では不便だけれど……」と古くからの名を惜しむ声も多い。

**'Ima no azana de wa fuben da keredo ...' to furuku kara no na o oshimu koe mo ōi.**

There are also many who are sorry to see the old names go, saying, 'The old locality names are impractical but ...'.

26.4.6.2.1.4 *Differences*

The contrast expressed by **ga** can be so weak that S1 **ga** is more like a preamble to S2, translatable as 'and', or rendered just with a colon.

a 竹内さんは病院に運ばれたが、頭などを強く打ち、重体。

 **Takeuchi-san wa byōin ni hakobareta ga, atama nado o tsuyoku uchi, jūtai.**

 Takeuchi-san was taken to hospital; he's in intensive care, having hit his head and elsewhere severely.

b 両親は離婚するが、母親は作家と再婚する。

 **Ryōshin wa rikon suru ga, hahaoya wa sakka to saikon suru.**

 The parents are getting divorced, and the mother is remarrying a writer.

26.4.6.2.2 **-nagara (mo), -tsutsu (mo), noni, ga** and **keredomo**

-**nagara**/-**tsutsu** (**mo**) and **noni** express a stronger contrast than **ga** and **keredomo**, in the sense of 'even though'. -**nagara**/-**tsutsu** (**mo**) are mostly used in the written (or formal spoken) language, usually about third persons, whereas the others are more colloquial. -**nagara**/-**tsutsu** (**mo**) express a factual contrast, whereas **noni** indicates a more subjective or emotional contrast. This is particularly evident in the use of **noni** in unfinished sentences, where it expresses disappointment or regret (26.4.5.2).

## 26.4.7 mon(o)

**mon(o)** also expresses a contrast that is mostly used in newpaper style language.

### 26.4.7.1 *Clause 1* **mono no** *clause 2*

In this construction, **mono no** means 'whereas', 'while' (see 26.4.5, 26.4.1, 26.4.3).

a 株価は上昇しているものの、景気は低迷が続いている。

 **Kabuka wa jōshō shite iru mono no, keiki wa teimei ga tsuzuite iru.**

 Although share prices are rising, the recession is continuing.

b 風雪の影響で一部の路線に遅れが出たものの、大きな混乱はなかった。

**Fūsetsu no eikyō de ichibu no rosen ni okure ga deta mono no, ōki na konran wa nakatta.**

As a result of the snow and wind, there were delays on some lines, but no major disruptions.

c 県内景気はテンポは緩慢なものの、回復傾向を持続している。

**Kennai keiki wa tenpo wa kanman na mono no, kaifuku keikō o jizoku shite iru.**

Business in the prefecture is slow (*lit.* "in tempo"), but the recovery trend continues.

---

26.4.7.2 *Clause 1* **mono o** *clause 2*

This means 'but', 'although', and is used typically in the form -**ba ii mono o** 'should have . . . , but' (see 26.1.1).

a 「心外」なら断わればいいものを受けてしまった。

**'Shingai' nara kotowareba ii mono o ukete shimatta.**

If he thought it 'unexpected' he should have turned it
   [= the premiership] down, but ended up taking it on.

*Note* – the combination **mono o** itself can also be **mono** [lexical N] + **o** [case particle], or [nominalizer] + **o** [case particle] (see 5.6.2).

## 26.5 Purpose and reason

### 26.5.1 **no ni**

**no ni** has two uses: attaching Adj/**na**-Adj predicates like **ii** and **benri**, it indicates purpose 'good/convenient for doing', and attaching other predicates it means 'for', 'in order to' (see 22.3, 2.4.12).

#### 26.5.1.1 *Verb* **no ni ii/benri**

This means 'good/convenient for doing'.

a カップルがお互いの相性を見るのにいい。

**Kappuru ga o-tagai no aishō o miru no ni ii.**

It [= rally driving]'s useful for couples to see how compatible they are.

b 生物の遺伝を考えるのにいい例だ。

**Seibutsu no iden o kangaeru no ni ii rei da.**

It [= blood type]'s a good example for considering the genetics of organisms.

c 国立公園で夏のキャンピングを楽しむのに便利。

**Kokuritsu kōen de natsu no kyanpingu o tanoshimu no ni benri.**

It's [a] handy [place] for enjoying summer camping in the [nearby] national park.

---

| 26.5.1.2 | *With other predicates* |

Here, the meaning is 'for', 'in order to'. Note that with some predicates, the valency of the verb determines the use of **ni** (see example c).

a 缶は持ち運ぶのに軽い方がいい。

**Kan wa mochihakobu no ni karui hō ga ii.**

Cans are better light for carrying about.

b この味を見つけるのに四年かかったそうだ。

**Kono aji o mitsukeru no ni yonen kakatta sō da.**

Apparently it took four years to discover this taste.

c 若い女性を集めるのに困らない。

**Wakai josei o atsumeru no ni komaranai.** (cf., N **ni komaru**
'have a shortage of/problem')

We have no problem recruiting young women.

---

| **26.5.2** | **kara** |

In S1 **kara** S2, **kara** basically indicates the reason for the action or state of S2. In use 26.5.2.1, **node** can also be used in some cases (see 26.5.3).

The forms preceding **kara** are usually plain final forms, although **desu/-masu** forms are common in speech, in which case the final predicate also uses matching **desu/-masu** forms. With adjective and nouns, plain forms are often used in S1 even though the final predicate may be polite.

26.5.2.1 *Clause 1* **kara**, *clause 2*

S1 **kara** gives the reason or cause for S2 'as', 'since', 'so'. In some uses (a, c and d), **kara** can be replaced by **node**. However, this is not possible in examples b and e (where the reason is emphasized); in examples g and h, where S2 is a subjective statement, an invitation, emphatic statement, etc., it is also better to use **kara** (see 26.5.3).

*Note* – in example b the negative predicate is a negation not of **urete iru**, but of the whole clause, **kakaku ga yasui kara urete iru**.

a 安かったからずいぶん売れた。
   **Yasukatta kara zuibun ureta.**
   Because they were cheap, they sold pretty well.

b 価格が安いから売れているのではない。
   **Kakaku ga yasui kara urete iru no de wa nai.**
   The reason it's selling is not because the price is low.

c 添加物もないから新鮮でおいしい。
   **Tenkabutsu mo nai kara shinsen de oishii.**
   There are no additives, so it's fresh and tasty.

d 仕事は楽しいから、ストレスはまったくない。
   **Shigoto wa tanoshii kara, sutoresu wa mattaku nai.**
   I enjoy the work, so I'm not stressed at all.

e 好きだから憎かった。
   **Suki da kara nikukatta.**
   I hated him [precisely] because I like him.

f 学校だと、みんなと一緒だから勉強がはかどる。
   **Gakkō da to, minna to issho da kara benkyō ga hakadoru.**
   In school, one makes progress with one's studies because one does things with the others.

g VTRが壊れたそうですね。安くしますから買いませんか。
   **Buitīāru ga kowareta sō desu ne. Yasuku shimasu kara kaimasen ka.**
   I hear that your video's broken down. I'll make it cheap, so how about buying one?

h 本当のことだから怒りませんよ。
   **Hontō no koto da kara okorimasen yo.**
   It's the truth, so I'm not getting upset.

## 26.5.2.2 Idiomatic use

In this use only a weak reason is implied.

a いいから早く買いに行けよ。

**Ii kara hayaku kai ni ike yo.**

Just get on with it and go buy it.

b 1937年12月生まれだからもう75歳。

**Sen kyūhyaku sanjūnana-nen jūnigatsu umare da kara mō
nanajūgo-sai.**

He was born in December 1937, which makes him already 75.

## 26.5.2.3 Clause 1 **no wa,** clause 2 **kara** copula

Ending a cleft sentence, **kara** indicates 'the reason why' (see 26.5.4.1.3).

a 小説を書くきっかけとなったのは、外国語で小説を読んだか
らです。

**Shōsetsu o kaku kikkake to natta no wa, gaikokugo de
shosetsu o yonda kara desu.**

The reason why I started writing novels is because I read novels in
foreign languages.

b 研究者たちが注目するのは、単に珍しいからではない。原始の地
球で起きた巨大マンガン鉱床の誕生が、ここで再現されている
可能性が高いからだ。

**Kenkyūsha-tachi ga chūmoku suru no wa, tan ni mezurashii
kara de wa nai. Genshi no chikyū de okita kyodai mangan
kōshō no tanjō ga, koko de saigen sarete iru kanōsei ga
takai kara da.**

The reason why researchers pay attention [to the mineral deposit] is
not just because it's unusual. It is because there is a strong
possibility that the birth of gigantic manganese deposits that
happened in prehistoric times has been replicated here.

## 26.5.2.4 Clause 1 **kara**

Without S2, the implication can be that it is understood from the context
or situation, or it can appeal to the listener in the sense of 'you see'.

a 人は人、自分は自分だから。

**Hito wa hito, jibun wa jibun da kara.**

Others can do as they like, I go my own way (*lit.* "People are people, I am I, you see").

b 人間はしょせん、不幸の中でしか真実を学ぶことはできないのだから。

**Ningen wa shosen, fukō no naka de shika shinjitsu o manabu koto wa dekinai no da kara.**

Ultimately, people can only learn the truth from a position of being unhappy, you see.

c 何しろ突然でしたから。

**Nanishiro totsuzen deshita kara.**

[His death] was so unexpected, you see.

d ちょっと待ってください。お茶を入れてきますから。

**Chotto matte kudasai. O-cha o irete kimasu kara.**

Please wait a little. I'll make some tea.

| 26.5.2.5 | *Clause 1* **no/n da kara**, *clause 2* |

This is a more emphatic variant of **kara** (see also 26.5.3).

a 一人で暮らすのだから、そんなに広い部屋はいらない。

**Hitori de kurasu no da kara, sonna ni hiroi heya wa iranai.**

As he will be living alone, he doesn't need such a large room.

b 日本人なんだから、いつでも帰れる。

**Nihonjin nan da kara, itsu demo kaereru.**

I'm Japanese, so I can always go back home.

| 26.5.2.6 | *Clause 1* **kara koso** *clause 2* |

Here, the reason is emphasized in the sense of 'precisely because', 'for the very reason that' (see 11.4.1).

a この本は私がこの村の住人じゃなかったからこそ書けた。

**Kono hon wa watashi ga kono mura no jūnin ja nakatta kara koso kaketa.**

I was able to write this book precisely because I wasn't living in this village.

b 物価が安いからこそぜいたくに暮らせる。
**Bukka ga yasui kara koso zeitaku ni kuraseru.**
It's for the very reason that things are cheap that you can live in luxury.

*Clause I* **kara ni wa** *clause 2*

This indicates a reason in the sense that S2 is expected as a consequence
of the action of S1 'so', 'since'.

a やると言ったからにはやる。
**Yaru to itta kara ni wa yaru.**
I said I'll do it, so I will.

b 反対するからには理由があるのだろう。
**Hantai suru kara ni wa riyū ga aru no darō.**
Since you oppose it, you must have a reason.

*Clause I* **kara to itte** *clause 2-negative*

Followed by a negative S2, this indicates that something is not going to
happen just because of the state or result of S2 'not . . . just because',
'doesn't necessarily mean that', 'may be . . . but that doesn't mean that'
(see also 21.2).

The idea of 'not necessarily' can be reinforced by **to wa kagiranai** 'not
necessarily'.

a 子供ができたからといって、変わるものではない。
**Kodomo ga dekita kara to itte, kawaru mono de wa nai.**
This [sharing of responsibilities] is not going to change just because
   I got pregnant.

b 努力したからといって全員が試合に出場できるとは限らない。
**Doryoku shita kara to itte zen'in ga shiai ni shutsujō dekiru
   to wa kagiranai.**
Having tried hard doesn't necessarily guarantee that everyone can play
   in the match.

c 人口が増えないからといって新たな施設がいらないわけではない。
**Jinkō ga fuenai kara to itte arata na shisetsu ga iranai wake
   de wa nai.**
Just because the population is not growing doesn't mean that we don't
   need any new facilities.

node

In S1 **node** S2, **node** indicates the reason for the action or state of S2.

The forms preceding **node** are usually plain noun-modifying forms, although **desu/-masu** forms can be used in speech.

26.5.3.1 *Clause 1* **node**, *clause 2*

This indicates a reason 'as', 'because', 'so'. In all examples, **node** can be replaced by **kara** (see 26.5.2).

a 飲んでいたので、はっきり覚えていない。
**Nonde ita node, hakkiri oboete inai.**
As I'd been drinking, I can't remember clearly.

b 彼女に振られたので、女の子の友達がいません。
**Kanojo ni furareta node, onna no ko no tomodachi ga imasen.**
Because I got dumped by my girlfriend, I have no female friends.

c うちは夫婦仲が悪いので、よくケンカをする。
**Uchi wa fūfu-naka ga warui node, yoku kenka o suru.**
We often have arguments, because we're not on good terms as
 a couple.

d 通勤に便利なのでここに引っ越した。
**Tsūkin ni benri na node koko ni hikkoshita.**
We've moved here because it's convenient for commuting to work.

e 明日は休みなので、山へでも行こうと思っている。
**Ashita wa yasumi na node, yama e demo ikō to omotte iru.**
Tomorrow is a holiday, so I'm thinking of making a trip to the
 mountains or somewhere.

26.5.3.2 *Clause 1* **node** (...) *in unfinished sentences*

Where the situation makes clear what the S2 verb would be, it can be omitted. **kara** can also be used in the same way.

a 「どうしてもおふろに入りたかったので」と汗をぬぐっていた。
**'Dōshite mo ofuro ni hairi-takatta node' to ase o nugutte ita.**
He was wiping off the sweat [after the bath], saying 'I just *had* to take
 a bath, you see'.

b 「それ以上はプライバシーにかかわるので……」と言葉を切
  った。
  **'Sore ijō wa puraibashī ni kakawaru node …' to kotoba o kitta.**
  He cut short his words, saying '[Saying] anything more would infringe
  on their privacy, so …'.

**tame**

**tame** expresses two basic meanings: purpose and cause or reason.

When used adverbially as **tame ni** V, or to modify a N as **tame no** N, it
usually expresses purpose.

When used to connect two clauses, S1 and S2, i.e. in the form S1 **tame**
S2, when **tame** (**ni**) is attached to plain V-past, and when completing a
cleft sentence in the form **tame da**, it can express either a cause or reason.

**tame** is formally a N, and therefore preceded by N-modifying forms and
followed by forms of the copula: when used adverbially, by **ni**, when
modifying N, by **no**, and as a predicate, by **da**, etc.

### 26.5.4.1 *Reason or cause*

26.5.4.1.1 Clause 1 **tame** clause 2 (+ copula)

This indicates a reason or cause 'because', 'due to', 'of'. When used in the
sense of 'because' (examples a–c), **tame** can be replaced by **kara** or **node**,
but not in the meaning of 'due to', 'of' (example d).

a カメは昼行性であるためコツコツ進む。
  **Kame wa chūkōsei de aru tame kotsukotsu susumu.**
  Because the tortoise is diurnal, it moves slowly but steadily.

b 平地が少ないため、建設コストは割高だ。
  **Heichi ga sukunai tame, kensetsu kosuto wa waridaka da.**
  As there is not much flat ground, the construction costs are
  comparatively high.

c 東京―北京間は遠回り飛行のため、四時間かかっている。
  **Tōkyō - Pekin-kan wa tōmawari hikō no tame, yo-jikan
  kakatte iru.**
  The sector Tokyo–Beijing is a circuitous flying route, and so it takes
  four hours.

d 長女の結ちゃん（4）は、約一時間後に病院で一酸化中毒のため
死亡した。

**Chōjo no Yui-chan (4) wa, yaku ichi-jikan-go ni byōin de
issanka chūdoku no tame shibō shita.**

Yui-chan (4), their eldest daughter, died about one hour later in
hospital of monoxide poisoning.

---

26.5.4.1.2 Verb/adjective-**ta tame (ni)**

In this use, **tame (ni)** can be replaced by **kara** or **node**.

a 人間は脳を持ってしまったために社会というものを作った。

**Ningen wa nō o motte shimatta tame ni shakai to iu
mono o tsukutta.**

Because humans acquired a brain, they created what's known as society.

b 気温の高い日が多かったため、家庭用の需要が落ち込んだ。

**Kion no takai hi ga ōkatta tame, kateiyō no juyō ga ochikonda.**

Because there were many warm days, domestic demand fell.

---

26.5.4.1.3 Cleft sentence **tame da**

This means 'the reason why . . . is because'. **kara** (but not **node**) can be
used in the same way (see 26.5.2.3).

a ペットショップがはやるのは、新年を身ぎれいにして迎えさせた
いという飼い主が増えているためでしょう。

**Pettoshoppu ga hayaru no wa, shinnen o migirei ni shite
mukaesasetai to iu kainushi ga fuete iru tame deshō.**

The reason why grooming parlours (*lit.* "pet shops") are popular is
probably because there are more and more owners who want to
have [their pet] enter the New Year neat and tidy.

b 実が腐らなかったのは、土質が乾燥していたためだ。

**Mi ga kusaranakatta no wa, doshitsu ga kansō shite ita
tame da.**

The reason why the seed didn't rot was because the soil was dry.

---

26.5.4.2 *Verb-**ru**/adjective-**i**/na-adjective-**na**/noun* **no tame ni/no**

When used adverbially in the form **tame ni** predicate, or to modify a noun
in the form of **tame no N**, **tame** usually indicates purpose. In the sentences
below, **tame** is not interchangeable with **noni** (see 26.5.1).

a 元気なうちは人のために働きたい。
   **Genki na uchi wa hito no tame ni hatarakitai.**
   While I'm healthy I want to work for [the benefit of] others.

b まさに相撲をやるために生まれてきたような力士。
   **Masa ni sumō o yaru tame ni umarete kita yō na rikishi.**
   He's a wrestler who just seems to have been born to do sumo.

c けがをしないためのトレーニング法とは何か。
   **Kega o shinai tame no torēningu-hō to wa nani ka.**
   [He teaches them things like] [What are the] ways of training in order
   to prevent injury.

## 26.6 Addition

### 26.6.1 shi

Attached to clauses (after final forms of V/Adj and **na**-Adj/N + copula),
**shi** signals an addition 'and (moreover)'. It can be used more than once in
a sentence.

a 自分の家は狭いし汚いなどといわず、···
   **Jibun no ie wa semai shi kitanai nado to iwazu...**
   Don't say that your house is small and messy and so on...[as an
   excuse for not inviting foreigners]

b 娘さんと結婚します。しかし養子にはならないし、会社も継ぎ
   ません。
   **Musume-san to kekkon shimasu. Shikashi yōshi ni wa naranai
   shi, kaisha mo tsugimasen.**
   I'll marry your daughter. But I won't be an adopted son, and I won't
   succeed to the company.

c 若いんだし、別にカタにはまることはないし、カッコつけて生き
   たっていいと思う。
   **Wakai n da shi, betsu ni kata ni hamaru koto wa nai shi,
   kakko tsukete ikitatte ii to omou.**
   I think it's OK to make themselves look smart – they are young, and
   there's no need for them to conform.

d この事件はほぼ終息したし、二度と起こることはない。
   **Kono jiken wa hobo shūsoku shita shi, nido to okoru
   koto wa nai.**
   This incident has more or less ended, and will never happen again.

## 26.7 Range of activities

### 26.7.1 -tari

The conjunctive particle **-tari** is attached to the **-ta** base, i.e. the form of V/Adj and **na**-Adj/N that **-ta** attaches to. It indicates a range of actions or activities that are performed by the same agent (subject). After words indicating a state, **-tari suru** means 'often', 'tend to'.

Although **-tari** is mostly used in the pattern *A*-**tari** *B*-**tari suru** 'do things/ things are like *A* and/or *B*', **-tari suru** can be used by itself (with the implication of 'things like'), and examples without **suru** are found too.

#### 26.7.1.1 *Clause-verb (=action)*-**tari**

This indicates a range of activities (not all are mentioned, i.e. others are usually implied), in the sense of 'do things such as'. In textbooks, etc. this use of **-tari** is often characterized as 'alternative', but examples such as b and d should make it clear that the actions are *not* alternate (and at any rate there are many examples with only one **-tari**!).

a たまの休日には本を読んだりゴルフに興じたりする。
**Tama no kyūjitsu ni wa hon o yondari gorufu ni kyōjitari suru.**
On his rare days off he does things like reading books and enjoying golf.

b 例えば、盲導犬は人にほえたり、かみついたりすることがない。
**Tatoeba, mōdōken wa hito ni hoetari, kamitsuitari suru koto ga nai.**
For instance, guide dogs don't do things like barking at people or biting them.

c 特に慌てたりする同僚はいなかった。
**Toku ni awatetari suru dōryō wa inakatta.**
There weren't any colleagues who were particularly flustered.

d 産業の本来の役割は、物やサービスを作ったり、販売することである。
**Sangyō no honrai no yakuwari wa, mono ya sābisu o tsukuttari, hanbai suru koto de aru.**
The original role of industry is to make things and services, and sell [them].

e 二十八日は音楽を聞いたり、読書をして過ごされた。
   **Nijūhachi-nichi wa ongaku o kiitari, dokusho o shite sugosareta.**
   The 28th she [= member of Imperial family] spent doing things like
   listening to music and reading.

26.7.1.2 *Clause-adjective/**na**-adjective/noun (=state)* **-tari**

In this use, **-tari** indicates a tendency.

a 都会にいれば田舎が贅沢だったりする。
   **Tokai ni ireba inaka ga zeitaku dattari suru.**
   If you're in the city, the countryside tends to be a luxury.

b 何とか職を見つけたいが、いい職は倍率が五百倍だったりする。
   **Nantoka shoku o mitsuke-tai ga, ii shoku wa bairitsu ga
   gohyaku-bai dattari suru.**
   I'd like to find a job somehow, but the application ratio for good jobs
   is often 500 to one.

c 恋人という関係は友達という関係とは違う問題がたくさん生じて
   きます。例えば、嫉妬だったり、束縛だったり。
   **Koibito to iu kankei wa tomodachi to iu kankei to wa chigau
   mondai ga takusan shōjite kimasu. Tatoeba, shitto dattari,
   sokubaku dattari.**
   In a relationship of lovers, all sorts of problems different from a
   relationship of friends arise. For instance, it may be jealousy, or
   [imposing] restraint.

## 26.8 Conjunctive forms and particles compared

Conjunctive forms and particles join clauses in the sense of 'and'. They
include the following: **-te**, stem forms, **shi**, **-tari** (see 25, 26.6.1, 26.7).

26.8.1 *Stem forms*

Stem forms of V and Adj always mean 'and' when joining clauses into
compound sentences.

a 二人組は車で逃走し、夫婦にけがはなかった。
   **Futari-gumi wa kuruma de tōsō shi, fūfu ni kega wa nakatta.**
   The gang of two took flight, and the couple were not injured.

b 札幌は日の出は早く、日没は遅い。

**Sapporo wa hinode wa hayaku, nichibotsu wa osoi.**

In Sapporo, the sunrise is early, and the sunset is late.

With VN only, it is also common to drop **shi,** the conjunctive form of **suru.** However, this is found only in the written language, such as newspapers (see 1.9).

c 車はそのまま逃走、女性にけがはなかった。

**Kuruma wa sono mama tōsō, josei ni kega wa nakatta.**

The car drove off without stopping, and the woman was not hurt.

## 26.8.2 -te/de

-te/de can also be used in the same way in the sense of 'and' (example a), but depending on the context can indicate a wider range of meanings when forming compound S. In example b, the implication is one of reason 'and therefore', and in example c, the implication is one of time sequence 'since/after being born' (see 25).

a スポーツ好きで、とりわけ「素潜り」が得意。

**Supōtsu-zuki de, toriwake 'sumoguri' ga tokui.**

He likes sports, and is especially good at skin diving.

b 実験やスライド映写を多用して、分かりやすい。

**Jikken ya suraido eisha o tayō shite, wakariyasui.**

It [= the course] uses a lot of experiments and slide projections, and is therefore easy to follow.

c それも生まれてはじめての体験だった。

**Sore mo umarete hajimete no taiken datta.**

Also, it [= cutting glass] was a first for me (*lit.* "first time since I was born").

## 26.8.3 shi

Used between clauses, **shi** signals an addition 'and', 'and (moreover)'. It is used when giving reasons, excuses, etc. (often more than one). Example a has two instances of **shi** attached to the two reasons (or motivations) given.

Examples b and c have only one instance of **shi,** but give a second reason in different form, using **N** + **wa/mo,** respectively.

Example b is a politician's reply to being asked about the influence of a scandal on the stock market, and example c explains why the speaker thinks that in times of recession live shows don't necessarily prosper.

a 若いんだし、別にカタにはまることはないし、カッコつけて生きたっていいと思う。

**Wakai n da shi, betsu ni kata ni hamaru koto wa nai shi, kakko tsukete ikitatte ii to omou.**

I think it's OK to make themselves look smart – they are young, and there's no need for them to conform.

b この事件はほぼ終息したし、二度と起こることはない。

**Kono jiken wa hobo shūsoku shita shi, nido to okoru koto wa nai.**

This incident has more or less ended, and will never happen again.

c 家で寝転がってテレビでも見ている方が楽だし、お金もかからない。

**Ie de nekorogatte terebi demo mite iru hō ga raku da shi, o-kane mo kakaranai.**

Lying down at home watching TV is easier, and doesn't cost anything either.

### 26.8.4 -tari

In its use after V only, -tari indicates a range of actions or activities that are performed by the same person, in which use it often translates as 'and'.

-tari is mostly used twice in a sentence [A-tari B-tari suru ('do things/things are like A and/or B')], -tari suru can be used by itself (with the implication of 'things like'), and examples without suru (example b) are found too.

a 例えば、盲導犬は人にほえたり、かみついたりすることがない。

**Tatoeba, mōdōken wa hito ni hoetari, kamitsuitari suru koto ga nai.**

For instance, guide dogs don't do things like barking at people and/or biting them.

b 産業の本来の役割は、物やサービスを作ったり、販売することである。

**Sangyō no honrai no yakuwari wa, mono ya sābisu o tsukuttari, hanbai suru koto de aru.**

The original role of industry is to make things and services, and sell [them].Nem. Sequi duciisq uibera inciate esciminia pore, te optati derspita num quistis conemol orrores cilibea sequae solute

**659**

# Chapter 27

# Abbreviations: truncations and ellipsis

## 27.1 Truncations

Where English uses initial capital letters to shorten lengthy terms to acronyms (United Nations → UN, North Atlantic Treaty Organization → NATO, etc.), Japanese generally cuts the number of *kanji* in Sino-Japanese words, or equivalent units in Native-Japanese and Western-Japanese (English-style acronyms are found with the names of some companies, such as **Nippon Hōsō Kyōkai = NHK**).

### 27.1.1 Sino-Japanese truncations

As most Sino-Japanese compounds consist of multiples of two or three *kanji*, this typically involves cutting the units after the first *kanji* of each unit of meaning, generally resulting in a two-*kanji* truncation:

a 国際連合 **Kokusai Rengō** → 国連 'UN'

b 温帯性低気圧 **ontai-sei teikiatsu** → 温低 'extratropical cyclone'

In the written media, it is common to give the Japanese translation first, with the English acronym added after it (in round brackets).

c 国際通貨基金 **Kosusai Tsūka Kikin** (IMF)

In the spoken media, the order is reversed, with the Japanese translation added after the acronym.

## 27.1.2 *Native-Japanese truncations*

With Native-Japanese words, truncations are far less common, although the names of some common restaurant dishes use a similar principle, except that some of the units remain uncut:

a 天ぷらどんぶり **tenpura donburi** → 天どん **tendon** 'tempura on rice'

b ねぎまぐろ **negi maguro** → ねぎま **negima** 'tuna [mashed] with leeks in broth'

## 27.1.3 *Native-Japanese truncations and Sino-Japanese 'conversions'*

In general terminology, Native-Japanese *kanji* units are often pronounced in their Sino-Japanese pronuncation (examples a and b), but sometimes also partly retain their Native-Japanese pronunciation (example c):

a 名古屋ー神戸 **Nagoya-Kōbe** 'Nagoga-Kōbe' → 名神 **Meishin** [motorway]

b 早稲田大学 **Waseda Daigaku** 'Waseda University' → 早大 **Sōdai**

c 横浜国立大学 **Yokohama Kokuritsu Daigaku** 'Yokohama National University' → 横国大 **Yokokokudai**

## 27.1.4 *Western-Japanese truncations*

Similar processes are also applied to Western-Japanese nouns (including so-called 'Japlish').

Here, the unit is mostly 2 + 2 'moras' or Japanese syllables/*kana* (examples a and b). Shorter 2 + 1 (example c), 1 + 2 (example d) and 1 + 1 (example e) units are also found, but these are very much exceptions to the rule.

a エアコンディショナー **eakondishonā** 'air conditioner' → エアコン **eakon**

b ワードプロセッサー **wādopurosessā** 'word processor' → ワープロ **wāpuro**

c インドパキスタン **Indo Pakisutan** 'India and Pakistan' → インパ
   (or 印パ) **In-Pa**

d レモンスカッシュ **remon sukasshu** 'lemon squash' → レスカ **resuka**

e ベースアップ **bēsu appu** 'rise in basic pay' → ベア **bea**

---

| 27.1.5 | *Mixed-Japanese truncations* |

These combinations tend to use a *kanji* representing the first morpheme
of a Sino-Japanese compound (example a) or a *kanji* representing a whole
Native-Japanese word (example b) with, usually, the first two 'moras' or
Japanese syllables/*kana*.

a 短期プライムレート **tanki puraimu rēto** 'short-term prime rate'
   → 短プラ **tanpura**

b 生コンクリート **nama konkurīto** 'raw concrete' → 生コン **namakon**

---

## 27.2 Ellipsis

Ellipsis in Japanese is a somewhat tricky issue, because it's sometimes
not clear whether something is omitted or whether it's not needed in the
first place. Personal pronouns, which are frequently absent (e.g. example
27.2.1 a) are a case in point. They exist, but are only used when required
for purposes such as clarification, emphasis, etc. They are therefore *not*
included under ellipsis.

Also, when compared to English, Japanese 'lacks' certain grammatical
features, such as the article (definite and indefinite), and relative pronouns,
which therefore by definition cannot be ellipted.

Ellipsis here refers to a sentence where some part (ranging from a case or
adverbial particle to a predicate) is missing, the meaning of which can,
however, easily be recovered, either from the context or because that part
tends to be omitted customarily (see 2.1.3).

Where a verb would be repeated in English, it is usually ellipted (or sub-
stituted with words like 'do' or auxiliaries such as 'will' 'might', etc. in
English. In Japanese, where there is a sense of 'also', this can be conveyed
by using the adverbial particle **mo** (see 11.2.1.1.2). Where an addition is

indicated, the *first* verb can be omitted (see example 27.2.3 g), because in Japanese the object of a sentence comes before the verb.

Note also the use of the adverb **sō**: 'in that way', 'so' to substitute for a full predicate, normally used (just like 'so' in English) when replying to others' comments.

a 「日本は世界的な視野を持たなければいけないと思います」。
　「私もそう思います」。
**'Nihon wa sekai-teki na shiya o motanakereba ikenai to omoimasu.' 'Watashi mo sō omoimasu.'**
'I think that Japan needs to view things globally.' 'I think so too.'

## 27.2.1 Ellipsis of particle

The case particles **o**, **wa** and **ga** are often ellipted in informal speech; ellipted o and wa are often indicated by comma intonation (and by a comma in writing) (see 2.2.1.2, 11.3.4.1.2, 2.1.2).

a たばこ、やめなきや。(= ellipsis of **o**)
**Tabako, yamenakya.**
I must stop smoking (*lit.* "stop tobacco").

b 仕事、ありませんか。(= ellipsis of **wa**)
**Shigoto, arimasen ka.**
Isn't there any work?

c 今夜はお父さん帰ってこないの。(= ellipsis of **ga**)
**Kon'ya wa otōsan kaette konai no.**
Tonight, hubby's not coming home.

## 27.2.2 Ellipsis of noun

A noun can be ellipted in Japanese in a way similar to English to avoid unneccessary repetition. However, whereas in English the second noun is usually ellipted, in Japanese it is the first one.

In example a, the noun after the first **gotoki** is ellipted (omitted) because it is identical to the second one.

Counters [number + counter] can also be used without the noun they count where the context makes it clear which noun they refer to (example b) (see 4.2.5)

a 政治家と官僚が対等であるかのごとき、争っているかのごとき状
態は自然ではない。
**Seijika to kanryō ga taitō de aru ka no gotoki, arasotte iru ka
no gotoki jōtai wa shizen de wa nai.**
A state of affairs where politicians and administrators seem on an
equal footing, and seem to compete, is unnatural.

b 精密なイラストは・・・息をのむほど美しい。一枚を仕上げるのに
一カ月くらいかかるそうだ。
**Seimitsu na irasuto wa ... iki o nomu hodo utsukushii.
Ichi-mai o shiageru no ni ik-kagetsu kurai kakaru
sō da.**
The accurate illustrations ... are breathtakingly beautiful. Apparently it
takes about a month to finish one.

## 27.2.3 Ellipsis of predicate (whole or part)

The predicate (or part of it) that may be assumed to be ellipted is given
in brackets below (see 10.2.4.2.2, 17.2.2.2, 2.1.3, 2.6.2, 2.4.3, 11.2.1.1.2,
11.4.3.6, 2.2.1.3, 11.3.4.2.2).

Where the ellipsis occurs not at the end of the sentence but in some other
part, the position where ellipsis takes place is also given in (empty) [ ].

a まさか取締役になるとは。(思わなかった, etc.)
**Masaka torishimari-yaku ni naru to wa. [omowanakatta. etc.]**
I'd never [have thought] that I'd be executive president.

b ちょっと口にしては次々と灰皿へ。(入れる, etc.)
**Chotto kuchi ni shite wa tsugitsugi to haizara e. [ireru, etc.]**
He smokes them briefly [each time], and then one after the other
[stubs them out] in the ashtray.

c おふくろに花束を! (贈ろう, etc.)
**Ofukuro ni hanataba o! [okurō, etc.]**
Flowers for Mum!

d ヨーロッパのブランドものはモノトーンで大人っぽく、私にはど
うも。(似合わない, etc.)
**Yōroppa no burando-mono wa monotōn de otona-ppoku,
watashi ni wa dōmo. [niawanai, etc.]**
European designer clothes are in plain colours and have a grown-up
feel about them, and are not quite [right] for me.

e そんなに焦らなくても、まだ若いのだから。(いい, etc.)

**Sonna ni aseranakute mo [ ], mada wakai no da kara. [ii, etc.]**

You needn't fret so much, because you're still young.

f たばこ、やめなきゃ。(いけない, etc.)

**Tabako, yamenakya. [ikenai, etc.]**

I must stop smoking.

g 肉は動物を殺してまで、と思うので、食べることが少なくなりました。(は食べたくない, etc.)

**Niku wa dōbutsu o koroshite made [ ], to omou node, taberu koto ga sukunaku narimashita. [wa tabetakunai, etc.]**

I don't eat much meat now, because I feel that [I don't want to eat it] if it means killing animals.

h 会社に入ってからは、まずレンズの技術を、次にレンズ以外のことを極めるのが夢となった。(= 極める)

**Kaisha ni haitte kara wa, mazu renzu no gijutsu o [ ], tsugi ni renzu igai no koto o kiwameru no ga yume to natta. [kiwameru]**

After I entered the company, my dream was first to master lens technology, and then things other than lenses.

# Chapter 28

# Stylistic effects and point of view

## 28.1   Inversion

In an inverted sentence the order of constituents is reversed, usually to place emphasis on the part that is brought to the beginning of the sentence. It is not really possible to imitate the effect of this in English translation, where the word order is different.

a 何だその言い方は。
   **Nan da sono iikata wa.**
   What sort of language is this! (= Mind your language!)

b 「覚えておけ」とぐらい言ってやれ、松井クン。
   **'Oboete oke' to gurai itte yare, Matsui-kun.**
   Matsui-kun, at least tell them, 'Remember this'.

c 「（プレゼントを）やらなくちゃいかんな、そりゃ」
   とニヤリ。
   **'(Purezento o) yaranakucha ikan na, sorya' to niyari.**
   'I'll have to give her (a [birthday] present), won't I', he smirked.
    (**sorya = sore wa**)

d 喫煙者率—日本になじんだ？外国たばこ
   **Kitsuensha-ritsu ---Nihon ni najinda? gaikoku tabako.**
   Percentage of smokers [of foreign brands is rising]:
    foreign cigarettes – have people got used to them?

e 世界へ広げよう、五輪の感動。
   **Sekai e hirogeyō, gorin no kandō.**
   The excitement of the Olympics – let's spread it around the world.

## 28.2 Repetition and emphasis

Repetition is used quite extensively in Japanese. It is used either for emphasis, or in a number of grammatical structures that also indicate some form of emphasis.

### 28.2.1 Emphasis by simple repetition

#### 28.2.1.1 Repetition of noun

a 不況、不況と言われているが、企業にとっては今がチャンス。
   **Fukyō, fukyō to iwarete iru ga, kigyō ni totte wa ima ga chansu.**
   It's said that it's a bad recession, but for business now it is a time of opportunity.

b 企業も「リストラ、リストラ」とキズの入ったレコードのように
   繰り返す。
   **Kigyō mo 'risutora, risutora' to kizu no haitta rekōdo no yō ni kurikaesu.**
   Industry too repeats 'restructuring' like a broken record.

#### 28.2.1.2 Repetition of [noun + case particle]

These are idiomatic expressions, such as **hi ni hi ni** 'by the day'.

a 技術は日に日に進歩している。
   **Gijutsu wa hi ni hi ni shinpo shite iru.**
   The technology is progressing by the day.

#### 28.2.1.3 Repetition of verb/adjective/**na**-adjective forms

a 知ってる知ってる。
   **Shitteru shitteru.**
   I know!

b 夫「平均支払額は四百十万円。結構、高い代償だ」妻「いや、
安い、安い。四件に一件は百万円以下です」

**Otto 'Heikin shiharai-gaku wa yonhyaku jūman-en. Kekkō,
takai daishō da' Tsuma 'Iya, yasui, yasui. Yonken ni ikken
wa hyakuman-en ika desu'**

Husband: 'The average amount paid is 4,100,000 yen. That's quite an
expensive [divorce] compensation.' Wife: 'No, it's quite cheap.
One in four settlements is 1 million or less.'

c ダメだ、ダメだと、いつも思ってますけれどね。

**Dame da, dame da, to itsumo omotte imasu keredo ne.**

I always think I'm no good, you see.

d 行けども行けども、景色は一向に変わらない。

**Ikedomo ikedomo, keshiki wa ikkō ni kawaranai.**

No matter how long you go on, the scenery doesn't
change at all.

---

### 28.2.2 | *Emphasis through grammatical structures*

This is expressed by structures like [V1-positive **ka** V1-negative **uchi**] 'barely
has . . . happened' and [V/Adj1-**ba** V/Adj2 **hodo**] 'the more . . . , the . . . -er'
(see 26.1.1, 26.2.8, 11.5.2; see also 9.1.2.3.1).

a 12月の声を聞くか聞かないうちに街は早くもクリスマス一色だ。

**Jūni-gatsu no koe o kiku ka kikanai uchi ni machi wa hayaku
mo kurisumasu isshoku da.**

December having barely arrived, the town has swiftly taken on an
atmosphere of Christmas.

b 組織が大きければ大きいほど決定は遅い。

**Soshiki ga ōkikereba ōkii hodo kettei wa osoi.**

The larger an organization is, the longer it takes to
make decisions.

c 犯人は憎んでも憎んでも憎みきれない。極刑をもって償ってもら
う以外ない。

**Hannin wa nikunde mo nikunde mo nikumi-kirenai. Kyokkei
o motte tsugunatte morau igai nai.**

There's no limit to my hatred for the culprit [who killed my little
daughter]. This [crime] can be atoned for only by the maximum
penalty.

d　野球の審判には逆らえない。スーパープレーヤーだろうと、常勝
　　の名監督だろうと関係ない。

**Yakyū no shinpan ni wa sakaraenai. Sūpāpureyā darō to, jōshō no mei-kantoku darō to kankei nai.**

You can't contradict a baseball umpire. It doesn't matter whether you're a superplayer or a famous coach who always wins.

**28.3　Onomatope (sound symbolism)**

Onomatope refers to words whose pronunciation (sound) suggests the nature of their action or state (in English, apart from animal sounds such as 'bow-wow', sound symbolism includes, for example, words beginning with 'sl-' suggesting something unpleasant, as in 'slime', 'slink', 'slither', 'slovenly', 'slug').

Japanese typically uses onomatope where English uses other forms of expression; compare the English translations. For instance, **baribari no gijutsusha** (**baribari** can refer to a tearing or crunching sound, but in the context of work indicates 'energetic' or 'being at the forefront of things') could also be expressed as **dai-ikkyu** 'first rank' **no gijutsusha**, but the onomatope version is more idiomatic. In example 28.3.1 c, the onomatope **burari** (describing a state of 'dangling') modifies **aruku** 'to walk', describing the way of walking.

In Japanese, a number of typical sound patterns can be distinguished; the most common ones are given in the following list:

| (C1-)V-C2-V × 2* | **kasa-kasa** 'rustle', **gata-gata** 'clatter' **goro-goro** (sound of thunder/stomach/purring cat etc.) **pika-pika** (glitter of light), **kucha-kucha** 'wrinkled', **yobo-yobo** 'tottering', **zuki-zuki** 'throbbing (with pain)', **atsu-atsu** 'piping hot', **ira-ira** 'jittery' |
|---|---|
| (C-)Vn-to | **chan-to** 'properly', **un-to** 'lots' |
| (C-)Vt-to | **sat-to** 'suddenly', **jit-to** 'still', **at-to** 'instantly' |
| (C-)V-CCC-ri | **yukkuri** 'slowly', **shikkari** 'firm', **uttori** 'vacantly' |
| C-Vn-C-V-ri | **nonbiri** 'leisurely', **bon'yari** 'vacant', **hin'yari** 'chilly' |

*Note* – * In this column, C stands for consonant and V for vowel; C1 and C2 being first and second consonant, respectively. Vn indicates vowel followed by **n**, and so on.

Japanese onomatope can act grammatically as outlined in the following sections.

669

### 28.3.1 As adverb (see 10.1.4)

Depending on the item, onomatope can be used as adverbs without particles, or with the addition of the particle of manner, **to**, or the adverbial form of the copula, **ni**.

Those ending in **to** already have **to** 'built in'.

a　成績表はちゃんと提出していただきます。
　　**Seiseki-hyō wa chanto teishutsu shite itadakimasu.**
　　We get them to submit their transcripts properly.

b　頭の中がぴかぴかと光った。
　　**Atama no naka ga pikapika to hikatta.**
　　There was a flash of light inside my head.

c　ぶらりと歩くと時がゆっくり流れていくようだ。
　　**Burari to aruku to toki ga yukkuri nagarete iku yō da.**
　　When one walks aimlessly, time seems to flow slowly.

d　ゴルフをしないとよぼよぼになる。
　　**Gorufu o shinai to yoboyobo ni naru.**
　　If I don't play golf, I become decrepit.

### 28.3.2 As noun-modifiers

This requires the addition of **no**, **na**, or **to shita** (see 6.6.6, 6.6.7.2).

a　しゃきっとした歯ごたえは暑い夏にも向く。(しゃきっ **shaki'**
　　'crisp')
　　**Shakit-to shita hagotae wa atsui natsu ni mo muku. [to** after
　　**shaki'** doubles the consonant]
　　The crisp texture is right for the hot summer, too.

b　漠とした不安に襲われる。
　　**Baku to shita fuan ni osowareru.**
　　One gets attacked by a vague feeling of unease.

c　大学は・・・工学科を出た。ばりばりの技術者でもあった。
　　**Daigaku wa ... kōgakka o deta. Baribari no gijutsusha de mo
　　atta.**
　　At university, he graduated from the ... engineering department.
　　　He was also a first-rate technician.

## 28.3.3 As noun

Unusually, some onomatope can be used as nouns, with case particles attached, in cases where the onomatope is understood to indicate some object (in example a, **iraira** stands for something like **iraira no kimochi** 'feeling of being irate', and in example b, **atsuatsu** stands for something like **atsuatsu no tabemono** 'a dish that is piping hot'.

a いらいらが高じて虐待に走るケースすら出ている。
   **Iraira ga kōjite gyakutai ni hashiru kēsu sura dete iru.**
   There are even cases emerging in which irritation is aggravated and turns into abuse.

b アツアツを頂く。
   **Atsuatsu o itadaku.**
   I dig into the piping hot [dish].

## 28.3.4 As predicate

This requires the addition of the copula, or forms of **suru/shite iru**.

a 電話の声の調子もしっかりしていた。
   **Denwa no koe no chōshi mo shikkari shite ita.**
   The tone of his voice on the phone was steady, too.

## 28.4 Classicisms

A form of language based on classical Japanese (essentially the language of the Heian period, around the year 1000) called *bungo* (文語) was the standard written form of Japanese between the Meiji restoration (1868) and the end of the Second World War.

Around the turn of the twentieth century, the Tokyo vernacular, *kōgo* (口語) became dominant in some newspapers and popular fiction as a result of the so-called *genbun itchi* ('one form for spoken and written language') movement, but *bungo's* influence has continued (in much reduced form) to the present day. For instance, *haiku* (17-syllable poem) and *waka* (31-syllable poem) writing is still very popular, with weekend newspapers carrying competitive selections of recent creations every week; these forms of poetry often use classical grammar.

### 28.4.1 Classical forms

In everyday Japanese texts (and to an extent, conversation, too), certain classicisms crop up occasionally, including the following (the classical language had separate forms for final and noun-modifying uses, which have subsequently fallen together). See Table 28.1 for some common equivalents.

For examples, see 17, 6.2.3, 6.2.4 (-ki, -shi), 17.1.1.2 (nashi), 17.1.2.1 (-nu), 17.1.2.3 (-zu, ni arazu), 17.1.5.4 (zaru).

**Table 28.1** Common classical forms with colloquial equivalents

|  | Classical form | Colloquial equivalent |
| --- | --- | --- |
| Noun-modifying | Adj-**ki** | Adj-**i** |
|  | **-nu** | **-nai** |
|  | **-zaru** | **-nai** |
| Final | Adj-**shi** | Adj-**i** |
|  | **-zu** | **-nai** |
|  | **ni arazu** | **de wa nai** |
| Conjunctive | **-zu** | **-nai de** |

### 28.4.2 Classical copula

There is also a classical copula, **nari**, which is still occasionally found in the written style, and has a noun-modifying positive form, **naru** N, and a N-modifying negative form, **naranu** N.

a 「君、星よりもはるかなり」
   **'Kimi, hoshi yori mo haruka <u>nari</u>'** [= song title]
   'You are more distant than the stars'

**naru** N is also found in a number of idiomatic expressions, which include **ōi naru** N 'big' and **ika naru** N **mo**, a more formal variant of **donna** N **demo**, 'no matter which N', 'no N whatsoever'.

b 日本の方が豊かと考えるのは大いなる誤解だね。
   **Nihon no hō ga yutaka to kangaeru no wa <u>ōi naru</u> gokai da ne.**
   It's a grave misunderstanding to think that Japan is more affluent
      [than China].

c NATOの拡張にはいかなる国も拒否権を行使できない。

**NATO no kakuchō ni wa <u>ikanaru</u> kuni mo kyohi-ken o kōshi dekinai.**

No country whatsover can exercise the right to veto an expansion of NATO.

### 28.4.3 | Idiomatic uses of classical forms

Classical forms also survive in a number of idiomatic patterns, which include the following: **naranu** (see 17.1.5.2), **-nu uchi** (see 26.2.8.1.2 g), **-zaru o enai** (see 17.2.2.5), **-zu ni wa irarenai** (see 17.2.3), **-neba** (**naranai**) (see 17.2.2.2 a and h), **-bekarazu** (see 9.4.1).

## 28.5 Point of view

Compared to languages like English, Japanese is said to have certain characteristics that can be said to give it a more speaker-centred point of view. The most typical of these characteristics are briefly described in this section.

### 28.5.1 | Subjective adjectives

These are adjectives that are typically used to refer to the feelings of the speaker (or grammatical subject) rather than some objective state: **samui** 'I'm cold', **hazukashii** 'I feel ashamed', etc.

a ⋯隊員らは「寒い、寒い」を連発。

**. . . tai-in-ra wa 'Samui, samui' o renpatsu.**

. . . the corps members kept saying '[I am/feel] cold'.

b 悠揚迫らぬ富士の威容に、人間の浅知恵が恥ずかしい。

**Yūyō semaranu Fuji no iyō ni, ningen no asajie ga hazukashii.**

Before the serene dignity of Mt Fuji, one feels ashamed of mankind's insensitivity [= lots of chimneys spoiling the view].

### 28.5.2 | Use of passive where English uses active

Cases where Japanese uses a passive construction whereas English would use the active voice include the so-called 'adversative passive' (where the patient (subject) is adversely affected by the action of the verb), as in example a.

In other instances, as in example b, the speaker does not see things from the barber's point of view (i.e. 'the barber told me . . .' in the active voice), but focusses on himself (i.e. 'I was told by the barber . . .' in the passive voice).

a　お金を無造作に置いていたが、まさか、取られるとは思っていなかった。

**Okane o muzōsa ni oite ita ga, masaka, torareru to wa omowanakatta.**

I put the money down casually, but it never occurred to me that someone would steal it (*lit.* "I would get it stolen").

b　今年5月に理容師と相談したら、縛ってみてはと勧められてやってみた。

**Kotoshi gogatsu ni riyō-shi to sōdan shitara, shibatte mite wa to susumerarete yatte mita.**

When I consulted with my barber in May this year, he suggested (*lit.* "I was suggested to by him") that I might tie up [my hair], so I gave it a try.

### 28.5.3 *Use of transitive and intransitive verbs*

Japanese uses a large number of transitive and intransitive verb pairs (see 7.3). When a transitive verb is used, the implication is that the subject is responsible for the action of the verb; but the corresponding intransitive verb implies that something happens for which nobody is overtly responsible or to be blamed.

a　厚さはわずかに0.5ミリ。手に取ると壊れてしまいそうだ。

**Atsusa wa wazuka ni rei-ten gomiri. Te ni toru to kowarete shimai-sō da.**

They [the earthenware teacups] are only 0.5 mm thick. They look as if they'll break when you take them in your hand.

b　三年前の作品をみると、壊してしまいたい気持ちになる。

**Sannen-mae no sakuhin o miru to, kowashite shimai-tai kimochi ni naru.**

When I look at things [= pottery I made] three years ago, I feel I want to break them.

The above distinction is not a problem in itself, but differences in point of view are seen in the way things are expressed; for instance, where English uses expressions such as 'they catch the offender' or 'the offender gets caught', Japanese uses neither the active/transitive, nor the passive, but the intransitive.

In example d, an ageing player explains his diminishing performance by saying that the reason is not that 'the ball doesn't fly as it used to' (**bōru ga tobanaku natta**), where English would use a transitive or causative expression.

c 犯人は無差別に発砲したのでしょうか。早く捕まってくれないと
不安です。

**Hannin wa mu-sabetsu ni happō shita no deshō ka. Hayaku tsukamatte kurenai to fuan desu.**

The culprit presumably fired the gun indiscriminately. If he doesn't get caught soon, I'll be worried.

d ボールが飛ばなくなったわけではない。体力より気力が落ちて
いる。

**Bōru ga tobanaku natta wake de wa nai. Tairyoku yori kiryoku ga ochite iru.**

It's not that [I can't get the golf] ball to fly [the distance] any more. It's my mental rather than physical strength that's diminished.

## 28.5.4 *Performative verbs*

Performative verbs are mainly verbs of giving and receiving (**ageru/yaru/sashiageru, kureru/kudasaru, morau/itadaku**, etc.), which can be used by themselves, or attached to the conjunctive form of other verbs (V-te **ageru**, V-te **kureru**, V-te **morau**, etc.) to indicate for whose benefit the action of the verb is performed. In English, the difference is often left to the context.

a 働くということは、雇ってもらっているとか、働いてやっている
と考えるのではなく、会社とどこまでイーブンな関係になれる
かだ。

**Hataraku to iu koto wa, yatotte moratte iru to ka, hataraite yatte iru to kangaeru no de wa naku, kaisha to doko made ībun na kankei ni nareru ka da.**

Working is not about feeling that someone is [doing you a favour by] employing you, or you are [doing someone the favour of] working for them, but to what degree you can get on an even footing with your company.

The choice of performative verbs depends on who gives to whom. Additionally, the notion of ingroup/outgroup comes into play. This requires that persons with whom the speaker identifies (the speaker's family or members of his company, etc.) are treated on a par with the speaker when addressing listeners belonging to other groups.

**Table 28.2** Performatives and noun phrase marking

|  | Noun phrase 1 | Noun phrase 2 | Noun phrase 3 | Verb |
|---|---|---|---|---|
| **ageru** 'give' | Giver-**ga/wa** | Recipient-**ni** | Thing-**o/wa** | **ageru** |
| **kureru** 'give' | Giver-**ga/wa** | Recipient-**ni** | Thing-**o/wa** | **kureru** |
| **morau** 'receive' | Recipient-**ga/wa** | Giver-**ni/kara** | Thing-**o/wa** | **morau** |

The difference in use between the three types of performatives makes it quite clear who gives what to whom; for this reason, some, or even all, of the NPs below can be ellipted or omitted (they can also appear in a different order).

**yaru** and **sashiageru** work in the same way as **ageru**, **kudasaru** as **kureru**, and **itadaku** as **morau**.

### 28.5.4.1 | **ageru** *(sashiageru)*, **yaru**

The examples that follow use **ageru** only, but **sashiageru** can be used in the same way (superpolite equivalent, see Table 16.1).

**yaru** is a verb that is mostly used in the sense of **suru** by itself (example a). It can also be used to 'give' to people of lower status than the speaker, but in fact **ageru** is often used in such cases (see 28.5.4.1.3 b, where a mother gives money to her high-school-student son). However, **yaru** is used for giving (water, feed, etc.) to plants, animals, etc. (examples b and c, but see 28.5.4.1.5 a, where **ageru** is used for giving to a cat!).

a 来年も一生懸命やるだけだ。
   **Rainen mo isshōkenmei yaru dake da.**
   Next year too we'll all work as hard as we can, that's all.

b 五—七日に一回を目安にたっぷり水をやる。
   **Itsuka kara nanoka ni ik-kai o meyasu ni tappuri mizu o yaru.**
   You water it (*lit.* "give it water") once every five to seven days or so.

c 「鶏に餌をやる少年」

**'Niwatori ni esa o yaru shōnen'**

'Boy feeding chickens' [= Title of a photograph]

All noun phrases present

a リンダさんは週に二回学校に行っているので、代わりにマイクさんが哺乳瓶で赤ちゃんに母乳をあげる。

**Rinda-san wa shū ni ni-kai gakkō ni itte iru node, kawari ni Maiku-san ga honyū-bin de aka-chan ni bonyū o ageru.**

As Linda goes to school twice a week, Mike gives the baby a bottle feed instead.

Noun phrases 2 and 3 present

a 虫歯になるので、娘にはアメをあげないでください。

**Mushiba ni naru node, musume ni ame o agenai de kudasai.**

Please don't give my daughter any sweets as she'll get tooth decay.

b もし拾った人がいたら、その人に幸せをあげたと思えばいいよ。

**Moshi hirotta hito ga itara, sono hito ni shiawase o ageta to omoeba ii yo.**

If someone picked up [your wallet], you should just think that you've given happiness to that person.

Noun phrase 2 present

a 保育園では、たまに戸外へ出て、菓子をあげることはよくある。

**Hoiku-en de wa, tama ni kogai e dete, kashi o ageru koto wa yoku aru.**

In the kindergarten, we occasionally go out and often give [the children] sweets.

b その際、高校生の二男に「残った分はあげる」と留守中の生活費として二万円を渡したところ・・・

**Sono sai, kōkō-sei no jinan ni 'Nokotta bun wa ageru' to rusu-chū no seikatsu-hi to shite niman-en o watashita tokoro . . .**

On that occasion, when she gave her second son, a high-school student, 20,000 yen as living expenses during their absence with the words 'You can keep any that's left over . . .'

28.5.4.1.4 Noun phrase 3 present

a 三千六百円になるから、お母さんにあげる。

**Sanzen roppyaku-en ni naru kara, Okāsan ni ageru.**

[The prize] will come to 3,600 yen, so I'll give it to you [= Mum].

28.5.4.1.5 **ageru** in relative clauses

In a relative clause, the number of required NPs is fewer. In the example below, NP3 cannot be mentioned inside the relative clause (shown by [ ]) as it is identical with the modified noun **neko** (see 22.1).

a 魚屋は時田の家に顔を出したが、いつも魚をあげていたネコがいない。

**Sakana-ya wa Tokita no ie ni kao o dashita ga, [itsumo sakana o agete ita] neko ga inai.**

The fishmonger visited Tokita's place, but the cat he always used to give fish to wasn't there.

28.5.4.1.6 Verb-**te ageru** (-te yaru, -te sashiageru)

Here, the number of required NPs depends on the valency of the verb to which -**te ageru** is attached. -**te yaru** can be used to those of lower status, and -**te sashiageru** of higher status (see 7.2, 15.1.1, 15.1.2, 16.3, Table 16.1).

a お菓子を買ってあげる。

**Okashi o katte ageru.**

I'll buy you sweets.

b 今度、一緒に連れていってあげるからね。

**Kondo, issho ni tsurete itte ageru kara ne.**

[Grown-up grandson to grandfather:] I'll take you [back to your birthplace] one of these days, OK?

c 日本でもボランティア活動が増えてきましたが、まだまだ
"してあげる" という恩に着せたような意識が強いようです。

**Nihon de mo borantia katsudō ga fuete kimashita ga, madamada 'shite ageru' to iu on ni kiseta yō na ishiki ga tsuyoi yō desu.**

Voluntary work has increased in Japan too, but the feeling of doing others a favour in the sense of 'I'm doing it *for* you' still seems to be strong.

d テーブルでお母さんやお父さんが子供たちに絵本を読んてあげる
　姿も目立つ。

**Tēburu de o-kāsan ya o-tōsan ga kodomo-tachi ni ehon o
yonde ageru sugata mo medatsu.**

At the table you see mothers and fathers reading picture books to
their children.

e 「外国人に道を聞かれたらどうする」「場所が分かれば教えてあ
　げる」

**'Gaikoku-jin ni michi o kikaretara dō suru' 'Basho ga
wakareba oshiete ageru'**

'What do you do if a foreigner asks you the way?' 'If I know the
location, I'll tell him.'

f 同居してあげる、と恩着せがましく言われてありがたがる親が多
　いからだろう。

**Dōkyo shite ageru, to onkise-gamashiku iwarete ariga-tagaru
oya ga ōi kara darō.**

This is probably because there are many parents who feel gratified
when told patronizingly [by their children], 'We'll live with you'.

### 28.5.4.2 kureru (kudasaru)

**kudasaru** is used in the same way, for subjects + **ga/wa** who are of higher
status.

### 28.5.4.2.1 kureru

a 同情するなら金をくれ。

**Dōjō suru nara kane o kure.**

If you feel sorry for me give me some money.

b 父親は一日に一ドル小遣いをくれる。

**Chichioya wa ichinichi ni ichi-doru kozukai o kureru.**

The father gives them one dollar pocket money a day [in story about
children spending time with divorced parents].

c 愚痴を繰り返していても、だれもあなたを救い出してはく
　れない。

**Guchi o kurikaeshite ite mo, dare mo anata o sukui-dashite
wa kurenai.**

If you just keep complaining, no one is going to help you.

d 上位にいると、「すぐ手紙をくれる」という。
**Jōi ni iru to, 'Sugu tegami o kureru' to iu.**
When he is among the leaders [in a tournament], '[Grandma] sends
me a letter right away', he says.

e チョコレートでもくれるのかな。 (**demo** here replaces **o**)
**Chokorēto demo kureru no ka na.**
Maybe [my daughters] will give me chocolates or something.

28.5.4.2.2 | **kureru** in relative clauses

The NP (NP1) that is identical to the modified N (**hito**) cannot be mentioned inside the relative clause (shown by [ ]) (see 22.1).

a 一日も早く病気を克服し、メッセージをくれた人に会いに行
きたい。
**Ichinichi mo hayaku byōki o kokufuku shi, [messēji o kureta]
hito ni ai ni ikitai.**
I want to defeat my illness as quickly as possible, and go and meet the
people who've sent me messages.

28.5.4.2.3 | **-te kureru**

When attached to V-**te**, **kureru** indicates that the action of the verb is
performed for the benefit of first or third persons; in the case of third
persons, the implication is that the speaker sympathizes or takes sides with
them (see 15.3).

Example a needs some explanation. Here, -**te kureru** is used by the father
of an Olympic gold medallist, who won in front of a largely local audience
in an area where he used to go and practise and which was like a second
home to the athlete.

a みんなが応援してくれました。
**Minna ga ōen shite kuremashita.**
Everyone cheered him on.

b 今の会社は女性に仕事を任せてくれない。
**Ima no kaisha wa josei ni shigoto o makasete kurenai.**
The company I am with now doesn't let women take responsibility for
the work.

c 祖父は何も財産を残してくれませんでした。
**Sofu wa nani mo zaisan o nokoshite kuremasen deshita.**
My grandfather didn't leave me any money.

**28.5.4.3** **morau/itadaku** *(moraeru/itadakeru = potential)*

With **morau** (itadaku is used with givers of higher status), either **ni** or **kara** can be used to mark NP2.

**28.5.4.3.1** **morau**

a 複数のボーイフレンドからプレゼントをもらった若い女性が、要らない品を持ち込んでいる例も多い。

**Fukusū no bōifurendo kara purezento o moratta wakai josei ga, iranai shina o mochikonde iru rei mo ōi.**

There are also many cases where young women, who received presents from several boyfriends, bring in things they don't need [= to pawn].

**28.5.4.3.2** **morau** in relative clauses

The NP that is identical with the modified N (**mono**) cannot be mentioned inside the relative clause (shown by [ ]).

a 皆様（記者団）から何かもらえるものがあったら、喜んでいただきます。

**[Mina-sama (kisha-dan) kara nani ka moraeru] mono ga attara, yorokonde itadakimasu.**

If there's anything I can get from you [press corps], I'll accept it gladly.

**28.5.4.3.3** Verb-**te morau** (Verb-**te moraeru** = potential)

-**te itadaku** is used with givers who are higher in status (see 15.5, 15.6).

In example a, a husband tells his new wife, who wishes to retain her maiden name, to change it, i.e. his interests are indicated by the verb **kaeru** + -**te morau**, 'have things changed for his benefit'.

Example b shows the words of a father about a suspect accused of having killed his young daughter and who is currently being tried in court. **tsugunau** 'make up for the crime' is used with -**te morau**, for the speaker's (and his group/family's) benefit.

a 僕の名字にちゃんと変えてもらわないと、田舎の両親に何て言われるか······。

**Boku no myōji ni chanto kaete morawanai to, inaka no ryōshin ni nan te iwareru ka...**

Unless you change your surname to mine, God knows what my traditional-minded parents will say to me...

b 犯人は憎んでも憎んでも憎みきれない。極刑をもって償ってもら
う以外ない。

**Hannin wa nikunde mo nikunde mo nikumi-kirenai. Kyokkei o
motte tsugunatte morau igai nai.**

I hate the culprit more than words can express. This [crime] can be
atoned for only by the maximum penalty.

c 安さだけでは顧客に満足してもらえない時代になった。

**Yasu-sa dake de wa kokyaku ni manzoku shite moraenai jidai
ni natta.**

It's (*lit.* "it's become") an age where cheapness isn't enough to satisfy
customers.

# Index